WEBSTER'S REFERENCE LIBRARY

CONCISE EDITION
SPELLING
GRAMMAR & USAGE

**GEDDES &
GROSSET**

Published 2002 by Geddes & Grosset

© 2002 Geddes & Grosset
David Dale House, New Lanark ML11 9DJ, Scotland

This book is not published by the original publishers of Webster's Dictionary or
by their successors

ISBN 1 84205 271 3

Printed and bound in Europe

Contents

Spelling

aard'vark
aback
aba'cus
ab'a'lo'ne
aban'don
aban'doned
aban'don'ment
abase
abased
abase'ment
abashed
abas'ing
abate
abat'ed
abate'ment
abat'ing
ab'at'toir
ab'axial
ab'bé
ab'bess
ab'bey
ab'bot
ab'bre'vi'ate
ab'bre'vi'at'ed
ab'bre'vi'at'ing
ab'bre'vi'a'tion
ab'di'cate
ab'di'cat'ed
ab'di'cat'ing
ab'di'ca'tion
ab'do'men
ab'dom'i'nal
ab'duct
ab'duc'tion
ab'duc'tor
abed
ab'er'rance
ab'er'ran'cy
ab'er'rant
ab'er'ra'tion
abet
abet'ting
abet'ment
abet'ted
abet'ter
abet'tor
abey'ance
abey'ant
ab'hor
ab'horred
ab'hor'rence
ab'hor'rent
ab'hor'ring

abide
abid'ed
abid'ing
abil'i'ties
abil'i'ty
ab'ject
ab'ject'ly
ab'ject'ness
ab'ju'ra'tion
ab'jure
ab'jured
ab'jur'ing
ab'late
ab'lat'ed
ab'lat'ing
ab'la'tion
ab'la'tive
abla'ze
able
able-bod'ied
ab'lu'tion
ab'ne'gate
ab'ne'gat'ed
ab'ne'gat'ing
ab'ne'ga'tion
ab'nor'mal
ab'nor'mal'i'ties
ab'nor'mal'i'ty
ab'nor'mal'ly
aboard
abode
abol'ish
abol'ish'able
abol'ish'ment
ab'o'li'tion
ab'o'li'tion'ism
ab'o'li'tion'ist
abom'i'na'ble
abom'i'na'bly
abom'i'nate
abom'i'nated
abom'i'nat'ing
abom'i'na'tion
ab'orig'i'nal
ab'orig'i'ne
abort
abort'ed
abor'ti'fa'cient
abor'tion
abor'tion'ist
abort'ive'ly
abor'tive
abound

about
above
above'board
ab'ra'ca'dab'ra
abrade
abrad'ed
abrad'ing
abra'sion
abra'sive
abreast
abridge
abridged
abridge'ment
abridg'ing
abroad
ab'ro'gate
ab'ro'gat'ed
ab'ro'gat'ing
ab'ro'ga'tion
abrupt
abrupt'ly
abrupt'ness
ab'scess
ab'scessed
ab'scis'sa
absciss'ae
ab'scis'sas
ab'scis'sion
ab'scond
ab'seil
ab'seil'ing
ab'sence
ab'sent
ab'sen'tee
ab'sen'tee'ism
ab'sent'ly
ab'sent-mind'ed
ab'sinth
ab'sinthe
ab'so'lute
ab'so'lute'ly
ab'so'lu'tion
ab'so'lut'ism
ab'solve
ab'solved
ab'solv'ing
ab'sorb
ab'sorb'able
ab'sorb'en'cy
ab'sorb'ent
ab'sorb'ing'ly
ab'sorp'tion
ab'sorp'tive

ab'stain
ab'stain'er
ab'ste'mi'ous
ab'ste'mi'ous'ness
ab'sten'tion
ab'sti'nence
ab'sti'nent
ab'stract
ab'stract'ed
ab'stract'ed'ly
ab'strac'tion
ab'stract'ly
ab'struse
ab'surd
ab'sur'di'ties
ab'sur'di'ty
ab'surd'ly
ab'surd'ness
abun'dance
abun'dant
abun'dant'ly
abuse
abused
abus'er
abus'ing
abu'sive
abu'sive'ly
abu'sive'ness
abut
abut'ment
abut'ted
abut'ting
abys'mal
abys'mal'ly
abyss
aca'cia
ac'a'dem'ic
ac'a'dem'i'cal
aca'demi'cal'ly
ac'a'de'mi'cian
acad'e'mies
acad'e'my
acan'thi
acan'thus
a cap'pel'la
ac'cede
ac'ced'ed
ac'ced'ing
ac'ce'le'ran'do
ac'cel'er'ant
ac'cel'er'ate
ac'cel'er'at'ed
ac'cel'er'at'ing

ac'cel'er'a'tion
ac'cel'er'a'tor
ac'cent
ac'cen'tu'ate
ac'cen'tu'at'ed
ac'cen'tu'at'ing
ac'cen'tu'a'tion
ac'cept
ac'cept'abil'ity
ac'cept'able
ac'cept'ably
ac'cep'tance
ac'cept'ed
ac'cept'er
ac'cept'or
ac'cess
ac'ces'si'bil'i'ty
ac'ces'si'ble
ac'ces'si'bly
ac'ces'sion
ac'ces'so'ry
ac'ci'dence
ac'ci'dent
ac'ci'den'tal
ac'ci'den'tal'ly
ac'cident-prone
ac'claim
ac'cla'ma'tion
ac'clai'm'ing
ac'cli'mate
ac'cli'mat'ed
ac'cli'ma'ti'za'tion
ac'cli'ma'tize
ac'cli'ma'tized
ac'cli'ma'tiz'ing
ac'cli'ma'tion
ac'cliv'i'ties
ac'cliv'i'ty
ac'co'lade
ac'com'mo'date
ac'com'mo'dat'ed
ac'com'mo'dat'ing
ac'com'mo'da'tion
ac'com'mo'da'tive
ac'com'pa'nied
ac'com'pa'ni'ment
ac'com'pa'nist
ac'com'pa'ny
ac'com'pa'ny'ing
ac'com'plice
ac'com'plish
ac'com'plished
ac'com'plish'ing

ac'com'plish'ment
ac'cord
ac'cor'dance
ac'cord'ing
ac'cord'ing'ly
ac'cor'di'on
ac'cor'di'on'ist
ac'cost
ac'couche'ment
ac'count
ac'count'abil'i'ty
ac'count'able
ac'count'ably
ac'coun'tan'cy
ac'coun'tant
ac'count'ing
ac'cou'tre'ments
ac'cred'it
ac'cred'i'ta'tion
ac'cred'it'ed
ac'cred'it'ing
ac'cre'tion
ac'cre'tive
ac'cru'al
ac'crue
ac'crued
ac'cru'ing
ac'cul'tur'a'tion
ac'cu'mu'late
ac'cu'mu'lat'ed
ac'cu'mu'lat'ing
ac'cu'mu'la'tion
ac'cu'mu'la'tive
ac'cu'ra'cy
ac'cu'rate
ac'cu'rate'ly
ac'cu'rate'ness
ac'curs'ed
ac'curst
ac'cu'sa'tion
ac'cu'sa'tive
ac'cu'sa'to'ry
ac'cuse
ac'cused
ac'cus'er
ac'cus'ing
ac'cus'ing'ly
ac'cus'tom
ac'cus'tomed
aceph'a'lous
acer'bic
acer'bi'ty
ac'e'tate

ace'tic
acet'i'fy
ac'e'tone
acet'y'lene
ache
ached
achiev'able
achieve
achieved
achieve'ment
achiev'er
achiev'ing
ach'ing
ach'ro'mat'ic
ac'id
acid'ic
acid'i'fied
acid'i'fy
acid'i'fy'ing
acid'i'ty
ac'i'do'sis
acid'u'late
acid'u'la'tion
acid'u'lous
ac'knowl'edge
ac'knowl'edge'able
ac'knowl'edged
ac'knowl'edg'ing
ac'knowl'edge'ment
ac'me
ac'ne
ac'o'lyte
ac'o'nite
acorn
acous'tic
acous'ti'cal
acous'tics
ac'quaint
ac'quain'tance
ac'quain'tance'ship
ac'quaint'ed
ac'qui'esce
ac'qui'esced
ac'qui'es'cence
ac'qui'es'cent
ac'qui'es'cing
ac'quire
ac'quired
ac'quire'ment
ac'quir'ing
ac'qui'si'tion
ac'quis'i'tive
ac'quit

ac'quit'ting
ac'quit'tal
ac'quit'tance
ac'quit'ted
acre
acre'age
ac'rid
acrid'i'ty
Ac'ri'lan
ac'ri'mo'ni'ous
ac'ri'mo'ny
ac'ro'bat
ac'ro'bat'ic
ac'ro'bat'ics
ac'ro'nym
ac'ro'pho'bia
acrop'o'lis
across
acros'tic
acryl'ic
act'ing
ac'ti'nide
ac'tin'i'um
ac'tion
ac'tion'able
ac'tion'ably
ac'ti'vate
ac'ti'vat'ed
ac'ti'vat'ing
ac'ti'va'tion
ac'ti'va'tor
ac'tive
ac'tive'ly
ac'tive'ness
ac'tiv'ism
ac'tiv'ist
ac'tiv'i'ties
ac'tiv'i'ty
ac'tor
ac'tress
ac'tu'al
ac'tu'al'i'ties
ac'tu'al'i'ty
ac'tu'al'iza'tion
ac'tu'al'ize
ac'tu'al'ly
ac'tu'ar'i'al
ac'tu'ar'ies
ac'tu'ary
ac'tu'ate
ac'tu'at'ed
ac'tu'at'ing
ac'tu'a'tion

ac'tu'a'tor
acu'ity
acu'men
acu'pres'sure
acu'punc'ture
acute
acute'ly
acute'ness
ad'age
ada'gio
ad'a'mant
ad'a'man'tine
adapt
adapt'abil'i'ty
adapt'able
ad'ap'ta'tion
adapt'er
adap'tive
adapt'or
ad'dend
ad'den'da
ad'den'dum
ad'der
ad'dict
ad'dic'ted
ad'dic'tion
ad'dic'tive
ad'di'tion
ad'di'tion'al
ad'di'tive
ad'dle
ad'dress
ad'dress'ee
ad'duce
ad'e'noid
ad'e'noi'dal
adept
adept'ly
ad'e'qua'cy
ad'e'quate
ad'e'quate'ly
ad'here
ad'hered
ad'her'ence
ad'her'ent
ad'her'ing
ad'he'sion
ad'he'sive
ad'he'sive'ness
ad hoc
adi'a'bat'ic
adieu
adieus

adieux
ad in'fi'ni'tum
adi'os
ad'i'pose
ad'i'pos'i'ty
ad'ja'cen'cies
ad'ja'cent
ad'ja'cent'ly
ad'jec'ti'val
ad'jec'ti'val'ly
ad'jec'tive
ad'join
ad'join'ing
ad'journ
ad'journ'ment
ad'judge
ad'judged
ad'judg'ing
ad'ju'di'cate
ad'ju'di'cat'ed
ad'ju'di'cat'ing
ad'ju'di'ca'tion
ad'ju'di'ca'tive
ad'ju'di'ca'tor
ad'junct
ad'junc'tive
ad'ju'ra'tion
ad'jure
ad'jured
ad'jur'ing
ad'just
ad'just'able
ad'just'er
ad'just'ment
ad'jus'tor
ad'ju'tan'cy
ad'ju'tant
ad-lib
ad-libbed
ad-lib'bing
ad'min'is'ter
ad'min'is'trate
ad'min'is'tra'tion
ad'min'is'tra'tive
ad'min'is'tra'tor
ad'mir'a'ble
ad'mi'ra'bly
ad'mi'ral
ad'mi'ral'ty
ad'mi'ra'tion
ad'mire
ad'mired
ad'mir'er

ad'mir'ing
ad'mir'ing'ly
ad'mis'si'bil'i'ty
ad'mis'si'ble
ad'mis'sion
ad'mit
ad'mit'tance
ad'mit'ted
ad'mit'ted'ly
ad'mit'ting
ad'mix'ture
ad'mon'ish
ad'mo'ni'tion
ad'mon'i'to'ry
ad nau'se'am
ado
ado'be
ad'o'les'cence
ad'o'les'cent
adopt
adopt'able
adopt'er
adop'tion
adop'tive
ador'able
ador'ably
ad'o'ra'tion
adore
adored
ador'ing
ador'ing'ly
adorn
adorn'ment
ad're'nal
adren'a'line
adrift
adroit
adroit'ly
adroit'ness
ad'sorb
ad'sor'bent
ad'sorp'tion
ad'u'late
ad'u'lat'ing
ad'u'la'tion
ad'u'la'to'ry
adult
adul'ter'ant
adul'ter'ate
adul'ter'at'ed
adul'ter'at'ing
adul'ter'a'tion
adul'ter'er

adul'ter'ess
adul'ter'ous
adul'tery
adult'hood
ad va'lo'rem
ad'vance
ad'vanced
ad'vance'ment
ad'vanc'ing
ad'van'tage
ad'van'taged
ad'van'ta'geous
ad'van'ta'geous'ly
ad'van'tag'ing
ad'vent
ad'ven'ti'tious
ad'ven'ture
ad'ven'tur'er
ad'ven'ture'some
ad'ven'tur'ing
ad'ven'tur'ous
ad'ven'tur'ous'ly
ad'verb
ad'ver'bi'al
ad'ver'bi'al'ly
ad'ver'sar'ies
ad'ver'sary
ad'verse
ad'verse'ly
ad'verse'ness
ad'ver'si'ties
ad'ver'si'ty
ad'vert
ad'ver'tence
ad'ver'tent
ad'ver'tise
ad'ver'tised
ad'ver'tise'ment
ad'ver'tis'er
ad'ver'tis'ing
ad'vice
ad'vis'abil'i'ty
ad'vis'able
ad'vis'ably
ad'vise
ad'vised
ad'vis'ed'ly
ad'vise'ment
ad'vis'er
ad'vis'ing
ad'vi'so'ry
ad'vo'caat
ad'vo'ca'cy

9

ad'vo'cate
ad'vo'cat'ed
ad'vo'cat'ing
ad'vo'ca'tion
aegis
aeo'lian
ae'on
ae'o'ni'an
aer'ate
aer'at'ed
aer'at'ing
aer'a'tion
aer'a'tor
ae'ri'al
ae'ri'al'ist
ae'rie
ae'ries
aer'o'bat'ics
aer'obe
aer'o'bic
aer'o'bi'cal'ly
aer'o'bics
aero'dy'nam'ic
aero'dy'nam'i'cal'ly
aero'dy'nam'ics
aer'o'log'i'cal
aer'ol'o'gist
aero'nau'ti'cal
aero'naut'ics
aero'plane
aero'sol
aero'space
ae'ry
aes'thete
aes'thet'ic
aes'thet'i'cal'ly
aes'thet'i'cism
aes'thet'ics
aes'ti'vate
aes'ti'vated
aes'ti'vat'ing
aes'ti'va'tion
afar
af'fa'bil'i'ty
af'fa'ble
af'fa'bly
af'fair
af'fect
af'fec'ta'tion
af'fect'ed
af'fect'ed'ly
af'fect'ed'ness
af'fect'ing

af'fect'ing'ly
af'fec'tion
af'fec'tion'ate
af'fec'tion'ate'ly
af'fec'tive
af'fen'pin'scher
af'fer'ent
af'fi'ance
af'fi'da'vit
af'fil'i'ate
af'fil'i'at'ed
af'fil'i'at'ing
af'fil'i'a'tion
af'fin'i'ties
af'fin'i'ty
af'firm
af'fir'ma'tion
af'fir'ma'tive
af'fir'ma'tive'ly
af'fix
af'fla'tus
af'flict
af'flic'tion
af'flu'ence
af'flu'ent
af'ford
af'for'es'ta'tion
af'fray
af'fright
af'front
Af'ghan
afi'cio'na'do
afield
aflame
afloat
afoot
afore'men'tioned
afore'said
afore'thought
afraid
afresh
Af'ri'can
Af'ri'kaans
Af'ro-Amer'i'can
af'ter
af'ter'birth
af'ter'burn'er
af'ter'care
af'ter'ef'fect
af'ter'glow
af'ter'life
af'ter'math
af'ter'most

af'ter'noon
af'ter'shave
af'ter'taste
af'ter'thought
af'ter'ward
af'ter'wards
again
against
agape
agar
ag'ate
aga've
aged
age'ing
age'ism
age'ist
age'less
agen'cies
agen'cy
agen'da
agent
ag'glom'er'ate
ag'glom'er'at'ing
ag'glom'er'a'tion
ag'glu'ti'nate
ag'glu'ti'nat'ing
ag'glu'ti'na'tion
ag'glu'ti'na'tive
ag'gran'dize
ag'gran'dized
ag'gran'dize'ment
ag'gran'diz'ing
ag'gra'vate
ag'gra'vat'ed
ag'gra'vat'ing
ag'gra'va'tion
ag'gre'gate
ag'gre'gat'ed
ag'gre'gat'ing
ag'gre'ga'tion
ag'gre'ga'tive
ag'gress
ag'gres'sion
ag'gres'sive
ag'gres'sive'ly
ag'gres'sive'ness
ag'gres'sor
ag'grieve
ag'grieved
ag'griev'ing
aghast
ag'ile
ag'ile'ly

agil'i'ty
ag'i'tate
ag'i'tat'ed
ag'i'tat'ing
ag'i'ta'tion
ag'i'ta'tor
ag'it'prop
agleam
ag'nos'tic
ag'nos'ti'cism
agog
ag'o'nies
ag'o'nize
ag'o'nized
ag'o'niz'ing
ag'o'niz'ing'ly
ag'o'ny
ag'o'ra'pho'bia
ag'o'ra'pho'bic
agrar'i'an
agrar'i'an'ism
agree
agree'abil'i'ty
agree'able
agree'ably
agreed
agree'ing
agree'ment
ag'ri'cul'tur'al
ag'ri'cul'tur'al'ist
ag'ri'cul'ture
ag'ri'cul'tur'ist
ag'ro'nom'ic
ag'ro'nom'i'cal
agron'o'mist
agron'o'my
aground
ague
ahead
ahoy
aide-de-camp
aide-me'moire
ai'grette
ai'le'ron
ail'ing
ail'ment
aimed
aim'less
aim'less'ly
aï'o'li
air'borne
air'brush
air'bus

air-con'di'tion
air-con'di'tioned
air con'di'tion'er
air con'di'tion'ing
air-cooled
air'craft
air'crew
air'drop
air'dropped
air'drop'ping
Aire'dale
air'field
air'foil
air'head
air'i'est
air'i'er
air'i'ly
air'i'ness
air'ing
air'less
air'lift
air'line
air'lin'er
air'mail
air'man
air'play
air'port
air pres'sure
air'ship
air'sick
air'sick'ness
air'space
air'strip
air'tight
air'wave
air'way
air'wor'thi'ness
air'wor'thy
airy
aisle
ajar
akim'bo
akin
al'a'bas'ter
à la carte
alac'ri'ty
à la King
à la mode
alarm
alarm'ing
alarm'ist
alas
Alas'kan

al'ba'core
al'ba'tross
al'be'it
al'bi'nism
al'bi'no
al'bi'nos
al'bum
al'bu'men
al'bu'min
al'bu'min'ous
al'che'mist
al'che'my
al'co'hol
al'co'hol'ic
al'co'hol'ism
al'cove
al'der
al'der'man
alert
alert'ness
alex'ia
al'fal'fa
al'fres'co
al'ga
al'gae
al'ge'bra
al'ge'bra'ic
al'ge'bra'i'cal
al'ge'bra'ist
al'go'rithm
alias
alia'ses
al'i'bi
alien
alien'able
alien'ate
alien'at'ed
alien'at'ing
alien'ation
alien'ism
alien'ist
alight
alight'ed
alight'ing
align
align'ment
alike
al'i'ment
al'i'men'tal
al'i'men'ta'ry
al'i'men'ta'tion
al'i'mo'ny
al'i'phat'ic

al'i'quant
al'i'quot
alit
alive
al'ka'li
al'ka'lies
al'ka'line
al'ka'lin'i'ty
al'ka'lis
al'ka'li'za'tion
al'ka'lize
al'ka'lized
al'ka'liz'ing
al'ka'loid
al'ka'loi'dal
all-around
al'lay
al'layed
al'lay'ing
al'le'ga'tion
al'lege
al'leged
al'leg'ed'ly
al'le'giance
al'leg'ing
al'le'gor'ic
al'le'gor'i'cal
al'le'gor'i'cal'ly
al'le'go'ries
al'le'go'ry
al'le'gret'to
al'le'gret'tos
al'le'gro
al'le'gros
al'le'lu'ia
al'ler'gen
al'ler'gic
al'ler'gies
al'ler'gist
al'ler'gy
al'le'vi'ate
al'le'vi'at'ed
al'le'vi'at'ing
al'le'vi'a'tion
al'le'vi'a'tive
al'le'vi'a'to'ry
al'ley
al'leys
al'ley'way
al'li'ance
al'lied
al'lied
al'lies

al'li'ga'tor
al'lit'er'ate
al'lit'er'at'ed
al'lit'er'at'ing
al'lit'er'a'tion
al'lit'er'a'tive
al'lo'cate
al'lo'cat'ed
al'lo'cat'ing
al'lo'ca'tion
al'lo'path'ic
al'lo'pa'thy
al'lot
al'lot'ment
al'lot'ta'ble
al'lot'ted
al'lot'ting
all-over
al'low
al'low'able
al'low'ably
al'low'ance
al'low'ed'ly
al'low'ing
al'loy
all-round
all-right
all'spice
all-star
all-time
al'lude
al'lud'ed
al'lud'ing
al'lure
al'lured
al'lure'ment
al'lur'ing
al'lur'ing'ly
al'lu'sion
al'lu'sive
al'lu'sive'ly
al'lu'via
al'lu'vi'al
al'lu'vi'um
al'ly
al'ly'ing
al'ma ma'ter
al'ma'nac
al'mighty
al'mond
al'most
alms
al'oe

11

aloft
alo'ha
alone
alone'ness
along
along'side
aloof
aloof'ness
alo'pe'cia
aloud
al'paca
al'pen'stock
al'pha
al'pha'bet
al'pha'bet'ic
al'pha'bet'i'cal
al'pha'bet'i'cal'ly
al'pha'bet'ize
al'pha'bet'iz'ing
al'pha'nu'mer'ic
al'pine
al'ready
al'right
Al'sa'tian
al'so
al'so-ran
al'tar
al'tar'piece
al'ter
al'ter'abil'i'ty
al'ter'able
al'ter'ation
al'ter'ative
al'ter'cate
al'ter'ca'tion
al'tered
al'ter ego
al'ter'ing
al'ter'nate
al'ter'nat'ed
al'ter'nate'ly
al'ter'nat'ing
al'ter'na'tion
al'ter'na'tive
al'ter'na'tive'ly
al'ter'na'tor
al'though
al'tim'e'ter
al'ti'tude
al'to
al'to'geth'er
al'tru'ism
al'tru'ist

al'tru'is'tic
al'um
alu'mi'na
alu'mi'nium
alu'mi'nous
alum'na
alum'nae
alum'ni
alum'nus
al've'o'lar
al'ways
alys'sum
amal'gam
amal'gam'ate
amal'gam'ation
aman'u'en'ses
aman'u'en'sis
am'a'ryl'lis
amass
amass'ment
am'a'teur
am'a'teur'ish
am'a'teur'ism
am'a'to'ry
amaze
amazed
amaze'ment
amaz'ing
amaz'ing'ly
am'bas'sa'dor
am'bas'sa'do'ri'al
am'bas'sa'dress
am'ber
am'ber'gris
am'bi'ance
am'bi'dex'ter'i'ty
am'bi'dex'trous
am'bi'ence
am'bi'ent
am'bi'gu'ities
am'bi'gu'ity
am'big'u'ous
am'big'u'ous'ly
am'bi'tion
am'bi'tious
am'bi'tious'ly
am'bi'tious'ness
am'biv'a'lence
am'biv'a'lent
am'ble
am'bled
am'bling
am'bro'sia

am'bro'sial
am'bu'lance
am'bu'lant
am'bu'late
am'bu'lat'ed
am'bu'lat'ing
am'bu'la'to'ry
am'bus'cade
am'bush
am'bush'ment
ame'lio'ra'ble
ame'lio'rate
ame'lio'rat'ed
ame'lio'rat'ing
ame'lio'ra'tion
ame'lio'ra'tive
ame'lio'ra'tor
amen
ame'na'bil'i'ty
ame'na'ble
ame'na'ble'ness
ame'na'bly
amend
amend'able
amend'ment
ame'ni'ty
amen'or'rhoea
amerce
amerce'ment
amer'cea'ble
Amer'i'can
Amer'i'ca'na
Amer'i'can'ism
Amer'i'can'iza'tion
Amer'i'can'ize
Amer'i'can'ized
Amer'i'can'iz'ing
am'er'i'ci'um
am'e'thyst
ami'a'bil'i'ty
ami'a'ble
ami'a'bly
am'i'ca'bil'i'ty
am'i'ca'ble
am'i'ca'bly
amid
amid-ships
amidst
ami'go
ami'gos
ami'no acid
amiss
am'i'ty

am'me'ter
am'mo'nia
am'mo'ni'ac
am'mo'ni'um
am'mu'ni'tion
am'ne'sia
am'ne'si'ac
am'ne'sic
am'nes'ties
am'nes'ty
am'ni'o'cen'te'ses
am'ni'o'cen'te'sis
am'ni'on
am'ni'ot'ic
amoe'ba
amoe'bae
amoe'bas
amoe'bic
amoe'boid
amok
among
amongst
amor'al
am'o'rous
am'o'rous'ly
am'o'rous'ness
amor'phous
am'or'ti'za'tion
am'or'tize
am'or'tized
am'or'tiz'ing
amount
amour
amour prop're
am'per'age
am'pere
am'per'sand
am'phet'amine
am'phib'i'an
am'phib'i'ous
am'phi'the'atre
am'pho'ra
am'pho'rae
am'ple
am'ple'ness
am'pli'fi'ca'tion
am'pli'fied
am'pli'fi'er
am'pli'fy
am'pli'fy'ing
am'pli'tude
am'ply
am'poule

am'pule
am'pu'tate
am'pu'tat'ed
am'pu'tat'ing
am'pu'ta'tion
am'pu'tee
amuck
am'u'let
amuse
amused
amuse'ment
amus'ing
amus'ing'ly
an'a'bol'ic
anach'ro'nism
anach'ro'nis'tic
anach'ro'nous
an'a'con'da
anaemia
anaemic
an'aes'the'sia
an'aes'the'si'ol'o'gist
an'aes'thet'ic
an'aes'the'tist
an'aes'the'tize
an'aes'the'tiz'ing
an'a'gram
an'a'gram'mat'ic
an'a'gram'mat'i'cal
anal
ana'lep'tic
an'al'ge'sia
an'al'ge'sic
an'a'log
an'a'log'i'cal
anal'o'gies
anal'o'gize
anal'o'gous
an'a'logue
anal'o'gy
anal'y'ses
anal'y'sis
an'a'lyst
an'a'lyt'ic
an'a'ly'sa'tion
an'a'lyse
an'a'lysed
an'a'lys'ing
an'a'paest
an'ar'chic
an'ar'chi'cal
an'ar'chism
an'ar'chist

an'ar'chis'tic
an'ar'chy
anath'e'ma
anath'e'ma'tize
an'a'tom'i'cal
an'a'tom'i'cal'ly
anat'o'mies
anat'o'mist
anat'o'mi'za'tion
anat'o'mize
anat'o'mized
anat'o'mizing
anat'o'my
an'ces'tor
an'ces'tral
an'ces'tress
an'ces'tries
an'ces'try
an'chor
an'chor'age
an'cho'rite
an'chor'man
an'cho'vies
an'chovy
an'cient
an'cient'ness
an'cil'lary
an'dan'te
an'dan'ti'no
and'i'ron
an'dro'gen
an'drog'y'nous
an'drog'y'ny
an'droid
an'ec'do'tal
an'ec'dote
an'ec'dot'i'cal
an'e'mom'e'ter
anem'o'ne
an'er'oid
an'eu'rism
an'eu'rysm
anew
an'gel
an'gel'ic
an'gel'i'ca
an'gel'i'cal'ly
an'ger
an'gi'na
an'gi'nal
an'gi'na pec'to'ris
an'gio'gram
an'gle

angler
An'gli'can
An'gli'can'ism
An'gli'cism
an'gli'ci'za'tion
An'gli'cize
an'gling
An'glo-Irish
An'glo-Catholic
An'glo-ma'nia
An'glo'phile
An'glo'phobe
An'glo'pho'bia
An'glo-Sax'on
an'go'ra
an'gos'tu'ra
an'gri'ly
an'gri'ness
an'gry
angst
ang'strom
ang'strom unit
an'guish
an'guished
an'gu'lar
an'gu'lar'i'ty
an'gu'la'tion
an'hy'dride
an'hy'drous
an'i'line
an'i'mad'ver'sion
an'i'mad'vert
an'i'mal
an'i'mal'ism
an'i'mal'i'ty
an'i'mal'ize
an'i'mate
an'i'mat'ed
an'i'mat'ing
an'i'ma'tion
an'i'ma'tor
an'i'mism
an'i'mis'tic
an'i'mos'ities
an'i'mos'i'ty
an'i'mus
an'ion
an'ise
ani'seed
an'i'sette
ankh
an'kle
an'klet

an'ky'lose
an'ky'lo'ses
an'ky'lo'sis
anna
an'nal
an'nal'ist
an'nal'is'tic
an'nals
an'neal
an'ne'lid
an'nex
an'nex'a'tion
an'ni'hi'late
an'ni'hi'lat'ed
an'ni'hi'lat'ing
an'ni'hi'la'tion
an'ni'hi'la'tor
an'ni'ver'sa'ries
an'ni'ver'sa'ry
an'no Do'mi'ni
an'no'tate
an'no'tat'ed
an'no'tat'ing
an'no'ta'tion
an'no'ta'tor
an'nounce
an'nounced
an'nounce'ment
an'nounc'er
an'nounc'ing
an'noy
an'noy'ance
an'nu'al
an'nu'al'ly
an'nu'i'tant
an'nu'i'ty
an'nul
an'nu'lar
an'nulled
an'nul'ling
an'nul'ment
an'nun'ci'ate
an'nun'ci'at'ing
an'nun'ci'a'tion
an'nun'ci'a'tor
an'ode
an'od'ize
an'o'dyne
anoint
anoint'ment
anom'a'lies
anom'a'lism
anom'a'lis'tic

anom'a'lous
anom'a'ly
anon
an'o'nym'i'ty
anon'y'mous
anony'mously
an'o'rak
an'orex'ia ner'vo'sa
an'orex'ic
an'oth'er
an'ser'ine
an'swer
an'swer'able
ant'ac'id
an'tag'o'nism
an'tag'o'nist
an'tag'o'nis'tic
an'tag'o'nize
an'tag'o'niz'ing
Ant'arc'tic
an'te
ant'eat'er
an'te-bel'lum
an'te'cede
an'te'ced'ed
an'te'ced'ence
an'te'ced'ent
an'te'ced'ing
an'te'cham'ber
an'te'date
an'te'di'lu'vi'an
an'te'lope
an'te me'ri'di'em
an'te'na'tal
an'ten'na
an'ten'nae
an'ten'nas
an'te'pe'nult
an'te'ri'or
an'te'room
an'them
an'ther
ant'hill
an'thol'o'gies
an'thol'o'gist
an'thol'o'gy
an'thra'cite
an'thrax
an'thro'po'cen'tric
an'thro'poid
an'thro'po'log'ic
an'thro'po'log'i'cal
an'thro'pol'o'gist

an'thro'pol'o'gy
an'thro'pom'e'try
an'thro'po'mor'phic
an'ti'bac'te'ri'al
an'ti'bal'lis'tic
an'ti'bi'ot'ic
an'ti'bod'ies
an'ti'body
an'tic
An'ti'christ
an'tic'i'pate
an'tic'i'pat'ed
an'tic'i'pat'ing
an'tic'i'pa'tion
an'tic'i'pa'tive
an'tic'i'pa'to'ry
an'ti'cler'i'cal
an'ti'cli'mac'tic
an'ti'cli'max
an'ti'clock'wise
an'ti'co'ag'u'lant
an'ti'cy'clone
an'ti'dot'al
an'ti'dote
an'ti'freeze
an'ti'gen
an'ti'grav'i'ty
an'ti'he'ro
an'ti'he'roes
an'ti'his'ta'mine
an'ti'log
an'ti'log'a'rithm
an'ti'ma'cas'sar
an'ti'mat'ter
an'ti'mis'sile
an'ti'mo'ny
an'ti'pas'to
an'ti'pa'thet'ic
an'tip'a'thies
an'tip'a'thy
an'ti'per'son'nel
an'ti'per'spi'rant
an'ti'pode
an'tip'o'des
an'tip'o'de'an
an'ti'pope
an'ti'quar'i'an
an'ti'quar'ies
an'ti'quary
an'ti'quate
an'ti'quat'ed
an'ti'quat'ing
an'tique

an'tiqued
an'tique'ness
an'tiqu'ing
an'tiq'ui'ty
an'tir'rhi'num
an'ti-Se'mit'ic
an'ti-Sem'i'tism
an'ti'sep'sis
an'ti'sep'tic
an'ti'sep'ti'cal'ly
an'ti'se'rum
an'ti'slav'ery
an'ti'so'cial
an'ti'stat'ic
an'tith'e'ses
an'tith'e'sis
an'ti'thet'i'cal
an'ti'tox'ic
an'ti'tox'in
an'ti'trust
an'ti'viv'i'sec'tion'ism
an'ti'viv'i'sec'tion'ist
ant'ler
ant'lered
an'to'nym
anus
an'vil
anx'i'e'ties
anx'i'e'ty
anx'ious
anx'ious'ly
anx'ious'ness
any'bod'ies
any'body
any'how
any'more
any'one
any'place
any'thing
any'way
any'where
any'wise
aor'ta
aor'tal
aor'tic
apace
apart
apart'heid
apart'ment
ap'a'thet'ic
ap'a'thet'i'cal'ly
ap'a'thy
ape'ri'ent

aper'i'tif
ap'er'ture
apex
apex'es
apha'sia
aphid
aphi'des
aphis
aph'o'rism
aph'o'rist
aph'o'ris'tic
aph'ro'dis'i'ac
api'ar'i'an
api'ar'ies
api'a'rist
api'ary
ap'i'cal
api'ces
api'cul'tur'al
api'cul'ture
api'cul'tur'ist
apiece
ap'ish
aplen'ty
aplomb
apoc'a'lypse
apoc'a'lyp'tic
apoc'o'pe
apoc'ry'pha
ap'o'deic'tic
ap'o'dic'tic
ap'o'gee
apo'lit'i'cal
apol'o'get'ic
apol'o'get'i'cal
apol'o'get'i'cal'ly
apol'o'get'ics
apol'o'gies
apol'o'gist
apol'o'gize
apol'o'gized
apol'o'giz'ing
apol'o'gy
ap'o'plec'tic
ap'o'plexy
apos'ta'sies
apos'ta'sy
apos'tate
apos'ta'tize
a pos'te'ri'o'ri
apos'tle
apos'to'late
ap'os'tol'ic

ap'os'tol'i'cal
apos'trophe
apoth'e'car'ies
apoth'e'cary
ap'o'thegm
apo'them
apo'the'o'ses
apoth'e'o'sis
apoth'e'o'size
ap'pal
ap'palled
ap'pal'ling
ap'pa'rat'us
ap'pa'rat'us'es
ap'par'el
ap'par'ent
ap'par'ent'ly
ap'pa'ri'tion
ap'peal
ap'peal'able
ap'peal'ing'ly
ap'pear
ap'pear'ance
ap'pease
ap'peased
ap'pease'ment
ap'peas'er
ap'peasing
ap'pel'lant
ap'pel'late
ap'pel'la'tion
ap'pel'la'tive
ap'pend
ap'pen'dage
ap'pen'dant
ap'pen'dec'to'my
ap'pen'di'ces
ap'pen'di'ci'tis
ap'pen'dix
ap'pen'dix'es
ap'per'cep'tion
ap'per'tain
ap'pe'tite
ap'pe'tiz'er
ap'pe'tiz'ing
ap'plaud
ap'plause
ap'ple
ap'ple'cart
ap'ple'jack
ap'ple'sauce
ap'pli'ance
ap'pli'ca'bil'i'ty

ap'pli'ca'ble
ap'pli'cant
ap'pli'ca'tion
ap'pli'ca'tor
ap'pli'ca'to'ry
ap'plied
ap'pli'qué
ap'ply
ap'ply'ing
ap'pog'gia'tu'ra
ap'point
ap'poin'tee
ap'point'ive
ap'point'ment
ap'por'tion
ap'por'tion'ment
ap'pose
ap'posed
ap'pos'ing
ap'po'site
ap'po'si'tion
ap'pos'i'tive
ap'prais'al
ap'praise
ap'praised
ap'prais'er
ap'prais'ing
ap'pre'ci'a'ble
ap'pre'ci'a'bly
ap'pre'ci'ate
ap'pre'ci'at'ing
ap'pre'ci'a'tion
ap'pre'ci'a'tive
ap'pre'hend
ap'pre'hen'si'ble
ap'pre'hen'sion
ap'pre'hen'sive
ap'pren'tice
ap'pren'tice'ship
ap'prise
ap'prised
ap'pris'ing
ap'proach
ap'proach'able
ap'pro'ba'tion
ap'pro'ba'to'ry
ap'pro'pri'ate
ap'pro'pri'at'ed
ap'pro'pri'ate'ly
ap'pro'pri'ate'ness
ap'pro'pri'at'ing
ap'pro'pri'a'tion
ap'prov'al

ap'prove
ap'proved
ap'prov'ing
ap'prov'ing'ly
ap'prox'i'mate
ap'prox'i'mate'ly
ap'prox'i'ma'tion
ap'pur'te'nance
ap'pur'te'nant
après-ski
ap'ri'cot
a pri'o'ri
apron
ap'ro'pos
apse
apt
ap'ti'tude
apt'ly
apt'ness
aqua
aqua'cul'ture
aqua'lung
aqua'ma'rine
aqua'naut
aqua'plane
aquar'ia
aquar'i'um
aquat'ic
aqua vi'tae
aq'ue'duct
aque'ous
aq'ui'line
Ar'ab
ar'a'besque
Ara'bi'an
ar'a'ble
arach'nid
ar'ba'lest
ar'bi'ter
ar'bit'ra'ment
ar'bi'trari'ly
ar'bi'trary
ar'bi'trate
ar'bi'trat'ed
ar'bi'trat'ing
ar'bi'tra'tion
ar'bi'tra'tor
ar'bo're'al
ar'bo're'ta
ar'bo're'tum
ar'bour
ar'bu'tus
arc

ar'cade
ar'cane
arced
ar'chae'o'log'i'cal
ar'chae'o'log'i'cal'ly
ar'chae'ol'o'gist
ar'chae'ol'o'gy
ar'cha'ic
ar'cha'ism
arch'an'gel
arch'bish'op
arch'dea'con
arch'di'oc'e'san
arch'di'o'cese
arch'du'cal
arch'duch'ess
arch'duke
arch'en'e'mies
arch'en'e'my
arch'er
ar'chery
ar'che'typ'al
ar'che'type
arch'fiend
ar'chi'epis'co'pal
ar'chi'pel'a'go
ar'chi'pel'a'gos
ar'chi'tect
ar'chi'tec'ton'ic
ar'chi'tec'tur'al
ar'chi'tec'tur'al'ly
ar'chi'tec'ture
ar'chi'val
ar'chive
ar'chi'vist
arch'ly
arch'way
arc'ing
Arc'tic
ar'cu'ate
ar'dent
ar'dent'ly
ar'dour
ar'du'ous
ar'ea
are'na
Ar'gen'tin'i'an
ar'go'sy
ar'got
ar'gu'able
ar'gu'ably
ar'gue
ar'gued

ar'gu'ing
ar'gu'ment
ar'gu'men'ta'tion
ar'gu'men'ta'tive
aria
Ar'i'an
ar'id
arid'i'ty
Ar'i'es
aright
arise
aris'en
aris'ing
ar'is'toc'ra'cies
ar'is'toc'ra'cy
aris'to'crat
aris'to'crat'ic
arith'me'tic
ar'ith'met'i'cal
ar'ith'met'i'cal'ly
arith'me'ti'cian
arm
ar'ma'da
ar'ma'dil'lo
ar'ma'ment
ar'ma'ture
arm'chair
armed
Ar'me'nian
arm'ful
arm'hole
ar'mies
arm'ing
ar'mi'stice
ar'moire
ar'mour
ar'moured
ar'mour'ies
ar'moury
arm'pit
ar'my
aro'ma
ar'o'mat'ic
ar'o'mat'i'cal
arose
around
arous'al
arouse
aroused
arous'ing
ar'peg'gio
ar'raign
ar'raign'ment

ar'range
ar'ranged
ar'range'ment
ar'rang'ing
ar'rant
ar'ras
ar'ray
ar'ray'al
ar'rears
ar'rear'age
ar'rest
ar'rest'er
ar'ri'val
ar'rive
ar'rived
ar'riv'ing
ar'ri'viste
ar'ro'gance
ar'ro'gant
ar'ro'gant'ly
ar'ro'gate
ar'ro'gat'ed
ar'ro'ga'tion
ar'ron'disse'ment
ar'row
ar'row'head
ar'row'root
ar'royo
ar'se'nal
ar'se'nic
ar'son
ar'son'ist
ar'te'fact
ar'te'ri'al
ar'ter'ies
ar'te'ri'o'scle'ro'sis
ar'tery
ar'te'sian
art'ful
art'ful'ly
ar'thrit'ic
ar'thri'tis
ar'thro'pod
ar'ti'choke
ar'ti'cle
ar'tic'u'lar
ar'tic'u'late
ar'tic'u'lat'ed
ar'tic'u'late'ly
ar'tic'u'late'ness
ar'tic'u'lat'ing
ar'tic'u'la'tion
ar'tic'u'la'tor

ar'ti'fact
ar'ti'fice
ar'ti'fi'cial
ar'ti'fi'ci'al'i'ty
ar'ti'fi'cial'ly
ar'til'lery
ar'til'lery'man
ar'ti'ness
ar'ti'san
art'ist
ar'tiste
ar'tis'tic
ar'tis'ti'cal'ly
art'ist'ry
art'less
art'less'ly
art'less'ness
art'work
arty
as'bes'tos
as'bes'to'sis
as'cend
as'cend'ance
as'cend'an'cy
as'cend'ant
as'cend'ence
as'cend'en'cy
as'cend'ent
as'cen'sion
as'cent
as'cer'tain
as'cer'tain'able
as'cer'tain'ment
as'cet'ic
as'cet'i'cism
as'cot
as'crib'able
as'cribe
as'cribed
as'crib'ing
as'crip'tion
asep'sis
asep'tic
asex'u'al
asex'u'al'i'ty
ash
ashamed
asham'ed'ly
ash'en
ash'es
ash'i'er
ash'i'est
ashore

ash'ram
ash'tray
ashy
Asian
Asi'at'ic
aside
as'i'nine
as'i'nin'i'ty
askance
askew
asleep
aso'cial
as'par'a'gus
as'pect
as'pen
as'per'i'ty
as'perse
as'persed
as'pers'ing
as'per'sion
as'phalt
as'phyx'ia
as'phyx'i'ate
as'phyx'i'at'ed
as'phyx'i'at'ing
as'phyx'i'a'tion
as'pic
as'pi'dis'tra
as'pi'rant
as'pi'rate
as'pi'rat'ed
as'pi'rat'ing
as'pi'ra'tion
as'pi'ra'tor
as'pire
as'pi'rin
as'pir'ing
as'sail
as'sail'able
as'sail'ant
as'sas'sin
as'sas'si'nate
as'sas'si'nat'ed
as'sas'si'nat'ing
as'sas'si'na'tion
as'sault
as'say
as'say'er
as'se'gai
as'sem'blage
as'sem'ble
as'sem'bled
as'sem'bler

as'sem'blies
as'sem'bling
as'sem'bly
as'sem'bly'man
as'sent
as'sen'ta'tion
as'sert
as'ser'tion
as'ser'tive
as'ser'tive'ness
as'sess
as'sess'able
as'sess'ment
as'sess'or
as'set
as'sev'er'ate
as'sev'er'at'ed
as'sev'er'at'ing
as'sev'er'a'tion
as'si'du'i'ty
as'sid'u'ous
as'sid'u'ous'ly
as'sid'u'ous'ness
as'sign
as'sign'able
as'sign'ably
as'sig'na'tion
as'sign'ment
as'sim'i'la'ble
as'sim'i'late
as'sim'i'lat'ed
as'sim'i'lat'ing
as'sim'i'la'tion
as'sist
as'sis'tance
as'sis'tant
as'size
as'so'ci'ate
as'so'ci'at'ed
as'so'ci'at'ing
as'so'ci'a'tion
as'so'ci'a'tive
as'so'nance
as'so'nant
as'sort
as'sor'ted
as'sort'ment
as'suage
as'suaged
as'suage'ment
as'suag'ing
as'sua'sive
as'sume

as'sumed
as'sum'ing
as'sump'tion
as'sur'ance
as'sure
as'sured
as'sur'ed'ly
as'sur'ed'ness
as'sur'ing
as'ter
as'ter'isk
astern
as'ter'oid
asth'ma
asth'mat'ic
asth'mat'i'cal'ly
as'tig'mat'ic
astig'ma'tism
astir
as'ton'ish
as'ton'ish'ing
as'ton'ish'ing'ly
as'ton'ish'ment
as'tound
as'tound'ed
as'tound'ing
astrad'dle
as'tra'khan
as'tral
astray
astride
as'trin'gen'cy
as'trin'gent
as'tro'dome
as'tro'labe
as'trol'o'ger
as'tro'log'ic
as'tro'log'i'cal
as'tro'log'i'cal'ly
as'trol'o'gy
as'tro'naut
as'tro'nau'ti'cal
as'tro'nau'tics
as'tron'o'mer
as'tro'nom'ic
as'tro'nom'i'cal
as'tro'nom'i'cal'ly
as'tron'o'my
as'tro'phys'i'cist
as'tro'phys'ics
as'tu'cious
as'tute
as'tute'ly

as'tute'ness
asun'der
asy'lum
asym'met'ric
asym'met'ri'cal
asym'me'try
at'a'vism
at'a'vis'tic
ate
at'el'ier
athe'ism
athe'ist
athe'is'tic
athe'is'ti'cal
ath'ero'scle'ro'sis
athirst
ath'lete
ath'let'ic
ath'let'i'cal'ly
ath'let'i'cism
ath'let'ics
athwart
at'las
at'las'es
at'mos'phere
at'mos'pher'ic
at'mos'pher'i'cal
at'mos'pher'ics
at'oll
at'om
atom'ic
atom'i'cal
at'om'ism
at'om'ize
at'om'ized
at'om'iz'er
at'om'iz'ing
atonal
ato'nal'i'ty
atone
atoned
atone'ment
aton'ing
atria
atri'um
atro'cious
atro'cious'ly
atroc'i'ties
atroc'i'ty
atro'phic
at'ro'phied
at'ro'phies
at'ro'phy

at'ro'phy'ing
at'tach
at'ta'ché
at'tached
at'tach'ment
at'tack
at'tack'er
at'tain
at'tain'able
at'tain'der
at'tain'ment
at'taint
at'tar
at'tempt
at'tend
at'tend'ance
at'tend'ant
at'ten'tion
at'ten'tive
at'ten'tive'ly
at'ten'u'ate
at'ten'u'at'ed
at'ten'u'at'ing
at'ten'u'a'tion
at'test
at'tes'ta'tion
at'tic
at'tire
at'tired
at'tire'ment
at'tir'ing
at'ti'tude
at'ti'tu'di'nize
at'tract
at'trac'tion
at'trac'tive
at'trac'tive'ly
at'trac'tive'ness
at'tri'but'able
at'tri'bute
at'tri'but'ed
at'tri'but'ing
at'trib'u'tive
at'tri'bu'tion
at'trit'ed
at'tri'tion
at'tune
at'tuned
at'tun'ing
atyp'i'cal
au'ber'gine
au'burn
auc'tion

17

auc'tion'eer
au'da'cious
au'da'cious'ly
au'dac'i'ty
au'di'bil'i'ty
au'di'ble
au'di'bly
au'di'ence
au'dio
au'dio'phile
au'di'ovi'su'al
au'dio'vi'su'als
au'dit
au'di'tion
au'dit'or
au'di'to'ri'um
au'di'to'ry
aught
aug'ment
aug'men'ta'tion
au grat'in
au'gur
au'gured
au'gur'ing
au'gust
au'gust'ly
au na'tu'rel
aunt
au pair
au'ra
au'ral
au'ral'ly
au're'ate
au're'ole
au're'o'my'cin
au re'voir
au'ri'cle
au'ric'u'lar
au'ro'ra
au'ro'ras
au'ro'ra aus'tra'lis
au'ro'ra bo're'al'is
au'ro'rae
aus'pice
aus'pic'es
aus'pi'cious
aus'pi'cious'ly
aus'tere
aus'tere'ly
aus'ter'i'ties
aus'ter'i'ty
Aus'tra'lian
Aus'tri'an

au'then'tic
au'then'ti'cate
au'then'ti'cat'ed
au'then'ti'cat'ing
au'then'ti'ca'tion
au'then'tic'i'ty
au'thor
au'thor'ess
au'thor'i'tar'i'an
au'thor'i'ta'tive
au'thor'i'ta'tive'ly
au'thor'i'ta'tive'ness
au'thor'i'ties
au'thor'i'ty
au'thor'i'za'tion
au'thor'ize
au'thor'ized
au'thor'iz'ing
au'thor'ship
au'tism
au'tis'tic
au'to'bahn
au'to'bi'og'ra'pher
au'to'bio'graph'ic
au'to'bio'graph'i'cal
au'to'bi'og'ra'phies
au'to'bi'og'ra'phy
au'toc'ra'cies
au'toc'ra'cy
au'to'crat
au'to'crat'ic
au'to'crat'i'cal'ly
au-to-da-fé
au'to'graph
au'tom'a'ta
au'to'mate
au'to'mat'ed
au'to'mat'ic
au'to'mat'i'cal
au'to'mat'i'cal'ly
au'to'mat'ing
au'to'ma'tion
au'tom'a'tism
au'tom'a'ton
au'to'mo'bile
au'to'mo'tive
au'to'nom'ic
au'ton'o'mies
au'ton'o'mous
au'ton'o'my
au'to'pi'lot
au'top'sies
au'top'sy

au'tos-da-fe
au'to'sug'ges'tion
au'tumn
au'tum'nal
aux'il'ia'ries
aux'il'ia'ry
avail
avail'abil'i'ty
avail'able
avail'ably
av'a'lanche
av'a'lanch'ing
avant-garde
av'a'rice
av'a'ri'cious
av'a'ri'cious'ly
avast
avenge
avenged
aveng'er
aveng'ing
av'e'nue
aver
av'er'age
av'er'aged
av'er'ag'ing
aver'ment
averred
aver'ring
averse
averse'ly
aver'sion
aver'sive
aver'sively
avert
avert'able
avi'ar'ies
avi'ary
avi'ate
avi'a'tion
avi'a'tor
avi'a'trix
av'id
avid'i'ty
av'id'ly
av'id'ness
av'o'ca'do
av'o'ca'tion
avoid
avoid'able
avoid'ance
av'oir'du'pois
avow

avow'al
avowed
avow'ed'ly
avun'cu'lar
await
awake
awaked
awak'en
awak'en'ing
awak'ing
award
aware
aware'ness
awash
away
awe
awed
aweigh
awe'some
awe-strick'en
awe-struck
aw'ful
aw'ful'ly
aw'ful'ness
awhile
aw'ing
awk'ward
awk'ward'ly
awk'ward'ness
awn'ing
awoke
awry
axe
ax'es
ax'i'al
ax'ile
ax'il'lary
ax'i'om
ax'i'o'mat'ic
ax'i'o'mat'i'cal
ax'i'om'at'i'cal'ly
ax'is
ax'le
aya'tol'lah
azal'ea
az'i'muth
Az'tec
az'ure
bab'bitt
bab'ble
bab'bled
bab'bling
babe

ba'bel
ba'bied
ba'bies
ba'boon
ba'bush'ka
ba'by
ba'by'hood
ba'by'ing
ba'by'ish
ba'by-sat
ba'by-sit
ba'by-sit'ter
ba'by-sit'ting
bac'ca'lau're'ate
bac'ca'rat
bac'cha'nal
bac'cha'na'lia
bac'cha'na'li'an
bach'e'lor
bach'e'lor'hood
ba'cil'li
ba'cil'lus
back
back'ache
back'bite
back'board
back'bone
back'break'ing
back'cloth
back'comb
back'date
back'dat'ed
back'dat'ing
back'door
back'drop
back'er
back'field
back'fire
back'fired
back'fir'ing
back'gam'mon
back'ground
back'hand
back'hand'ed
back'ing
back'lash
back'less
back'list
back'log
back'most
back'pack
back-pedal
back-ped'alled

back-ped'al'ling
back'rest
back'sent
back'side
back'slap'ping
back'slid'den
back'slide
back'slid'er
back'space
back'spaced
back'spac'ing
back'spin
back'stage
back'stairs
back'stitch
back'stop
back'stroke
back'talk
back'track
back-up
back'up
back'ward
back'ward'ness
back'wards
back'wash
back'water
back'woods
back'woods'man
back'yard
ba'con
bac'ter'ia
bac'te'ri'al
bac'te'ri'ci'dal
bac'te'ri'cide
bac'te'ri'o'log'i'cal
bac'te'ri'ol'o'gist
bac'te'ri'ol'o'gy
bac'ter'i'um
bade
badge
bad'ger
bad'i'nage
bad'lands
bad'ly
bad'min'ton
bad'mouth
bad'ness
baf'fle
baf'fled
baf'fling
bag
bag'a'telle
ba'gel

bag'ful
bag'gage
bagged
bag'gi'er
bag'ging
bag'ging
bag'gy
ba'gnio
bag'pipe
ba'guette
bail
bail'able
bail'iff
bail'i'wick
bait
baize
bake
baked
bak'er
bak'er'ies
bak'er'y
bak'ing
bak'sheesh
bal'a'lai'ka
bal'ance
bal'anced
bal'anc'er
bal'anc'ing
bal'co'nies
bal'co'ny
bald
bal'der'dash
bald'headed
bald'ing
bald'ly
bald'ness
bale
baled
ba'leen
bale'ful
bale'ful'ly
bal'ing
balk
balk'i'est
balky
bal'lad
bal'last
ball'boy
ball'cock
bal'le'ri'na
bal'let
bal'let'ic
bal'let'o'mane

bal'lis'tic
bal'lis'ti'cian
bal'lis'tics
bal'loon
bal'lot
bal'lot'ed
bal'lot'ing
ball'park
ball'point
ball'room
bal'ly'hoo
balm
balm'i'er
balmy
bal'sa
bal'sam
bal'us'ter
bal'us'trade
bam'bi'no
bam'boo
bam'boo'zle
bam'boo'zled
bam'boo'zling
ban
ba'nal
ba'nal'i'ty
ba'nana
band'age
band'aged
band'ag'ing
ban'dana
ban'dan'na
band'box
ban'deaux
ban'de'role
ban'di'coot
ban'died
ban'dit
ban'dit'ry
band'lead'er
band'mas'ter
ban'do'leer
ban'do'lier
bands'man
band'stand
band'wag'on
ban'dy
ban'dy'ing
ban'dy-legged
bane
bane'ful
ban'gle
ban'ish

ban'ish'ment
ban'is'ter
ban'jo
bank'book
bank'er
bank'ing
bank'roll
bank'rupt
bank'rupt'cies
bank'rupt'cy
banned
ban'ner
ban'ning
ban'nis'ter
banns
ban'quet
ban'quet'ed
banq'uet'ing
ban'quette
ban'shee
ban'tam
ban'tam'weight
ban'ter
ban'ter'ing'ly
ban'yan
ban'zai
bao'bab
bap'tism
bap'tis'mal
Bap'tist
bap'tis'tery
bap'tise
bap'tised
bap'tis'ing
bar
bar'a'thea
bar'bar'i'an
bar'bar'ic
bar'ba'rism
bar'bar'i'ties
bar'bar'i'ty
bar'ba'rous
bar'be'cue
bar'be'cued
bar'be'cu'ing
barbed
bar'bel
bar'bell
bar'ber
bar'ber'shop
bar'bi'can
bar'bi'tal
bar'bi'tu'rate

bar'ca'role
bare
bare'back
bare'faced
bare'foot
bare'head'ed
bare'ly
bare'ness
bar'gain
barge
barged
barg'ing
barite
bar'i'tone
bar'i'um
bar'keeper
bar'ley
bar'maid
bar'man
bar mitz'vah
bar'na'cle
barn'storm
barn'yard
bar'o'graph
ba'rom'et'er
baro'met'ric
baro'met'ri'cal'ly
bar'on
bar'on'age
bar'on'ess
bar'on'et
bar'on'et'cies
bar'on'et'cy
ba'ro'ni'al
bar'on'ies
bar'ony
ba'roque
bar'rack
bar'ra'cou'ta
bar'ra'cu'da
bar'rage
barred
bar'rel
bar'relled
bar'rel'ling
bar'rel-or'gan
bar'ren
bar'ren'ly
bar'ren'ness
bar'rette
bar'ri'cade
bar'ri'cad'ed
bar'ri'cad'ing

bar'ri'er
bar'ring
bar'ris'ter
bar'room
bar'row
bar'ten'der
bar'ter
bar'ter'er
bary'on
ba'ry'ta
ba'ry'tes
ba'sal
bas'al'ly
ba'salt
ba'sal'tic
base
base'ball
base'born
based
base'less
base'line
base'man
base'ment
base'ness
ba'ses
bash'ful
bash'ful'ly
bash'ful'ness
ba'sic
ba'si'cal'ly
ba'sil
ba'sil'i'ca
bas'i'lisk
ba'sin
bas'ing
ba'sis
bask
bas'ket
bas'ket'ball
bas'ket'ful
bas'ket'ry
bas'ket'work
bas-re'lief
bass
bas'set hound
bas'si'net
bas'so
bas'soon
bas'soon'ist
bas'sos
bas'tard
bas'tard'ize
bas'tard'ly

baste
bast'ed
bast'ing
bat
batch
bate
bat'ed
bath
bathe
bathed
bath'er
ba'thet'ic
bath'ing
ba'thos
bath'robe
bath'room
bath'tub
bathy'scaph
bathy'sphere
ba'tik
bat'ing
ba'tiste
bat'man
bat'on
bat'tal'ion
bat'ted
bat'ten
bat'ter
bat'ter
bat'tery
bat'ti'er
bat'ti'est
bat'ting
bat'tle
bat'tle-axe
bat'tled
bat'tle'dress
bat'tle'field
bat'tle'ment
bat'tle'ship
bat'tling
bat'ty
bau'ble
baud
baux'ite
bawd
bawd'i'er
bawd'i'est
bawd'i'ly
bawdy
bawl
bay'ber'ries
bay'ber'ry

bay'o'net
bay'o'net'ing
bay'o'net'ed
bay'ou
ba'zaar
ba'zoo'ka
bdel'li'um
beach
beach'comb'er
beach'head
bea'con
bead'ed
bead'i'er
bead'i'est
bead'ing
bead'like
bead'y
bea'gle
beak'er
beamed
bean'bag
bear
bear'able
bear'ably
bear'bait'ing
beard
beard'ed
beard'less
bear'er
bear'ing
bear'ish
bear'ish'ness
bear'skin
beast
beast'li'ness
beast'ly
beat
beat'en
beat'er
be'atif'ic
be'at'i'fi'ca'tion
be'at'i'fied
be'at'i'fy
be'at'i'fy'ing
beat'ing
be'at'i'tude
beat'nik
beat up
beat-up
beau
beau geste
beau monde
beaus

beau'te'ous
beau'ti'cian
beau'ties
beau'ti'fi'ca'tion
beau'ti'fied
beau'ti'ful
beau'ti'ful'ly
beau'ti'fy
beauty
beaux
beaux-arts
bea'ver
be'bop
be'calm
be'came
be'cause
beck'on
be'cloud
be'come
be'com'ing
bed
be'daz'zle
be'daz'zled
be'daz'zle'ment
be'daz'zling
bed'bug
bed'cham'ber
bed'clothes
bed'ded
bed'ding
be'decked
be-dev'il
be'dev'illed
be'dev'il'ling
be'dev'il'ment
bed'fel'low
be'dim
be'dimmed
be'dim'ming
bed'lam
Bed'ou'in
bed'pan
bed'post
be'drag'gle
be'drag'gling
bed'rid'den
bed'rock
bed'roll
bed'room
bed'side
bed'sore
bed'spread
bed'stead

bed'time
beech
beech'nut
bedew
beef
beef'cake
beef'eat'er
beef'i'er
beef'i'est
beef'steak
beefy
bee'hive
bee'keep'er
bee'keep'ing
bee'line
beep
beer
bees'wax
beet
bee'tle
beeves
be'fall
be'fall'en
be'fall'ing
be'fell
be'fit
be'fit'ted
be'fit'ting
be'fog
be'fogged
be'fog'ging
be'fore
be'fore'hand
be'friend
be'fud'dle
be'fud'dled
be'fud'dling
be'gan
be'gat
be'get
be'get'ting
beg'gar
beg'gar'ly
begged
beg'ging
be'gin
be'gin'ner
be'gin'ning
be'gone
be'go'nia
be'got
be'got'ten
be'got'ten

be'grime
be'grudge
be'grudged
be'grudg'ing
be'guile
be'guiled
be'guil'ing
be'guine
be'gun
be'half
be'have
be'haved
be'hav'ing
be'hav'iour
be'hav'iour'al
be'hav'iour'ism
be'hav'iour'ist
be'hav'iour'is'tic
be'head
be'head'ing
be'held
be'he'moth
be'hest
be'hind
be'hind'hand
be'hold
be'hold'en
be'hold'er
be'hold'ing
be'hoove
be'hove
be'hoved
be'hov'ing
beige
be'ing
be'la'bour
be'lat'ed
be'lat'ed'ly
be'lay
be'layed
be'lay'ing
belch
be'lea'guer
bel'fries
bel'fry
Bel'gian
be'lie
be'lied
be'lief
be'liev'able
be'lieve
be'lieved
be'liev'er

be'liev'ing
be'lit'tle
be'lit'tled
be'lit'tling
bel'la'don'na
belle
belles let'tres
bell'hop
bell'li'cose
bell'li'cos'i'ty
bel'lied
bel'lies
bel'lig'er'ence
bel'lig'er'en'cy
bel'lig'er'ent
bel'lig'er'ent'ly
bel'low
bel'lows
bell'tow'er
bel'ly
bel'ly'ache
bel'ly'ach'ing
bel'ly'ful
bel'ly'ing
be'long
be'long'ings
be'loved
be'low
belt'ed
belt'way
be'ly'ing
be'mire
be'mired
be'mir'ing
be'moan
be'muse
be'mused
be'mus'ing
bench'mark
bend
bend'ing
be'neath
ben'e'dict
bene'dic'tion
bene'dic'to'ry
bene'fac'tion
bene'fac'tor
bene'fac'tress
ben'e'fice
ben'e'ficed
be'nef'i'cence
be'nef'i'cent
ben'e'fi'cial

ben'e'fi'cial'ly
ben'e'fi'ci'a'ries
ben'e'fi'ci'a'ry
ben'e'fic'ing
ben'e'fit
ben'e'fit'ed
ben'e'fit'ing
be'nev'o'lence
be'nev'o'lent
be'nev'o'lent'ly
Ben'gali
be'night'ed
be'nign
be'nig'nan'cy
be'nig'nant
be'nig'ni'ty
be'nign'ly
bent
be'numb
ben'zene
ben'zine
ben'zol
be'queath
be'quest
be'rate
be'rat'ed
be'rat'ing
be'reave
be'reaved
be'reave'ment
be'reav'ing
be'reft
be'ret
ber'ga'mot
ber'i'beri
ber'ke'li'um
ber'ret'ta
ber'ries
ber'ry
ber'serk
berth
ber'yl
be'ryl'li'um
be'seech
be'seeched
be'seech'ing
be'seech'ing'ly
be'set
be'set'ting
be'side
be'sides
be'siege
be'sieged

be'sieg'er
be'sieg'ing
be'smear
be'smirch
be'sot'ted
be'sought
be'speak
be'speak'ing
be'spoke
be'spok'en
best
bes'tial
bes'ti'al'i'ty
bes'tial'ly
be'stir
be'stirred
be'stir'ring
best-look'ing
be'stow
be'stow'al
be'strid'den
be'stride
be'strid'ing
be'strode
best-sell'er
bet
be'ta
be'take
be'tak'en
be'tak'ing
be'ta'tron
be'tel
bête noir
beth'el
be'tide
be'tid'ed
be'tid'ing
be'to'ken
be'took
be'tray
be'tray'al
be'tray'er
be'troth
be'troth'al
be'trothed
bet'ted
bet'ter
bet'ter-look'ing
bet'ter'ment
bet'ting
bet'tor
be'tween
be'twixt

bev'el
bev'elled
bev'el'ling
bev'er'age
bev'ies
bevy
be'wail
be'ware
be'wil'der
be'wil'der'ing'ly
be'wil'der'ment
be'witch
be'witch'ing
be'witch'ment
be'yond
be'zique
bhang
bi'an'nu'al
bi'an'nual'ly
bi'as
bi'ased
bi'as'ing
bi'ath'lon
bi'ax'i'al
bi'be'lot
Bi'ble
Bib'li'cal
bib'li'cal'ly
bib'li'og'ra'pher
bib'lio'graph'ic
bib'li'og'ra'phies
bib'li'og'ra'phy
bib'lio'ma'nia
bib'lio'ma'ni'ac
bib'li'o'phile
bib'u'lous
bi'cam'er'al
bi'car'bon'ate
bi'cen'te'na'ries
bi'cen'te'n'ary
bi'cen'ten'ni'al
bi'ceps
bi'chlo'ride
bick'er
bi'cus'pid
bi'cy'cle
bi'cy'cled
bi'cy'cler
bi'cy'cling
bi'cy'clist
bid
bid'da'ble
bid'den

bid'der
bid'ding
bide
bid'ed
bi'det
bid'ing
bi'en'ni'al
bi'en'ni'al'ly
bi'en'ni'um
bier
bi'fo'cal
bi'fo'cals
bi'fur'cate
bi'fur'cat'ed
bi'fur'cat'ing
bi'fur'ca'tion
big
big'a'mist
big'a'mous
big'a'mous'ly
big'a'my
big'ger
big'gest
big'gish
big-heart'ed
bight
big'ot
big'ot'ed
big'ot'ry
big'wig
bi'jou
bi'joux
bike
bik'er
bi'ki'ni
bi'la'bi'al
bi'lat'er'al
bi'lat'er'al'ly
bil'ber'ries
bil'ber'ry
bile
bilge
bil'har'zia
bi'lin'gual
bil'ious
bil'ious'ness
bill'board
billed
bil'let
bil'let-doux
bil'let'ed
bil'let'ing
bil'lets-doux

bil'liards
bill'ing
bil'lion
bil'lion'aire
bil'lionth
bil'low
bil'lowed
bil'lowy
bil'ly goat
bim'bo
bi'met'al'lism
bi'month'ly
bi'na'ry
bind
bind'er
bind'er'ies
bind'ery
bind'ing
bind'weed
binge
bin'go
bin'na'cle
bi'noc'u'lar
bi'no'mi'al
bi'o'chem'i'cal
bi'o'chem'ist
bi'o'chem'is'try
bio'de'grad'able
bi'o'ecol'o'gy
bi'o'en'gi'neer'ing
bi'o'gen'e'sis
bi'og'ra'pher
bio'graph'ic
bio'graph'i'cal
bio'graph'i'cal'ly
bi'og'ra'phies
bi'og'ra'phy
bi'o'log'i'cal
bio'log'i'cal'ly
bi'ol'o'gist
bi'ol'o'gy
bi'o'met'rics
bi'o'me'try
bi'on'ic
bi'on'ics
bi'o'nom'ics
bio'phys'ics
bi'op'sies
bi'op'sy
bio'rhythm
bio'syn'the'sis
bi'o'tin
bi'par'ti'san

bi'par'tite
bi'ped
bi'plane
bi'po'lar
bi'ra'cial
birch
bird-bath
bird-brained
bird'cage
birdie
bird'lime
bird'seed
bird's-eye
bi'ret'ta
birth'day
birth'mark
birth'place
birth-rate
birth'right
birth'stone
bis'cuit
bi'sect
bi'sec'tion
bi'sec'tor
bi'sex'u'al
bi'sex'u'al'i'ty
bish'op
bish'op'ric
bis'muth
bi'son
bisque
bis'tro
bit
bitch
bitch'i'er
bitch'i'est
bitch'i'ly
bitch'i'ness
bitchy
bite
bit'ing
bit'ten
bit'ter
bit'ter'ly
bit'tern
bit'ter'ness
bit'ter'sweet
bit'ti'er
bit'ti'est
bit'ty
bi'tu'men
bi'tu'mi'nous
bi'va'lence

bi'va'lent
bi'valve
bi'val'vu'lar
biv'ouac
biv'ouacked
biv'ouack'ing
bi'week'lies
bi'week'ly
bi'zarre
bi'zarre'ness
blab
blabbed
blab'ber
blab'bing
black
black'ball
black'ber'ries
black'berry
black'bird
black'board
black'en
black-eyed
black'guard
black'head
black'jack
black'list
black'ly
black'mail
black'mail'er
black'ness
black'out
black'smith
black'thorn
black'top
blad'der
blade
blad'ed
blame'able
blame
blamed
blame'less
blame'wor'thy
blam'ing
blanch
blanc'mange
bland
blan'dish
blan'dish'ment
bland'ly
bland'ness
blank
blan'ket
blan'ket'ed

blan'ket'ing
blank'ly
blank'ness
blare
blared
blar'ing
blar'ney
bla'sé
blas'pheme
blas'phemed
blas'phem'er
blas'phe'mies
blas'phem'ing
blas'phem'ous
blas'phe'my
blast
blast'ed
blast'off
bla'tan'cy'
bla'tant
bla'tant'ly
blaze
blazed
blaz'er
blaz'ing
bleach
bleach'er
bleak
bleak'ly
bleak'ness
blear'i'ness
bleary
bleat
bled
bleed
bleed'ing
bleep
blem'ish
blend
blend'er
bless
bless'ed
bless'ed
bles'sing
blest
blew
blight
blind
blind'er
blind'fold
blind'ing
blind'ly
blind'ness

blink
blink'er
bliss
bliss'ful
bliss'ful'ly
blis'ter
blithe
blithe'ly
blitz
blitz'krieg
bliz'zard
bloat'ed
blob
bloc
block
block'ade
block'ad'ed
block'ad'ing
block'age
block'bus'ter
block'head
block'house
blond
blonde
blond'ness
blood
blood'bath
blood'curd'ling
blood'hound
blood'ied
blood'i'er
blood'i'est
blood'i'ly
blood'less
blood'let'ting
blood'shed
blood'shot
blood'stained
blood'stream
blood'suck'er
blood'thirst'i'ness
blood'thirsty
bloody
bloody'ing
bloom
bloom'ers
bloom'ing
bloop'er
blos'som
blot
blotch
blotch'i'er
blotch'i'est

blotchy
blot'ted
blot'ter
blot'ting
blouse
blou'son
blow
blow-dried
blow-dries
blow-dry
blow'dry'er
blow'er
blow'flies
blow'fly
blow'i'er
blow'i'est
blow'ing
blown
blow'torch
blowy
blub'ber
blud'geon
blue
blue'bell
blue'ber'ries
blue'berry
blue'bird
blue-blood'ed
blue'bot'tle
blue-col'lar
blue'grass
blue'ness
blue-nose
blue'print
blu'est
blue'stock'ing
blu'ing
blu'ish
blun'der
blun'der'buss
blun'der'ing
blunt'ly
blunt'ness
blur
blurb
blurred
blur'ring
blur'ry
blurt
blush
blushed
blush'er
blush'ing

blus'ter
blus'ter'ing'ly
blus'ter'ous
blus'tery
boa
boar
board
board'er
board'room
board'walk
boast
boast'ful
boast'ful'ly
boast'ful'ness
boast'ing'ly
boat
boat'er
boat'house
boat'ing
boat'man
boat'swain
bob
bobbed
bob'bin
bob'bing
bob'ble
bob'bled
bob'bling
bob'by pin
bob'by socks
bob'cat
bob'o'link
bob'sled
bob'white
bode
bod'ed
bo'de'ga
bod'ice
bod'ies
bod'i'less
bodi'ly
bod'ing
bod'kin
body
body'build'er
body'build'ing
body'guard
body'work
Boer
bog
bo'gey
bog'gle
bog'gled

bog'gling
bog'gy
bo'gus
bogy
bo'gey'man
bo'he'mi'an
boil'er
boil'er'suit
boil'ing point
bois'ter'ous
bois'ter'ous'ness
bo'la
bo'las
bold
bold'face
bold'ly
bold'ness
bo'le'ro
bol'lard
boll wee'vil
boll'worm
bo'lo
bo'lo'gna
bo'lo'ney
bol'ster
bol'ster'er
bolt
bolt'ed
bomb
bom'bard
bom'bar'dier
bom'bard'ment
bom'bast
bom'bas'tic
bom'bas'ti'cal'ly
bom'ba'zine
bombe
bomb'er
bomb'proof
bomb'shell
bomb'sight
bo'na fide
bo'nan'za
bon'bon
bond'age
bond'ed
bond'holder
bond'sman
bone
bone chi'na
boned
bone'head
bon'fire

bon'go
bon'ho'mie
bon'i'er
bon'ing
bon mot
bon'net
bon'ny
bon'sai
bo'nus
bo'nus'es
bon voy'age
bony
boo'by
boo'dle
boo'gie-woo'gie
book'bind'er
book'bind'ing
book'case
book'end
book'ie
book'ish
book'keep'er
book'keep'ing
book'let
book-mak'er
book'mark
book'mo'bile
book'plate
book'sell'er
book'shelf
book'worm
boor
boor'ish
boost
boost'er
boot'black
boo'tee
booth
boo'tie
boot'leg
boot'legged
boot'leg'ger
boot'leg'ging
boo'ty
booze
booz'er
booz'i'er
booz'i'est
boozy
bo'rax
bor'der
bor'dered
bor'der'land

bor'der'line
bore
bored
bore'dom
bor'er
bo'ric
bor'ing
born
borne
bor'ough
bor'row
bor'row'er
borsch
borscht
bor'zoi
bos'om
boss'i'est
boss'i'ness
bossy
bo'sun
bo'tan'ic
bo'tan'i'cal
bot'a'nist
bot'a'nize
bot'a'ny
botch
botch'i'est
botchy
both
both'er
both'er'some
bo tree
bot'tle
bot'tled
bot'tle'ful
bot'tle'neck
bot'tling
bot'tom
bot'tom'less
bot'tom'most
bot'u'lism
bou'clé
bou'doir
bouf'fant
bou'gain'vil'laea
bough
bought
bought
bouil'lon
boul'der
bou'le'vard
bounce
bounced

bounc'er
bounc'ing
bound
bound'aries
bound'ary
bound'less
boun'te'ous
boun'ties
boun'ti'ful
boun'ty
bou'quet
bou'quet gar'ni
bou'quets gar'nis
bour'bon
bour'geois
bour'geoi'sie
bourse
bout
bou'tique
bou'ton'niere
bo'vine
bowd'ler'ize
bowd'ler'ized
bowd'ler'iz'ing
bow'el
bow'er
bow'er'ies
bow'ery
bow'ie
bow'ing
bow'knot
bowl
bow'leg
bow'legged
bowl'er
bowl'ful
bow'line
bowl'ing
bow'string
box'car
box'er
box'ful
box'ing
boy
boy'cott
boy'friend
boy'hood
boy'ish
boy'ish'ly
boy'sen'ber'ries
boy'sen'berry
bra
brace

braced
brace'let
brac'er
brac'es
brac'ing
brack'en
brack'et
brack'et'ed
brack'et'ing
brack'ish
brad
brad'ded
brad'ding
bra'd'ing
brag
brag'ga'do'cio
brag'gart
bragged
brag'ging
Brah'min
braid
brain
brain'child
brain'i'er
brain'i'est
brain'less
brain'pow'er
brain'storm
brain'storm'ing
brain'wash
brain'wash'ing
brainy
braise
braised
brais'ing
brake
brak'ing
bram'ble
bram'bly
bran
branch
branched
brand
brand'er
bran'died
bran'dies
bran'dish
brand-new
bran'dy
brass
brass'i'er
bras'siere
brassy

brat
brat'tish
brat'ty
brat'wurst
bra'va'do
brave
braved
brave'ly
brave'ness
brav'er'ies
brav'ery
brav'ing
bra'vo
bra'vu'ra
brawl
brawl'er
brawn
brawn'i'er
brawn'i'ness
brawny
braze
bra'zen
bra'zier
Bra'zil'ian
breach
bread
bread'bas'ket
bread'board
bread'ed
bread'fruit
bread'line
breadth
bread'win'ner
break
break'able
break'age
break'away
break'down
break'er
break-even
break'fast
break'ing
break'neck
break'out
break'through
break-up
break'wa'ter
bream
breast
breast'bone
breast-fed
breast-feed
breast-feed'ing

breast'plate
breast'stroke
breath
breathe
breathed
breath'er
breath'ing
breath'less
breath'less'ness
breath'tak'ing
breathy
bred
breech
breech'es
breech'load'er
breed
breed'er
breed'ing
breed'ing
breeze
breez'i'ness
breezy
breth'ren
Bre'ton
breve
bre'vet
bre'vet'ted
bre'vet'ting
bre'vi'a'ries
bre'vi'a'ry
brev'i'ty
brew
brew'er
brew'er'ies
brew'ery
bri'ar
brib'able
bribe
bribed
brib'er'ies
brib'ery
brib'ing
bric-a-brac
brick
brick'lay'er
brick'work
brick'yard
brid'al
bride
bride'groom
brides'maid
bridge
bridge'head

bridge'work
bri'dle
bri'dled
bri'dling
brief
brief'case
brief'ing
brief'ly
brief'ness
bri'er
brig
bri'gade
brig'a'dier
brig'and
brig'an'tine
bright
bright'en
bright'ly
bright'ness
bril'liance
bril'lian'cy
bril'liant
bril'lian'tine
bril'liant'ly
brim
brim'ful
brimmed
brim'ming
brim'stone
brine
bring
bring'ing
brink
brink'man'ship
briny
brioche
bri'quet
bri'quette
brisk
bris'ket
brisk'ly
brisk'ness
bris'tle
bris'tled
bris'tli'er
bris'tli'est
bris'tling
bris'tly
britch'es
Brit'ish
Brit'on
brit'tle
broach

broached	broth'er-in-law	buck'et	bulk'i'er
broach'ing	broth'er'li'ness	buck'et'ful	bulk'i'er
broad'cast	broth'er'ly	buck'le	bulk'i'est
broad'cast'ed	brougham	buck'ram	bulk'i'ness
broad'cast'er	brought	buck'shot	bulky
broad'cast'ing	brou'ha'ha	buck'skin	bull
broad'cloth	brow	buck'tooth	bull'dog
broad'en	brow'beat	buck'wheat	bull'doze
broad'ly	brow'beat'en	bu'col'ic	bull'dozed
broad'mind'ed	brown	bud	bull'doz'er
broad'ness	brown'ie	bud'ded	bull'doz'ing
broad'side	browse	Bud'dha	bul'let
broad'sword	browsed	Bud'dhism	bul'le'tin
bro'cade	brows'ing	Bud'dhist	bul'let-proof
bro'cad'ed	bru'cel'lo'sis	bud'dies	bull'fight
bro'cad'ing	bru'in	bud'ding	bull'fight'er
broc'co'li	bruise	bud'dy	bull'finch
bro'chette	bruised	budge	bull'frog
bro'chure	bruis'er	bud'ger'i'gar	bull'head'ed
broil	bruis'ing	budg'et	bul'lied
broil'er	bruit	bud'get'ary	bul'lies
broke	brunch	buf'fa'lo	bul'lion
bro'ken	bru'nette	buf'fa'loed	bull'ock
bro'ken-down	brush	buf'fa'loes	bull'ring
bro'ken-heart'ed	brush-off	buff'er	bull's-eye
bro'ker	brush'wood	buf'fet	bull'terrier
bro'ker'age	brush'work	buf'foon	bul'ly
bro'mide	brusque	buf'foon'ery	bul'ly'ing
bron'chi	brusque'ly	bug	bul'rush
bron'chi'al	brusque'ness	bug'bear	bul'wark
bron'chit'ic	brut	bugged	bum
bron'chi'tis	bru'tal	bug'ger	bum'ble-bee
bron'cho'scope	bru'tal'i'ties	bug'gery	bummed
bronchus	bru'tal'i'ty	bug'gies	bum'ming
bron'co	bru'tal'i'za'tion	bug'ging	bump'er
bron'to'sau'rus	bru'tal'ize	bug'gy	bump'i'er
bronze	bru'tal'ized	bu'gle	bump'i'est
bronzed	bru'tal'iz'ing	bu'gler	bump'i'ness
bronz'ing	bru'tal'ly	bu'gling	bump'kin
brooch	brute	build	bump'tious
brood	brut'ish	build'er	bumpy
brood'i'er	brut'ish'ness	built	bunch
brood'i'est	bub'ble	bulb	bunchy
brood'ing	bub'bled	bul'bous	bun'co
broody	bub'bli'er	Bul'gar'i'an	bun'combe
brook	bub'bli'est	bulge	bun'dle
broom	bub'bling	bulged	bun'dled
broom'stick	bub'bly	bul'gi'er	bun'dling
broque	bu'bon'ic	bul'gi'est	bun'ga'low
broth	buc'ca'neer	bulg'ing	bun'gle
broth'el	buck	bul'gur	bun'gled
broth'er	buck'a'roo	bulgy	bun'gler
broth'er'hood	buck'board	bulk'head	bun'gling

bun'ion
bun'ker
bun'kum
bun'nies
bun'ny
bun'ting
buoy
buoy'an'cy
buoy'ant
bur'ble
bur'bled
bur'bling
bur'den
bur'den'some
bu'reau
bu'reauc'ra'cies
bu'reauc'ra'cy
bu'reau'crat
bu'reau'crat'ic
bu'reaus
bu'reaux
bur'geon
bur'gess
bur'gher
bur'glar
bur'glar'ies
bur'glar'ize
bur'glar'ized
bur'glar'iz'ing
bur'glary
bur'gle
bur'gled
bur'gling
bur'go'mas'ter
buri'al
bur'ied
bu'rin
bur'lap
bur'lesque
bur'lesqued
bur'lesqu'ing
bur'li'er
bur'li'est
bur'li'ness
bur'ly
Bur'mese
burn
burned
burn'er
burn'ing
bur'nish
bur'noose
bur'nous

burnt
burp
burr
burred
bur'ring
bur'ro
bur'row
bur'sa
bur'sar
bur'sa'ry
bur'si'tis
burst
burst'ing
bury
bury'ing
bus
bus'bies
bus'boy
bus'by
bus'es
bush
bush-ba'by
bush'el
bush'i'er
bush'i'est
bush'ing
bush'man
bush'mas'ter
bush'men
bush'whack
bushy
bus'ied
busi'er
busi'ly
busi'ness
busi'ness'like
busi'ness'man
bus'tard
bus'tle
bus'tled
bus'tling
busy
busy'bod'ies
busy'body
busy'ing
bu'tane
butch
butch'er
butch'ery
but'ler
butt
butte
but'ter

but'ter'cup
but'ter'fin'gered
but'ter'fin'gers
but'ter'flies
but'ter'fly
but'ter'milk
but'ter'scotch
but'ter'wort
but'tery
but'tock
but'ton
but'ton'hole
but'ton'hol'ing
but'tress
bu'tyl
bux'om
buy
buy'er
buy'ing
buzz
buz'zard
buzz'er
buzz'word
bye'law
by'gone
by'law
by-line
by'pass
bypath
by-prod'uct
by'stand'er
byte
by'way
by'word
ca'bal
ca'balled
ca'bal'le'ro
ca'bal'ling
ca'bana
cab'a'ret
cab'bage
cab'bie
cab'by
cab'in
cab'i'net
cable
ca'bled
ca'ble'gram
ca'bling
ca'boose
cab'ri'o'let
ca'cao
cache

cached
ca'chet
cach'ing
ca'chou
cack'le
cack'led
cack'ling
ca'coph'o'nous
ca'coph'o'ny
cac'ti
ca'dav'er'ous
cad'die
cad'died
cad'dies
cad'dish
cad'dy
cad'dy'ing
ca'dence
ca'den'za
ca'det
cadge
cadged
cadg'ing
cad'mi'um
cad're
ca'du'ceus
Cae'sar'e'an
cae'su'ra
cae'su'rae
ca'fé
ca'fé au lait
caf'e'te'ria
caf'feine
caf'tan
cage
caged
ca'gey
ca'gi'er
ca'gi'est
ca'gi'ly
cag'ing
ca'gy
cai'man
cais'son
cai'tiff
ca'jole
ca'joled
ca'jol'ing
Ca'jun
cake
caked
cak'ing
cal'a'bash

cal'a'boose
cal'a'mine
ca'lam'i'ties
ca'lam'i'tous
ca'lam'i'ty
cal'ci'fi'ca'tion
cal'ci'fied
cal'ci'fy
cal'ci'fy'ing
cal'ci'mine
cal'ci'um
cal'cu'la'bil'i'ty
cal'cu'la'ble
cal'cu'late
cal'cu'la'ted
cal'cu'lat'ing
cal'cu'la'tion
cal'cu'la'tor
cal'cu'li
cal'cu'lus
cal'dron
cal'en'dar
cal'ends
calf
cal'i'bre
cal'i'brate
cal'i'brat'ed
cal'i'brat'ing
cal'i'bra'tion
cal'i'co
cal'i'coes
cal'i'for'ni'um
ca'liph
cal'lig'ra'pher
cal'lig'ra'phy
call'ing
cal'li'ope
cal'li'per
cal'lis'then'ics
cal'lous
cal'lused
cal'lous'ly
cal'lous'ness
cal'low
cal'lus
calm
calm'ly
calm'ness
ca'lo'ric
cal'o'rie
cal'o'ries
cal'o'rif'ic
ca'lum'ni'ate

ca'lum'ni'at'ed
ca'lum'ni'at'ing
ca'lum'ni'a'tion
cal'um'nies
cal'um'ny
calve
calved
calves
calv'ing
ca'ly'ces
ca'lyp'so
ca'lyx
ca'ma'ra'de'rie
cam'ber
cam'bric
Cam'bo'di'an
came
cam'el
ca'mel'lia
ca'mel'o'pard
cam'eo
cam'era
cam'era ob'scu'ra
cam'i'sole
cam'o'mile
cam'ou'flage
cam'ou'flaged
cam'ou'flag'ing
cam'paign
cam'paign'er
cam'pa'ni'le
cam'pa'ni'li
camp'er
camp'fire
cam'phor
cam'phor'a'ted
cam'pus
cam'pus'es
cam'shaft
can
Ca'na'di'an
ca'nal
can'a'pé
ca'nard
ca'nar'ies
ca'nary
ca'nas'ta
can'can
can'cel
can'cel'la'tion
can'celled
can'cel'ling
can'cer

can'cer'ous
can'de'la
can'de'la'bra
can'de'la'brum
can'des'cence
can'des'cent
can'did
can'di'da'cies
can'di'da'cy
can'di'date
can'did'ly
can'died
can'died
can'dies
can'dle
can'dled
can'dle'stick
can'dling
can'dour
can'dy
cane
caned
ca'nine
can'ing
can'is'ter
can'ker
can'na'bis
canned
can'ner'ies
can'nery
can'ni'bal
can'ni'bal'ism
can'ni'bal'ize
can'ni'bal'iz'ing
can'ni'ly
can'ni'ness
can'ning
can'non
can'non'ade
can'non'ball
can'not
can'ny
ca'noe
ca'noed
ca'noe'ing
ca'noe'ist
can'on
ca'non'i'cal
can'on'iza'tion
can'on'ize
can'on'iz'ing
can'o'pied
can'o'pies

can'o'py
can'o'py'ing
can'ta'bi'le
can'ta'lope
can'ta'loup
can'ta'loupe
can'tan'ker'ous
can'ta'ta
can'teen
can'ter
can'ti'le'ver
can'to
can'ton
Can'ton'ese
can'ton'ment
can'tor
can'vas
can'vass
can'vass'er
can'yon
cap
ca'pa'bil'i'ties
ca'pa'bil'i'ty
ca'pa'ble
ca'pa'bly
ca'pa'cious
ca'pac'i'tate
ca'pac'i'tat'ed
ca'pac'i'tat'ing
ca'pac'i'ties
ca'pac'i'tor
ca'pac'i'ty
ca'per
cap'ful
cap'il'lar'ies
cap'il'lar'i'ty
cap'il'lar'y
cap'i'tal
cap'i'tal'ism
cap'i'tal'ist
cap'i'tal'is'tic
cap'i'tal'iza'tion
cap'i'tal'ize
cap'i'tal'ly
cap'i'ta'tion
ca'pit'u'late
ca'pit'u'lat'ed
ca'pit'u'lat'ing
ca'pit'u'la'tion
ca'pon
capped
cap'ping
ca'pric'cio

ca'price
ca'pri'cious
ca'pri'cious'ly
cap'ri'ole
cap'ri'oled
cap'ri'ol'ing
cap'si'cum
cap'size
cap'siz'ing
cap'stan
cap'su'lar
cap'sule
cap'tain
cap'tain'cy
cap'tion
cap'tious
cap'ti'vate
cap'ti'vat'ed
cap'ti'vat'ing
cap'ti'va'tion
cap'tive
cap'tiv'i'ty
cap'tor
cap'ture
cap'tured
cap'tur'ing
ca'pu'chin
cap'y'bara
car'a'cole
car'a'cul
ca'rafe
car'a'mel
car'a'mel'ize
car'a'mel'ized
car'a'mel'iz'ing
car'at
car'a'van
car'a'van'sa'ries
car'a'van'sa'ry
car'a'van'se'rai
car'a'way
car'bide
car'bine
car'bo'hy'drate
car'bol'ic
car'bon
car'bo'na'ceous
car'bon'ate
car'bon'at'ed
car'bon'at'ing
car'bo'na'tion
car'bon di'ox'ide
car'bon'if'er'ous

car'bon'iza'tion
car'bon'ize
car'bon'ized
car'bon mon'ox'ide
Car'bo'run'dum
car'boy
car'bun'cle
car'bu're'ttor
car'cass
car'cin'o'gen
car'ci'no'gen'ic
car'ci'no'ma
car'ci'no'ma'ta
car'da'mom
card'board
car'di'ac
car'di'gan
car'di'nal
car'dio'gram
car'dio'graph
car'di'og'ra'phy
car'di'ol'o'gy
car'dio'vas'cu'lar
card'sharp
care
cared
ca'reen
ca'reer
care'free
care'ful
care'ful'ly
care'ful'ness
care'less
care'less'ly
care'less'ness
ca'ress
ca'ress'ing'ly
car'et
care'tak'er
care'worn
car'go
Car'ib'be'an
car'i'bou
car'i'ca'ture
car'i'ca'tured
car'i'ca'turing
car'i'ca'tur'ist
car'ies
car'il'lon
car'ing
car'mine
car'nage
car'nal

car'nal'i'ty
car'nal'ly
car'na'tion
car'ne'lian
car'ni'val
car'ni'vore
car'niv'o'rous
car'ol
car'olled
car'ol'ling
car'om
ca'rot'id
ca'rous'al
ca'rouse
ca'roused
ca'rous'ing
car'pel
car'pen'ter
car'pen'try
car'pet
car'pet'bag
car'pet'bag'ger
car'pet'ed
car'pet'ing
car'port
car'rel
car'riage
car'ried
car'ri'er
car'ri'on
car'ob
car'rot
car'roty
car'rou'sel
car'ry
car'ry'ing
car'sick
cart'age
carte blanche
car'tel
car'te'lize
car'ti'lage
car'ti'lag'i'nous
car'tog'ra'pher
car'to'graph'ic
car'tog'ra'phy
car'ton
car'toon
car'tridge
cart'wheel
carve
carved

carv'ing
cary'at'id
cary'at'i'des
ca'sa'ba
cas'cade
cas'cad'ed
cas'cad'ing
cas'cara
case
case-book
cased
case-hard'ened
case'load
case'ment
ca'se'ous
case'work
case'work'er
ca'shew
cash'ier
cash'mere
cas'ing
ca'si'no
cask
cas'ket
cas'sa'ba
cas'sa'va
cas'se'role
cas'sette
cas'sock
cas'so'war'ies
cas'so'wary
cast
cas'ta'nets
cast'away
caste
cas'tel'lat'ed
cast'er
cas'ti'gate
cas'ti'gat'ed
cas'ti'gat'ing
cas'ti'ga'tion
cast'ing
cast'off
cast off
cast-off
cast iron
cas'tle
cas'tor
cas'trate
cas'trat'ed
cas'trat'ing
cas'tra'tion
ca'su'al

ca'su'al'ly
ca'su'al'ness
ca'su'al'ties
ca'su'al'ty
ca'su'ist
ca'su'is'tic
ca'su'ist'ry
cat'a'clysm
cat'a'clys'mal
cat'a'clys'mic
cat'a'comb
cat'a'falque
cat'a'lep'sies
cat'a'lep'sy
cat'a'lep'tic
cat'a'logue
cat'a'logued
cat'a'logu'ing
ca'tal'y'sis
cat'a'lyst
cat'a'lyt'ic
cat'a'lyse
cat'a'lys'ing
cat'a'ma'ran
cat'amount
cat'a'pult
cat'a'ract
ca'tarrh
ca'tarrh'al
ca'tas'tro'phe
cat'a'stroph'ic
cat'call
catch
catch'all
catch'er
catch'i'er
catch'ing
catch'ment area
catch'phrase
catch-up
catch'word
catchy
cat'e'chism
cat'e'chist
cat'e'chi'za'tion
cat'e'chize
cat'e'chized
cat'e'chiz'ing
cat'e'gor'i'cal
cat'e'gor'i'cal'ly
cat'e'go'ries
cat'e'go'rize
cat'e'go'riz'ing

cat'e'go'ry
ca'ter
ca'ter'er
cat'er'pil'lar
cat'er'waul
cat'fish
cat'gut
ca'thar'sis
ca'thar'tic
ca'the'dral
Cath'er'ine wheel
cath'e'ter
cath'e'ter'ize
cath'e'ter'ized
cath'e'ter'iz'ing
cath'ode
Cath'o'lic
cath'o'lic
Ca'thol'i'cism
cath'o'lic'i'ty
ca'thol'i'cize
cat'kin
cat'mint
cat'nip
cat-o'-nine-tails
cat's-eye
cat'sup
cat'ter'ies
cat'tery
cat'ti'er
cat'ti'est
cat'ti'ness
cat'tle
cat'tle'man
cat'ty
cat'walk
Cau'ca'sian
Cau'ca'soid
cau'cus
cau'cus'es
cau'cus'ing
caught
caul
caul'dron
cau'li'flow'er
caulk
caus'al
cau'sal'i'ty
cau'sa'tion
cause
cause cé'lè'bre
caused
cause'less

cause'way
caus'ing
caus'tic
caus'ti'cal'ly
cau'ter'ies
cau'ter'iza'tion
cau'ter'ize
cau'ter'ized
cau'ter'iz'ing
cau'tery
cau'tion
cau'tion'ary
cau'tious
cau'tious'ly
cau'tious'ness
cav'al'cade
cav'a'lier
cav'al'ry
cave
ca've'at
caved
cave'man
cav'er
cav'ern
cav'ern'ous
cav'i'ar
ca'vi'are
ca'vies
cav'il
cav'illed
cav'il'ling
cav'ing
cav'i'ties
cav'i'ty
ca'vort
ca'vy
cay'enne
cay'man
cay'use
cease
ceased
cease'fire
cease'less
cease'less'ly
ceas'ing
ce'ca
ce'dar
cede
ced'ed
ce'dil'la
ced'ing
ceil'ing
cel'e'brant

cel'e'brate
cel'e'brat'ing
cel'e'bra'tion
cel'e'bra'tor
ce'leb'ri'ties
ce'leb'ri'ty
ce'ler'i'ty
cel'ery
ce'les'tial
cel'i'ba'cy
cel'i'bate
cell
cel'lar
cel'list
cel'lo
cel'lo'phane
cel'lu'lar
cel'lu'loid
cel'lu'lose
Celt'ic
ce'ment
cem'e'ter'ies
cem'e'tery
ceno'taph
cen'ser
cen'sor
cen'so'ri'al
cen'so'ri'ous
cen'sor'ship
cen'sur'able
cen'sure
cen'sured
cen'sur'er
cen'sur'ing
cen'sus
cen'sus'ing
cent
cen'taur
cen'te'nar'i'an
cen'te'na'ries
cen'te'na'ry
cen'ten'ni'al
cen'tre
cen'tre'board
cen'tred
cen'tre'fold
cen'tre'piece
cen'tes'i'mal
cen'ti'grade
cen'ti'gram
cen'ti'li'tre
cen'ti'me'tre
cen'ti'pede

31

cen'tral
cen'tral'iza'tion
cen'tral'ize
cen'tral'ized
cen'tral'iz'ing
cen'tral'ly
cen'trif'u'gal
cen'tri'fuge
cen'tr'ing
cen'trip'e'tal
cen'tro'bar'ic
cen'tu'ries
cen'tu'ri'on
cen'tu'ry
ce'phal'ic
ce'ram'ic
ce're'al
cer'e'bel'lum
ce're'bral
cer'e'bric
ce're'bro'spi'nal
ce're'bro'vas'cu'lar
cer'e'brum
cer'e'mo'ni'al
cer'e'mo'nies
cer'e'mo'ni'ous
cer'e'mo'ni'ous'ly
cer'e'mo'ny
ce'rise
ce'ri'um
cer'tain
cer'tain'ly
cer'tain'ties
cer'tain'ty
cer'ti'fi'a'ble
cer'tif'i'cate
cer'ti'fi'ca'tion
cer'ti'fied
cer'ti'fi'er
cer'ti'fy
cer'ti'fy'ing
cer'ti'tude
ce'ru'le'an
cer'vi'cal
cer'vi'ces
cer'vix
cae'sar'e'an
ces'sa'tion
cess'pit
cess'pool
cae'su'ra
cae'su'rae
ce'ta'cean

chafe
chafed
chaff
chaf'finch
chaf'ing
cha'grin
cha'grined
cha'grin'ing
chain
chain-smok'er
chair'man
chair'man'ship
chair'men
chair'per'son
chair'wom'an
chaise longue
chal'et
chal'ice
chalk
chalk'i'er
chalk'i'est
chalky
chal'lenge
chal'lenged
chal'leng'er
chal'leng'ing
chamb'er
cham'ber'lain
cham'ber'maid
cham'bray
cha'me'leon
cham'ois
cham'o'mile
cham'pagne
cham'pi'on
cham'pi'on'ship
chance
chanced
chan'cel'lor
chanc'i'er
chanc'i'est
chanc'ing
chancy
chan'de'lier
chan'dler
change
change'able
changed
change'ful
change'less
change'ling
chang'ing
chan'nel

chan'nelled
chan'nel'ling
chan'teuse
chan'tey
chan'ti'cleer
cha'os
cha'ot'ic
cha'ot'i'cal'ly
chap
chap'ar'ral`
cha'peau
chap'el
chap'er'on
chap'er'one
chap'er'oned
chap'er'on'ing
chap'lain
chapped
chap'ping
chap'ter
char
char'a'banc
char'ac'ter
char'ac'ter'is'tic
char'ac'ter'is'ti'cal'ly
char'ac'ter'iza'tion
char'ac'ter'ize
char'ac'ter'ized
char'ac'ter'iz'ing
cha'rade
char'coal
charge
charge'able
charged
char'gé d'af'faires
char'ger
char'ging
chari'er
chari'est
char'i'ot
char'i'o'teer
cha'ris'ma
char'is'mat'ic
char'i'ta'ble
char'i'ta'bly
char'i'ties
char'i'ty
char'la'tan
char'lotte
charm
charm'er
charm'ing
charm'ing'ly

char'nel house
charred
char'ring
char'ter
char'treuse
chary
chase
chased
chas'er
chas'ing
chasm
chas'sis
chaste
chas'ten
chaste'ness
chas'tise
chas'tise'ment
chas'tis'ing
chas'ti'ty
chat
cha'teau
cha'teaux
chat'ted
chat'tel
chat'ter
chat'ter'box
chat'ter'er
chat'ti'er
chat'ti'est
chat'ti'ly
chat'ti'ness
chat'ting
chat'ty
chauf'feur
chau'vin'ism
chau'vin'ist
chau'vin'is'tic
cheap
cheap'en
cheap'ly
cheap'ness
cheap'skate
cheat
cheat'er
check
check'er'board
check'ers
check'list
check'mate
check'out
check'point
check'room
ched'dar

cheek
cheek'bone
cheek'i'er
cheek'i'est
cheek'i'ness
cheeky
cheep
cheer'ful
cheer'ful'ly
cheer'ful'ness
cheer'i'er
cheer'i'ly
cheer'i'ness
cheer-lead'er
cheer'less
cheery
cheese
cheese'burg'er
cheese'cake
cheese'cloth
cheese'par'ing
chee'tah
chef
chef d'oeu'vre
chem'i'cal
chem'i'cal'ly
che'mise
chem'ist
chem'is'try
che'mo'ther'a'py
che'nille
cheong'sam
cheque
cheque'book
cheque'red
cher'ish
che'root
cher'ries
cher'ry
cher'ub
che'ru'bic
cher'ubs
chess
chess'man
ches'ter'field
chest'i'er
chest'nut
chesty
che'val glass
chev'ron
chew
chew'er
chew'i'er

chew'i'est
chewy
chez
chiar'oscu'ro
chic
chi'cane
chi'ca'nery
Chi'ca'no
chi'chi
chick'a'dee
chick'en
chick'en'pox
chick-pen
chick'weed
chi'cle
chic'o'ry
chide
chid'ed
chid'ing
chief
chief'ly
chief'tain
chif'fon
chif'fo'nier
chig'ger
chi'gnon
chil'blain
child
child'bear'ing
child'birth
child'hood
child'ish
child'ish'ly
child'ish'ness
child'less
child'like
chil'dren
chill
chil'li
chill'i'er
chill'i'est
chill'i'ness
chill'ing
chilly
chi'mae'ra
chime
chi'me'ra
chim'ing
chim'ney
chim'pan'zee
chin
chi'na
chin'chil'la

Chi'nese
chink
chinned
chin'ning
chintz
chintzy
chin'wag
chip
chip'board
chip'munk
chipped
chip'per
chip'ping
chi'rog'ra'pher
chi'rog'ra'phy
chi'ro'man'cy
chi'rop'o'dist
chi'rop'o'dy
chi'ro'prac'tic
chi'ro'prac'tor
chirp
chirp'i'er
chirp'i'est
chirpy
chis'el
chis'elled
chis'el'ler
chis'el'ling
chit
chit'chat
chit'ter'lings
chiv'al'ric
chiv'al'rous
chiv'al'rous'ly
chiv'al'ry
chive
chiv'ied
chiv'vied
chiv'vy
chiv'vy'ing
chivy
chiv'y'ing
chlo'ride
chlo'ri'nate
chlo'ri'nat'ed
chlo'ri'nat'ing
chlo'ri'na'tion
chlo'rine
chlo'ro'form
chlo'ro'phyll
chock-a-block
chock'full
choc'o'late

choice
choice'ness
choir'boy
choke
choked
chok'er
chok'ing
cho'ler
chol'era
cho'ler'ic
cho'les'ter'ol
choose
choos'i'er
choos'i'est
choos'ing
choosy
chop
chopped
chop'per
chop'pi'er
chop'pi'est
chop'pi'ness
chop'ping
chop'py
chop'stick
chop su'ey
cho'ral
cho'rale
cho'ral'ly
chord
chore
cho'rea
cho'reo'graph
cho're'og'ra'pher
cho'reo'graph'ic
cho're'og'ra'phy
cho'ris'ter
chor'tle
chor'tled
chor'tling
cho'rus
cho'rus'es
cho'rus'ing
chose
cho'sen
chow
chow'der
chow mein
chris'ten
Chris'ten'dom
chris'ten'ing
Chris'tian
Chris'tian'i'ty

Chris'tian'ize
Chris'tian'ized
Christ'like
Christ'mas
Christ'mas'sy
Christ'mas'tide
chro'mat'ic
chro'mat'i'cal'ly
chro'mat'ics
chro'ma'tog'ra'phy
chrome
chro'mi'um
chro'mo'litho'graph
chro'mo'some
chron'ic
chron'i'cal'ly
chron'i'cle
chron'i'cled
chron'i'cler
chron'i'cling
chro'nol'o'ger
chro'no'log'i'cal
chro'no'log'i'cal'ly
chro'nol'o'gies
chro'nol'o'gy
chro'nom'e'ter
chry'sal'i'des
chrys'a'lis
chry'san'the'mum
chub'bi'er
chub'bi'est
chub'bi'ness
chub'by
chuck'full
chuck'le
chuck'ling
chukka
chum'my
chunk
chunk'i'er
chunk'i'est
chunky
church
church'go'er
church'li'ness
church'man
church'war'den
church'yard
chur'lish
chur'lish'ness
churn
churn'ing
chute

chut'ney
ci'ca'da
ci'ca'tri'ces
ci'ca'trix
ci'ce'ro'ne
ci'der
ci'gar
cig'a'rette
cil'ia
cil'i'ary
cel'i'ate
cil'i'um
cinch
cin'cho'na
cinc'ture
cin'der
cin'e'ma
cin'e'mat'o'graph
cin'e'ma'tog'ra'pher
cin'e'ma'tog'ra'phy
ci'né'ma vé'ri'té
cin'er'ar'i'um
cin'na'bar
cin'na'mon
ci'pher
cir'ca
cir'cle
cir'cled
cir'clet
cir'cling
cir'cuit
cir'cu'itous
cir'cuit'ry
cir'cu'lar
cir'cu'lar'iza'tion
cir'cu'lar'ize
cir'cu'lar'iz'ing
cir'cu'late
cir'cu'lat'ed
cir'cu'lat'ing
cir'cu'la'tion
cir'cu'la'tive
cir'cu'la'to'ry
cir'cum'am'bi'ent
cir'cum'cise
cir'cum'cised
cir'cum'cis'ing
cir'cum'ci'sion
cir'cum'fer'ence
cir'cum'flex
cir'cum'flu'ent
cir'cum'fuse
cir'cum'lo'cu'tion

cir'cum'loc'u'to'ry
cir'cum'nav'i'gate
cir'cum'nav'i'ga'tion
cir'cum'scribe
cir'cum'scrip'tion
cir'cum'spect
cir'cum'spec'tion
cir'cum'spect'ly
cir'cum'stance
cir'cum'stan'tial
cir'cum'stan'ti'ate
cir'cum'stan'ti'a'tion
cir'cum'vent
cir'cum'ven'tion
cir'cus
cir'cus'es
cir'rho'sis
cir'rus
cis'al'pine
cis'soid
cis'tern
cit'a'del
ci'ta'tion
cite
cit'ed
cit'ies
cit'ing
cit'i'zen
cit'i'zen'ries
cit'i'zen'ry
cit'i'zen'ship
cit're'ous
ci'tric acid
cit'ron
cit'ro'nel'la
cit'rus
city
civ'et
civ'ic
civ'ics
civ'il
ci'vil'ian
ci'vil'i'ties
ci'vil'i'ty
civ'i'li'za'tion
civ'i'lize
civ'i'lized
civ'i'liz'ing
civ'il'ly
clad
cla'dis'tics
claim
claim'able

claim'ant
clair'voy'ance
clair'voy'ant
clam
clam'bake
clam'ber
clammed
clam'mi'er
clam'mi'est
clam'mi'ness
clam'ming
clam'my
clam'our
clam'or'ous
clamp
clamp'er
clan
clan'des'tine
clang
clan'gour
clan'gour'ous
clank
clan'nish
clans'man
clap
clap'board
clapped
clap'per
clap'ping
clap-trap
claque
clar'et
clar'i'fi'ca'tion
clar'i'fied
clar'i'fy
clar'i'fy'ing
clar'i'net
clar'i'net'tist
clar'i'on
clar'i'ty
clash
clasp
clasp-knife
class
clas'sic
clas'si'cal
clas'si'cal'ly
clas'si'cism
clas'si'cist
class'i'er
clas'si'est
clas'si'fi'ca'tion
clas'si'fied

clas'si'fy
clas'si'fy'ing
class'less
class'mate
class-room
classy
clat'ter
claus'al
clause
claus'tro'pho'bia
claus'tro'pho'bic
clav'i'chord
clav'i'cle
claw
clay
clay'ey
clean
clean-cut
clean'er
clean'li'ness
clean'ly
clean'ness
cleanse
cleansed
cleans'er
cleans'ing
clear
clear'ance
clear-cut
clear'ing
clear'ly
clear'ness
clear-sight'ed
cleat
cleav'age
cleave
cleaved
cleav'er
cleav'ing
clef
cleft
cle'ma'tis
clem'en'cy
clem'ent
clench
clere'sto'ries
clere'sto'ry
cler'gies
cler'gy
cler'gy'man
cler'ic
cler'i'cal
cler'i'cal'ism

clerk
clev'er
clev'er'ly
clev'er'ness
clev'is
clew
cli'ché
click
cli'ent
cli'en'tele
cliff
cliff-hang'er
cli'mac'ter'ic
cli'mac'tic
cli'mate
cli'ma'tic
cli'mat'i'cal
cli'max
climb
climb'er
clime
clinch
clinch'er
cling
cling'ing
clin'ic
clin'i'cal
clin'i'cal'ly
cli'ni'cian
clink
clink'er
clink'er-built
clin'quant
clip
clip'board
clipped
clip'per
clip'ping
clique
cliqu'ish
cli'to'ris
clo'aca
clo'acae
cloak
cloak'room
clob'ber
clock
clock'wise
clock'work
clod
clod'dish
clod'hop'per
clog

clogged
clog'ging
cloi'son'né
clois'ter
clois'tered
clois'tral
clone
cloned
clon'ing
close
closed
close'ly
close'ness
clos'est
clos'et
clos'et'ed
clos'et'ing
close-up
clos'ing
clo'sure
clot
cloth
clothe
clothed
clothes'horse
clothes'pin
cloth'ier
cloth'ing
clot'ted
clot'ting
clo'ture
cloud
cloud'burst
cloud'ed
cloud'i'er
cloud'i'est
cloud'i'ness
cloud'less
cloudy
clout
clove
clo'ven
clo'ver
clown
clown'ish
cloy
cloy'ing'ly
club
club'able
club'ba'ble
clubbed
club'bing
club'foot

club'house
cluck
clue
clump
clum'si'er
clum'si'est
clum'si'ly
clum'si'ness
clum'sy
clung
clus'ter
clutch
clut'ter
coach
coach'man
co'ag'u'late
co'ag'u'lat'ed
co'ag'u'lat'ing
co'ag'u'la'tion
coal
coa'lesce
co'alesced
co'ales'cence
co'ales'cent
co'alesc'ing
coal'field
co'ali'tion
coarse
coarse'ly
coars'en
coarse'ness
coast
coast'al
coast'er
coast'guard
coast'line
coat
coat dress
co'ati-mun'di
coat'ing
coat'tail
co-au'thor
coax
co'ax'i'al
coax'ing'ly
co'balt
cob'ble
cob'bler
cob'ble'stone
cob'nut
CO'BOL
co'bra
cob'web

co'ca
co'caine
coc'cyx
co'chi'neal
cock
cock'ade
cock-a-hoop
cock-a-leek'ie
cock'a'too
cock'a'trice
cock'crow
cock'er'el
cock'er spaniel
cock'eye
cock'eyed
cock'fight
cock'fight'ing
cock'i'er
cock'i'est
cock'i'ly
cock'i'ness
cock'le
cock'le'bur
cock'le'shell
cock'ney
cock'pit
cock'roach
cocks'comb
cock'sure
cock'tail
cocky
co'coa
co'co'nut
co'coon
cod'dle
cod'dled
cod'dling
code
cod'ed
co'deine
co'dex
cod'fish
cod'ger
co'di'ces
cod'i'cil
cod'i'fi'ca'tion
cod'i'fied
cod'i'fy
cod'i'fy'ing
cod'ing
co'ed'u'ca'tion
co'ed'u'ca'tion'al
co'ef'fi'cient

co'equal
co'erce
co'erced
co'erc'ing
co'er'cion
co'er'cive
co'ex'ist
co'ex'ist'ence
co'ex'tend
cof'fee
cof'fer
cof'fin
co'gen'cy
co'gent
co'gent'ly
cog'i'tate
cog'i'tat'ed
cog'i'tat'ing
cog'i'ta'tive
co'gnac
cog'nate
cog'na'tion
cog'ni'tion
cog'ni'tive
cog'ni'zance
cog'ni'zant
co'hab'it
co'hab'i'ta'tion
co'here
co'hered
co'her'ence
co'her'en'cy
co'her'ent
co'her'ent'ly
co'her'ing
co'he'sion
co'he'sive
co'he'sive'ness
co'hort
coif
coif'feur
coif'fure
coil
coin
coin'age
co'in'cide
co'in'cid'ed
co'in'ci'dence
co'in'ci'dent
co'in'ci'den'tal
co'in'ci'den'tal'ly
co'in'cid'ing
coi'tion

coi'tus
coke
co'la
col'an'der
cold
cold-blood'ed
cold'ly
cold'ness
cole'slaw
col'ic
col'icky
col'i'se'um
co'li'tis
col'lab'o'rate
col'lab'o'rat'ed
col'lab'o'rat'ing
col'lab'o'ra'tion
col'lab'o'ra'tor
col'lage
col'lapse
col'lapsed
col'laps'ible
col'laps'ing
col'lar
col'lar'bone
col'late
col'lat'ed
col'lat'er'al
col'lat'ing
col'la'tion
col'league
col'lect
col'lect'ed
col'lect'ible
col'lec'tion
col'lec'tive
col'lec'tive'ly
col'lec'ti'vism
col'lec'ti'vist
col'lec'tiv'i'ty
col'lec'tiv'iza'tion
col'lec'tiv'ize
col'lec'tor
col'leen
col'lege
col'le'gian
col'le'giate
col'lide
col'lid'ed
col'lid'ing
col'lie
col'lier'ies
col'liery

col'li'mate
col'lin'ear
col'li'sion
col'lo'cate
col'lo'ca'tion
col'loid
col'lo'qui'al
col'lo'qui'al'ism
col'lo'qui'al'ly
col'lo'quy
col'lude
col'lu'sion
col'lu'sive
co'logne
co'lon
col'o'nel
co'lo'nial
co'lo'nial'ism
co'lo'nial'ist
col'o'nies
col'o'nist
col'o'ni'za'tion
col'o'nize
col'o'niz'ing
col'on'nade
col'o'ny
col'our
col'or'ation
col'or'a'tu'ra
col'our-blind
col'oured
col'our'fast
col'our'ful
col'our'ing
col'our'ist
col'our'less
co'los'sal
co'los'sus
co'los'to'mies
co'los'to'my
colt
colt'ish
Co'lum'bi'an
col'um'bine
co'lum'bi'um
col'umn
co'lum'nar
col'um'nist
co'ma
co'ma'tose
comb
com'bat
com'bat'ant

com'bat'ed
com'bat'ing
com'bat'ive
comb'er
com'bi'na'tion
com'bi'na'tive
com'bine
com'bined
com'bin'ing
com'bus'ti'ble
com'bus'tion
com'bus'tive
come
come'back
co'me'di'an
co'me'di'enne
com'e'dies
com'e'dy
come'li'ness
come'ly
co'mes'ti'ble
com'et
come'up'pance
com'fort
com'fort'able
com'fort'ably
com'fort'er
com'fort'less
com'ic
com'i'cal
com'i'cal'ly
com'ing
com'i'ty
com'ma
com'mand
com'man'dant
com'man'deer
com'mand'er
com'mand'ment
com'man'do
com'man'dos
com'mem'o'rate
com'mem'o'rat'ed
com'mem'o'rat'ing
com'mem'o'ra'tion
com'mem'o'ra'tive
com'mence
com'mence'ment
com'menc'ing
com'mend
com'mend'able
com'mend'ably
com'men'da'tion

com'men'su'rate
com'men'su'ra'tion
com'ment
com'men'tar'ies
com'men'tary
com'men'tate
com'men'tat'ed
com'men'tat'ing
com'men'ta'tor
com'merce
com'mer'cial
com'mer'cial'ism
com'mer'cial'iza'tion
com'mer'cial'ize
com'mer'cial'ly
com'min'gle
com'min'gled
com'min'gling
com'mis'er'ate
com'mis'er'at'ed
com'mis'er'at'ing
com'mis'er'a'tion
com'mis'sar
com'mis'sar'i'at
com'mis'sar'ies
com'mis'sary
com'mis'sion
com'mis'sioned
com'mis'sion'er
com'mit
com'mit'ment
com'mit'tal
com'mit'ted
com'mit'tee
com'mit'ting
com'mode
com'mo'di'ous
com'mod'i'ties
com'mod'i'ty
com'mo'dore
com'mon
com'mon'al'ty
com'mon'er
com'mon'ly
com'mon'place
com'mons
com'mon'weal
com'mon'wealth
com'mo'tion
com'mu'nal
com'mune
com'muned
com'mu'ni'ca'ble

com'mu'ni'cant
com'mu'ni'cate
com'mu'ni'cat'ed
com'mu'ni'cat'ing
com'mu'ni'ca'tion
com'mu'ni'ca'tive
com'mun'ing
com'mun'ion
com'mu'ni'qué
com'mun'ism
com'mun'ist
com'mu'nis'tic
com'mu'ni'ties
com'mu'ni'ty
com'mu'nize
com'mu'niz'ing
com'mut'able
com'mu'ta'tion
com'mute
com'mut'ed
com'mu'ter
com'mut'ing
com'pact
com'pact'ly
com'pact'ness
com'pac'tor
com'pa'nies
com'pan'ion
com'pan'ion'able
com'pan'ion'ship
com'pan'ion'way
com'pa'ny
com'pa'ra'bil'ity
com'pa'ra'ble
com'pa'ra'bly
com'par'a'tive
com'par'a'tive'ly
com'pare
com'pared
com'par'ing
com'par'i'son
com'part'ment
com'part'men'tal'ize
com'part'ment'ed
com'pass
com'pas'sion
com'pas'sion'ate
com'pas'sion'ate'ly
com'pat'i'bil'i'ty
com'pat'i'ble
com'pat'i'bly
com'pa'tri'ot
com'peer

com'pel
com'pelled
com'pel'ling
com'pen'dia
com'pen'di'um
compendiums
com'pen'sate
com'pen'sat'ing
com'pen'sa'tion
com'pen'sa'tive
com'pen'sa'to'ry
com'pete
com'pet'ed
com'pe'tence
com'pe'ten'cy
com'pe'tent
com'pe'tent'ly
com'pet'ing
com'pe'ti'tion
com'pet'i'tive
com'pet'i'tor
com'pi'la'tion
com'pile
com'piled
com'pil'er
com'pil'ing
com'pla'cence
com'pla'cen'cy
com'pla'cent
com'pla'cent'ly
com'plain
com'plain'ant
com'plaint
com'plai'sance
com'plai'sant
com'plai'sant'ly
com'ple'ment
com'ple'men'ta'ry
com'plete
com'plet'ed
com'plete'ly
com'plete'ness
com'plet'ing
com'ple'tion
com'plex
com'plex'ion
com'plex'i'ties
com'plex'i'ty
com'pli'ance
com'pli'an'cy
com'pli'ant
com'pli'cate
com'pli'cat'ed

com'pli'cat'ing
com'pli'ca'tion
com'plic'i'ties
com'plic'i'ty
com'plied
com'pli'ment
com'pli'men'ta'ri'ly
com'pli'men'ta'ry
com'ply
com'ply'ing
com'po'nent
com'port
com'port'ment
com'pose
com'posed
com'pos'er
com'pos'ing
com'pos'ite
com'po'si'tion
com'pos'i'tor
com'pos men'tis
com'post
com'po'sure
com'pote
com'pound
com'pre'hend
com'pre'hen'si'bil'i'ty
com'pre'hen'si'ble
com'pre'hen'si'bly
com'pre'hen'sion
com'pre'hen'sive
com'press
com'press'ible
com'press'ing
com'pres'sion
com'pres'sor
com'prise
com'prised
com'pris'ing
com'pro'mise
com'pro'mised
com'pro'mis'ing
comp'trol'ler
com'pul'sion
com'pul'sive
com'pul'sive'ly
com'pul'so'ry
com'punc'tion
com'pu'ta'tion
com'pute
com'put'ed
com'put'er
com'put'er'iza'tion

com'put'er'ize
com'put'er'iz'ing
com'put'ing
com'rade
con
con'cat'e'na'tion
con'cave
con'cav'i'ties
con'cav'i'ty
con'ceal
con'ceal'ment
con'cede
con'ced'ed
con'ced'ing
con'ceit
con'ceit'ed
con'ceiv'able
con'ceiv'ably
con'ceive
con'ceived
con'ceiv'ing
con'cen'trate
con'cen'trat'ed
con'cen'trat'ing
con'cen'tra'tion
con'cen'tric
con'cen'tri'cal
con'cept
con'cep'tion
con'cep'tu'al
con'cep'tu'al'iza'tion
con'cep'tu'al'ize
con'cern
con'cerned
con'cern'ment
con'cert
con'cert'ed
con'cer'ti
con'cer'ti'na
con'cer'to
con'ces'sion
con'ces'sion'aire
conch
con'cierge
con'cil'i'ate
con'cil'i'at'ed
con'cil'i'at'ing
con'cil'i'a'tion
con'cil'i'a'to'ry
con'cise
con'cise'ly
con'cise'ness
con'ci'sion

con'clave
con'clude
con'clud'ed
con'clud'ing
con'clu'sion
con'clu'sive
con'clu'sive'ly
con'coct
con'coc'tion
con'com'i'tant
con'cord
con'cord'ance
con'cord'ant
con'cor'dat
con'course
con'crete
con'cret'ed
con'cret'ing
con'cre'tion
con'cu'bine
con'cu'pis'cent
con'cur
con'curred
con'cur'rence
con'cur'rent
con'cur'rent'ly
con'cur'ring
con'cuss
con'cus'sion
con'cus'sive
con'demn
con'dem'na'ble
con'dem'na'tion
con'dem'na'to'ry
con'den'sa'tion
con'dense
con'densed
con'dens'er
con'dens'ing
con'de'scend
con'de'scend'ing
con'de'scend'ing'ly
con'de'scen'sion
con'dign
con'di'ment
con'di'tion
con'di'tion'al
con'di'tion'al'ly
con'di'tioned
con'di'tion'er
con'di'tion'ing
con'dole
con'doled

con'do'lence
con'dol'ing
con'dom
con'do'min'i'um
con'do'na'tion
con'done
con'doned
con'don'ing
con'dor
con'duce
con'duced
con'duc'ing
con'du'cive
con'duct
con'duct'ance
con'duc'tion
con'duc'tive
con'duc'tor
con'duc'tress
con'duit
cone
co'ney
con'fec'tion
con'fec'tion'er
con'fec'tion'ery
con'fed'er'a'cies
con'fed'er'a'cy
con'fed'er'ate
con'fed'er'a'tion
con'fer
con'fer'ence
con'ferred
con'fer'ring
con'fess
con'fessed
con'fes'sion
con'fes'sion'al
con'fes'sor
con'fet'ti
con'fi'dant
con'fi'dante
con'fide
con'fid'ed
con'fi'dence
con'fi'dent
con'fi'den'tial
con'fi'den'ti'al'i'ty
con'fi'den'tial'ly
con'fi'dent'ly
con'fid'ing
con'fig'u'ra'tion
con'fine
con'fined

con'fine'ment
con'fin'ing
con'firm
con'fir'ma'tion
con'fir'ma'tive
con'fir'ma'to'ry
con'firmed
con'fis'cate
con'fis'cat'ed
con'fis'cat'ing
con'fis'ca'tion
con'fis'ca'tor
con'fis'ca'to'ry
con'fla'gra'tion
con'flate
con'flat'ed
con'flat'ing
con'fla'tion
con'flict
con'flict'ing
con'flic'tion
con'flu'ence
con'flu'ent
con'flux
con'form
con'form'able
con'form'ance
con'for'ma'tion
con'form'ist
con'form'i'ty
con'found
con'found'ed
con'front
con'fron'ta'tion
con'fuse
con'fused
con'fused'ly
con'fus'ing
con'fu'sion
con'fu'ta'tion
con'fute
con'fut'ed
con'fut'ing
con'ga
con'geal
con'geal'ment
con'gen'ial
con'ge'ni'al'i'ty
con'gen'ial'ly
con'gen'i'tal
con'gen'i'tal'ly
con'ger eel
con'gest

con'ges'tion
con'ges'tive
con'glom'er'ate
con'glom'er'at'ed
con'glom'er'at'ing
con'glom'er'a'tion
con'grat'u'late
con'grat'u'lat'ed
con'grat'u'lat'ing
con'grat'u'la'tion
con'grat'u'la'to'ry
con'gre'gate
con'gre'gat'ed
con'gre'gat'ing
con'gre'ga'tion
con'gre'ga'tion'al
con'gress
con'gres'sion'al
con'gress'man
con'gress'wom'an
con'gru'ence
con'gru'en'cy
con'gru'ent
con'gru'ent'ly
con'gru'i'ty
con'gru'ous
con'gru'ous'ly
con'gru'ous'ness
con'ic
con'i'cal
co'nies
co'ni'fer
co'nif'er'ous
con'jec'tur'al
con'jec'ture
con'jec'tured
con'jec'tur'ing
con'join
con'joint
con'joint'ly
con'ju'gal
con'ju'gal'ly
con'ju'gate
con'ju'gat'ed
con'ju'gat'ing
con'ju'ga'tion
con'ju'ga'tive
con'junc'tion
con'junc'tive
con'junc'ti'vi'tis
con'jur'a'tion
con'jure
con'jured

con'jur'er
con'jur'ing
con'jur'or
con'nect
con'nec'tion
con'nec'tive
con'nec'tor
conned
con'ning
con'nip'tion
con'niv'ance
con'nive
con'nived
con'niv'ing
con'nois'seur
con'no'ta'tion
con'no'ta'tive
con'note
con'not'ed
con'not'ing
con'nu'bi'al
con'quer
con'quer'able
con'quer'or
con'quest
con'quis'ta'dor
con'san'guin'e'ous
con'san'guin'i'ty
con'science
con'sci'en'tious
con'sci'en'tious'ly
con'sci'en'tious'ness
con'scion'able
con'scious
con'scious'ly
con'scious'ness
con'script
con'scrip'tion
con'se'crate
con'se'crat'ed
con'se'crat'ing
con'se'cra'tion
con'se'cra'tor
con'sec'u'tive
con'sec'u'tive'ly
con'sen'sus
con'sent
con'se'quence
con'se'quent
con'se'quen'tial
con'se'quent'ly
con'ser'va'tion
con'ser'va'tion'ist

con'serv'a'tism
con'serv'a'tive
con'ser'va'tive'ly
con'ser'va'toire
con'serv'a'to'ries
con'serv'a'to'ry
con'serve
con'served
con'serv'ing
con'sid'er
con'sid'er'able
con'sid'er'ably
con'sid'er'ate
con'sid'er'ate'ly
con'sid'er'a'tion
con'sid'er'ing
con'sign
con'sign'er
con'sign'ment
con'sign'or
con'sist
con'sist'ence
con'sist'en'cies
con'sist'en'cy
con'sist'ent
con'sist'ent'ly
con'sis'to'ry
con'sol'able
con'so'la'tion
con'sol'a'to'ry
con'sole
con'soled
con'sol'i'date
con'sol'i'dat'ed
con'sol'i'dat'ing
con'sol'i'da'tion
con'sol'ing
con'som'mé
con'so'nant
con'sort
con'sor'tia
con'sor'ti'um
con'spic'u'ous
con'spic'u'ous'ly
con'spic'u'ous'ness
con'spir'a'cies
con'spir'a'cy
con'spir'a'tor
con'spir'a'to'ri'al
con'spire
con'spired
con'spir'er
con'spir'ing

con'sta'ble
con'stab'u'lar'ies
con'stab'u'lary
con'stan'cy
con'stant
con'stant'ly
con'stel'la'tion
con'ster'na'tion
con'sti'pate
con'sti'pa'tion
con'stit'u'en'cies
con'stit'u'en'cy
con'stit'u'ent
con'sti'tute
con'sti'tu'tion
con'sti'tu'tion'al
con'sti'tu'tion'al'ism
con'sti'tu'tion'al'i'ty
con'sti'tu'tion'al'ly
con'strain
con'strained
con'straint
con'strict
con'stric'tion
con'stric'tive
con'stric'tor
con'stru'able
con'struct
con'struc'tion
con'struc'tive
con'struc'tive'ly
con'struc'tor
con'strue
con'strued
con'stru'ing
con'sul
con'su'lar
con'su'late
con'sul'ship
con'sult
con'sul'tan'cies
con'sul'tan'cy
con'sult'ant
con'sul'ta'tion
con'sul'ta'tive
con'sum'able
con'sume
con'sumed
con'sum'er
con'sum'er'ism
con'sum'ing
con'sum'mate
con'sum'mat'ed

con'sum'mat'ing
con'sum'ma'tion
con'sump'tion
con'sump'tive
con'tact
con'ta'gion
con'ta'gious
con'ta'gious'ness
con'tain
con'tain'er
con'tain'ment
con'tam'i'nant
con'tam'i'nate
con'tam'i'nat'ed
con'tam'i'nat'ing
con'tam'i'na'tion
con'tem'plate
con'tem'plat'ed
con'tem'plat'ing
con'tem'pla'tion
con'tem'pla'tive
con'tem'pla'tive'ly
con'tem'po'ra'ne'ous
con'tem'po'rar'ies
con'tem'po'rary
con'tempt
con'tempt'ible
con'tempt'ibly
con'temp'tu'ous
con'temp'tu'ous'ly
con'tend
con'tend'er
con'tent
con'tent'ed
con'tent'ed'ly
con'tent'ed'ness
con'ten'tion
con'ten'tious
con'tent'ment
con'ter'mi'nous
con'test
con'test'able
con'test'ant
con'text
con'tex'tu'al
con'tex'ture
con'ti'gu'ities
con'ti'gu'ity
con'tig'u'ous
con'tig'u'ous'ly
con'ti'nence
con'ti'nen'cy
con'ti'nent

con'ti'nen'tal
con'tin'gen'cies
con'tin'gen'cy
con'tin'gent
con'tin'u'al
con'tin'u'al'ly
con'tin'u'ance
con'tin'u'a'tion
con'tin'ue
con'tin'ued
con'tin'u'ing
con'ti'nu'i'ty
con'tin'u'ous
con'tin'u'ous'ly
con'tin'u'um
con'tort
con'tor'tion
con'tor'tion'ist
con'tour
con'tra
con'tra'band
con'tra'bass
con'tra'cep'tion
con'tra'cep'tive
con'tract
con'tract'ed
con'trac'tile
con'trac'tion
con'trac'tive
con'trac'tor
con'trac'tu'al
con'tra'dict
con'tra'dic'tion
con'tra'dic'to'ry
con'tra'dis'tinc'tion
con'tral'to
con'trap'tion
con'tra'pun'tal
con'tra'ri'ly
con'tra'ri'ness
con'tra'ri'wise
con'tra'ry
con'trast
con'trast'ing'ly
con'tra'vene
con'tra'ven'ing
con'tra'ven'tion
con'tre'temps
con'trib'ut'able
con'trib'ute
con'trib'ut'ed
con'trib'ut'ing
con'tri'bu'tion

con'trib'u'tor
con'trib'u'tory
con'trite
con'trite'ly
con'trite'ness
con'tri'tion
con'triv'ance
con'trive
con'trived
con'triv'ing
con'trol
con'trol'la'ble
con'trolled
con'trol'ler
con'trol'ling
con'tro'ver'sial
con'tro'ver'sies
con'tro'ver'sy
con'tro'vert
con'tu'ma'cy
con'tu'me'ly
con'tuse
con'tused
con'tus'ing
con'tu'sion
co'nun'drum
con'ur'ba'tion
con'va'lesce
con'va'lesced
con'va'les'cence
con'va'les'cent
con'vec'tion
con'vec'tor
con'vene
con'vened
con'ven'er
con'ven'ience
con'ven'ient
con've'nient'ly
con'ven'ing
con've'nor
con'vent
con'ven'tion
con'ven'tion'al
con'ven'tion'al'ism
con'ven'tion'al'i'ty
con'ven'tion'al'ize
con'ven'tion'al'ly
con'verge
con'ver'gence
con'ver'gent
con'verg'ing
con'ver'sant

con'ver'sa'tion
con'ver'sa'tion'al
con'ver'sa'tion'a'list
con'verse
con'versed
con'verse'ly
con'vers'ing
con'ver'sion
con'vert
con'vert'er
con'vert'ible
con'ver'tor
con'vex
con'vex'i'ty
con'vey
con'vey'able
con'vey'ance
con'vey'anc'ing
con'vey'er
con'vey'or
con'vict
con'vic'tion
con'vince
con'vinced
con'vinc'i'ble
con'vinc'ing
con'vinc'ing'ly
con'viv'i'al
con'viv'i'al'ity
con'vo'cation
con'voke
con'voked
con'vok'ing
con'vo'lute
con'vo'lut'ed
con'vo'lute'ly
con'vo'lut'ing
con'vo'lu'tion
con'voy
con'vulse
con'vulsed
con'vuls'ing
con'vul'sion
con'vul'sive
con'vul'sive'ly
co'ny
cook
cook'e'ry
cook'ie
cook'ing
Cook's tour
cool
cool'ant

cool'er
cool'ish
cool'ly
cool'ness
coop
coop'er'age
co'op'er'ate
co'op'er'at'ed
co'op'er'at'ing
co'op'er'a'tion
co'op'er'a'tive
co-opt
co'or'di'nate
co'or'di'nat'ed
co'or'di'nat'ing
co'or'di'na'tion
co'or'di'na'tor
cop
co'part'ner
cope
coped
cop'ied
cop'i'er
cop'ies
co'pi'lot
cop'ing
co'pi'ous
co'pi'ous'ly
cop'per
cop'per'plate
cop'pery
cop'pice
cop'ra
copse
cop'u'la
cop'u'late
cop'u'lat'ed
cop'u'lat'ing
cop'u'la'tion
cop'u'la'tive
copy
copy'book
copy'ing
copy'right
copy'writ'er
co'quet
co'quet'ry
co'quette
co'quett'ish
cor'a'cle
cor'al
cord'age
cor'dial

cor'dial'i'ty
cor'dial'ly
cord'ite
cord'less
cor'don
cor'do'van
cor'du'roy
core
cored
cor'gi
co'ri'an'der
cor'ing
cork'screw
cor'mo'rant
corn
corn'cob
cor'nea
cor'ne'al
cor'ner
cor'ner'back
cor'ner'stone
cor'net
corn'field
corn'flakes
corn'flow'er
cor'nice
corn'i'er
corn'i'est
corn'meal
corn' starch
cor'nu'co'pia
corny
co'rol'la
cor'ol'lar'ies
cor'ol'lary
co'ro'na
cor'o'nar'ies
cor'o'nary
cor'o'na'tion
cor'o'ner
cor'o'net
cor'po'ra
cor'po'ral
cor'po'rate
cor'po'rate'ly
cor'po'ra'tion
cor'po'ra'tism
cor'po'ra'tive
cor'po're'al
corps
corps de bal'let
corpse
cor'pu'lence

cor'pu'lent
cor'pus
cor'pus'cle
cor'pus'cu'lar
cor'ral
cor'ralled
cor'ral'ling
cor'rect
cor'rect'able
cor'rec'tion
cor'rec'tion'al
cor'rec'tive
cor'rect'ly
cor'rect'ness
cor're'late
cor're'lat'ed
cor're'lat'ing
cor're'la'tion
cor'rel'a'tive
cor're'spond
cor're'spond'ence
cor're'spond'ent
cor're'spond'ing
cor're'spond'ing'ly
cor'ri'dor
cor'ri'gen'da
cor'ri'gen'dum
cor'ri'gi'bil'i'ty
cor'ri'gi'ble
cor'rob'o'rate
cor'rob'o'rat'ed
cor'rob'o'rat'ion
cor'rob'o'ra'tive
cor'rob'o'ra'to'ry
cor'rode
cor'rod'ed
cor'rod'ing
cor'ro'sion
cor'ro'sive
cor'ru'gate
cor'ru'gat'ed
cor'ru'gat'ing
cor'ru'ga'tion
cor'rupt
cor'rupt'ibil'i'ty
cor'rupt'ible
cor'rup'tion
cor'rupt'ly
cor'rupt'ness
cor'sage
cor'sair
cor'set

cor'tege
cor'tex
cor'ti'cal
cor'ti'ces
cor'ti'sone
co'run'dum
cor'us'cate
cor'vette
co'se'cant
co'si'er
co'sig'na'to'ry
co'si'ly
co'sine
co'si'ness
cos let'tuce
cos'met'ic
cos'met'i'cal'ly
cos'me'tol'o'gist
cos'mic
cos'mi'cal'ly
cos'mog'o'nist
cos'mog'o'ny
cos'mog'ra'pher
cos'mog'ra'phics
cos'mog'ra'phy
cos'mol'o'gist
cos'mol'o'gy
cos'mo'naut
cos'mo'pol'i'tan
cos'mop'o'lite
cos'mos
cos'mo'tron
cos'set
co-star
co-starred
co-star'ring
cos'tive
cost'li'er
cost'ly
cos'tume
cos'tumed
cos'tum'er
cos'tum'ing
co'sy
cot
co'tan'gent
cote
co'te'rie
co'til'lion
cot'tage
cot'ter
cot'ton
cot'ton'tail

cot'ton'wood
cot'tony
couch
couch'ant
couch'grass
cou'gar
cough
coun'cil
coun'cil'lor
coun'sel
coun'selled
coun'sel'ling
coun'sel'lor
count
count'able
count'down
coun'te'nance
coun'te'nanced
coun'te'nanc'ing
count'er
coun'ter'act
coun'ter'ac'tive
coun'ter'at'tack
coun'ter'bal'ance
coun'ter'charge
coun'ter'claim
coun'ter'claim'ant
coun'ter'clock'wise
coun'ter'cul'ture
coun'ter'es'pi'o'nage
coun'ter'feit
coun'ter'feit'er
coun'ter'foil
coun'ter'in'tel'li'gence
coun'ter'ir'ri'tant
coun'ter'mand
coun'ter'meas'ure
coun'ter'of'fen'sive
coun'ter'pane
coun'ter'part
coun'ter'point
coun'ter'poise
coun'ter'proof
coun'ter'pro'pos'al
coun'ter'sign
coun'ter'sig'na'ture
coun'ter'sink
coun'ter'spy
coun'ter'ten'or
coun'ter'weight
coun'tess
coun'ties
count'less

coun'tries
coun'tri'fied
coun'try
coun'try'fied
coun'try'man
coun'try'side
coun'try'wom'an
coun'ty
coup
coup de grâce
coup d'é'tat
coupé
cou'ple
coup'ler
coup'let
coup'ling
cou'pon
cour'age
cou'ra'geous
cou'ra'geous'ly
cour'i'er
course
coursed
cours'er
cours'ing
cour'te'ous
cour'te'ous'ly
cour'te'sies
cour'te'sy
court'house
cour'ti'er
court'li'ness
court'ly
court-mar'tial
court'room
court'ship
court'yard
cous'in
cou'ture
cou'tu'rier
cov'e'nant
cov'er
cov'er'age
cov'er'all
cov'ered
cov'er'ing
cov'er'less
cov'er'let
cov'ert
cov'ert'ly
cov'er-up
cov'et
cov'et'ous

cov'et'ous'ly
cov'et'ous'ness
cov'ey
cow'ard
cow'ard'ice
cow'ard'li'ness
cow'ard'ly
cow'boy
cow'er
cow'er'ing
cow'hand
cowl
co-work'er
cow'pox
cow'rie
cow'ry
cow'slip
cox'comb
cox'swain
coy
coy'ly
coy'ness
coy'o'te
coy'pu
coz'en
coz'en'er
crab
crabbed
crab'bing
crab'by
crack'down
crack'er
crack'er'jack
crack'ing
crack'le
crack'led
crack'ling
crack-up
cra'dle
cra'dled
cra'dling
craft'i'er
craft'i'est
craft'i'ly
crafts'man
crafts'man'ship
crafty
crag
crag'ged
crag'gi'ness
crag'gy
cram
crammed

cram'ming
cram'pon
cran'ber'ries
cran'ber'ry
crane
craned
crane'fly
crania
cran'ing
cra'ni'um
crank'case
crank'i'er
crank'i'est
crank'i'ly
crank'i'ness
crank'shaft
cranky
cran'nied
cran'nies
cran'ny
crash
crash-land
crass
crass'ly
crass'ness
crate
crat'ed
cra'ter
cra'tered
crat'ing
cra'vat
crave
craved
cra'ven
crav'ing
craw
crawl
cray'fish
cray'on
craze
crazed
cra'zi'er
cra'zi'est
cra'zi'ness
craz'ing
cra'zy
creak
creak'i'er
creak'i'est
creak'i'ly
creaky
cream
cream'er'ies

cream'ery
cream'i'er
cream'i'est
cream'i'ness
creamy
crease
creased
creas'ing
creasy
cre'ate
cre'at'ed
cre'at'ing
cre'a'tion
cre'a'tive
cre'ative'ly
cre'a'tiv'i'ty
cre'a'tor
crea'ture
crèche
cre'dence
cre'den'tial
cre'den'za
cred'i'bil'i'ty
cred'i'ble
cred'i'bly
cred'it
cred'it'abil'i'ty
cred'it'able
cred'it'a'bly
cred'i'tor
cre'do
cre'du'li'ty
cred'u'lous
creed
creek
creel
creep
creep'er
creep'i'er
creep'i'est
creep'i'ness
creep'ing
creepy
cre'mate
cre'mat'ed
cre'mat'ing
cre'ma'tion
crem'a'to'ria
cre'ma'to'ri'um
cre'ma'to'ry
crème de la crème
crème de menthe
cren'el'ate

cren'el'at'ed
cren'el'at'ing
cren'el'la'tion
Cre'ole
cre'o'sote
crepe
crepe de Chine
crêpe su'zette
crept
cre'pus'cu'lar
cres'cen'do
cres'cent
cress
crest
crest'ed
crest'fall'en
crest'less
cre'tin
cre'tin'ism
cre'tin'ous
cre'tonne
cre'vasse
crev'ice
crew
crew'ed
crew'man
crib
crib'bage
cribbed
crib'bing
crick
crick'et
cried
cri'er
cries
crime
crim'i'nal
crim'i'nal'i'ty
crim'i'nal'ly
crim'i'nol'o'gist
crim'i'nol'o'gy
crimp
crim'son
cringe
cringed
cring'ing
crin'kle
crin'kled
crin'kli'er
crin'kli'est
crin'kling
crin'kly
crin'o'line

crip'ple
crip'pled
crip'pling
cri'ses
cri'sis
crisp
crisp'i'er
crisp'i'est
crisp'ly
crisp'ness
crispy
criss-cross
cri'te'ria
cri'te'ri'on
crit'ic
crit'i'cal
crit'i'cal'ly
crit'i'cism
crit'i'ciz'able
crit'i'cize
crit'i'cized
crit'i'cizing
cri'tique
croak
croak'i'er
croak'i'est
croaky
cro'chet
cro'cheted
cro'chet'ing
crock
crock'ery
croc'o'dile
cro'cus
crois'sant
crone
cro'nies
cro'ny
crook
crook'ed
crook'ed'ly
croon
croon'er
crop
cropped
crop'ping
cro'quet
cro'quette
cross
cross'bar
cross'bones
cross'bow
cross'breed

cross-coun'try
cross-eye
cross-eyed
cross-ex'am'ine
cross-fire
cross'hatch
cross'ing
cross-legged
cross'ly
cross-over
cross-pol'li'nate
cross-pol'li'na'tion
cross-ref'er'ence
cross'wind
cross'word
crotch'et'i'ness
crotch'ety
crouch
croup
crou'pi'er
crou'ton
crow
crow'bar
crowd
crown
crow's-feet
cru'ces
cru'cial
cru'ci'al'i'ty
cru'ci'ble
cru'ci'fied
cru'ci'fix
cru'ci'fix'ion
cru'ci'form
cru'ci'fy
cru'ci'fy'ing
crude
crude'ly
crude'ness
crud'est
cru'di'tés
cru'di'ties
cru'di'ty
cru'el
cru'el'ly
cru'el'ness
cru'el'ties
cru'el'ty
cru'et
cruise
cruised
cruis'er
cruis'ing

crul'ler
crumb
crum'ble
crum'bli'er
crum'bli'est
crum'bling
crum'bly
crum'mi'est
crum'my
crum'pet
crum'ple
crum'pled
crum'pling
crunch
crunch'i'er
crunchy
cru'sade
cru'sad'er
crush
crush'er
crush'ing
crust
crus'ta'cean
crust'i'er
crust'i'est
crust'i'ly
crusty
crutch
crux
cry
cry'ing
cry'o'gen'ics
crypt
cryp'tic
cryp'ti'cal'ly
cryp'to'gram
cryp'to'graph
crys'tal
crys'tal'line
crys'tal'li'za'tion
crys'tal'lize
cube
cubed
cu'bic
cu'bi'cal
cu'bi'cle
cub'ing
cub'ism
cuck'old
cuck'oo
cu'cum'ber
cud'dle
cud'dled

cud'dle'some
cud'dling
cud'gel
cud'gelled
cud'gel'ling
cue
cued
cue'ing
cui'sine
cul-de-sac
cu'li'nary
cull
cul'mi'nate
cul'mi'nat'ed
cul'mi'nat'ing
cul'mi'na'tion
cu'lottes
cul'pa'bil'i'ty
cul'pa'ble
cul'pa'bly
cul'prit
cult
cul'tist
cul'ti'vate
cul'ti'vat'ed
cul'ti'vat'ing
cul'ti'va'tion
cul'ti'va'tor
cul'tur'al
cul'ture
cul'tured
cul'tur'ing
cul'vert
cum'ber
cum'ber'some
cum'brance
cum'brous
cum'in
cum lau'de
cum'mer'bund
cu'mu'late
cu'mu'la'tion
cu'mu'la'tive
cu'mu'li
cu'mu'lo'nim'bus
cu'mu'lous
cu'mu'lus
cu'ne'i'form
cun'ning
cun'ning'ly
cun'ning'ness
cup
cup'board

cup'ful
cu'pid'i'ty
cu'po'la
cupped
cup'ping
cur
cur'abil'i'ty
cur'able
Cu'ra'çao
cu'ra're
cu'rate
cur'a'tive
cu'ra'tor
curb
curb'ing
curb'stone
curd
cur'dle
cur'dled
cur'dling
cure
cure-all
cured
curet
curette
cur'few
cur'ing
cu'rio
cu'ri'o'sa
cu'ri'os'i'ties
cu'ri'os'i'ty
cu'ri'ous
cu'ri'ous'ly
cu'ri'ous'ness
curl
curl'er
curl'ew
curl'i'cue
curl'i'er
curl'i'est
curl'i'ness
curl'ing
curly
cur'rant
cur'ren'cies
cur'ren'cy
cur'rent
cur'rent'ly
cur'ric'u'la
cur'ric'u'lar
cur'ric'u'lum
cur'ric'u'lum vi'tae
cur'ried

cur'rish
cur'ry
cur'ry'ing
curse
curs'ed
curs'ed'ness
curs'ing
cur'sive
cur'so'ri'ly
cur'so'ry
curt
cur'tail
cur'tail'ment
cur'tain
curt'ly
curt'ness
curt'sied
curt'sies
curt'sy
curt'sy'ing
cur'va'ceous
cur'va'ture
curve
curved
cur'vi'lin'e'ar
curv'ing
cush'i'er
cush'i'est
cush'ion
cushy
cusp
cus'pid
cus'pi'dor
cuss
cuss'ed
cuss'ed'ness
cus'tard
cus'to'di'al
cus'to'di'an
cus'to'dy
cus'tom
cus'tom'ary
cus'tom'er
cus'tom'ize
cus'tom'ized
cus'tom'iz'ing
cut
cut-and-dried
cu'ta'ne'ous
cut'back
cute
cute'ness
cut'est

cu'ti'cle
cut'lass
cut'lery
cut'let
cut-off
cut-rate
cut-throat
cut'ting
cut'tle'fish
cy'a'nide
cy'ber'net'ics
cy'cla'men
cy'cle
cy'cled
cyc'lic
cy'cli'cal
cy'cling
cyc'list
cy'clone
cy'clo'pe'dia
cy'clo'ra'ma
cy'clo'ram'ic
cy'clo'tron
cyg'net
cyl'in'der
cy'lin'dric
cy'lin'dri'cal
cym'bal
cyn'ic
cyn'i'cal
cyn'i'cal'ly
cyn'i'cism
cy'no'sure
cy'pher
cy'press
cyst
cys'tic
czar
czar'e'vitch
czar'ist
czar'ri'na
Czech
dab
dabbed
dab'bing
dab'ble
dab'bled
dab'bler
dab'bling
da ca'po
da'cha
dachs'hund
dac'tyl

dac'tyl'ic
dad'dies
dad'dy
daf'fo'dil
daf'fy
dag'ger
da'guerreo'type
dahl'ia
dai'lies
dain'ti'er
dain'ti'est
dain'ti'ly
dain'ti'ness
dain'ty
dai'qui'ri
dair'ies
dai'ry
dairy'man
da'is
dai'sies
dai'sy
dal'li'ance
dal'lied
dal'ly
dal'ly'ing
dam
dam'age
dam'aged
dam'ag'ing
dam'ask
dammed
dam'ming
damn
dam'na'ble
dam'na'bly
dam'na'tion
damned
damned'est
damp'en
damp'er
damp'ness
dam'sel
dam'son
dan
dance
danced
danc'ing
dan'de'li'on
dan'der
dan'dies
dan'di'fied
dan'di'fy
dan'di'fy'ing

dan'dle
dan'dled
dan'dling
dan'druff
dan'dy
dan'dy'ism
dan'ger
dan'ger'ous
dan'ger'ous'ly
dan'gle
dan'gled
dan'gling
Dan'ish
dank
dank'ness
dan*seur*
dan*seuse*
daph'nia
dap'per
dap'ple
dap'pled
dap'pling
dare
dared
dare'dev'il
dare'dev'il'ry
dar'ing
dar'ing'ly
dark
dark'en
dark'ish
dark'ling
dark'ly
dark'ness
dark'room
dar'ling
dar'ling'ness
dash'board
dash'ing
das'tard
das'tard'li'ness
das'tard'ly
da'ta
dat'able
date
dat'ed
date'less
date'line
dat'ing
da'tive
da'tum
daub
daugh'ter

daugh'ter-in-law
daunt'less
dau'phin
dau'phine
dav'en'port
dav'it
daw'dle
daw'dled
daw'dler
daw'dling
dawn
dawn'ing
day'break
day'dream
day'light
day'time
daze
dazed
daz'ed'ly
daz'ing
daz'zle
daz'zled
daz'zling
dea'con
dea'con'ess
de'ac'ti'vate
de'ac'ti'vat'ed
de'ac'ti'va'ting
de'ac'ti'va'tion
dead
dead'beat
dead'en
dead-end
dead-eye
dead'head
dead'li'er
dead'li'est
dead'line
dead'li'ness
dead'lock
dead'ly
dead'pan
dead-weight
dead'wood
deaf
deaf'en
deaf'en'ing
deaf'en'ing'ly
deaf-mute
deaf'ness
deal
deal'er
deal'ing

dealt
dean
dean'er'ies
dean'ery
dean'ship
dear
dear'ly
dear'ness
dearth
death
death'bed
death'blow
death'less
death'ly
de'ba'cle
de'bar
de'bark
de'bar'ka'tion
de'bar'ment
de'barred
de'bar'ring
de'base
de'based
de'base'ment
de'bas'ing
de'bat'able
de'bate
de'bat'ed
de'bat'er
de'bat'ing
de'bauch
de'bauched
de'bau'chee
de'bauch'er
de'bauch'ery
de'bauch'ment
de'ben'ture
de'bil'i'tate
de'bil'i'tat'ed
de'bil'i'tat'ing
de'bil'i'ta'tion
de'bil'i'ties
de'bil'i'ty
deb'it
deb'it'ed
deb'it'ing
deb'o'nair
de'brief
de'bris
debt
debt'or
de'bug
de'bugged

de'bug'ging
de'bunk
de'but
deb'u'tante
de'cade
dec'a'dence
dec'a'dent
dec'a'dent'ly
de'caf'fein'at'ed
dec'a'gon
dec'a'gram
deca'he'dra
dec'a'he'dron
de'cal
de'camp
de'camp'ment
de'cant
de'cant'er
de'cap'i'tate
de'cap'i'tat'ed
de'cap'i'tat'ing
de'cap'i'ta'tion
dec'a'pod
de'cath'lete
de'cath'lon
de'cay
de'cease
de'ceased
de'ce'dent
de'ceit
de'ceit'ful
de'ceit'ful'ly
de'ceit'ful'ness
de'ceive
de'ceived
de'ceiv'er
de'ceiv'ing
de'cel'er'ate
de'cel'er'at'ed
de'cel'er'at'ing
de'cel'er'a'tion
de'cen'cies
de'cen'cy
de'cen'ni'al
de'cent
de'cent'ly
de'cen'tral'iza'tion
de'cen'tral'ize
de'cen'tral'ized
de'cen'tral'iz'ing
de'cep'tion
de'cep'tive
de'cep'tive'ly

dec'i'bel
de'cide
de'cid'ed
de'cid'ed'ly
de'cid'ing
de'cid'u'ous
deci'lit'er
dec'i'mal
dec'i'mal'iza'tion
dec'i'mal'ize
dec'i'mal'ized
dec'i'mal'iz'ing
dec'i'mate
dec'i'mat'ed
dec'i'mat'ing
dec'i'ma'tion
deci'me'tre
de'ci'pher
de'ci'pher'able
de'ci'sion
de'ci'sive
de'ci'sive'ly
de'ci'sive'ness
de'claim
dec'la'ma'tion
de'clam'a'tory
dec'la'ra'tion
de'clar'a'tive
de'clar'a'to'ry
de'clare
de'clared
de'clar'ing
de'clas'si'fied
de'clas'si'fy
de'clas'si'fy'ing
de'clen'sion
de'clin'able
dec'li'na'tion
de'cline
de'clined
de'clin'ing
de'cliv'i'ties
de'cliv'i'tous
de'cliv'i'ty
de'code
de'cod'ed
de'cod'er
de'cod'ing
dé'colle'tage
dé'col'le'té
de'com'mis'sion
de'com'pose
de'com'posed

de'com'pos'ing
de'com'po'si'tion
de'com'press
de'com'pres'sion
de'con'ges'tant
de'con'tam'i'nate
de'con'tam'i'nat'ed
de'con'tam'i'nat'ing
de'con'tam'i'na'tion
de'con'trol
de'con'trolled
de'con'trol'ling
de'cor
dec'o'rate
dec'o'rat'ed
dec'o'rat'ing
dec'o'ra'tion
dec'o'ra'tive
dec'o'ra'tor
dec'o'rous
dec'o'rous'ly
de'co'rum
de'coy
de'crease
de'creased
de'creas'ing
de'creas'ing'ly
de'cree
de'creed
de'cree'ing
de'cre'ment
de'crep'it
de'crep'it'ly
de'crep'i'tude
de'cre'scen'do
de'cri'al
de'cried
de'cry
de'cry'ing
ded'i'cate
ded'i'cat'ed
ded'i'cat'ing
ded'i'ca'tion
ded'i'ca'to'ry
de'duce
de'duc'ible
de'duct
de'duct'ible
de'duc'tion
de'duc'tive
deed
deem
deep

deep'en
deep'ly
deep'ness
deep-root'ed
deep-seat'ed
deer
deer'stalk'er
de-es'ca'late
de-es'ca'lat'ed
de-es'ca'lat'ing
de-es'ca'la'tion
de'face
de'faced
de'face'ment
de'fac'ing
de fac'to
de'fal'cate
de'fal'ca'tion
def'a'ma'tion
de'fam'a'to'ry
de'fame
de'famed
de'fam'ing
de'fault
de'fault'er
de'feat
de'feat'ism
de'feat'ist
def'e'cate
def'e'cat'ed
def'e'cat'ing
def'e'ca'tion
de'fect
de'fec'tion
de'fec'tive
de'fec'tive'ly
de'fec'tor
de'fend
de'fence
de'fence'less
de'fence'less'ness
de'fend'ant
de'fend'er
de'fen'si'bil'i'ty
de'fen'si'ble
de'fen'sive
de'fens'ive'ly
de'fer
def'er'ence
def'er'en'tial
def'er'en'tial'ly
de'fer'ment
de'ferred

de'fer'ring
de'fi'ance
de'fi'ant
de'fi'ant'ly
de'fi'cien'cies
de'fi'cien'cy
de'fi'cient
def'i'cit
de'fied
de'file
de'filed
de'file'ment
de'fil'ing
de'fin'able
de'fine
de'fined
de'fin'ing
def'i'nite
def'i'nite'ly
def'i'ni'tion
de'fin'i'tive
de'fin'i'tive'ly
de'flate
de'flat'ed
de'flat'ing
de'flat'ion
de'fla'tion'ary
de'flect
de'flec'tion
de'flec'tive
de'flec'tor
de'flow'er
de'fo'li'ant
de'fo'li'ate
de'fo'li'at'ed
de'fo'li'at'ing
de'fo'li'a'tion
de'for'est
de'for'est'a'tion
de'form
de'for'ma'tion
de'formed
de'form'i'ties
de'form'i'ty
de'fraud
de'fray
de'fray'al
de'fray'ment
de'frock
de'frost
deft
deft'ly
deft'ness

de'funct
de'fuse
de'fused
de'fus'ing
de'fy
de'fy'ing
de'gauss
de'gen'er'a'cy
de'gen'er'ate
de'gen'er'at'ed
de'gen'er'ate'ly
de'gen'er'at'ing
de'gen'er'a'tion
de'gen'er'a'tive
de'grad'able
deg'ra'da'tion
de'grade
de'grad'ed
de'grad'ing
de'gree
de'his'cence
de'his'cent
de'hu'man'iza'tion
de'hu'man'ize
de'hu'man'ized
de'hu'man'iz'ing
de'hu'mid'i'fy
de'hy'drate
de'hy'drat'ed
de'hy'drat'ing
de'hy'dra'tion
de'-ice
de'-ic'er
de'i'fi'ca'tion
de'i'fied
de'i'fy
de'i'fy'ing
deign
de-ion'ize
de-ion'ized
de-ion'iz'ing
de'ism
de'ist
de'is'tic
de'is'ti'cal
de'i'ties
de'i'ty
dé'jà vu
de'ject'ed
de'jec'ted'ly
de'jec'tion
de ju're
de'lay

de'lec'ta'ble
de'lec'ta'bly
de'lec'ta'tion
del'e'gate
del'e'gat'ed
del'e'gat'ing
del'e'ga'tion
de'lete
de'let'ed
del'e'te'ri'ous
de'let'ing
de'le'tion
delft
delft'ware
de'lib'er'ate
de'lib'er'at'ed
de'lib'er'ate'ly
de'lib'er'at'ing
de'lib'er'a'tion
de'lib'er'a'tive
del'i'ca'cies
del'i'ca'cy
del'i'cate
del'i'cate'ly
del'i'ca'tes'sen
de'li'cious
de'li'cious'ly
de'li'cious'ness
de'light
de'light'ed
de'light'ed'ly
de'light'ful
de'light'ful'ly
de'lim'it
de'lim'i'ta'tion
de'lin'e'ate
de'lin'e'at'ed
de'lin'e'at'ing
de'lin'e'a'tion
de'lin'e'a'tor
de'lin'quen'cies
de'lin'quen'cy
de'lin'quent
del'i'quesce
de'lir'i'ous
de'lir'i'ous'ly
de'lir'i'um
de'lir'i'um tre'mens
de'liv'er
de'liv'er'ance
de'liv'er'er
de'liv'er'ies
de'liv'ery

de'louse
de'loused
de'lous'ing
del'phin'i'um
del'ta
del'toid
de'lude
de'lud'ed
de'lud'ing
del'uge
del'uged
del'ug'ing
de'lu'sion
de'lu'sive
de'lu'sive'ly
de'lu'so'ry
de'luxe
delve
delv'ing
de'mag'ne'ti'za'tion
de'mag'ne'tize
de'mag'ne'tized
de'mag'ne'tiz'ing
dem'a'gog'ic
dem'a'gog'i'cal
dem'a'gogue
dem'a'gogu'ery
dem'a'gogy
de'mand
de'mar'cate
de'mar'ca'tion
de'mean
de'mean'our
de'ment'ed
de'men'tia
de'mer'it
de'mesne
dem'i'god
dem'i'john
de'mil'i'tar'iza'tion
de'mil'i'ta'rize
demi'mon'daine
demi'monde
de'mise
de'mised
de'mis'ing
dem'i'tasse
demo
de'mo'bi'li'za'tion
de'mo'bi'lize
de'mo'bi'lized
de'mo'bi'liz'ing
de'moc'ra'cies

de'moc'ra'cy
dem'o'crat
dem'o'crat'ic
dem'o'crat'i'cal'ly
de'moc'ra'ti'za'tion
de'moc'ra'tize
de'moc'ra'tized
de'moc'ra'tiz'ing
de'mog'ra'pher
dem'o'graph'ic
de'mog'ra'phy
de'mol'ish
dem'o'li'tion
de'mon
de'mo'ni'ac
de'mo'ni'a'cal
de'mo'ni'a'cal'ly
de'mon'ic
de'mon'ol'o'gy
de'mon'stra'ble
de'mon'stra'bly
dem'on'strate
dem'on'strat'ed
dem'on'strat'ing
dem'on'stra'tion
de'mon'stra'tive
dem'on'strat'or
de'mor'al'iza'tion
de'mor'al'ize
de'mor'al'ized
de'mor'a'liz'ing
de'mote
de'mot'ed
de'mot'ic
de'mot'ing
de'mo'tion
de'mur
de'mure
de'mure'ly
de'mure'ness
de'murred
de'mur'ring
de'mys'ti'fied
de'mys'ti'fy
de'mys'ti'fy'ing
de'na'tion'al'iza'tion
de'na'tion'a'lize
de'na'tion'a'lized
de'na'tion'al'iz'ing
de'nat'u'ral'iza'tion
de'nat'u'ra'lize
de'nat'u'ral'ized
de'nat'u'ral'iz'ing

de'na'zi'fi'ca'tion
de'na'zi'fied
de'na'zi'fy
de'na'zi'fy'ing
den'gue
de'ni'al
de'nied
de'nier
den'i'grate
den'i'grat'ed
den'i'grat'ing
den'i'gra'tion
den'im
den'i'zen
denomination
de'mo'ni'ac
denominational
de'nom'i'na'tor
de'no'ta'tion
de'note
de'not'ed
de'not'ing
de'noue'ment
de'nounce
de'nounced
de'nounc'ing
dense
dense'ly
den'si'ties
den'si'ty
den'ti'frice
den'tin
den'tine
den'tist'ry
den'ture
de'nude
de'nud'ed
de'nud'ing
de'nun'ci'a'tion
de'nun'ci'a'tion
de'ny
de'ny'ing
de'odor'ant,
de'odor'ize
de'odor'ized
de'odor'iz'ing
de'ox'i'dize
de'ox'i'dized
de'ox'i'diz'ing
de'ox'y'gen'at'ed
de'ox'y'gen'at'ing
de'ox'y'gen'a'tion
de'par'ture
de'pend'able

de'pend'ably
de'pen'dant
de'pen'dence
de'pen'den'cies
de'pen'den'cy
de'pen'dent
de'pict
de'pict'ed
de'pict'ing
de'pic'tion
de'pil'a'to'ry
de'plete
de'plet'ed
de'plet'ing
de'ple'tion
de'plor'able
de'plor'ably
de'plore
de'plored
de'plor'ing
de'ploy
de'ploy'ment
de'pol'ar'ize
de'pop'u'late
de'pop'u'lat'ed
de'pop'u'lat'ing
de'pop'u'la'tion
de'port
de'por'ta'tion
de'port'ment
de'pos'able
de'pose
de'posed
de'pos'ing
de'pos'it
de'pos'it'ed
de'pos'it'ing
dep'o'si'tion
de'pos'i'tor
de'pos'i'to'ry
de'pot
de'pra'va'tion
de'prave
de'praved
de'prav'ing
de'prav'i'ty
dep're'cate
dep're'cat'ed
dep're'cat'ing
dep're'ca'tion
dep're'ca'to'ry
de'pre'ci'ate
de'pre'ci'at'ed

de'pre'ci'at'ing
de'pre'ci'a'tion
de'pre'ci'a'to'ry
dep're'date
dep're'dat'ed
dep're'dat'ing
dep're'da'tion
de'press
de'pres'sant
de'pressed
de'press'ing'ly
de'pres'sion
de'pres'sive
dep'ri'va'tion
de'prive
de'prived
de'priv'ing
depth
dep'u'tate
dep'u'ta'tion
de'pute
de'put'ed
dep'u'ties
de'put'ing
dep'u'tize
dep'u'tized
dep'u'tiz'ing
dep'u'ty
de'raign
de'raign'ment
de'rail
de'rail'ment
de'range
de'ranged
de'range'ment
de'rang'ing
der'bies
der'by
der'e'lict
der'e'lic'tion
de'ride
de'rid'ing
de ri'gueur
de'ri'sion
de'ri'sive
de'ri'sive'ly
de'ri'so'ry
de'riv'able
der'i'va'tion
de'riv'a'tive
de'rive
de'rived
de'riv'ing

der'ma'ti'tis
der'ma'to'log'i'cal
der'ma'tol'o'gist
der'ma'tol'o'gy
der'mis
der'nier cri
der'o'gate
der'o'gat'ed
der'o'gat'ing
der'o'ga'tion
de'rog'a'to'ri'ly
de'rog'a'to'ry
der'rick
der'ring-do
der'rin'ger
der'vish
de'sal'i'nate
des'cant
de'scend
de'scend'ant
de'scend'ed
de'scend'ent
de'scend'ing
de'scent
de'scrib'able
de'scribe
de'scribed
de'scrib'ing
de'scried
de'scrip'tion
de'scrip'tive
de'scrip'tive'ly
de'scry
de'scry'ing
des'e'crate
des'e'crat'ed
des'e'crat'ing
des'e'cra'tion
de'seg're'gate
de'seg're'gat'ed
de'seg're'gat'ing
de'seg're'ga'tion
de'sen'si'tize
de'sen'si'tized
de'sen'si'tiz'ing
de'sert
des'ert
de'sert'ed
de'sert'er
de'ser'tion
de'serve
de'served
de'serv'ed'ly

de'serv'ing
des'ha'bille
des'ic'cate
des'ic'cated
des'ic'cat'ing
des'ic'ca'tion
de'sid'er'a'ta
de'sid'er'a'tum
de'sign
des'ig'nate
des'ig'nat'ed
des'ig'nat'ing
des'ig'na'tion
de'signed
de'sign'ed'ly
de'signer
de'sign'ing
de'sir'abil'i'ty
de'sir'able
de'sir'ably
de'sire
de'sired
de'sir'ing
de'sir'ous
de'sist
des'o'late
des'o'lat'ed
des'o'lat'ing
des'o'la'tion
de'spair
de'spair'ing
de'spair'ing'ly
des'patch
des'per'a'do
des'per'a'does
des'per'ate
des'per'ate'ly
des'per'a'tion
des'pi'ca'ble
des'pi'ca'bly
de'spise
de'spised
de'spis'ing
de'spite
de'spoil
de'spoil'ment
de'spo'li'a'tion
de'spond
de'spond'ence
de'spond'en'cy
de'spond'ent
de'spon'dent'ly
des'pot

49

des'pot'ic
des'pot'i'cal'ly
des'pot'ism
des'sert
des'sert'spoon
des'ti'na'tion
des'tine
des'tined
des'ti'nies
des'tin'ing
des'ti'ny
des'ti'tute
des'ti'tu'tion
de'stroy
de'stroy'er
de'struct'i'bil'i'ty
de'struc'ti'ble
de'struc'tion
de'struc'tive
de'struc'tive'ly
de'struc'tive'ness
des'ue'tude
des'ul'to'ri'ly
des'ul'to'ry
de'tach
de'tach'able
de'tached
de'tach'ment
de'tail
de'tain
de'tain'ee
de'tain'er
de'tain'ment
de'tect
de'tect'able
de'tec'tion
de'tec'tive
de'tec'tor
dé'tente
de'ten'tion
de'ten'tion
de'ter
de'ter'gent
de'te'ri'o'rate
de'te'ri'o'rat'ed
de'te'ri'o'rat'ing
de'te'ri'o'ra'tion
de'ter'min'able
de'ter'mi'nant
de'ter'mi'nate
de'ter'mi'na'tion
de'ter'mine
de'ter'mined

de'ter'mined'ly
de'ter'min'er
de'ter'min'ing
de'ter'min'ism
de'ter'min'is'tic
de'terred
de'ter'rence
de'ter'rent
de'ter'ring
de'test
de'test'able
de'tes'ta'tion
de'throne
de'throne'ment
det'o'nate
det'o'nat'ed
det'o'nat'ing
det'o'na'tion
det'o'na'tor
de'tour
de'tox'i'fi'cation
de'tract
de'trac'tion
de'trac'tor
det'ri'ment
det'ri'men'tal
de'tri'tus
de trop
deuce
deu'te'ri'um
Deut'sch'mark
de'val'u'ate
de'val'u'at'ed
de'val'u'at'ing
de'val'u'a'tion
de'value
dev'as'tate
dev'as'tat'ed
dev'as'tat'ing
dev'as'tat'ing'ly
dev'as'ta'tion
de'vel'op
de'vel'oped
de'vel'op'er
de'vel'op'ing
de'vel'op'ment
de'vel'op'men'tal
de'vi'ance
de'vi'ant
de'vi'ate
de'vi'at'ed
de'vi'at'ing
de'vi'a'tion

de'vi'a'tion'ism
de'vice
dev'il
dev'il'ish
dev'il'ish'ly
dev'illed
dev'il'ling
dev'il-may-care
dev'il'ment
dev'il'ry
dev'il'ries
dev'il'tries
dev'il'try
de'vi'ous
de'vi'ous'ness
de'vis'able
de'vis'al
de'vise
de'vised
de'vi'see
de'vis'ing
de'vi'sor
de'void
dev'o'lu'tion
de'volve
de'volved
de'volv'ing
de'vote
de'vot'ed
dev'o'tee
de'vote'ment
de'vot'ing
de'vo'tion
de'vo'tion'al
de'vour
de'vour'ing
de'vout
de'vout'ly
de'vout'ness
dew
dew'berry
dew'i'er
dew'i'est
dew'i'ness
dew'lap
dewy
dew'y-eyed
dex'ter'i'ty
dex'ter'ous
dex'ter'ous'ly
dex'trose
dex'trous
dhow

di'a'be'tes
di'a'bet'ic
di'a'bol'ic
di'a'bol'i'cal
di'a'bol'i'cal'ly
di'a'crit'ic
di'a'crit'i'cal
di'a'dem
di'ag'nose
di'ag'nosed
di'ag'no'ses
di'ag'nos'ing
di'ag'no'sis
di'ag'nos'tic
di'ag'nos'ti'cian
di'ag'o'nal
di'ag'o'nal'ly
di'a'gram
di'a'grammed
di'a'gram'ming
di'a'gram'matic
di'a'gram'mat'i'cal
di'al
di'a'lect
di'a'lec'tal
di'a'lec'tic
di'a'lec'ti'cal
di'a'lec'ti'cian
di'alled
di'al'ling
di'al'y'sis
di'a'man'té
di'am'e'ter
di'a'met'ric
di'a'met'ri'cal'ly
dia'mond
di'a'pa'son
dia'per
di'aph'a'nous
di'a'phragm
di'a'ries
di'a'rist
di'ar'rhoea
di'a'ry
di'as'to'le
di'as'tol'ic
di'as'tro'phism
di'a'ther'my
di'a'ton'ic
di'a'tribe
dice
diced
dic'ey

di'cho'tic
di'cho'tom'ic
di'chot'o'mies
di'chot'o'mous
di'chot'o'my
dic'i'er
dic'i'est
dic'ing
dick'ey
dic'ta
dic'tate
dic'tat'ed
dic'tat'ing
dic'ta'tion
dic'ta'tor
dic'ta'to'ri'al
dic'ta'to'ri'al'ly
dic'ta'tor'ship
dic'tion
dic'tion'ar'ies
dic'tion'ary
dic'tum
did
di'dac'tic
di'dac'ti'cal
di'dac'ti'cal'ly
di'dac'ti'cism
die
died
die-hard
die'sel
di'et
di'e'tary
di'e'tet'ic
di'e'tet'ics
di'eti'cian
dif'fer
dif'fer'ence
dif'fer'ent
dif'fer'en'tial
dif'fer'en'ti'ate
dif'fer'en'ti'a'tion
dif'fer'ent'ly
dif'fi'cult
dif'fi'cul'ties
dif'fi'cul'ty
dif'fi'dence
dif'fi'dent
dif'fi'dent'ly
dif'fuse
dif'fused
dif'fuse'ly
dif'fuse'ness

dif'fus'ing
dif'fu'sion
dig
di'gest
di'gest'ibil'i'ty
di'gest'ible
di'ges'tion
di'ges'tive
dig'ger
dig'ging
dig'gings
dig'it
dig'it'al
dig'i'tal'is
dig'i'ti'za'tion
dig'i'tize
dig'i'tized
dig'i'tiz'ing
dig'ni'fied
dig'ni'fy
dig'ni'fy'ing
dig'ni'tar'ies
dig'ni'tary
dig'ni'ties
dig'ni'ty
di'gress
di'gres'sion
di'gres'sive
di'he'dral
di'lap'i'date
di'lap'i'dat'ed
di'lap'i'dat'ing
di'lap'i'da'tion
dil'a'ta'tion
di'late
di'lat'ed
di'lat'ing
di'la'tion
dil'a'to'ri'ly
dil'a'to'ry
di'lem'ma
dil'et'tan'te
dil'et'tan'ti
dil'et'tan'tism
dil'i'gence
dil'i'gent
dil'i'gent'ly
dil'ly-dal'lied
dil'ly-dal'ly
dil'ly-dal'ly'ing
di'lute
di'lut'ed
di'lut'ing

di'lu'tion
di'lu'vi'al
dim
di'men'sion
di'men'sion'al
di'min'ish
di'min'ish'ing
di'min'u'en'do
dim'i'nu'tion
di'min'u'tive
dim'i'ty
dim'ly
dimmed
dim'mer
dim'ming
dim'ness
dim'ple
dim-wit'ted
din
di'nar
dine
dined
din'er
di'nette
din'ghies
din'ghy
din'gi'ness
din'gy
din'ing
dinned
din'ner
din'ning
di'no'saur
di'oc'e'san
di'o'cese
di'o'rama
di'ox'ide
dip
diph'the'ria
diph'thong
di'plo'ma
di'plo'ma'cies
di'plo'ma'cy
dip'lo'mat
dip'lo'mat'ic
dip'lo'mat'i'cal'ly
dipped
dip'ping
dip'so'ma'nia
dip'so'ma'ni'ac
dip'tych
dire
di'rect

di'rec'tion
di'rec'tion'al
di'rec'tive
di'rect'ly
di'rect'ness
di'rec'tor
di'rec'to'rate
di'rec'to'ri'al
di'rec'to'ries
di'rec'tor'ship
di'rec'to'ry
dire'ness
dirge
di'ri'gi'ble
dirndl
dirt'ied
dirt'i'ly
dirt'i'ness
dirty
dirty'ing
dis'abil'i'ty
dis'able
dis'abled
dis'able'ment
dis'abling
dis'abuse
dis'abused
dis'abus'ing
dis'ad'van'tage
dis'ad'van'taged
dis'ad'van'ta'geous
dis'ad'van'tag'ing
dis'af'fect
dis'af'fect'ed
dis'af'fec'tion
dis'agree
dis'agree'able
dis'agree'ably
dis'agreed
dis'agree'ing
dis'agree'ment
dis'al'low
dis'al'low'ance
dis'ap'pear
dis'ap'pear'ance
dis'ap'point
dis'ap'point'ing'ly
dis'ap'point'ment
dis'ap'pro'ba'tion
dis'ap'pro'ba'tion
dis'ap'prov'al
dis'ap'prove
dis'ap'proved

dis'ap'prov'ing
dis'ap'prov'ing'ly
dis'arm
dis'ar'ma'ment
dis'ar'range
dis'ar'ranged
dis'ar'range'ment
dis'ar'rang'ing
dis'ar'ray
dis'as'sem'ble
dis'as'so'ci'ate
dis'as'ter
dis'as'trous
dis'as'trous'ly
dis'avow
dis'avow'al
dis'band
dis'band'ment
dis'bar
dis'bar'ment
dis'barred
dis'bar'ring
dis'be'lief
dis'be'lieve
dis'be'lieved
dis'be'liev'er
dis'be'liev'ing
dis'burse
dis'bursed
dis'burse'ment
dis'burs'er
dis'burs'ing
disc
dis'card
dis'cern
dis'cern'ible
dis'cern'ibly
dis'cern'ing
dis'cern'ment
dis'charge
dis'charged
dis'char'ger
dis'charg'ing
dis'ci'ple
dis'ci'pli'nar'i'an
dis'ci'pli'nary
dis'ci'pline
dis'ci'plined
dis'ci'plin'ing
dis'claim
dis'claim'er
dis'close
dis'closed

dis'closing
dis'closure
dis'coid
dis'col'or'a'tion
dis'col'our
dis'com'bob'u'late
dis'com'bob'u'lat'ed
dis'com'bob'u'lat'ing
dis'com'bob'u'lation
dis'com'fit
dis'com'fit'ed
dis'com'fit'ing
dis'com'fi'ture
dis'com'fort
dis'com'mode
dis'com'mod'ed
dis'com'mod'ing
dis'com'pose
dis'com'posed
dis'com'pos'ing
dis'com'po'sure
dis'con'cert
dis'con'cert'ed
dis'con'cert'ing
dis'con'cert'ing'ly
dis'con'nect
dis'con'nect'ed
dis'con'nec'tion
dis'con'so'late
dis'con'so'late'ly
dis'con'tent
dis'con'tent'ed
dis'con'tent'ed'ly
dis'con'tent'ment
dis'con'tin'u'ance
dis'con'tin'u'a'tion
dis'con'tin'ue
dis'con'tin'ued
dis'con'tin'u'ing
dis'con'ti'nu'i'ties
dis'con'ti'nu'ity
dis'con'tin'u'ous
dis'cord
dis'cord'ance
dis'cor'dan'cy
dis'cor'dant
dis'cord'ant'ly
dis'co'theque
dis'count
dis'cour'age
dis'cour'age'ment
dis'cour'ag'ing
dis'course

dis'coursed
dis'cours'ing
dis'cour'te'ous
dis'cour'te'ous'ly
dis'cour'te'sies
dis'cour'te'sy
dis'cov'er
dis'cov'er'able
dis'cov'er'er
dis'cov'er'ies
dis'cov'ery
dis'cred'it
dis'cred'it'able
dis'creet
dis'creet'ly
dis'crep'an'cies
dis'crep'an'cy
dis'crep'ant
dis'crete
dis'cre'tion
dis'cre'tion'ary
dis'crim'i'nate
dis'crim'i'nat'ed
dis'crim'i'nate'ly
dis'crim'i'nat'ing
dis'crim'i'na'tion
dis'crim'i'na'to'ry
dis'cur'sive
dis'cur'sive'ness
dis'cus
dis'cuss
dis'cus'sion
dis'dain
dis'dain'ful
dis'dain'ful'ly
dis'ease
dis'eased
dis'eas'ing
dis'em'bark
dis'em'bar'ka'tion
dis'em'bark'ment
dis'em'bod'ied
dis'em'bodi'ment
dis'em'body
dis'em'body'ing
dis'em'bow'el
dis'em'bow'elled
dis'em'bow'el'ling
dis'em'bow'el'ment
dis'en'able
dis'en'chant
dis'en'chant'ment
dis'en'cum'ber

dis'en'fran'chise
dis'en'fran'chised
dis'en'fran'chis'ing
dis'en'gage
dis'en'gaged
dis'en'gage'ment
dis'en'gag'ing
dis'en'tan'gle
dis'en'tan'gled
dis'en'tan'gle'ment
dis'en'tan'gling
dis'equi'lib'ri'um
dis'es'tab'lish
dis'es'tab'lish'ment
dis'fa'vour
dis'fig'ure
dis'fig'ured
dis'fig'ure'ment
dis'fig'ur'ing
dis'fran'chise
dis'fran'chised
dis'fran'chise'ment
dis'fran'chis'ing
dis'gorge
dis'gorged
dis'gorg'ing
dis'grace
dis'graced
dis'grace'ful
dis'grace'ful'ly
dis'grac'ing
dis'grun'tle
dis'grun'tled
dis'grun'tle'ment
dis'grun'tling
dis'guise
dis'guised
dis'guis'ing
dis'gust
dis'gust'ed
dis'gust'ed'ly
dis'gust'ing
dis'gust'ing'ly
dis'ha'bille
dis'har'mo'nies
dis'har'mo'ny
dis'heart'en
dis'heart'en'ing
di'shev'elled
dish'i'er
dish'i'est
dis'hon'est
dis'hon'es'ties

dis'hon'est'ly
dis'hon'es'ty
dis'hon'our
dis'hon'our'able
dis'hon'our'ably
dishy
dis'il'lu'sion
dis'il'lu'sion'ment
dis'in'cen'tive
dis'in'cli'na'tion
dis'in'cline
dis'in'clined
dis'in'clin'ing
dis'in'fect
dis'in'fect'ant
dis'in'fec'tion
dis'in'for'ma'tion
dis'in'gen'u'ous
dis'in'gen'u'ous'ly
dis'in'her'it
dis'in'her'i'tance
dis'in'te'grate
dis'in'te'grat'ed
dis'in'te'grat'ing
dis'in'te'gra'tion
dis'in'ter
dis'in'ter'est
dis'in'ter'es'ted
dis'in'ter'est'ed'ly
dis'in'ter'est'ed'ness
dis'in'ter'ment
dis'in'terred
dis'in'ter'ring
dis'join
dis'joint
dis'joint'ed
dis'junc'tion
disk
dis'lik'able
dis'like
dis'liked
dis'lik'ing
dis'lo'cate
dis'lo'cat'ing
dis'lo'ca'tion
dis'lodge
dis'lodged
dis'lodg'ing
dis'lodge'ment
dis'loy'al
dis'loy'al'ly
dis'loy'al'ty
dis'mal

dis'mal'ly
dis'man'tle
dis'man'tled
dis'man'tling
dis'may
dis'mem'ber
dis'mem'ber'ment
dis'miss
dis'mis'sal
dis'mis'sive
dis'mis'sive'ly
dis'mount
dis'obe'di'ence
dis'obe'di'ent
dis'obe'di'ent'ly
dis'obey
dis'oblig'ing
dis'or'der
dis'or'dered
dis'or'der'li'ness
dis'or'der'ly
dis'or'ga'ni'za'tion
dis'or'gan'ize
dis'or'gan'ized
dis'ori'en'tate
dis'ori'en'tat'ed
dis'ori'en'ta'tion
dis'ori'ent'ed
dis'own
dis'par'age
dis'par'aged
dis'par'age'ment
dis'par'ag'ing
dis'par'ag'ing'ly
dis'pa'rate
dis'pa'rate'ly
dis'par'i'ties
dis'par'i'ty
dis'pas'sion
dis'pas'sion'ate
dis'pas'sion'ate'ly
dis'patch
dis'patch'er
dis'pel
dis'pelled
dis'pel'ling
dis'pen'sa'bil'i'ty
dis'pen'sa'ble
dis'pen'sa'ries
dis'pen'sa'ry
dis'pen'sa'tion
dis'pense
dis'pensed

dis'pens'er
dis'pens'ing
dis'pers'al
dis'perse
dis'persed
dis'pers'ing
dis'per'sion
dispir'it'ed
dispir'it'ed'ly
dispir'it'ing
dis'place
dis'placed
dis'place'ment
dis'plac'ing
dis'play
dis'please
dis'pleas'ing
dis'pleas'ure
dis'port
dis'pos'able
dis'pos'al
dis'pose
dis'pos'ing
dis'po'si'tion
dis'pos'sess
dis'pos'ses'sion
dis'pro'por'tion
dis'pro'por'tion'ate
dis'pro'por'tion'ate'ly
dis'prove
dis'prov'ing
dis'put'able
dis'pu'tant
dis'pu'ta'tion
dis'pu'ta'tious
dis'pute
dis'put'ed
dis'put'ing
dis'qual'i'fi'ca'tion
dis'qual'i'fied
dis'qual'i'fy
dis'qual'i'fy'ing
dis'qui'et
dis'qui'etude
dis'qui'si'tion
dis're'gard
dis're'pair
dis'rep'u'ta'ble
dis're'pute
dis're'spect
dis're'spect'ful
dis're'spect'ful'ly
dis'robe

dis'robed
dis'rob'ing
dis'rupt
dis'rupt'er
dis'rup'tion
dis'rup'tive
dis'sat'is'fac'tion
dis'sat'is'fac'to'ry
dis'sat'is'fied
dis'sat'is'fy
dis'sat'is'fy'ing
dis'sect
dis'sect'ed
dis'sec'tion
dis'sem'blance
dis'sem'ble
dis'sem'bled
dis'sem'bling
dis'sem'i'nate
dis'sem'i'nat'ed
dis'sem'i'nat'ing
dis'sem'i'na'tion
dis'sen'sion
dis'sent
dis'sent'er
dis'sen'tient
dis'sent'ing
dis'sen'tious
dis'ser'tate
dis'ser'ta'ted
dis'ser'ta'ting
dis'ser'ta'tion
dis'serve
dis'served
dis'serv'ice
dis'serv'ing
dis'si'dence
dis'si'dent
dis'sim'i'lar
dis'sim'i'lar'i'ty
dis'sim'i'late
dis'sim'i'lat'ed
dis'sim'i'lat'ing
dis'sim'i'la'tion
dis'si'mil'i'tude
dis'sim'u'late
dis'sim'u'lat'ed
dis'sim'u'lat'ing
dis'sim'u'la'tion
dis'si'pate
dis'si'pat'ed
dis'si'pat'ing
dis'si'pa'tion

dis'so'ci'ate
dis'so'ci'at'ed
dis'so'ci'at'ing
dis'so'ci'a'tion
dis'sol'u'ble
dis'so'lute
dis'so'lu'tion
dis'solv'a'ble
dis'solve
dis'solv'ing
dis'so'nance
dis'so'nant
dis'suade
dis'suad'ed
dis'suad'ing
dis'sua'sion
dis'sua'sive
dis'taff
dis'tal
dis'tance
dis'tanced
dis'tanc'ing
dis'tant
dis'tant'ly
dis'taste
dis'taste'ful
dis'taste'ful'ly
dis'tem'per
dis'tend
dis'ten'sion
dis'ten'tion
dis'til
dis'til'late
dis'til'la'tion
dis'tilled
dis'till'er
dis'till'er'ies
dis'till'ery
dis'till'ing
dis'tinct
dis'tinc'tion
dis'tinc'tive
dis'tinc'tive'ly
dis'tinc'tive'ness
dis'tinct'ly
dis'tin'gué
dis'tin'guish
dis'tin'guish'able
dis'tin'guished
dis'tort
dis'tor'ted
dis'tor'tion
dis'tract

dis'tract'ed'ly
dis'tract'ing
dis'trac'tion
dis'trait
dis'traught
dis'tress
dis'tress'ful
dis'tress'ing
dis'tress'ing'ly
dis'trib'ute
dis'trib'ut'ed
dis'trib'ut'ing
dis'tri'bu'tion
dis'trib'u'tor
dis'trict
dis'trust
dis'trust'ful
dis'turb
dis'turb'ance
dis'turbed
dis'un'ion
dis'u'nite
dis'u'ni'ted
dis'u'ni'ting
dis'u'ni'ty
dis'use
dis'used
dis'us'ing
ditch
dith'er
dith'y'ramb
dith'y'ram'bic
dit'ta'nies
dit'ta'ny
dit'to
dit'to'ing
dit'ty
di'u'ret'ic
di'ur'nal
di'va
di'va'gate
di'va'ga'tion
di'va'lent
di'van
dive
dived
di'verge
di'verged
di'ver'gence
di'ver'gent
di'verg'ing
di'vers
di'verse

di'ver'si'fi'ca'tion
di'ver'si'fied
di'ver'si'fy
di'ver'si'fy'ing
di'ver'sion
di'ver'sion'ary
di'ver'si'ties
di'ver'si'ty
di'vert
di'ver'ti'men'ti
di'ver'ti'men'to
di'ver'tisse'ment
div'est
di'vide
di'vid'ed
div'i'dend
di'vid'er
di'vid'ing
div'i'na'tion
di'vine
di'vine'ly
div'ing
di'vin'i'ties
di'vin'i'ty
di'vis'i'ble
di'vi'sion
di'vi'sion'al
di'vi'sive
di'vi'sor
di'vorce
di'vor'cee
di'vorc'ing
div'ot
di'vulge
di'vulged
di'vul'gence
di'vulg'ing
div'vied
div'vy
div'vy'ing
diz'zied
diz'zi'est
diz'zi'ly
diz'zi'ness
diz'zy
diz'zy'ing
do
doc'ile
do'cile'ly
do'cil'i'ty
dock'et
dock'et'ed
dock'et'ing

doc'tor
doc'tor'al
doc'tor'ate
doc'tri'naire
doc'tri'nal
doc'trine
doc'u'ment
doc'u'men'tary
doc'u'men'ta'tion
dod'der
dod'dery
dodge
dodg'ing
do'do
do'does
does
doesn't
dog
doge
dog-eared
dog'fight
dog'ged
dogged
dog'ged'ly
dog'ged'ness
dog'ger'el
doggie bag
dog'ging
dog'gone
dog'ma
dog'mat'ic
dog'mat'i'cal
dog'ma'ti'cal'ly
dog'ma'tism
dog'ma'tist
dog'ma'tize
dog'ma'tized
dog'ma'tiz'ing
do-good'er
dog'watch
doi'lies
doi'ly
do'ing
dol'ce
dol'drums
dole
doled
dole'ful
dole'ful'ly
do'li'cho'ce'phal'ic
dol'ing
dol'lar
dol'lies

dol'lop
dol'ly
dol'o'mite
dol'or'ous
dol'phin
dolt
dolt'ish
do'main
dome
domed
do'mes'tic
do'mes'ti'cal'ly
do'mes'ti'cate
do'mes'ti'cat'ed
do'mes'ti'cat'ing
do'mes'ti'ca'tion
do'mes'tic'i'ties
do'mes'tic'i'ty
dom'i'cile
dom'i'ciled
dom'i'cil'ing
dom'i'nance
dom'i'nancy
dom'i'nant
dom'i'nate
dom'i'nat'ing
domi'na'tion
dom'i'neer
dom'i'neer'ing
dom'ing
do'min'ion
dom'i'no
dom'i'noes
don
do'nate
do'nat'ed
do'nat'ing
do'na'tion
do'na'tor
done
don'jon
don'key
don'key-work
donned
don'ning
do'nor
do'nut
doo'dle
doom
dooms'day
door
door'jamb
door'knob

door'man
dope
doped
dop'ey
dop'i'ness
dop'ing
dop'pel'gäng'er
do'ries
dor'man'cy
dor'mant
dor'mer
dor'mered
dor'mice
dor'mi'to'ries
dor'mi'to'ry
dor'mouse
dor'sal
do'ry
dos'age
dose
dosed
do-si-do
dos'ing
dos'si'er
dost
dot
dot'age
dote
dot'ed
doth
dot'ing
dot'ted
dot'ter'el
dot'tier
dot'tiest
dot'ting
dou'ble
dou'ble-breast'ed
dou'ble-cross
dou'bled
dou'ble-deck'er
dou'ble en'ten'dre
dou'ble-faced
dou'ble'head'er
dou'ble-joint'ed
doub'let
dou'ble-time
dou'bling
dou'bloon
doub'ly
doubt
doubt'ful
doubt'ful'ly

doubt'less
douche
douched
douch'ing
dough
dough'i'er
dough'i'est
dough'nut
dough'ti'ness
dough'ty
dough'y
dour
dour'ness
douse
doused
dous'ing
dove
dove'cote
dove'tail
dow'a'ger
dowd'i'ly
dow'di'ness
dow'dy
dow'el
dow'eled
dow'el'ing
dow'er
down
down'grade
down'grad'ed
down'grad'ing
down'heart'ed
downi'ness
down'stream
down'town
down'trod'den
downy
dow'ries
dow'ry
dowse
dowsed
dows'ing
dox'ol'o'gy
doy'en
doy'enne
doze
dozed
doz'en
doz'enth
dozing
drab
drab'ness
drachm

drach'ma
drach'mae
dra'co'ni'an
draft
draft'ee
drag
dra'gée
dragged
drag'ging
drag'net
drag'on
drag'on'flies
drag'on'fly
dra'goon
drain
drain'age
drake
dram
dra'ma
dra'ma'tic
dra'mat'i'cal'ly
dra'mat'ics
dram'a'tist
dram'a'ti'za'tion
dram'a'tize
drank
drape
draped
draper
dra'per'ies
dra'pery
draping
dras'tic
drast'i'cal'ly
draught
draught'i'er
draughts'man
draughty
draw
draw'bridge
draw'er
draw'ing
drawl
drawn
dread
dread'ful
dread'ful'ly
dread'nought
dream
dreamed
dream'er
dream'i'est
dream'i'ly

dream'ing
dreamt
dreamy
drear'i'er
drear'i'ly
drear'i'ness
dreary
dredge
dredged
dredg'er
dredg'ing
dregs
dreg'gy
drench
dress
dres'sage
dressed
dress'er
dress'i'est
dres'sing
dressy
drew
drib'ble
drib'bled
drib'bling
drib'let
dried
dri'er
dri'est
drift
drift'age
drift'er
drill'ing
dri'ly
drink
drink'a'ble
drink'er
drink'ing
drip
dripped
drip'ping
drip'py
drive
driv'el
driv'elled
driv'el'ing
driv'en
driv'ing
driz'zle
driz'zled
driz'zling
driz'zly
droll

droll'ery
drol'ly
drom'e'dar'ies
drom'e'dary
drone
droned
dron'ing
drool
droop
droop'ing'ly
droop'y
drop
drop'let
dropped
drop'per
drop'ping
drop'sy
dro'soph'i'la
dross
drought
drought'i'est
droughty
drove
drowned
drowse
drows'i'ly
drows'ing
drow'sy
drub
drubbed
drub'bing
drudge
drudg'ery
drudg'ing
drug
drugged
drug'ging
drug'gist
dru'id
drum
drummed
drum'mer
drum'ming
drunk
drunk'ard
drunk'en
drunk'en'ly
drunk'en'ness
dru'pa'ceous
drupe
dry
dry'ad

dry'ads
dry'a'des
dry'er
dry'est
dry'ing
dry'ly
dry'ness
du'al
du'al'ism
du'al'is'tic
du'al'i'ty
dub
dubbed
dub'bin
dub'bing
du'bi'e'ty
du'bi'ous
du'bi'ous'ly
du'cal
du'cat
duch'ess
duchy
duck'i'est
duck'ling
ducky
duc'tile
duct'less
dude
dudg'eon
du'el
du'elled
du'el'ling
du'el'list
du'en'na
du'et
duf'fel
duf'fel-bag
duff'er
duf'fle
dug
du'gong
dug'out
duke'dom
dul'cet
dul'ci'mer
dull
dull'ard
dull'ness
dul'ly
dulse
du'ly
dumb
dumb'bell

dumb'found
dumb'ness
dumb'wait'er
dum'found
dum'mies
dum'my
dump'i'er
dump'i'ness
dump'ling
dumpy
dun
dunce
dun'der'head
dune
dun'ga'ree
dun'geon
dung'hill
dun'lin
dun'nage
dunned
dun'ning
du'o'dec'i'mal
du'o'de'nal
du'o'de'num
duo'logue
dupe
duped
dup'ing
du'ple
du'plex
du'pli'cate
du'pli'cat'ed
du'pli'cat'ing
du'pli'ca'tion
du'pli'ca'tor
du'plic'i'ties
du'plic'i'ty
du'ra'bil'i'ty
du'ra'ble
Du'ral'u'min
dur'ance
du'ra'tion
du'ress
dur'ing
durst
dusk
dusk'i'ness
dusky
dust'er
dust'i'er
dust'i'ness
dust'less
dusty

du'te'ous
du'ti'a'ble
du'ties
du'ti'ful
du'ti'ful'ly
du'ty
dwarf
dwarf'ish
dwell
dwelled
dwell'ing
dwelt
dwindle
dwin'dled
dwin'dling
dye
dyed
dye'ing
dy'er
dye'stuff
dy'ing
dyke
dy'nam'ic
dy'nam'i'cal'ly
dy'nam'ics
dy'na'mism
dy'na'mist
dy'na'mite
dy'na'mit'er
dy'na'mo
dy'na'mo'tor
dy'nast
dy'nas'tic
dy'nas'ties
dy'nas'ty
dy'na'tron
dyne
dy'node
dys'en'tery
dys'func'tion
dys'lex'ia
dys'lex'ic
dys'men'or'rhoea
dys'pep'sia
dys'pep'tic
dys'phag'ic
dys'tro'phic
dys'tro'phy
dys'uria
dys'uric
each
ea'ger
ea'ger'ly

ea'ger'ness
ea'gle
ea'gle-eyed
ea'glet
ear
ear'ache
ear'drum
ear'ful
earl
earl'dom
ear'li'er
ear'li'est
ear'li'ness
ear'lobe
ear'ly
ear'mark
earn
ear'nest
ear'nest'ly
ear'nest'ness
earn'ings
ear'ring
ear'shot
ear-split'ting
earth
earth'bound
earth'en
earth'en'ware
earth'i'ness
earth'li'ness
earth'ly
earth'quake
earth'shaking
earth'work
earth'worm
earthy
ear'wig
ear'wigged
ear'wig'ging
ease
eased
ea'sel
ease'ment
eas'i'er
eas'i'est
eas'i'ly
eas'i'ness
eas'ing
east
east'bound
Eas'ter
east'er'lies
east'er'ly

east'ern
east'ern'er
east'er'nize
east'er'nized
east'er'niz'ing
east'ern'most
east'ward
easy
easy'go'ing
eat
eat'able
eat'en
eat'er'ies
eat'ery
eat'ing
eau de Co'logne
eau-de-vie
eaves
eaves'drop
eaves'dropped
eaves'drop'per
eaves'drop'ping
ebb
ebb'ing
eb'on
eb'ony
ebul'lience
ebul'lient
eb'ul'li'tion
ec'cen'tric
ec'cen'tri'cal'ly
ec'cen'tric'i'ties
ec'cen'tric'i'ty
ec'cle'si'as'tic
ec'cle'si'as'ti'cal
ech'e'lon
echid'na
echo
ech'oed
ech'oes
ech'o'ing
echo'lo'ca'tion
eclair
eclamp'sia
éclat
ec'lec'tic
ec'lec'ti'cal'ly
ec'lec'ti'cism
eclipse
eclipsed
eclips'ing
eclip'tic
ec'logue

ec'o'log'ic
ec'o'log'i'cal
ecol'o'gist
ecol'o'gy
eco'nom'ic
eco'nomi'cal
eco'nom'i'cal'ly
eco'nom'ics
econ'o'mies
econ'o'mist
econ'o'mize
econ'o'miz'ing
econ'o'my
eco'sys'tem
ec'ru
ec'sta'sies
ec'sta'sy
ec'stat'ic
ec'stat'i'cal
ec'stat'i'cal'ly
ec'to'morph
ec'top'ic
ec'to'plasm
ec'u'men'ic
ec'u'men'i'cal
ec'u'men'ism
ec'ze'ma
ec'zem'a'tous
e'da'cious
ed'died
ed'dies
ed'dy
ed'dy'ing
edel'weiss
ede'ma
eden'tate
edge
edged
edg'i'er
edg'i'est
edg'i'ness
edg'ing
edgy
ed'i'bil'i'ty
ed'i'ble
edict
ed'i'fi'ca'tion
ed'i'fice
ed'i'fied
ed'i'fy
ed'i'fy'ing
ed'it
edi'tion

ed'i'tor
ed'i'to'ri'al
ed'i'to'ri'al'ize
ed'i'to'ri'al'iz'ing
ed'i'to'ri'al'ly
ed'u'ca'ble
ed'u'cate
ed'u'cat'ed
ed'u'cat'ing
ed'u'ca'tion
ed'u'ca'tion'al
ed'u'ca'tion'al'ist
ed'u'ca'tion'al'ly
ed'u'ca'tion'ist
ed'u'ca'tive
ed'u'ca'tor
educe
educed
educ'i'ble
educ'ing
educ'tion
eel
eely
e'en
e'er
ee'rie
ee'ri'ly
ee'ri'ness
ef'face
ef'faced
ef'face'ment
ef'fac'ing
ef'fect
ef'fec'tive
ef'fec'tive'ly
ef'fec'tive'ness
ef'fec'tu'al
ef'fec'tu'al'ly
ef'fec'tu'ate
ef'fec'tu'at'ed
ef'fec'tu'at'ing
ef'fem'i'na'cy
ef'fem'i'nate
ef'fem'i'nate'ly
ef'fen'di
ef'fer'vesce
ef'fer'ves'cence
ef'fer'ves'cent
ef'fer'vesc'ing
ef'fete
ef'fi'ca'cies
ef'fi'ca'cious
ef'fi'ca'cious'ly

ef'fi'ca'cy
ef'fi'cien'cy
ef'fi'cient
ef'fi'cient'ly
ef'fi'gies
ef'fi'gy
ef'flo'resce
ef'flo'resced
ef'flo'res'cence
ef'flo'res'cent
ef'flo'resc'ing
ef'flu'ence
ef'flu'ent
ef'flu'vi'al
ef'flu'vi'um
ef'fort
ef'fort'less
ef'fron'ter'ies
ef'fron'tery
ef'ful'gence
ef'ful'gent
ef'fuse
ef'fused
ef'fus'ing
ef'fu'sion
ef'fu'sive
ef'fu'sive'ly
egal'i'tar'i'an
egal'i'tar'i'an'ism
egg'nog
egg'plant
egg'shell
eg'lan'tine
ego
ego'cen'tric
ego'cen'tric'i'ty
ego'ism
ego'ist
ego'is'tic
ego'ma'nia
ego'ma'ni'ac
ego'tism
ego'tist
ego'tis'tic
ego'tis'ti'cal
egre'gious
egress
egres'sion
egret
Egyp'tian
Egyp'tol'o'gist
Egyp'tol'o'gy
ei'der

ei'der'down
eight
eight'een
eight'eenth
eight'fold
eighth
eight'ies
eight'i'eth
eighty
ein'stein'i'um
ei'ther
ejac'u'late
ejac'u'lat'ed
ejac'u'lat'ing
ejac'u'la'tion
ejac'u'la'to'ry
eject
ejec'tion
eject'ment
ejec'tor
eke
eked
ek'ing
elab'o'rate
elab'o'rat'ed
elab'o'rate'ly
elab'o'rate'ness
elab'o'rat'ing
elab'o'ra'tion
élan
eland
elapse
elapsed
elaps'ing
elas'tic
elas'ti'cal
elas'tic'i'ty
elate
elat'ed
elat'ing
ela'tion
el'bow
eld'er
el'der'ber'ries
el'der'ber'ry
eld'er'li'ness
eld'er'ly
eld'est
elect
elec'tion
elec'tion'eer
elec'tive
elec'tor

elec'tor'al
elec'tor'ate
elec'tric
elec'tri'cal
elec'tri'cal'ly
elec'tri'cian
elec'tric'i'ty
elec'tri'fi'ca'tion
elec'tri'fied
elec'tri'fy
elec'tri'fy'ing
elec'tro
elec'tro'analy'sis
elec'tro'cute
elec'tro'cut'ed
elec'tro'cut'ing
elec'tro'cu'tion
elec'trode
elec'tro'dy'nam'ics
elec'trol'y'sis
elec'tro'lyte
elec'tro'lyt'ic
elec'tro'lyze
elec'tro'lyzed
elec'tro'lyz'ing
elec'tro'mag'net
elec'tro'mag'net'ic
elec'tro'mag'net'ism
elec'tro'mo'tive
elec'tron
elec'tron'ic
elec'tron'i'cal'ly
elec'tron'ics
elec'tro'plate
elec'tro'plat'ed
elec'tro'plat'ing
elec'tro'ther'a'py
elec'trum
elec'tuary
el'ee'mosy'nary
el'e'gance
el'e'gan'cy
el'e'gant
el'e'gant'ly
ele'gi'ac
el'e'gies
el'e'gize
el'e'giz'ing
el'e'gy
el'e'ment
el'e'men'tal
el'e'men'ta'ri'ly
el'e'men'ta'ry

el'e'phant
el'e'phan'ti'a'sis
el'e'phan'tine
el'e'vate
el'e'vat'ed
el'e'vat'ing
el'e'va'tion
el'e'va'tor
elev'en
elev'enth
elf
elf'in
elic'it
elide
elid'ed
elid'ing
el'i'gi'bil'i'ty
el'i'gi'ble
elim'i'nate
elim'i'nat'ed
elim'i'nat'ing
elim'i'na'tion
eli'sion
elite
elit'ism
elit'ist
elix'ir
el'lipse
el'lip'ses
el'lip'sis
el'lip'soid
el'lip'tic
el'lip'ti'cal
el'lip'ti'cal'ly
el'o'cu'tion
el'o'cu'tion'ary
el'o'cu'tion'ist
elon'gate
elon'gat'ed
elon'gat'ing
elon'ga'tion
elope
eloped
elope'ment
elop'ing
el'o'quence
el'o'quent
elo'quent'ly
else
else'where
elu'ci'date
elu'ci'dat'ed
elu'ci'dat'ing

elu'ci'da'tion
elude
elud'ed
elud'ing
elu'sion
elu'sive
elu'sive'ly
elu'sive'ness
elu'so'ry
el'ver
elves
ema'ci'ate
ema'ci'at'ed
ema'ci'a'tion
em'a'nate
em'a'nat'ed
em'a'nat'ing
em'a'na'tion
eman'ci'pate
eman'ci'pat'ed
eman'ci'pat'ing
eman'ci'pa'tion
eman'ci'pa'tion'ist
eman'ci'pa'tor
emas'cu'late
emas'cu'lat'ed
emas'cu'lating
emas'cu'la'tion
em'balm
em'balm'er
em'balm'ment
em'bank'ment
em'bar'go
em'bar'goed
em'bar'goes
em'bar'go'ing
em'bark
em'bar'ka'tion
em'bark'ment
em'bar'rass
em'bar'rass'ed
em'bar'rass'ing
em'bar'ras'sing'ly
em'bar'rass'ment
em'bas'sies
em'bas'sy
em'bat'tle
em'bat'tled
em'bat'tle'ment
em'bat'tling
em'bed
em'bed'ded
em'bed'ding

em'bel'lish
em'bel'lish'ment
em'ber
em'bez'zle
em'bez'zled
em'bez'zle'ment
em'bez'zler
em'bez'zling
em'bit'ter
em'bit'ter'ment
em'bla'zon
em'blaz'on'ment
em'blem
em'blem'at'ic
em'blem'at'i'cal
em'blem'a'ti'cal'ly
em'bod'ied
em'bodi'ment
em'bod'y
em'body'ing
em'bold'en
em'bo'lism
em'bo'lus
em'boss
em'boss'ment
em'bou'chure
em'brace
em'brac'ing
em'bra'sure
em'bro'cate
em'bro'ca'tion
em'broi'der
em'broi'der'ies
em'broi'dery
em'broil
em'broil'ment
em'bryo
em'bry'o'log'i'cal
em'bry'ol'o'gist
em'bry'ol'o'gy
em'bry'on'ic
em'bry'os
em'cee
em'ceed
em'cee'ing
emend
emen'da'ble
emen'da'tion
em'er'ald
emerge
emerged
emer'gence
emer'gen'cies

emer'gen'cy
emer'gent
emerg'ing
emer'i'tus
emer'sion
em'ery
eme'sis
emet'ic
em'etine
em'i'grant
em'i'grate
em'i'grat'ing
em'i'gra'tion
émi'gré
em'i'nence
émi'nence grise
em'i'nen'cy
em'i'nent
em'i'nent do'main
em'i'nent'ly
emir'ate
em'is'sar'ies
em'is'sary
emis'sion
emis'sive
emit
emit'ted
emit'ting
emol'lient
emol'u'ment
emote
emot'ed
emot'ing
emo'tion
emo'tion'al
emo'tion'al'ism
emo'tion'al'ly
emo'tive
em'pan'el
em'pa'thet'ic
em'path'ic
em'pa'thize
em'pa'thized
em'pa'thiz'ing
em'pa'thy
em'per'or
em'pha'ses
em'pha'sis
em'pha'size
em'pha'sized
em'pha'siz'ing
em'phat'ic
em'phat'i'cal'ly

em'phy'se'ma
em'pire
em'pir'i'cal
em'pir'i'cal'ly
em'pir'i'cism
em'pir'i'cist
em'place'ment
em'plane
em'planed
em'plan'ing
em'ploy
em'ploy'able
em'ploy'ee
em'ploy'er
em'ploy'ment
em'po'ria
em'po'ri'um
em'pow'er
em'press
emp'tied
emp'ties
emp'ti'ness
emp'ty
emp'ty'ing
em'py're'al
em'py're'an
emu
em'u'late
em'u'lat'ing
em'u'la'tion
em'u'lous
emul'si'fi'ca'tion
emul'si'fied
emul'si'fi'er
emul'si'fy
emul'si'fy'ing
emul'sion
emul'sive
emul'soid
en'able
en'abled
en'abling
en'act
en'ac'tion
en'act'ment
enam'el
enam'elled
enam'el'ling
enam'el'ware
en'am'our
en'am'oured
en bloc
en'camp

en'camp'ment
en'cap'su'late
en'cap'su'lat'ing
en'cap'sule
en'cap'sul'at'ed
en'case
en'cased
en'cas'ing
en'ceinte
en'ceph'a'li'tis
en'chain
en'chant
en'chant'ing
en'chant'ing'ly
en'chant'ment
en'chant'ress
en'chi'la'da
en'cir'cle
en'cir'cled
en'cir'cle'ment
en'cir'cling
en'clave
en'close
en'closed
en'clos'ing
en'clo'sure
en'code
en'cod'ed
en'cod'ing
en'co'mia
en'co'mi'um
en'com'pass
en'core
en'cored
en'cor'ing
en'coun'ter
en'cour'age
en'cour'aged
en'cour'age'ment
en'cour'ag'ing
en'cour'ag'ing'ly
en'croach
en'croach'ment
en'crust
en'crus'ta'tion
en'cum'ber
en'cum'brance
en'cyc'li'cal
en'cy'clo'pae'dia
en'cy'clo'pae'dic
en'cy'clo'pe'dia
en'cy'clo'pe'dic
en'dan'ger

en'dan'ger'ment
en'dear
en'dear'ing'ly
en'dear'ment
en'deav'our
en'dem'ic
en'dem'i'cal
end'ing
en'dive
end'less
end'less'ly
en'do'crine
en'do'crin'ol'o'gist
en'do'cri'nol'o'gy
en'dog'a'mous
en'dog'enous
en'do'morph
en'dor'phin
en'dorse
en'dor'see
en'dorse'ment
en'dor'ser
en'dors'ing
en'do'scope
en'dos'co'pies
en'dos'co'py
endow
en'dow'ment
en'due
en'dued
en'du'ing
en'dur'able
en'dur'ance
en'dure
en'dur'ing
en'dur'ing'ness
en'e'ma
en'e'mies
en'e'my
en'er'get'ic
en'er'get'i'cal'ly
en'er'gies
en'er'gize
en'er'gized
en'er'gi'zer
en'er'giz'ing
en'er'gy
en'er'vate
en'er'vat'ed
en'er'vat'ing
en'er'va'tion
en'face'ment
en'fant ter'ri'ble

en'fee'ble
en'fee'bled
en'fee'ble'ment
en'fee'bling
en'fold
en'force
en'force'able
en'forced
en'force'ment
en'forc'ing
en'fran'chise
en'fran'chised
en'fran'chise'ment
en'fran'chis'ing
en'gage
en'gaged
en'gage'ment
en'gag'ing
en'gag'ing'ly
en'gen'der
en'gine
en'gi'neer
en'gi'neer'ing
En'glish
en'gorge
en'gorged
en'gorge'ment
en'gorg'ing
en'grave
en'graved
en'grav'er
en'grav'ing
en'gross
en'grossed
en'gross'ing
en'gross'ment
en'gulf
en'gulf'ment
en'hance
en'hanced
en'hance'ment
en'hanc'ing
enig'ma
en'ig'mat'ic
en'ig'mat'i'cal
en'ig'ma'ti'cal'ly
en'join
en'join'ment
en'joy
en'joy'able
en'joy'ably
en'joy'ment
en'large

en'larged
en'large'ment
en'larg'er
en'larg'ing
en'light'en
en'light'en'ment
en'list
en'list'ed
en'list'ment
en'liv'en
en masse
en'mesh
en'mi'ties
en'mi'ty
en'no'ble
en'no'bled
en'no'ble'ment
en'no'bling
en'nui
enor'mi'ties
enor'mi'ty
enor'mous
enor'mous'ly
enough
en pas'sant
en'plane
en'planed
en'plan'ing
en plein
en'quire
en'quired
en'quir'er
en'quir'ies
en'quir'ing
en'quiry
en'rage
en'raged
en'rag'ing
en'rapt
en'rap'ture
en'rap'tured
en'rap'tur'ing
en'rich
en'rich'ment
en'rol
en'rolled
en'rol'ling
en'rol'ment
en route
en'sconce
en'sconced
en'sconc'ing
en'semble

en'shrine
en'shrined
en'shrin'ing
en'shroud
en'sign
en'si'lage
en'si'laged
en'si'lag'ing
en'slave
en'slaved
en'slave'ment
en'slav'ing
en'snare
en'snared
en'snare'ment
en'snar'ing
en'sue
en'sued
en'su'ing
en suite
en'sure
en'sured
en'sur'ing
en'tab'la'ture
en'tail
en'tail'ment
en'tan'gle
en'tan'gled
en'tan'gle'ment
en'tan'gling
en'tente
en'tente cor'diale
en'ter
en'ter'ic
en'ter'ing
en'ter'i'tis
en'ter'prise
en'ter'pris'ing
en'ter'tain
en'ter'tain'er
en'ter'tain'ing
en'ter'tain'ing'ly
en'ter'tain'ment
en'thral
en'thralled
en'thral'ing
en'thral'ment
en'throne
en'throned
en'throne'ment
en'thron'ing
en'thuse
en'thused

en'thu'si'asm
en'thu'si'ast
en'thu'si'as'tic
en'thu'si'as'ti'cal'ly
en'thus'ing
en'tice
en'ticed
en'tice'ment
en'tic'ing
en'tic'ing'ly
en'tire
en'tire'ly
en'tire'ness
en'tire'ty
en'ti'ties
en'ti'tle
en'ti'tled
en'ti'tle'ment
en'ti'tling
en'ti'ty
en'tomb
en'tomb'ment
en'to'mo'log'i'cal
en'to'mol'o'gist
en'to'mol'o'gy
en'tou'rage
en'to'zoa
en'to'zo'an
en'tr'acte
en'trails
en'train
en'train'ment
en'trance
en'trant
en'trap
en'trap'ment
en'trapped
en'trap'ping
en'treat
en'treat'ment
en'treaty
en'tre'chat
en'trée
en'trench
en'trench'ment
en'tre'pre'neur
en'tre'pre'neur'ial
en'tries
en'tro'py
en'trust
en'trust'ment
en'try
en'twine

en'twined
en'twin'ing
enu'mer'ate
enu'mer'at'ed
enu'mer'at'ing
enu'mer'a'tion
enu'mer'a'tor
enun'ci'ate
enun'ci'at'ed
enun'ci'at'ing
enun'ci'a'tion
en'u're'sis
en'vel'op
en've'lope
en'vel'op'ing
en'vi'a'ble
en'vi'able
en'vied
en'vies
en'vi'ous
en'vi'ous
en'vi'ous'ly
en'vi'ous'ness
en'vi'rons
en'vi'ron'ment
en'vi'ron'ment
en'vi'ron'men'tal
en'vi'ron'men'tal
en'vi'ron'men'tal'ism
en'vi'ron'men'tal'ist
en'vi'ron'men'tal'ly
en'vis'age
en'vis'ag'ing
en'vi'sion
en'voi
en'voy
en'vy
en'vy'ing
en'zy'mat'ic
en'zyme
eo'lian
eo'lith
eon
ep'au'let
ep'au'lette
epergne
ephed'rine
ephem'er'al
ep'ic
ep'i'cal
ep'i'cen'tre
ep'i'cure
Epi'cu're'an

ep'i'cu're'an'ism
ep'i'cur'ism
ep'i'cy'cle
ep'i'dem'ic
ep'i'de'mi'ol'o'gist
ep'i'de'mi'ol'o'gy
ep'ider'mal
ep'i'der'mic
ep'i'der'mis
epi'dia'scope
epi'du'ral
ep'i'glot'tis
ep'i'gram
ep'i'gram'mat'ic
ep'i'graph
ep'i'lep'sy
ep'i'lep'tic
ep'i'logue
epis'co'pa'cy
Epis'co'pal
Epis'co'pa'lian
Epis'co'pa'lian'ism
epis'co'pate
ep'i'sode
ep'i'sod'ic
ep'i'sod'i'cal
epis'te'mol'o'gy
epis'tle
epis'to'la'ry
ep'i'taph
ep'i'thet
epit'o'me
epit'o'mize
ep'och
ep'och'al
epon'y'mous
epon'y'mous'ly
ep'oxy
ep'si'lon
equa'bil'i'ty
equa'ble
equa'ble'ness
equa'bly
equal
equal'i'tar'i'an
equal'i'ties
equal'i'ty
equal'iza'tion
equal'ize
equal'ized
equal'i'zer
equal'iz'ing
equalled

equal'ling
equal'ly
equal'ness
equa'nim'i'ty
equate
equat'ed
equat'ing
equa'tion
equa'tion'al
equa'tor
equa'to'ri'al
equer'ries
equer'ry
eques'tri'an
eques'tri'enne
equi'dis'tance
equi'dis'tant
equi'lat'er'al
equil'i'brate
equil'i'brat'ed
equil'i'brat'ing
equil'i'bra'tion
equi'lib'ria
equi'lib'ri'um
equine
equi'noc'tial
equi'nox
equip
eq'ui'page
equip'ment
equi'poise
equipped
equip'ping
eq'ui'ta'ble
eq'ui'ta'bly
eq'ui'ties
eq'ui'ty
equiv'a'lence
equiv'a'lent
equiv'o'cal
equiv'o'cate
equiv'o'cat'ed
equiv'o'cat'ing
equiv'o'ca'tion
era
erad'i'ca'ble
erad'i'cate
erad'i'cat'ed
erad'i'cat'ing
erad'i'ca'tion
erad'i'ca'tor
eras'a'ble
erase

erased
eras'er
eras'ing
eras'ure
er'bi'um
ere
erect
erect'able
erec'ter
erec'tile
erec'tion
erec'tive
erect'ly
erect'ness
erec'tor
er'e'mite
er'e'mit'ic'al
er'go
er'go'nom'ic
er'go'nom'i'cal'ly
er'go'nom'ics
er'gon'o'mist
er'gos'ter'ol
er'got
er'i'ca
er'i'ca'ceous
er'mine
erne
erode
erod'ed
erod'ing
erog'e'nous
ero'sion
ero'sive
erot'ic
erot'i'ca
erot'i'cal'ly
erot'i'cism
err
er'rand
er'rant
er'rant'ry
er'ra'ta
er'rat'ic
er'rat'i'cal'ly
er'ra'tum
err'ing'ly
er'ro'ne'ous
er'ro'ne'ous'ly
er'ror
er'ror'less
er'satz
erst'while

er'u'dite
er'u'dite'ness
er'u'di'tion
erupt
erup'tion
erup'tive
ery'sip'e'las
eryth'ro'cyte
es'ca'lade
es'ca'late
es'ca'lat'ed
es'ca'lat'ing
es'ca'la'tion
es'ca'la'tor
es'cal'lop
es'ca'pade
es'cape
es'caped
es'ca'pee
es'ca'ping
es'cap'ism
es'cap'ist
es'ca'pol'o'gist
es'ca'pol'o'gy
es'car'got
es'ca'role
es'carp'ment
es'cheat
es'chew
es'chew'al
es'cort
es'cri'toire
es'crow
es'cu'do
es'cutch'eon
Es'ki'mo
es'o'ter'ic
es'o'ter'i'cal
es'pa'drille
es'pal'ier
es'par'to
es'pe'cial
es'pe'cial'ly
Es'pe'ran'to
es'pied
es'pi'o'nage
es'pla'nade
es'pous'al
es'pouse
es'poused
es'pous'ing
es'pres'so
es'prit de corps

es'py
es'py'ing
es'quire
es'say
es'say'ist
es'sence
es'sen'tial
es'sen'tial'ly
es'tab'lish
es'tab'lish'ment
es'tate
es'teem
es'ter
es'te'rase
es'ti'ma'ble
es'ti'ma'bly
es'ti'mate
es'ti'mat'ed
es'ti'mat'ing
es'ti'ma'tion
es'ti'ma'tor
es'trange
es'tranged
es'trange'ment
es'trang'ing
es'tray
es'treat
es'tu'ar'ies
es'tu'ary
et cet'era
etch
etch'ing
eter'nal
eter'nal'ly
eter'ni'ties
eter'ni'ty
eter'ni'za'tion
eter'nize
eth'a'nol
ether
ethe're'al
ethe're'al'iza'tion
ethe're'al'ize
ethe're'al'ly
eth'ic
eth'i'cal
eth'i'cal'ly
eth'ics
Ethi'o'pi'an
eth'nic
eth'ni'cal
eth'ni'cal'ly
eth'no'cen'tric

eth'no'cen'tri'cal'ly
eth'no'cen'tric'i'ty
eth'no'graph'i'cal
eth'no'graph'ic
eth'no'gra'phi'cal'ly
eth'nog'ra'phy
eth'no'log'i'cal
eth'no'log'i'cal'ly
eth'nol'o'gist
eth'nol'o'gy
eth'no'mu'si'col'o'gy
ethos
eth'yl
ethyl'ic
eti'o'log'i'cal
eti'ol'o'gy
et'i'quette
étude
ety'mo'log'i'cal
ety'mo'log'i'cal'ly
ety'mol'o'gies
ety'mol'o'gist
ety'mol'o'gy
eu'ca'lyp'ti
eu'ca'lyp'tus
Eu'cha'rist
Eu'cha'ris'tic
Eu'cha'ris'ti'cal
eu'chre
eu'demon
eu'gen'ic
eu'gen'i'cal'ly
eu'gen'ics
eu'lo'gies
eu'lo'gis'tic
eu'lo'gize
eu'lo'gized
eu'lo'giz'ing
eu'lo'gy
eu'nuch
eu'phe'mism
eu'phe'mist
eu'phe'mis'tic
eu'phe'mis'ti'cal
eu'phe'mis'ti'cal'ly
eu'phe'mize
eu'phe'mized
eu'phe'miz'ing
eu'phon'ic
eu'phon'i'cal
eu'pho'ni'ous
eu'pho'ni'um
eu'pho'nies

eu'pho'ny
eu'pho'ria
eu'phor'ic
Eu'ra'sian
eu're'ka
eu'rhyth'mics
eu'rhyth'mies
eu'rhyth'my
Eu'ro'pe'an
Eu'ro'pe'an'ize
eu'ro'pi'um
eu'tha'na'sia
evac'u'ant
evac'u'ate
evac'u'at'ed
evac'u'at'ing
evac'u'a'tion
evac'u'a'tor
evac'u'ee
evade
evad'ed
evad'ing
eval'u'ate
eval'u'at'ed
eval'u'at'ing
eval'u'a'tion
eval'u'a'tor
ev'a'nesce
ev'a'nesced
ev'a'nesc'ence
ev'a'nes'cent
ev'a'nesc'ing
evan'gel'ic
evan'gel'i'cal
evan'gel'i'cal'ism
evan'gel'i'cal'ly
evan'ge'lism
evan'ge'list
evan'ge'lis'tic
evan'ge'lis'ti'cal'ly
evan'ge'li'za'tion
evan'ge'lize
evan'ge'lized
evan'ge'liz'ing
evap'o'rate
evap'o'rat'ed
evap'o'rat'ing
evap'o'ra'tion
evap'o'ra'tor
eva'sion
eva'sive
eva'sive'ly
eva'sive'ness

even
even-hand'ed
even-hand'ed'ly
even-hand'ed'ness
eve'ning
even'ly
event'ful
event'ful'ly
even'tu'al
even'tu'al'i'ty
even'tu'al'ly
even'tu'ate
even'tu'at'ed
even'tu'at'ing
ev'er'green
ev'er'last'ing
ever'last'ing'ly
ever'sion
evert
ev'ery'body
ev'ery'day
ev'ery'one
ev'ery'thing
ev'ery'where
evict
evic'tion
evic'tor
ev'i'dence
ev'i'denced
ev'i'denc'ing
ev'i'dent
ev'i'den'tial
ev'i'dent'ly
evil
evil'do'er
evil'ly
evil-mind'ed
evil'ness
evince
evinced
evin'ci'ble
evinc'ing
evis'cer'ate
evis'cer'at'ed
evis'cer'at'ing
evis'cer'a'tion
ev'o'ca'tion
evoc'a'tive
evoc'a'tive'ly
evoke
evoked
evok'ing
ev'o'lu'tion

ev'o'lu'tion'al
ev'o'lu'tion'ary
ev'o'lu'tion'ism
ev'o'lu'tion'ist
evolve
evolved
evolve'ment
evolv'ing
ewe
ew'er
ex'ac'er'bate
ex'ac'er'bat'ed
ex'ac'er'bat'ing
ex'ac'er'ba'tion
ex'act
ex'act'able
ex'act'ing
ex'act'ing'ly
ex'act'i'tude
ex'act'ly
exact'ness
ex'ag'ger'ate
ex'ag'ger'at'ed
exag'ger'at'ed'ly
ex'ag'ger'at'ing
ex'ag'ger'a'tion
ex'alt
ex'al'ta'tion
ex'alt'ed
ex'am
ex'am'i'na'tion
ex'am'ine
ex'am'ined
ex'am'in'er
ex'am'in'ing
ex'am'ple
ex'am'pled
ex'am'pling
ex'as'per'ate
ex'as'per'at'ed
ex'as'per'at'ing
ex'as'per'a'tion
ex ca'the'dra
ex'ca'vate
ex'ca'vat'ed
ex'ca'vat'ing
ex'ca'va'tion
ex'ca'va'tor
ex'ceed
ex'ceed'ed
ex'ceed'ing
ex'ceed'ing'ly
ex'cel

ex'celled
ex'cel'lence
ex'cel'len'cies
ex'cel'len'cy
ex'cel'lent
ex'cel'lent'ly
ex'cel'ling
ex'cel'si'or
ex'cept
ex'cept'ing
ex'cep'tion
ex'cep'tion'able
ex'cep'tion'al
ex'cep'tion'al'ly
ex'cerpt
ex'cerp'tion
ex'cess
ex'ces'sive
ex'ces'sive'ly
ex'change
ex'change'abil'i'ty
ex'change'able
ex'changed
ex'chang'ing
ex'cheq'uer
ex'cis'able
ex'cise
ex'cised
ex'cis'ing
ex'ci'sion
ex'cit'abil'i'ty
ex'cit'able
ex'cit'ably
ex'ci'ta'tion
ex'cite
ex'cit'ed
ex'cit'ed'ly
ex'cite'ment
ex'cit'ing
ex'cit'ing'ly
ex'claim
ex'cla'ma'tion
ex'clam'a'to'ry
ex'clud'able
ex'clude
ex'clud'ed
ex'clud'ing
ex'clu'sion
ex'clu'sive
ex'clu'sive'ly
ex'clu'sive'ness
ex'clu'siv'i'ty
ex'com'mu'ni'ca'ble

ex'com'mu'ni'cant
ex'com'mu'ni'cate
ex'com'mu'ni'cat'ed
ex'com'mu'ni'cat'ing
ex'com'mu'ni'ca'tion
ex'co'ri'ate
ex'co'ri'at'ed
ex'co'ri'at'ing
ex'co'ri'a'tion
ex'cre'ment
ex'cre'men'tal
ex'cres'cence
ex'cres'cent
ex'cre'ta
ex'cre'tal
ex'crete
ex'cret'ed
ex'cret'ing
ex'cre'tion
ex'cre'to'ry
ex'cru'ci'ate
ex'cru'ci'at'ing
ex'cru'ci'a'ting'ly
ex'cru'ci'a'tion
ex'cul'pate
ex'cul'pat'ed
ex'cul'pat'ing
ex'cul'pa'tion
ex'cul'pa'to'ry
ex'cur'sion
ex'cur'sion'al
ex'cur'sion'ary
ex'cur'sive
ex'cus'able
ex'cus'ably
ex'cus'a'to'ry
ex'cuse
ex'cused
ex'cus'ing
ex'e'cra'ble
ex'e'cra'bly
ex'e'crate
ex'e'crat'ed
ex'e'crat'ing
ex'e'cra'tion
ex'e'cra'tive
ex'e'cra'tor
ex'ec'ut'able
ex'e'cute
ex'e'cut'ed
ex'e'cut'er
ex'e'cut'ing
ex'e'cu'tion

ex'e'cu'tion'er
ex'ec'u'tive
ex'ec'u'tor
ex'ec'u'trix
ex'e'ge'ses
ex'e'ge'sis
ex'em'plar
ex'em'pla'ri'ly
ex'em'pla'ry
ex'em'pli'fi'ca'tion
ex'em'pli'fied
ex'em'pli'fy
ex'em'pli'fy'ing
ex'empt
ex'emp'tion
ex'er'cise
ex'er'cised
ex'er'cis'er
ex'er'cis'ing
ex'ert
ex'er'tion
ex'fo'li'ate
ex'fo'li'at'ed
ex'fo'li'at'ing
ex'fo'li'a'tion
ex gra'tia
ex'ha'la'tion
ex'hale
ex'haled
ex'hal'ing
ex'haust
ex'haust'ed
ex'haust'ible
ex'haust'ing
ex'haus'tion
ex'haus'tive
ex'haus'tive'ly
ex'hib'it
ex'hib'it'ed
ex'hib'it'ing
ex'hi'bi'tion
ex'hi'bi'tion'ism
ex'hi'bi'tion'ist
ex'hib'i'tor
ex'hil'a'rate
ex'hil'a'rat'ed
ex'hil'a'rat'ing
ex'hil'a'ra'tion
ex'hil'a'ra'tive
ex'hort
ex'hor'ta'tion
ex'hor'ta'tive
ex'hor'ta'to'ry

ex'hort'ing'ly
ex'hu'ma'tion
ex'hume
ex'humed
ex'hum'ing
ex'i'gen'cies
ex'i'gen'cy
ex'i'gent
ex'i'gent'ly
ex'ig'u'ous
ex'ile
ex'iled
ex'il'ing
ex'ist
ex'ist'ence
ex'ist'ent
ex'is'ten'tial
ex'is'ten'tial'ism
ex'is'ten'tial'ist
ex'it
ex li'bris
ex'o'dus
ex of 'fi'cio
ex'og'a'mous
ex'og'a'my
ex'og'e'nous
ex'on'er'ate
ex'on'er'at'ed
ex'on'er'at'ing
ex'on'er'a'tion
ex'on'er'a'tive
ex'or'bi'tance
ex'or'bi'tant
ex'or'bi'tant'ly
ex'or'cise
ex'or'cised
ex'or'cis'ing
ex'or'cism
ex'or'cist
ex'o'skel'e'ton
ex'o'tic
ex'ot'i'ca
ex'ot'i'cal'ly
ex'ot'i'cism
ex'pand
ex'pand'abil'ity
ex'pand'able
ex'pand'er
ex'panse
ex'pan'si'bil'i'ty
ex'pan'si'ble
ex'pan'sion
ex'pan'sion'ism

ex'pan'sion'ist
ex'pan'sive
ex'pan'sive'ly
ex'pan'sive'ness
ex'pa'ti'ate
ex'pa'ti'at'ed
ex'pa'ti'at'ing
ex'pa'ti'a'tion
ex'pa'tri'ate
ex'pa'tri'at'ed
ex'pa'tri'at'ing
ex'pa'tri'a'tion
ex'pect
ex'pect'able
ex'pect'ably
ex'pect'an'cy
ex'pect'ant
ex'pec'ta'tion
ex'pect'ing'ly
ex'pec'to'rant
ex'pec'to'rate
ex'pec'to'rat'ed
ex'pec'to'rat'ing
ex'pec'to'ra'tion
ex'pe'di'ence
ex'pe'di'en'cy
ex'pe'di'ent
ex'pe'dite
ex'pe'dit'ed
ex'pe'dit'er
ex'pe'dit'ing
ex'pe'di'tion
ex'pe'di'tion'ary
ex'pe'di'tious
ex'pe'di'tious'ly
ex'pel
ex'pelled
ex'pel'ling
ex'pend
ex'pend'abil'i'ty
ex'pend'able
ex'pend'i'ture
ex'pense
ex'pen'sive
ex'pens'ive'ly
ex'pe'ri'ence
ex'pe'ri'enced
ex'pe'ri'enc'ing
ex'pe'ri'en'tial
ex'per'i'ment
ex'per'i'men'tal
ex'per'i'men'tal'ist
ex'per'i'men'tal'ly

ex'per'i'men'ta'tion
ex'per'i'ment'er
ex'pert
ex'per'tise
ex'pert'ly
ex'pert'ness
ex'pi'ate
ex'pi'at'ed
ex'pi'at'ing
ex'pi'a'tion
ex'pi'a'to'ry
ex'pi'ra'tion
ex'pir'a'to'ry
ex'pire
ex'pired
ex'pir'ing
ex'pi'ry
ex'plain
ex'plain'able
ex'pla'na'tion
ex'plan'a'to'ry
ex'ple'tive
ex'pli'ca'ble
ex'pli'cate
ex'pli'cat'ed
ex'pli'cat'ing
ex'pli'ca'tion
ex'pli'ca'tive
ex'plic'it
ex'plic'it'ly
ex'plic'it'ness
ex'plode
ex'plod'ed
ex'plod'ing
ex'ploit
ex'ploit'able
ex'ploi'ta'tion
ex'ploit'er
ex'ploit'ive
ex'plo'ra'tion
ex'plo'ita'tive
ex'plor'a'to'ry
ex'plore
ex'plor'er
ex'plo'sion
ex'plo'sive
ex'plo'sive'ly
ex'plo'sive'ness
ex'po'nent
ex'po'nen'tial
ex'po'nen'tial'ly
ex'port
ex'port'able

ex'por'ta'tion
ex'port'er
ex'pose
ex'po'sé
ex'posed
ex'pos'er
ex'pos'ing
ex'po'si'tion
ex'pos'i'tor
ex'pos'i'to'ry
ex post fac'to
ex'pos'tu'late
ex'pos'tu'lat'ed
ex'pos'tu'lat'ing
ex'pos'tu'la'tion
ex'pos'tu'la'to'ry
ex'po'sure
ex'pound
ex'press
ex'press'ible
ex'pres'sion
ex'pres'sion'ism
ex'pres'sion'ist
ex'pres'sion'less
ex'pres'sive
ex'pres'sive'ly
ex'press'ly
ex'press'way
ex'pro'pri'ate
ex'pro'pri'at'ed
ex'pro'pri'at'ing'
ex'pro'pri'a'tion
ex'pul'sion
ex'pul'sive
ex'punge
ex'punged
ex'pung'ing
ex'pur'gate
ex'pur'gat'ed
ex'pur'gat'ing
ex'pur'ga'tion
ex'pur'ga'to'ry
ex'qui'site
ex'qui'site'ly
ex'qui'site'ness
ex'tant
ex'tem'po'ra'ne'ous
ex'tem'po're
ex'tem'po'ri'za'tion
ex'tem'po'rize
ex'tem'po'rized
ex'tem'po'riz'ing
ex'tend

ex'tend'able
ex'tend'ed
ex'tend'ible
ex'ten'si'ble
ex'ten'sion
ex'ten'sive
ex'ten'sive'ly
ex'ten'sor
ex'tent
ex'ten'u'ate
ex'ten'u'at'ed
ex'ten'u'at'ing
ex'ten'u'a'tion
ex'te'ri'or
ex'ter'mi'nate
ex'ter'mi'nat'ed
ex'ter'mi'nat'ing
ex'ter'mi'na'tion
ex'ter'mi'na'tor
ex'ter'nal
ex'ter'nal'iza'tion
ex'ter'nal'ize
ex'ter'nal'ized
ex'ter'nal'iz'ing
ex'ter'nal'ly
ex'ter'ri'to'ri'al
ex'tinct
ex'tinc'tion
ex'tin'guish
ex'tin'guish'able
ex'tin'guish'er
ex'tin'guish'ment
ex'tir'pate
ex'tir'pat'ed
ex'tir'pat'ing
ex'tir'pa'tion
ex'tol
ex'tolled
ex'tol'ling
ex'tol'ment
ex'tort
ex'tor'ter
ex'tor'tion
ex'tor'tion'ary
ex'tor'tion'ate
ex'tor'tion'er
ex'tor'tion'ist
ex'tor'tive
ex'tra
ex'tract
ex'trac'tion
ex'trac'tive
ex'trac'tor

ex'tra'cur'ric'u'lar
ex'tra'dit'able
ex'tra'dite
ex'tra'dit'ed
ex'tra'dit'ing
ex'tra'di'tion
ex'tra'mar'i'tal
ex'tra'mu'ral
ex'tra'ne'ous
ex'traor'di'nari'ly
ex'traor'di'nary
ex'trap'o'late
ex'trap'o'la'tion
ex'tra'sen'so'ry
ex'tra'ter'res'tri'al
ex'tra'ter'ri'to'ri'al
ex'trav'a'gance
ex'trav'a'gan'cy
ex'trav'a'gant
ex'trav'a'gant'ly
ex'trav'a'gan'za
ex'treme
ex'treme'ly
ex'trem'ism
ex'trem'ist
ex'trem'i'ties
ex'trem'i'ty
ex'tri'cate
ex'tri'cat'ed
ex'tri'cat'ing
ex'tri'ca'tion
ex'trin'sic
ex'tro'ver'sion
ex'tro'vert
ex'trude
ex'trud'ed
ex'trud'ing
ex'tru'sion
ex'u'ber'ance
ex'u'ber'ant
ex'u'ber'ant'ly
ex'u'da'tion
ex'ude
ex'ud'ed
ex'ud'ing
ex'ult
ex'ult'ant
ex'ul'tant'ly
ex'ul'ta'tion
ex'ult'ing'ly
ex'ur'ban'ite
ex'ur'bia
eye

eye'ball
eye'brow
eyed
eye'ful
eye'glass'es
eyeing
eye'let
eye-open'er
eye'piece
eye'sight
eye'sore
eye-teeth
eye-tooth
eye'wash
eye'wit'ness
ey'ing
ey'rie
fa'ble
fa'bled
fab'ric
fab'ri'cate
fab'ri'cat'ed
fab'ri'cat'ing
fab'ri'ca'tion
fab'ri'ca'tor
fab'u'list
fab'u'lous
fab'u'lous'ly
fa'cade
face
face cloth
faced
face'less
face'lift
face-sav'ing
fac'et
fa'ce'tious
fa'ce'tious'ly
fac'et'ted
fa'cial
fa'cial'ly
fac'ile
fac'ile'ly
fa'cil'i'tate
fa'cil'i'tat'ed
fa'cil'i'tat'ing
fa'cil'i'ties
fa'cil'i'ty
fac'ing
fac'sim'i'le
fact
fac'tion
fac'tion'al

fac'tion'al'ism
fac'ti'tious
fac'tor
fac'to'ries
fac'to'ry
fac'to'tum
fac'tu'al
fac'tu'al'ly
fac'ul'ty
fad
fad'di'er
fad'di'est
fad'dist
fad'dy
fade
fade-out
fad'ed
fade'less
fad'ing
fae'cal
fae'ces
fag
fagged
fag'ging
fag'got
fa'ience
fail'ing
faille
fail-safe
fail'ure
fain
faint
faint-heart'ed
faint'ly
faint'ness
fair
fair'ground
fair'ies
fair'ly
fair-mind'ed
fair'ness
fair'way
fair-weath'er
fairy
fair'y'land
fait ac'com'pli
faith'ful
faith'ful'ly
faith'ful'ness
faith'less
fake
faked
fak'er

fak'ing
fa'kir
fal'con
fal'con'er
fal'con'ry
fal'der'al
fall
fal'la'cies
fal'la'cious
fal'la'cy
fall'en
fal'li'bil'i'ty
fal'li'ble
fall'ing
Fal'lo'pi'an tube
fall'out
fal'low
false
false'hood
false'ly
false'ness
fal'set'to
fal'si'fi'ca'tion
fal'si'fied
fal'si'fy
fal'si'fy'ing
fal'si'ties
fal'si'ty
fal'ter
fal'ter'ing
fame
famed
fa'mil'ial
fa'mil'ial
fa'mil'iar
fa'mil'iar'i'ty
fa'mil'iar'iza'tion
fa'mil'iar'ize
fa'mil'iar'ized
fa'mil'iar'iz'ing
fa'mil'iar'ly
fam'i'lies
fam'i'ly
fam'ine
fam'ish
fam'ished
fa'mous
fa'mous'ly
fan
fa'nat'ic
fa'nat'i'cal
fa'nat'i'cal'ly
fa'nat'i'cism

fa'nat'i'cize
fan'cied
fan'ci'er
fan'cies
fan'ci'est
fan'ci'ful
fan'ci'ful'ly
fan'ci'ly
fan'ci'ness
fan'cy
fan'cy'ing
fan'dan'go
fan'fare
fang
fanged
fan'light
fanned
fan'ning
fan'tail
fan'ta'sia
fan'ta'sies
fan'ta'size
fan'ta'sized
fan'ta'siz'ing
fan'tas'tic
fan'tas'ti'cal
fan'tas'ti'cal'ly
fan'tas'ti'cal'ness
fan'ta'sy
far
far'ad
far'a'day
far'a'way
farce
farced
far'ci'cal
farc'ing
fare
fared
fare'well
far'fetched
fa'ri'na
far'i'na'ceous
far'ing
farm'er
farm'ing
farm'stead
faro
far'ra'go
far'ra'goes
far-reach'ing
far'ri'er
far'row

far'see'ing
far'sight'ed
far'sight'ed'ness
far'ther
far'ther'most
far'thest
far'thin'gale
fas'ces
fas'cia
fas'ci'cle
fas'ci'cled
fas'ci'nate
fas'ci'nat'ed
fas'ci'nat'ing
fas'ci'nat'ing'ly
fas'ci'na'tion
fas'cism
fas'cist
fas'cis'tic
fash'ion
fash'ion'able
fash'ion'able'ness
fash'ion'ably
fas'ten
fas'ten'er
fas'ten'ing
fas'tid'i'ous
fas'tid'i'ous'ly
fas'tid'i'ous'ness
fast'ness
fat
fa'tal
fa'tal'ism
fa'tal'ist
fa'tal'is'tic
fa'tal'i'ties
fa'tal'i'ty
fa'tal'ly
fate
fat'ed
fate'ful
fa'ther
fa'ther'hood
fa'ther-in-law
fa'ther'land
fa'ther'less
fa'ther'li'ness
fa'ther'ly
fa'thers-in-law
fath'om
fath'om'able
fath'om'less
fat'i'ga'bil'i'ty

fat'i'ga'ble
fa'tigue
fa'tigued
fa'tig'uing
fat'less
fat'ness
fatly
fat'ted
fat'ten
fat'ter
fat'test
fat'ti'er
fat'ties
fat'ti'est
fat'ti'ness
fat'ting
fat'ty
fa'tu'i'ties
fa'tu'i'ty
fat'u'ous
fat'u'ous'ly
fau'cet
fault
fault'find'ing
fault'i'er
fault'i'ly
fault'i'ness
fault'less
fault'less'ly
faulty
faun
fau'na
fau'nae
fau'nas
faute de mieux
faux pas
fa'vour
fa'vour'able
fa'vour'able'ness
fa'vour'ably
fa'voured
fa'voured'ness
fa'vour'ing
fa'vour'ite
fa'vour'it'ism
fawn
faze
fazed
faz'ing
fe'al'ties
fe'al'ty
fear
fear'ful

fear'ful'ly
fear'ful'ness
fear'less
fear'less'ly
fear'less'ness
fear'some
fear'some'ness
fea'si'bil'i'ty
fea'si'ble
fea'si'ble'ness
fea'si'bly
feast
feat
feath'er
feath'er'bed'ding
feath'er'brain
feath'er'brained
feath'ered
feath'er'weight
feath'ery
fea'ture
fea'tured
fea'ture'less
fea'tur'ing
fe'brile
feck'less
fe'cund
fe'cun'date
fe'cun'dat'ed
fe'cun'dat'ing
fe'cun'da'tion
fe'cun'di'ty
fed
fed'er'al
fed'er'al'ism
fed'er'al'ist
fed'er'al'iza'tion
fed'er'al'ize
fed'er'al'ized
fed'er'al'iz'ing
fed'er'al'ly
fed'er'ate
fed'er'at'ed
fed'er'at'ing
fe'do'ra
fee'ble
fee'ble'mind'ed
fee'bler
fee'bly
feed
feed'back
feed'er
feed'ing

feel
feel'er
feel'ing
feet
feign
feigned
feign'er
feign'ing
feint
feist'i'est
feisty
feld'spar
fe'lic'i'tate
fe'lic'i'tat'ed
fe'lic'i'tat'ing
fe'lic'i'ta'tion
fe'lic'i'ties
fe'lic'i'tous
fe'lic'i'ty
fe'line
fe'lin'i'ty
fell
fel'la'tio
fel'low
fel'low'ship
fel'on
fel'o'nies
fe'lo'ni'ous
fel'o'ny
felt
fe'male
fem'i'nine
fem'i'nine'ness
fem'i'nin'ity
fem'i'nism
fem'i'nist
fem'i'nis'tic
fem'i'ni'za'tion
fem'i'nize
fem'i'nized
fem'i'niz'ing
femme fa'tale
fem'o'ra
fem'o'ral
fe'mur
fence
fenced
fenc'er
fenc'ing
fen'der
fen'nel
Fens
fe'ral

fer'ment
fer'men'ta'tion
fer'mi'um
fern
fe'ro'cious
fe'ro'cious'ly
fe'ro'cious'ness
fe'ro'ci'ty
fer'ret
fer'ret'ed
fer'ret'ing
fer'ried
fer'ries
fer'ro'con'crete
fer'ro'mag'net'ic
fer'rous
fer'ru'gi'nous
fer'rule
fer'ry
fer'ry'boat
fer'ry'ing
fer'tile
fer'tile'ness
fer'til'i'ty
fer'til'i'za'tion
fer'ti'lize
fer'ti'lized
fer'ti'liz'er
fer'ti'liz'ing
fer'ule
fer'ven'cy
fer'vent
fer'vent'ly
fer'vid
fer'vid'ness
fer'vour
fes'tal
fes'ter
fes'ti'val
fes'tive
fes'tive'ness
fes'tiv'i'ties
fes'tiv'i'ty
fes'toon
fe'ta
fe'tal
fetch
fetch'ing
fetch'ing'ly
fete
fet'ed
fe'ti'cide
fet'id

fet'id'ness
fet'ing
fet'ish
fet'ish'ism
fet'ish'ist
fet'lock
fet'ter
fet'tle
feud
feu'dal
feu'dal'ism
feu'dal'is'tic
feu'dal'iza'tion
feu'dal'ize
feud'ist
fe'ver
fever'few
fe'ver'ish
fe'ver'ish'ly
fe'ver'ish'ness
fe'ver'ous
few
fey
fez
fez'zes
fi'an'cé
fi'an'cée
fi'as'co
fi'at
fib
fibbed
fib'ber
fib'bing
fi'bre
fi'bred
fi'bre'glass
fi'bril
fi'broid
fi'bro'sis
fi'bro'si'tis
fi'brous
fib'u'la
fib'u'lae
fiche
fi'chu
fick'le
fick'le'ness
fic'tion
fic'tion'al
fic'tion'al'iza'tion
fic'tion'al'ized
fic'tion'al'iz'ing
fic'ti'tious

fic'ti'tious'ness
fid'dle
fid'dled
fid'dler
fid'dle'sticks
fid'dling
fi'del'i'ty
fidg'et
fid'get'ing
fidg'ety
fi'du'ci'ary
fief
field
field'er
field mouse
field'work
fiend
fiend'ish
fierce
fierce'ly
fierce'ness
fi'er'i'er
fier'i'est
fier'i'ly
fier'i'ness
fiery
fi'es'ta
fife
fif'teen
fif'teenth
fif'ties
fif'ti'eth
fif'ty
fight
fight'er
fight'ing
fig'ment
figu'ral
fig'ur'ate
fig'u'ra'tion
fig'u'ra'tive
fig'u'ra'tive'ly
fig'ure
fig'ured
fig'ure'head
fig'ure'less
fig'ur'ine
fig'ur'ing
fil'a'ment
fil'a'men'ta'ry
fil'a'ment'ed
fil'a'men'tous
filch

file
filed
fi'let
fil'i'al
fil'i'al'ly
fil'i'bus'ter
fil'i'gree
fil'i'greed
fil'i'gree'ing
fil'ing
Fil'i'pi'no
fill'er
fil'let
fil'let'ed
fil'let'ing
fil'lies
fill'ing
fil'lip
fil'ly
film'i'er
film'i'est
film'i'ness
filmy
fil'ter
fil'ter'able
filth
filth'i'er
filth'i'est
filth'i'ness
filthy
fil'tra'tion
fin
fi'na'gle
fi'na'gled
fi'na'gler
fi'na'gling
fi'nal
fi'na'le
fi'nal'ist
fi'na'li'ties
fi'nal'i'ty
fi'nal'ize
fi'nal'ized
fi'nal'iz'ing
fi'nal'ly
fi'nance
fi'nanced
fi'nan'cial
fi'nan'cial'ly
fin'an'cier
fi'nanc'ing
finch
find

fin de siè'cle
find'ing
fine
fine'ness
fine'ly
fin'er
fin'er'ies
fin'ery
fine'spun
fi'nesse
fi'nessed
fi'nes'sing
fin'est
fin'ger
fin'ger'board
fin'ger'ing
fin'ger'nail
fin'ger'print
fin'ger'tip
fin'ial
fin'ick'ing
fin'icky
fin'is
fin'ish
fin'ished
fin'ish'er
fi'nite
fi'nite'ly
fi'nite'ness
fink
fin'less
Finn
finned
fin'ning
Finn'ish
fir
fire
fire'arm
fire'ball
fire'bomb
fire'break
fire'crack'er
fired
fire-fight'er
fire'flies
fire'fly
fire'guard
fire'light
fire'man
fire'place
fire'plug
fire'pow'er
fire'proof

fire'trap
fire'wa'ter
fire'wood
fire'works
fir'ing
fir'kin
firm
fir'ma'ment
firm'ly
firm'ness
first
first'born
first'hand
first'ly
first-rate
first-string
fis'cal
fis'cal'ly
fish'er'ies
fish'er'man
fish'ery
fish'i'er
fish'i'est
fish'ing
fish'wife
fishy
fis'sion
fis'sion'able
fis'sure
fis'sured
fis'sur'ing
fist'ful
fist'i'cuffs
fit
fit'ful
fit'ful'ly
fit'ful'ness
fit'ly
fit'ness
fit'ted
fit'ter
fit'test
fit'ting
fit'ting
fit'ting'ly
fit'ting'ly
five'fold
fix
fix'able
fix'ate
fix'at'ed
fix'a'tion
fix'a'tive

fixed
fix'ed'ly
fix'er
fix'ing
fix'ings
fix'i'ty
fix'ture
fizz
fiz'zi'er
fiz'zi'est
fiz'zle
fiz'zled
fiz'zling
fiz'zy
fjord
flab'ber'gast
flab'bi'er
flab'bi'est
flab'bi'ly
flab'bi'ness
flab'by
flac'cid
flack
flag
flag'el'lant
flag'el'late
flag'el'lat'ed
flag'el'lat'ing
flag'el'la'tion
fla'geo'let
flagged
flag'ging
fla'gi'tious
flag'on
fla'grant
fla'grant'ly
flail
flair
flake
flaked
flak'i'er
flak'i'est
flak'i'ness
flak'ing
flaky
flam'bé
flam'boy'ance
flam'boy'an'cy
flam'boy'ant
flam'boy'ant'ly
flame
flamed
fla'men'co

flam'ing
flam'ing'ly
fla'min'go
flam'ma'ble
flange
flank
flank'er
flan'nel
flan'nel'ette
flap
flapped
flap'per
flap'ping
flare
flared
flare-up
flar'ing
flash'back
flash'i'er
flash'i'est
flash'i'ness
flashy
flask
flat
flat'foot
flat'foot'ed
flat'iron
flat'ly
flat'ness
flat'ted
flat'ten
flat'ter
flat'ter
flat'ter'er
flat'ter'ies
flat'ter'ing'ly
flat'tery
flat'test
flat'ting
flat'u'lence
flat'u'len'cy
flat'u'lent
fla'tus
flat'ware
flat'worm
flaunt
flaunt'ed
flaunt'ing'ly
flaunty
flau'tist
fla'vour
fla'voured
fla'vour'ing

fla'vour'less
flawed
flaw'less
flax
flax'en
flax'seed
flea
flea'bag
flea'bane
flea'bite
flea-bit'ten
flexion
fled
fledge
fledged
fledg'ing
fledg'ling
flee
fleece
fleeced
fleec'i'ness
fleec'ing
fleecy
flee'ing
fleet
fleet'ing
fleet'ing'ly
fleet'ly
fleet'ness
Flem'ish
flesh'i'er
flesh'i'ness
flesh'i'est
flesh'ly
fleshy
fleur-de-lis
flew
flex'i'bil'i'ty
flex'i'ble
flex'i'bly
flex'ure
flib'ber'ti'gib'bet
flick'er
flick'er'ing
fli'er
flies
flight
flight'i'er
flight'i'est
flight'i'ly
flight'i'ness
flight'less
flighty

flim'flam
flim'flammed
flim'flam'ming
flim'si'er
flim'si'est
flim'si'ly
flim'si'ness
flim'sy
flinch
flinch'ing
fling
fling'ing
flint'i'ness
flinty
flip
flip-flop
flip'pan'cy
flip'pant
flip'pant'ly
flipped
flip'per
flip'ping
flirt
flir'ta'tion
flir'ta'tious
flit
flit'ted
flit'ter
flit'ting
float
float'able
float'a'tion
float'er
float'ing
floc'cu'lence
floc'cu'lent
flocked
floe
flog
flogged
flog'ger
flog'ging
flood
flood'gate
flood'light
flood'light'ed
flood'light'ing
flood'lit
floor
floor'board
floor'ing
floo'zies
floo'zy

flop
flopped
flop'pi'er
flop'pies
flop'pi'est
flop'pi'ness
flop'ping
flop'py
flo'ra
flo'rae
flo'ral
flo'res'cence
flo'res'cent
flo'ret
flo'ri'cul'ture
flo'ri'cul'tur'ist
florid
flo'rid'i'ty
flor'id'ness
flo'rist
floss
flossy
flo'ta'tion
flo'til'la
flot'sam
flounce
flounced
flounc'ing
floun'der
flour'ish
flour'ish'ing
floury
flout
flout'er
flow
flow'er
flow'ered
flow'er'et
flow'er'ing
flow'er'pot
flow'ery
flown
flu
flub
flubbed
flub'bing
fluc'tu'ate
fluc'tu'at'ed
fluc'tu'at'ing
fluc'tu'a'tion
flue
flu'en'cy
flu'ent

flu'ent'ly
fluff
fluf'fi'er
fluf'fi'est
fluff'i'ness
fluffy
flu'id
flu'id'i'ty
flu'id'ness
flu'id ounce
fluke
fluky
flum'mox
flung
flun'key
flun'kies
flun'ky
flu'o'resce
flu'o'resced
flu'o'res'cence
flu'o'res'cent
flu'o'resc'ing
fluor'i'dat'ed
fluor'i'dat'ing
fluor'i'da'tion
flu'o'ride
fluor'o'scope
flur'ried
flur'ries
flur'ry
flur'ry'ing
flus'ter
flute
flut'ed
flut'ing
flut'ist
flut'ter
flut'ter'ing
flut'tery
flux
fly
fly'blown
fly'by
fly-by-night
fly'er
flying
fly'leaf
fly'leaves
fly'pa'per
fly'weight
fly'wheel
foal
foam

foam'i'er
foam'i'est
foam'i'ness
foamy
fob
fobbed
fob'bing
fo'cal
fo'cal'ize
fo'cal'ized
fo'cal'iz'ing
fo'cal'ly
fo'ci
fo'cus
fo'cused
fo'cus'es
fo'cus'er
fo'cus'ing
fod'der
foe
foehn
foe'tal
foe'tid
foe'ti'cide
foe'tus
fog
fog'bound
fo'gey
fogged
fog'gi'er
fog'gi'est
fog'gi'ly
fog'gi'ness
fog'ging
fog'gy
fo'gies
fo'gy
fo'gy'ish
föhn
foi'ble
foist
fold'er
fol'de'rol
fo'li'a'ceous
fo'li'age
fo'li'ate
fo'li'at'ed
fo'li'at'ing
fo'li'a'tion
fo'lio
folk
folk'lore
folk'si'ness

folk'sy
fol'li'cle
fol'lic'u'lar
fol'lies
fol'low
fol'low'er
fol'low'ing
fol'ly
fo'ment
fo'men'ta'tion
fo'ment'er
fon'dant
fon'dle
fon'dled
fon'dling
fond'ly
fond'ness
fon'due
food'stuff
fool'er'ies
fool'ery
fool'har'di'ness
fool'hardy
fool'ish
fool'ish'ly
fool'ish'ness
fool'proof
fools'cap
foot
foot'age
foot'ball
foot'bridge
foot'fall
foot'hold
foot'lights
foot'ling
foot'loose
foot'man
foot'note
foot'path
foot'print
foot'slog'ging
foot'sore
foot'step
foot'wear
foot'work
fop
fop'pery
fop'pish
for'age
for'aged
for'ag'ing
for'ay

for'bade
for'bear
for'bear'ance
for'bear'ing
for'bid
for'bid'dance
for'bid'den
for'bid'ding
for'bid'ding'ly
for'bore
for'borne
force
force'able
forced
force-fed
force-feed
force-feed'ing
force'ful
force'ful'ly
force'less
force'meat
for'ceps
for'ci'ble
for'ci'bly
forc'ing
ford'able
fore
fore'arm
fore'bear
fore'bode
fore'bod'ed
fore'bod'ing
fore'cast
fore'cast'ed
fore'cast'er
fore'cast'ing
fore'castle
fore'close
fore'closed
fore'clos'ing
fore'clo'sure
fore'deck
fore'doomed
fore'fa'ther
fore'feet
fore'fin'ger
fore'foot
fore'front
fore'gath'er
fore'go
fore'goes
fore'go'ing
fore'gone

fore'ground
fore'hand
fore'hand'ed
fore'head
for'eign
for'eign'er
fore'knew
fore'know
fore'know'ing
fore'know'ledge
fore'known
fore'leg
fore'lock
fore'man
fore'mast
fore'most
fore'name
fore'noon
fo'ren'sic
fore'or'dain
fore'or'di'na'tion
fore'part
fore'play
fore'quar'ter
fore'run'ner
fore'sail
fore'saw
fore'see
fore'see'able
fore'see'ing
fore'seen
fore'shad'ow
fore'shore
fore'short'en
fore'sight
fore'skin
for'est
fore'stall
for'est'a'tion
for'es'ter
for'est'ry
fore'taste
fore'tell
fore'tell'er
fore'tell'ing
fore'thought
fore'to'ken
fore'told
for'ev'er
for'ev'er'more
fore'warn
fore'went
fore'wing

fore'woman
fore'word
for'feit
for'fei'ture
for'gath'er
for'gave
forge
forged
forg'er
for'ger'ies
for'gery
for'get
for'get'ful
for'get'ful'ness
for'get'ta'ble
for'get'ting
forg'ing
for'giv'able
for'giv'ably
for'give
for'giv'en
for'give'ness
for'giv'ing
for'go
for'go'ing
for'gone
for'got
for'got'ten
forked
fork'lift
for'lorn
for'lorn'ly
for'mal
for'mal'de'hyde
for'mal'ism
for'mal'i'ties
for'mal'i'ty
for'mal'iza'tion
for'mal'ize
for'mal'ized
for'mal'iz'ing
for'mal'ly
for'mat
for'ma'tion
form'a'tive
for'mat'ted
for'mat'ting
for'mer
for'mer'ly
form'fit'ting
for'mi'da'ble
for'mi'da'bly
form'less

form'less'ness
for'mu'la
for'mu'lae
for'mu'la'ic
for'mu'lar'ies
for'mu'lary
for'mu'las
for'mu'late
for'mu'lat'ed
for'mu'lat'ing
for'mu'la'tion
for'mu'la'tor
for'ni'cate
for'ni'cat'ed
for'ni'cat'ing
for'ni'ca'tion
for'ni'ca'tor
for'sake
for'sak'en
for'swear
for'swear'ing
for'swore
for'sworn
for'syth'ia
fort
forte
for'te
forth
forth'com'ing
forth'right
forth'with
for'ties
for'ti'eth
for'ti'fi'cation
for'ti'fied
for'ti'fy
for'ti'fy'ing
for'tis'si'mo
for'ti'tude
fort'night
for'tress
for'tu'i'tous
for'tu'itous'ly
for'tu'i'tous'ness
for'tu'nate
for'tu'nate'ly
for'tune
for'tune tell'er
for'ty
fo'rum
fo'rums
for'ward
for'ward'ness

for'went
fos'sil
fos'sil'iza'tion
fos'sil'ized
fos'sil'iz'ing
fos'ter
fos'tered
fos'ter'ing
fought
foul
foul'ard
foul-mouthed
foul-up
found
foun'da'tion
foun'da'tion'al
found'er
found'ling
found'ries
found'ry
fount
foun'tain
four
four flush
four'fold
four-post'er
four'score
four'some
four'teen
four'teenth
fourth
fourth'ly
fowl
fox'glove
fox-hound
fox'i'er
fox'i'est
fox'i'ly
fox'i'ness
fox-trot
fox-trot'ted
fox-trot'ting
foxy
foy'er
fra'cas
frac'tion
frac'tion'al
frac'tion'al'ly
frac'tious
frac'ture
frac'tured
frac'tur'ing
frag'ile

fra'gil'i'ty
frag'ment
frag'men'tal
frag'men'tary
frag'men'ta'tion
frag'ment'ize
fra'grance
fra'grant
fra'grant'ly
frail
frail'ness
frail'ties
frail'ty
frame
framed
frame'work
fram'ing
franc
fran'chise
fran'chised
fran'chise'ment
fran'chis'ing
fran'gi'ble
fran'gi'pan'i
fran'gi'pan'ni
Fran'glais
frank
frank'furt'er
frank'in'cense
frank'ly
frank'ness
fran'tic
fran'ti'cal'ly
frap'pe
fra'ter'nal
fra'ter'nal'ly
fra'ter'ni'ties
fra'ter'ni'ty
frat'er'ni'za'tion
frat'er'nize
frat'er'nized
frat'er'niz'ing
frat'ri'cid'al
frat'ri'cide
fraud
fraud'u'lence
fraud'u'lent
fraud'u'lent'ly
fraught
fraz'zle
fraz'zled
freak
freak'i'er

freak'i'est
freak'ish
freak'ish'ly
freaky
freck'le
freck'led
freck'led
freck'ling
freck'ly
free
free'bie
free'boot'er
free'dom
free'lance
free'lanced
free'lanc'ing
free'load'er
free'ly
free'man
free'mar'tin
fre'er
free'sia
free'spo'ken
fre'est
free-stand'ing
free'style
free'think'er
free'way
free'wheel
freewill
freeze
freeze-dried
freeze-dry
freeze-frame
freez'er
freez'ing
freight
freight'age
freight'er
French
French fries
French'i'fied
French'i'fy
French'i'fy'ing
fre'net'ic
fre'net'i'cal'ly
fren'zied
fren'zied'ly
fren'zies
fren'zy
fren'zy'ing
fre'quen'cies
fre'quen'cy

fre'quent
fre'quen'ta'tive
fre'quent'ly
fres'co
fres'coed
fres'coes
fres'co'ing
fresh
fresh'en
fresh'et
fresh'ly
fresh'ness
fresh'wa'ter
fret
fret'ful
fret'ful'ly
fret'saw
fret'ted
fret'ting
fret'work
fri'a'ble
fri'ar
fri'ar'ies
fri'ary
fric'as'see
fric'as'seed
fric'as'see'ing
fric'a'tive
fric'tion
fric'tion'al
fric'tion'less
fridge
fried
friend
friend'less
friend'li'er
friend'li'est
friend'li'ness
friend'ly
friend'ship
fries
frieze
fri'gate
fright
fright'en
fright'en'ing
fright'en'ing'ly
fright'ful
fright'ful'ly
frig'id
fri'gid'i'ty
frig'id'ness
frill

fril'li'er
frill'i'est
frilli'ness
frilly
fringe
fringed
fring'ing
frip'per'ies
frip'pery
frisk
frisk'i'er
frisk'i'est
frisk'i'ness
frisky
fris'son
frit'ter
fri'vol'i'ties
fri'vol'i'ty
friv'o'lous
friv'o'lous'ly
frizz
friz'zi'er
friz'zi'est
friz'zi'ness
friz'zle
friz'zled
friz'zling
friz'zy
frock
frog
frogged
frog'ging
frog'man
frol'ic
frol'icked
frol'ick'ing
frol'ic'some
front
front'age
fron'tal
fron'tier
fron'tis'piece
front man
frost
frost'bit
frost'bite
frost'bit'ing
frost-bit'ten
frost'ed
frost'i'er
frost'i'est
frost'i'ly
frost'i'ness

frost'ing
frosty
froth
froth'i'er
froth'i'est
froth'i'ness
frothy
frou'frou
fro'ward
frown
frow'zy
frowzi'ness
froze
fro'zen
fro'zen'ness
fruc'ti'fi'ca'tion
fruc'ti'fy
fruc'tose
fru'gal
fru'gal'i'ties
fru'gal'i'ty
fru'gal'ly
fruit
fruit'cake
fruit flies
fruit fly
fruit'ful
fruit'ful'ly
fruit'ful'ness
fruit'i'er
fruit'i'est
fru'i'tion
fruit'less
frui'ty
frump
frump'ish
frumpy
frus'trate
frus'trat'ed
frus'trat'ing
frus'tra'tion
fry
fry'er
fry'ing
fuch'sia
fud'dle
fud'dled
fud'dling
fud'dy-dud'dy
fudge
fudged
fudg'ing
fu'el

fu'elled
fu'el'ling
fu'gi'tive
fugue
Füh'rer
ful'cra
ful'crum
ful'fil
ful'filled
ful'fil'ling
ful'fil'ment
full
full'back
full-blood'ed
full-blown
full-fledged
full-length
full'ness
ful'ly
ful'mi'nate
ful'mi'nat'ed
ful'mi'nat'ing
ful'mi'na'tion
ful'some
ful'some'ly
fum'ble
fum'bled
fum'bler
fum'bling
fume
fumed
fu'mi'gate
fu'mi'gat'ed
fu'mi'gat'ing
fu'mi'ga'tion
fu'mi'ga'tor
fum'ing
fum'ing'ly
func'tion
func'tion'al
func'tion'al'ism
func'tion'al'ist
func'tion'al'ly
func'tion'ar'ies
func'tion'ary
func'tion'less
fund
fun'da'ment
fun'da'men'tal
fun'da'men'tal'ism
fun'da'men'tal'ist
fun'da'men'tal'ly
fund-rais'er

fund-rais'ing
fu'ner'al
fu'ne'ra'ry
fu'ne're'al
fun'gal
fun'gi
fun'gi'cid'al
fun'gi'cide
fun'goid
fun'gus
fu'nic'u'lar
funk
funk'i'er
funk'i'est
funky
fun'nel
fun'nelled
fun'nel'ling
fun'ni'er
fun'nies
fun'ni'est
fun'ni'ly
fun'ni'ness
fun'ny
fur
fur'be'low
fur'bish
fur'cate
fu'ries
fu'ri'ous
fu'ri'ous'ly
furl
fur'less
fur'long
fur'lough
fur'nace
fur'nish
fur'nish'ings
fur'ni'ture
fu'rore
furred
fur'ri'er
fur'ri'est
fur'ring
fur'row
fur'ry
fur'ther
fur'ther'ance
fur'ther'more
fur'ther'most
fur'thest
fur'tive
fur'tive'ly

fu'ry
fuse
fused
fu'se'lage
fu'si'bil'i'ty
fu'si'ble
fu'sil
fu'si'lier
fu'sil'lade
fu'sil'lad'ed
fu'sil'lad'ing
fus'ing
fu'sion
fu'sion'ism
fuss
fuss'er
fus'si'er
fus'si'est
fus'si'ly
fuss'i'ness
fuss'pot
fussy
fus'tian
fus'tic
fust'i'er
fust'i'est
fusty
fu'tile
fu'til'i'ties
fu'til'i'ty
fu'ton
fu'ture
fu'tur'ism
fu'tur'is'tic
fu'tu'ri'ties
fu'tu'ri'ty
fuzz
fuz'zi'er
fuz'zi'est
fuz'zi'ly
fuzz'i'ness
fuzzy
gab
gabbed
gab'bing
gab'ble
gab'bled
gab'bling
gab'by
gab'er'dine
ga'ble
ga'bled
ga'bling

gad
gad'a'bout
gad'ded
gad'ding
gad'fly
gad'get
gad'get'ry
ga'do'lin'i'um
Gael
Gael'ic
gaff
gaffe
gag
ga'ga
gagged
gag'ging
gag'gle
gai'e'ties
gai'e'ty
gai'ly
gain
gain'er
gain'ful
gainfully
gain'said
gain'say
gain'say'ing
gait
gai'ter
ga'la
ga'lac'tic
gal'an'tine
gal'ax'ies
gal'axy
gale
gall
gal'lant
gal'lant'ly
gal'lant'ries
gal'lant'ry
gal'le'on
gal'ler'ies
gal'lery
gal'ley
gal'li'cism
gal'li'mau'fry
gall'ing
gal'li'um
gal'li'vant
gal'lon
gal'lop
gal'loped
gal'lop'ing

gal'lows
gall'stone
ga'lore
ga'losh'es
gal'van'ic
gal'va'nize
gal'va'nized
gal'va'niz'ing
gal'va'nom'e'ter
gam'bit
gam'ble
gam'bled
gam'bler
gam'bling
gam'bol
gam'bolled
gam'bol'ling
game
game'ly
games'man'ship
game'ster
ga'mete
gam'in
ga'mine
gam'i'ness
gam'ing
gam'ma
gam'ma glob'u'lin
gam'mon
gam'ut
gamy
gan'der
gang'land
gan'glia
gan'gling
gan'gli'on
gan'gly
gan'grene
gan'gre'nous
gang'ster
gan'net
gant'let
gan'tries
gan'try
gaol
gaol'er
gap
gape
gaped
gape'worm
gap'ing
gapped
gap'ping

gap'py
ga'rage
ga'raged
ga'rag'ing
gar'bage
gar'ble
gar'bled
gar'bling
gar'çon
gar'den
gar'den'er
gar'de'nia
gar'gan'tu'an
gar'gle
gar'gled
gar'gling
gar'goyle
gar'ish
gar'ish'ly
gar'ish'ness
gar'land
gar'lic
gar'ment
gar'ner
gar'net
gar'nish
gar'nish'ee
gar'nish'eed
gar'nish'ee'ing
gar'nish'ment
gar'ni'ture
ga'rotte
ga'rot'ted
ga'rot'ting
gar'ret
gar'ri'son
gar'rote
gar'rot'ed
gar'rot'ing
gar'ru'lous
gar'ru'lous'ly
gar'ter
gas
gas'bag
gas'e'ous
gas'es
gas'hold'er
gas'i'fi'ca'tion
gas'i'fied
gas'i'fy
gas'i'fy'ing
gas'ket
gas'light

gas'om'e'ter
gassed
gasser
gas'ses
gas'si'er
gas'si'est
gas'si'ness
gas'sing
gas'sy
gas'tric
gas'tri'tis
gas'tro-en'ter'i'tis
gas'tro'en'ter'ol'o'gy
gas'tro'in'tes'ti'nal
gas'tro'nom'ic
gas'tron'o'my
gas'works
gat
gath'er
gath'er'ing
gauche
gauche'ness
gau'che'rie
gau'cho
gaud'i'er
gaud'i'est
gaud'i'ly
gaud'i'ness
gaudy
gauge
gauged
gaug'ing
gaunt
gaunt'let
gauze
gauz'i'ness
gauzy
gave
gav'el
ga'votte
gawk
gawk'i'er
gawk'i'est
gawk'i'ly
gawk'i'ness
gawky
gay'e'ty
gay'ly
gay'ness
gaze
ga'ze'bo
gazed
ga'zelle

ga'zette
gaz'et'teer
gaz'ing
gaz'pa'cho
gear
gear'box
gear'shift
gear'wheel
gecko
geck'oes
geese
gei'sha
gel
gel'a'tin
gel'a'tine
ge'la'ti'nize
ge'lat'i'nous
ge'la'tion
geld
geld'ed
geld'ing
gel'id
ge'lid'i'ty
gel'ig'nite
gelled
gel'ling
gelt
gem
gem'i'nate
gem'i'nat'ed
gem'i'nate'ly
gem'i'nat'ing
gem'i'na'tion
gemmed
gem'ming
gem'o'log'i'cal
gem'ol'o'gist
gem'ol'o'gy
gem'stone
gen'darme
gen'der
gene
ge'ne'a'log'i'cal
ge'ne'al'o'gies
ge'ne'al'o'gist
ge'ne'al'o'gy
gen'era
gen'er'al
gen'er'al'ist
gen'er'al'i'ties
gen'er'al'i'ty
gen'er'al'iza'tion
gen'er'al'ize

gen'er'al'ized
gen'er'al'iz'ing
gen'er'al'ly
gen'er'ate
gen'er'at'ed
gen'er'at'ing
gen'er'a'tion
gen'er'a'tive
gen'er'a'tor
ge'ner'ic
ge'ner'i'cal
gen'er'os'i'ties
gen'er'os'i'ty
gen'er'ous
gen'er'ous'ly
gen'e'ses
gen'e'sis
ge'net'ic
ge'net'i'cal'ly
ge'net'i'cist
ge'net'ics
gen'ial
ge'ni'al'i'ty
ge'nial'ly
ge'nie
ge'nii
gen'i'tal
gen'i'ta'lia
gen'i'tals
gen'i'tive
gen'ius
gen'ius'es
gen'o'ci'dal
gen'o'cide
genre
gent
gen'teel
gen'teel'ly
gen'tian
gen'tile
gen'til'i'ty
gen'tle
gent'le'folk
gen'tle'man
gen'tle'man'ly
gent'le'ness
gent'ler
gen'tlest
gen'tle'wom'an
gen'tly
gen'tri'fi'ca'tion
gen'try
gen'u'flect

gen'u'flec'tion
gen'u'ine
gen'u'ine'ly
gen'u'ine'ness
genus
geo'cen'tric
geo'cen'tri'cal'ly
geo'chem'i'cal
geo'chem'ist
geo'chem'is'try
ge'ode
geo'des'ic
geod'e'sy
ge'o'gra'pher
geo'graph'ic
geo'graph'i'cal
geo'graph'i'cal'ly
ge'o'gra'phies
ge'o'gra'phy
geo'log'ic
geo'log'i'cal
geo'log'i'cal'ly
ge'ol'o'gies
ge'ol'o'gist
ge'ol'o'gy
ge'o'mag'net'ic
geo'mag'ne'tism
geo'met'ric
geo'met'ri'cal
geo'met'ri'cal'ly
geom'e'tries
ge'om'e'try
geo'phys'i'cal
geo'phys'i'cist
geo'phys'ics
geo'pol'i'tic
geo'po'lit'i'cal
geo'po'lit'i'cal'ly
geo'pol'i'tics
geor'gette
geo'ther'mal
ge'ra'ni'um
ger'bil
ger'i'at'ric
ger'i'a'tri'cian
ger'i'at'rics
ger'i'at'rist
Ger'man
ger'mane
Ger'man'ic
ger'ma'ni'um
ger'mi'cid'al
ger'mi'cide

ger'm'inal
ger'mi'nate
ger'mi'nat'ed
ger'mi'nat'ing
ger'mi'na'tion
ger'on'tol'o'gist
ger'on'tol'o'gy
ger'ry'man'der
ger'und
ge'stalt
ges'tate
ges'tat'ed
ges'tat'ing
ges'ta'tion
ges'tic'u'late
ges'tic'u'lat'ed
ges'tic'u'lat'ing
ges'tic'u'la'tion
ges'tic'u'la'to'ry
ges'tur'al
ges'ture
ges'tured
ges'tur'ing
ge'sund'heit
get
get'ting
gey'ser
Gha'nai'an
ghast'li'er
ghast'li'est
ghast'li'ness
ghast'ly
gher'kin
ghet'to
ghet'tos
ghost
ghost'li'est
ghost'li'ness
ghost'ly
ghost-write
ghost-writ'er
ghost-writ'ing
ghost-writ'ten
ghoul
ghoul'ish
ghoul'ish'ly
gi'ant
gib'ber
gib'ber'ish
gib'bet
gib'bon
gib'bous
gibe

gib'ing'ly
gib'let
gib'lets
gid'di'er
gid'di'est
gid'di'ly
gid'di'ness
gid'dy
gift'ed
gi'gan'tic
gi'gan'tism
gig'gle
gig'gling
gig'gly
gig'o'lo
gild
gild'ed
gill
gilt
gilt-edged
gim'crack
gim'let
gim'mick
gim'mick'ry
gim'mick'y
gin
gin'ger
gin'ger'bread
gin'ger'li'ness
gin'ger'ly
gin'gery
ging'ham
gin'gi'vi'tis
gin'seng
gip'sies
gip'sy
gi'raffe
gird
gird'er
gir'dle
gir'dled
gir'dling
girl
girl'friend
girl'hood
gir'lie
girl'ish
girth
gist
give
give-away
giv'en
giv'ing

giz'zard
gla'cé
gla'cial
gla'ci'a'tion
gla'cier
glad
glad'den
glad'der
glad'dest
glade
glad'i'a'tor
glad'i'a'to'ri'al
glad'i'o'la
glad'i'o'li
glad'i'o'lus
glad'i'o'lus'es
glad'ly
glad'ness
glam'or'isa'tion
glam'or'ise
glam'or'ised
glam'or'is'ing
glam'or'ous
glam'or'ous'ness
glam'our
glance
glanced
glanc'ing
glan'du'lar
glare
glared
glar'i'ness
glar'ing
glar'ing'ly
glas'*nost*
glas'nos'tian
glass
glass'blow'ing
glass'ful
glass'ine
glass'i'er
glass'i'est
glass'i'ly
glass'i'ness
glass'ware
glassy
glau'co'ma
glaze
glazed
gla'zier
glaz'ing
gleam
gleam'ing

gleamy
glean
glean'er
glean'ing
glee
glee'ful
glee'ful'ly
glee'ful'ness
glib
glib'best
glib'ly
glib'ness
glide
glid'ed
glid'ing
glim'mer
glimpse
glimpsed
glimps'ing
glis'san'do
glis'ten
glit'ter
glit'tery
gloam'ing
gloat
gloat'er
gloat'ing
glob
glob'al
glob'al'ly
globe
globe'trot'ter
globe'trot'ting
glob'u'lar
glob'ule
glock'en'spiel
gloom
gloom'i'er
gloom'i'est
gloom'i'ly
gloom'i'ness
gloomy
glo'ried
glo'ries
glo'ri'fi'ca'tion
glo'ri'fied
glo'ri'fy
glo'ri'fy'ing
glo'ri'ous
glo'ri'ous'ly
glo'ry
glo'ry'ing
gloss

glos'sa'ries
glos'sa'ry
gloss'i'er
gloss'i'ly
gloss'i'ness
glossy
glot'tal
glot'tis
glove
glow
glow'er
glow'ing
glow-worm
glu'cose
glue
glued
glue'ing
glu'ey
glu'ing
glum
glum'ly
glum'mer
glum'mest
glut
glu'ten
glu'ten'ous
glu'ti'nous
glut'ted
glut'ting
glut'ton
glut'ton'ous
glut'tony
glyc'er'in
glyc'er'ine
gnarl
gnarled
gnash
gnat
gnaw
gnawed
gnaw'ing
gneiss
gnome
gno'mic
gnu
go
goad
goad'ed
go-ahead
goal
goal'ie
goal'keep'er
goal'post

goat
goat'ee
goat'herd
goat'skin
gob
gob'bet
gob'ble
gob'bled
gob'bler
gob'bling
gob'let
gob'lin
go-cart
god
god-aw'ful
god'child
god'chil'dren
god'daugh'ter
god'dess
god'fa'ther
god-fear'ing
god'for'sak'en
god'head
god'less
god'less'ness
god'li'ness
god'ly
god'moth'er
god'par'ent
god'send
god'son
goes
go'fer
go-get'ter
gog'gle
gog'gled
gog'gle-eyed
gog'gling
go-go
go'ing
go'ing-over
go'ings-on
goi'tre
gold
gold'dig'ger
gold'en
gold'en'rod
gold'finch
gold'fish
gold'smith
golf
golf'er
gol'ly

go'nad
gon'do'la
gon'do'lier
gone
gon'er
gon'or'rhoea
goo
good
good-by
goodbye
good-heart'ed
good-hu'moured
good'ish
good-look'ing
good'ly
good-na'tured
good'ness
good-tem'pered
goody-goody
goo'ey
goo'i'er
goo'i'est
goose
goose'ber'ries
goose'ber'ry
goosed
goose-step
goose-stepped
goose-step'ping
goos'ing
go'pher
Gor'dian knot
gore
gored
gorge
gorged
gor'geous
gor'geous'ly
gor'geous'ness
gorg'ing
gor'gon
gor'gon'zo'la
gor'i'er
gor'i'est
go'ril'la
gor'ing
gorse
gory
gos'hawk
gos'ling
gos'pel
gos'sa'mer
gos'sip

gos'siped
gos'sip'er
gos'sip'ing
gos'sipy
got
gouache
gouge
gouged
goug'ing
gou'jon
gou'lash
gourd
gour'mand
gour'met
gout
gouty
gov'ern
gov'ern'able
gov'ern'ess
gov'ern'ment
gov'ern'men'tal
gov'er'nor
gov'ern'or'ship
gown
gowned
goy
goy'in
grab
grabbed
grab'ber
grab'bing
grace
graced
grace'ful
grace'ful'ly
grace'less
grac'ing
gra'cious
gra'cious'ly
gra'cious'ness
grack'le
gra'da'tion
grade
grad'ed
gra'di'ent
grad'ing
grad'u'al
grad'u'al'ly
grad'u'al'ness
grad'u'ate
grad'u'at'ed
grad'u'at'ing
grad'u'a'tion

graf'fi'ti
graft
graft'age
graft'er
graft'ing
gra'ham
grail
grain
grain'i'ness
grainy
gram
gram'mar
gram'mar'i'an
gram'mat'i'cal
gram'ma'ti'cal'ly
gramme
gram'pus
gra'na'ries
gra'na'ry
grand
grand'dad'dy
grand'child
grand'chil'dren
grand'daugh'ter
gran'dee
gran'deur
grand'fat'her
gran'dil'o'quence
gran'dil'o'quent
gran'dil'o'quent'ly
gran'di'ose
gran'di'ose'ly
grand'ly
grand mal
grand'moth'er
grand'pa
grand'par'ent
grand'son
grange
gran'ite
gran'nies
gran'ny
gra'no'la
gran'u'lar
gran'u'lar'i'ty
gran'u'late
gran'u'lat'ed
gran'u'lat'ing
gran'u'la'tion
gran'ule
grape
grape'fruit
grape'vine

graph
graph'ic
graph'i'cal
graph'i'cal'ly
graph'ite
graph'ol'o'gist
graph'ol'o'gy
grap'nel
grap'ple
grap'pled
grap'pler
grap'pling
grasp'ing
grass
grass'hop'per
gras'si'er
grass'i'est
grass'land
grassy
grate
grat'ed
grate'ful
grate'ful'ly
grat'er
grat'i'fi'ca'tion
grat'i'fied
grat'i'fy
grat'i'fy'ing
grat'ing
gra'tis
grat'i'tude
gra'tu'i'ties
gra'tu'i'tous
gra'tu'i'tous'ly
gra'tu'i'ty
gra'va'men
gra'vam'i'na
grave
graved
grav'el
grav'elled
grav'el'ling
grav'el'ly
grave'ly
grav'en
grave'ness
grav'er
grav'est
grave'stone
grave'yard
gravid
gra'vies
grav'ing

grav'i'tate
grav'i'tat'ed
grav'i'tat'ing
grav'i'ta'tion
grav'i'ta'tion'al
grav'i'ties
grav'i'ty
gra'vy
gray'ling
graze
grazed
graz'ing
grease
greased
grease'paint
greas'i'er
greas'i'est
greas'i'ness
greas'ing
greasy
great
great'coat
great'ly
great'ness
grebe
greed
greed'i'er
greed'i'est
greed'i'ly
greed'i'ness
greedy
Greek
green
green'back
green'ery
green'gage
green'horn
green'house
green'ing
green'ish
green'ness
greet
greet'ing
gre'gar'i'ous
gre'gar'i'ous'ly
gre'gar'i'ous'ness
grem'lin
gre'nade
gren'a'dier
gren'a'dine
grew
grey
grey'hound

grey'ish
grey'ness
grid
grid'dle
grid'i'ron
grief
grief-strick'en
griev'ance
grieve
grieved
griev'ing
griev'ous
griev'ous'ly
grif'fin
grif'fon
grill
gril'lage
grille
grilse
grim
grim'ace
grim'aced
grim'ac'ing
gri'mal'kin
grime
grim'i'ness
grim'ly
grim'mer
grim'mest
grim'ness
grimy
grin
grind
grind'er
grind'ing
grind'ing'ly
grind'stone
grinned
grin'ning
grip
gripe
griped
grip'er
grip'ing
grippe
gripped
grip'ping
gris'li'ness
gris'ly
grist
gris'tle
gris'tly
grit

grit'ted
grit'ti'er
grit'ti'est
grit'ti'ness
grit'ting
grit'ty
griz'zle
griz'zled
griz'zlies
griz'zling
griz'zly
groan
gro'cer
gro'cer'ies
gro'cery
grog
grog'gi'er
grog'gi'est
grog'gi'ly
grog'gi'ness
grog'gy
gro'gram
groin
grom'met
groom
groove
grooved
groov'er
groov'i'er
groov'i'est
groov'ing
groov'y
grope
groped
grop'ing
gros'grain
gross
gross'ly
gross'ness
gro'tesque
gro'tesque'ly
gro'tesque'ness
grot'to
grot'toes
grouch
grouch'i'ly
grouch'i'ness
grouchy
ground
ground'ing
ground'less
ground'nut
ground'sheet

ground'work
group
group'ie
group'ing
grouse
groused
grous'ing
grove
grovel
grov'elled
grov'el'ling
grow
grow'er
grow'ing
growl
growl'er
growl'ing
grown
grown-up
growth
grub
grubbed
grub'bi'er
grub'bi'est
grub'bi'ness
grub'bing
grub'by
grub'stake
grudge
grudged
grudg'ing
grudg'ing'ly
gru'el
gru'el'ling
grue'some
gruff
gruff'ly
gruff'ness
grum'ble
grum'bled
grum'bling
grump'i'er
grump'i'est
grump'i'ly
grump'i'ness
grumpy
grunt
grunt'ed
grunt'ing
gryph'on
guar'an'tee
guar'an'teed
guar'an'teeing

guar'an'tied
guar'an'ties
guar'an'tor
guar'an'ty
guar'an'ty'ing
guard
guard'ed
guard'ed'ly
guard'house
guard'i'an
guard'ian'ship
guard-rail
guards'man
gua'va
gu'ber'na'to'ri'al
gudg'eon
guer'ril'la
guess
guess'ing
guess'work
guest
guff
guf'faw
guid'ance
guide
guide'book
guid'ed
guide'line
guid'ing
gui'don
guild
guil'der
guild'hall
guile
guile'ful
guile'less
guil'le'mot
guil'lo'tine
guil'lo'tined
guil'lo'tin'ing
guilt
guilt'i'er
guilt'i'est
guilt'i'ly
guilt'i'ness
guilt'less
guilty
guin'ea
guise
gui'tar
gui'tar'ist
gu'lag
gulf

gull
gul'let
gul'li'bil'i'ty
gul'li'ble
gul'li'bly
gul'lies
gul'ly
gum
gum'bo
gum'boil
gum'drop
gummed
gum'mi'er
gum'mi'est
gum'mi'ness
gum'ming
gum'my
gump'tion
gum'shoe
gun
gun'boat
gun dog
gun'fight
gun'fire
gun'man
gun'met'al
gunned
gun'ner
gun'nery
gun'ning
gun'ny
gun'point
gun'pow'der
gun'run'ner
gun'run'ning
gun'shot
gun'shy
gun'smith
gun'wale
gup'pies
gup'py
gur'gle
gur'gled
gur'gling
gur'nard
gu'ru
gush'er
gush'i'er
gush'i'est
gush'i'ness
gush'ing
gushy
gus'set

gus'ta'to'ry
gust'i'er
gust'i'est
gust'i'ly
gust'i'ness
gus'to
gusty
gut
gut'less
guts'y
gut'ted
gut'ter
gut'ting
gut'tur'al
gut'tur'al'ly
guy
guz'zle
guz'zled
guz'zling
gym
gym'kha'na
gym'na'si'um
gym'na'si'ums
gym'nast
gym'nas'tic
gy'nae'co'log'i'cal
gy'nae'col'o'gist
gy'nae'col'o'gy
gyp
gypped
gyp'ping
gyp'sies
gyp'sum
gyp'sy
gy'rate
gy'rat'ed
gy'rat'ing
gy'ra'tion
gy'ra'tor
gy'ro'com'pass
gy'rom'e'ter
gy'ro'plane
gy'ro'scope
gy'ro'sta'bi'liz'er
gy'ro'sta'tics
ha'be'as cor'pus
hab'er'dash'er
hab'er'dash'ery
ha'bil'i'ment
hab'it
ha'bi'tabil'i'ty
hab'it'able
hab'i'tat

hab'i'ta'tion
ha'bit'u'al
ha'bit'u'al'ly
ha'bit'u'al'ness
ha'bit'u'ate
ha'bit'u'at'ed
ha'bit'u'a'tion
ha'bit'ué
ha'ci'en'da
hack
hack'le
hack'led
hack'ling
hack'ney
hack'neyed
hack'saw
had
had'dock
had'n't
hae'ma'tol'o'gy
hae'mo'glo'bin
hae'mo'phil'ia
hae'mo'phil'i'ac
haem'or'rhage
haem'or'rhaged
haem'or'rhag'ing
haem'or'rhoid
haf'ni'um
hag
hag'gard
hag'gard'ness
hag'gis
hag'gle
hag'gled
hag'gler
hag'gling
ha'gi'og'ra'phy
hagi'ol'o'gy
hag'rid'den
hail
hail'storm
hair
hair'ball
hair'breadth
hair'do
hair'dress'er
hair'i'er
hair'i'est
hair'piece
hair-rais'ing
hair'split'ting
hair'style
hairy

Hai'tian
hake
haled
half
half-caste
half-hearted
half-life
half-lives
half-tim'bered
half-wit'ted
hal'i'but
hal'ing
hal'i'to'sis
hall
hal'le'lu'jah
hall'mark
hal'loo
hal'low
hal'lowed
hal'lu'ci'nate
hal'lu'ci'nat'ed
hal'lu'ci'nat'ing
hal'lu'ci'na'tion
hal'lu'ci'na'to'ry
hal'lu'ci'no'gen'ic
ha'lo
halo'gen
halt
hal'ter
hal'ting
hal'va
hal'vah
halve
halved
halves
halves
hal'ving
hal'yard
ham
ham'burg'er
ham'let
hammed
ham'mer
ham'ming
ham'mock
ham'per
ham'ster
ham'string
ham'string'ing
ham'strung
hand'bag
hand'ball
hand'bill

hand'cuff
hand'ed
hand'ful
hand'i'cap
hand'i'capped
hand'i'cap'per
hand'i'cap'ping
hand'i'craft
hand'i'er
hand'i'est
hand'i'ly
hand'i'ness
hand'i'work
hand'ker'chief
han'dle
han'dle'bar
han'dled
han'dling
hand'made
hand'maid
hand-picked
hand'rail
hand'some
hand'some'ly
hand'some'ness
hand'som'est
hands-on
hand'stand
hand'writ'ing
hand'writ'ten
handy
handy'man
hang
hang'ar
hanged
hang'er
hang'er-on
hang'ing
hang'man
hang'nail
hang'over
hank'er
han'ky-pan'ky
han'som
hap
hap'haz'ard
hap'haz'ard'ly
hap'less
hap'pen
hap'pen'ing
hap'pen'stance
hap'pi'er

hap'pi'est
hap'pi'ly
hap'pi'ness
hap'py
ha'ra-ki'ri
ha'rangue
ha'rangued
ha'rangu'ing
har'ass
har'ass'ment
har'bin'ger
har'bour
har'bour mas'ter
hardball
hard-bit'ten
hard'board
hard-boiled
hard'en
hard'en'er
hardheart'ed
hard-hit'ting
har'di'er
har'di'est
har'di'hood
har'di'ly
har'd'iness
hard'ly
hard pal'ate
hard-pressed
hard'ware
hard'wood
har'dy
hare
harebell
hare'brained
hared
hare'lip
har'em
har'i'cot
har'ing
hark
har'ken
har'le'quin
har'lot
har'lot'ry
harm'ful
harm'ful'ly
harm'ful'ness
harm'less
harm'less'ly
harm'less'ness
har'mon'ic
har'mon'i'ca

har'mon'i'cal'ly
har'mon'ics
har'mo'nies
har'mo'ni'ous
har'mo'ni'ous'ly
har'mo'ni'um
har'mo'nize
har'mo'nized
har'mo'niz'ing
har'mo'ny
har'ness
har'pies
harp'ist
har'poon
harp'si'chord
har'py
har'ri'dan
har'ried
har'ri'er
har'row
har'ry
har'ry'ing
harsh
harsh'ly
harsh'ness
har'te'beest
har'um-scar'um
har'vest
har'ves'ter
has
has-been
hash'eesh
hash'ish
has'n't
has'sle
has'sled
has'sling
has'sock
haste
has'ten
hast'i'er
hast'i'est
hast'i'ly
hast'i'ness
hast'y
hat
hatch
hatch'back
hatch'er'ies
hatch'ery
hatch'et
hatch'et man
hatch'way

hate
hat'ed
hate'ful
hate'ful'ly
hate'ful'ness
hath
hat'ing
ha'tred
hat'ter
haugh'ti'er
haugh'ti'est
haugh'ti'ly
haugh'ti'ness
haugh'ty
haul
haul'age
haunch
haunch'es
haunt
haunt'ed
haunt'ing
haunt'ing'ly
haus'frau
haute cou'ture
haute cui'sine
haute école
hau'teur
haut monde
have
ha'ven
have-not
haven't
hav'er'sack
hav'ing
hav'oc
Ha'wai'ian
hawk
hawk'er
hawk'ish
haw'ser
haw'thorn
hay
haz'ard
haz'ard'ous
haz'ard'ous'ness
haze
hazed
ha'zel
ha'zel'nut
haz'ier
haz'i'est
ha'zi'ly
ha'zi'ness

haz'ing
ha'zy
head
head'ache
head'board
head'dress
head'first
head'fore'most
head'gear
head-hunt'er
head'ier
head'i'est
head'i'ly
head'i'ness
head'ing
head'less
head'light
head'line
head'lined
head'lin'ing
head'long
head'man
head'master
head'mis'tress
head'phone
head'quar'ters
head'shrink'er
head'word
head'work
heady
heal
heal'er
health
health'ful
health'ful'ly
health'i'er
health'i'est
health'i'ly
health'i'ness
healthy
heap
heaped
hear
heard
hear'er
hear'ing
heark'en
hear'say
hearse
heart
heart'ache
heart'beat
heart'break

heart'break'ing
heart'bro'ken
heart'burn
heart'en
hearth
hearth'stone
heart'i'er
heart'i'est
heart'i'ly
heart'i'ness
heart'less
heart'less'ly
heart'less'ness
heart'rend'ing
hearts'ease
heart'sick
heart'throb
heart-warm'ing
hearty
heat
heat'ed
heat'ed'ly
heat'er
heath
hea'then
heath'er
heave
heaved
heav'en
heav'en'ly
heav'en-sent
heav'en'ward
heavi'er
heavi'est
heavi'ly
heavi'ness
heav'ing
heavy
heavy-du'ty
heavy-hand'ed
heavy-heart'ed
heav'y'weight
He'bra'ic
He'brew
heck
heck'le
heck'led
heck'ler
heck'ling
hec'tare
hec'tic
hec'ti'cal'ly
hec'to'gram

hec'to'li'tre
hec'to'me'tre
hec'tor
hedge
hedged
hedge'hog
hedg'er
hedge'row
hedg'ing
he'don'ism
he'don'ist
he'don'is'tic
heed
heed'ful
heed'less
heel
heft'i'er
heft'i'est
hefty
he'gem'o'ny
he'gi'ra
heif'er
height
height'en
hei'nous
hei'nous'ness
heir
heir'ess
heir'loom
heist
he'ji'ra
held
he'li'cal
hel'i'cop'ter
he'li'port
he'li'um
he'lix
he'lix'es
hel'lion
hell'ish
hell'ish'ly
hell'ish'ness
hel'lo
helm
hel'met
hel'met'ed
helm'less
helms'man
help'er
help'ful
help'ful'ly
help'ful'ness
help'ing

help'less
help'less'ly
help'less'ness
hel'ter-skel'ter
hem
he-man
hem'i'sphere
hem'i'spher'i'cal
hem'lock
hemmed
hem'ming
hem'stich
hence
hence'forth
hench'man
hen'na
hep'a'ti'tis
hep'tag'on
hep'tag'o'nal
her
her'ald
he'ral'dic
her'ald'ry
herb
her'ba'ceous
herb'al
herb'al'ist
her'bi'cide
herb'i'vore
her'biv'o'rous
her'cu'le'an
herd
herds'man
here
here'af'ter
here'by
he'red'i'tar'i'ly
he'red'i'tary
he'red'i'ty
here'in
her'e'sies
her'e'sy
her'e'tic
he'ret'i'cal
here'to'fore
here'with
her'it'a'bil'i'ty
her'it'a'ble
her'it'age
her'maph'ro'dite
her'maph'ro'dit'ism
her'met'ic
her'met'i'cal'ly

her'mit
her'nia
her'ni'al
he'ro
he'roes
he'ro'ic
he'ro'i'cal'ly
her'o'in
her'o'ine
her'o'ism
her'on
her'pes
her'pe'tol'o'gy
her'ring
her'ring'bone
hers
her'self
hertz
hes'i'tance
hes'i'tan'cy
hes'i'tant
hes'i'tant'ly
hes'i'tate
hes'i'tat'ed
hes'i'tat'ing
hes'i'ta'tion
hes'sian
het'er'o'dox
het'er'o'doxy
het'er'o'ge'ne'i'ty
het'er'o'ge'ne'ous
het'er'o'sex'u'al
het'er'o'sex'u'al'i'ty
heu'ris'tic
hew
hewed
hew'ing
hewn
hex'ad
hex'a'gon
hex'ag'o'nal
hexa'gram
hey
hi'a'tus
hi'ba'chi
hi'ber'nate
hi'ber'nat'ed
hi'ber'nat'ing
hi'ber'na'tion
hi'bis'cus
hic'cup
hic'cupped
hick

hick'o'ry
hic'up'ping
hid
hid'den
hide
hide'bound
hid'e'ous
hid'e'ous'ly
hid'e'ous'ness
hid'ing
hi'er'ar'chi'cal
hi'er'ar'chic
hi'er'ar'chi'cal'ly
hi'er'ar'chies
hi'er'ar'chy
hi'er'o'glyph
hi'er'o'glyph'ic
high
high-ball
high'brow
high-class
high'er-up
high-fli'er
high-flown
high-fly'ing
high-grade
high-hand'ed
high-lev'el
high'light
high'ly
high-mind'ed
high'ness
high-oc'tane
high-pow'ered
high-pres'sure
high-pres'sured
high-pres'sur'ing
high-rise
high-spir'it'ed
high-tech
high-ten'sion
high-toned
high'way
high'way'man
hi'jack
hi'jack'er
hi'jack'ing
hike
hiked
hik'er
hik'ing
hi'lar'i'ous
hi'lar'i'ous'ly

hi'lar'i'ous'ness
hi'lar'i'ty
hill'bil'lies
hill'bil'ly
hill'i'er
hill'i'est
hill'ock
hilly
Hi'ma'la'yan
him'self
hind
hin'der
hind'er'er
Hin'di
hind'most
hind'quar'ter
hin'drance
hind'sight
Hin'du
Hin'du'ism
Hin'du'sta'ni
hinge
hinged
hing'ing
hin'ter'land
hip
hipped
hip'pie
hip'po'drome
hip'po'pot'a'mi
hip'po'pot'a'mus
hip'py
hire
hired
hire'ling
hir'ing
hir'sute
his
His'pan'ic
hiss
his'ta'mine
his'to'ri'an
his'tor'ic
his'tor'i'cal
his'tor'i'cal'ly
his'tor'i'cal'ness
his'to'ries
his'to'ry
his'tri'on'ic
his'tri'on'i'cal'ly
his'tri'on'ics
hit
hit-and-miss

hitch
hitch'hike
hitch'hiked
hitch'hik'er
hitch'hik'ing
hith'er
hith'er'to
hit-or-miss
hit'ter
hit'ting
hive
hived
hiv'ing
hoard
hoard'er
hoard'ing
hoar'frost
hoari'er
hoari'est
hoar'i'ness
hoarse
hoarse'ly
hoarse'ness
hoary
hoax
hoax'er
hob
hob'bies
hob'ble
hob'bled
hob'bling
hob'by
hob'by'ist
hob'gob'lin
hob'nail'ed
hob'nob
hob'nobbed
hob'nob'bing
hock'ey
ho'cus-po'cus
hod
hodge'podge
hoe
hoed
hoe'down
hoe'ing
hog
hogged
hog'ging
hog'gish
hogs'head
hog-tie
hog'wash

hoi pol'loi
hoist
hoist'ing
hoi'ty-toi'ty
ho'kum
hold
hold'all
hold'ing
hole
holed
hol'er
holey
hol'i'day
ho'li'er
hol'li'es
ho'li'est
ho'li'ness
hol'ing
hol'low
hol'low'ness
hol'ly
hol'ly'hock
hol'o'caust
hol'o'gram
hol'o'graph
hol'ster
ho'ly
hom'age
hom'bre
hom'burg
home'com'ing
home-grown
home'less
home'less'ness
home'li'ness
home'ly
ho'meo'path
ho'meo'path'ic
ho'me'op'a'thy
home'spun
home'stead
home'ward
home'wards
home'work
homey
ho'mi'cid'al
ho'm'i'cide
hom'i'let'ics
hom'i'lies
hom'i'ly
hom'i'ness
hom'i'ny
ho'mo'ge'ne'i'ty

ho'mo'ge'neous
ho'mog'e'nize
ho'mog'e'nized
ho'mog'e'niz'ing
ho'mog'e'nous
hom'o'graph
ho'mol'o'gous
hom'o'nym
ho'mo'pho'bia
ho'mo'pho'bic
hom'o'phone
Ho'mo sa'pi'ens
ho'mo'sex'u'al
ho'mo'sex'u'al'i'ty
hone
honed
hon'est
hon'es'ties
hon'est'ly
hon'es'ty
hon'ey
hon'ey'comb
hon'ey'dew
hon'eyed
hon'ey'moon'er
hon'ey'suck'le
hon'ing
honk
honky-tonk
hon'our
hon'our'able
hon'our'ably
hon'o'rar'i'um
hon'or'ary
hon'or'if'ic
hooch
hood
hood'ed
hood'lum
hoo'doo
hood'wink
hoo'ey
hoof
hoofed
hoof'er
hoofs
hook
hooked
hook'er
hook'ey
hooky
hoo'li'gan
hoo'li'gan'ism

hoop
hooped
hoop'la
hoo'ray
hoot
hoo'te'nan'ny
hooting
hooves
hop
hope
hoped
hope'ful
hope'ful'ly
hope'ful'ness
hope'less
hope'less'ly
hope'less'ness
hop'head
hop'ing
hopped
hop'per
hop'ping
hop'scotch
horde
hord'ed
hord'ing
ho'ri'zon
hor'i'zon'tal
hor'i'zon'tal'ly
hor'mon'al
hor'mone
horn
horn'blende
horned
hor'net
horn'ier
horn'i'est
horn'swog'gle
horny
hor'ol'o'ges
ho'rol'o'gist
ho'rol'o'gy
hor'o'scope
hor'ren'dous
hor'ri'ble
hor'ri'bly
hor'rid
hor'rid'ly
hor'rid'ness
hor'ri'fic
hor'rif'i'cal'ly
hor'ri'fi'ca'tion
hor'ri'fied

hor'ri'fy
hor'ri'fy'ing
hor'ri'fy'ing'ly
hor'ror
hors de com'bat
hors d'oeu'vre
horse
horse'back
horsed
horse'flies
horse'fly
horse'hair
horse'man
horse'play
horse'pow'er
horse'rad'ish
hors'es
horse'shoe
horse'whip
horse'whipped
horse'whip'ping
hors'ey
hors'i'er
hors'i'est
hors'ing
horsy
hor'ta'to'ry
hor'ti'cul'tur'al
hor'ti'cul'ture
hor'ti'cul'tur'ist
ho'san'na
hose
hosed
ho'siery
hos'ing
hos'pice
hos'pi'ta'ble
hos'pi'ta'bly
hos'pi'tal
hos'pi'tal'i'ties
hos'pi'tal'i'ty
hos'pi'tal'iza'tion
hos'pi'tal'ize
hos'pi'tal'ized
hos'pi'tal'iz'ing
host
hos'tage
hos'tel
hos'tel'ry
host'ess
hos'tile
hos'tile'ly
hos'til'i'ties

hos'til'i'ty
hot
hot-blood'ed
ho'tel
ho'te'lier
hot'foot
hot'head
hot-head'ed
hot'house
hot'ly
hot'ted
hot'ter
hot'test
hot'ting
hound
hour
hour'glass
houri
hour'ly
house
house'boat
house'bound
house'break'er
house'break'ing
house'bro'ken
house'coat
housed
house'hold
house'keep'er
house'maid
house'man
house'proud
house'room
hous'es
house-train
house'warm'ing
house'wife
house'wives
house'work
hous'ing
hove
hov'el
hov'er
hov'er'ing
how
how'dah
how'dy
how'ev'er
how'itz'er
howl
howl'er
hoy'den
hoy'den'ish

hub
hub'ble-bub'ble
hub'bub
hu'bris
huck'le'ber'ries
huck'le'ber'ry
huck'ster
hud'dle
hud'dled
hud'dling
hue
huff
huf'fi'er
huf'fi'est
huf'fi'ly
huff'i'ness
huffy
hug
huge
huge'ly
huge'ness
hugged
hug'ger
hug'ging
hu'la
hu'la-hu'la
hulk'ing
hull
hul'la'ba'loo
hul'lo
hum
hu'man
hu'mane
hu'mane'ly
hu'mane'ness
hu'man'ism
hu'man'is'tic
hu'man'i'tar'i'an
hu'man'i'tar'i'an'ism
hu'man'i'ties
hu'man'i'ty
hu'man'iza'tion
hu'man'ize
hu'man'ized
hu'man'iz'ing
hu'man'kind
hu'man'ly
hu'man'oid
hum'ble
hum'bled
hum'ble'ness
hum'bling
hum'bly

hum'bug
hum'ding'er
hum'drum
hu'meri
hu'mer'us
hu'mid
hu'mid'i'fied
hu'mid'i'fi'er
hu'mid'i'fy
hu'mid'i'fy'ing
hu'mid'i'ty
hu'mi'dor
hu'mil'i'ate
hu'mil'i'at'ed
hu'mil'i'at'ing
hu'mil'i'a'tion
hu'mil'i'ty
hummed
hum'mer
hum'ming
hum'ming'bird
hum'mock
hu'mour
hu'mor'ist
hu'mour'less
hu'mor'ous
hu'mor'ous'ly
hu'mor'ous'ness
hump
hump'back
humped
humpy
hu'mus
hunch
hunch'back
hun'dred
hun'dredth
hun'dred'weight
hung
Hun'gar'i'an
hun'ger
hun'gri'er
hun'gri'est
hun'gri'ly
hun'gri'ness
hun'gry
hunt
hunt'er
hunt'ing
hunt'ress
hunts'man
hur'dle
hur'dled

hur'dler
hur'dling
hur'dy-gur'dy
hurl
hurl'er
hur'ly-bur'ly
hur'rah
hur'ray
hur'ri'cane
hur'ried
hur'ried'ly
hur'ry
hur'ry'ing
hurt
hurt'ful
hurt'ing
hur'tle
hur'tled
hur'tling*
hus'band
hus'band'ry
husk'er
husk'i'er
husk'ies
husk'i'est
husk'i'ly
husk'i'ness
husky
hus'sar
hus'sies
hus'sy
hus'tings
hus'tle
hus'tled
hus'tler
hus'tling
hut
hutch
hy'a'cinth
hy'ae'na
hy'brid
hy'brid'iza'tion
hy'brid'ize
hy'brid'ized
hy'brid'iz'ing
hy'dran'gea
hy'drant
hy'drate
hy'drated
hy'drating
hy'dra'tion
hy'drau'lic
hy'drau'li'cal'ly

hy'drau'lics
hy'dro'car'bon
hy'dro'ce'phal'ic
hy'dro'ceph'a'lus
hy'dro'chlo'ric
hy'dro'dy'nam'ic
hy'dro'dy'nam'ics
hy'dro'e'lec'tric
hy'dro'elec'tric'ity
hy'dro'foil
hy'dro'gen
hy'drog'e'nous
hy'drol'y'sis
hy'drom'e'ter
hy'drop'a'thy
hy'dro'pho'bia
hy'dro'plane
hy'dro'planed
hy'dro'plan'ing
hy'dro'pon'ics
hy'dro'ther'a'pist
hy'dro'ther'a'py
hy'drous
hy'drox'ide
hy'e'na
hy'giene
hy'gien'ic
hy'gien'i'cal'ly
hy'gien'ist
hy'grom'e'ter
hy'men
hy'me'ne'al
hy'me'ne'al'ly
hymn
hym'nal
hym'na'ries
hym'na'ry
hym'no'dy
hype
hyped
hy'per'ac'tive
hy'per'bo'la
hy'per'bo'le
hy'per'bol'ic
hy'per'bo'lize
hy'per'bo'lized
hy'per'bo'liz'ing
hy'per'crit'i'cal
hy'per'sen'si'tive
hy'per'sen'si'tiv'i'ty
hy'per'ten'sion
hy'per'thy'roid'ism
hy'per'ven'ti'late

hy'per'ven'ti'lat'ed
hy'per'ven'ti'lat'ing
hy'per'ven'ti'la'tion
hy'phen
hy'phen'ate
hy'phen'at'ed
hy'phen'at'ing
hyp'ing
hyp'no'sis
hy'pno'ther'a'py
hyp'not'ic
hyp'no'tism
hyp'no'tist
hyp'no'tize
hyp'no'tized
hyp'no'tiz'ing
hy'po'chon'dria
hy'po'chon'dri'ac
hy'poc'ri'sies
hy'poc'ri'sy
hyp'o'crite
hy'po'crit'i'cal
hy'po'der'mic
hy'po'gly'cae'mia
hy'po'sen'si'tize
hy'po'ten'sion
hyp'ot'e'nuse
hyp'oth'e'cate
hy'poth'e'cat'ed
hy'poth'e'cat'ing
hy'poth'e'ca'tion
hy'po'ther'mia
hy'poth'e'ses
hy'poth'e'sis
hy'poth'e'size
hy'poth'e'sized
hy'poth'e'siz'ing
hy'po'thet'i'cal
hy'po'thet'i'cal'ly
hys'ter'ec'to'mies
hys'ter'ec'to'my
hys'ter'e'sis
hys'te'ria
hys'ter'ic
hys'ter'i'cal
hys'ter'i'cal'ly
hys'ter'ics
iamb
iam'bic
ibex
ibid
ibi'dem
ibis

ice
ice'berg
ice'bound
ice'break'er
ice'cap
ice cream
iced
Ice'lan'dic
ice-skate
ice-skat'ed
ice-skat'ing
ich'neu'mon
ich'thy'o'log'i'cal
ich'thy'ol'o'gist
ich'thy'ol'o'gy
ici'cle
ic'i'er
ic'i'est
ic'i'ly
ici'ness
ic'ing
icon
icon'o'clasm
icon'o'clast
icon'o'clas'tic
ico'nog'raphy
icy
idea
ide'al
ide'al'ism
ide'al'ist
ide'al'is'tic
ide'al'iza'tion
ide'al'ize
ide'al'ized
ide'al'iz'ing
ide'al'ly
ide'ate
ide'ation
idée fixe
idées fixes
iden'ti'cal
iden'ti'cal'ly
iden'ti'cal'ness
iden'ti'fi'able
iden'ti'fi'ably
iden'ti'fi'ca'tion
iden'ti'fied
iden'ti'fy
iden'ti'fy'ing
iden'ti'ties
iden'ti'ty
ideo'log'i'cal

ideo'log'i'cal'ly
ide'ol'o'gies
ide'ol'o'gist
ide'ol'o'gy
ides
id'i'o'cies
id'i'o'cy
id'i'om
id'i'o'mat'ic
id'i'o'mat'i'cal'ly
id'i'o'syn'cra'sies
id'i'o'syn'cra'sy
id'i'o'syn'crat'ic
id'i'ot
id'i'ot'ic
id'i'ot'i'cal'ly
idle
idled
idle'ness
idler
idlest
idling
idly
idol
idol'a'ter
idol'a'tries
idol'a'trous
idol'a'try
idol'iza'tion
idol'ize
idol'ized
idol'iz'ing
idyll
idyl'lic
idyl'lic'al'ly
ig'loo
ig'ne'ous
ig'nes fat'ui
ig'nis fat'u'us
ig'nit'a'bil'i'ty
ig'nit'able
ig'nite
ig'nit'ed
ig'nit'er
ig'nit'ing
ig'ni'tion
ig'no'bil'i'ty
ig'no'ble
ig'no'ble'ness
ig'no'bly
ig'no'min'ies
ig'no'min'i'ous
ig'no'min'i'ous'ly

ig'no'miny
ig'no'ra'mus
ig'no'rance
ig'no'rant
ig'no'rant'ly
ig'nore
ig'nored
ig'nor'ing
igua'na
ikon
ill
ill-ad'vised
ill-bred
il'le'gal
il'le'gal'i'ties
il'le'gal'i'ty
il'le'gal'ly
il'leg'i'bil'i'ty
il'leg'i'ble
il'leg'i'ble'ness
il'leg'i'bly
il'le'git'i'ma'cies
il'le'git'i'ma'cy
il'le'git'i'mate
il'le'git'i'mate'ly
ill-fat'ed
ill-fa'voured
ill-got'ten
il'lib'er'al
il'lic'it
il'lim'it'able
il'lit'er'a'cy
il'lit'er'ate
ill'ness
il'log'i'cal
il'log'i'cal'ly
ill-tempered
ill-timed
il'lu'mi'nate
il'lu'mi'nat'ed
il'lu'mi'nat'ing
il'lu'mi'na'tion
il'lu'mi'na'tor
il'lu'mine
il'lu'mined
il'lu'min'ing
ill-us'age
il'lu'sion
il'lu'sion'ist
il'lu'sive
il'lu'sive'ness
il'lu'so'ri'ness
il'lu'so'ry

il'lus'trate
il'lus'trat'ed
il'lus'trat'ing
il'lus'tra'tion
il'lus'tra'tive
il'lus'tra'tor
il'lus'tri'ous
il'lus'tri'ous'ness
im'age
im'aged
im'a'ge'ri'al
im'age'ries
im'age'ry
imag'in'able
imag'in'ably
imag'i'nari'ly
imag'i'nary
imag'i'na'tion
imag'i'na'tive
imag'i'na'tive'ly
imag'ine
imag'ined
ima'gi'nes
im'ag'ing
imag'in'ing
ima'go
imam
im'bal'ance
im'be'cile
im'be'cil'ic
im'be'cil'i'ty
im'bed
im'bed'ded
im'bed'ding
im'bibe
im'bibed
im'bib'ing
im'bro'glio
im'bue
im'bued
im'bu'ing
im'i'tate
im'i'tat'ed
im'i'tat'ing
im'i'ta'tion
im'i'ta'tive
im'i'ta'tor
im'mac'u'la'cy
im'mac'u'late
im'mac'u'late'ly
im'mac'u'late'ness
im'ma'nence
im'ma'nen'cy

im'ma'nent
im'ma'nent'ly
im'ma'te'ri'al
im'ma'te'ri'al'i'ty
im'ma'te'ri'al'ness
im'ma'ture
im'ma'ture'ly
im'ma'ture'ness
im'ma'tu'ri'ty
im'meas'ur'able
im'meas'ur'ably
im'me'di'a'cies
im'me'di'a'cy
im'me'di'ate
im'me'di'ate'ly
im'me'mo'ri'al
im'mense
im'mense'ly
im'mense'ness
im'men'si'ty
im'merge
im'merged
im'mer'gence
im'merg'ing
im'merse
im'mersed
im'mers'ing
im'mer'sion
im'mi'grant
im'mi'grate
im'mi'grat'ed
im'mi'grat'ing
im'mi'gra'tion
im'mi'gra'tor
im'mi'nence
im'mi'nent
im'mo'bile
im'mo'bil'i'ty
im'mo'bi'lize
im'mo'bi'lized
im'mo'bi'liz'ing
im'mod'er'ate
im'mod'er'ate'ly
im'mod'est
im'mod'est'ly
im'mod'es'ty
im'mo'late
im'mo'lat'ed
im'mo'lat'ing
im'mo'la'tion
im'mo'la'tor
im'mor'al
im'mo'ral'i'ties

im'mo'ral'i'ty
im'mor'al'ly
im'mor'tal
im'mor'tal'i'ty
im'mor'tal'ize
im'mor'tal'ized
im'mor'tal'iz'ing
im'mor'tal'ly
im'mov'abil'i'ty
im'mov'able
im'mov'ably
im'mune
im'mu'ni'ties
im'mu'ni'ty
im'mu'ni'za'tion
im'mu'nize
im'mu'nized
im'mu'niz'ing
im'mu'nol'o'gy
im'mure
im'mured
im'mur'ing
im'mu'ta'bil'i'ty
im'mu'ta'ble
im'mu'ta'ble'ness
im'mu'ta'bly
im'pact
im'pact'ed
im'pac'tion
im'pair
im'pair'ment
im'pa'la
im'pale
im'paled
im'pale'ment
im'pal'ing
im'pal'pa'bil'i'ty
im'pal'pa'ble
im'pan'el
im'pan'eled
im'pan'el'ing
im'part
im'par'tial
im'par'ti'al'i'ty
im'par'tial'ly
im'par'tial'ness
im'pass'abil'i'ty
im'pass'able
im'pass'able'ness
im'pass'ably
im'passe
im'pas'si'bil'i'ty
im'pas'si'ble

im'pas'si'ble'ness
im'pas'sion
im'pas'sioned
im'pas'sioned'ness
im'pas'sive
im'pas'sive'ly
im'pas'sive'ness
im'pas'siv'i'ty
im'pa'tience
im'pa'tient
im'pa'tient'ly
im'peach
im'peach'able
im'peach'ment
im'pec'ca'bil'i'ty
im'pec'ca'ble
im'pec'ca'bly
im'pe'cu'ni'ous
im'pe'cu'ni'ous'ness
im'pede
im'ped'ed
im'ped'i'ment
im'ped'i'men'ta
im'ped'ing
im'pel
im'pelled
im'pel'ling
im'pend
im'pend'ing
im'pen'e'tra'bil'i'ty
im'pen'e'tra'ble
im'pen'e'tra'bly
im'pen'i'tence
im'pen'i'tent
im'per'a'tive
im'per'a'tive'ness
im'per'cep'ti'bil'i'ty
im'per'cep'ti'ble
im'per'cep'ti'bly
im'per'cep'tive
im'per'fect
im'per'fec'tion
im'per'fect'ly
im'per'fect'ness
im'pe'ri'al
im'pe'ri'al'ism
im'pe'ri'al'ist
im'pe'ri'al'is'tic
im'pe'ri'al'is'ti'cal'ly
im'pe'ri'al'ly
im'per'il
im'per'illed
im'pe'ril'ling

im'per'il'ment
im'pe'ri'ous
im'pe'ri'ous'ly
im'pe'ri'ous'ness
im'per'ish'abil'i'ty
im'per'ish'able
im'per'ma'nence
im'per'ma'nen'cy
im'per'ma'nent
im'per'ma'nent'ly
im'per'me'abil'i'ty
im'per'me'able
im'per'son'al
im'per'son'al'ly
im'per'son'ate
im'per'son'at'ed
im'per'son'at'ing
im'per'son'a'tion
im'per'son'a'tor
im'per'ti'nence
im'per'ti'nent
im'per'ti'nent'ly
im'per'turb'able
im'per'turb'ably
im'per'vi'ous
im'per'vi'ous'ly
im'per'vi'ous'ness
im'pe'ti'go
im'pet'u'os'i'ty
im'pet'u'ous
im'pet'u'ous'ly
im'pet'u'ous'ness
im'pe'tus
im'pi'e'ties
im'pi'e'ty
im'pinge
im'pinged
im'pinge'ment
im'ping'ing
im'pi'ous
im'pi'ous'ly
im'pi'ous'ness
im'plac'abil'i'ty
im'plac'able
im'plac'able'ness
im'plac'a'bly
im'plant
im'plan'ta'tion
im'plant'er
im'plau'si'bil'i'ty
im'ple'ment
im'plau'si'ble
im'plau'si'bly

im'plead
im'ple'men'tal
im'pli'cate
im'pli'cat'ed
im'pli'cat'ing
im'pli'ca'tion
im'plic'it
im'plic'it'ly
im'plic'it'ness
im'plied
im'plode
im'plod'ed
im'plod'ing
im'plo'ra'tion
im'plore
im'plored
im'plor'ing
im'plo'sion
im'plo'sive
im'ply
im'ply'ing
im'po'lite
im'po'lite'ly
im'po'lite'ness
im'pol'i'tic
im'pol'i'tic'ly
im'pon'der'a'ble
im'port
im'port'able
im'por'tance
im'por'tant
im'por'tant'ly
im'por'ta'tion
im'port'er
im'por'tu'nate
im'por'tune
im'por'tuned
im'por'tun'ing
im'por'tu'ni'ties
im'por'tu'ni'ty
im'pose
im'posed
im'pos'ing
im'pos'ing'ly
im'po'si'tion
im'pos'si'bil'i'ties
im'pos'si'bil'i'ty
im'pos'si'ble
im'pos'si'bly
im'post
im'post'er
im'pos'tor
im'pos'ture

im'po'tence
im'po'ten'cy
im'po'tent
im'po'tent'ly
im'pound
im'pound'age
im'pov'er'ish
im'pov'er'ish'ment
im'prac'ti'ca'bil'i'ty
im'prac'ti'ca'ble
im'prac'ti'ca'ble'ness
im'prac'ti'cal
im'pre'cate
im'pre'cat'ed
im'pre'cat'ing
im'pre'ca'tion
im'pre'cise
im'pre'ci'sion
im'preg'na'bil'i'ty
im'preg'na'ble
im'preg'na'ble'ness
im'preg'nate
im'preg'nat'ed
im'preg'nat'ing
im'preg'na'tion
im'preg'na'tor
im'pre'sa'rio
im'press
im'press'ible
im'pres'sion
im'pres'sion'able
im'pres'sion'ably
im'pres'sion'ism
im'pres'sion'ist
im'pres'sion'is'tic
im'pres'sive
im'pres'sive'ly
im'pres'sive'ness
im'press'ment
im'pri'ma'tur
im'print
im'prin'ter
im'pris'on
im'pris'on'ment
im'prob'a'bil'i'ties
im'prob'a'bil'i'ty
im'prob'a'ble
im'prob'a'ble'ness
im'prob'a'bly
im'promp'tu
im'prop'er
im'prop'er'ly
im'prop'er'ness

im'pro'pri'e'ties
im'pro'pri'e'ty
im'prov'abil'i'ty
im'prov'able
im'prove
im'proved
im'prove'ment
im'prov'i'dence
im'prov'i'dent
im'prov'i'dent'ly
im'prov'ing
im'prov'i'sa'tion
im'prov'i'sa'tion'al
im'pro'vise
im'pro'vised
im'pro'vis'ing
im'pru'dence
im'pru'dent
im'pru'dent'ly
im'pu'dence
im'pu'dent
im'pu'dent'ly
im'pugn
im'pug'na'tion
im'pugn'er
im'pulse
im'pul'sion
im'pul'sive
im'pul'sive'ly
im'pul'sive'ness
im'pu'ni'ty
im'pure
im'pure'ness
im'pu'ri'ties
im'pu'ri'ty
im'pu'ta'tion
im'pute
im'put'ed
im'put'ing
in'a'bil'i'ty
in ab'sen'tia
in'ac'ces'si'bil'i'ty
in'ac'ces'si'ble
in'ac'ces'si'bly
in'ac'cu'ra'cies
in'ac'cu'ra'cy
in'ac'cu'rate
in'ac'tion
in'ac'ti'vate
in'ac'ti'va'tion
in'ac'tive
in'ac'tive'ly
in'ac'tiv'i'ty

in'ad'e'qua'cies
in'ad'e'qua'cy
in'ad'e'quate
in'ad'e'quate'ly
in'ad'mis'si'ble
in'ad'mis'si'bly
in'ad'vert'ence
in'ad'vert'en'cy
in'ad'vert'ent
in'ad'ver'tent'ly
in'ad'vis'able
in'al'ien'abil'i'ty
in'al'ien'able
in'al'ien'ably
in'al'ter'able
in'amo'ra'ta
in'ane
inane'ly
in'ane'ness
in'an'i'mate
in'an'i'ty
in'ap'pli'ca'ble
in'ap'pre'cia'bly
in'ap'pro'pri'ate
in'ap'pro'pri'ate'ly
in'apt
in'ap'ti'tude
in'apt'ly
in'ar'tic'u'late
in'ar'tic'u'late'ly
in'as'much as
in'at'ten'tion
in'at'ten'tive
in'au'di'ble
in'au'di'bly
in'au'gu'ral
in'au'gu'rate
in'au'gu'rat'ed
in'au'gu'rat'ing
in'au'gu'ra'tion
in'aus'pi'cious
in'aus'pi'cious'ly
in'born
in'bred
in'breed
in'breed'ing
in'built
in'cal'cu'la'bil'i'ty
in'cal'cu'la'ble
in'cal'cu'la'bly
in'can'des'cence
in'can'des'cent
in'can'ta'tion

in'ca'pa'ble
in'ca'pa'bly
in'ca'pac'i'tate
in'ca'pac'i'tat'ed
in'ca'pac'i'tat'ing
in'ca'pac'i'ta'tion
in'ca'pac'i'ties
in'ca'pac'i'ty
in'car'cer'ate
in'car'cer'at'ed
in'car'cer'at'ing
in'car'cer'a'tion
in'car'nate
in'car'nat'ed
in'car'nat'ing
in'car'na'tion
in'cau'tious
in'cen'di'aries
in'cen'di'ary
in'cense
in'censed
in'cens'ing
in'cen'tive
in'cep'tion
in'cer'ti'tude
in'ces'sant
in'ces'sant'ly
in'cest
in'ces'tu'ous
inch
in'cho'ate
in'ci'dence
in'ci'dent
in'ci'den'tal
in'ci'den'tal'ly
in'cin'er'ate
in'cin'er'at'ed
in'cin'er'at'ing
in'cin'er'a'tion
in'cin'er'a'tor
in'cip'i'ent
in'cise
in'cised
in'cis'ing
in'ci'sion
in'ci'sive
in'ci'sor
in'ci'ta'tion
in'cite
in'cit'ed
in'cite'ment
in'cit'ing
in'ci'vil'ity

in'clem'en'cy
in'clem'ent
in'cli'na'tion
in'cline
in'clined
in'clin'ing
in'clude
in'clud'ed
in'clud'ing
in'clu'sion
in'clu'sive
in'cog'ni'to
in'cog'ni'zant
in'co'her'ence
in'co'her'ent
in'co'her'ent'ly
in'com'bus'ti'ble
in'come
in'com'ing
in'com'mode
in'com'mo'di'ous
in'com'mu'ni'ca'do
in'com'pa'ra'ble
in'com'pa'ra'bly
in'com'pat'i'bil'i'ty
in'com'pat'i'ble
in'com'pe'tence
in'com'pe'ten'cy
in'com'pe'tent
in'com'pe'tent'ly
in'com'plete
in'com'plete'ly
in'com'ple'tion
in'com'pre'hen'si'ble
in'com'pre'hen'sion
in'con'ceiv'able
in'con'ceiv'a'bly
in'con'clu'sive
in'con'gru'i'ties
in'con'gru'i'ty
in'con'gru'ous
in'con'gru'ous'ly
in'con'se'quen'tial
in'con'se'quen'tial'ly
in'con'sid'er'able
in'con'sid'er'ate
in'con'sis'ten'cies
in'con'sis'ten'cy
in'con'sis'tent
in'con'sol'able
in'con'spic'u'ous
in'con'sol'a'bly
in'con'spic'u'ous'ly

in'con'stan'cy
in'con'stant
in'con'test'abil'i'ty
in'con'test'able
in'con'ti'nence
in'con'ti'nen'cy
in'con'ti'nent
in'con'trol'la'ble
in'con'tro'vert'ible
in'con'tro'vert'ibly
in'con'ven'ience
in'con'ven'ienced
in'con'ven'ienc'ing
in'con'ven'ient
in'cor'po'rate
in'cor'po'rat'ed
in'cor'po'rat'ing
in'cor'po'ra'tion
in'cor'po're'al
in'cor'rect
in'cor'rect'ly
in'cor'ri'gi'bil'i'ty
in'cor'ri'gi'ble
in'cor'ri'gi'ble'ness
in'cor'ri'gi'bly
in'cor'rupt'i'bil'i'ty
in'cor'rupt'i'ble
in'cor'rupt'i'bly
in'creas'able
in'crease
in'creased
in'creas'ing
in'creas'ing'ly
in'cred'i'bil'i'ty
in'cred'i'ble
in'cred'i'bly
in'cre'du'li'ty
in'cred'u'lous
in'cred'u'lous'ly
in'cre'ment
in'cre'men'tal
in'crim'i'nate
in'crim'i'nat'ed
in'crim'i'nat'ing
in'crim'i'na'tion
in'crust
in'crus'ta'tion
in'cu'bate
in'cu'bat'ed
in'cu'bat'ing
in'cu'ba'tion
in'cu'ba'tor
in'cu'bi

in'cu'bus
in'cul'cate
in'cul'cat'ed
in'cul'cat'ing
in'cul'ca'tion
in'cul'pate
in'cul'pat'ed
in'cul'pat'ing
in'cul'pa'tion
in'cum'ben'cy
in'cum'bent
in'cur
in'cur'able
in'cur'ably
in'cu'ri'ous
in'cu'ri'ous'ly
in'curred
in'cur'ring
in'cur'sion
in'cur'sive
in'debt'ed
in'debt'ed'ness
in'de'cen'cy
in'de'cent
in'de'cent'ly
in'de'ci'pher'able
in'de'ci'sion
in'de'ci'sive
in'de'ci'sive'ness
in'de'co'rous
in'de'co'rum
in'deed
in'de'fat'i'ga'ble
in'de'fat'i'ga'bly
in'de'fea'si'ble
in'de'fen'si'bil'i'ty
in'de'fen'si'ble
in'de'fen'si'bly
in'de'fin'able
in'de'fin'ably
in'def'i'nite
in'def'i'nite'ly
in'del'i'ble
in'del'i'bly
in'del'i'ca'cy
in'del'i'cate
in'dem'ni'fi'ca'tion
in'dem'ni'fied
in'dem'ni'fy
in'dem'ni'fy'ing
in'dem'ni'ties
in'dem'ni'ty
in'dent

in'den'ta'tion
in'den'ted
in'den'ture
in'den'tur'ing
in'de'pend'ence
in'de'pend'en'cy
in'de'pend'ent
in'de'pen'dent'ly
in'de'scrib'abil'i'ty
in'de'scrib'able
in'de'scrib'ably
in'de'struct'i'bil'i'ty
in'de'struct'i'ble
in'de'ter'min'able
in'de'ter'mi'na'cy
in'de'ter'mi'nate
in'de'ter'mi'na'tion
in'dex
In'di'an
in'di'cate
in'di'cat'ed
in'di'cat'ing
in'di'ca'tion
in'dic'a'tive
in'di'ca'tor
in'di'ces
in'dict
in'dict'able
in'dict'ment
in'dif'fer'ence
in'dif'fer'ent
in'dif'fer'ent'ly
in'di'gence
in'dig'e'nous
in'di'gent
in'di'gest'i'bil'i'ty
in'di'gest'i'ble
in'di'gest'i'ble'ness
in'di'ges'tion
in'dig'nant
in'dig'nant'ly
in'dig'na'tion
in'dig'ni'ties
in'dig'ni'ty
in'di'go
in'di'rect
in'di'rec'tion
in'di'rect'ly
in'dis'cern'ible
in'dis'ci'pline
in'dis'creet
in'dis'crete
in'dis'cre'tion

in'dis'crim'i'nate
in'dis'crim'i'nate'ly
in'dis'crim'i'nat'ing
in'dis'crim'i'na'tion
in'dis'pen'sa'bil'i'ty
in'dis'pen'sa'ble
in'dis'pen'sa'ble'ness
in'dis'posed
in'dis'po'si'tion
in'dis'put'able
in'dis'put'ably
in'dis'sol'u'bil'i'ty
in'dis'sol'u'ble
in'dis'tinct
in'dis'tinct'ly
in'dis'tin'guish'able
in'di'um
in'di'vid'u'al
in'di'vid'u'a'list
in'di'vid'u'al'is'tic
in'di'vid'u'al'i'ty
in'di'vid'u'al'ize
in'di'vid'u'al'ized
in'di'vid'u'al'iz'ing
in'di'vid'u'al'ly
in'di'vis'i'ble
in'doc'tri'nate
in'doc'tri'nat'ed
in'doc'tri'nat'ing
in'doc'tri'na'tion
In'do-Eu'ro'pe'an
in'do'lence
in'do'lent
in'dom'i'ta'bil'i'ty
in'dom'i'ta'ble
in'dom'i'ta'bly
In'do'ne'sian
in'door
in'doors
in'drawn
in'du'bi'ta'bil'i'ty
in'du'bi'ta'ble
in'du'bi'ta'bly
in'duce
in'duced
in'duce'ment
in'duc'ing
in'duct
in'duct'ance
in'duct'ee
in'duc'tion
in'duc'tive
in'dulge

in'dulged
in'dul'gence
in'dul'gent
in'dul'gent'ly
in'dulg'ing
in'dus'tri'al
in'dus'tri'al'ism
in'dus'tri'al'ist
in'dus'tri'al'iza'tion
in'dus'tri'al'ize
in'dus'tries
in'dus'tri'ous
in'dus'tri'ous'ly
in'dus'try
in'e'bri'ate
in'e'bri'at'ed
in'e'bri'at'ing
in'e'bri'a'tion
in'ed'i'ble
in'ef'fa'bil'i'ty
in'ef'fa'ble
in'ef'fa'bly
in'ef'fec'tive
in'ef'fec'tive'ly
in'ef'fec'tive'ness
in'ef'fec'tu'al
in'ef'fec'tu'al'ly
in'ef'fi'ca'cious
in'ef'fi'ca'cy
in'ef'fi'cien'cy
in'ef'fi'cient
in'ef'fi'cient'ly
in'el'e'gant
in'el'i'gi'bil'i'ty
in'el'i'gi'ble
in'eluc'ta'ble
in'ept
in'ept'i'tude
in'equal'i'ties
in'e'qual'i'ty
in'eq'ui'ta'ble
in'eq'ui'ties
in'eq'ui'ty
in'erad'i'ca'ble
in'erad'i'ca'bly
in'er'rant
in'ert
in'er'tia
in'er'tial
in'es'cap'a'ble
in'es'sen'tial
in'es'ti'ma'ble
in'es'ti'ma'bly

in'ev'i'ta'bil'i'ties
in'ev'i'ta'bil'i'ty
in'ev'i'ta'ble
in'ev'i'ta'bly
in'ex'act
in'ex'cus'able
in'ex'cus'ably
in'ex'haust'i'bil'i'ty
in'ex'haust'i'ble
in'ex'o'ra'bil'i'ty
in'ex'o'ra'ble
in'ex'o'ra'bly
in'ex'pen'sive
in'ex'pe'ri'ence
in'ex'pe'ri'enced
in'ex'pert
in'ex'pi'a'ble
in'ex'pi'a'bly
in'ex'pli'ca'bil'i'ty
in'ex'pli'ca'ble
in'ex'pli'ca'bly
in'ex'press'i'bil'i'ty
in'ex'press'i'ble
in'ex'press'i'bly
in'ex'pres'sive
in'ex'tin'guish'able
in ex'tre'mis
in'ex'tri'ca'bil'i'ty
in'ex'tri'ca'ble
in'ex'tri'ca'bly
in'fal'li'bil'i'ty
in'fal'li'ble
in'fal'li'bly
in'fa'mies
in'fa'mous
in'fa'my
in'fan'cies
in'fan'cy
in'fant
in'fant'hood
in'fan'ti'cide
in'fan'tile
in'fan'tine
in'fan'tries
in'fan'try
in'fan'try'man
in'farc'tion
in'fat'u'ate
in'fat'u'at'ed
in'fat'u'at'ing
in'fat'u'a'tion
in'fect
in'fec'tion

in'fec'tious
in'fec'tive
in'fe'lic'i'ty
in'fer
in'fer'able
in'fer'ence
in'fer'en'tial
in'fe'ri'or
in'fe'ri'or'i'ty
in'fer'nal
in'fer'no
in'fer'nos
in'ferred
in'fer'ring
in'fer'tile
in'fer'til'i'ty
in'fest
in'fes'ta'tion
in'fi'del
in'fi'del'i'ties
in'fi'del'i'ty
in'field
in'field'er
in'fight'er
in'fight'ing
in'fil'trate
in'fil'trat'ed
in'fil'trat'ing
in'fil'tra'tion
in'fil'tra'tor
in'fi'nite
in'fi'nite'ly
in'fi'nite'ness
in'fin'i'tes'i'mal
in'fin'i'tes'i'mal'ly
in'fin'i'ties
in'fin'i'tive
in'fin'i'tive'ly
in'fin'i'ty
in'firm
in'fir'ma'ries
in'fir'ma'ry
in'fir'mi'ties
in'fir'mi'ty
in'flame
in'flamed
in'flam'ing
in'flam'ma'bil'i'ty
in'flam'ma'ble
in'flam'ma'ble'ness
in'flam'ma'tion
in'flam'ma'to'ry
in'flat'able

in'flate
in'flat'ed
in'flat'ing
in'fla'tion
in'fla'tion'ary
in'flect
in'flec'tion
in'flec'tion'less
in'flec'tive
in'flex'i'bil'i'ty
in'flex'i'ble
in'flex'i'bly
in'flict
in'flict'a'ble
in'flic'tion
in'flo'res'cence
in'flow
in'flu'ence
in'flu'enced
in'flu'enc'ing
in'flu'en'tial
in'flu'en'za
in'flux
in'form
in'for'mal
in'for'mal'i'ty
in'for'mal'ly
in'form'ant
in'for'ma'tion
in'for'ma'tion'al
in'for'ma'tive
in'for'ma'to'ry
in'formed
in'for'mer
in'frac'tion
in'fra dig
in'fran'gi'bil'i'ty
in'fran'gi'ble
in'fran'gi'bly
in'fra'red
in'fra'son'ic
in'fra'struc'ture
in'fre'quen'cy
in'fre'quent
in'fre'quent'ly
in'fringe
in'fringed
in'fringe'ment
in'fring'ing
in'fu'ri'ate
in'fu'ri'at'ed
in'fu'ri'at'ing
in'fu'ri'a'tion

in'fuse
in'fused
in'fus'i'ble
in'fus'ing
in'fu'sion
in'gen'ious
in'ge'nious'ly
in'ge'nue
in'ge'nu'i'ty
in'gen'u'ous
in'gen'u'ous'ly
in'gest
in'ges'tion
in'gle
in'gle'nook
in'glo'ri'ous
in'glo'ri'ous'ly
in'got
in'grain
in'grate
in'gra'ti'ate
in'gra'ti'at'ed
in'gra'ti'at'ing
in'gra'ti'a'tion
in'grat'i'tude
in'gre'di'ent
in'gress
in'grow'ing
in'grown
in'hab'it
in'hab'it'able
in'hab'it'ant
in'hab'i'ta'tion
in'hab'it'ed
in'hal'ant
in'ha'la'tion
in'ha'la'tor
in'hale
in'haled
in'hal'ing
in'har'mon'ic
in'har'mo'ny
in'here
in'hered
in'her'ence
in'her'ent
in'her'ent'ly
in'her'ing
in'her'it
in'her'i'tance
in'her'i'tor
in'hib'it
in'hib'i'ter

in'hi'bi'tion	in'nate	in'quired	in'sert
in'hib'i'tive	in'nate'ly	in'quir'er	in'sert'er
in'hib'i'to'ry	in'ner	in'quir'ies	in'ser'tion
in'hos'pi'ta'ble	in'ner'most	in'quir'ing	in'set
in'hos'pi'tal'i'ty	in'ner'sole	in'quir'ing'ly	in'set'ting
in'hu'man	in'ner'vate	in'quiry	in'shore
in'hu'mane	in'ner'vat'ed	in'qui'si'tion	in'side
in'hu'man'i'ty	in'ner'vat'ing	in'quis'i'tive	in'sid'er
in'hu'ma'tion	in'ner'va'tion	in'quis'i'tive'ly	in'sid'i'ous
in'im'i'cal	in'ning	in'quis'i'tive'ness	in'sid'i'ous'ly
in'im'i'ta'ble	inn'keep'er	in'quis'i'tor	in'sight
in'im'i'ta'bly	in'no'cence	in'quis'i'to'ri'al	in'sig'nia
in'iq'ui'ties	in'no'cent	in'road	in'sig'nif'i'cance
in'iq'ui'tous	in'no'cent'ly	in'sa'lu'bri'ous	in'sig'nif'i'cant
in'iq'ui'ty	in'noc'u'ous	in'sane	in'sig'nif'i'cant'ly
in'i'tial	in'noc'u'ous'ly	in'sane'ly	in'sin'cere
in'i'tialed	in'no'vate	in'san'i'tary	in'sin'cere'ly
in'i'tial'ing	in'no'vat'ed	in'san'i'ties	in'sin'cer'i'ties
in'i'tial'ly	in'no'vat'ing	in'san'i'ty	in'sin'cer'i'ty
in'i'ti'ate	in'no'va'tion	in'sa'tia'bil'i'ty	in'sin'u'ate
in'i'ti'at'ed	in'no'va'tive	in'sa'tia'ble	in'sin'u'at'ed
in'i'ti'at'ing	in'no'va'tor	in'sa'tia'bly	in'sin'u'at'ing
in'i'ti'a'tion	in'no'va'to'ry	in'sa'ti'ate	in'sin'u'a'tion
in'i'ti'a'tive	in'nu'en'do	in'scribe	in'sin'u'a'tor
in'i'ti'a'tor	in'nu'en'does	in'scribed	in'sip'id
in'ject	in'nu'en'dos	in'scrib'ing	in'si'pid'i'ty
in'jec'tion	in'nu'mer'a'ble	in'scrip'tion	in'sip'id'ly
in'jec'tor	in'nu'mer'a'bly	in'scrip'tive	in'sip'id'ness
in'ju'di'cious	in'nu'mer'ous	in'scru'ta'bil'i'ty	in'sist
in'junc'tion	in'nu'tri'tion	in'scru'ta'ble	in'sis'tence
in'jure	in'ob'serv'ance	in'scru'ta'bly	in'sis'tent
in'jured	in'ob'serv'ant	in'seam	in'sis'tent'ly
in'ju'ries	in'oc'u'lant	in'sect	in si'tu
in'jur'ing	in'oc'u'late	in'sec'ti'cid'al	in'so'bri'e'ty
in'ju'ri'ous	in'oc'u'lat'ed	in'sec'ti'cide	in'so'cia'bil'i'ty
in'ju'ry	in'oc'u'lat'ing	in'sec'ti'vore	in'so'cia'ble
in'jus'tice	in'oc'u'la'tion	in'sec'tiv'o'rous	in'so'cia'bly
ink'blot	in'of'fen'sive	in'se'cure	in'so'far
ink'i'er	in'op'er'a'ble	in'se'cure'ly	in'sole
ink'ling	in'op'er'a'tive	in'se'cu'ri'ty	in'so'lence
inky	in'op'por'tune	in'sem'i'nate	in'so'lent
in'laid	in'op'por'tu'ni'ty	in'sem'i'nat'ed	in'so'lent'ly
in'land	in'or'di'nate	in'sem'i'nat'ing	in'sol'u'bil'i'ty
in-law	in'or'di'nate'ly	in'sem'i'na'tion	in'sol'u'ble
in'lay	in'or'gan'ic	in'sen'sate	in'sol'u'bly
in'lay'ing	in'o'scu'late	in'sen'si'bil'i'ty	in'solv'able
in'let	in'pa'tient	in'sen'si'ble	in'sol'ven'cy
in lo'co pa'ren'tis	in'pour	in'sen'si'tive	in'sol'vent
in'mate	in'put	in'sen'si'tiv'i'ty	in'som'nia
in me'mo'ri'am	in'put'ting	in'sen'ti'ent	in'som'ni'ac
in'most	in'quest	in'sep'a'ra'bil'i'ty	in'so'much
inn	in'qui'e'tude	in'sep'a'ra'ble	in'sou'ci'ance
in'nards	in'quire	in'sep'a'ra'bly	in'sou'ci'ant

in'spect
in'spec'tion
in'spec'tor
in'spec'tor'ate
in'spi'ra'tion
in'spi'ra'tion'al
in'spire
in'spired
in'spir'ing
in'spir'it
in'sta'bil'i'ties
in'sta'bil'i'ty
in'sta'ble
in'stall
in'stal'la'tion
in'stalled
in'stall'ing
in'stall'ment
in'stal'ment
in'stance
in'stant
in'stan'ta'ne'ous
in'stan'ta'neous'ly
in'stan'ter
in'stant'ly
in'state
in'stat'ed
in'state'ment
in'stat'ing
in'stead
in'step
in'sti'gate
in'sti'gat'ed
in'sti'gat'ing
in'sti'ga'tion
in'sti'ga'tor
in'stil
in'stil'la'tion
in'stilled
in'stil'ling
in'stinct
in'stinc'tive
in'stinc'tive'ly
in'stinc'tu'al
in'sti'tute
in'sti'tut'ed
in'sti'tut'ing
in'sti'tu'tion
in'sti'tu'tion'al
in'sti'tu'tion'al'ism
in'sti'tu'tion'al'ize
in'sti'tu'tion'al'ized
in'sti'tu'tion'al'iz'ing

in'struct
in'struc'tion
in'struc'tive
in'struc'tor
in'stru'ment
in'stru'men'tal
in'stru'men'ta'list
in'stru'men'ta'tion
in'sub'or'di'nate
in'sub'or'di'na'tion
in'sub'stan'tial
in'sub'stan'ti'al'i'ty
in'suf'fer'able
in'suf'fer'ably
in'suf'fi'cience
in'suf'fi'cien'cy
in'suf'fi'cient
in'suf'fi'cient'ly
in'su'lar
in'su'lar'i'ty
in'su'late
in'su'lat'ed
in'su'lat'ing
in'su'la'tion
in'su'la'tor
in'su'lin
in'sult
in'sult'ing'ly
in'su'per'able
in'sup'port'able
in'sup'press'ible
in'sur'abil'i'ty
in'sur'able
in'sur'ance
in'sure
in'sured
in'sur'er
in'sur'gence
in'sur'gen'cy
in'sur'gent
in'sur'ing
in'sur'mount'able
in'sur'rec'tion
in'sur'rec'tion'ist
in'sus'cep'ti'ble
in'swing
in'swinger
in'tact
in'ta'glio
in'take
in'tan'gi'bil'i'ty
in'tan'gi'ble
in'tan'gi'ble'ness

in'tan'gi'bly
in'te'ger
in'te'gral
in'te'gral'ly
in'te'grant
in'te'grate
in'te'grat'ed
in'te'grat'ing
in'te'gra'tion
in'teg'ri'ty
in'tegu'ment
in'tel'lect
in'tel'lec'tu'al
in'tel'lec'tu'al'ism
in'tel'lec'tu'al'ize
in'tel'lec'tu'al'ly
in'tel'li'gence
in'tel'li'gent
in'tel'li'gent'ly
in'tel'li'gent'sia
in'tel'li'gi'bil'i'ty
in'tel'li'gi'ble
in'tel'li'gi'bly
in'tem'per'ance
in'tem'per'ate
in'tend
in'tend'ant
in'tense
in'tense'ly
in'tense'ness
in'ten'si'fi'ca'tion
in'ten'si'fied
in'ten'si'fi'er
in'ten'si'fy
in'ten'si'fy'ing
in'ten'sion
in'ten'si'ties
in'ten'si'ty
in'ten'sive
in'ten'sive'ly
in'tent
in'ten'tion
in'ten'tion'al
in'ten'tion'al'ly
in'tent'ly
in'ter
in'ter'act
in'ter'ac'tion
in'ter'ac'tive
in'ter alia
in'ter'bred
in'ter'breed
in'ter'breed'ing

in'ter'ca'late
in'ter'ca'la'tion
in'ter'cede
in'ter'ced'ed
in'ter'ced'ing
in'ter'cept
in'ter'cep'tion
in'ter'cept'or
in'ter'ces'sion
in'ter'ces'sor
in'ter'change
in'ter'change'able
in'ter'change'ably
in'ter'changed
in'ter'chang'ing
in'ter'con'nect
in'ter'con'nec'tion
in'ter'con'ti'nen'tal
in'ter'course
in'ter'cul'tur'al
in'ter'cross
in'ter'de'part'men'tal
in'ter'de'pend'ence
in'ter'de'pend'ent
in'ter'dict
in'ter'dic'tion
in'ter'dis'ci'pli'nary
in'ter'est
in'ter'est'ed
in'ter'est'ing
in'ter'est'ing'ly
in'ter'face
in'ter'faith
in'ter'fere
in'ter'fered
in'ter'fer'ence
in'ter'fer'ing
in'ter'fer'on
in'ter'ga'lac'tic
in'ter'im
in'te'ri'or
in'ter'ject
in'ter'jec'tion
in'ter'jec'to'ry
in'ter'lace
in'ter'laced
in'ter'lac'ing
in'ter'lard
in'ter'lay'er
in'ter'leaf
in'ter'leave
in'ter'line
in'ter'link

in'ter'lock
in'ter'lo'cu'tion
in'ter'loc'u'tor
in'ter'loc'u'to'ry
in'ter'lope
in'ter'loped
in'ter'lop'er
in'ter'lop'ing
in'ter'lude
in'ter'lu'nar
in'ter'lu'na'ry
in'ter'mar'riage
in'ter'mar'ry
in'ter'me'di'ar'ies
in'ter'me'di'ary
in'ter'me'di'ate
in'ter'me'di'at'ing
in'ter'me'di'a'tion
in'ter'me'di'a'tor
in'ter'ment
in'ter'mez'zi
in'ter'mez'zo
in'ter'mi'na'ble
in'ter'mi'na'bly
in'ter'min'gle
in'ter'min'gled
in'ter'min'gling
in'ter'mis'sion
in'ter'mit
in'ter'mit'ted
in'ter'mit'tence
in'ter'mit'ten'cy
in'ter'mit'tent
in'ter'mit'tent'ly
in'ter'mit'ting
in'ter'mix
in'ter'mix'ture
in'tern
in'ter'nal
in'ter'nal'i'za'tion
in'ter'nal'ize
in'ter'nal'ized
in'ter'nal'iz'ing
in'ter'nal'ly
in'ter'na'tion'al
in'ter'na'tion'al'ism
in'ter'na'tion'al'i'ty
in'ter'na'tion'al'ize
in'ter'na'tion'al'ized
in'ter'na'tion'al'iz'ing
in'ter'na'tion'al'ly
in'terne
in'ter'ne'cine

in'tern'ee
in'tern'ist
in'tern'ment
in'tern'ship
in'ter'nun'cio
in'ter'of'fice
in'ter'pen'e'trate
in'ter'pen'e'tra'tion
in'ter'per'son'al
in'ter'plan'e'tary
in'ter'play
in'ter'po'late
in'ter'po'la'tion
in'ter'po'la'tor
in'ter'pose
in'ter'posed
in'ter'pos'ing
in'ter'po'si'tion
in'ter'pret
in'ter'pre'ta'tion
in'ter'pre'ta'tive
in'ter'pret'er
in'ter'pre'tive
in'ter'ra'cial
in'terred
in'ter'reg'na
in'ter'reg'num
in'ter're'late
in'ter're'lat'ed
in'ter're'lat'ing
in'ter'rel'a'tion'ship
in'ter'ring
in'ter'ro'gate
in'ter'ro'gat'ed
in'ter'ro'gat'ing
in'ter'ro'ga'tion
in'ter'rog'a'tive
in'ter'ro'ga'tor
in'ter'rupt
in'ter'rup'tion
in'ter'scho'las'tic
in'ter'sect
in'ter'sec'tion
in'ter'space
in'ter'sperse
in'ter'spersed
in'ter'spers'ing
in'ter'sper'sion
in'ter'stel'lar
in'ter'stice
in'ter'sti'tial
in'ter'tid'al
in'ter'twine

in'ter'twined
in'ter'twin'ing
in'ter'val
in'ter'vene
in'ter'vened
in'ter'ven'ing
in'ter'ven'tion
in'ter'view
in'ter'view'ee
in'ter'view'er
in'ter'weave
in'ter'weav'ing
in'ter'wove
in'ter'wo'ven
in'tes'tate
in'tes'ti'nal
in'tes'tine
in'ti'ma'cies
in'ti'ma'cy
in'ti'mate
in'ti'mate
in'ti'mated
in'ti'mate'ly
in'ti'mate'ly
in'ti'mate'ness
in'ti'mat'ing
in'ti'ma'tion
in'tim'i'date
in'tim'i'dat'ed
in'tim'i'dat'ing
in'tim'i'da'tion
in'to
in'tol'er'a'ble
in'tol'er'a'bly
in'tol'er'ance
in'tol'er'ant
in'tol'er'ant'ly
in'tomb
in'to'nate
in'to'nat'ed
in'to'nat'ing
in'to'na'tion
in'tone
in'toned
in'ton'ing
intox'icant
in'tox'i'cate
in'tox'i'cat'ed
in'tox'i'cat'ing
in'tox'i'ca'tion
in'trac'ta'bil'i'ty
in'trac'ta'ble
in'tra'mu'ral

in'tra'mu'ral'ly
in'tran'si'gence
in'tran'si'gen'cy
in'tran'si'gent
in'tran'si'tive
in'tra'u'ter'ine
in'tra've'nous
in'tra've'nous'ly
in'trench
in'trep'id
in'tre'pid'i'ty
in'trep'id'ly
in'tri'ca'cies
in'tri'ca'cy
in'tri'cate
in'tri'cate'ly
in'trigue
in'trigued
in'trigu'ing
in'trig'uing'ly
in'trin'sic
in'trin'si'cal'ly
in'tro'duce
in'tro'duced
in'tro'duc'ing
in'tro'duc'tion
in'tro'duc'to'ry
in'tro'spect
in'tro'spec'tion
in'tro'spec'tive
in'tro'ver'sion
in'tro'vert
in'trude
in'trud'ed
in'trud'er
in'trud'ing
in'tru'sion
in'tru'sive
in'tu'it
in'tu'it'ed
in'tu'it'ing
in'tu'i'tion
in'tu'i'tive
in'tu'itive'ly
in'tu'mes'cence
in'tu'mes'cent
in'un'date
in'un'dat'ed
in'un'dat'ing
in'un'da'tion
in'ure
in'ured
in'ur'ing

in'vade
in'vad'ed
in'vad'er
in'vad'ing
in'val'id
in'va'lid
in'val'i'date
in'val'i'dat'ed
in'val'i'dat'ing
in'val'i'da'tion
in'va'lid'ism
in'val'id'i'ty
in'valu'a'ble
inval'uably
in'vari'a'bil'i'ty
in'vari'a'ble
in'vari'ably
in'var'i'ant
in'va'sion
in'va'sive
in'vec'tive
in'veigh
in'vei'gle
in'vent
in'ven'tion
in'ven'tive
in'ven'tive'ness
in'ven'tor
in'ven'to'ried
in'ven'to'ries
in'ven'to'ry
in'ven'to'ry'ing
in'verse
in'ver'sion
in'vert
in'ver'te'brate
in'vert'ed
in'vest
in'ves'ti'gate
in'ves'ti'gat'ed
in'ves'ti'gat'ing
in'ves'ti'ga'tion
in'ves'ti'ga'tive
in'ves'ti'gat'or
in'ves'ti'ga'to'ry
in'ves'ti'ture
in'vest'ment
in'ves'tor
in'vet'er'ate
in'vid'i'ous
in'vig'or'ate
in'vig'or'at'ed
in'vig'or'at'ing

in'vig'or'a'tion
in'vin'ci'bil'i'ty
in'vin'ci'ble
in'vin'ci'bly
in'vi'o'la'bil'i'ty
in'vi'o'la'ble
in'vi'o'la'bly
in'vi'o'late
in'vis'i'bil'i'ty
in'vis'i'ble
in'vis'i'bly
in'vi'ta'tion
in'vite
in'vit'ed
in'vit'ing
in'vit'ing'ly
in'vo'ca'tion
in'voice
in'voiced
in'voic'ing
in'voke
in'voked
in'vok'ing
in'vol'un'tar'i'ly
in'vol'un'tary
in'vo'lute
in'vo'lu'tion
in'volve
in'volved
in'volve'ment
in'volv'ing
in'vul'ner'a'bil'i'ty
in'vul'ner'a'ble
in'ward
in'ward'ly
in'wards
in'weave
in'weaved
in'weav'ing
in'wove
in'wov'en
in'wrought
io'dine
ion
ion'ic
ion'i'za'tion
ion'ize
io'ta
ip'e'cac
ip'so fac'to
Ira'ni'an
Iraqi
iras'ci'bil'i'ty

iras'ci'ble
irate
ir'i'des'cence
ir'i'des'cent
irid'i'um
iris
iris'es
Irish
irk
irk'some
iron
iron'clad
iron'er
iron'hand'ed
iron'heart'ed
iron'ic
iron'i'cal
iron'i'cal'ly
iro'nies
iron'stone
iron'ware
iron'work
iro'ny
ir'ra'di'ate
ir'ra'di'at'ed
ir'ra'di'at'ing
ir'ra'di'a'tion
ir'rad'i'ca'ble
ir'ra'tion'al
ir'ra'tion'al'ity
ir'ra'tion'al'ly
ir're'claim'a'ble
ir'rec'on'cil'a'bil'i'ty
ir'rec'on'cil'a'ble
ir'rec'on'cil'ably
ir're'cov'er'able
ir're'deem'able
ir're'deem'ably
ir're'duc'i'ble
ir'ref'u'ta'ble
ir'reg'u'lar
ir'reg'u'lar'i'ties
ir'reg'u'lar'i'ty
ir'reg'u'lar'ly
ir'rel'e'vance
ir'rel'e'van'cies
ir'rel'e'van'cy
ir'rel'e'vant
ir'rel'e'vant'ly
ir're'li'gious
ir're'me'di'a'ble
ir're'mis'si'ble
ir're'mov'a'ble

ir'rep'a'ra'ble
ir're'place'a'ble
ir're'press'ible
ir're'press'ibly
ir're'proach'able
ir're'sist'i'bil'i'ty
ir're'sist'i'ble
ir're'sist'i'bly
ir'res'o'lute
ir'res'o'lu'tion
ir're'spec'tive
ir're'spon'si'bil'i'ty
ir're'spon'si'ble
ir're'spon'si'bly
ir're'spon'sive
ir're'triev'a'bil'i'ty
ir're'triev'able
ir're'triev'ably
ir'rev'er'ence
ir'rev'er'ent
ir'rev'er'ent'ly
ir're'vers'i'bil'i'ty
ir're'vers'i'ble
ir're'vers'ibly
ir'rev'o'ca'bil'i'ty
ir'rev'o'ca'ble
ir'rev'o'ca'bly
ir'ri'gate
ir'ri'gat'ed
ir'ri'gat'ing
ir'ri'ga'tion
ir'ri'ta'bil'i'ty
ir'ri'ta'ble
ir'ri'ta'bly
ir'ri'tant
ir'ri'tate
ir'ri'tat'ed
ir'ri'tat'ing
ir'ri'tat'ing'ly
ir'ri'ta'tion
ir'rupt
isin'glass
Is'lam
Is'lam'ic
Is'lam'ism
is'land
is'land'er
isle
is'let
iso'bar
iso'late
iso'lat'ed
iso'lat'ing

iso'la'tion
iso'la'tion'ism
iso'la'tion'ist
iso'met'ric
iso'met'ri'cal
isos'ce'les
iso'therm
iso'ther'mal
iso'ton'ic
iso'tope
iso'top'ic
Is'rae'li
Is'ra'el'ite
is'su'ance
is'sue
is'sued
is'su'ing
isth'mus
Ital'ian
ital'ic
ital'i'ci'za'tion
ital'i'cize
ital'i'cized
ital'i'ciz'ing
itch
itch'i'ness
itchy
item
item'ize
item'ized
item'iz'ing
it'er'ate
it'er'a'tion
itin'er'ant
itin'er'ar'ies
itin'er'ary
itin'er'ate
itin'er'a'tion
ivied
ivies
ivo'ries
ivo'ry
ivy
jab
jabbed
jab'ber
jab'bing
ja'bot
ja'cinth
jack'al
jack'a'napes
jack'ass
jack'boot

jack'daw
jack'et
jack'et'ed
jack'ham'mer
jack-in-the-box
jack-knife
jack-knifed
jack-knif'ing
jack-knives
jack-of-all-trades
jack-o'-lan'tern
jack'pot
jack rab'bit
jac'quard
jade
jad'ed
jad'ing
jag
jagged
jag'ged
jag'ging
jag'uar
jai alai
jail
jail'bird
jail'break
jail'er
ja'lop'ies
jal'opy
jal'ou'sie
jam
jamb
jam'bo'ree
jammed
jam'mer
jam'ming
jan'gle
jan'gled
jan'gling
jan'i'tor
jan'i'to'ri'al
Jap'a'nese
jar
jar'di'niere
jar'ful
jar'gon
jarred
jar'ring
jas'mine
jaun'dice
jaun'diced
jaunt
jaun'ti'ly

jaun'ti'ness
jaun'ty
Ja'va'nese
jave'lin
jaw'bone
jaw'break'er
jay'walk
jay'walk'er
jazz
jaz'zi'er
jaz'zi'est
jazz'i'ly
jazz'i'ness
jazzy
jeal'ous
jeal'ous'ies
jeal'ous'ly
jeal'ousy
jeans
jeer
jeer'er
jeer'ing'ly
je'june
jel'lied
jel'lies
jel'li'fy
jel'ly
jel'ly'fish
jen'ny
jeop'ar'dize
jeop'ar'dized
jeop'ar'diz'ing
jeop'ar'dy
jer'e'mi'ad
jerk
jerk'i'er
jerk'i'est
jerk'i'ly
jer'kin
jerk'i'ness
jerky
jerry-built
jer'sey
jes'sa'mine
jest'er
jet
jet lag
jet'lin'er
jet-pro'pelled
jet'sam
jet'ted
jet'ties
jet'ting

jet'ti'son
jet'ty
jeu d'es'prit
Jew
jew'el
jew'elled
jew'el'ler
jew'ell'ery
Jew'ish
Jew'ish'ness
Jew'ry
jew's-harp
jib
jibbed
jib'bing
jibe
jif'fies
jif'fy
jig
jigged
jig'ging
jig'gle
jig'gled
jig'gling
jig'gly
jig'saw
ji'had
jilt'er
jin'gle
jin'gled
jin'gling
jin'go'ism
jin'go'is'tic
jink
jinx
jit'ney
jit'ter'bug
jit'ter'bug'ging
jit'ters
jit'tery
jive
jived
jiv'ing
job
jobbed
job'ber
job'bing
job'hold'er
job'less
jock'ey
jock'ey'ing
jock'strap
jo'cose

jo'cose'ly
jo'cos'i'ty
joc'u'lar
joc'u'lar'i'ty
joc'u'lar'ly
joc'und
jo'cun'di'ty
jodh'pur
jog
jogged
jog'ger
jog'ging
jog'gle
jog'gled
jog'gling
joie de vi'vre
join
join'er
join'ery
joint
joint'ed
joint'ly
joist
jo'jo'ba
joke
joked
jok'er
joke'ster
jok'ing
jok'ing'ly
jol'li'er
jol'li'est
jol'li'ty
jol'ly
jolt
jolt'ing'ly
jolty
jon'quil
Jor'da'ni'an
joss stick
jos'tle
jos'tled
jos'tling
jot
jot'ted
jot'ting
joule
jour'nal
jour'nal'ese
jour'nal'ism
jour'nal'ist
jour'nal'is'tic
jour'ney

jour'ney'man
joust
jo'vi'al
jo'vi'al'i'ty
jo'vi'al'ly
jowl
joy'ful
joy'ful'ly
joy'less
joy'ous
joy'ous'ly
joy'rid'den
joy'ride
joy'rid'ing
joy'rode
joy'stick
ju'bi'lance
ju'bi'lant
ju'bi'la'tion
ju'bi'lee
Ju'da'ic
Ju'da'i'cal
Ju'da'ism
judge
judged
judge'ment
judg'ing
judg'ment
ju'di'cial
ju'di'cial'ly
ju'di'ci'ary
ju'di'cious
ju'di'cious'ly
ju'do
jug
jugged
jug'ger'naut
jug'gle
jug'gled
jug'gler
jug'gling
jug'u'lar
juice
juic'er
juic'i'er
juic'i'est
juic'i'ness
juicy
ju'jit'su
ju'ju
ju'jube
juke'box
ju'lep

ju'li'enne
jum'ble
jum'bled
jumb'ling
jum'bo
jump
jump'er
jump'i'er
jump'i'est
jump'i'ness
jump'ing
jumpy
junc'tion
junc'ture
jun'gle
jun'ior
ju'ni'per
junk
jun'ket
jun'ket'ing
junk'ie
junky
jun'ta
ju'ries
ju'ris'dic'tion
ju'ris'dic'tion'al
ju'ris'pru'dence
ju'ris'pru'dent
ju'ris'pru'den'tial
jur'ist
ju'ror
ju'ry
just
just'ice
jus'tice'less
jus'ti'fi'able
jus'ti'fi'ably
jus'ti'fi'ca'tion
jus'ti'fi'ca'to'ry
jus'ti'fied
jus'ti'fy
jus'ti'fy'ing
just'ly
just'ness
jut
jute
jut'ted
jut'ting
ju'venes'cence
ju've'nescent
ju've'nile
ju've'nil'i'ty
jux'ta'pose

jux'ta'posed
jux'ta'pos'ing
jux'ta'po'si'tion
ka'bob
kaf'tan
kale
ka'lei'do'scope
ka'lei'do'scop'ic
ka'mi'ka'ze
kan'ga'roo
ka'o'lin
ka'o'line
ka'pok
ka'put
kar'a'kul
kar'at
ka'ra'te
kar'ma
ka'ty'did
kay'ak
kayo
ke'bab
kedge
kedged
ked'ge'ree
kedg'ing
keel
keel'haul
keel'son
keen
keen'ly
keen'ness
keep
keep'er
keep'ing
keep'sake
keg
keg'ler
kelp
kel'pie
ken
ken'nel
ken'nelled
ke'no
Ke'nyan
ke'pi
kept
ker'a'tin
ker'chief
ker'nel
ker'o'sene
kes'trel
ketch

ketch'up	kindest	kit'ty	knot'hole
ke'tone	kind-heart'ed	ki'wi	knot'less
ket'tle	kin'dle	ki'wi'fruit	knot'ted
ket'tle'drum	kin'dled	klatch	knot'ti'er
key	kind'li'est	klax'on	knot'ti'est
key'board	kind'li'ness	klep'to'ma'nia	knot'ting
keyed	kin'dling	klep'to'ma'ni'ac	knot'ty
key'hole	kind'ness	knack	knout
key'note	kin'dred	knap'sack	know
key'not'ing	kin'e'mat'ic	knave	know'able
key'punch	kin'e'mat'i'cal	knav'ery	know-how
key'stone	kin'e'mat'ics	knav'ish	know'ing
khaki	kin'e'scope	knead	know'ing'ly
kha'lif	ki'net'ic	knee	know-it-all
khan	ki'net'ics	knee'cap	knowl'edge
kib'butz	kin'folk	kneed	knowl'edge'able
kib'itz'er	king	knee-deep	knowl'edge'ably
ki'bosh	king'bolt	knee'ing	known
kick'back	king'dom	kneel	know-noth'ing
kick-off	king'fish'er	kneeled	knuck'le
kid	king'li'ness	kneel'ing	knuck'led
kid'ded	king'ly	knell	knuck'le-dust'er
kid'die	king'pin	knelt	knuck'ling
kid'ding	king-size	knew	knurl
kid'dish	king-sized	knick'er'bock'ers	knurly
kid'dish'ness	kink	knick'ers	ko'a'la
kid'nap	kink'i'er	knick'knack	kohl
kid'nap'er	kink'i'est	knife	kohl'ra'bi
kid'napped	kinky	knifed	ko'la
kid'nap'per	kins'folk	knife-edge	ko'lin'sky
kid'nap'ping	kin'ship	knif'ing	kook
kid'ney	kins'man	knight	kook'a'bur'ra
kill	kins'wom'an	knight-er'rant	kook'ie
kill'deer	ki'osk	knight'hood	kook'i'er
kill'er	kip	knight'ly	kook'i'est
kill'ing	kip'per	knit	kooky
kill'joy	kirsch	knit'ted	ko'peck
kiln	kis'met	knit'ter	ko'pek
kilo	kiss	knit'ting	Ko'ran
ki'lo'byte	kiss'able	knit'wear	Ko'ran'ic
kil'o'cy'cle	kit	knives	Ko're'an
kil'o'gram	kitch'en	knob	ko'sher
ki'lo'hertz	kitch'en'ette	knobbed	kow-tow
kil'o'li'tre	kitch'en'ware	knob'bi'er	kraal
kil'o'me'tre	kite	knob'by	krim'mer
kil'o'volt	kit'ed	knock	kro'na
kil'o'watt	kith	knock'down	kro'ne
kilt	kit'ing	knock'er	kro'ner
kilt'er	kitsch	knock-knee	ku'dos
ki'mo'no	kit'ten	knock-kneed	ku'miss
kin	kit'ten'ish	knock'out	kum'mel
kind	kit'ties	knoll	kum'quat
kin'der'gar'ten	kit'ti'wake	knot	kung fu

Kurd'ish
kurled
Ku'waiti
kwash'i'or'kor
kyle
ky'pho'sis
ky'phot'ic
laa'ger
lab
la'bel
la'bell'er
la'belled
la'bel'ling
la'bi'al
la'bi'ate
la'bile
la'bi'o'den'tal
la'bi'um
lab'o'ra'to'ries
lab'o'ra'to'ry
la'bour
la'boured
la'bour'er
la'bour-in'ten'sive
la'bo'ri'ous
la'bo'ri'ous'ly
la'bour-sav'ing
la'bur'num
lab'y'rinth
lab'y'rin'thi'an
lab'y'rin'thine
lace
laced
lac'er'ate
lac'er'at'ed
lac'er'at'ing
lac'er'a'tion
lach'ry'mal
lach'ry'mose
lach'ry'mose'ly
lac'i'er
lac'i'est
lac'ing
lack
lack'a'dai'si'cal
lack'ey
lack'lus'tre
la'con'ic
la'con'i'cal'ly
lac'quer
la'crosse
lac'tate
lac'tat'ed

lac'tat'ing
lac'ta'tion
lac'te'al
lac'tic
lac'tose
la'cu'na
la'cus'trine
lacy
lad
lad'der
lad'die
lade
lad'ed
lad'en
la-di-da
la'dies
la'dle
ladle'ful
la'dy
la'dy'bug
la'dy-in-wait'ing
la'dy-killer
la'dy'like
la'dy'ship
la'dy's-slip'per
lag
la'ger
lag'gard
lagged
lag'ging
la'goon
laid
laid-back
lain
lair
lais'sez-faire
la'i'ty
lake
lake'side
lal'la'tion
lam
la'ma
la'ma'sery
lamb
lam'baste
lam'bast'ed
lam'bast'ing
lam'bent
lam'bent'ly
lam'bre'quin
lamb'skin
la'mé
lame

lamed
lame'ness
la'ment
lam'en'ta'ble
lam'en'ta'bly
lam'en'ta'tion
lam'i'nate
lam'i'nat'ed
lam'i'nat'ing
lam'i'na'tion
lam'ing
lammed
lam'ming
lamp'black
lamp'light
lamp'lit
lam'poon
lamp'post
lam'prey
lamp'shade
lance
lanced
lan'ce'o'late
lan'cet
lanc'ing
lan'dau
land'ed
land'fall
land'hold'er
land'ing
land'la'dies
land'la'dy
land'less
land'less'ness
land'locked
land'lord
land'lub'ber
land'mark
land'mass
land'own'er
land'own'ing
land'scape
land'scaped
land'scap'er
land'scap'ing
land'slide
land'slip
land'ward
lane
lang syne
lan'guage
lan'guid
lan'guid'ly

lan'guish
lan'guish'ing
lan'guor
lan'guor'ous
lank'i'er
lank'i'est
lank'i'ness
lank'ness
lanky
lan'o'lin
lan'tern
lan'tha'nide
lan'tha'num
lan'yard
la'pel
lap'ful
lap'i'dary
lap'in
lap'is la'zu'li
Lapp
lapped
lap'pet
lap'ping
lapse
lapsed
laps'ing
lap'wing
lar'board
lar'ce'nous
lar'ce'ny
larch
lar'der
large
large'ly
large'ness
larg'er
large-scale
lar'gess
lar'gesse
larg'est
lar'ghet'to
larg'ish
lar'go
lar'i'at
lark'spur
lar'va
lar'vae
lar'val
la'ryn'ge'al
la'ryn'ges
la'ryn'gi'tis
lar'ynx
las'civ'i'ous

las'civ'i'ous'ly
la'ser
lash
lash'ing
lass
las'si'tude
las'so
las'soes
last-ditch
last'ing
last'ly
latch
latch'key
late
late'com'er
la'teen
late'ly
la'ten'cy
late'ness
la'tent
la'tent'ly
lat'er
lat'er'al
lat'er'al'ly
lat'est
la'tex
lath
lathe
lath'er
lath'ery
lath'ing
Lat'in
Lat'in-A'mer'i'can
Lat'in'ate
La'ti'no
lat'i'tude
lat'i'tu'di'nal
lat'i'tu'di'nar'i'an
la'trine
lat'ter
lat'ter'ly
lat'tice
lat'ticed
lat'tice'work
lat'tic'ing
Lat'vi'an
laud
laud'a'ble
laud'a'bly
lau'da'num
laud'a'tive
laud'a'to'ry
laugh

laugh'a'ble
laugh'a'bly
laugh'ing
laugh'ing'ly
laugh'ing'stock
laugh'ter
launch
launch'er
laun'der
laun'der'ette
laun'dress
laun'dries
laun'dry
lau're'ate
lau'rel
la'va
lav'a'liere
lav'a'to'ries
lav'a'to'ry
lav'en'der
lav'ish
lav'ish'ly
lav'ish'ness
law
law-abid'ing
law'break'er
law'break'ing
law'ful
law'ful'ly
law'ful'ness
law'less
law'less'ness
law'mak'er
law'mak'ing
lawn
lawn mow'er
law'ren'ci'um
law'suit
law'yer
lax
lax'a'tive
lax'i'ty
lax'ness
lay
lay'about
lay'er
lay'ette
lay'ing
lay'man
lay'off
lay'out
lay'over
laze

lazed
laz'i'er
la'zi'est
la'zi'ly
la'zi'ness
laz'ing
la'zy
la'zy'bones
lea
leach
lead
lead'en
lead'er
lead'er'ship
lead-in
lead'ing
leaf
leaf'age
leaf'i'ness
leaf'less
leaf'let
leaf'let'ted
leaf'let'ting
leaf'stalk
leak
leak'age
leak'i'er
leak'i'est
leak'i'ness
leaky
lean
lean'ing
lean'ness
leant
lean-to
leap
leaped
leap'frog
leap'frogged
leap'frog'ging
leap'ing
leapt
learn
learned
learn'er
learn'ing
learnt
leary
lease
leased
lease'hold
lease'hold'er
leash

leas'ing
least
least'ways
least'wise
leath'er
leath'er'neck
leath'ery
leave
leav'en
leaves
leave-tak'ing
leav'ing
Leb'a'nese
lech'er
lech'er'ous
lech'ery
lec'tern
lec'ture
lec'tured
lec'tur'er
lec'ture'ship
lec'tur'ing
led
ledge
ledg'er
lee
leech
leek
leer
leer'ing'ly
leery
lee'ward
lee'way
left
left-hand'ed
left'ies
left'ism
left'ist
left'over
left'ward
left-wing
lefty
leg
leg'a'cies
leg'a'cy
le'gal
le'gal'ism
le'gal'ist
le'gal'is'tic
le'gal'is'ti'cal'ly
le'gal'i'ties
le'gal'i'ty
le'gal'i'za'tion

le'gal'ize
le'gal'ized
le'gal'iz'ing
le'gal'ly
leg'ate
leg'a'tee
le'ga'tion
le'ga'to
leg'end
leg'end'ary
leg'er'de'main
legged
leg'gi'er
leg'gi'est
leg'ging
leg'gy
leg'gy
leg'horn
leg'i'bil'i'ty
leg'i'ble
leg'i'bly
le'gion
le'gion'ary
le'gion'naire
leg'is'late
leg'is'lat'ed
leg'is'lat'ing
leg'is'la'tion
leg'is'la'tive
leg'is'la'tor
leg'is'la'ture
le'git'i'ma'cy
le'git'i'mate
le'git'i'mat'ed
le'git'i'mate'ly
le'git'i'mat'ing
le'git'i'ma'tion
le'git'i'mi'za'tion
le'git'i'mize
le'git'i'mized
le'git'i'miz'ing
leg'less
le'gume
le'gu'mi'nous
lei
leis
lei'sure
lei'sure'li'ness
lei'sure'ly
leit'mo'tif
leit'mo'tiv
lem'ma
lem'ma'ta

lem'ming
lem'on
lem'on'ade
le'mur
lend
lend'er
lend'ing
length
length'en
length'i'er
length'i'est
length'i'ly
length'i'ness
length'ways
length'wise
lengthy
le'ni'ence
le'ni'en'cy
le'ni'ent
le'nient'ly
len'i'tive
len'i'ty
lens
Lent
lent
len'til
le'o'nine
leop'ard
le'o'tard
lep'er
lep're'chaun
lep'ro'sy
lep'rous
les'bi'an
les'bi'an'ism
lese-maj'es'ty
le'sion
less
les'see
less'en
less'er
les'son
les'sor
lest
let
let'down
le'thal
le'thal'ly
le'thar'gic
le'thar'gi'cal
leth'ar'gy
let'ter
let'ter bomb

let'tered
let'ter'er
let'ter'head
let'ter'ing
let'ter'press
let'ters pa'tent
let'ting
let'tuce
let'up
leu'kae'mia
leu'ko'cyte
lev'ee
lev'el
lev'el-head'ed
lev'el'ling
lev'elled
leveller
lev'el'ly
lev'el'ness
lev'er
lev'er'age
lev'er'et
le'vi'a'than
lev'ied
lev'ies
lev'i'tate
lev'i'tat'ed
lev'i'tat'ing
lev'i'ta'tion
lev'i'ty
levy
levy'ing
lewd
lewd'ly
lewd'ness
lex'i'cal
lex'i'cog'ra'pher
lex'i'co'graph'ic
lex'i'cog'ra'phy
lex'i'con
li'a'bil'i'ties
li'a'bil'i'ty
li'a'ble
li'aise
li'aised
li'ais'ing
li'ai'son
li'a'na
li'ar
li'ba'tion
li'bel
li'bel'ler
li'belled

li'bel'ling
li'bel'lous
li'bel'ous
lib'er'al
lib'er'al'ism
lib'er'al'i'ty
lib'er'al'i'za'tion
lib'er'al'ize
lib'er'al'ized
lib'er'al'iz'ing
lib'er'al'ly
lib'er'ate
lib'er'at'ed
lib'er'at'ing
lib'er'a'tion
lib'er'a'tor
Li'be'ri'an
lib'er'tar'i'an
lib'er'ties
lib'er'tine
lib'er'tin'ism
lib'er'ty
li'bid'in'al
li'bid'i'nous
li'bid'i'nous'ness
li'bi'do
li'brar'i'an
li'brar'ies
li'brary
li'bret'ti
li'bret'tist
li'bret'to
Lib'y'an
lice
li'cence
li'cense
li'censed
li'cens'ee
li'cens'er
li'cens'ing
li'cen'ti'ate
li'cen'tious
li'cen'tious'ness
li'chee
li'chen
lic'it
lick
lid
lid'ded
lido
lie
lied
lied'er

liege
lien
lieu
lieu'ten'an'cy
lieu'ten'ant
life
life'blood
life'boat
life'buoy
life cy'cle
life'guard
life'less
life'like
life'line
life'sav'er
life-size
life'style
life'time
lift-off
lig'a'ment
lig'a'ture
light
light'en
light'er
light-fin'gered
light-foot'ed
light-head'ed
light-heart'ed
light-heart'ed'ly
light'house
light'ing
light'ly
light-mind'ed
light'ness
light'ning
light'ship
light'weight
light-year
lig'nite
lik'able
like
like'able
liked
like'li'er
like'li'est
like'li'hood
like'ly
lik'en
like'ness
like'wise
lik'ing
li'lac
lil'ies

lilt'ing
lily
lily-liv'ered
limb
lim'ber
lim'bo
lime
lim'eade
limed
lime'light
lim'er'ick
lime'stone
lim'ey
lim'ing
lim'it
lim'it'a'ble
lim'i'ta'tion
lim'i'ta'tive
lim'it'ed
lim'it'ing
lim'it'less
limn
lim'ner
lim'ou'sine
limp
lim'pet
lim'pid
lim'pid'ness
limp'ing'ly
limp'ly
limy
lin'age
linch'pin
lin'den
line
lin'e'age
lin'e'al
lin'e'a'ment
lin'e'ar
lined
line'man
lines'man
lin'en
lin'er
lin'ger
lin'ge'rie
lin'ger'ing'ly
lin'go
lin'goes
lin'gua fran'ca
lin'gual
lin'guist
lin'guis'tic

lin'guis'ti'cal'ly
lin'guis'tics
lin'i'ment
lin'ing
link
link'age
linked
link'er
link-up
lin'net
li'no'le'um
lin'seed
lint
lin'tel
lint'i'er
linty
li'on
li'on'ess
li'on'heart'ed
li'on'i'za'tion
li'on'ize
li'on'ized
li'on'iz'ing
lip
lip'py
lip-read
lip-read'ing
lip'stick
lip'-synch
liq'ue'fac'tion
liq'ue'fi'a'ble
liq'ue'fied
liq'ue'fy
liq'ue'fy'ing
li'queur
liq'uid
liq'ui'date
liq'ui'dat'ed
liq'ui'dat'ing
liq'ui'da'tion
liq'ui'da'tor
li'quid'i'ty
liq'uid'ize
liq'uid'ized
liq'uid'iz'ing
liq'uid'ness
liq'uor
liquo'rice
li'ra
li're
lisle
lisp
lis'som

lis'some
lis'some'ness
lis'som'ness
list
lis'ten
lis'ten'er
lis'te'ri'o'sis
list'ing
list'less
list'less'ly
list'less'ness
lit
lit'a'nies
lit'a'ny
li'tchi
li'tre
lit'er'a'cy
lit'er'al
lit'er'al'ism
lit'er'al'i'ty
lit'er'al'ness
lit'er'ar'i'ness
lit'er'ary
lit'er'ate
lit'e'ra'ti
lit'er'a'ture
lithe
lithe'some
lithe'someness
lith'i'um
litho'graph
li'thog'ra'pher
lith'o'graph'ic
li'thog'ra'phy
li'thog'ra'phy
Lith'u'a'ni'an
lit'i'gant
lit'i'gate
lit'i'gat'ed
lit'i'gat'ing
lit'i'ga'tion
li'ti'gious
lit'mus
li'to'tes
lit'ter
lit'ter'bug
lit'tle
lit'to'ral
li'tur'gic
li'tur'gi'cal
lit'ur'gies
lit'ur'gist
lit'ur'gy

liv'a'ble
live
live'abil'ity
live'a'ble
lived
live-in
live'li'er
live'li'est
live'li'hood
live'li'ness
live'long
live'ly
liv'en
liv'er
liv'er'ied
liv'er'ies
liv'er'ish
liv'er'wurst
liv'ery
lives
live'stock
liv'id
li'vid'i'ty
liv'id'ly
liv'ing
liz'ard
lla'ma
load
load'ed
loaf
loaf'er
loam
loamy
loan
loath
loathe
loathed
loath'ing
loath'some
loaves
lob
lo'bar
lobbed
lob'bied
lob'bies
lob'bing
lob'by
lob'by'ing
lob'by'ist
lobe
lobed
lo'be'lia
lo'bot'o'mies

lo'bot'o'my
lob'ster
lo'cal
lo'cale
lo'cal'i'ties
lo'cal'i'ty
lo'cal'i'za'tion
lo'cal'ize
lo'cal'ized
lo'cal'iz'ing
lo'cal'ly
lo'cate
lo'cat'ed
lo'cat'ing
lo'ca'tion
lo'ca'tor
lo'ci
lock
lock'a'ble
lock'er
lock'et
lock'jaw
lock'out
lock'smith
lock'up
lo'co'mo'tion
lo'co'mo'tive
lo'cum te'nens
lo'cum te'nen'tes
lo'cus
lo'cust
lo'cu'tion
lode
lode'star
lode'stone
lodge
lodged
lodge'ment
lodg'er
lodg'ing
lodg'ment
loess
loft'i'er
loft'i'est
loft'i'ly
loft'i'ness
lofty
log
lo'gan'ber'ries
lo'gan'ber'ry
log'a'rithm
log'a'rith'mic
log'book

loge
logged
log'ger
log'ger'head
log'gia
log'gie
log'ging
log'ic
log'i'cal
log'i'cal'ly
log'i'cal'ness
lo'gi'cian
lo'gis'tic
lo'gis'ti'cal
lo'gis'tics
lo'go
log'roll'ing
lo'gy
loin
loin'cloth
loi'ter
loi'ter'er
loll
loll'i'pop
lol'lop
lol'loped
lol'lop'ing
lone
lone'li'er
lone'li'est
lone'li'ness
lone'ly
lon'er
lone'some
long'bow
lon'gev'i'ty
long'hair
long'hand
long'ing
long'ing'ly
lon'gi'tude
lon'gi'tu'di'nal
lon'gi'tu'di'nal'ly
long johns
long-lived
long-play'ing
long-range
long'shore'man
long-sight'ed
long-suf'fer'ing
long-term
long-wind'ed
loo'fah

look
look-alike
look'er-on
look'out
loom
loon'i'er
loon'ies
loon'i'est
loon'i'ness
loony
loop
loop'hole
loop'y
loose
loosed
loose-leaf
loose'ly
loos'en
loose'ness
loos'er
loos'est
loos'ing
loot
loot'ed
loot'er
lop
lope
loped
lop'er
lop'ing
lopped
lop'ping
lop'sid'ed
lo'qua'cious
lo'qua'cious'ness
lo'quac'i'ty
lord'li'est
lord'li'ness
lord'ly
lor'do'sis
lord'ship
lore
lor'gnette
lor'ries
lor'ry
lo'ry
los'a'ble
lose
los'er
los'ing
loss
lost
lot

loth
lo'thar'io
lo'tion
lot'ted
lot'ter'ies
lot'tery
lot'ting
lo'tus
lo'tus-eat'er
louche
loud
loud'ly
loud'mouthed
loud'ness
loud'speak'er
lounge
lounged
loung'ing
lour
louring
louse
lous'i'er
lous'i'est
lous'i'ness
lousy
lout
lout'ish
lout'ish'ness
lou'ver
lov'abil'i'ty
lov'able'ness
lov'ably
love
love'able
love'bird
love child
love chil'dren
loved
love'less
love'less
love'li'er
love'li'est
love'li'ness
love'ly
love'mak'ing
lov'er
lov'ing
lov'ing
lov'ing'ly
lov'ing'ness
low
low'born
low'boy

low'brow
low-down
low'er
low'er
low'er'case
low'er-class
low'er'ing
low-keyed
low'land
low-lev'el
low'li'er
low'li'est
low'li'ness
low'ly
low-ly'ing
low-mind'ed
low-pres'sure
low-spir'it'ed
low-ten'sion
lox
loy'al
loy'al'ist
loy'al'ly
loy'al'ties
loy'al'ty
loz'enge
lu'au
lub'ber
lu'bri'cant
lu'bri'cate
lu'bri'cat'ed
lu'bri'cat'ing
lu'bri'ca'tion
lu'bri'ca'tor
lu'bri'cious
lu'cid
lu'cid'i'ty
lu'cid'ly
lu'cid'ness
luck
luck'i'er
luck'i'est
luck'i'ly
luck'i'ness
luck'less
lucky
lu'cra'tive
lu'cra'tive'ness
lu'cre
lu'cu'brate
lu'cu'bra'tion
lu'di'crous
lu'di'crous'ly

lu'di'crous'ness
lug
lug'gage
lugged
lug'ger
lug'ging
lu'gu'bri'ous
lu'gu'bri'ous'ly
luke'warm
lull
lull'a'bies
lull'a'by
lum'ba'go
lum'bar
lum'ber
lum'ber'ing
lum'ber'jack
lu'men
lu'mi'nar'ies
lu'mi'nary
lu'mi'nes'cence
lu'mi'nes'cent
lu'mi'nos'i'ty
lu'mi'nous
lu'mi'nous'ness
lum'mox
lump'i'er
lump'i'est
lump'i'ness
lumpy
lu'na'cies
lu'na'cy
lu'nar
lu'nate
lu'na'tic
lunch
lunch'eon
lunch'time
lunge
lunged
lung'ing
lunk'head
lu'pin
lu'pine
lu'pus
lurch
lure
lured
lu'rid
lu'rid'ly
lu'rid'ness
lur'ing
lurk

lurk'er
lus'cious
lus'cious'ly
lus'cious'ness
lush
lush'ness
lust
lus'tre
lus'tre'less
lust'ful
lust'ful'ness
lust'i'er
lust'i'est
lust'i'ly
lust'i'ness
lus'trous
lusty
lute
lu'te'tium
lux'u'ri'ance
lux'u'ri'ant
lux'uri'ant'ly
lux'u'ri'ate
lux'u'ri'at'ed
lux'u'ri'at'ing
lux'u'ri'a'tion
lux'u'ries
lux'u'ri'ous
lux'uri'ous'ly
lux'u'ry
ly'ce'um
ly'chee
lych'gate
ly'ing
ly'ing-in
lymph
lym'phat'ic
lynch
lynch'ing
lynch'pin
lynx
ly'on'naise
lyre
ly'ric
lyr'i'cal
lyr'i'cal'ly
lyr'i'cism
lyr'i'cist
ma'ca'bre
mac'ad'am
mac'ad'am'ize
ma'caque
mac'a'ro'ni

105

mac'a'roon
ma'caw
mace
maced
mac'er'ate
mac'er'at'ed
mac'er'at'ing
mac'er'a'tion
ma'chair
ma'chete
mach'i'nate
mach'i'nat'ed
mach'i'nat'ing
mach'i'na'tion
ma'chine
ma'chined
ma'chin'ery
ma'chin'ing
ma'chin'ist
ma'chis'mo
ma'cho
mack'er'el
mack'i'naw
mack'in'tosh
mac'ra'mé
mac'ro'bi'ot'ic
mac'ro'cosm
ma'cron
mac'ro'scop'ic
mad
mad'am
mad'ame
mad'den
mad'en'ing'ly
mad'der
mad'dest
made
mad'e'moi'selle
mad'ern'ing'ly
mad'ly
mad'man
mad'ness
mad'ras
mad'ri'gal
mad'wom'an
mael'strom
maes'tro
mag'a'zine
ma'gen'ta
mag'got
mag'goty
ma'gi
mag'ic

mag'i'cal
mag'i'cal'ly
ma'gi'cian
mag'icked
mag'ick'ing
mag'is'te'ri'al
mag'is'te'ri'al'ly
mag'is'tra'cies
mag'is'tra'cy
mag'is'trate
mag'ma
mag'na'nim'i'ty
mag'nan'i'mous
mag'nan'i'mous'ly
mag'nate
mag'ne'sia
mag'ne'si'um
mag'net
mag'net'ic
mag'net'i'cal'ly
mag'net'ism
mag'net'ize
mag'net'ized
mag'net'iz'ing
mag'ne'to
mag'ne'tom'e'ter
mag'ni'fi'ca'tion
mag'nif'i'cence
mag'nif'i'cent
mag'nif'i'cent'ly
mag'ni'fied
mag'ni'fi'er
mag'ni'fy
mag'ni'fy'ing
mag'nil'o'quent
mag'ni'tude
mag'no'lia
mag'num
mag'num opus
mag'pie
ma'gus
ma'ha'ra'jah
ma'ha'ra'ni
ma'hat'ma
mah-jongg
ma'hog'a'ny
ma'hout
maid
maid'en
maid'en'hair
maid'en'head
maiden name
maid of hon'our

maid'ser'vant
mail'a'ble
mail'lot
maim
main
main'frame
main'land
main'line
main'lined
main'lin'ing
main'ly
main'mast
main'sail
main'spring
main'stay
main'stream
main'tain
main'tain'a'ble
main'te'nance
maître d'hô'tel
maize
ma'jes'tic
ma'jes'ti'cal
ma'jes'ti'cal'ly
maj'es'ties
maj'es'ty
ma'jol'i'ca
ma'jor
ma'jor-do'mos
ma'jor'ette
ma'jor'i'ties
ma'jor'i'ty
mak'able
make
make'able
make-be'lieve
make'fast
ma'ker
make'shift
make-up
make'weight
mak'ing
mal'ab'sorp'tion
ma'lac'ca
mal'a'chite
mal'ad'ap'ta'tion
mal'a'dapt'ed
mal'ad'just'ed
mal'ad'just'ment
mal'ad'min'is'ter
mal'a'droit
mal'a'droit'ness
mal'a'dy

ma'laise
mal'a'prop
mal'a'prop'ism
mal'ap'ro'pos
ma'lar'ia
ma'lar'i'al
ma'lar'key
mal'con'tent
mal de mer
male
mal'e'dic'tion
mal'e'dic'to'ry
mal'e'fac'tion
mal'e'fac'tor
ma'lef'ic
ma'lef'i'cent
ma'lev'o'lence
ma'lev'o'lent
ma'lev'o'lent'ly
mal'fea'sance
mal'fea'sant
mal'for'ma'tion
mal'formed
mal'func'tion
mal'ice
ma'li'cious
ma'li'cious'ly
ma'lign
ma'lig'nan'cies
ma'lig'nan'cy
ma'lig'nant
ma'lig'nant'ly
ma'lig'ni'ty
ma'lign'ly
ma'lin'ger
ma'lin'ger'er
mall
mal'lard
mal'lea'bil'i'ty
mal'lea'ble
mal'lea'ble'ness
mal'let
mal'low
malm'sey
mal'nour'ished
mal'nu'tri'tion
mal'oc'clu'sion
mal'o'dour
mal'o'dor'ous
mal'prac'tice
mal'prac'ti'tion'er
malt
Mal'tese

mal'tose
mal'treat
mal'treat'ment
malty
ma'ma
mam'ba
mam'bo
mam'ma
mam'mal
mam'ma'li'an
mam'ma'ries
mam'ma'ry
mam'mo'gram
mam'mon
mam'moth
mam'my
man
man'a'cle
man'a'cled
man'a'cling
man'age
man'age'abil'i'ty
man'age'able
man'age'able'ness
man'age'ably
man'aged
man'age'ment
man'ag'er
man'ag'er'ess
man'a'ge'ri'al
man'ag'er ship
man'ag'ing
man'a'kin
ma'ña'na
man'a'tee
man'da'mus
man'da'rin
man'date
man'dat'ed
man'dat'ing
man'da'to'ri'ly
man'da'to'ry
man'di'ble
man'do'lin
man'do'line
man'drake
man'drel
man'drill
mane
man-eat'er
man-eat'ing
ma'nège
man'ful

man'ful'ly
man'ga'nese
mange
man'ger
man'gi'ness
man'gle
man'gled
man'gling
man'go
man'goes
man'grove
man'gy
man'han'dle
man'han'dled
man'han'dling
man'hole
man'hood
man-hour
man'hunt
ma'nia
ma'ni'ac
ma'ni'a'cal
ma'ni'a'cal'ly
man'ic
man'i'cure
man'i'cured
man'i'cur'ing
man'i'cur'ist
man'i'fest
man'i'fes'ta'tion
man'i'fest'ly
man'i'fes'to
man'i'fes'tos
man'i'fold
man'i'kin
ma'nil'la
ma'nille
man'i'oc
ma'nip'u'la'ble
ma'nip'u'late
ma'nip'u'lat'ed
ma'nip'u'lat'ing
ma'nip'u'la'tion
ma'nip'u'la'tive
ma'nip'u'la'tor
ma'nip'u'la'to'ry
man'i'to
man'i'tou
man'i'tu
man'kind
man'li'er
man'li'est
man'like

man'li'ness
man'ly
man-made
man'na
manned
man'ne'quin
man'ner
man'nered
man'ner'ism
man'ner'ly
man'ni'kin
man'ning
man'nish
man'nish'ly
man'ni'tol
ma'noeu'vr'able
ma'noeu'vre
man-of-war
ma'nom'e'ter
man'or
ma'no'ri'al
man'pow'er
man'que
man'sard
manse
man'ser'vant
man'sion
man-sized
man'slaugh'ter
man slay'er
man'tel
man'tel'piece
man'tel shelf
man'tel shelves
man'til'la
man'tis
man'tle
man'tra
man'u'al
man'u'al'ly
man'u'fac'ture
man'u'fac'tured
man'u'fac'tur'er
man'u'fac'tur'ing
man'u'mis'sion
ma'nure
man'u'script
many
many-sid'ed
Mao'ri
map
ma'ple
mapped

map'ping
ma'quis
mar
mar'a'bou
mar'a'bout
ma'ra'ca
mar'a'schi'no
mar'a'thon
ma'raud
ma'raud'er
ma'raud'ing
mar'ble
mar'bled
mar'bling
mar'bly
mar'cel
mar'celled
mar'cel'ling
mar'cel wave
march
march'er
mar'chion'ess
mar'ga'rine
mar'ga'ri'ta
mar'gin
mar'gi'nal
mar'gin'al'ly
mar'gue'rite
ma'ri'a'chi
ma'ri'cu'ture
mar'i'gold
ma'ri'jua'na
ma'rim'ba
ma'ri'na
mar'i'nade
mar'i'nad'ed
mar'i'nad'ing
mar'i'nate
mar'i'nat'ed
mar'i'nat'ing
ma'rine
mar'i'ner
mar'i'on'ette
mar'i'tal
mar'i'time
mar'jo'ram
marked
mark'ed'ly
mark'er
mar'ket
mar'ket'abil'i'ty
mar'ket'able
mar'ket'ed

mar'ket'ing
mar'ket'place
mark'ing
marks'man
marks'man'ship
mar'lin
mar'line
mar'line'spike
mar'ma'lade
mar'mo'set
mar'mot
ma'roon
mar'quee
mar'quess
mar'que'try
mar'quis
mar'quise
mar'qui'sette
marred
mar'riage
mar'riage'a'ble
mar'ried
mar'ring
mar'rons gla'cés
mar'row
mar'row'bone
mar'row'fat
mar'rowy
mar'ry
mar'ry'ing
marsh
mar'shal
mar'shalled
mar'shal'ling
marsh'i'er
marsh'i'est
marsh'i'ness
marsh'mal'low
marshy
mar'su'pi'al
mar'ten
mar'tial
mar'tin
mar'ti'net
mar'ti'ni
mar'tyr
mar'tyr'dom
mar'tyred
mar'tyr'ing
mar'vel
mar'velled
mar'vel'ling
mar'vel'lous

mar'vell'ous'ly
mar'zi'pan
mas'cara
mas'cot
mas'cu'line
mas'cu'lin'i'ty
mas'cu'lin'ize
mash
mashed
mash'er
mask
masked
mask'er
mas'och'ism
mas'och'ist
mas'och'is'tic
ma'son
ma'son'ic
ma'son'ry
masque
mas'quer'ade
mas'quer'ad'ed
mas'quer'ad'ing
mas'sa'cre
mas'sa'cred
mas'sa'cring
mas'sage
mas'saged
mas'sag'ing
mas'seur
mas'seuse
mas'sif
mas'sive
mas'sive'ly
mass-pro'duce
mass-pro'duced
mass-pro'duc'ing
mass-pro'duc'tion
mast
mas'tec'to'mies
mas'tec'to'my
mas'ter
mas'ter'ful
mas'ter'ly
mas'ter'mind
mas'ter'piece
mas'ter'stroke
mas'tery
mast'head
mas'ti'cate
mas'ti'ca'ting
mas'ti'ca'tion
mas'tiff

mas'to'don
mas'toid
mas'tur'bate
mas'tur'ba'tion
mat
mat'a'dor
match
match'less
match'mak'er
match'mak'ing
mate
mat'ed
ma'te'ri'al
ma'te'ri'al'ism
ma'te'ri'al'ist
ma'te'ri'al'is'tic
ma'te'ri'al'is'ti'cal'ly
ma'te'ri'al'iza'tion
ma'te'ri'al'ize
ma'te'ri'al'ized
ma'te'ri'al'iz'ing
ma'te'ri'al'ly
ma'te'ri'el
ma'ter'nal
ma'ter'nal'is'tic
ma'ter'nal'ly
ma'ter'ni'ty
math'e'mat'i'cal
math'e'mat'i'cal'ly
math'e'ma'ti'cian
math'e'mat'ics
mat'i'nee
mat'ing
mat'ins
ma'tri'arch
ma'tri'ar'chal
ma'tri'ar'chal'ism
ma'tri'ar'chies
ma'tri'ar'chy
ma'tri'ces
ma'tri'cide
ma'tric'u'lant
ma'tric'u'lat'ed
ma'tric'u'lat'ing
ma'tric'u'la'tion
ma'tri'lin'e'al
mat'ri'mo'ni'al
mat'ri'mo'ny
ma'trix
ma'tron
ma'tron'ly
matt
matte

mat'ted
mat'ter
mat'ting
mat'tock
mat'tress
mat'u'rate
mat'u'rat'ing
mat'u'ra'tion
ma'ture
ma'tured
ma'tur'ing
ma'tu'ri'ty
mat'zo
maud'lin
maul
mau'so'le'um
mauve
ma'ven
mav'er'ick
mawk'ish
mawk'ish'ness
max'im
max'i'ma
max'i'mal
max'i'mi'za'tion
max'i'mize
max'i'mized
max'i'miz'ing
max'i'mum
may'be
Mayday
May Day
may'flies
may'flow'er
may'fly
may'hem
may'on'naise
may'or
may'or'al
may'or'al'ty
may'or'ess
maze
maz'ing
ma'zur'ka
ma'zy
mea cul'pa
mead
mead'ow
mead'ow'lark
mea'gre
mea'gre'ness
meal
meal'i'ness

mealy
mealy bug
mealy-mouthed
mean
me'an'der
mean'ing
mean'ing'ful
mean'ing'ful'ly
mean'ing'less
mean'ly
mean'ness
meant
mean'time
mean'while
mea'sles
meas'li'er
mea'sli'est
mea'sly
meas'ur'abil'i'ty
meas'ur'able
meas'ur'ably
meas'ure
meas'ured
meas'ure'ment
meas'ur'er
mea'sur'ing
meat
meat'i'er
meat'i'est
meat'i'ness
meaty
me'chan'ic
me'chan'i'cal
me'chan'i'cal'ly
mech'an'ism
mech'a'nis'tic
mech'a'ni'za'tion
mech'a'nize
mech'a'nized
mech'a'niz'ing
med'al
med'alled
me'dal'lion
med'al'list
med'dle
med'dled
med'dler
med'dle'some
med'dling
me'dia
me'di'al
me'di'an
me'di'ate

me'di'at'ed
me'di'at'ing
me'di'a'tion
me'di'a'tor
me'di'a'to'ry
med'ic
med'i'ca'ble
med'i'cal
med'i'cal'ly
me'di'ca'ment
med'i'cate
med'i'cat'ed
med'i'cat'ing
med'i'ca'tion
me'dic'i'nal
me'dic'i'nal'ly
med'i'cine
me'di'e'val
me'di'e'val'ism
me'di'o'cre
me'di'oc'ri'ties
me'di'oc'ri'ty
med'i'tate
med'i'tat'ed
med'i'tat'ing
med'i'ta'tion
med'i'ta'tive
med'i'ta'tive'ly
med'i'ta'tor
me'di'um
me'di'ums
med'lar
med'ley
meek
meek'ly
meek'ness
meer'schaum
meet
meet'ing
meet'ing house
mega'byte
mega'cy'cle
mega'death
mega'hertz
mega'lith
meg'a'lo'ma'nia
meg'a'lo'ma'ni'ac
meg'a'lop'o'lis
mega'phone
mega'ton
mega'watt
mei'osis
mel'a'mine

mel'an'cho'lia
mel'an'chol'ic
mel'an'chol'i'ness
mel'an'choly
me'lange
mel'a'nin
mel'a'no'ma
me'lee
mel'io'ra'ble
mel'io'rate
mel'io'rat'ed
mel'io'rat'ing
mel'io'ra'tion
mel'io'ra'tor
mel'lif'lu'ent
mel'lif'lu'ous
mel'low
me'lo'de'on
me'lod'ic
me'lod'i'cal'ly
mel'o'dies
me'lo'di'ous
me'lo'di'ous'ness
mel'o'dra'ma
mel'o'dra'mat'ic
mel'o'dra'mat'i'cal'ly
mel'o'dy
mel'on
melt
melt'able
melt'ed
melt'ing
mem'ber
mem'ber'less
mem'ber'ship
mem'brane
mem'bra'nous
me'men'to
me'men'toes
memo
mem'oir
mem'o'ra'bil'ia
mem'o'ra'ble
mem'o'ra'bly
mem'o'ran'da
mem'o'ran'dum
me'mo'ri'al
me'mo'ri'al'i'za'tion
me'mo'ri'al'ize
me'mo'ri'al'ized
me'mo'ri'al'iz'ing
me'mo'ri'al'ly
mem'o'ries

mem'o'ri'za'tion
mem'o'rize
mem'o'rized
mem'o'riz'ing
mem'o'ry
mem'sa'hib
men
men'ace
men'aced
men'ac'ing
men'ac'ing'ly
mé'nage
mé'nage à tois
me'nag'er'ie
mend
mend'a'ble
men'da'cious
men'dac'i'ty
men'de'le'vi'um
men'di'cant
men'folk
me'ni'al
me'ni'al'ly
men'in'gi'tis
me'nis'cus
men'o'pau'sal
men'o'pause
men'sal
men'ses
men'stru'al
men'stru'ate
men'stru'at'ed
men'stru'at'ing
men'stru'a'tion
men'sur'a'ble
men'su'ra'tion
mens'wear
men'tal
men'tal'i'ties
men'tal'i'ty
men'tal'ly
men'thol
men'tho'lat'ed
men'tion
men'tion'a'ble
men'tor
menu
me'phit'ic
mer'can'tile
mer'can'til'ism
mer'ce'nar'ies
mer'ce'nary
mer'cer'ize

mer'cer'ized
mer'chan'dise
mer'chan'dised
mer'chan'dis'er
mer'chan'dis'ing
mer'chant
mer'cies
mer'ci'ful
mer'ci'ful'ly
mer'ci'less
mer'ci'less'ly
mer'cu'ri'al
mer'cu'ro'chrome
mer'c'ury
mer'cy
mere
mere'ly
mer'e'tri'cious
mer'e'tri'cious'ness
mer'gan'ser
merge
merged
mer'gence
merg'er
merg'ing
me'rid'i'an
me'ringue
me'ri'no
mer'it
mer'i'ted
mer'it'ed'ly
mer'it'ing
mer'it'less
mer'i'toc'ra'cies
mer'i'toc'ra'cy
mer'i'to'ri'ous
mer'maid
mer'man
mer'ri'er
mer'ri'est
mer'ri'ly
mer'ri'ment
mer'ri'ness
mer'ry
mer'ry-go-round
mer'ry'mak'er
mer'ry'mak'ing
me'sa
mé'sal'li'ance
mes'arch
mes'cal
mes'ca'line
mes'dames

me'shuga
mesh'work
mes'mer'ic
mes'mer'i'cal'ly
mes'mer'ism
mes'mer'i'za'tion
mes'mer'ize
mes'mer'ized
mes'mer'iz'ing
me'son
mes'quite
mess
mes'sage
mes'sen'ger
mess'i'er
mess'i'est
mes'sieurs
mess'i'ly
mess'i'ness
messy
mes'ti'zo
met
me'tabo'lic
me'tabo'li'cal'ly
me'tabo'lism
me'tabo'lize
me'tabo'lized
me'tabo'liz'ing
met'al
met'alled
me'tal'lic
met'al'ling
met'al'lize
met'al'lized
met'al'liz'ing
met'al'loid
met'al'lur'gic
met'al'lur'gi'cal
met'al'lur'gist
met'al'lur'gy
met'al'work
meta'mor'phic
meta'mor'phism
meta'mor'phose
meta'mor'phosed
meta'mor'pho'ses
meta'mor'phos'ing
meta'mor'pho'sis
met'a'phor
met'a'phor'ic
met'a'phor'i'cal
met'a'phor'i'cal'ly
meta'phys'ic

meta'phys'i'cal
meta'phys'ics
me'tas'ta'sis
meta'tar'sal
meta'tar'sus
me'tath'e'sis
met'a'zo'an
mete
met'ed
me'tem'psy'cho'sis
me'te'or
me'te'or'ic
me'te'or'ite
me'te'or'oid
me'te'or'o'log'i'cal
me'te'or'ol'o'gist
me'te'or'ol'o'gy
me'ter
meth'a'done
meth'ane
meth'a'nol
meth'od
me'thod'i'cal
me'thod'i'cal'ly
Meth'od'ism
Meth'od'ist
meth'od'ize
meth'od'o'log'i'cal
meth'od'ol'o'gies
meth'od'ol'o'gist
meth'od'ol'o'gy
me'tic'u'lous
me'tic'u'lous'ly
me'tic'u'lous'ness
mé'tier
met'ing
meto'nym
meto'nym'ic'al
me'ton'y'my
me'tre
met'ric
met'ri'cal
met'ri'cal'ly
met'ri'ca'tion
met'ro
met'ro'nome
met'ro'nom'ic
me'trop'o'lis
met'ro'pol'i'tan
met'tle
met'tle'some
mew
Mex'i'can

mez'za'nine
mez'zo
mez'zo-so'pra'no
mi'aow
mi'as'ma
mi'as'ma'ta
mi'ca
mice
mi'cro
mi'cro'a'nal'y'sis
mi'crobe
mi'cro'bi'al
mi'cro'bi'o'log'i'cal
mi'cro'bi'ol'o'gist
mi'cro'bi'ol'o'gy
mi'cro'chip
mi'cro'com'put'er
mi'cro'copy
mi'cro'cosm
mi'cro'dot
mic'ro'elec'tron'ics
mi'cro'fiche
mi'cro'film
mi'cro'gram
mi'cro'groove
mi'crom'e'ter
mi'cro'mi'cron
mi'cro'mil'li'me'ter
mi'cron
mi'cro'or'gan'ism
mi'cro'phone
mi'cro'pho'to'graph
mi'cro'pro'ces'sor
mi'cro'read'er
mi'cro'scope
mi'cro'scop'ic
mi'cro'scop'i'cal'ly
mi'cros'co'py
mi'cro'sec'ond
mi'cro'sur'gery
mi'cro'wave
mic'tu'rate
mic'tu'rat'ed
mic'tu'rat'ing
mic'tu'ri'tion
mid'day
mid'dies
mid'dle
mid'dle-aged
midd'lebrow
mid'dle'man
mid'dle'weight
mid'dling

mid'dy
midge
midg'et
mid'land
mid'most
mid'night
mid'point
mid'riff
mid'sec'tion
mid'ship'man
midst
mid'stream
mid'sum'mer
mid'term
mid'way
mid'wife
mid'wife'ry
mid'wives
mid'year
mien
miffed
might'i'er
might'i'est
might'i'ly
might'i'ness
mighty
mi'graine
mi'grant
mi'grate
mi'grat'ed
mi'grat'ing
mi'gra'tion
mi'gra'tor
mi'gra'to'ry
mi'ka'do
mike
milch
mild
mil'dew
mil'dewy
mild'ly
mild'ness
mile'age
mil'er
mile'stone
mi'lieu
mi'lieus
mi'lieux
mil'i'tan'cy
mil'i'tant
mil'i'tant'ness
mil'i'tar'i'ly
mil'i'ta'rism

mil'i'tar'ist
mil'i'ta'ris'tic
mil'i'ta'ris'ti'cal'ly
mil'i'ta'ri'za'tion
mil'i'ta'rize
mil'i'tary
mil'i'tate
mil'i'tat'ed
mil'i'tat'ing
mi'li'tia
mi'li'tia'man
milk
milk'er
milk'i'er
milk'i'est
milk'i'ness
milk'maid
milk'man
milk'sop
milk'weed
milky
mill
mil'len'nia
mil'len'ni'al
mil'len'ni'um
mill'er
mil'let
mil'li'gram
mil'li'li'tre
mil'li'me'tre
mil'li'ner
mil'li'nery
mill'ing
mil'lion
mil'lion'aire
mil'lionth
mil'li'pede
mil'li'sec'ond
mill'pond
mill'wright
mime
mimed
mim'eo'graph
mim'er
mim'ic
mim'i'cal
mim'icked
mim'ick'er
mim'ick'ing
mim'ic'ries
mim'ic'ry
mim'ing
mi'mo'sa

min'a'ret
mi'na'to'ry
mince
minced
mince'meat
minc'er
minc'ing
minc'ing'ly
mind
mind-bog'gling
mind'ed
mind'er
mind'ful
mind'less
mine
mined
mine'field
min'er
min'er'al
min'er'al'i'za'tion
min'er'al'ize
min'er'al'ized
min'er'al'iz'ing
min'er'al'og'i'cal
min'er'al'o'gist
min'er'al'o'gy
min'e'stro'ne
mine'sweep'er
min'gi'er
min'gi'est
min'gle
min'gled
min'gling
min'gy
mini
min'i'a'ture
min'i'a'tur'i'za'tion
min'i'a'tur'ize
min'i'a'tur'ized
min'i'a'tur'iz'ing
min'im
min'i'ma
min'i'mal
min'i'mal'ly
min'i'mi'za'tion
min'i'mize
min'i'mized
min'i'miz'ing
min'i'mum
min'ing
min'ing
min'ion
min'is'cule

mini'skirt
min'is'ter
min'is'te'ri'al
min'is'trant
min'is'tra'tion
min'is'tries
min'is'try
min'now
mi'nor
mi'nor'i'ties
mi'nor'i'ty
mi'no'taur
min'strel
mint'age
min'u'end
min'u'et
mi'nus
mi'nus'cule
min'ute
mi'nute
min'ut'ed
mi'nute'ly
min'ute'man
min'ut'est
mi'nu'tia
mi'nu'ti'ae
min'ut'ing
minx
mir'a'cle
mi'rac'u'lous
mi'rac'u'lous'ly
mi'rage
mire
mired
mir'ing
mir'ror
mir'rored
mir'ror'ing
mirth
mirth'ful'ly
mirth'ful'ness
mirth'less
mirth'less'ly
miry
mis'ad'ven'ture
mis'ad'vise
mis'al'li'ance
mis'an'thrope
mis'an'throp'ic
mis'an'thro'py
mis'ap'pli'ca'tion
mis'ap'plied
mis'ap'ply

mis'ap'ply'ing
mis'ap'pre'hend
mis'ap'pre'hen'sion
mis'ap'pro'pri'ate
mis'ap'pro'pri'at'ed
mis'ap'pro'pri'at'ing
mis'ap'pro'pri'a'tion
mis'be'have
mis'be'haved
mis'be'hav'ing
mis'be'ha'viour
mis'belief
mis'believ'er
mis'cal'cu'late
mis'cal'cu'lat'ed
mis'cal'cu'lat'ing
mis'cal'cu'la'tion
mis'cal'cu'la'tor
mis'call
mis'car'ried
mis'car'riage
mis'car'ry
mis'car'ry'ing
mis'cast
mis'ce'ge'na'tion
mis'cel'la'ne'ous
mis'cel'la'nies
mis'cel'la'ny
mis'chance
mis'chief
mis'chie'vous
mis'chie'vous'ly
mis'ci'bil'i'ty
mis'ci'ble
mis'con'ceive
mis'con'ceived
mis'con'ceiv'ing
mis'con'cep'tion
mis'con'duct
mis'con'struc'tion
mis'con'strue
mis'con'strued
mis'con'stru'ing
mis'count
mis'cre'ant
mis'cue
mis'cued
mis'cu'ing
mis'deal
mis'deal'ing
mis'dealt
mis'deed
mis'de'mean'or

mis'di'rect
mis'di'rec'tion
mis'do'ing
mise-en-scène
mis'em'ploy
mis'em'ploy'ment
mi'ser
mis'er'a'ble
mis'er'a'ble'ness
mis'er'a'bly
mi'se're're
mis'er'ies
mi'ser'li'ness
mi'ser'ly
mis'ery
mis'es'ti'mate
mis'fea'sance
mis'fire
mis'fired
mis'fit
mis'fit'ted
mis'fit'ting
mis'for'tune
mis'giv'ing
mis'gov'ern
mis'gov'ern'ment
mis'guid'ance
mis'guide
mis'guid'ed
mis'guid'ing
mis'han'dle
mis'han'dled
mis'han'dling
mis'hap
mis'hear
mis'heard
mis'hear'ing
mish'mash
mis'in'form
mis'in'form'ant
mis'in'for'ma'tion
mis'in'form'er
mis'in'ter'pret
mis'in'ter'pre'ta'tion
mis'in'ter'pret'er
mis'judge
mis'judged
mis'judg'ing
mis'judg'ment
mis'laid
mis'lay
mis'lay'ing
mis'lead

mis'lead'er
mis'lead'ing
mis'lead'ing'ly
mis'led
mis'man'age
mis'man'aged
mis'man'age'ment
mis'man'ag'ing
mis'match
mis'match'ed
mis'match'ing
mis'name
mis'named
mis'nam'ing
mis'no'mer
mi'so'gam'ist
mi'sog'a'my
mi'sog'y'nist
mi'sog'y'nous
mi'sog'y'ny
mis'place
mis'placed
mis'place'ment
mis'plac'ing
mis'play
mis'print
mis'pri'sion
mis'prize
mis'pro'nounce
mis'pro'nounced
mis'pro'nounc'ing
mis'pro'nun'ci'a'tion
mis'quo'ta'tion
mis'quote
mis'quot'ed
mis'quot'ing
mis'read
mis'read'ing
mis'rep're'sent
mis'rep're'sen'ta'tion
mis'rep're'sen'ta'tive
mis'rule
mis'ruled
mis'rul'ing
miss
mis'sal
mis'shape
mis'shaped
mis'shap'en
mis'shap'ing
mis'sile
miss'ing
mis'sion

mis'sion'ar'ies
mis'sion'ary
mis'sis
mis'sive
mis'spell
mis'spelled
mis'spel'ling
mis'spelt
mis'spend
mis'spend'ing
mis'spent
mis'state
mis'stat'ed
mis'state'ment
mis'stat'ing
mis'step
mis'sus
mist
mis'tak'a'ble
mis'take
mis'tak'en
mis'tak'en'ly
mis'tak'en'ness
mis'tak'ing
mis'ter
mist'i'er
mist'i'est
mist'i'ly
mis'time
mis'timed
mis'tim'ing
mist'i'ness
mis'tle'toe
mis'took
mis'tral
mis'treat
mis'treat'ment
mis'tress
mis'tri'al
mis'trust
mis'trust'ful
mis'trust'ful'ly
mis'trust'ing'ly
misty
mis'un'der'stand
mis'un'der'stand'ing
mis'un'der'stood
mis'us'age
mis'use
mis'used
mis'us'ing
mis'val'ue
mit'i'gate

mit'i'gat'ed
mit'i'gat'ing
mit'i'ga'tion
mit'i'ga'tive
mit'i'ga'tor
mit'i'ga'to'ry
mi'to'sis
mi'tre
mitt
mit'ten
mix
mixed
mix'er
mix'ing
mix'ture
miz'zen
miz'zen'mast
mne'mon'ic
mne'mon'ics
moa
moan
moan'er
moat
mob
mobbed
mob'bing
mob'bish
mo'bile
mo'bil'i'ty
mo'bi'li'za'tion
mo'bi'lize
mo'bi'lized
mo'bi'liz'ing
mob'oc'ra'cy
mob'ster
moc'ca'sin
mo'cha
mock
mock'er
mock'ery
mock'ing'bird
mock'ing'ly
mock-up
mod'al
mo'dal'i'ty
mod'al'ly
mode
mod'el
mod'elled
mod'el'ling
mo'dem
mod'er'ate
mod'er'at'ed

mod'er'ate'ly
mod'er'ate'ness
mod'er'at'ing
mod'er'a'tion
mod'er'a'tor
mod'ern
mod'ern'ism
mod'ern'ist
mod'ern'ist'ic
mo'der'ni'ty
mod'ern'i'za'tion
mod'ern'ize
mod'ern'ized
mod'ern'iz'ing
mod'est
mod'est'ly
mod'es'ty
mod'i'cum
mod'i'fi'a'ble
mod'i'fi'ca'tion
mod'i'fied
mod'i'fi'er
mod'i'fy
mod'i'fy'ing
mod'ish
mod'ish'ly
mod'ish'ness
mo'diste
mod'u'lar
mod'u'late
mod'u'lat'ed
mod'u'lat'ing
mod'u'la'tion
mod'u'la'to'ry
mod'ule
mo'dus o'pe'ran'di
mo'dus vi'ven'di
mo'gul
mo'hair
mo'hi'can
moi'e'ty
moi're
moi'ré
moist
mois'ten
moist'en'er
mois'ture
mois'tur'ize
mois'tur'ized
mois'tur'iz'er
mois'tur'iz'ing
mo'lar
mo'las'ses

mole
mo'lec'u'lar
mol'e'cule
mole'hill
mole'skin
mo'lest
mo'les'ta'tion
mo'lest'er
moll
mol'li'fi'ca'tion
mol'li'fied
mol'li'fi'er
mol'li'fy
mol'li'fy'ing
mol'lusc
mo'lyb'de'num
mol'ly'cod'dle
mol'ten
mom
mo'ment
mo'men'tar'i'ly
mo'men'tary
mo'men'tous
mo'men'tum
mom'ma
mon'ad
mo'nad'ic
mo'nad'i'cal
mon'arch
mo'nar'chal
mo'nar'chic
mo'nar'ch'ical
mo'nar'chic'al'ly
mon'ar'chies
mon'ar'chism
mon'ar'chist
mon'ar'chy
mon'as'te'ri'al
mon'as'ter'ies
mon'as'tery
mo'nas'tic
mo'nas'ti'cal
mo'nas'ti'cism
mon'au'ral
mon'au'ral'ly
mon'e'tar'i'ly
mon'e'tar'ism
mon'e'tar'ist
mon'e'tary
mon'e'ti'za'tion
mon'e'tize
mon'e'tized
mon'e'tiz'ing

mon'ey
mon'eyed
mon'ger
Mon'gol
Mon'go'lian
mon'gol'oid
mon'goose
mon'grel
mon'ied
mon'ies
mon'i'ker
mon'ism
mo'nis'tic
mo'nis'ti'cal'ly
mo'ni'tion
mon'i'tor
mon'i'tored
mon'i'to'ri'al
mon'i'tor'ing
monk
mon'key
mon'keyed
mon'key'ing
mon'key tricks
monk'ish
mono
mono'chro'mat'ic
mono'chrome
mono'chro'mic
mono'chro'mi'cal
mono'chro'mi'cal'ly
mon'o'cle
mon'o'cline
mon'o'cli'nal
mono'cot'y'le'don
mo'nod'ic
mon'o'dist
mon'o'dy
mon'oe'cious
mo'nog'a'mist
mo'nog'a'mous
mo'nog'a'my
mono'gram
mono'gram'mat'ic
mono'grammed
mono'gram'ming
mono'graph
mo'nog'ra'pher
mono'graph'ic
mono'lith
mono'lith'ic
mono'log'ist
mono'logue

113

mono'ma'nia
mono'ma'ni'ac
mono'me'tal'lic
mono'met'al'lism
mo'no'mi'al
mono'nu'cle'o'sis
mono'plane
mo'nop'o'lies
mo'nop'o'lis'tic
mo'nop'o'li'za'tion
mo'nop'o'lize
mo'nop'o'lized
mo'nop'o'liz'er
mo'nop'o'liz'ing
mo'nop'o'ly
mono'rail
mono'so'di'um
glu'ta'mate
mono'syl'lab'ic
mono'syl'lable
mono'the'ism
mono'the'ist
mono'the'is'tic
mono'tone
mo'not'o'nous
mo'not'o'nous'ly
mo'not'o'ny
mono'type
mon'ox'ide
mon'sieur
mon'soon
mon'ster
mon'stros'i'ties
mon'stros'i'ty
mon'strous
mon'strous'ly
mon'tage
month
month'lies
month'ly
mon'u'ment
mon'u'men'tal
mon'u'men'tal'ly
mooch
mooch'er
mood
mood'i'er
mood'i'est
mood'i'ly
mood'i'ness
moody
moon
moon'beam

moon'less
moon'light
moon'light'ing
moon'lit
moon'scape
moon'shine
moor
moor'ing
moose
moot
moot point
mop
mope
moped
mo'ped
mop'ing
mopped
mop'pet
mop'ping
mo'quette
mo'raine
mor'al
mo'rale
mor'al'ist
mor'al'is'tic
mor'al'i'ties
mo'ral'i'ty
mor'al'i'za'tion
mor'al'ize
mor'al'ized
mor'al'iz'er
mor'al'iz'ing
mor'al'ly
mo'rass
mor'a'to'ria
mor'a'to'ri'um
mo'ray
mor'bid
mor'bid'i'ty
mor'bid'ly
mor'bid'ness
mor'dan'cy
mor'dant
more
more'over
mo'res
mor'ga'nat'ic
morgue
mor'i'bund
mor'nay sauce
morn'ing
morn'ing-glory
Mo'roc'can

mo'ron
mo'ron'ic
mo'ron'i'cal'ly
mo'rose
mo'rose'ly
mo'rose'ness
mor'pheme
mor'phia
mor'phine
mor'pho'log'ic
mor'pho'log'i'cal
mor'phol'o'gist
mor'phol'o'gy
mor'row
mor'sel
mor'tal
mor'tal'i'ties
mor'tal'i'ty
mor'tal'ly
mor'tar
mor'tar'board
mort'gage
mort'gaged
mort'ga'gee
mort'ga'ger
mort'gag'ing
mort'gag'or
mor'ti'cian
mor'ti'fi'ca'tion
mor'ti'fied
mor'ti'fy
mor'ti'fy'ing
mor'tise
mor'tised
mor'tis'ing
mor'tu'ar'ies
mor'tu'ary
mo'sa'ic
mo'sey
mo'seyed
mo'sey'ing
Mos'lem
mosque
mos'qui'to
mos'qui'toes
mos'qui'tos
moss
moss'back
moss'i'er
moss'i'est
moss'like
mossy
most

most'ly
mote
mo'tel
mo'tet
moth'ball
moth-eat'en
moth'er
moth'er'hood
moth'er-in-law
moth'er'land
moth'er'less
moth'er'li'ness
moth'er'ly
moth'er-of-pearl
moth'er-to-be
mo'tif
mo'tile
mo'til'i'ty
mo'tion
mo'tion'less
mo'tion'less'ness
mo'ti'vate
mo'ti'vat'ed
mo'ti'vat'ing
mo'ti'va'tion
mo'ti'va'tion'al
mo'tive
mot'ley
mo'tor
mo'tor'bike
mo'tor'boat
mo'tor'bus
mo'tor'cade
mo'tor'car
mo'tor court
mo'tor'cy'cle
mo'tor'cy'cled
mo'tor'cy'cling
mo'tor'cy'clist
mo'tor'ist
mo'tor'i'za'tion
mo'tor'ize
mo'tor'ized
mo'tor'iz'ing
mot'tle
mot'tled
mot'tling
mot'to
mot'toes
moue
mould
mould'a'ble
mould'er

114

mould'i'er
mould'i'est
mould'i'ness
mould'ing
mouldy
moult
moult'er
mound
mount
mount'a'ble
moun'tain
moun'tain'eer
moun'tain'ous
moun'tain'side
moun'te'bank
mount'ing
mourn
mourn'er
mourn'ful
mourn'ful'ly
mourn'ing
mouse
mous'er
mous'ey
mous'i'er
mous'i'est
mous'sa'ka
mousse
mous'tache
mousy
mouth
mouthed
mouth'ful
mouth'i'ness
mouth'piece
mouth'wash
mouth'wa'ter'ing
mouthy
mou'ton
mov'abil'i'ty
mov'able
mov'ably
move
move'able
moved
move'ment
mov'er
mov'ie
mov'ie'go'er
mov'ing
mov'ing'ly
mow
mowed

mow'er
mow'ing
mown
moz'za'rel'la
much
much'ness
mu'ci'lage
mu'ci'lag'i'nous
muck
muck'i'er
muck'i'est
muck'rake
muck'raked
muck'rak'er
muck'rak'ing
mucky
mu'cos'i'ty
mu'cous
mu'cus
mud
mud'ded
mud'died
mud'di'er
mud'di'est
mud'di'ness
mud'ding
mud'dle
mud'dled
mud'dle'head'ed
mud'dler
mud'dling
mud'dy
mud'dy'ing
mud'guard
mu'ez'zin
muff
muf'fin
muf'fle
muf'fled
muf'fler
muf'fling
muf'ti
mug
mugged
mug'ger
mug'gi'ness
mug'ging
mug'gy
mug'wump
muk'luk
mu'lat'to
mu'lat'toes
mul'ber'ries

mul'ber'ry
mulch
mulct
mu'le'teer
mul'ish
mul'ish'ness
mull
mul'lah
mul'let
mul'li'gan
mul'li'ga'taw'ny
mul'lion
mul'lioned
mul'ti'col'oured
mul'ti'far'i'ous
mul'ti'far'i'ous'ness
mul'ti'lat'er'al
mul'ti'lev'el
mul'ti'lin'gual
mul'ti'mil'lion'aire
mul'ti'na'tion'al
mul'ti'no'mial
mul'ti'par'ity
mul'ti'par'tite
mul'ti'ple
mul'ti'ple-choice
mul'ti'plex
mul'ti'pli'a'ble
mul'ti'pli'cand
mul'ti'pli'ca'tion
mul'ti'plic'i'ty
mul'ti'plied
mul'ti'pli'er
mul'ti'ply
mul'ti'ply'ing
mul'ti'ra'cial
mul'ti'tude
mul'ti'tu'di'nous
mum
mum'ble
mum'bled
mum'bler.
mum'bling
mum'bo jum'bo
mummed
mum'mer
mum'mies
mum'mi'fi'ca'tion
mum'mi'fied
mum'mi'fy
mum'mi'fy'ing
mum'ming
mum'my

munch
mun'dane
mu'nic'i'pal
mu'ni'ci'pal'i'ties
mu'nic'i'pal'i'ty
mu'nic'i'pal'ly
mu'nif'i'cence
mu'nif'i'cent
mu'nif'i'cent'ly
mu'ni'tion
mu'on
mu'ral
mu'ral'ist
mur'der
mur'der'er
mur'der'ess
mur'der'ous
mur'der'ous'ly
mu'ri'at'ic ac'id
murk
murk'i'er
murk'i'est
murk'i'ness
murky
mur'mur
mur'mur'er
mur'mur'ing
mur'rain
mus'cat
mus'ca'tel
mus'cle
mus'cle-bound
mus'cled
mus'cling
mus'cly
mus'cu'lar
mus'cu'lar'i'ty
mus'cu'la'ture
muse
mused
mus'er
mu'se'um
mush
mushi'ly
mush'i'ness
mush'room
mushy
mu'sic
mu'si'cal
mu'si'cale
mu'si'cal'ly
mu'si'cal'ness
mu'si'cian

mu'si'cian'ship	mut'tered	nag'ging	nar'row-mind'ed
mus'ing	mut'ter'ing	nai'ad	nar'row-mind'edness
musk	mut'ton	nai'ads	nar'row'ness
mus'kel'lunge	mu'tu'al	nai'ades	nar'wal
mus'ket	mu'tu'al'i'ty	nail	nar'whal
mus'ket'eer	mu'tu'al'ly	nain'sook	nar'whale
mus'ket'ry	muu'muu	na'ïve	na'sal
musk'i'ness	muz'zle	na'ïve'ly	na'sal'i'ty
musk'mel'on	muz'zled	na'ïve'ness	na'sal'ize
musk'rat	muz'zling	na'ïve'té	na'sal'ized
musky	muzzy	na'ïve'ty	na'sal'iz'ing
Mus'lim	my'col'o'gist	na'ked	na'sal'ly
mus'lin	my'col'o'gy	na'ked'ly	nas'cence
mus'quash	my'na	na'ked'ness	nas'cen'cy
muss	my'o'pia	nam'by-pam'by	nas'cent
mus'sel	my'op'ic	name	nas'ti'er
mussy	myr'i'ad	named	nas'ti'est
mus'tang	myrrh	name'less	nas'ti'ly
mus'tard	myr'tle	name'ly	nas'ti'ness
mus'ter	my'self	name'sake	na'stur'tium
must'i'er	mys'ter'ies	nam'ing	nas'ty
must'i'est	mys'te'ri'ous	nan'keen	na'tal
mus'ti'ly	mys'te'ri'ous'ly	nan'nies	na'tal'i'ty
mus'ti'ness	mys'tery	nan'ny	na'tant
mus'ty	mys'tic	nano'sec'ond	na'ta'to'ri'al
mu'ta'bil'i'ty	mys'ti'cal	nap	na'ta'to'ri'um
mu'ta'ble	mys'ti'cal'ly	na'palm	na'tion
mu'ta'ble'ness	mys'ti'cism	nape	na'tion'al
mu'ta'bly	mys'ti'fi'ca'tion	naph'tha	na'tion'al'ism
mu'tant	mys'ti'fied	naph'tha'lene	na'tion'al'ist
mu'tate	mys'ti'fy	nap'kin	na'tion'al'is'tic
mu'tat'ed	mys'ti'fy'ing	napped	na'tion'al'i'ties
mu'tat'ing	mys'tique	nap'ping	na'tion'al'i'ty
mu'ta'tion	myth	nar'cism	na'tion'al'i'za'tion
mu'ta'tion'al	myth'ic	nar'cis'si	na'tion'al'ize
mute	myth'i'cal	nar'cis'sism	na'tion'al'ized
mut'ed	myth'i'cal'ly	nar'cis'sist	na'tion'al'iz'ing
mute'ly	myth'o'log'ic	nar'cis'sis'tic	na'tion'al'ly
mute'ness	myth'o'log'i'cal	nar'cis'sus	na'tion'hood
mu'ti'late	my'thol'o'gist	nar'co'sis	na'tion-state
mu'ti'lat'ed	my'thol'o'gy	nar'cot'ic	na'tion'wide
mu'ti'lat'ing	myx'o'ma'to'sis	nar'cot'ism	na'tive
mu'ti'la'tion	nab	nar'co'tize	na'tive'ly
mu'ti'la'tor	nabbed	nar'co'tized	na'tive'ness
mu'ti'neer	nab-bing	nar'co'tiz'ing	na'tiv'ism
mut'ing	na'bob	nar'rate	na'tiv'i'ties
mu'ti'nied	na'celle	nar'ra'ted	na'tiv'i'ty
mu'ti'nies	na'cre	nar'ra'ting	nat'ter
mu'ti'nous	na'cre'ous	nar'ra'tion	nat'ti'er
mu'ti'ny	na'dir	nar'ra'tive	nat'ti'est
mu'ti'ny'ing	nag	nar'ra'tor	nat'ti'ly
mutt	nagged	nar'row	nat'ti'ness
mut'ter	nag'ger	nar'row'ly	nat'ty

nat'u'ral
nat'u'ral'ism
nat'u'ral'ist
nat'u'ral'is'tic
nat'u'ral'i'za'tion
nat'u'ral'ize
nat'u'ral'ized
nat'u'ral'iz'ing
nat'u'ral'ly
nat'u'ral'ness
na'ture
naught
naugh'ti'er
naugh'ti'est
naugh'ti'ly
naugh'ti'ness
naugh'ty
nau'sea
nau'se'ate
nau'se'at'ed
nau'se'at'ing
nau'seous
nau'seous'ness
nau'ti'cal
nau'ti'cal'ly
nau'ti'lus
nau'ti'lus'es
na'val
nave
na'vel
na'vies
nav'i'ga'bil'i'ty
nav'i'ga'ble
nav'i'ga'ble'ness
nav'i'gate
nav'i'gat'ed
nav'i'gat'ing
nav'i'ga'tion
nav'i'ga'tion'al
nav'i'ga'tor
na'vy
na'wab
nay
neap
near
near'by
near'ly
near'ness
near-sight'ed
neat
neat'ly
neat'ness
neb'u'la

neb'u'lae
neb'u'lar
neb'u'los'i'ty
neb'u'lous
neb'u'lous'ness
nec'es'sar'ies
nec'es'sar'i'ly
nec'es'sary
ne'ces'si'tes
ne'ces'si'tate
ne'ces'si'ta'ted
ne'ces'si'ta'ting
ne'ces'si'ty
neck
neck'er'chief
neck'lace
neck'line
neck'tie
ne'crol'o'gies
ne'crol'o'gy
nec'ro'man'cer
nec'ro'man'cy
ne'crop'o'lis
nec'tar
nec'tar'ine
nee
need
need'ful
need'ful'ly
need'i'er
need'i'est
need'i'ness
nee'dle
nee'dled
nee'dle'point
need'less
need'less'ly
nee'dle'wom'an
nee'dle'work
nee'dling
needy
ne'er
ne'er-do-well
ne'far'i'ous
ne'far'i'ous'ness
ne'gate
ne'ga'ted
ne'ga'ting
ne'ga'tion
neg'a'tive
neg'a'tive'ly
neg'a'tive'ness
neg'a'tiv'ism

neg'a'tiv'i'ty
ne'glect
ne'glect'ful
ne'glect'ful'ly
neg'li'gee
neg'li'gence
neg'li'gent
neg'li'gent'ly
neg'li'gi'bil'i'ty
neg'li'gi'ble
neg'li'gi'bly
ne'go'ti'a'bil'i'ty
ne'go'ti'a'ble
ne'go'ti'ate
ne'go'ti'at'ed
ne'go'ti'at'ing
ne'go'ti'a'tion
ne'go'ti'a'tor
Ne'gress
Ne'gro
Ne'groes
Ne'groid
neigh
neigh'bour
neigh'bour'hood
neigh'bour'ing
neigh'bour'li'ness
neigh'bour'ly
nei'ther
nem'a'tode
nem'e'sis
neo'clas'sic
neo'clas'si'cal
neo'clas'si'cism
neo'co'lo'nial'ism
neo'lith
Neo'lith'ic
neo'logi'cal
ne'ol'o'gism
ne'ol'o'gy
ne'on
neo'na'tal
ne'o'nate
neo'phyte
neo'prene
neph'ew
ne'phri'tis
ne plus ul'tra
nep'o'tism
nep'o'tist
nep'tu'ni'um
nerve
nerved

nerve'less
nerve-rack'ing
nerve-wrack'ing
nerv'ing
nerv'ous
ner'vous'ly
nerv'ous'ness
nervy
nerv'i'ness
nes'tle
nes'tled
nest'ling
net
neth'er
neth'er'most
neth'er world
net'ted
net'ting
net'tle
net'tled
net'tle'some
net'tling
net'work
neu'ral
neu'ral'gia
neu'ras'the'nia
neu'riti'c
neu'ri'tis
neu'ro'log'i'cal
neu'rol'o'gist
neu'rol'o'gy
neu'ron
neu'rone
neu'ro'ses
neu'ro'sis
neu'rot'ic
neu'rot'i'cal'ly
neu'ter
neu'tral
neu'tral'ism
neu'tral'ist
neu'tral'i'ty
neu'tral'iza'tion
neu'tral'ize
neu'tral'ized
neu'tral'iz'er
neu'tral'iz'ing
neu'tral'ly
neu'tron
nev'er
nev'er'more
nev'er'the'less
new

new'born
new'com'er
new'el
new'fan'gled
new'ish
new'ly
new'ly'wed
new'ness
news
news'cast'er
news'let'ter
news'pa'per
news'pa'per'man
news'print
news'reel
news'room
news'stand
news'wor'thy
newsy
newt
next
nex'us
ni'a'cin
nib'ble
nib'bled
nib'bling
nice
nice'ly
nice'ness
ni'ce'ties
ni'ce'ty
niche
nick
nick'el
nick'el'o'de'on
nick'name
nick'named
nick'nam'ing
nic'o'tine
nic'o'tin'ic
nic'tate
nic'ti'tate
niece
nif'ti'est
nif'ty
nig'gard
nig'gard'li'ness
nig'gard'ly
nig'gle
nig'gled
nig'gling
nigh
night

night'cap
night'clothes
night'club
night'dress
night'fall
night'gown
night'ie
night'in'gale
night'life
night'ly
night'mare
night'mar'ish
night'shade
night'shirt
night'time
ni'hil'ism
ni'hil'ist
ni'hil'is'tic
nil
nim'ble
nim'ble'ness
nim'bly
nim'bus
nin'com'poop
nine
nine'teen
nine'teenth
nine'ties
nine'ti'eth
nine'ty
nin'nies
nin'ny
ninth
ni'o'bi'um
nip
nipped
nip'per
nip'ping
nip'ple
nip'py
nir'va'na
nisi
nit
nit-pick
nit-pick'ing
ni'trate
ni'tra'tion
ni'tric
ni'tro'gen
ni'trog'e'nous
ni'tro'glyc'er'in
ni'tro'glyc'er'ine
ni'trous

nit'ty-grit'ty
nit'wit
no
no'bel'i'um
no'bil'i'ty
no'ble
no'ble'man
no'ble'ness
no'bler
no'blesse oblige
no'blest
no'ble'wom'an
no'bly
no'bod'ies
no'body
noc'tur'nal
noc'turne
nod
nod'al
nod'ded
nod'ding
node
nod'u'lar
nod'ule
no'el
noes
nog'gin
noise
noised
noise'less
noise'less'ly
nois'i'er
nois'i'est
nois'i'ly
nois'i'ness
nois'ing
noi'some
noisy
no'mad
no'mad'ic
no'mad'i'cal'ly
no'mad'ism
nom de guerre
nom de plume
no'men'cla'ture
nom'i'nal
nom'i'nal'ly
nom'i'nate
nom'i'nat'ed
nom'i'nat'ing
nom'i'na'tion
nom'i'na'tive
nom'i'nee

noms de guerre
noms de plume
non'age
no'na'gen'ar'i'an
non'ag'gres'sion
non'al'co'hol'ic
non'aligned
non'align'ment
nonce
non'cha'lance
non'cha'lant
non'cha'lant'ly
non-com
non'com'bat'ant
non'com'mis'sioned
non'com'mit'tal
non'com'mit'tal'ly
non com'pos men'tis
non'con'duc'tor
non'con'form'ist
non'con'form'i'ty
non'con'trib'u'to'ry
non'co'op'er'a'tion
non'de'script
none
non'en'ti'ties
non'en'ti'ty
non'es'sen'tial
none'such
none'the'less
non'event
non'ex'is'tence
non'ex'is'tent
non'fic'tion
non'flam'ma'ble
non'hu'man
non'in'ter'ven'tion
non'iron
non'mem'ber
non'met'al
non'me'tal'lic
non-nu'cle'ar
non'pa'reil
non'par'ti'san
non'pay'ment
non'plus
non'plussed
non'plus'sing
non'prof'it
non'pro'lif'er'a'tion
non'res'i'dence
non'res'i'den'cy
non'res'i'dent

non're'sis'tance
non're'stric'tive
non'sched'uled
non'sec'tar'i'an
non'sense
non'sen'si'cal
non'sen'si'cal'ly
non se'qui'tur
non'shrink
non'smok'er
non'smok'ing
non'stan'dard
non'start'er
non'stick
non'stop
non'sup'port
non'un'ion
non'ver'bal
non'vi'o'lence
non'vi'o'lent
non'vi'o'lent'ly
noo'dle
nook
noon
noon'day
noon'time
noose
nor
nor'mal
nor'mal'cy
nor'mal'i'ty
nor'mal'i'za'tion
nor'mal'ize
nor'mal'ized
nor'mal'iz'ing
nor'mal'ly
nor'ma'tive
north'bound
north'east
north'east'er
north'east'er'ly
north'east'ern
north'east'ward
north'er'li'ness
nor'ther'ly
north'ern
north'ern'er
north'ern'most
north'ward
north'ward'ly
north'wards
north'west
north'west'er'ly

north'west'ern
north'west'ward
Nor'we'gian
nose
nose'bleed
nosed
nose dive
nose'gay
nos'ey
nosh
nos'i'er
nos'i'est
nos'i'ly
nos'i'ness
nos'ing
nos'tal'gia
nos'tal'gic
nos'tal'gi'cal'ly
nos'tril
nos'trum
nosy
not
no'ta be'ne
no'ta'bil'i'ties
no'ta'bil'i'ty
no'ta'ble
no'ta'ble'ness
no'ta'bly
no'ta'ries
no'ta'ri'za'tion
no'ta'rize
no'ta'rized
no'ta'riz'ing
no'ta'ry
no'ta'ry pu'blic
no'ta'tion
no'ta'tion'al
notch
notched
note
note'book
not'ed
not'ed'ly
note'pad
note'pa'per
note'wor'thi'ness
note'wor'thy
noth'ing
noth'ing'ness
no'tice
no'tice'a'ble
no'tice'a'bly
no'ticed

no'tic'ing
no'ti'fi'able
no'ti'fi'ca'tion
no'ti'fied
no'ti'fy
no'ti'fy'ing
not'ing
no'tion
no'tion'al
no'to'ri'e'ty
no'to'ri'ous
no'to'ri'ous'ly
no'to'ri'ous'ness
not'with'stand'ing
nou'gat
nought
noun
nour'ish
nour'ish'ing
nour'ish'ment
nou'veau riche
nou'veaux riches
no'va
nov'el
nov'el'ette
nov'el'ist
nov'el'is'tic
nov'el'ties
nov'el'ty
no've'na
nov'ice
no'vi'ti'ate
now
now'a'days
no'where
no'wise
nox'ious
noz'zle
nth
nu'ance
nub
nub'bin
nu'bile
nu'cle'ar
nu'cle'ate
nu'clei
nu'cle'on
nu'cle'onics
nu'cle'us
nude
nude'ness
nudge
nudged

nudg'ing
nud'ism
nud'ist
nu'di'ty
nu'ga'to'ry
nug'get
nui'sance
nuke
nuked
nuk'ing
null
nul'li'fi'ca'tion
nul'li'fied
nul'li'fier
nul'li'fy
nul'li'fy'ing
nul'li'ty
numb
num'ber
num'ber'less
numb'ly
numb'ness
numb'skull
nu'mer'a'ble
num'er'ab'ly
nu'mer'a'cy
nu'mer'al
nu'mer'ate
nu'mer'at'ed
nu'mer'at'ing
nu'mer'a'tion
nu'mer'a'tor
nu'mer'i'cal
nu'mer'i'cal'ly
numerol'ogy
nu'mer'ous
nu'mis'mat'ic
nu'mis'ma'tist
nun
nun'cio
nun'ner'ies
nun'nery
nup'tial
nup'tial'ly
nurse
nursed
nurse'maid
nurs'er'ies
nurs'ery
nurs'ing
nur'ture
nur'tured
nur'tur'ing

119

nut
nut'crack'er
nut'hatch
nut'meg
nu'tri'ent
nu'tri'ment
nu'tri'tion
nu'tri'tion'al
nu'tri'tion'al'ly
nu'tri'tion'ist
nu'tri'tious
nu'tri'tive
nut'shell
nut'ti'er
nut'ti'est
nut'ty
nuz'zle
nuz'zled
nuz'zling
ny'lon
nymph
nym'pho'ma'nia
nym'pho'ma'ni'ac
oaf
oaf'ish
oak
oak'en
oa'kum
oar
oar'lock
oars'man
oases
oa'sis
oat
oath
oat'meal
ob'bli'ga'to
ob'du'ra'cy
ob'du'rate
ob'du'rate'ly
ob'du'rate'ness
obe'di'ence
obe'di'ent
obe'di'ent'ly
obei'sance
obei'sant
ob'e'lisk
obese
obese'ness
obes'i'ty
obey
ob'fus'cate
ob'fus'ca'ted

ob'fus'ca'ting
ob'fus'ca'tion
obi
obit'u'ar'ies
obit'u'ary
ob'ject
ob'jec'tion
ob'jec'tion'able
ob'jec'tion'ably
ob'jec'tive
ob'jec'tive'ly
ob'jec'tive'ness
ob'jec'tiv'i'ty
ob'ject'less
ob'ject'or
ob'jet d'art
ob'jur'gate
ob'jur'gat'ed
ob'jur'gat'ing
ob'jur'ga'tion
ob'jur'ga'to'ry
obligato
ob'late
ob'la'tion
ob'li'gate
ob'li'gat'ed
ob'li'gat'ing
ob'li'ga'tion
ob'lig'a'to'ry
oblige
obliged
oblig'ing
oblig'ing'ly
ob'lique
ob'lique'ly
ob'liq'ui'ty
ob'lit'er'ate
ob'lit'er'at'ed
ob'lit'er'at'ing
ob'lit'er'a'tion
ob'lit'er'a'tive
ob'liv'i'on
ob'liv'i'ous
ob'long
ob'lo'quy
ob'nox'ious
ob'nox'ious'ly
oboe
obo'ist
ob'scene
ob'scene'ly
ob'scene'ness
ob'scen'i'ties

ob'scen'i'ty
ob'scu'ran'tism
ob'scu'ran'tist
ob'scure
ob'scured
ob'scure'ness
ob'scur'ing
ob'scu'ri'ty
ob'se'qui'ous
ob'se'qui'ous'ly
ob'se'qui'ous'ness
ob'se'quy
ob'serv'a'ble
ob'serv'a'bly
ob'ser'vance
ob'ser'vant
ob'ser'va'tion
ob'ser'va'tion'al
ob'ser'va'to'ries
ob'ser'va'to'ry
ob'serve
ob'served
ob'serv'er
ob'serv'ing
ob'sess
ob'ses'sion
ob'ses'sion'al
ob'ses'sion'al'ly
ob'ses'sive
ob'ses'sive'ly
ob'sid'i'an
ob'so'les'cence
ob'so'les'cent
ob'so'lete
ob'so'lete'ness
ob'sta'cle
ob'stet'ric
ob'stet'ri'cal
ob'ste'tri'cian
ob'stet'rics
ob'sti'na'cy
ob'sti'nate
ob'sti'nate'ly
ob'sti'nate'ness
ob'strep'er'ous
ob'strep'er'ous'ness
ob'struct
ob'struc'tion
ob'struc'tion'ism
ob'struc'tion'ist
ob'struc'tive
ob'struc'tive'ness
ob'struc'tor

ob'tain
ob'tain'a'ble
ob'tain'ment
ob'trude
ob'trud'ed
ob'trud'ing
ob'tru'sion
ob'tru'sive
ob'tru'sive'ly
ob'tuse
ob'tuse'ness
ob'verse
ob'verse'ly
ob'vert
ob'vi'ate
ob'vi'at'ed
ob'vi'at'ing
ob'vi'a'tion
ob'vi'ous
ob'vi'ous'ly
ob'vi'ous'ness
ob'vo'lute
oc'a'ri'na
oc'ca'sion
oc'ca'sion'al
oc'ca'sion'al'ly
oc'ci'dent
oc'ci'den'tal
oc'clude
oc'clud'ed
oc'clud'ing
oc'clu'sion
oc'clu'sive
oc'cult
oc'cult'ism
oc'cult'ist
oc'cu'pan'cy
oc'cu'pant
oc'cu'pa'tion
oc'cu'pa'tion'al
oc'cu'pa'tion'al'ly
oc'cu'pied
oc'cu'pi'er
oc'cu'py
oc'cu'py'ing
oc'cur
oc'curred
oc'cur'rence
oc'cur'rent
oc'cur'ring
ocean
oce'an'ic
oce'a'no'graph'i'cal

oce'a'nog'ra'pher
oce'a'no'graph'ic
oce'a'nog'ra'phy
oce'lot
ochre
ochry
o'clock
oc'ta'gon
oc'tag'o'nal
oc'tag'o'nal'ly
oc'ta'he'dra
oc'ta'he'dral
oc'ta'he'dron
oc'tane
oc'tave
oc'ta'vo
oc'tet
oc'to'ge'nar'i'an
oc'to'pus
oc'to'roon
oc'u'lar
oc'u'list
odd
odd'ball
odd'i'ties
odd'i'ty
odd'ment
odd'ness
ode
odi'ous
odi'ous'ness
odi'um
odom'e'ter
odor'if'er'ous
odor'ous
odour
odoor'less
od'ys'sey
of
off
of'fal
off beat
off'col'our
of'fence
of'fence'less
of'fend
of'fend'er
of'fen'sive
of'fen'sive'ly
of'fer
of'fer'er
of'fer'ing
of'fer'to'ri'al

of'fer'to'ries
of'fer'to'ry
off'hand
off'hand'ed'ness
of'fice
of'fice'hold'er
of'fic'er
of'fi'cial
of'fi'cial'dom
of'fi'cial'ly
of'fi'ci'ate
of'fi'ci'at'ed
of'fi'ci'at'ing
of'fi'ci'a'tion
of'fi'ci'a'tor
of'fi'cious
of'fi'cious'ly
off'ing
off'load
off'set
off'set'ting
off'shoot
off'shore
off'side
off'spring
off'stage
off-the-record
of'ten
of'ten'times
ogle
ogled
ogler
ogling
ogre
ogre'ish
ohm
ohm'age
ohm'ic
ohm'me'ter
oil
oil'cloth
oil'field
oil'i'er
oil'i'est
oil'i'ness
oil'man
oil'skin
oily
oint'ment
okra
old
old'en
old'er

old'est
old-fash'ioned
old'ish
old'ness
old'ster
old-tim'er
old-world
ole'ag'i'nous
ole'an'der
oleo'mar'ga'rine
ol'fac'tion
ol'fac'to'ry
ol'i'garch
ol'i'gar'chic
oli'gar'chi'cal
oli'gar'chies
ol'i'gar'chy
ol'i'gop'o'ly
ol'ive
oliv'en'ite
oma'sum
om'buds'man
ome'ga
om'elette
omen
om'i'nous
om'i'nous'ly
omis'sion
omit
omit'ted
omit'ting
om'ni'bus
om'nip'o'tence
om'nip'o'tent
om'nip'o'tent'ly
om'ni'pres'ence
om'ni'pres'ent
om'nis'cience
om'nis'cient
om'niv'or'ous
once
on'com'ing
one
one-piece
on'er'ous
one'self
one-sid'ed
one-up'man'ship
one-way
on'go'ing
on'ion
on'iony
on'look'er

on'ly
on'o'mat'o'poe'ia
on'o'mat'o'poe'ic
on'rush'ing
on'set
on'shore
on'slaught
on'to
on'tol'ogy
onus
on'ward
on'yx
oo'dles
oomph
ooze
oozed
oo'zi'ness
ooz'ing
oo'zy
opac'i'ty
opal
opal'es'cence
opal'es'cent
opaque
opaque'ly
open
open'er
open-hand'ed
open-hand'ed'ness
open house
open'ing
open'ly
open-mind'ed
open-mind'ed'ness
open-mouthed
open'ness
open ses'a'me
open'work
opera
op'er'a'bil'i'ty
op'er'a'ble
op'er'a'bly
op'er'ate
op'er'at'ed
op'er'at'ic
op'er'at'ing
op'er'a'tion
op'er'a'tion'al
op'er'a'tive
op'er'a'tor
op'er'et'ta
oph'thal'mic
oph'thal'mol'o'gist

oph'thal'mol'o'gy
opi'ate
opine
opined
opin'ion
opin'ion'at'ed
opi'um
opos'sum
op'po'nent
op'por'tune
op'por'tune'ly
op'por'tun'ism
op'por'tun'ist
op'por'tun'is'tic
op'por'tu'ni'ties
op'por'tu'ni'ty
op'pos'able
op'pose
op'posed
op'pos'er
op'pos'ing
op'po'site
op'po'site'ness
op'po'si'tion
op'press
op'pres'sion
op'pres'sive
op'pres'sive'ly
op'pres'sor
op'pro'bri'ous
op'pro'bri'um
op'pugn
op'tic
op'ti'cal
op'ti'cian
op'tics
op'ti'mal
op'ti'mism
op'ti'mist
op'ti'mis'tic
op'ti'mis'ti'cal'ly
op'ti'mi'za'tion
op'ti'mize
op'ti'mized
op'ti'miz'ing
op'ti'mum
op'tion
op'tion'al
op'to'met'ric
op'tom'e'trist
op'tom'e'try
op'u'lence
op'u'lent

op'u'lent'ly
opus
opus'es
or'a'cle
orac'u'lar
oral
oral'ly
or'ange
or'ange'ries
or'ange'ry
orang u'tan
orate
orat'ed
orat'ing
ora'tion
or'a'tor
or'a'tor'i'cal
or'a'to'ries
or'a'to'rio
or'a'to'ry
or'bic'u'lar
or'bit
or'bit'al
or'chard
or'ches'tra
or'ches'tral
or'ches'trate
or'ches'trat'ed
or'ches'trat'ing
or'ches'tra'tion
or'chid
or'dain
or'dain'er
or'dain'ment
or'deal
or'der
or'dered
or'der'lies
or'der'li'ness
or'der'ly
or'di'nal
or'di'nance
or'di'nand
or'di'nar'i'ly
or'di'nar'i'ness
or'di'nary
or'di'na'tion
ord'nance
or'dure
ore
oreg'a'no
or'gan
or'gan'die

or'gan'ic
or'gan'i'cal'ly
or'gan'ism
or'gan'ist
or'gan'iz'a'ble
or'gan'i'za'tion
or'gan'i'za'tion'al
or'gan'ize
or'gan'ized
or'gan'iz'er
or'gan'iz'ing
or'gasm
or'gas'mic
or'gi'as'tic
or'gi'as'ti'cal'ly
or'gies
or'gy
or'iel
ori'ent
Ori'en'tal
ori'en'tate
ori'en'tat'ed
ori'en'tat'ing
ori'en'ta'tion
ori'en'teer'ing
or'i'fice
ori'ga'mi
or'i'gin
orig'i'nal
orig'i'nal'i'ty
orig'i'nal'ly
orig'i'nate
orig'i'nat'ed
orig'i'nat'ing
orig'i'na'tion
orig'i'na'tive
orig'i'na'tor
ori'ole
or'i'son
or'mo'lu
or'na'ment
or'na'men'tal
or'na'men'ta'tion
or'nate
or'nate'ly
or'nate'ness
or'nith'ic
or'ni'tho'log'ic
or'ni'tho'log'i'cal
or'ni'thol'o'gist
or'ni'thol'o'gy
oro'tund
oro'tun'di'ty

or'phan
or'phan'age
or'tho'don'tic
or'tho'don'tics
or'tho'don'tist
or'tho'dox
or'tho'dox'ies
or'tho'dox'ly
or'tho'dox'ness
or'tho'doxy
or'thog'o'nal
or'tho'graph'ic
or'thog'ra'phy
or'tho'pae'dic
or'tho'pae'dics
or'tho'pae'dist
or'to'lan
os'cil'late
os'cil'lat'ed
os'cil'lat'ing
os'cil'la'tion
os'cil'la'tor
os'cil'la'to'ry
os'cil'lo'scope
os'cu'late
os'cu'la'tion
osier
os'mi'um
os'mo'sis
os'mot'ic
os'prey
os'si'fi'ca'tion
os'si'fied
os'si'fy
os'si'fy'ing
os'ten'si'ble
os'ten'si'bly
os'ten'sive
os'ten'sive'ly
os'ten'ta'tion
os'ten'ta'tious
os'ten'ta'tious'ly
os'te'o'path
os'te'o'path'ic
os'te'op'a'thy
os'te'o'po'ro'sis
os'tra'cism
os'tra'cize
os'tra'cized
os'tra'ciz'ing
os'trich
oth'er
oth'er'ness

oth'er'wise
oti'ose
ot'ter
ouch
ought
ounce
our
ours
our'selves
ou'sel
oust
oust'er
out
out'bid
out'bid'ded
out'bid'ding
out'board
out'bound
out'brave
out'break
out'build'ing
out'burst
out'cast
out'class
out'come
out'cries
out'cry
out'dat'ed
out'did
out'dis'tance
out'dis'tanced
out'dis'tanc'ing
out'do
out'do'ing
out'done
out'door
out'doors
out'er
out'er'most
out'er space
out'face
out'field
out'field'er
out'fit
out'fit'ter
out'flank
out'flow
out'fox
out'go'ing
out'grew
out'grow
out'grow'ing
out'grown

out'growth
out'house
out'ing
out'land'ish
out'last
out'law
out'lay
out'let
out'line
out'lined
out'lin'ing
out'live
out'lived
out'liv'ing
out'look
out'ly'ing
out'ma'noeu'vre
out'mod'ed
out'num'ber
out-of-date
out-of-the-way
out'pa'tient
out'post
out'pour'ing
out'put
out'put'ting
out'rage
out'raged
out'ra'geous
out'ra'geous'ly
out'rag'ing
out'ran
out'range
out'rank
ou'tré
out'rid'er
out'rig'ger
out'right
out'run
out'run'ning
out'sell
out'sel'ling
out'set
out'shine
out'shin'ing
out'shone
out'side
out'sid'er
out'size
out'skirts
out'smart
out'sold
out'spo'ken

out'spok'en'ness
out'spread
out'stand'ing
out'stand'ing'ly
out'stay
out'strip
out'stripped
out'strip'ping
out'vote
out'vot'ed
out'vot'ing
out'ward
out'ward'ly
out'wards
out'wear
out'weigh
out'wit
out'wit'ted
out'wit'ting
out'worn
ou'zel
ou'zo
ova
oval
oval'ness
ovar'i'an
ova'ries
ova'ry
ovate
ova'tion
ov'en
oven'proof
over
over'act
over'ac'tive
over'age
over'all
over'anx'ious
over'anx'ious'ly
over'ate
over'awe
over'bal'ance
over'bal'anced
over'bal'ancing
over'bear'ing
over'board
over'came
over'cast
over'charge
over'charged
over'charg'ing
over'coat
over'come

over'com'ing
over'com'pen'sa'tion
over'con'fi'dence
over'crowd'ed
over'crowd'ing
over'do
over'does
over'do'ing
over'done
over'dose
over'draft
over'drawn
over'dressed
over'drive
over'due
over'eat
over'eat'en
over'eat'ing
over'em'pha'sis
over'em'pha'size
over'em'pha'sized
over'es'ti'mate
over'es'ti'mat'ed
over'es'ti'mat'ing
over'ex'ert
over'ex'er'tion
over'flow
over'flowing
over'gen'er'ous
over'grown
over'growth
over'hand
over'hang
over'hang'ing
over'haul
over'haul'ing
over'head
over'hear
over'heard
over'hear'ing
over'heat
over'hung
over'in'dul'gence
over'joyed
over'kill
over'laid
over'lain
over'land
over'lap
over'lapped
over'lap'ping
over'lay
over'lay'ing

over'leaf	over'state	ox'ford	pad'dy
over'load	over'stat'ed	ox'i'da'tion	pad'lock
over'look	over'state'ment	ox'ide	pa'dre
over'lord	over'stat'ing	ox'i'dize	pae'an
over'ly	over'step	ox'i'dized	pae'di'at'ric
over'manned	over'stepped	ox'i'diz'ing	pae'di'at'ri'cian
over'man'ning	over'stepping	ox'tail	pae'di'at'rics
over'much	overt	oxy'a'cet'y'lene	pae'dol'o'gy
over'night	over'take	ox'y'gen	pa'el'la
over'night	over'tak'en	ox'y'gen'ate	pa'gan
over'paid	over'tak'ing	ox'y'gen'at'ed	pa'gan'ism
over'pass	over'tax	ox'y'gen'at'ing	page
over'play	over-the-coun'ter	ox'y'gen'a'tion	pag'eant
over'pop'u'lat'ed	over'threw	oxy'mo'ron	pag'eant'ry
over'pop'u'la'tion	over'throw	oyez	page'boy
over'pow'er	over'throw'ing	oys'ter	paged
over'priced	over'thrown	oy'ster'catch'er	pag'i'nate
over'ran	over'time	ozone	pag'i'na'tion
over'rate	overt'ly	pab'u'lum	pag'ing
over'rat'ed	over'tone	pace	pa'go'da
over'rat'ing	over'took	paced	paid
over'reach	over'ture	pace'mak'er	pail
over're'act	over'turn	pac'er	pail'ful
over'rid'den	over'val'ue	pace'setter	pain
over'ride	over'val'ued	pachy'derm	pain'ful
over'rid'ing	over'val'uing	pachy'der'ma'tous	pain'ful'ly
over'rode	over'view	pachy'teñe	pain'kill'er
over'rule	over'ween'ing	pa'cif'ic	pain'less
over'run	over'weight	pa'cif'i'ca'tion	pain'less'ly
over'run'ning	over'whelm	pa'cif'i'ca'to'ry	pains'tak'ing
over'saw	over'whelm'ing'ly	pac'i'fied	pains'tak'ing'ly
over'sea	over'work	pac'i'fi'er	paint
over'seas	over'worked	pac'i'fist	paint'er
over'see'ing	over'work'ing	pac'i'fy	paint'ing
over'seen	over'wrought	pac'i'fy'ing	paint'work
over'seer	ovip'a'rous	pac'ing	pair
over'sell	ovi'pos'i'tor	pack'age	pais'ley
over'sell'ing	ovoid	pack'aged	Pa'ki'stani
over'sexed	ovu'late	pack'ag'er	pal
over'shad'ow	ovu'lat'ed	pack'ag'ing	pal'ace
over'shoe	ovu'lat'ing	pack'er	Pa'laeo'cene
over'shoot	ovu'la'tion	pack'et	pa'lae'og'ra'phy
overs'hoot'ing	ovum	pack'ing	pa'lae'o'lith
over'shot	owe	pack'sad'dle	Pa'laeo'lith'ic
over'sight	owed	pact	pa'lae'on'tol'ogy
over'sim'pli'fied	ow'ing	pad	pa'lae'on'tol'o'gist
over'sim'pli'fy	owl	pad'ded	Pa'lae'o'zo'ic
over'sim'pli'fy'ing	owl'ish	pad'dies	pa'lan'quin
over'size	owl'ish'ly	pad'ding	pal'at'a'bil'i'ty
over'sleep	own'er	pad'dle	pal'at'a'ble
over'sleep'ing	own'er'ship	pad'dled	pal'at'a'bly
over'slept	ox	pad'dling	pal'ate
over'sold	ox'en	pad'dock	pa'la'tial

pa'la'tial'ly
pal'a'tine
pa'lav'er
pale
paled
pale'ly
pale'ness
Pal'es'tin'ian
pal'ette
pal'i'mo'ny
pal'in'drome
pal'ing
pal'ing
pal'i'sade
pal'i'sad'ed
pal'i'sad'ing
pall
pal'la'di'um
pall'bear'er
palled
pal'let
pal'li'asse
pal'li'ate
pal'li'at'ed
pal'li'at'ing
pal'li'a'tion
pal'lia'tive
pal'lid
pal'ling
pal'lor
palm
pal'mate
pal'met'to
palm'ist
palm'is'try
pal'o'mi'no
pal'pa'bil'i'ty
pal'pa'ble
pal'pa'bly
pal'pate
pal'pat'ed
pal'pat'ing
pal'pa'tion
pal'pi'tate
pal'pi'tat'ed
pal'pi'tat'ing
pal'pi'ta'tion
pal'sied
pal'sy
pal'tri'ness
pal'try
pam'pas
pam'per

pam'phlet
pam'phle'teer
pan
pan'a'ce'a
pa'nache
Pan'a'ma'ni'an
pan'a'tela
pan'cake
pan'chro'mat'ic
pan'cre'as
pan'cre'at'ic
pan'da
pan'dem'ic
pan'de'mo'ni'um
pan'der
pan'der'er
pane
pan'e'gy'ric
pan'el
pan'el'led
pan'el'ling
pan'el'list
pang
pan'han'dled
pan'han'dler
pan'han'dling
pan'ic
pan'icked
pan'ick'ing
pan'icky
pan'ic-strick'en
panned
pan'nier
pan'ning
pan'o'ply
pan'o'rama
pan'o'ram'ic
pan'o'ram'i'cal'ly
pan'pipe
pan'sies
pan'sy
pan'ta'loon
pan'the'ism
pan'the'ist
pan'the'is'tic
pan'the'on
pan'ther
pan'ties
pant'ile
pan'to'mime
pan'to'mimed
pan'to'mim'ic
pan'to'mim'ing

pan'to'mim'ist
pan'tries
pan'try
pan'ty
pant'y'hose
pan'zer
pap
pa'pa
pa'pa'cy
pa'pal
pa'paw
pa'pa'ya
pa'per
pa'per'back
pa'per'er
pa'per knife
pa'per knives
pa'per'weight
pa'per'work
pa'pery
pa'pier-mâ'ché
pa'pil'la
pa'poose
pap'ri'ka
pa'py'ri
pa'py'rus
par
par'a'ble
pa'rab'o'la
para'bo'lic
par'a'chute
par'a'chut'ed
par'a'chut'ing
par'a'chut'ist
pa'rade
pa'rad'ed
par'a'digm
pa'rad'ing
par'a'dise
par'a'di'si'a'cal
par'a'dox
par'a'dox'i'cal
para'dox'i'cal'ly
par'af'fin
par'a'gon
par'a'graph
par'a'keet
par'al'lac'tic
par'al'lax
par'al'lel
par'al'leled
par'al'lel'ing
par'al'lel'o'gram

pa'ral'y'sis
par'a'lyt'ic
par'a'ly'sa'tion
par'a'lyse
par'a'lysed
par'a'lys'ing
par'a'med'ic
pa'ram'e'ter
para'mil'i'tary
par'a'mount
par'a'mour
par'a'noia
para'noi'ac
par'a'noid
para'nor'mal
par'a'pet
par'a'pher'nal'ia
par'a'phrase
par'a'phrased
par'a'phras'ing
par'a'ple'gia
par'a'ple'gic
par'a'psy'chol'o'gy
par'a'site
par'a'sit'ic
par'a'sit'i'cal
par'a'sit'i'cal'ly
par'a'sit'ism
par'a'sol
para'troop'er
para'troops
par avion
par'boil
par'cel
par'celled
par'cel'ling
parch
parch'ment
par'don
par'don'able
par'don'ably
par'doned
par'don'ing
pare
pared
par'e'gor'ic
par'ent
par'ent'age
pa'ren'tal
pa'ren'the'ses
pa'ren'the'sis
par'en'thet'ic
par'en'thet'i'cal

par'en'thet'i'cal'ly
par'ent'hood
pa're'sis
par ex'cel'lence
par'fait
pa'ri'ah
par'i-mu'tu'el
par'ing
par'ish
pa'rish'ion'er
par'i'ty
park
par'ka
par'lance
par'lay
par'layed
par'lay'ing
par'ley
par'leyed
par'ley'ing
par'lia'ment
par'lia'men'tar'i'an
par'lia'men'ta'ry
par'lour
par'lous
pa'ro'chi'al
pa'ro'chi'al'ism
par'o'died
par'o'dist
par'o'dy
par'o'dy'ing
pa'role
pa'roled
pa'rol'ee
pa'rol'ing
pa'rot'id
par'ox'ysm
par'ox'ys'mal
par'quet
par'queted
par'quet'ing
par'quet'ry
par'ra'keet
par'ri'cide
par'ried
par'rot
par'roted
par'rot'ing
par'ry
par'ry'ing
parse
parsed
par'si'mo'ni'ous

par'si'mo'ny
pars'ing
par'sley
pars'nip
par'son
par'son'age
par'take
par'tak'en
par'ta'ker
par'tak'ing
part'ed
par'the'no'gen'e'sis
par'tial
par'ti'al'i'ty
par'tial'ly
par'tic'i'pant
par'tic'i'pate
par'tic'i'pat'ed
par'tic'i'pat'ing
par'tic'i'pa'tion
par'tic'i'pa'tive
par'tic'i'pa'tor
par'tic'i'pa'tory
par'ti'c'i'ple
par'ti'cle
par'ti'col'oured
par'tic'u'lar
par'tic'u'lar'i'ty
par'tic'u'lar'ize
par'tic'u'lar'ly
par'tic'u'late
par'tied
par'ties
part'ing
par'ti'san
par'ti'san'ship
par'tite
par'ti'tion
par'ti'tioned
par'ti'tion'ing
par'ti'tive
part'ly
part'ner
part'ner'ship
par'took
par'tridge
par'tu'ri'ent
par'tu'ri'tion
par'ty
par'ty'ing
par've'nu
pas'chal
pas de deux

pa'sha
pass
pass'a'ble
pass'a'bly
pass'age
pas'sage'way
pas'sé
passed
pas'sen'ger
passe-par'tout
pass'er-by
pas'ser'ine
pas'sim
pass'ing
pas'sion
pas'sion'ate
pas'sion'ate'ly
pas'sion'ate'ness
pas'sion'flow'er
pas'sion fruit
pas'sion'less
pas'sive
pas'siv'i'ty
pass'port
pass'word
past
pas'ta
paste
paste'board
pas'ted
pas'tel
pas'teur'i'za'tion
pas'teur'ize
pas'teur'ized
pas'teur'iz'ing
pas'tiche
past'i'er
past'i'est
pas'tille
pas'time
past'i'ness
pas'ting
past mas'ter
pas'tor
pas'to'ral
pas'tor'ate
pas'tra'mi
pas'tries
pas'try
pas'tur'age
pas'ture
pas'tured
pas'tur'ing

pasty
pat
patch
patch'i'er
patch'i'est
pa'tchou'li
pa'tchou'ly
patch'work
patchy
pate
pâ'té
pâ'té de foie gras
pa'tel'la
pa'tel'lae
pa'ten'cy
pat'ent
pat'ent'ee
pat'ent'ly
pa'ter'fa'mil'i'as
pat'er'nal
pa'ter'nal'ism
pa'ter'nal'ist
pa'ter'nal'is'tic
pa'ter'ni'ty
pa'ter'noster
pa'thet'ic
pa'thet'i'cal'ly
patho'gen'ic
path'o'log'ic
path'o'log'i'cal
pa'tho'log'i'cal'ly
pa'thol'o'gist
pa'thol'o'gy
pa'thos
path'way
pa'tience
pa'tient
pa'tient'ly
pat'i'na
pa'tio
pat'ois
pa'tri'arch
pa'tri'ar'chal
pa'tri'ar'chies
pa'tri'ar'chy
pa'tri'cian
pat'ri'cide
pat'ri'mo'nies
pat'ri'mo'ny
pa'tri'ot
pa'tri'ot'ic
pa'tri'ot'i'cal'ly
pa'tri'ot'ism

pa'trol
pa'trolled
pa'trol'ler
pa'trol'ling
pa'tron
pa'tron'age
pa'tron'ess
pa'tron'ize
pa'tron'ized
pa'tron'iz'ing
pa'tron'iz'ing'ly
pat'ro'nym'ic
pat'sies
pat'sy
pat'ted
pat'ter
pat'tern
pat'terned
pat'ties
pat'ting
pat'ty
pau'ci'ty
paunch
paunch'i'er
paunch'i'est
paunch'i'ness
paunchy
pau'per
pau'per'ism
pau'per'ize
pause
paused
paus'ing
pave
paved
pave'ment
pa'vil'ion
pav'ing
paw
pawn
pawn'bro'ker
pay
pay'able
pay'ee
pay'er
pay'ing
pay'load
pay'mas'ter
pay'ment
pay'off
pay'o'la
pay'roll
pea

peace
peace'able
peace'ably
peace corps
peace'ful
peace'ful'ly
peace'keep'ing
peace'mak'er
peach
peach'i'er
peach'i'est
peachy
pea'cock
pea'fowl
pea'hen
peak
peak'ed
peal
pea'nut
pear
pearl
pearly
peas'ant
peas'ant'ry
pea'shoot'er
peat
peaty
peb'ble
peb'bled
peb'bli'er
peb'bli'est
peb'bling
peb'bly
pe'can
pec'ca'dil'lo
pec'ca'dil'loes
pec'ca'ries
pec'ca'ry
peck
pec'tin
pec'to'ral
pec'u'late
pec'u'la'tion
pe'cu'liar
pe'cu'li'ar'i'ties
pe'cu'li'ar'i'ty
pe'cu'liar'ly
pe'cu'ni'ary
ped'a'gog'ic
ped'a'gog'i'cal
ped'a'gog'i'cal'ly
ped'a'gogue
ped'a'go'gy

ped'al
ped'alled
ped'al'ling
ped'ant
pe'dan'tic
pe'dan'ti'cal'ly
ped'ant'ry
ped'dle
ped'dled
ped'dler
ped'dling
ped'er'ast
ped'es'tal
ped'i'cure
ped'i'cur'ist
ped'i'gree
ped'i'greed
ped'i'ment
pe'dom'e'ter
peek
peek'a'boo
peel
peel'ing
peep
peep'hole
peer
peer'age
peer'ess
peer'less
peeve
peeved
peev'ing
peev'ish
peev'ish'ly
pee'wit
peg
pegged
peg'ging
pei'gnoir
pe'jo'ra'tive
pe'koe
pel'age
pe'lag'ic
pelf
pel'i'can
pel'la'gra
pel'let
pell-mell
pel'lu'cid
pe'lo'ta
pel'vic
pel'vis
pem'mi'can

pen
pe'nal
pe'nal'i'za'tion
pe'nal'ize
pe'nal'ized
pe'nal'iz'ing
pen'al'ties
pen'al'ty
pen'ance
pence
pen'chant
pen'cil
pen'cilled
pen'cil'ling
pend'ant
pend'en'cy
pend'ent
pend'ent'ly
pend'ing
pen'du'lous
pen'du'lum
pen'e'tra'bil'i'ty
pen'e'tra'ble
pen'e'tra'bly
pen'e'trate
pen'e'trat'ed
pen'e'trat'ing
pen'e'tra'tion
pen'e'tra'tive
pen'guin
pen'i'cil'lin
pen'in'su'la
pen'in'su'lar
pe'nis
pen'i'tence
pen'i'tent
pen'i'ten'tial
pen'i'ten'tia'ries
pen'i'ten'tia'ry
pen'i'tent'ly
pen'knife
pen'knives
pen'man'ship
pen'nant
penned
pen'nies
pen'ni'less
pen'ning
pen'ny
pen'ny-an'te
pen'ny-pinch'er
pen'ny'worth
pe'no'log'i'cal

pe'nol'o'gist
pe'nol'o'gy
pen pal
pen'push'er
pen'sion
pen'sion'a'ble
pen'sion'er
pen'sive
pen'sive'ly
pen'sive'ness
pen'ta'cle
pen'ta'gon
pen'tag'o'nal
pen'ta'gram
pen'tam'e'ter
pen'tath'lete
pen'tath'lon
Pen'te'cos'tal
pent'house
pen'tom'ic
pent up
pe'nult
pen'ul'ti'mate
pe'num'bra
pe'nu'ri'ous
pen'u'ry
pe'o'nies
pe'o'ny
peo'ple
peo'pled
peo'pling
pep
pep'lum
pepped
pep'per
pep'per'corn
pep'per'i'ness
pep'per'mint
pep'pery
pep'pi'er
pep'pi'ness
pep'ping
pep'py
pep'sin
pep'tic
per
per'ad'ven'ture
per'am'bu'late
per'am'bu'lat'ed
per'am'bu'lat'ing
per'am'bu'la'tion
per'am'bu'la'to'ry
per an'num

per'cale
per cap'i'ta
per'ceiv'a'ble
per'ceiv'a'bly
per'ceive
per'ceived
per'ceiv'ing
per'cent
per'cent'age
per'cen'tile
per'cept
per'cep'ti'bil'i'ty
per'cep'ti'ble
per'cep'ti'bly
per'cep'tion
per'cep'tive
per'cep'tive'ly
per'cep'tive'ness
per'cep'tu'al
perch
per'chance
per'cip'i'ence
per'cip'i'ent
per'co'late
per'co'lat'ed
per'co'lat'ing
per'co'la'tion
per'co'la'tor
per'cus'sion
per'cus'sive
per di'em
per'di'tion
per'du'ra'ble
per'e'gri'na'tion
per'e'grine
per'emp'to'ri'ly
per'emp'to'ri'ness
per'emp'to'ry
per'en'ni'al
per'en'ni'al'ly
per'e'stroika
per'e'stroi'kan
per'fect
per'fect'er
per'fect'i'bil'i'ity
per'fect'i'ble
per'fec'tion
per'fec'tion'ism
per'fec'tion'ist
per'fec'tive
per'fect'ly
per'fid'i'ous
per'fi'dy

per'fo'rate
per'fo'rat'ed
per'fo'rat'ing
per'fo'ra'tion
per'fo'ra'tor
per'force
per'form
per'form'a'ble
per'for'mance
per'form'er
per'fume
per'fumed
per'fum'ery
per'fum'ing
per'func'to'ri'ly
per'func'to'ri'ness
per'func'to'ry
per'go'la
per'haps
peri'gee
per'il
per'iled
per'il'ing
per'il'ous
per'il'ous'ly
pe'rim'e'ter
per'i'met'ric
per'i'met'ri'cal
peri'na'tal
pe'ri'nea
pe'ri'ne'um
pe'ri'od
pe'ri'od'ic
pe'ri'od'i'cal
pe'ri'od'i'cal'ly
pe'ri'o'dic'i'ty
peri'pa'tet'ic
pe'riph'er'al
periph'er'al'ly
pe'riph'er'ies
pe'riph'ery
pe'riph'ra'sis
peri'scope
peri'scopic
per'ish
per'isha'bil'i'ty
per'isha'ble
per'isha'ble'ness
per'ish'a'bly
peri'stal'sis
peri'stal'tic
peri'style
peri'to'ne'um

per'i'to'ni'tis
peri'wig
per'i'win'kle
per'jure
per'jured
per'jur'er
per'ju'ries
per'jur'ing
per'ju'ri'ous
per'ju'ry
perk
perk'i'er
perk'i'est
perky
perma'frost
per'ma'nence
per'ma'nen'cies
per'ma'nen'cy
per'ma'nent
per'ma'nent'ly
per'man'ga'nate
per'me'a'bil'i'ty
per'me'a'ble
per'me'a'bly
per'me'ate
per'me'at'ed
per'me'at'ing
per'me'a'tion
per'me'a'tive
per'mis'si'bil'i'ty
per'mis'si'ble
per'mis'si'bly
per'mis'sion
per'mis'sive
per'mis'sive'ness
per'mit
per'mit'ted
per'mit'ting
per'mu'ta'tion
per'mute
per'ni'cious
per'nick'e'ty
per'o'rate
per'o'ra'tion
per'ox'ide
per'pen'dic'u'lar
per'pe'trate
per'pe'trat'ed
per'pe'trat'ing
per'pe'tra'tion
per'pe'tra'tor
per'pet'u'al
per'pet'u'al'ly

per'pet'u'ate
per'pet'u'at'ed
per'pet'u'at'ing
per'pet'u'a'tion
per'pet'u'a'tor
per'pe'tu'i'ty
per'plex
per'plexed
per'plex'ing
per'plex'i'ties
per'plex'i'ty
per'qui'site
per'ron
per'ry
per'salt
perse
per se
per'se'cute
per'se'cut'ed
per'se'cut'ing
per'se'cu'tion
per'se'cu'tive
per'se'cu'tor
per'se'ver'ance
per'se'vere
per'se'vered
per'se'ver'ing
Per'sian
per'si'flage
per'sim'mon
per'sist
per'sist'ence
per'sis'ten'cy
per'sist'ent
per'sis'tent'ly
per'son
per'so'na
per'son'able
per'so'nae
per'son'age
per'so'na gra'ta
per'son'al
per'son'al'i'ties
per'son'al'i'ty
per'son'al'iza'tion
per'son'al'ize
per'son'al'ized
per'son'al'iz'ing
per'son'al'ly
per'so'na non gra'ta
per'son'ate
per'son'at'ed
per'son'at'ing

per'son'a'tion
per'son'a'tor
per'son'i'fi'ca'tion
per'son'i'fied
per'son'i'fy
per'son'i'fy'ing
per'son'nel
per'spec'tive
per'spi'ca'cious
per'spi'cac'i'ty
per'spi'cu'i'ty
per'spic'u'ous
per'spi'ra'tion
per'spire
per'spired
per'spir'ing
per'suad'a'ble
per'suade
per'suad'ed
per'suad'ing
per'sua'sion
per'sua'sive
per'sua'sive'ly
pert
per'tain
per'ti'na'cious
per'ti'nac'i'ty
per'ti'nence
per'ti'nent
per'ti'nent'ly
pert'ly
pert'ness
per'turb
per'turb'a'ble
per'tur'ba'tion
pe'ruke
pe'rus'al
pe'ruse
pe'rused
pe'rus'ing
Pe'ru'vi'an
per'vade
per'vad'ed
per'vad'er
per'vad'ing
per'va'sion
per'va'sive
per'verse
per'verse'ly
per'verse'ness
per'ver'sion
per'ver'si'ty
per'vert

per'vert'ed
per'vi'ous
pe'se'ta
pesk'i'er
pesk'i'est
pesk'i'ness
pes'ky
pe'so
pes'sa'ries
pes'sa'ry
pes'si'mism
pes'si'mist
pes'si'mis'tic
pes'si'mis'ti'cal'ly
pes'ter
pest'i'cide
pes'tif'er'ous
pes'ti'lence
pes'ti'lent
pes'ti'len'tial
pes'tle
pet
pet'al
pet'al'ine
pet'alled
pet'al-like
pe'tard
pe'ter
pet'i'ole
pe'tit bour'geois
pe'tite
pe'tite bour'geoi'sie
pe'tite'ness
pe'tit four
pe'ti'tion
pe'ti'tion'ary
pe'ti'tioned
pe'ti'tion'er
pe'ti'tion'ing
pe'tit lar'ce'ny
pe'tits fours
pet'rel
pet'ri'fac'tion
pet'ri'fi'ca'tion
pet'ri'fied
pet'ri'fy
pet'ri'fy'ing
pet'ro'chem'i'cal
pe'tro'chem'is'try
pe'trog'ra'phy
pet'rol
pet'ro'la'tum
pe'tro'le'um

pe'trol'o'gy
pet'ted
pet'ti'coat
pet'ti'er
pet'ti'est
pet'ti'fog
pet'ti'fogged
pet'ti'fog'ging
pet'ti'ly
pet'ting
pet'tish
pet'tish'ness
pet'ty
pet'u'lance
pet'u'lan'cy
pet'u'lant
pet'u'lant'ly
pe'tu'nia
pew
pe'wit
pew'ter
pe'yo'te
pfen'nig
pha'e'ton
pha'lan'ger
pha'lan'ges
pha'lanx
phal'li
phal'lic
phal'lus
phan'ta'sies
phan'tasm
phan'tas'ma'go'ria
phan'tas'ma'gor'ic
phan'tas'mal
phan'ta'sy
phan'tom
phar'aoh
Phar'i'see
phar'ma'ceu'tic
phar'ma'ceu'ti'cal
phar'ma'ceu'tics
phar'ma'cies
phar'ma'cist
phar'ma'col'o'gist
phar'ma'col'o'gy
phar'ma'co'poe'ia
phar'ma'co'poe'ial
phar'ma'cy
phar'yn'gi'tis
phar'ynx
phase
phased

129

phas'ing
pheas'ant
phe'no'bar'bi'tal
phe'nom'e'na
phe'nom'e'nal
phe'nom'e'nal'ly
phe'nom'e'non
phew
phi'al
phi'lan'der
phi'lan'der'er
phil'an'throp'ic
phil'an'throp'i'cal
phi'lan'thro'pies
phi'lan'thro'pist
phi'lan'thro'py
phil'a'tel'ic
phi'lat'e'list
phi'lat'e'ly
phil'har'mon'ic
phi'lip'pic
Phil'ip'pine
phil'o'den'dron
phil'o'lo'gi'an
phil'o'log'i'cal
phi'lol'o'gist
phi'lol'o'gy
phi'los'o'pher
phil'o'soph'ic
phil'o'soph'i'cal
philo'soph'i'cal'ly
phi'los'o'phies
phi'los'o'phize
phi'los'o'phy
phil'tre
phle'bi'tis
phle'bot'o'my
phlegm
phleg'mat'ic
phleg'mat'i'cal
pho'bia
pho'bic
phoe'be
phoe'nix
phon
pho'nate
pho'na'tion
pho'na'tory
phone
phoned
pho'neme
pho'ne'mic
pho'net'ic

pho'net'i'cal'ly
pho'ne'ti'cian
pho'net'ics
phoney
phonic
phon'ics
phon'i'er
phon'i'est
pho'ni'ness
phon'ing
pho'no'graph
pho'no'log'ic
pho'no'log'i'cal
pho'nol'o'gy
pho'ny
phoo'ey
phos'phate
phos'pho'resce
phos'pho'resced
phos'pho'res'cence
phos'pho'res'cent
phos'pho'resc'ing
phos'pho'rus
pho'to
pho'to'cop'ied
pho'to'cop'i'er
pho'to'cop'ies
pho'to'copy
pho'to'cop'y'ing
pho'to'en'grave
pho'to'en'grav'ing
pho'to'gen'ic
pho'to'graph
pho'tog'ra'pher
pho'to'graph'ic
pho'to'graph'i'cal'ly
pho'tog'ra'phy
pho'to'gra'vure
pho'to'sen'si'tive
Pho'to'stat
pho'to'stat'ted
pho'to'stat'ting
pho'to'syn'the'sis
phras'al
phrase
phrased
phra'se'ol'o'gy
phras'ing
phre'nol'o'gist
phre'nol'o'gy
phy'lac'ter'ies
phy'lac'tery
phy'log'e'ny

phy'lum
phys'ic
phys'i'cal
phys'i'cal'ly
phy'si'cian
phys'i'cist
phys'ics
phys'i'og'nom'i'cal
phys'i'og'no'mies
phys'i'og'no'mist
phys'i'og'no'my
phys'i'o'graph'ic
phys'i'og'ra'phy
phys'i'o'log'i'cal
phys'i'ol'o'gist
phys'i'ol'o'gy
phys'io'ther'a'pist
phys'i'o'ther'a'py
phy'sique
pi
pi'a'nis'si'mo
pi'a'nist
pi'ano
pi'an'o'for'te
pi'az'za
pi'ca
pic'a'dor
pic'a'resque
pic'ca'lil'li
pic'co'lo
pick
pick'a'back
pick'axe
picked
pick'er
pick'er'el
pick'et
pick'et'ed
pick'et'er
pick'et'ing
pick'i'er
pick'i'est
pick'ing
pick'le
pick'led
pick'ling
pick-me-up
pick'pock'et
pick'up
picky
pic'nic
pic'nicked
pic'nick'er

pic'nick'ing
pic'to'ri'al
pic'ture
pic'tured
pic'tur'esque
pic'tur'esque'ly
pic'tur'ing
pic'ul
pid'dle
pid'dled
pid'dling
pidg'in
pie
pie'bald
piece
pieced
piece'meal
piece'work
piec'ing
pied-à-terre
pie-eyed
pier
pierce
pierced
pierc'ing
pierc'ing'ly
pi'e'ty
pif'fle
pig
pi'geon
pigeon breast
pi'geon'hole
pi'geon'holed
pi'geon'hol'ing
pi'geon-toed
pigged
pig'ger'ies
pig'gery
pig'ging
pig'gish
pig'gy'back
pig'head'ed
pig'let
pig'ment
pig'men'ta'tion
pig'mies
pig'my
pig'sties
pig'sty
pig'tail
pike
pik'er
pike'staff

pi'laf
pi'laff
pi'las'ter
pi'lau
pi'law
pilch
pil'chard
pile
piles
piled
pil'fer
pil'fer'age
pil'fer'er
pil'grim
pil'grim'age
pil'ing
pill
pil'lage
pil'laged
pil'lag'er
pil'lag'ing
pil'lar
pil'lared
pil'lion
pil'lo'ried
pil'lo'ries
pil'lo'ry
pil'lo'ry'ing
pil'low
pi'lot
pi'lot'age
pi'lot'ed
pi'lot'ing
pi'men'to
pim'ple
pim'pled
pim'ply
pin
pin'a'fore
pin'ball
pince-nez
pin'cers
pinch
pinch'er
pin'cush'ion
pine
pine'ap'ple
pine cone
pined
pin'feath'er
ping pong
pin'head
pin'ing

pin'ion
pin'ioned
pin'ion'ing
pink
pink'ie
pink'ish
pinky
pin'na'cle
pin'nate
pinned
pin'ning
pi'noch'le
pin'prick
pint
pin'to
pint-size
pint-sized
pin'wheel
pi'o'neer
pi'ous
pi'ous'ness
pip
pipe
piped
pipe'line
pip'er
pi'pette
pip'ing
pipped
pip'pin
pip'ping
pip-squeak
pi'quan'cy
pi'quant
pi'quant'ness
pique
piqued
pi'quing
pi'ra'cy
pi'ra'nha
pi'rate
pi'rat'ed
pi'rat'i'cal
pi'rat'ing
pi'rogue
pir'ou'ette
pir'ou'et'ted
pir'ou'et'ting
pis'ca'to'ri'al
pis'ta'chio
piste
pis'til
pis'til'late

pis'tol
pis'toled
pis'tol'ing
pis'ton
pit
pit-a-pat
pitch
pitch black
pitch'blende
pitch'er
pitch'fork
pitchy
pit'e'ous
pit'e'ous'ly
pit'fall
pit'head
pith'e'can'thro'pi
pith'e'can'thro'pus
pith'i'er
pith'i'est
pith'i'ness
pithy
piti'a'ble
piti'ably
pit'ied
piti'ful
piti'ful'ly
piti'less
piti'less'ly
pit'man
pi'ton
pit'tance
pit'ted
pit'ter-pat'ter
pit'ting
pi'tu'itar'ies
pi'tu'i'tar'y
pity
pit'y'ing
pity'ing'ly
piv'ot
piv'ot'al
piv'ot'al'ly
piv'ot'ed
piv'ot'ing
pix'ie
pix'ie'ish
pixy
pi'zazz
piz'za
piz'zazz
piz'ze'ri'a
piz'zi'ca'to

plac'a'bil'i'ty
plac'a'ble
plac'a'bly
plac'ard
pla'cate
pla'cat'ed
pla'cat'ing
pla'ca'tion
pla'ca'tive
pla'ca'to'ry
place
pla'ce'bo
plac'ed
place'ment
pla'cen'ta
pla'cen'tal
plac'er
plac'id
pla'cid'i'ty
plac'id'ly
plac'id'ness
plac'ing
plack'et
pla'gia'rism
pla'gia'rist
pla'gia'ris'tic
pla'gia'rize
pla'gia'rized
pla'gia'riz'er
pla'gia'riz'ing
pla'gia'ry
plague
plagued
pla'guing
plaice
plaid
plain
plain'ly
plain'ness
plain'song
plain'spo'ken
plaint
plain'tiff
plain'tive
plain'tive'ly
plait
plait'ing
plan
plane
planed
plan'et
plan'e'tar'i'um
plan'e'tary

131

plan'e'toid	plau'si'bly	plen'i'tude	plum'met'ed
plan'gent	play	plen'te'ous	plum'met'ing
plan'ing	play'act'ing	plen'ti'ful	plum'mi'er
plan'ish	play'back	plen'ti'ful'ly	plum'mi'est
plank'ing	play'bill	plen'ty	plump
plank'ton	play'boy	pleth'o'ra	plump'ish
plan'less	play'er	pleu'ri'sy	plump'ly
planned	play'ful	plex'us	plump'ness
plan'ner	play'ful'ly	pli'a'bil'i'ty	plun'der
plan'ning	play'ground	pli'a'ble	plun'der'er
plant	play'house	pli'a'ble'ness	plunge
plant'a'ble	play'let	pli'a'bly	plunged
plan'tain	play'mate	pli'an'cy	plung'er
plan'ta'tion	play-off	pli'ant	plung'ing
plant'er	play'room	pli'ant'ly	plu'per'fect
plan'ti'grade	play'wright	pli'ant'ness	plu'ral
plaque	pla'za	plied	plu'ral'ism
plas'ma	plea	pli'ers	plu'ral'ist
plas'ter	pleach	plight	plu'ral'is'tic
plas'ter'board	plead	plim'soll	plu'ral'i'ties
plas'tered	plead'a'ble	plod	plu'ral'i'ty
plas'ter'er	plead'ed	plod'ded	plu'ral'iza'tion
plas'ter'ing	plead'ing	plod'der	plu'ral'ize
plas'tic	plead'ing'ly	plod'ding	plu'ral'ly
plas'ti'cal'ly	pleas'ant	plop	plus
plas'tic'i'ty	pleas'ant'ly	plopped	plus fours
plat	pleas'ant'ries	plop'ping	plush
plat du jour	pleas'ant'ry	plo'sive	plush'i'er
plate	please	plot	plush'i'est
pla'teau	pleased	plot'ted	plush'i'ness
pla'teaux	pleas'ing	plot'ter	plushy
plat'ed	pleas'ing'ly	plot'ting	plu'toc'ra'cies
plate'ful	pleas'ur'able	plov'er	plu'toc'ra'cy
plate'let	pleas'ur'ably	ploy	plu'to'crat
plat'en	pleas'ure	pluck	plu'to'crat'ic
plat'form	plea'sured	pluck'i'er	plu'to'ni'um
plat'ing	plea'sur'ing	pluck'i'est	plu'vi'al
plat'i'num	pleat	pluck'i'ly	ply
plat'i'tude	pleat'ed	pluck'i'ness	ply'ing
plat'i'tu'di'nal	pleb	plucky	ply'wood
plat'i'tu'di'nize	plebe	plug	pneu'mat'ic
plat'i'tu'di'nous	ple'be'ian	plugged	pneu'mat'i'cal'ly
pla'ton'ic	pleb'i'scite	plug'ging	pneu'mo'co'ni'o'sis
pla'ton'i'cal'ly	plec'trum	plum	pneu'mo'nia
pla'toon	pled	plum'age	poach
plat'ted	pledge	plumb	poach'er
plat'ter	pledged	plumb'er	pock
plat'ting	pledg'ee	plumb'ing	pock'et
platy'pus	pledg'ing	plumb line	pock'et'book
plau'dit	ple'na'ry	plume	pock'et'ed
plau'si'bil'i'ty	ple'nip'o'tent	plumed	pock'et'ful
plau'si'ble	pleni'po'ten'tia'ries	plum'ing	pock'et'ing
plau'si'ble'ness	plen'i'po'ten'ti'ary	plum'met	pock'et'knife

pock'et'knives
pock'mark
pod
pod'ded
pod'ding
po'di'a'trist
po'di'a'try
po'di'um
pod'like
po'em
po'e'sies
po'e'sy
po'et
po'et'as'ter
po'et'ess
po'et'ic
po'et'i'cal
po'et'i'cal'ly
po'et'ize
po'et' lau're'ate
po'et'ry
po'go stick
po'grom
poi
poign'an'cy
poign'ant
poig'nant'ly
poin'ci'ana
poin'set'tia
point
point-blank
point'ed
point'edly
point'er
poin'til'lism
poin'til'list
point'less
point'less'ly
poise
poised
pois'ing
poi'son
poi'soned
poi'son'er
poi'son'ing
poi'son'ous
poke
poked
pok'er
pok'i'er
pok'i'est
pok'ing
poky

po'lar
po'lar'i'ties
po'lar'i'ty
po'lar'i'za'tion
po'lar'ize
po'lar'ized
po'lar'iz'ing
pol'der
pole
pole'axe
pole'cat
poled
po'lem'ic
po'lem'i'cal
po'lem'i'cist
pole vault
po'lice
po'liced
po'lice'man
po'lice'wom'an
pol'i'cies
po'lic'ing
pol'i'cy
pol'i'cy'hold'er
pol'ing
po'lio
pol'i'o'my'e'li'tis
Po'lish
pol'ish
pol'ish'er
po'lite
po'lite'ly
po'lite'ness
pol'i'tic
po'lit'i'cal
po'lit'i'cal'ly
pol'i'ti'cian
po'lit'i'ci'za'tion
po'lit'i'cize
po'lit'i'cized
po'lit'i'ciz'ing
pol'i'tick'ing
po'lit'i'co
pol'i'tics
pol'i'ties
pol'i'ty
pol'ka
pol'kaed
pol'ka'ing
poll
pol'lard
pol'len
poll'er

pol'li'nate
pol'li'nat'ed
pol'li'nat'ing
pol'li'na'tion
pol'li'na'tor
pol'li'wog
poll'ster
pol'lu'tant
pol'lute
pol'lut'ed
pol'lu'ter
pol'lut'ing
pol'lu'tion
po'lo
pol'o'naise
po'lo'ni'um
pol'ter'geist
pol'troon
poly'an'drous
poly'an'dry
poly'an'thi
poly'an'thus
poly'chro'mat'ic
poly'chro'mat'ic
poly'chrome
poly'es'ter
poly'eth'yl'ene
po'lyg'a'mist
po'lyg'a'mous
po'lyg'a'my
pol'y'glot
poly'gon
po'lyg'o'nal
poly'graph
po'lyg'y'nous
po'lyg'y'ny
poly'he'dron
poly'mer
po'ly'mer'i'za'tion
po'ly'mer'ize
poly'mor'phism
Poly'ne'sian
poly'no'mi'al
pol'yp
poly'phon'ic
pol'y'sty'rene
poly'syl'lab'ic
poly'syl'la'ble
poly'tech'nic
poly'the'ism
poly'the'ist
poly'the'is'tic
poly'un'sat'u'rat'ed

poly'ure'thane
po'made
po'man'der
pome'gran'ate
pom'e'lo
pom'mel
pom'melled
pom'mel'ling
pom'pa'dour
pom'pa'no
pom-pom
pom'pon
pom'pos'i'ty
pomp'ous
pomp'ous'ly
pon'cho
pon'der
pon'der'a'ble
pon'der'ous
pon'der'ous'ly
pon'gee
pongy
pon'iard
po'nies
pon'tiff
pon'tif'i'cal
pon'tif'i'cal'ly
pon'tif'i'cate
pon'tif'i'cat'ed
pon'tif'i'cat'ing
pon'toon
po'ny
po'ny tail
poo'dle
pooh
pooh-pooh
poop
poor
poor'ish
poor'ly
pop
pop'corn
pop'ery
pop'eyed
pop'in'jay
pop'ish
pop'lar
pop'lin
pop'pa'dom
popped
pop'per
pop'pies
pop'ping

pop'py
pop'py'cock
pop'u'lace
pop'u'lar'i'ty
pop'u'lar'i'za'tion
pop'u'lar'ize
pop'u'lar'ized
pop'u'lar'iz'ing
pop'u'lar'ly
pop'u'late
pop'u'lat'ed
pop'u'lat'ing
pop'u'la'tion
pop'u'lism
pop'u'list
pop'u'lous
por'ce'lain
porch
por'cine
por'cu'pine
pore
pored
por'ing
pork
pork'er
por'no
por'nog'ra'pher
por'no'graph'ic
por'nog'ra'phy
po'ros'i'ty
po'rous
po'rous'ness
por'phy'ry
por'poise
por'ridge
port'a'bil'i'ty
port'a'ble
port'ably
por'tage
por'taged
por'tag'ing
por'tal
port'cul'lis
por'tend
por'tent
por'ten'tous
por'ten'tous'ly
por'ter
port'fo'lio
port'hole
por'ti'co
por'ti'coes
por'tion

por'tioned
por'tion'ing
port'li'er
port'li'est
port'li'ness
port'ly
port'man'teau
port'man'teaux
por'trait
por'trait'ist
por'trai'ture
por'tray
por'tray'al
por'tray'er
Por'tu'guese
pose
posed
pos'er
pos'eur
po'sies
pos'ing
pos'it
pos'it'ed
pos'it'ing
po'si'tion
po'si'tioned
po'si'tion'ing
pos'i'tive
pos'i'tive'ly
pos'i'tive'ness
pos'i'tiv'ism
pos'i'tiv'ist
pos'i'tron
pos'se
pos'sess
pos'sessed
pos'ses'sion
pos'ses'sive
pos'ses'sive'ness
pos'ses'sor
pos'si'bil'i'ties
pos'si'bil'i'ty
pos'si'ble
pos'si'bly
pos'sum
post
post'age
post'al
post'card
post'date
post'dat'ed
post'dat'ing
post'er

pos'te'ri'or
pos'te'ri'or'i'ty
pos'ter'i'ty
pos'tern
post'fix
post'gla'cial
post'grad'u'ate
post'haste
post'hu'mous
post'hu'mous'ly
pos'til
post'il'ion
pos'til'lion
post'in'dus'tri'al
post'ing
post'lude
post'man
post'mark
post'mas'ter
post me'rid'i'em
post'mis'tress
post'mor'tem
post'na'sal
post'na'tal
post-paid
post'par'tum
post'pon'a'ble
post'pone
post'poned
post'pone'ment
post'pon'ing
post'pran'di'al
post'script
pos'tu'lant
pos'tu'late
pos'tu'lat'ed
pos'tu'lat'ing
pos'tu'la'tion
pos'tu'la'tor
pos'ture
pos'tured
pos'tur'ing
post'war
po'sy
pot
po'ta'ble
pot'ash
po'tas'si'um
po'ta'to
po'ta'toes
pot'bel'lied
pot'bel'lies
pot'bel'ly

pot'boil'er
po'teen
po'ten'cy
po'tent
po'ten'tate
po'ten'tial
po'ten'ti'al'i'ties
po'ten'ti'al'i'ty
po'ten'tial'ly
po'tent'ly
po'theen
pot'herb
pot'hole
po'tion
pot'luck
pot'pour'ri
pot'sherd
pot'tage
pot'ted
pot'ter
pot'ter'ies
pot'tery
pot'ties
pot'ting
pot'ty
pouch
pouched
pouchy
pouf
pouffe
poul'tice
poul'try
pounce
pounced
pounc'ing
pound
pound'age
pour
pour'a'ble
pout
pov'er'ty
pov'er'ty-strick'en
pow'der
pow'dery
pow'er
pow'er'boat
pow'er'ful
pow'er'ful'ly
pow'er'ful'ness
pow'er'house
pow'er'less
pow'er'less'ness
pow'wow

pox
prac'ti'ca'bil'i'ty
prac'ti'ca'ble
prac'ti'ca'ble'ness
prac'ti'ca'bly
prac'ti'cal
prac'ti'cal'i'ties
prac'ti'cal'i'ty
prac'ti'cal'ly
prac'tice
prac'ticed
prac'tic'ing
prac'ti'tion'er
prae'di'al
prag'mat'ic
prag'mat'i'cal
prag'mat'i'cal'ly
prag'ma'tism
prag'ma'tist
prag'ma'tis'tic
prai'rie
praise
praised
praise'wor'thy
prais'ing
pra'line
prance
pranced
pranc'ing
prank
prank'ish
prank'ster
prate
prat'ed
prat'fall
prat'ing
prat'tle
prat'tled
prat'tling
prawn
prawn'er
pray
prayer
prayer'ful
preach
preach'er
preach'ment
preachy
pre'ad'o'les'cence
pre'ad'o'les'cent
pre'am'ble
pre'ar'range
pre'ar'ranged

pre'ar'range'ment
pre'ar'rang'ing
pre'as'signed
pre'can'cel
pre'can'cer'ous
pre'car'i'ous
pre'car'i'ous'ly
pre'car'i'ous'ness
pre'cau'tion
pre'cau'tion'ary
pre'cede
pre'ced'ed
prec'e'dence
prec'e'dent
pre'ced'ing
pre'cept
pre'cep'tive
pre'cep'tor
pre'cep'to'ri'al
pre'ces'sion
pre'cinct
pre'ci'os'i'ty
pre'cious
pre'cious'ness
prec'i'pice
pre'cip'i'tant
pre'cip'i'tate
pre'cip'i'tat'ed
pre'cip'i'tate'ly
pre'cip'i'tat'ing
pre'cip'i'ta'tion
pre'cip'i'ta'tive
pre'cip'i'ta'tor
pre'cip'i'tous
pre'cip'i'tous
pré'cis
pre'cise
pre'cise'ly
pre'cise'ness
pre'ci'sion
pre'ci'sion'ist
pre'clude
pre'clud'ed
pre'clud'ing
pre'clu'sion
pre'clu'sive
pre'co'cious
pre'co'cious'ly
pre'co'cious'ness
pre'coc'i'ty
pre'cog'ni'tion
pre'cog'ni'tive
pre'con'ceive

pre'con'ceived
pre'con'ceiv'ing
pre'con'cep'tion
pre'con'di'tion
pre'cook
pre'cur'sor
pre'cur'so'ry
pre'date
pred'a'tor
pred'a'to'ry
pre'de'cease
pred'e'ces'sor
pre'des'ti'nate
pre'des'ti'nat'ed
pre'des'ti'nat'ing
pre'des'ti'na'tion
pre'des'tine
pre'des'tined
pre'de'ter'mi'na'tion
pre'de'ter'mine
pre'de'ter'mined
pre'de'ter'min'er
pre'de'ter'min'ing
pred'i'ca'bil'i'ty
pred'i'ca'ble
pre'dic'ament
pred'i'cate
pred'i'cat'ed
pred'i'cat'ing
pred'i'ca'tion
pred'i'ca'tive
pre'dict
pre'dict'a'bil'i'ty
pre'dict'able
pre'dict'a'bly
pre'dic'tion
pre'dic'tive
pre'di'gest'ed
pre'di'lec'tion
pre'dis'pose
pre'dis'posed
pre'dis'pos'ing
pre'dis'po'si'tion
pre'dom'i'nance
pre'dom'i'nan'cy
pre'dom'i'nant
pre'dom'i'nant'ly
pre'dom'i'nate
pre'dom'i'nat'ed
pre'dom'i'nat'ing
pre'dom'i'na'tion
pre-em'i'nence
pre-em'i'nent

pre-em'i'nent'ly
pre-empt
pre-emp'tion
pre-emp'tive
pre-emp'tor
preen
pre-ex'ist
pre-ex'ist'ence
pre-ex'ist'ent
pre'fab'ri'cate
pre'fab'ri'cat'ed
pre'fab'ri'cat'ing
pre'fab'ri'ca'tion
pref'ace
pref'aced
pref'ac'ing
pref'a'to'ry
pre'fect
pre'fer
pre'fer'a'bil'i'ty
pref'er'a'ble
pref'er'a'ble'ness
pref'er'a'bly
pref'er'ence
pref'er'en'tial
pref'er'en'tial'ly
pre'fer'ment
pre'ferred
pre'fer'ring
pre'fig'ure
pre'fig'ured
pre'fig'ur'ing
pre'fix
pre'flight
pre'form
preg'na'bil'i'ty
preg'nan'cies
preg'nan'cy
preg'nant
pre'heat
pre'hen'sile
pre'his'tor'ic
pre'his'to'ry
pre'judge
pre'judged
pre'judg'ing
pre'judg'ment
prej'u'dice
prej'u'diced
prej'u'di'cial
prej'u'dic'ing
prel'ate
pre'lim'i'nar'ies

135

pre'lim'i'nar'i'ly
pre'lim'i'nary
prel'ude
prel'ud'ing
pre'ma'ri'tal
pre'ma'ture
pre'ma'ture'ly
pre'ma'ture'ness
pre'ma'tu'ri'ty
pre'med'i'cal
pre'med'i'tate
pre'med'i'tat'ed
pre'med'i'tat'ing
pre'med'i'ta'tion
pre'med'i'ta'tive
pre'men'stru'al
pre'mier
pre'miere
pre'mier'ship
prem'ise
prem'ised
prem'is'ing
pre'mi'um
pre'mo'ni'tion
pre'mon'i'to'ri'ly
pre'mon'i'to'ry
pre'na'tal
pre'na'tal'ly
pre'oc'cu'pa'tion
pre'oc'cu'pied
pre'oc'cu'py
pre'oc'cu'py'ing
pre'op'er'a'tive
pre'ordain
pre'paid
prep'a'ra'tion
pre'par'a'to'ri'ly
pre'par'a'to'ry
pre'pare
pre'pared
pre'par'ed'ness
pre'par'ing
pre'pay
pre'pay'ing
pre'pay'ment
pre'plan
pre'planned
pre'plan'ning
pre'pon'der'ance
pre'pon'der'an'cy
pre'pon'der'ant
pre'pon'der'ant'ly
pre'pon'der'ate

pre'pon'der'at'ed
pre'pon'der'at'ing
pre'pon'der'a'tion
prep'o'si'tion
pre'posi'tor
pre'pos'sess
pre'pos'sess'ing
pre'pos'ses'sion
pre'pos'ter'ous
pre'pos'ter'ous'ly
pre'po'ten'cy
pre'po'tent
pre'pu'bes'cent
pre'puce
pre're'cord
pre'req'ui'site
pre'rog'a'tive
pres'age
pres'aged
pres'ag'ing
Pres'by'te'ri'an
pres'by'ter'ies
pres'by'tery
pre'school
pre'scibe
pre'sci'ence
pre'sci'ent
pre'scribed
pre'scrib'ing
pre'script
pre'scrip'tion
pre'scrip'tive
pre'sea'son
pre'sea'son'al
pre'se'lect
pres'ence
pre'sent
pres'ent
pre'sent'a'bil'i'ty
pre'sent'a'ble
pre'sent'a'ble'ness
pre'sent'a'bly
pres'en'ta'tion
pre'sent'er
pre'sen'ti'ment
pres'ent'ly
pre'serv'able
pres'er'va'tion
pre'serv'a'tive
pre'serve
pre'served
pre'serv'er
pre'serv'ing

pre'side
pre'sid'ed
pres'i'den'cies
pres'i'den'cy
pres'i'dent
pres'i'dent-elect
pres'i'den'tial
pre'sid'ing
pre'sid'i'um
pre'sig'ni'fy
press
press'ing
press'man
press'mark
pres'sor
press'room
press-up
pres'sure
pres'sured
pres'sur'ing
pres'sur'i'za'tion
pres'su'rize
pres'su'rized
pres'su'riz'er
press'work
pres'ti'dig'i'ta'tion
pres'tige
pres'tig'ious
pres'tis'si'mo
pres'to
pre'stressed
pre'sum'a'ble
pre'sum'a'bly
pre'sume
pre'sumed
pre'sum'ing
pre'sump'tion
pre'sump'tive
pre'sump'tu'ous
pre'sump'tu'ous'ly
pre'sump'tu'ous'ness
pre'sup'pose
pre'sup'posed
pre'sup'pos'ing
pre'sup'po'si'tion
pre'tence
pre'tend
pre'tend'ed
pre'tend'er
pre'ten'sion
pre'ten'tious
pre'ten'tious'ness
pret'er'ite

pret'er'i'tion
pre'ter'nat'u'ral
pre'ter'nat'u'ral'ly
pre'test
pre'text
pretti'fi'ca'tion
pret'ti'er
pret'ti'est
pret'ti'fied
pret'ti'fy
pret'ti'fy'ing
pret'ti'ly
pret'ti'ness
pret'ty
pret'zel
pre'vail
pre'vail'ing
prev'a'lence
prev'a'lent
pre'var'i'cate
pre'var'i'cat'ed
pre'var'i'cat'ing
pre'var'i'ca'tion
pre'vent
pre'vent'a'bil'i'ty
pre'vent'a'ble
pre'ven'ta'tive
pre'ven'tion
pre'ven'tive
pre'view
pre'vi'ous
pre'vi'ous'ly
pre'vision
pre'war
prey
prey'er
price
priced
price'less
pric'ey
pric'i'er
pric'i'est
pric'ing
prick
prick'le
prick'led
prick'li'ness
prick'ling
prick'ly
pride
prid'ed
pride'ful'ly
prid'ing

pried
prie-dieu
priest
priest'ess
priest'hood
priest'li'ness
priest'ly
prig
prig'gish
prig'gish'ness
prim
pri'ma bal'le'ri'na
pri'ma'cy
pri'ma don'na
pri'ma fa'cie
pri'mal
pri'mar'ies
pri'mar'i'ly
pri'ma'ry
pri'mate
prime
primed
prime me'rid'i'an
prim'er
pri'me'val
prim'ing
prim'i'tive
prim'ly
primmed
prim'mer
prim'mest
prim'ming
prim'ness
pri'mo'gen'i'tor
pri'mo'gen'i'ture
pri'mor'di'al
prim'rose
prim'u'la
prim'u'lae
prince
prince'dom
prince'li'ness
prince'ly
prin'cess
prin'ci'pal
prin'ci'pal'i'ties
prin'ci'pal'i'ty
prin'ci'pal'ly
prin'ci'ple
prin'ci'pled
prin'ta'ble
print'er
prin'ting

prin'tout
pri'or
pri'or'ess
pri'o'ries
pri'or'i'ties
pri'or'i'ty
pri'ory
prism
pris'mat'ic
pris'on
pris'on'er
pris'on'er of war
pris'si'ness
pris'sy
pris'tine
pri'va'cy
pri'vate
pri'va'teer
pri'vate'ly
pri'va'tion
pri'vat'iza'tion
pri'vat'ize
pri'vat'ized
pri'vat'iz'ing
priv'et
priv'ies
priv'i'lege
priv'i'leged
priv'i'leg'ing
privy
prize
prized
prize'fight'er
priz'ing
prob'a'bil'i'ties
prob'a'bil'i'ty
prob'a'ble
prob'a'bly
pro'bate
pro'bat'ed
pro'bat'ing
pro'ba'tion
pro'ba'tion'al
pro'ba'tion'al'ly
pro'ba'tion'ary
pro'ba'tion'er
pro'ba'tive
pro'ba'to'ry
probe
probed
prob'ing
pro'bi'ty
prob'lem

prob'lem'at'ic
prob'lem'at'ical
pro'bos'cis
pro'ce'dur'al
pro'ce'dur'al'ly
pro'ce'dure
pro'ceed
pro'ceed'ing
pro'ceeds
proc'ess
pro'ces'sion
pro'ces'sion'al
pro'claim
proc'la'ma'tion
pro'cliv'i'ties
pro'cliv'i'ty
pro'con'sul
pro'cras'ti'nate
pro'cras'ti'nat'ed
pro'cras'ti'nat'ing
pro'cras'ti'na'tion
pro'cras'ti'na'tor
pro'cre'ant
pro'cre'ate
pro'cre'at'ed
pro'cre'at'ing
pro'cre'a'tion
pro'cre'a'tive
pro'cre'a'tor
pro'crus'te'an
proc'tor
proc'to'ri'al
pro'cur'a'ble
pro'cur'ance
proc'u'ra'tor
pro'cure
pro'cured
pro'cur'er
pro'cur'ing
pro'curement
prod
prod'ded
prod'der
prod'ding
prod'i'gal
prod'i'gal'i'ty
prod'i'gal'ly
prod'i'gies
pro'di'gious
pro'di'gious'ly
pro'di'gious'ness
prod'i'gy
pro'duce

pro'duced
pro'duc'er
pro'duc'ing
prod'uct
pro'duc'tion
pro'duc'tive
pro'duc'tive'ly
pro'duc'tiv'i'ty
pro'em
pro'fan'a'to'ry
pro'fane
pro'faned
pro'fane'ness
pro'fan'er
pro'fan'ing
pro'fan'i'ty
pro'fess
pro'fessed
pro'fess'ed'ly
pro'fes'sion
pro'fes'sion'al
pro'fes'sion'al'ism
pro'fes'sion'al'ly
pro'fes'sor
pro'fes'so'ri'al
pro'fes'so'ri'al'ly
pro'fes'sor'ship
prof'fer
prof'fered
prof'fer'ing
pro'fi'cien'cy
pro'fi'cient
pro'file
pro'filed
pro'fil'ing
prof'it
prof'it'a'bil'i'ty
prof'it'a'ble
prof'it'a'ble'ness
prof'it'a'bly
prof'it'ed
prof'it'eer
pro'fit'er'ole
prof'it'ing
prof'it'less
prof'li'ga'cy
prof'li'gate
pro for'ma
pro'found
pro'found'ly
pro'fun'di'ties
pro'fun'di'ty
pro'fuse

pro'fuse'ly
pro'fu'sion
pro'gen'i'tor
prog'e'ny
pro'ges'ter'one
prog'no'ses
prog'no'sis
prog'nos'tic
prog'nos'ti'cate
prog'nos'ti'cat'ed
prog'nos'ti'cat'ing
prog'nos'ti'ca'tion
prog'nos'ti'ca'tive
prog'nos'ti'ca'tor
pro'gram
pro'gramme
pro'grammed
pro'gram'mer
pro'gram'ming
prog'ress
pro'gres'sion
pro'gres'sive
pro'gres'sive'ly
pro'hib'it
pro'hi'bi'tion
pro'hi'bi'tion'ist
pro'hib'i'tive
pro'hib'i'tive'ly
pro'hib'i'to'ry
pro'ject
pro'jec'tile
pro'jec'tion
pro'jec'tion'ist
pro'jec'tive
pro'jec'tive'ly
pro'jec'tor
pro'lapse
pro'le'tar'i'an
pro'le'tar'i'at
pro'lif'er'ate
pro'lif'er'at'ed
pro'lif'er'at'ing
pro'lif'er'a'tion
pro'lif'er'a'tive
pro'lif'ic
pro'lif'i'ca'cy
pro'lif'i'cal'ly
pro'lif'ic'ness
pro'lix
pro'lix'i'ty
pro'loc'u'tor
pro'lo'gue
pro'long

pro'lon'ga'tion
prom
prom'e'nade
prom'e'nad'ed
prom'e'nad'er
prom'e'nad'ing
pro'me'thi'um
prom'i'nence
prom'i'nent
prom'i'nent'ly
pro'mis'cu'i'ty
pro'mis'cu'ous
pro'mis'cu'ous'ly
pro'mis'cu'ous'ness
prom'ise
prom'ised
prom'is'ing
prom'is'so'ry
prom'on'to'ries
prom'on'to'ry
pro'mot'a'ble
pro'mote
pro'mot'ed
pro'mot'er
pro'mot'ing
pro'mo'tion
pro'mo'tion'al
pro'mo'tive
prompt
prompt'er
promp'ti'tude
prompt'ly
prompt'ness
prom'ul'gate
prom'ul'gat'ed
prom'ul'gat'ing
prom'ul'ga'tion
prone
prone'ness
prong
pro'nom'i'nal
pro'noun
pro'nounce
pro'nounce'a'ble
pro'nounced
pro'nounce'ment
pro'nounc'ing
pron'to
pro'nun'ci'a'tion
proof
proof'read
proof'read'er
prop

prop'a'gan'da
prop'a'gan'dism
prop'a'gan'dist
prop'a'gan'dis'tic
prop'a'gan'dize
prop'a'gan'dized
prop'a'gan'diz'ing
prop'a'gate
prop'a'gat'ed
prop'a'gat'ing
prop'a'ga'tion
prop'a'ga'tion'al
prop'a'ga'tive
prop'a'ga'tor
pro'pane
pro'pel
pro'pel'lant
pro'pelled
pro'pel'ler
pro'pel'ling
pro'pen'si'ties
pro'pen'si'ty
prop'er
prop'er'ly
prop'er'tied
prop'er'ties
prop'er'ty
proph'e'cies
proph'e'cy
proph'e'sied
proph'e'sy
proph'e'sy'ing
proph'et
proph'et'ess
pro'phet'ic
pro'phet'i'cal'ly
pro'phy'lac'tic
pro'phy'lax'is
pro'pin'qui'ty
pro'pi'ti'ate
pro'pi'ti'a'tion
pro'pi'ti'a'to'ry
pro'pi'tious'ly
pro'pit'ti'at'ing
pro'po'nent
pro'por'tion
pro'por'tion'a'ble
pro'por'tion'a'bly
pro'por'tion'al
pro'por'tion'al'i'ty
pro'por'tion'al'ly
pro'por'tion'ate
pro'por'tion'ate'ly

pro'pos'al
pro'pose
pro'posed
pro'pos'er
pro'pos'ing
prop'o'si'tion
pro'pound
propped
prop'ping
pro'pri'etary
pro'pri'e'ties
pro'pri'etor
pro'pri'etor'ship
pro'pri'etress
pro'pri'ety
pro'pul'sion
pro'pul'sive
pro rata
pro'rate
pro'rat'ed
pro'rat'ing
pro'ra'tion
pro'sa'ic
pro'sa'i'cal'ly
pro'sa'ic'ness
pros and cons
pro'sce'ni'um
pro'scibe
pro'scribed
pro'scrib'er
pro'scrib'ing
pro'scrip'tion
pro'scrip'tive
prose
pros'e'cut'a'ble
pros'e'cute
pros'e'cut'ed
pros'e'cut'ing
pros'e'cu'tion
pros'e'cu'tor
pros'e'lyte
pros'e'ly'tism
pros'e'ly'tize
pros'e'ly'tized
pros'e'ly'tiz'ing
pros'pect
pro'spec'tive
pros'pec'tor
pro'spec'tus
pros'per
pros'pered
pros'per'ing
pros'per'i'ty

pros'per'ous
pros'ta'glan'din
pros'tate
pros'the'sis
pros'thet'ic
pros'tho'don'tics
pros'tho'don'tist
pros'ti'tute
pros'ti'tut'ed
pros'ti'tut'ing
pros'ti'tu'tion
pros'ti'tu'tor
pros'trate
pros'trat'ed
pros'trat'ing
pros'tra'tion
pros'y
pro'tac'tin'i'um
pro'tag'o'nist
pro'te'an
pro'tect
pro'tect'ing
pro'tec'tion
pro'tec'tion'ist
pro'tec'tion'ism
pro'tec'tive
pro'tec'tive'ly
pro'tec'tive'ness
pro'tec'tor
pro'tec'tor'ate
pro'té'gé
pro'té'gée
pro'tein
pro tem
pro tem'po're
pro'test
Prot'es'tant
Prot'es'tant'ism
prot'es'ta'tion
pro'test'er
pro'to'col
pro'ton
pro'to'plasm
pro'to'type
pro'to'zo'an
pro'tract
pro'trac'tile
pro'trac'tion
pro'trac'tive
pro'trac'tor
pro'trude
pro'trud'ent
pro'tru'sion

pro'tru'sive
pro'tu'ber'ance
pro'tu'ber'ant
proud
proud'ly
prov'able
prov'ably
prove
proved
prov'en
prov'e'nance
prov'en'der
prov'erb
prov'er'bi'al
prov'er'bi'al'ly
pro'vid'a'ble
pro'vide
pro'vid'ed
prov'i'dence
prov'i'dent
prov'i'den'tial
prov'i'den'tial'ly
pro'vid'er
pro'vid'ing
prov'ince
pro'vin'cial
pro'vin'cial'ism
pro'vin'cial'ist
pro'vin'ci'al'i'ty
pro'vin'cial'ize
pro'vin'cial'ized
pro'vin'cial'iz'ing
pro'vin'cial'ly
prov'ing
pro'vi'sion
pro'vi'sion'al
pro'vi'sion'al'ly
pro'vi'sion'ary
pro'vi'so
pro'vi'so'ry
prov'o'ca'tion
pro'voc'a'tive
pro'voc'a'tive'ly
pro'voke
pro'voked
pro'vok'ing
pro'vok'ing'ly
prov'ost
prow
prow'ess
prowl
prowl'er
prox'ies

prox'i'mal
prox'i'mate
prox'im'i'ty
prox'i'mo
proxy
prude
pru'dence
pru'dent
pru'den'tial
prud'ery
prud'ish
prud'ish'ness
prune
pruned
prun'ing
pru'ri'ence
pru'ri'en'cy
pru'ri'ent
Prus'sian
prus'sic
pry
pry'ing
psalm
psalm'book
psalm'ic
psalm'ist
pse'phol'o'gist
pse'phol'o'gy
pseu'do
pseu'do'nym
pseu'don'y'mous
pseu'do'sci'ence
pseu'do'sci'en'tif'ic
pshaw
pso'ri'a'sis
psych
psy'che
psych'e'del'ic
psy'chi'at'ric
psy'chi'a'trist
psy'chi'a'try
psy'chic
psy'chi'cal
psy'chi'cal'ly
psy'chi'a'tri'cal'ly
psy'cho
psy'cho'a'nal'y'sis
psy'cho'an'a'lyst
psy'cho'an'a'lyt'ic
psy'cho'an'a'lyt'i'cal
psy'cho'an'a'lyze
psy'cho'an'a'lyzed
psy'cho'an'a'lyz'ing

psy'cho'bi'ol'o'gy
psy'cho'dra'ma
psy'cho'dy'nam'ic
psy'cho'gen'e'sis
psy'cho'ge'net'ic
psy'cho'gen'ic
psy'cho'gen'i'cal'ly
psy'cho'log'ic
psy'cho'log'i'cal
psy'cho'log'i'cal'ly
psy'chol'o'gist
psy'chol'o'gy
psy'cho'met'ric
psy'cho'met'ri'cal'ly
psy'cho'mo'tor
psy'cho'neu'ro'ses
psy'cho'neu'ro'sis
psy'cho'neu'rot'ic
psy'cho'path
psy'cho'path'ic
psy'cho'path'i'cal'ly
psy'cho'path'o'log'ic
psy'cho'pa'thol'o'gist
psy'cho'pa'thol'o'gy
psy'chop'a'thy
psy'cho'ses
psy'cho'sis
psy'cho'so'mat'ic
psy'cho'ther'a'pist
psy'cho'ther'a'py
psy'chot'ic
psy'chot'i'cal'ly
psyl'lid
ptar'mi'gan
pter'o'dac'tyl
ptero'pod
ptero'saur
pto'maine
ptya'lin
pub
pu'ber'ty
pu'bes'cence
pu'bes'cen'cy
pu'bes'cent
pu'bic
pub'lic
pub'li'can
pub'li'ca'tion
pub'li'cist
pub'li'ci'ty
pub'li'cize
pub'li'cized
pub'li'ciz'ing

pub'lic'ly
pub'lic'ness
pub'lic-spir'it'ed
pub'lish
pub'lish'er
puce
puck
puck'er
puck'ish
pud'ding
pud'dle
pud'dled
pud'dling
pudg'i'ness
pudgy
pueb'lo
pu'er'ile
pu'er'il'i'ty
pu'er'per'al
puff
puff'ball
puff'i'er
puff'i'est
puf'fin
puff'i'ness
puffy
pug
pu'gil'ism
pu'gil'ist
pu'gil'is'tic
pug'na'cious
pug'na'cious'ness
pug'nac'i'ty
puis'sant
puke
puked
puk'ing
pul'chri'tude
pul'chri'tu'di'nous
pull
pul'let
pul'ley
pul'mo'nary
pul'mo'tor
pulp
pulp'i'ness
pul'pit
pulpy
pul'sar
pul'sate
pul'sat'ed
pul'sat'ing
pul'sa'tion

pul'sa'tor
pulse
pulsed
puls'ing
pul'ver'iz'a'ble
pul'ver'i'za'tion
pul'ver'ize
pul'ver'ized
pul'ver'iz'er
pul'ver'iz'ing
pu'ma
pum'ice
pum'mel
pum'melled
pum'mel'ling
pump
pump'a'ble
pump'er
pum'per'nick'el
pump'kin
pun
punch
punch'ball
punch-drunk
punch'i'er
punch'i'est
punchy
punc'til'io
punc'til'i'ous
punc'til'i'ous'ly
punc'tu'al
punc'tu'al'i'ty
punc'tu'al'ly
punc'tu'al'ness
punc'tu'ate
punc'tu'at'ed
punc'tu'at'ing
punc'tu'a'tion
punc'tur'a'ble
punc'ture
punc'tured
punc'tur'ing
pun'dit
pun'gen'cy
pun'gent
pun'gent'ly
pu'ni'er
pu'ni'est
pu'ni'ness
pun'ish
pun'ish'a'ble
pun'ish'ment
pu'ni'tive

punk
punned
pun'ning
pun'ster
pu'ny
pup
pu'pa
pu'pae
pu'pil
pup'pet
pup'pet'eer
pup'pet'ry
pup'pies
pup'py
pup'py'ish
pur'chas'a'ble
pur'chase
pur'chased
pur'chas'er
pur'chas'ing
pure
pure'bred
pu'ree
pure'ly
pure'ness
pur'ga'tion
pur'ga'tive
pur'ga'to'ri'al
pur'ga'to'ry
purge
purged
purg'ing
pu'ri'fi'ca'tion
pu'ri'fied
pu'ri'fi'er
pu'ri'fy
pu'ri'fy'ing
pur'ism
pur'ist
pu'ris'tic
pu'ri'tan
pu'ri'tan'i'cal
pu'ri'ty
purl
pur'lieus
pur'loin
pur'loin'er
pur'ple
pur'plish
pur'port
pur'port'ed'ly
pur'pose
pur'posed

pur'pose'ful
pur'pose'ful'ly
pur'pose'less
pur'pose'ly
pur'pos'ing
purr
purse
pursed
purs'er
purs'ing
pur'su'ance
pur'su'ant
pur'sue
pur'sued
pur'su'er
pur'su'ing
pur'suit
pu'ru'len'cy
pu'ru'lent
pu'ru'lent'ly
pur'vey
pur'vey'ance
pur'vey'or
pur'view
pus
push
push-but'ton
push'cart
push'er
push'i'er
push'i'est
push'i'ly
push'i'ness
push'over
pushy
pu'sil'la'nim'i'ty
pu'sil'lan'i'mous
puss
pus'sies
pussy
pussy'cat
pussy'foot
pussy'wil'low
pus'tule
put
pu'ta'tive
put-down
pu'tre'fac'tion
pu'tre'fied
pu'tre'fy
pu'tre'fy'ing
pu'tres'cent
pu'trid

pu'trid'ness
putsch
putt
putt'ed
put'tee
put'ter
putt'ing
put'ting
put'ty
puz'zle
puz'zled
puz'zle'ment
puz'zler
puz'zling
pye-dog
Pyg'mies
pyg'my
py'lon
py'or'rhoea
pyr'a'mid
py'ram'i'dal
pyre
py'ret'ic
py'rites
py'ro'ma'nia
py'ro'ma'ni'ac
py'ro'ma'ni'a'cal
py'rom'e'ter
py'ro'tech'nics
py'thon
Py'thon'esque
py'thon'ess
py'thon'ic
pyu'ria
pyx'id'ium
qua
quack
quack'ery
quad
quad'ran'gle
quad'ran'gu'lar
quad'rant
quad'ran'tal
quad'ra'phon'ic
quad'rate
quad'rat'ed
quad'rat'ic
quad'rat'ics
quad'ra'ture
qua'dren'ni'al
quad'ri'lat'er'al
qua'drille
quad'ril'lion

quad'ril'lionth
quad'ri'ple'gia
quad'ri'ple'gic
quad'ri'va'lent
quad'roon
qua'dru'ma'nous
quad'ru'ped
quad'ru'ple
quad'ru'pled
quad'ru'plet
quad'ru'pli'cate
quad'ru'pling
quaff
quag'mire
quail
quaint
quaint'ly
quaint'ness
quake
quaked
Quak'er
Quak'er'ism
quak'ing
qual'i'fi'a'ble
qual'i'fi'ca'tion
qual'i'fied
qual'i'fier
qual'i'fy
qual'i'fy'ing
qual'i'ta'tive
qual'i'ta'tive'ly
qual'i'ties
qual'i'ty
qualm
qualm'ish
quan'da'ries
quan'da'ry
quan'ta
quan'ti'fi'a'ble
quan'ti'fi'ca'tion
quan'ti'fied
quan'ti'fy
quan'ti'fy'ing
quan'ti'ta'tive
quan'ti'ties
quan'ti'ty
quan'tum
quar'an'tin'a'ble
quar'an'tine
quar'an'tined
quar'an'tin'ing
quar'rel
quar'relled

quar'rel'ling
quar'rel'some
quar'ried
quar'ries
quar'ry
quar'ry'ing
quart
quar'ter
quar'ter'back
quar'ter'deck
quar'ter'fi'nal
quar'ter'ing
quar'ter'lies
quar'ter'ly
quar'ter'mas'ter
quar'tet
quar'tette
quar'to
quartz
qua'sar
quash
qua'si
qua'si-ju'di'cial
qua'ter'nary
quat'rain
qua'ver
quav'er'ing'ly
quay
quay'side
queas'i'er
queas'i'est
quea'si'ly
quea'si'ness
quea'sy
queen
queen'li'ness
queen'ly
queer
queer'ly
queer'ness
quell
quench
quench'a'ble
que'ried
que'ries
quer'u'lous'ly
quer'u'ulous
que'ry
que'ry'ing
quest
quest'ing'ly
ques'tion
ques'tion'a'bil'i'ty

ques'tion'a'ble
ques'tion'a'ble'ness
ques'tion'a'bly
ques'tioned
ques'tion'er
ques'tion'ing
ques'tion'ing'ly
ques'tion'naire
queue
queued
queue'ing
queu'ing
quib'ble
quib'bled
quib'bling
quiche
quick
quick'en
quick-freeze
quick'ie
quick'lime
quick'ly
quick'ness
quick'sand
quick'sil'ver
quick'step
quick-tem'pered
quick-wit'ted
quid
quid pro quo
qui'es'cence
qui'es'cent
qui'et
qui'et'ed
qui'et'ing
qui'et'ism
qui'et'ly
qui'et'ness
qui'e'tude
quill
quilt
quilt'ing
quince
qui'nine
quin'quen'ni'al
quin'sy
quint
quin'tes'sence
quin'tes'sen'tial
quin'tet
quin'tette
quin'til'lion
quin'til'lion'th

quin'tu'ple
quin'tu'pled
quin'tu'plet
quin'tu'pling
quip
quipped
quip'ping
quip'ster
quire
quirk
quirk'i'er
quirk'i'est
quirk'i'ness
quirky
quis'ling
quit
quit'claim
quite
quits
quit'tance
quit'ted
quit'ter
quit'ting
quiv'er
quiv'ered
quiv'er'ing
qui vive
quix'ot'ic
quix'ot'i'cal'ly
quiz
quiz'mas'ter
quizzed
quiz'zes
quiz'zi'cal
quiz'zi'cal'ly
quiz'zing
quoit
quoits
quon'dam
quo'rum
quo'ta
quot'able
quo'ta'tion
quote
quot'ed
quoth
quo'tid'i'an
quo'tient
quot'ing
rab'bet
rab'bet'ed
rab'bet'ing
rab'bi

rab'bin'i'cal
rab'bin'i'cal'ly
rab'bis
rab'bit
rab'bit'ed
rab'bit'ing
rab'ble
rab'id
rab'id'ly
ra'bies
rac'coon
race
raced
race'horse
ra'ceme
rac'er
race'track
ra'cial
ra'cial'ism
ra'cial'ist
ra'cial'ly
rac'i'er
rac'i'est
rac'i'ly
rac'i'ness
rac'ing
rac'ism
rac'ist
rack
rack'et
rack'et'eer
rac'on'teur
ra'coon
racy
ra'dar
ra'di'al
ra'di'al'ly
ra'di'ance
ra'di'an'cy
ra'di'ant
ra'di'ant'ly
ra'di'ate
ra'di'at'ed
ra'di'at'ing
ra'di'a'tion
ra'di'a'tor
rad'i'cal
rad'i'cal'ism
rad'i'cal'ize
rad'i'cal'ized
rad'i'cal'iz'ing
rad'i'cal'ly
rad'i'cle

ra'dii
ra'dio
ra'di'o'ac'tive
ra'di'o'ac'tiv'i'ty
rad'io'car'bon
ra'di'oed
ra'di'o' fre'quen'cy
ra'di'o'gram
ra'di'o'graph
ra'di'og'ra'pher
ra'di'og'ra'phy
ra'di'o'ing
ra'dio'iso'tope
ra'di'ol'o'gist
ra'di'ol'o'gy
ra'di'os'copy
ra'di'o'tel'e'phone
ra'di'o'ther'a'pist
ra'di'o'ther'a'py
rad'ish
ra'di'um
ra'di'us
ra'don
raf'fia
raf'fish
raf'fish'ness
raf'fle
raf'fled
raf'fling
raft'er
rag
ra'ga
rag'a'muf'fin
rag'bag
rage
raged
ragged
rag'ged
rag'ged'ly
rag'ged'ness
rag'gedy
rag'ging
rag'ing
rag'lan
ra'gout
rag'tag
rag'time
rag'weed
raid
raid'er
rail
rail'ing
rail'lery

rail'road
rail'way
rai'ment
rain
rain'bow
rain'coat
rain'drop
rain'fall
rain'i'er
rain'i'est
rain'i'ly
rain'i'ness
rain'wa'ter
rainy
raise
raised
rai'sin
rais'ing
rai'son d'êt're
raj
ra'jah
rake
raked
rake-off
rak'ing
rak'ish
rak'ish'ness
ral'lied
ral'lies
ral'ly
ral'ly'ing
ram
ram'ble
ram'bled
ram'bler
ram'bling
ram'bunc'tious
ram'i'fi'ca'tion
ram'i'fied
ram'i'fy
ram'i'fy'ing
rammed
ram'ming
ram'page
ram'paged
ram'pag'ing
ram'pan'cy
ramp'ant
ram'pant'ly
rampart
ram'rod
ram'shack'le
ran

ranch
ranch'er
ranch'ing
ran'cid
ran'cid'i'ty
ran'cid'ness
ran'cor'ous
ran'cour
rand
rand'i'er
rand'i'est
ran'dom
ran'dom'ize
ran'dom'ly
ran'dom'ness
randy
rang
range
ranged
rang'er
rang'i'ness
rang'ing
rangy
ran'kle
ran'kled
ran'kling
ran'sack
ran'som
rant'er
rap
ra'pa'cious
ra'pa'cious'ly
ra'pac'i'ty
rape
rap'id
rap'id fire
ra'pid'i'ty
rap'id'ly
rap'id'ness
ra'pi'er
rap'ine
rap'ist
rapped
rap'per
rap'ping
rap'port
rap'proche'ment
rap'scal'lion
rapt
rapt'ly
rap'ture
rap'tur'ous
rap'tur'ous'ly

rare
rare'bit
rar'e'fac'tion
rar'e'fied
rar'e'fied
rar'e'fy
rar'e'fy'ing
rare'ly
rar'er
rar'est
rar'ing
rar'i'ties
rar'i'ty
ras'cal
ras'cal'i'ty
ras'cal'ly
rash
rash'er
rash'ly
rash'ness
rasp
rasp'ber'ry
rasp'ing'ly
raspy
Ras'ta
Ras'ta'far'i'an
rat
rat'able
ra'ta'fia
rat-a-tat
ratch'et
rate
rate'able
rat'ed
rath'er
rat'i'fi'ca'tion
rat'i'fied
rat'i'fi'er
rat'i'fy
rat'i'fy'ing
rat'ing
ra'tio
ra'ti'o'ci'na'tion
ra'tion
ra'tion'al
ra'tion'ale
ra'tion'al'ism
ra'tion'al'ist
ra'tion'al'is'tic
ra'tion'al'is'ti'cal'ly
ra'tion'al'i'ty
ra'tion'al'i'za'tion
ra'tion'al'ize

ra'tion'al'ized
ra'tion'al'iz'er
ra'tion'al'iz'ing
ra'tion'al'ly
ra'tios
rat'tan
rat'ted
rat'ter
rat'ti'er
rat'ti'est
rat'ti'ness
rat'ting
rat'tle
rat'tle'brain
rat'tled
rat'tler
rat'tle'snake
rat'tling
rat'ty
rau'cous
rau'cous'ly
raun'chi'er
raunch'i'est
raun'chy
rav'age
rav'aged
rav'ag'er
rav'ag'ing
rave
raved
rav'el
rav'elled
rav'el'ling
ra'ven
rav'en'ous
rav'en'ous'ly
ra'vine
rav'ing
ra'vi'o'li
rav'ish
rav'ish'ing
rav'ish'ing'ly
rav'ish'ment
raw
raw'boned
raw'hide
raw'ness
ray
ray'on
raze
razed
raz'ing
ra'zor

raz'zle-daz'zle
re
reach
reach'able
re'act
re'ac'tion
re'ac'tion'ar'ies
re'ac'tion'ary
re'ac'ti'vate
re'ac'ti'vat'ed
re'ac'ti'vat'ing
re'ac'ti'va'tion
re'ac'tive
re'ac'tor
read
read'a'bil'i'ty
read'a'ble
read'a'ble'ness
read'er
read'er'ship
read'ied
read'i'ly
read'i'ness
re'ad'just
re'ad'just'ment
ready
read'y'ing
ready-made
re'af'firm
re'a'gent
re'al
re'align'ment
re'al'ism
re'al'ist
re'al'is'tic
re'al'is'ti'cal'ly
re'al'i'ties
re'al'i'ty
re'al'iz'a'ble
re'al'i'za'tion
re'al'ize
re'al'ized
re'al'iz'ing
re'al'ly
realm
re'al'tor
re'al'ty
ream
ream'er
re'an'i'mate
re'an'i'mat'ed
re'an'i'mat'ing
re'an'i'ma'tion

reap
reap'er
re'ap'pear
re'ap'pear'ance
re'ap'por'tion
re'ap'por'tion'ment
re'ap'prais'al
re'ap'praise
re'ap'praised
re'ap'prais'ing
rear
rear ad'mi'ral
rear'guard
re'arm
re'ar'ma'ment
rear'most
re'ar'range
re'ar'ranged
re'ar'range'ment
re'ar'rang'ing
rea'son
rea'son'a'bil'i'ty
rea'son'a'ble
rea'son'a'ble'ness
rea'son'a'bly
rea'son'er
rea'son'ing
re'as'sem'ble
re'as'sem'bled
re'as'sem'bling
re'as'sem'bly
re'as'sert
re'as'sess'ment
re'as'sume
re'as'sump'tion
re'as'sur'ance
re'as'sure
re'as'sured
re'as'sur'ing
re'as'sur'ing'ly
re'bate
re'bat'ed
re'bat'ing
re'bel
re'belled
re'bel'ling
re'bel'lion
re'bel'lious
re'bel'li'ous'ly
re'bel'lious'ness
re'birth
re'born
re'bound

re'buff
re'build
re'build'ing
re'built
re'buke
re'buked
re'buk'ing
re'but
re'but'tal
re'but'ted
re'but'ter
re'but'ting
re'cal'ci'trance
re'cal'ci'tran'cy
re'cal'ci'trant
re'call
re'cant
re'can'ta'tion
re'cap
re'ca'pit'u'late
re'ca'pit'u'lat'ed
re'ca'pit'u'lat'ing
re'ca'pit'u'la'tion
re'capped
re'cap'ping
re'cap'ture
re'cap'tured
re'cap'tur'ing
re'cast
re'cede
re'ced'ed
re'ced'ing
re'ceipt
re'ceiv'a'ble
re'ceive
re'ceived
re'ceiv'er
re'ceiv'er'ship
re'ceiv'ing
re'cen'cy
re'cent
re'cent'ly
re'cent'ness
re'cep'ta'cle
re'cep'tion
re'cep'tion'ist
re'cep'tive
re'cep'tive'ly
re'cep'tive'ness
re'cep'tiv'i'ty
re'cess
re'ces'sion
re'ces'sion'al

re'ces'sion'ary
re'ces'sive
re'charge
re'charge'able
re'charged
re'charg'ing
re'cher'ché
re'cid'i'vism
re'cid'i'vist
rec'i'pe
re'cip'i'ence
re'cip'i'en'cy
re'cip'i'ent
re'cip'ro'cal
re'cip'ro'cal'ly
re'cip'ro'cate
re'cip'ro'cat'ed
re'cip'ro'cat'ing
re'cip'ro'ca'tion
re'cip'ro'ca'tive
rec'i'proc'i'ty
re'ci'sion
re'cit'al
rec'i'ta'tion
rec'i'ta'tive
re'cite
re'cit'ed
re'cit'ing
reck'less
reck'less'ly
reck'less'ness
reck'on
reck'on'ing
re'claim
re'claim'able
rec'la'ma'tion
re'cline
re'clined
re'clin'er
re'clin'ing
rec'luse
re'clu'sion
re'clu'sive
rec'og'ni'tion
rec'og'niz'a'ble
rec'og'niz'a'bly
rec'og'ni'zance
rec'og'nize
rec'og'nized
rec'og'niz'ing
re'coil
re'coil'less
rec'ol'lect

re'col'lect
rec'ol'lec'tion
rec'om'mend
rec'om'mend'able
rec'om'men'da'tion
rec'om'mend'er
re'com'mit
re'com'mit'tal
rec'om'pense
rec'om'pensed
rec'om'pens'ing
rec'on'cil'a'ble
rec'on'cil'a'bly
rec'on'cile
rec'on'ciled
rec'on'cile'ment
rec'on'cil'er
rec'on'cil'i'a'tion
rec'on'cil'ing
rec'on'dite
re'con'di'tion
re'con'firm
re'con'fir'ma'tion
re'con'nais'sance
re'con'noi'tre
re'con'noi'tred
re'con'sid'er
re'con'sid'er'a'tion
re'con'sti'tute
re'con'struct
re'con'struc'tion
re'cord
rec'ord
re'cord'er
re'cord'ing
re'count
re'coup
re'course
re'cov'er
re'cov'er'able
re'cov'er'ies
re'cov'ery
rec're'ant
re'cre'ate
re'cre'at'ed
re'cre'at'ing
re-cre'a'tion
rec're'a'tion
rec're'a'tion'al
rec're'a'tive
re'crim'i'nate
re'crim'i'nat'ed
re'crim'i'nat'ing

re'crim'i'na'tion
re'crim'i'na'tive
re'crim'i'na'to'ry
re'cruit
re'cruit'er
re'cruit'ment
rec'tal
rec'tan'gle
rec'tan'gu'lar
rec'ti'fi'a'ble
rec'ti'fi'ca'tion
rec'ti'fied
rec'ti'fi'er
rec'ti'fy
rec'ti'fy'ing
rec'ti'lin'e'ar
rec'ti'tude
rec'tor
rec'to'ries
rec'to'ry
rec'tum
re'cum'ben'cy
re'cum'bent
re'cum'bent'ly
re'cu'per'ate
re'cu'per'at'ed
re'cu'per'at'ing
re'cu'per'a'tion
re'cu'per'a'tive
re'cur
re'curred
re'cur'rence
re'cur'rent
re'cur'ring
re'cy'cle
red
red-blood'ed
red'den
red'der
red'dish
re'dec'o'rate
re'dec'o'rat'ed
re'dec'o'rat'ing
re'dec'o'ra'tion
re'ded'i'cate
re'ded'i'cat'ed
re'ded'i'cat'ing
re'ded'i'ca'tion
re'deem
re'deem'a'ble
re'deem'er
re'demp'tion
re'demp'tive

re'demp'to'ry
re'de'ploy
re'de'ploy'ment
re'de'sign
re'de'vel'op
re'de'vel'op'ment
red-hand'ed
red'head
red'head'ed
re'did
re'di'rect
re'di'rec'tion
re'dis'trib'ute
re'dis'trib'ut'ed
re'dis'trib'ut'ing
re'dis'tri'bu'tion
re'dis'trict
red-let'ter
red'ness
re'do
re'does
re'do'ing
red'o'lence
red'o'len'cy
red'o'lent
re'done
re'dou'ble
re'dou'bled
re'dou'bling
re'doubt
re'doubt'able
re'doubt'ably
re'dound
re'dress
re'duce
re'duced
re'duc'er
re'duc'i'ble
re'duc'ing
re'duc'tion
re'dun'dan'cies
re'dun'dan'cy
re'dun'dant
re'dun'dant'ly
re'du'pli'cate
re'du'pli'cat'ed
re'du'pli'cat'ing
re'dup'li'ca'tion
red'wood
re-echo
re-ech'oes
re-ech'o'ing
reed

reed'i'er
reed'i'est
re-ed'u'cate
re-ed'u'ca'tion
reedy
reef
reef'er
reef knot
reek
reel
re-elect
re-elec'tion
re-em'pha'size
re-em'pha'sized
re-em'pha'siz'ing
re-em'ploy
re-en'act
re-en'force
re-en'forced
re-en'force'ment
re-en'forc'ing
re-en'list
re-en'list'ment
re-en'ter
re-en'trance
re-en'try
re-es'tab'lish
re-es'tab'lish'ment
re-ex'am'i'na'tion
re-ex'am'ine
re-ex'am'ined
re-ex'am'in'ing
re'fec'to'ries
re'fec'to'ry
re'fer
re'fer'a'ble
ref'er'ee
ref'er'eed
ref'er'ee'ing
ref'er'ence
ref'er'enced
ref'er'enc'ing
ref'er'en'da
ref'er'en'dum
ref'er'ent
ref'er'en'tial
re'fer'ral
re'ferred
re'fer'ring
re'fill
re'fill'a'ble
re'fi'nance
re'fine

re'fined
re'fine'ment
re'fin'er'ies
re'fin'ery
re'fin'ing
re'fin'ish
re'fit
re'fit'ted
re'fit'ting
re'flat'ed
re'flat'ing
re'fla'tion
re'fla'tion'ary
re'flect
re'flec'tion
re'flec'tive
re'flec'tive'ly
re'flec'tor
re'flex
re'flex'ive
re'for'est
re'for'est'a'tion
re'form
ref'or'ma'tion
re'form'a'tive
re'form'a'to'ry
re'formed
re'form'er
re'form'ist
re'fract
re'frac'tion
re'frac'tive
re'frac'to'ri'ness
re'frac'to'ry
re'frain
re'fran'gi'ble
re'fresh
re'fresh'er
re'fresh'ing
re'fresh'ing'ly
re'fresh'ment
re'fried
re'frig'er'ant
re'frig'er'ate
re'frig'er'at'ing
re'frig'er'ation
re'frig'er'a'tor
ref'uge
ref'u'gee
re'ful'gence
re'ful'gent
re'fund
re'fur'bish

re'fus'al
re'fuse
ref'use
re'fused
re'fuse'nik
re'fus'ing
re'fut'a'ble
ref'u'ta'tion
re'fute
re'fut'ed
re'fut'ing
re'gain
re'gal
re'gale
re'galed
re'ga'lia
re'gal'ing
re'gal'ly
re'gard
re'gard'ful
re'gard'ing
re'gard'less
re'gat'ta
re'gen'cies
re'gen'cy
re'gen'er'a'cy
re'gen'er'ate
re'gen'er'at'ed
re'gen'er'at'ing
re'gen'er'a'tion
re'gen'er'a'tive
re'gent
reg'gae
reg'i'cide
re'gime
reg'i'men
reg'i'ment
reg'i'men'tal
reg'i'men'ta'tion
re'gion
re'gion'al
re'gion'al'ism
re'gion'al'ly
reg'is'ter
reg'is'tered
reg'is'trant
reg'is'trar
reg'is'tra'tion
reg'is'tries
reg'is'try
re'gress
re'gres'sion
re'gres'sive

re'gret
re'gret'ful
re'gret'ful'ly
re'gret'ful'ness
re'gret'ta'ble
re'gret'ta'bly
re'gret'ted
re'gret'ting
re'group
reg'u'lar
reg'u'lar'i'ties
reg'u'lar'i'ty
reg'u'lar'ize
reg'u'lar'ized
reg'u'lar'iz'ing
reg'u'lar'ly
reg'u'late
reg'u'lat'ed
reg'u'lat'ing
reg'u'la'tion
reg'u'la'tive
reg'u'la'tor
reg'u'la'to'ry
re'gur'gi'tate
re'gur'gi'tat'ed
re'gur'gi'tat'ing
re'gur'gi'ta'tion
re'ha'bil'i'tate
re'ha'bil'i'tat'ed
re'ha'bil'i'tat'ing
re'ha'bil'i'ta'tion
re'ha'bil'i'ta'tive
re'hash
re'hears'al
re'hearse
re'hearsed
re'hears'ing
re'house
re'housed
re'hous'ing
reign
re'im'burse
re'im'bursed
re'im'burse'ment
re'im'burs'ing
rein
re'in'car'nate
re'in'car'nat'ed
re'in'car'nat'ing
re'in'car'na'tion
rein'deer
re'in'fec'tion
re'in'force

re'in'forced
re'in'force'ment
re'in'forc'ing
re'in'state
re'in'stated
re'in'state'ment
re'in'stat'ing
re'in'sur'ance
re'in'ter'pre'ta'tion
re'in'vest
re'in'vest'ment
re'is'sue
re'it'er'ate
re'it'er'at'ed
re'it'er'at'ing
re'it'er'a'tion
re'it'er'a'tive
re'ject
re'jec'tion
re'joice
re'joiced
re'joic'ing
re'join
re'join'der
re'ju've'nate
re'ju've'nat'ed
re'ju've'nat'ing
re'ju've'na'tion
re'kin'dle
re'kin'dled
re'kin'dling
re'laid
re'lapse
re'lapsed
re'laps'ing
re'late
re'lat'ed
re'lat'ing
re'la'tion
re'la'tion'al
re'la'tion'ship
rel'a'tive
rel'a'tive'ly
rel'a'tiv'i'ty
re'lax
re'lax'ant
re'lax'a'tion
re'lay
re'lay'ing
re'lease
re'leased
re'leas'ing
rel'e'gate

rel'e'gat'ed
rel'e'gat'ing
rel'e'ga'tion
re'lent
re'lent'less
re'lent'less'ly
rel'e'vance
rel'e'van'cy
rel'e'vant
re'li'a'bil'i'ty
re'li'a'ble
re'li'a'ble'ness
re'li'a'bly
re'li'ance
re'li'ant
rel'ic
rel'ict
re'lied
re'lief
re'liev'a'ble
re'lieve
re'lieved
re'liev'ing
re'li'gion
re'li'gi'os'ity
re'li'gious
re'li'gious'ly
re'lin'quish
rel'i'quar'ies
rel'i'qua'ry
rel'ish
re'live
re'lived
re'liv'ing
re'load
re'lo'cate
re'lo'cat'ed
re'lo'cat'ing
re'lo'ca'tion
re'luc'tance
re'luc'tant
re'luc'tant'ly
re'ly
re'ly'ing
re'made
re'main
re'main'der
re'make
re'mak'ing
re'mand
re'mark
re'mark'a'ble
re'mark'a'ble'ness

re'mark'a'bly
re'mar'riage
re'mar'ried
re'mar'ry
re'mar'ry'ing
re'me'di'a'ble
re'me'di'al
rem'e'died
rem'e'dies
rem'e'dy
rem'e'dy'ing
re'mem'ber
re'mem'brance
re'mind
re'mind'er
rem'i'nisce
rem'i'nisced
rem'i'nis'cence
rem'i'nis'cent
rem'i'nisc'ing
re'miss
re'mis'sion
re'miss'ness
re'mit
re'mit'tance
re'mit'ted
re'mit'ting
rem'nant
re'mod'el
re'mod'elled
re'mod'el'ling
re'mon'strance
re'mon'strate
re'mon'strat'ed
re'mon'strat'ing
re'morse
re'morse'ful
re'morse'ful'ly
re'morse'less
re'morse'less'ly
re'mote
re'mote'ly
re'mote'ness
re'mount
re'mov'a'ble
re'mov'al
re'move
re'moved
re'mov'er
re'mov'ing
re'mu'ner'ate
re'mu'ner'at'ed
re'mu'ner'at'ing

re'mu'ner'a'tion
re'mu'ner'a'tive
ren'ais'sance
re'nal
re'name
re'named
re'nam'ing
re'nas'cence
re'nas'cent
rend
rend'ed
ren'der
ren'dez'vous
ren'dez'voused
ren'dez'vous'ing
rend'ing
ren'di'tion
ren'e'gade
re'nege
re'neged
re'neg'ing
re'new
re'new'al
ren'net
re'nom'i'nate
re'nounce
re'nounced
re'nounc'ing
ren'o'vate
ren'o'vat'ed
ren'o'vat'ing
ren'o'va'tion
ren'o'vat'or
re'nown
re'nowned
rent'al
re'nun'ci'a'tion
re'open
re'or'ga'ni'za'tion
re'or'ga'nize
re'or'ga'nized
re'or'ga'niz'ing
re'paid
re'pair
rep'a'ra'ble
rep'a'ra'tion
rep'ar'tee
re'past
re'pa'tri'ate
re'pa'tri'at'ed
re'pa'tri'at'ing
re'pa'tri'a'tion
re'pay

re'pay'able
re'pay'ing
re'pay'ment
re'peal
re'peat
re'peat'able
re'peat'ed
re'peat'ed'ly
re'peat'er
re'pel
re'pelled
re'pel'lent
re'pel'ling
re'pent
re'pent'ance
re'pent'ant
re'per'cus'sion
rep'er'toire
rep'er'to'ry
rep'e'ti'tion
rep'e'ti'tious
re'pet'i'tive
re'phrase
re'phrased
re'phras'ing
re'place
re'place'a'ble
re'placed
re'place'ment
re'plac'ing
rep'lay
re'plen'ish
re'plete
re'ple'tion
rep'li'ca
rep'li'cate
rep'li'cat'ed
rep'li'ca'tion
re'plied
re'plies
re'ply
re'ply'ing
re'point
re'port
re'port'able
re'port'age
re'port'ed'ly
re'port'er
rep'or'to'ri'al
re'pose
re'posed
re'pos'ing
re'pos'i'to'ries

re'pos'i'to'ry
re'pos'sess
re'pos'ses'sion
re'pot
re'pot'ted
re'pot'ting
rep're'hend
rep're'hen'si'ble
rep're'hen'sion
rep're'sent
rep're'sen'ta'tion
rep're'sen'ta'tion'al
rep're'sent'a'tive
re'press
re'pres'sion
re'pres'sive
re'prieve
re'prieved
re'priev'ing
re'pri'mand
re'print
re'pris'al
re'proach
re'proach'ful
re'proach'ful'ly
rep'ro'bate
rep'ro'ba'tion
re'pro'duce
re'pro'duced
re'pro'duc'ing
re'pro'duc'tion
re'pro'duc'tive
re'proof
re'prove
re'proved
re'prov'ing
re'prov'ing'ly
rep'tile
rep'til'i'an
re'pub'lic
re'pub'li'can
re'pub'li'can'ism
re'pu'di'ate
re'pu'di'at'ed
re'pu'di'at'ing
re'pu'di'a'tion
re'pug'nance
re'pug'nan'cy
re'pug'nant
re'pulse
re'pulsed
re'puls'ing
re'pul'sion

re'pul'sive
re'pul'sive'ly
rep'u'ta'bil'i'ty
rep'u'ta'ble
rep'u'ta'bly
rep'u'ta'tion
re'pute
re'put'ed
re'put'ed'ly
re'put'ing
re'quest
requi'em
re'qui'es'cat
re'quire
re'quired
re'quire'ment
re'quir'ing
req'ui'site
req'ui'si'tion
re'quit'al
re'quite
re'ran
rere'dos
re'route
re'rout'ed
re'rout'ing
re'run
re'run'ning
re'scind
re'scis'sion
res'cue
res'cued
res'cu'er
res'cu'ing
re'search
re'search'er
re'seat
re'sell
re'sell'ing
re'sem'blance
re'sem'ble
re'sem'bled
re'sem'bling
re'sent
re'sent'ful
re'sent'ful'ly
re'sent'ment
res'er'va'tion
re'serve
re'served
re'serv'ing
re'serv'ist
res'er'voir

re'set
re'set'ting
re'set'tle
re'set'tled
re'set'tle'ment
re'set'tling
re'shuf'fle
re'shuf'fled
re'shuf'fling
re'side
re'sid'ed
res'i'dence
res'i'den'cy
res'i'dent
res'i'den'tial
re'sid'ing
re'sid'u'al
res'i'due
re'sign
res'ig'na'tion
re'signed
re'sign'ed'ly
re'sil'ience
re'sil'ien'cy
re'sil'ient
res'in
res'in'ous
re'sist
re'sist'ance
re'sist'ant
re'sist'er
re'sist'i'ble
re'sis'tor
re'sold
res'o'lute
res'o'lute'ly
res'o'lu'tion
re'solve
re'solved
re'solv'ing
res'o'nance
res'o'nant
res'o'nate
res'o'nat'ed
res'o'nat'ing
res'o'na'tor
re'sort
re'sound
re'source
re'source'ful
re'spect
re'spect'abil'i'ty
re'spect'able

re'spec'ta'bly
re'spect'er
re'spect'ful
re'spect'ful'ly
re'spect'ful'ness
re'spect'ing
re'spec'tive
re'spec'tive'ly
res'pi'ra'tion
res'pi'ra'tor
res'pi'ra'to'ry
re'spire
re'spired
re'spir'ing
res'pite
re'splen'dence
re'splen'dent
re'splen'dent'ly
re'spond
re'spond'ent
re'sponse
re'spon'si'bil'i'ties
re'spon'si'bil'i'ty
re'spon'si'ble
re'spon'si'bly
re'spon'sive
re'spon'sive'ness
re'state
re'stat'ed
re'state'ment
re'stat'ing
res'tau'rant
res'tau'ra'teur
rest'ful
rest'ful'ly
res'ti'tu'tion
res'tive
res'tive'ness
rest'less
rest'less'ly
rest'less'ness
re'stock
res'to'ra'tion
re'stor'a'tive
re'store
re'stored
re'stor'er
re'stor'ing
re'strain
re'strained
re'straint
re'strict
re'strict'ed

re'stric'tion
re'stric'tive
re'struc'ture
re'struc'tured
re'struc'tur'ing
re'sult
re'sult'ant
ré'su'mé
re'sume
re'sumed
re'sum'ing
re'sump'tion
re'sur'face
re'sur'faced
re'sur'fac'ing
re'sur'gence
re'sur'gent
res'ur'rect
res'ur'rec'tion
re'sus'ci'tate
re'sus'ci'tat'ed
re'sus'ci'tat'ing
re'sus'ci'ta'tion
re'sus'ci'ta'tor
re'tail
re'tail'er
re'tain
re'tain'er
re'take
re'tak'en
re'tak'ing
re'tal'i'ate
re'tal'i'at'ed
re'tal'i'at'ing
re'tal'i'a'tion
re'tal'i'a'to'ry
re'tard
re'tard'ant
re'tar'da'tion
re'tard'ed
retch
re'tell
re'telling
re'ten'tion
re'ten'tive
re'ten'tiv'i'ty
re'think
re'think'ing
re'thought
ret'i'cence
ret'i'cent
re'tic'u'lar
ret'i'cule

ret'i'na
ret'i'nae
ret'i'nal
ret'i'nue
re'tire
re'tired
re'tire'ment
re'tir'ing
re'told
re'took
re'tort
re'touch
re'trace
re'traced
re'trac'ing
re'tract
re'tract'able
re'trac'tile
re'trac'tion
re'trac'tor
re'tread
re'treat
re'trench
re'trench'ment
re'tri'al
ret'ri'bu'tion
re'trib'u'tive
re'triev'al
re'trieve
re'trieved
re'triev'er
re'triev'ing
ret'ro'ac'tive
ret'ro'ac'tive'ly
ret'ro'fire
ret'ro'grade
ret'ro'gress
ret'ro'gres'sion
ret'ro'gres'sive
ret'ro'rock'et
ret'ro'spect
ret'ro'spec'tion
ret'ro'spec'tive
ret'ro'spec'tive'ly
re'trous'sé
re'turn
re'turn'a'ble
re'turn'ee
re'un'ion
re'u'nite
re'u'nit'ed
re'u'nit'ing
rev

re'val'u'a'tion
re'value
re'vamp
re'veal
rev'eil'le
rev'el
rev'e'la'tion
rev'elled
rev'el'ler
rev'el'ling
rev'el'ries
rev'el'ry
re'venge
re'venged
re'venge'ful
re'veng'ing
rev'e'nue
rev'e'nu'er
re'ver'ber'ate
re'ver'ber'at'ed
re'ver'ber'at'ing
re'ver'ber'a'tion
re'vere
re'vered
rev'er'ence
rev'er'enced
rev'er'enc'ing
rev'er'end
rev'er'ent
rev'er'en'tial
rev'er'ent'ly
rev'er'ie
re'ver'ing
re'ver'sal
re'verse
re'versed
re'vers'i'ble
re'vers'ing
re'ver'sion
re'vert
re'view
re'view'er
re'vile
re'viled
re'vil'ing
re'vise
re'vised
re'vis'ing
re'vi'sion
re'vi'sion'ism
re'vi'sion'ist
re'vis'it
re'vis'it'ed

re'vis'it'ing
re'vi'tal'iza'tion
re'vi'tal'ize
re'vi'tal'ized
re'vi'tal'iz'ing
re'viv'al
re'vi'val'ism
re'viv'al'ist
re'vive
re'vived
re'viv'i'fi'ca'tion
re'viv'i'fied
re'viv'i'fy
re'viv'i'fy'ing
re'viv'ing
rev'o'ca'ble
rev'o'ca'tion
re'voke
re'voked
re'vok'ing
re'volt
re'volt'ing'ly
rev'o'lu'tion
rev'o'lu'tion'ar'ies
rev'o'lu'tion'ary
rev'o'lu'tion'ist
rev'o'lu'tion'ize
re'volve
re'volved
re'volv'er
re'volv'ing
re'vue
re'vul'sion
revved
rev'ving
re'wak'en
re'ward
re'wind
re'wind'ing
re'wire
re'wired
re'wir'ing
re'work
re'wound
re'write
re'writ'ing
re'writ'ten
re'wrote
rhap'sod'ic
rhap'sod'i'cal'ly
rhap'so'dies
rhap'so'dist
rhap'so'dize

rhap'so'dized
rhap'so'diz'ing
rhap'so'dy
rhe'ni'um
rhe'o'stat
rhe'sus
rhet'o'ric
rhe'tor'i'cal
rhe'tor'i'cal'ly
rhet'o'ri'cian
rheum
rheu'mat'ic
rheu'ma'tism
rheu'ma'toid
rheumy
rhine'stone
rhi'ni'tis
rhi'noc'er'os
rhi'zome
rho'di'um
rho'do'den'dron
rhom'bo'he'dra
rhom'bo'he'dron
rhom'boid
rhom'bus
rhu'barb
rhyme
rhymed
rhym'ing
rhythm
rhyth'mic
rhyth'mi'cal
rhyth'mi'cal'ly
rib
rib'ald
rib'ald'ry
rib'and
ribbed
rib'bing
rib'bon
ri'bo'fla'vin
ri'bo'nu'cle'ic
rice
rich
rich'es
rich'ly
rich'ness
Rich'ter scale
rick
rick'et'i'ness
rick'ets
rick'ety
rick'shaw

ric'o'chet
ric'o'cheted
ric'o'chet'ing
ric'o'chet'ted
ric'o'chet'ting
rid
rid'dance
rid'ded
rid'den
rid'ding
rid'dle
rid'dled
rid'dling
ride
rid'er
ridge
ridged
ridg'ing
rid'i'cule
rid'i'culed
rid'i'cul'ing
ri'dic'u'lous
ri'dic'u'lous'ly
rid'ing
rife
rif'fle
rif'fled
rif'fling
riff'raff
ri'fle
ri'fled
ri'fle'man
ri'fling
rift
rig
rigged
rig'ger
rig'ging
right
right-an'gled
righ'teous
righ'teous'ness
right'ful
right'ful'ly
right-hand'ed
right'ism
right'ist
right'ly
right-of-way
right-wing'er
rig'id
ri'gid'i'ties
ri'gid'i'ty

rig'id'ly
rig'ma'role
rig'or
ri'gor mor'tis
rig'or'ous
rig'o'rous'ly
rig'our
rile
riled
ril'ing
rim
rim'less
rimmed
rim'ming
rind
ring
ring'ed
ring'er
ring'ing
ring'lead'er
ring'let
ring'mas'ter
ring'side
ring'worm
rinse
rinsed
rins'ing
ri'ot
ri'ot'ed
ri'ot'er
ri'ot'ing
ri'ot'ous
ri'ot'ous'ly
rip
ri'par'i'an
rip'en
ripe'ness
rip-off
ri'poste
ri'post'ed
ri'post'ing
ripped
rip'per
rip'ping
rip'ple
rip'pled
rip'pling
rise
ris'en
ris'er
ris'i'bil'i'ty
ris'i'ble
ris'ing

risk
risk'i'er
risk'i'est
risk'i'ness
risky
ri'sot'to
ris'qué
rite
rit'u'al
rit'u'al'ism
rit'u'al'ist
rit'u'al'is'tic
rit'ually
ritz'i'er
ritzy
ri'val
ri'valled
ri'val'ling
ri'val'ries
ri'val'ry
riv'en
riv'er
riv'er'side
riv'et
riv'et'ed
riv'et'er
riv'et'ing
Riv'i'er'a
roach
roach'es
road
road'bed
road'block
road'house
road'run'ner
road'side
road'ster
road'way
road'work
road'wor'thy
roam
roan
roar
roast
roast'er
rob
robbed
rob'ber
rob'ber'ies
rob'bery
rob'bing
robe
robed

rob'in
rob'ing
ro'bot
ro'bot'ic
ro'bot'ics
ro'bust
ro'bust'ly
ro'bust'ness
roc
rock
rock'a'bil'ly
rock-bound
rock'er
rock'et
rock'et'ed
rock'et'ing
rock'et'ry
rock'i'er
rock'i'est
rock'i'ness
rock'like
rock'ling
rocky
ro'co'co
rod
rode
ro'dent
ro'deo
roe
roent'gen
rogue
rogu'ery
rogu'ish
rogu'ish'ly
roist'er
role
role-play'ing
roll
roll call
roll'er
roll'er bear'ing
roll'er coast'er
roll'er skate
rol'lick
rol'lick'ing
roll'ing mill
ro'ly-po'ly
ro'maine
ro'man à clef
ro'mance
ro'manced
ro'manc'ing
Ro'ma'ni'an

ro'man'tic
ro'man'ti'cal'ly
ro'man'ti'cism
ro'man'ti'cist
ro'man'ti'cize
ro'man'ti'cized
ro'man'ti'ciz'ing
romp
romp'er
ron'do
rood
roof
roof'ing
roof'less
roof'top
rook
rook'er'ies
rook'ery
room
room'ful
room'i'er
room'i'est
room'i'ness
room'mate
roomy
roost
roost'er
root
root'less
rope
roped
rop'ey
rop'i'er
rop'ing
ropy
ror'qual
ro'sa'ceous
ro'sa'ries
ro'sa'ry
rose
ro'sé
ro'se'ate
rose'mary
ro'sette
rose'wood
ros'i'er
ros'i'est
ros'in
ros'i'ness
ros'ter
ros'tra
ros'trum
rosy

rot
ro'ta
ro'tate
ro'tat'ed
ro'tat'ing
ro'ta'tion
rote
ro'tis'ser'ie
ro'tor
rot'ted
rot'ten
rot'ter
rot'ting
ro'tund
ro'tun'da
ro'tun'di'ty
rou'ble
roué
rouge
rouged
rough
rough'age
rough'cast
rough'en
rough-hewed
rough-hewn
rough'house
rough'ly
rough'neck
rough'ness
rough'rid'er
rough'shod
roug'ing
rou'lade
rou'lette
round
round'a'bout
round-arm
round'ed
roun'de'lay
round'er
round'ly
round'up
round'worm
roupy
rouse
rous'edness
roused
rous'ing
roust
roust'a'bout
rout
route

rout'ed
rou'tine
rout'ine'ly
rou'tin'ist
roux
rove
roved
rov'er
rov'ing
row
row'an
row'boat
row'di'er
row'dies
row'di'est
row'di'ly
row'di'ness
row'dy
row'dy'ism
row'er
roy'al
roy'al'ist
roy'al'ly
roy'al'ties
roy'al'ty
rub
rubbed
rub'ber
rub'ber'ize
rub'ber'ized
rub'ber'iz'ing
rub'ber'neck
rub'bery
rub'bing
rub'bish
rub'bishy
rub'ble
ru'bel'la
ru'bi'cund
ru'bid'i'um
ru'bies
ruble
ru'bric
ru'by
ruche
ruched
ruch'ing
ruck
ruck'sack
ruck'us
ruc'tion
rud'der
rud'di'er

rud'di'est
rud'di'ness
rud'dy
rude
rude'ly
rude'ness
ru'di'ment
ru'di'men'tal
ru'di'men'ta'ry
rue
rued
rue'ful
rue'ful'ly
rue'ful'ness
ruff
ruf'fi'an
ruf'fian'ly
ruf'fle
ruf'fled
ruf'fling
rug
rug'by
rug'ged
rug'ged'ly
rug'ged'ness
ru'in
ru'in'a'tion
ru'ing
ru'in'ous
ru'in'ous'ly
rule
ruled
rul'er
rul'ing
rum
rum'ba
rum'ble
rum'bled
rum'bling
ru'mi'nant
ru'mi'nate
ru'mi'nat'ing
ru'mi'na'tion
ru'mi'na'tive
ru'mi'na'tive'ly
rum'mage
rum'mag'ing
rum'my
ru'mour
ru'mour'mon'ger
rum'ple
rum'pled
rum'pling

rum'pus
run
run'about
run'around
run'away
run'down
rune
rung
ru'nic
run'nel
run'ner
run'ner-up
run'ni'er
run'ni'est
run'ning
run'ny
run-on
runt
runt'i'est
runty
run'way
ru'pee
rup'ture
rup'tured
rup'tur'ing
ru'ral
ru'ral'i'za'tion
rur'al'ize
ru'ral'ized
ru'ral'ly
ruse
rush
rush hour
rusk
rus'set
Rus'sian
rus'tic
rus'ti'cate
rus'ti'cat'ed
rus'ti'cat'ing
rus'ti'ca'tion
rus'tic'i'ty
rust'i'er
rust'i'est
rust'i'ness
rus'tle
rus'tled
rus'tler
rus'tling
rust'proof
rusty
rut
rut'ted

rut'ting
ru'ta'ba'ga
ru'the'ni'um
ruth'less
ruth'less'ly
ruth'less'ness
rut'ted
rut'ti'est
rut'ting
rut'tish
rut'tish'ness
rut'ty
rye
rye'grass
sab'bat'i'cal
sa'ble
sa'bot
sab'o'tage
sab'o'taged
sab'o'tag'ing
sab'o'teur
sa'bre
sac
sac'cha'rin
sac'cha'rine
sac'er'do'tal
sa'chet
sack
sack'cloth
sack'ful
sack'ing
sa'cra
sac'ra'ment
sa'cred
sa'cred'ly
sa'cred'ness
sac'ri'fice
sac'ri'ficed
sac'ri'fi'cial
sac'ri'fic'ing
sac'ri'lege
sac'ri'le'gious
sac'ris'tan
sac'ris'ties
sac'ris'ty
sac'ro'il'i'ac
sac'ro'sanct
sac'ro'sanc'ti'ty
sa'crum
sad
sad'den
sad'der
sad'dest

sad'dle
sad'dled
sad'dler
sad'dling
sad'ism
sad'ist
sa'dis'tic
sa'dis'ti'cal'ly
sad'ly
sad'ness
sa'do'mas'och'ism
sa'do'mas'och'ist
sa'fa'ri
safe
safe-con'duct
safe-de'pos'it
safe'guard
safe'keep'ing
safe'ly
saf'er
saf'est
safe'ty
saf'flow'er
saf'fron
sag
sa'ga
sa'ga'cious
sa'ga'cious'ly
sa'gac'i'ty
sage
sage'brush
sage'ly
sage'ness
sagged
sag'ging
sa'go
sa'hib
said
sail
sail'ing
sail'or
saint
saint'ed
saint'hood
saint'li'er
saint'li'est
saint'li'ness
saint'ly
sa'ke
sa'laam
sa'la'cious
sa'la'cious'ness
sal'ad

sal'a'man'der
sa'la'mi
sal'ar'ied
sal'a'ries
sal'a'ry
sale
sale'abil'i'ty
sale'able
sales'man
sales'man'ship
sales'peo'ple
sales'per'son
sales'wom'an
sa'li'ence
sa'li'en'cy
sa'li'ent
sa'li'ent'ly
sa'li'ent'ness
sa'line
sa'lin'i'ty
sa'li'va
sal'i'vary
sal'i'vate
sal'i'vat'ed
sal'i'vat'ing
sal'i'va'tion
sal'lied
sal'low
sal'ly
sal'ly'ing
salm'on
sal'mo'nel'la
sa'lon
sa'loon
sal'sa
sa'lsi'fy
salt
salt'cel'lar
salt'ed
salt'i'er
salt'i'est
sal'tine
salt'i'ness
salt'pe'tre
salt'sha'ker
salt-wa'ter
salty
sa'lu'bri'ous
sal'u'tary
sal'u'ta'tion
sa'lu'ta'to'ry
sa'lute
sa'lut'ed

sa'lut'ing
sal'vage
sal'vage'a'ble
sal'vaged
sal'vag'ing
sal'va'tion
salve
salved
sal'ver
salv'ing
sal'vo
sal'voes
sal vo'la'ti'le
sa'mar'i'um
sam'ba
same
same'ness
sam'ite
sam'o'var
sam'pan
sam'ple
sam'pled
sam'pler
sam'pling
sam'u'rai
san'a'to'ria
san'a'to'ri'um
sanc'ti'fi'ca'tion
sanc'ti'fied
sanc'ti'fy
sanc'ti'fy'ing
sanc'ti'mo'ni'ous
sanc'ti'mo'ni'ous'ly
sanc'ti'mo'ny
sanc'tion
sanc'tion'a'ble
sanc'ti'ty
sanc'tu'ar'ies
sanc'tu'ary
sanc'tum
san'dal
san'dal'wood
sand'bag
sand'bagged
sand'bag'ging
sand-cast
sand-cast'ed
sand-cast'ing
sand'er
sand'i'er
sand'i'est
sand'i'ness
sand'pa'per

sand'pi'per
sand'wich
sand'wich man
sandy
sane
sane'ly
sane'ness
sang
sang'froid
san'gria
san'gui'nary
san'guine
san'i'tar'i'ly
san'i'tar'i'um
san'i'tary
san'i'ta'tion
san'i'tize
san'i'tized
san'i'tiz'ing
san'i'ty
sank
San'skrit
sap
sa'pi'ence
sa'pi'en'cy
sa'pi'ent
sa'pi'en'tial
sap'ling
sapped
sap'phire
sap'ping
sap'py
sap'suck'er
sar'a'band
sar'a'bande
sa'ran
sar'casm
sar'cas'tic
sar'cas'ti'cal'ly
sar'co'ma
sar'coph'a'gi
sar'coph'a'gus
sar'dine
sar'don'ic
sar'don'i'cal'ly
sa'ri
sa'rong
sar'sa'pa'ril'la
sar'to'ri'al
sash
sa'shay
sa'shi'mi
sas'sa'fras

sas'si'ness
sas'sy
sat
sa'tan'ic
sa'tan'i'cal
sa'tay
satch'el
sate
sat'ed
sa'teen
sat'el'lite
sa'ti'a'bil'i'ty
sa'ti'a'ble
sa'ti'a'ble'ness
sa'ti'a'bly
sa'ti'ate
sa'ti'at'ed
sa'ti'at'ing
sa'ti'a'tion
sa'ti'e'ty
sat'in
sat'ing
sat'in'wood
sat'iny
sat'ire
sa'tir'i'cal
sa'tir'i'cal'ly
sat'i'rist
sat'i'rize
sat'i'rized
sat'i'riz'ing
sat'is'fac'tion
sat'is'fac'to'ri'ly
sat'is'fac'to'ry
sat'is'fi'a'ble
sat'is'fied
sat'is'fy
sat'is'fy'ing
sat'su'ma
sat'u'ra'ble
sat'u'rate
sat'u'rat'ed
sat'u'rat'ing
sat'u'ra'tion
sat'ur'na'lia
sat'ur'nine
sa'tyr
sat'yr'i'a'sis
sa'tyr'ic
sauce
sauce'boat
sauce'pan
sau'cer

sauc'i'er
sauc'i'est
sau'ci'ness
sau'cy
sau'er'bra'ten
sau'er'kraut
sau'na
saun'ter
sau'sage
sau'té
sau'téed
sau'té'ing
sav'age
sav'aged
sav'age'ly
sav'age'ness
sav'age'ry
sav'ag'ing
sa'van'na
sa'van'nah
sa'vant
save
saved
sav'er
sav'ing
sav'iour
sa'voir-faire
sa'vour
sa'vou'ries
sa'vour'i'ly
sa'vour'i'ness
sa'voury
sa'voy cab'bage
sav'vy
saw
sawed
saw'ing
saw'mill
sawn
sax'o'phone
sax'o'phon'ist
say
say'ing
say-so
scab
scab'bard
scabbed
scab'bi'ness
scab'bing
scab'by
sca'bies
scads
scaf'fold

scaf'fold'ing
scal'a'wag
scald
scald'ing
scale
scaled
scal'ing
scal'lion
scal'lop
scalp
scal'pel
scalp'er
scaly
scamp
scamp'er
scam'pi
scan
scan'dal
scan'dal'i'za'tion
scan'dal'ize
scan'dal'ized
scan'dal'iz'ing
scan'dal'mon'ger
scan'dal'ous
scan'dal'ous'ly
Scan'di'na'vi'an
scan'di'um
scanned
scan'ner
scan'ning
scan'sion
scant
scant'i'er
scant'i'est
scant'i'ly
scant'i'ness
scant'ness
scanty
scape'goat
scap'u'la
scar
scar'ab
scarce
scarce'ly
scarce'ness
scar'ci'ties
scar'ci'ty
scare
scare'crow
scared
scare'mon'ger
scarf
scarfs

scar'i'er
scar'i'est
scar'i'fi'ca'tion
scar'i'fied
scar'i'fy
scar'i'fy'ing
scar'ing
scar'la'ti'na
scar'let
scarp
scarred
scar'ring
scarves
scary
scat
scathe
scathed
scath'ing
scath'ing'ly
scat'ted
scat'ter
scat'ter'brain
scat'ter'brained
scat'ting
scav'enge
scav'enged
scav'en'ger
scav'eng'ing
sce'nar'io
sce'nar'ist
scene
scen'ery
sce'nic
sce'ni'cal
scent
scep'tic
scep'ti'cal
scep'ti'cism
scep'ti'cist
scep'tre
sched'ule
sched'uled
sched'ul'ing
sche'ma
sche'ma'ta
sche'mat'ic
sche'mat'i'cal'ly
sche'ma'tize
sche'ma'tized
sche'ma'tiz'ing
scheme
schem'er
schem'ing

scher'zo
schism
schis'mat'ic
schis'mat'i'cal
schiz'oid
schiz'o'phre'nia
schiz'o'phren'ic
schmaltz
schmaltzy
schmalz
schnapps
schol'ar
schol'ar'li'ness
schol'ar'ly
schol'ar'ship
scho'las'tic
scho'las'ti'cal
scho'las'ti'cism
school
school board
school'child
school'chil'dren
school'ing
school'teach'er
school'work
schoon'er
sci'at'ic
sci'at'i'ca
sci'ence
sci'en'tif'ic
sci'en'tif'i'cal'ly
sci'en'tist
scim'i'tar
scin'til'la
scin'til'lant
scin'til'late
scin'til'lat'ed
scin'til'lat'ing
scin'til'la'tion
sci'on
scis'sors
scle'ro'sis
scoff
scoff'er
scoff'ing'ly
scoff'law
scold
scold'ing
scol'lop
sconce
scone
scoop
scoop'er

scoop'ful
scoot
scoot'er
scope
scor'bu'tic
scorch
scorched
scorch'er
scorch'ing
score
score'board
score'card
scored
score'keep'er
score'less
scor'er
scor'ing
scorn
scorn'er
scorn'ful
scorn'ful'ly
scorn'ful'ness
scor'pi'on
Scot
scotch
scot-free
Scot'tie
Scot'tish
scoun'drel
scoun'drel'ly
scour
scour'er
scourge
scourged
scourg'ing
scout
scout'ing
scout'mas'ter
scow
scowl
scrab'ble
scrab'bled
scrab'bling
scrag
scragged
scrag'gi'er
scrag'gi'est
scrag'ging
scrag'gly
scrag'gy
scram
scram'ble
scram'bled

scram'bler
scram'bling
scrammed
scram'ming
scrap
scrap'book
scrape
scraped
scrap'er
scra'pie
scrap'ing
scrapped
scrap'per
scrap'pi'er
scrap'pi'est
scrap'pi'ness
scrap'ping
scrap'py
scratch
scratch'i'ness
scratchy
scrawl
scrawn'i'er
scrawn'i'est
scrawn'i'ness
scrawny
scream
scream'er
scream'ing
scree
screech
screen
screen'er
screen'ing
screen'play
screen'writ'er
screw
screw'ball
screw'driv'er
screw'i'er
screw'i'est
screwy
scrib'ble
scrib'bled
scrib'bler
scrib'bling
scribe
scribed
scrib'ing
scrim'mage
scrim'maged
scrim'mag'er
scrim'mag'ing

scrimp'i'ness
scrimpy
scrim'shaw
script
scrip'tur'al
scrip'ture
script'writ'er
scriv'en'er
scrof'u'la
scroll
scroll'work
scrooge
scro'ta
scro'tum
scrounge
scrounged
scroung'er
scroung'ing
scrub
scrubbed
scrub'bi'er
scrub'bi'est
scrub'bing
scrub'by
scruff
scruf'fi'er
scruf'fi'est
scruf'fi'ly
scruff'i'ness
scruffy
scrump'tious
scrunch
scru'ple
scru'pu'los'i'ty
scru'pu'lous
scru'pu'lous'ly
scru'pu'lous'ness
scru'ta'ble
scru'ti'nize
scru'ti'niz'er
scru'ti'niz'ing'ly
scru'tin'nized
scru'ti'ny
scu'ba
scud
scud'ded
scud'ding
scuff
scuf'fle
scuf'fled
scuf'fling
scull
scul'ler'ies

scul'lery
sculpt
sculp'tor
sculp'tress
sculp'tur'al
sculp'ture
sculp'tured
sculp'tur'ing
scum
scum'my
scup'per
scurf
scur'ried
scur'ril'i'ty
scur'ri'lous
scur'ry
scur'ry'ing
scur'vi'ness
scur'vy
scut
scut'tle
scut'tle'butt
scut'tled
scut'tling
scythe
scythed
scyth'ing
sea
sea'board
sea'borne
sea'far'er
sea'far'ing
sea'food
sea front
sea'go'ing
sea'gull
sea'horse
seal
sea lam'prey
seal'ant
seal'skin
seam
sea'man
sea'man'ship
seam'i'ness
seam'less
seam'stress
seamy
se'ance
sea'plane
sea'port
sear
search

search'er
search'ing
search'ing'ly
search'light
sea'scape
sea'shell
sea'shore
sea'sick
sea'sick'ness
sea'side
sea'son
sea'son'a'ble
sea'son'al
sea'son'al'ly
sea'son'er
sea'son'ing
seat
seat'ing
sea'ward
sea'weed
sea'wor'thi'ness
sea'wor'thy
se'ba'ceous
se'cant
se'cede
se'ced'ed
se'ced'ing
se'ces'sion
se'ces'sion'ist
se'clude
se'clud'ed
se'clud'ed'ness
se'clud'ing
se'clu'sion
se'clu'sive
sec'ond
sec'on'dar'ies
sec'ond'ar'i'ly
sec'ond'ary
sec'ond-best
sec'ond-class
sec'ond'er
sec'ond-guess
sec'ond'hand
sec'ond'ly
sec'ond-rate
se'cre'cy
se'cret
sec're'tar'i'al
sec're'tar'i'at
sec're'tar'ies
sec're'tary
se'crete

155

se'cret'ed
se'cre'tin
se'cret'ing
se'cre'tion
se'cre'tive
se'cre'tive'ly
se'cret'ly
se'cre'to'ry
sect
sec'tar'i'an
sec'tar'i'an'ism
sec'tary
sec'tile
sec'til'ity
sec'tion
sec'tion'al
sec'tion'al'ism
sec'tion'al'ist
sec'tor
sec'to'ri'al
sec'u'lar
sec'u'lar'ism
sec'u'lar'i'za'tion
sec'u'lar'ize
sec'u'lar'ized
sec'u'lar'iz'ing
se'cur'a'ble
se'cure
se'cured
se'cure'ly
se'cure'ness
se'cur'ing
se'cu'ri'ties
se'cu'ri'ty
se'dan
se'date
se'dat'ed
se'date'ly
se'date'ness
se'dat'ing
se'da'tion
sed'a'tive
sed'en'tar'i'ness
sed'en'tary
sedge
sed'i'ment
sed'i'men'ta'ry
sed'i'men'ta'tion
se'di'tion
se'di'tion'ary
se'di'tious
se'duce
se'duce'a'ble

se'duced
se'duce'ment
se'duc'er
se'duc'i'ble
se'duc'ing
se'duc'tion
se'duc'tive
se'duc'tive'ly
se'du'li'ty
sed'u'lous
sed'u'lous'ness
see
seed
seed'bed
seed'cake
seed'er
seed'i'er
seed'i'est
seed'i'ly
seed'i'ness
seed'ling
seedy
see'ing
seek
seek'ing
seem
seem'ing
seem'ing'ly
seem'li'est
seem'li'ness
seem'ly
seen
seep
seep'age
seepy
se'er
seer'ess
seer'suck'er
see'saw
seethe
seethed
seeth'ing
see-through
seg'ment
seg'men'tal
seg'men'tary
seg'men'ta'tion
seg're'gate
seg're'gat'ed
seg're'gat'ing
seg're'ga'tion
seg're'ga'tion'ist
seine

seined
sein'ing
seis'mic
seis'mo'graph
seis'mog'ra'phy
seis'mol'o'gist
seis'mol'o'gy
seize
seized
seiz'ing
sei'zure
sel'dom
se'lect
se'lect'ed
se'lec'tion
se'lec'tive
se'lec'tive'ly
se'lec'tiv'i'ty
se'lec'tor
se'le'ni'um
self
self-abase'ment
self-ab'ne'ga'tion
self-ab'sorbed
self-abuse
self-ad'dressed
self-ad'just'ing
self-as'ser'tive
self-as'sur'ance
self-as'sured
self-cen'tred
self-com'posed
self-con'fessed
self-con'fi'dence
self-con'fi'dent
self-con'scious
self-con'scious'ly
self-con'tained
self-con'trol
self-con'trolled
self-cor'rect'ing
self-crit'i'cism
self-de'cep'tion
self-de'cep'tive
self-de'feat'ing
self-de'fence
self-de'lu'sion
self-de'ni'al
self-dis'ci'pline
self-ed'u'cat'ed
self-ef'fac'ing
self-em'ployed
self-es'teem

self-ev'i'dent
self-ev'i'dent'ly
self-ex'plan'a'to'ry
self-ex'pres'sion
self-ful'fil'ment
self-gov'ern'ing
self-gov'ern'ment
self-im'age
self-im'por'tance
self-im'por'tant
self-im'posed
self-in'duced
self-in'dul'gence
self-in'dul'gent
self-in'flict'ed
self-in'ter'est
self-in'ter'est'ed
self'ish
self'ish'ly
self'ish'ness
self'less
self'less'ly
self'less'ness
self-liq'ui'dat'ing
self-made
self-op'er'at'ing
self-pity
self-pitying
self-pol'li'na'tion
self-portrait
self-pos'sessed
self-pos'ses'sion
self-pres'er'va'tion
self-pro'pelled
self-pro'tec'tion
self-raising
self-re'al'i'za'tion
self-regard
self-re'li'ance
self-re'li'ant
self-re'spect
self-re'spec'ting
self-re'straint
self-righ'teous
self-ris'ing
self-rule
self-sac'ri'fice
self-sa'cri'fic'ing
self'same
self-sat'is'fac'tion
self-sat'is'fied
self-sat'is'fy'ing
self-serv'ice

self-serv'ing
self-start'er
self-styled
self-suf'fi'cien'cy
self-suf'fi'cient
self-sup'port
self-sup'port'ing
self-taught
self-willed
sell
sell'er
sell'ing
sell out
selt'zer
sel'vage
sel'vedge
selves
se'man'tic
se'man'ti'cal
se'man'tics
sem'a'phore
sem'blance
se'men
se'mes'ter
semi'an'nu'al
semi'an'nu'al'ly
semi'ar'id
semi'au'to'mat'ic
semi'cir'cle
semi'cir'cu'lar
semi'clas'sic
semi'clas'si'cal
semi'co'lon
semi'con'duct'ing
semi'con'duc'tor
semi'con'scious
semi'de'tached
semi'fi'nal
semi'fi'nal'ist
semi'flu'id
semi'for'mal
semi'liq'uid
semi'month'ly
sem'i'nal
sem'i'nar
semi'nar'i'an
sem'i'nar'ies
sem'i'nary
semi'of'fi'cial
se'mi'ot'ic
semi'per'ma'nent
semi'per'me'a'ble
semi'pre'cious

semi'pri'vate
semi'pro'fes'sion'al
semi'pub'lic
semi'skilled
semi'sol'id
Se'mite
Se'mit'ic
Se'mit'ics
semi'tone
semi'ton'ic
semi'trail'er
semi'trop'i'cal
semi'trop'ics
semi'week'ly
semi'year'ly
sem'o'li'na
sem'pli'ce
sem'pre
se'na'ry
sen'ate
sen'a'tor
sen'a'to'ri'al
send
send'er
send'ing
send-off
se'nes'cence
se'nes'cent
se'nile
se'nil'i'ty
sen'ior
sen'ior'i'ty
se'ñor
se'ño'ra
se'ño'ri'ta
se'ñors
sen'sate
sen'sa'tion
sen'sa'tion'al
sen'sa'tion'al'ism
sen'sa'tion'al'ist
sen'sa'tion'al'ly
sense
sensed
sense'less
sense'less'ly
sense'less'ness
sen'si'bil'i'ties
sen'si'bil'i'ty
sen'si'ble
sen'si'ble'ness
sen'si'bly
sens'ing

sen'si'tive
sen'si'tive'ly
sen'si'tiv'i'ties
sen'si'tiv'i'ty
sen'si'ti'za'tion
sen'si'tize
sen'si'tized
sen'si'tiz'er
sen'si'tiz'ing
sen'sor
sen'so'ri'al
sen'so'ry
sen'su'al
sen'su'al'ism
sen'su'al'i'ty
sen'su'al'i'za'tion
sen'su'al'ize
sen'su'al'ized
sen'su'al'iz'ing
sen'su'al'ly
sen'su'ous
sen'su'ous'ly
sent
sen'tence
sen'tenced
sen'tenc'ing
sen'ten'tial
sen'ten'tious
sen'ten'tiously
sen'tient
sen'ti'ment
sen'ti'men'tal
sen'ti'men'ta'list
sen'ti'men'tal'i'ties
sen'ti'men'tal'i'ty
sen'ti'men'tal'ize
sen'ti'men'tal'ized
sen'ti'men'tal'iz'ing
sen'ti'men'tal'ly
sen'ti'nel
sen'tries
sen'try
se'pal
sep'a'ra'bil'i'ty
sep'a'ra'ble
sep'a'ra'bly
sep'a'rate
sep'a'rat'ed
sep'ar'ate'ly
sep'a'rate'ness
sep'a'rat'ing
sep'a'ra'tion
sep'a'ra'tism

sep'a'ra'tist
sep'a'ra'tive
sep'a'ra'tor
se'pia
sep'oy
sep'sis
sep'ten'ni'al
sep'tet
sep'tic
sep'ti'cae'mia
sep'ti'cal'ly
sep'tic'i'ty
sep'tu'ple
sep'ul'chre
se'pul'chral
se'quel
se'quence
se'quen'tial
se'quen'tial'ly
se'ques'ter
se'ques'tered
se'ques'tra'ble
se'ques'trate
se'ques'trat'ed
se'ques'trat'ing
se'ques'tra'tion
se'quin
se'quinned
se'quoia
se'ra'pe
ser'aph
se'raph'ic
ser'a'phim
ser'aphs
Serb
Ser'bi'an
Ser'bo-Cro'at
Ser'bo-Cro'a'tian
ser'e'nade
ser'e'nad'ed
ser'e'nad'ing
ser'en'dip'i'ty
se'rene
se'rene'ly
se'ren'i'ty
serf
serf'dom
serge
ser'geant
se'ri'al
se'ri'al'i'za'tion
se'ri'al'ize
se'ri'al'ized

157

se'ri'al'iz'ing	set'tler	shack'le	shame'ful'ly
se'ri'al'ly	set'tling	shack'led	shame'less
se'ri'a'tim	set-to	shack'ling	shame'less'ly
se'ries	sev'en	shad	shame'less'ness
se'ri'ous	sev'en'teen	shade	sham'ing
se'ri'ous'ly	sev'en'teenth	shad'ed	shammed
se'ri'ous-mind'ed	sev'enth	shad'i'er	sham'mer
se'ri'ous'ness	sev'en'ties	shad'i'est	sham'ming
ser'mon	sev'en'ti'eth	shad'i'ly	sham'poo
ser'mon'ize	sev'en'ty	shad'i'ness	sham'pooed
ser'mon'ized	sev'er	shad'ing	sham'poo'ing
ser'mon'iz'er	sev'er'a'bil'i'ty	shad'ow	sham'rock
ser'mon'iz'ing	sev'er'a'ble	shad'owy	sha'mus
se'rous	sev'er'al	shady	shan'dies
ser'pent	sev'er'al'ly	shaft	shan'dy
ser'pen'tine	sev'er'ance	shaft'ing	shang'hai
ser'rate	se'vere	shag	shang'haied
ser'rat'ed	sev'ered	shag'gi'er	shang'hai'ing
ser'rat'ing	se'vere'ly	shag'gi'est	shank
ser'ra'tion	se'vere'ness	shag'gi'ly	shan't
ser'ried	se'ver'est	shag'gi'ness	shan'ties
se'rum	sev'er'ing	shag'gy	shan'tung
serv'ant	se'ver'i'ty	sha'green	shan'ty
serve	sew	shah	shap'able
served	sew'age	shak'a'ble	shape
serv'er	sewed	shake	shape'able
ser'vice	sew'er	shake'a'ble	shaped
serv'ice'a'bil'i'ty	sew'er'age	shak'en	shape'less
serv'ice'a'ble	sew'ing	shake off	shape'li'er
serv'ice'a'ble'ness	sewn	shak'er	shape'li'est
serv'ice'a'bly	sex	shak'i'er	shape'li'ness
serv'iced	sex'i'er	shak'i'est	shape'ly
ser'vice'man	sex'i'est	shak'i'ly	shap'er
serv'ic'ing	sex'i'ness	shak'i'ness	shap'ing
ser'vile	sex'ism	shak'ing	shard
ser'vile'ly	sex'ist	shaky	share
ser'vile'ness	sex'less	shale	share'crop
ser'vil'i'ty	sex'tant	shall	share'cropped
serv'ing	sex'tet	shal'lot	share'crop'per
ser'vi'tude	sex'ton	shal'low	share'crop'ping
ser'vo'mech'an'ism	sex'tu'ple	shal'low'ly	shared
ses'a'me	sex'tu'plet	shal'low'ness	share'hold'er
ses'qui'cen'ten'ni'al	sex'u'al	sham	shar'er
ses'sion	sex'u'al'i'ty	sha'man	shar'ing
set	sex'u'al'ly	sham'ble	shark
set'back	sexy	sham'bled	shark'skin
set piece	sfor'zan'do	sham'bles	sharp
set'tee	shab'bi'er	sham'bling	sharp'en
set'ter	shab'bi'est	shame	sharp'en'er
set'ting	shab'bi'ly	shamed	sharp'er
set'tle	shab'bi'ness	shame'faced	sharp-eyed
set'tled	shab'by	shame'faced'ly	sharp'ie
set'tle'ment	shack	shame'ful	sharp'ish

sharp'ly
sharp'ness
sharp'shoot'er
sharp-tongued
sharp-wit'ted
shat'ter
shat'ter'proof
shave
shaved
shav'en
shav'er
shav'ing
shawl
she
sheaf
shear
sheared
shear'ing
sheath
sheathe
sheathed
sheath'ing
sheath knife
sheath knives
sheaves
she'bang
shed
shed'ding
sheen
sheeny
sheep
sheep'fold
sheep'herd'er
sheep'ish
sheep'ish'ly
sheep'skin
sheer
sheer'ness
sheet
sheet'ing
sheik
sheik'dom
sheikh
sheikh'dom
shek'els
shelf
shell
shel'lac
shel'lacked
shel'lack'ing
shelled
shell'fish
shel'ly

shel'ter
shelve
shelved
shelves
shelv'ing
she'nan'i'gan
shep'herd
shep'herd'ess
sher'bet
sher'iff
sher'ries
sher'ry
shi'at'su
shib'bo'leth
shied
shield
shift
shift'i'er
shift'i'est
shift'i'ly
shift'i'ness
shift'less
shifty
shil'le'lagh
shil'ling
shilly-shall'ied
shilly-shally
shilly-shally'ing
shim'mer
shim'mery
shim'mied
shim'my
shin
shin'dig
shine
shined
shin'er
shin'gle
shin'gled
shin'gles
shin'gling
shin'gly
shin'i'er
shin'i'est
shin'i'ness
shin'ing
shinned
shin'ning
Shin'to
Shin'to'ism
shiny
ship
ship'board

ship'build'ing
ship'mate
ship'ment
ship'pa'ble
shipped
ship'per
ship'ping
ship'shape
ship'wreck
shirk
shirk'er
shirt
shirt'tail
shish ke'bab
shi'ver
shiv'ery
shoal
shock ab'sorb'er
shock'er
shock'ing
shock'ing'ly
shock'proof
shod
shod'di'er
shod'di'est
shod'di'ly
shod'di'ness
shod'dy
shoe
shoe'ing
shoe'mak'er
shoe'string
shone
shoo
shook
shoot
shoot'ing
shop
shop'keep'er
shop'lift'er
shop'lift'ing
shopped
shop'per
shop'ping
shop'worn
shore
shored
shore'line
shor'ing
shorn
short
short'age
short'bread

short'cake
short-change
short-changed
short-chang'ing
short-cir'cuit
short-cir'cuit'ed
short-cir'cuit'ing
short'com'ing
short'cut
short'cut'ting
short'en
short'en'ing
short'fall
short'hand
short-hand'ed
short-haul
short'horn
short-lived
short'ly
short'ness
short-range
short-sight'ed
short-sight'ed'ness
short-tem'pered
short-term
short-wind'ed
shot
shot'gun
shot'gunned
shot'gun'ning
should
shoul'der
shout
shout'ing
shove
shoved
shov'el
shov'el'ful
shov'elled
shov'el'ling
shov'ing
show
show'case
show'cased
show'cas'ing
show'down
showed
show'er
show'ery
show'i'er
show'i'est
show'i'ly
show'i'ness

show'ing
show'man
show'man'ship
shown
show-off
show'piece
show'room
showy
shrank
shrap'nel
shred
shred'ded
shred'der
shred'ding
shrew
shrewd
shrewd'ly
shrewd'ness
shrew'ish
shriek
shrift
shrike
shrill
shrill'ness
shril'ly
shrimp
shrine
shrink
shrink'a'ble
shrink'age
shrink'ing
shrive
shrived
shriv'el
shriv'elled
shriv'el'ling
shriv'en
shriv'ing
shroud
shrove
shrub
shrub'ber'ies
shrub'bery
shrug
shrugged
shrug'ging
shrunk
shrunk'en
shucks
shud'der
shud'dery
shuf'fle
shuf'fle'board

shuf'fled
shuf'fler
shuf'fling
shun
shunned
shun'ner
shun'ning
shunt
shush
shut
shut'down
shut-eye
shut'ter
shut'ting
shut'tle
shut'tle'cock
shut'tled
shut'tling
shy
shy'ing
shy'ly
shy'ness
Si'a'mese
sib'i'lance
sib'i'lant
sib'ling
sib'yl
sib'yl'line
sic
Si'cil'ian
sick
sick'bed
sick'en
sick'en'ing
sick'en'ing'ly
sick'le
sick'li'er
sick'li'est
sick'li'ness
sick'ly
sick'ness
sick'room
side'board
side'burns
side'car
sid'ed
side'kick
side'light
side'line
side'lined
side'lin'ing
si'de're'al
side-sad'dle

side'show
side-split'ting
side'step
side'stepped
side'step'ping
side'swipe
side'swiped
side'swip'ing
side'track
side'walk
side'ways
side'wind'er
sid'ing
si'dle
si'dled
si'dling
siege
sie'mens
si'en'na
si'er'ra
si'es'ta
sieve
sieved
siev'ing
sift'er
sift'ings
sigh
sigh'ing
sight
sight'ed
sight'less
sight'ly
sight-read'ing
sight'see'ing
sight'se'er
sign
sig'nal
sig'nalled
sig'nal'ling
sig'nal'ly
sig'nal'man
sig'na'to'ries
sig'na'to'ry
sig'na'ture
sign'board
sig'net
sig'nif'i'cance
sig'nif'i'cant
sig'nif'i'cant'ly
sig'ni'fi'ca'tion
sig'ni'fied
sig'ni'fy
sig'ni'fy'ing

si'gnor
si'gno'ra
si'gno're
si'gno'ri
si'gno'ri'na
si'gno'ri'ne
sign'post
Sikh
Sikh'ism
si'lage
si'lence
si'lenced
si'lenc'er
si'lenc'ing
si'lent
si'lent'ly
sil'hou'ette
sil'hou'et'ted
sil'hou'et'ting
sil'ica
sil'i'con
sil'i'cone
sil'i'co'sis
silk
silk'en
silk'i'er
silk'i'est
silk'i'ly
silk'i'ness
silk'worm
silky
sill
sil'li'er
sil'li'est
sil'li'ness
sil'ly
si'lo
silt
sil'ta'tion
silty
sil'ver
sil'ver'fish
sil'ver'i'ness
sil'ver'smith
sil'ver-tongued
sil'ver'ware
sil'very
sim'i'an
sim'i'lar
sim'i'lar'i'ties
sim'i'lar'i'ty
sim'i'lar'ly
sim'i'le

si'mil'i'tude
sim'mer
sim'per
sim'per'ing'ly
sim'ple
sim'ple-mind'ed
sim'ple-mind'ed'ness
sim'ple'ness
sim'pler
sim'plest
sim'ple'ton
sim'plex
sim'plic'i'ties
sim'plic'i'ty
sim'pli'fi'ca'tion
sim'pli'fied
sim'pli'fy
sim'pli'fy'ing
sim'plis'tic
sim'plis'ti'cal'ly
sim'ply
sim'u'late
sim'u'lat'ed
sim'u'lat'ing
sim'u'la'tion
sim'u'la'tive
sim'u'la'tor
si'mul'cast
si'mul'ta'ne'i'ty
si'mul'ta'ne'ous
si'mul'ta'ne'ous'ly
sin
since
sin'cere
sin'cere'ly
sin'cer'i'ty
sine
si'ne'cure
si'ne die
si'ne qua non
sin'ew
sin'ewy
sin'fo'nia
sin'ful
sin'ful'ly
sin'ful'ness
sing
sing'able
singe
singed
singe'ing
sing'er
sing'ing

sin'gle
sin'gle-breast'ed
sin'gled
sin'gle-hand'ed
sin'gle-hand'ed'ly
sin'gle-mind'ed
sin'gle-mind'ed'ly
sin'gle'ness
sin'gle-space
sin'gle-spaced
sin'gle-spac'ing
sin'gle'ton
sin'gle-track
sin'gling
sin'gly
sing'song
sin'gu'lar
sin'gu'lar'i'ties
sin'gu'lar'i'ty
sin'gu'lar'ly
Sin'hal'ese
sin'is'ter
sink
sink'able
sink'er
sink'hole
sink'ing
sin'less
sinned
sin'ner
sin'ning
sin'u'ate
sin'u'at'ed
sin'u'at'ing
sin'u'os'i'ty
sin'u'ous
sin'u'ous'ness
si'nus
si'nus'i'tis
sip
si'phon
sipped
sip'ping
sir
sire
sired
si'ren
sir'ing
sir'loin
si'roc'co
si'sal
sis'sies
sis'sy

sis'ter
sis'ter'hood
sis'ter-in-law
sis'ter'li'ness
sis'ter'ly
sit
si'tar
sit'com
sit-down
site
sit'ed
sit-in
sit'ing
sit'ter
sit'ting
sit'u'ate
sit'u'at'ed
sit'u'at'ing
sit'u'a'tion
six-pence
six-penny
six-shoot'er
six'teen
six'teenth
sixth
six'ties
six'ti'eth
six'ty
siz'a'ble
siz'a'ble'ness
siz'a'bly
size
size'able
size'able'ness
size'ably
sized
siz'ing
siz'zle
siz'zled
siz'zling
skate
skate'board
skat'ed
skat'er
skat'ing
skein
skel'e'tal
skel'e'ton
sketch
sketch'book
sketch'i'er
sketch'i'est
sketch'i'ly

sketch'i'ness
sketchy
skew
skew'bald
skew'er
ski
skid
skid'ded
skid'ding
skied
ski'er
skies
skiff
ski'ing
skil'ful
skil'ful'ly
skill
skilled
skil'let
skim
skimmed
skim'ming
skimp
skimp'i'er
skimp'i'est
skimp'i'ly
skimp'i'ness
skimp'y
skin
skin-deep
skin-dive
skin-dived
skin-diving
skin'flint
skin'head
skinned
skin'ni'er
skin'ni'est
skin'ning
skin'ny
skin'tight
skip
skipped
skip'per
skip'ping
skir'mish
skirt
skit
skit'ter
skit'tish
skoal
skol
skua

skul'dug'gery
skulk
skulk'er
skull
skull'cap
skunk
sky
sky'div'ing
sky-high
sky'jack
sky'jack'er
sky'light
sky'rock'et
sky'scrap'er
sky'ward
sky'writ'ing
slab
slabbed
slab'bing
slack
slack'en
slack'er
slack'ness
slag
slain
slake
slaked
slak'ing
sla'lom
slam
slammed
slam'mer
slam'ming
slan'der
slan'der'er
slan'der'ous
slang
slang'i'ly
slang'i'ness
slangy
slant
slant'ways
slant'wise
slap
slap'dash
slap'hap'py
slapped
slap'ping
slap'stick
slasher
slash'ing
slat
slate

slat'ed
slat'ing
slat'ted
slat'tern
slat'tern'li'ness
slat'tern'ly
slat'ting
slaugh'ter
slaugh'ter'house
Slav
slave
slaved
slav'er
slav'ery
Slav'ic
slav'ing
slav'ish
sla'vish'ly
Sla'von'ic
slay
slay'ing
sleaz'i'er
sleaz'i'est
slea'zi'ly
slea'zi'ness
slea'zy
sled
sled'ded
sled'ding
sledge
sledged
sledge'ham'mer
sledg'ing
sleek
sleek'ness
sleep
sleep'er
sleep'i'er
sleep'i'est
sleep'i'ly
sleep'i'ness
sleep'ing
sleep'less
sleep'less'ness
sleep'walk'er
sleep'walk'ing
sleepy
sleepy'head
sleet
sleety
sleeve
sleeved
sleeve'less

sleev'ing
sleigh
sleight
slen'der
slen'der'ize
slen'der'ness
slept
sleuth
slew
slice
sliced
slic'ing
slick
slick'er
slick'ness
slid
slide
slid'ing
slight
slight'ing'ly
slight'ly
slim
slime
slim'i'er
slim'i'est
slim'i'ness
slimmed
slim'mer
slim'mest
slim'ming
slim'ness
slimy
sling
sling'ing
slink
slink'i'er
slink'i'est
slink'ing
slinky
slip
slip'cov'er
slip'knot
slip'page
slipped
slip'per
slip'per'i'er
slip'per'i'est
slip'per'i'ness
slip'pery
slip'ping
slip'py
slip'shod
slip'stream

slip'way
slit
slith'er
slith'ery
slit'ting
sliv'er
slob
slob'ber
slob'bery
sloe
sloe-eyed
slog
slo'gan
slo'gan'eer
slogged
slog'ging
sloop
slop
slope
sloped
slop'ing
slopped
slop'pi'er
slop'pi'est
slop'pi'ly
slop'pi'ness
slop'ping
slop'py
sloshy
slot
sloth
sloth'ful
sloth'ful'ly
slot'ted
slot'ting
slouch
slouch'i'ly
slouchy
slough
sloughy
Slo'vak
slov'en
slov'en'li'ness
slov'en'ly
slow
slow'down
slow'ly
slow-mo'tion
slow'ness
slow'poke
slow-wit'ted
slow'worm
sludge

sludgy
slug
slug'gard
slug'gard'li'ness
slugged
slug'ging
slug'gish
slug'gish'ly
sluice
sluiced
sluic'ing
slum
slum'ber
slum'ber'er
slum'ber'ous
slummed
slum'ming
slum'my
slump
slumped
slung
slunk
slur
slurred
slur'ring
slur'ry
slush
slush'i'er
slush'i'est
slush'i'ness
slushy
slut
slut'tish
sly
sly'ly
sly'ness
smack
smack'ing
small
small'ish
small'ness
small'pox
small-scale
smarm'i'er
smarm'i'est
smarmy
smart
smart al'eck
smart'en
smart'ly
smart'ness
smash'ing
smat'ter'ing

smear
smear'i'ness
smeary
smell
smelled
smel'li'er
smel'li'est
smel'ling
smelly
smelt
smelt'er
smid'gen
smile
smiled
smi'ling
smi'ling'ly
smirch
smirk
smirk'ing'ly
smite
smith'er'eens
smith'ies
smithy
smit'ing
smit'ten
smock
smock'ing
smog
smog'gy
smoke
smoked
smoke'house
smoke'less
smok'er
smoke'stack
smok'i'er
smok'i'est
smok'i'ness
smok'ing
smoky
smooch
smoochy
smooth
smooth'en
smooth'ie
smooth'ly
smooth'ness
smoothy
smor'gas'bord
smote
smoth'er
smoul'der
smudge

smudged
smudg'i'ness
smudg'ing
smudgy
smug
smug'ger
smug'gest
smug'gle
smug'gled
smug'gler
smug'gling
smug'ly
smug'ness
smut
smut'ti'er
smut'ti'est
smut'ti'ness
smut'ty
snaf'fle
sna'fu
sna'fued
snag
snagged
snag'ging
snag'gy
snail
snake
snaked
snak'i'er
snak'i'est
snak'i'ly
snak'i'ness
snak'ing
snaky
snap
snap'drag'on
snapped
snap'per
snap'pi'er
snap'pi'est
snap'ping
snap'pish
snap'py
snap'shot
snare
snared
snar'ing
snarl
snarly
snatch
snatchy
snaz'zi'er
snaz'zi'est

snaz'zy
sneak
sneak'er
sneak'i'er
sneak'i'est
sneak'i'ly
sneak'i'ness
sneak'ing
sneaky
sneer
sneer'ing'ly
sneeze
sneezed
sneez'ing
sneezy
snick
snick'er
snide
sniff
snif'fer
snif'fi'er
snif'fi'est
snif'fi'ly
snif'fle
snif'fled
snif'fling
snif'fy
snif'ter
snig'ger
snip
snipe
sniped
snip'er
snip'ing
snipped
snip'pet
snip'pi'ness
snip'ping
snip'py
snitch
snitch'er
sniv'el
sniv'elled
sniv'el'ling
snob
snob'bery
snob'bi'er
snob'bi'est
snob'bish
snob'bish'ness
snob'by
snook
snook'er

snoop	snug'gest	so'da	sol'emn
snoop'er	snug'ging	so'dal'i'ty	so'lem'ni'ty
snoopy	snug'gle	sod'den	sol'em'ni'za'tion
snoot'i'er	snug'gled	sod'den'ness	sol'em'nize
snoot'i'est	snug'gling	sod'ding	sol'em'nized
snoot'i'ness	snug'ly	so'di'um	sol'em'niz'ing
snooty	snug'ness	sod'omy	sol'emn'ly
snooze	so	so'fa	sol'emn'ness
snoozed	soak	soft	sole'ness
snooz'ing	soak'ing	soft'ball	so'le'noid
snore	soap	sof'ten	so'le'noi'dal
snored	soap'i'ness	soft'en'er	sol-fa
snor'ing	soap'suds	soft-head'ed	so'lic'it
snor'kel	soapy	soft-heart'ed	so'lic'i'ta'tion
snor'kelled	soar	soft'ie	so'lic'it'ed
snor'kel'ling	soaring	soft'ly	so'lic'it'ing
snort	sob	soft'ness	so'lic'i'tor
snort'ed	sobbed	soft-ped'al	so'lic'i'tous
snot	sob'bing	soft-ped'alled	so'lic'i'tous'ly
snot'ti'er	so'ber	soft-ped'all'ing	so'lic'i'tude
snot'ti'est	so'ber'ly	soft-spo'ken	sol'id
snot'ti'ness	so'ber'ness	soft'ware	sol'i'dar'i'ty
snot'ty	so'bri'e'ty	soft'wood	so'lid'i'fi'ca'tion
snout	so'bri'quet	softy	so'lid'i'fied
snow	soc'cer	sog'gi'er	so'lid'i'fy
snow'ball	so'cia'bil'i'ty	sog'gi'est	so'lid'i'fy'ing
snow'blow'er	so'cia'ble	sog'gi'ness	so'lid'i'ty
snow'bound	so'cia'ble'ness	sog'gy	sol'id'ly
snow'capped	so'cia'bly	soi-di'sant	sol'id'ness
snow'fall	so'cial	soi'gné	sol'id'state
snow'field	so'cial'ism	soi'gnée	so'lil'o'quies
snow'flake	so'cial'ist	soil	so'lil'o'quize
snow'i'er	so'cial'is'tic	soi'ree	so'lil'o'quized
snowiest	so'cial'ite	so'journ	so'lil'o'quiz'ing
snow'i'ness	so'ci'al'i'ty	sol'ace	so'lil'o'quy
snow'man	so'cial'i'za'tion	sol'aced	sol'ing
snow'mo'bile	so'cial'ize	sol'ac'ing	sol'i'taire
snow'plough	so'cial'ized	so'lar	sol'i'tar'i'ness
snow'shoe	so'cial'iz'ing	so'lar'i'um	sol'i'tary
snowy	so'cial'ly	so'lar'i'za'tion	sol'i'tude
snub	so'ci'e'tal	so'lar'ize	so'lo
snubbed	so'ci'e'ties	so'lar'ized	so'loed
snub'bing	so'ci'e'ty	so'lar'iz'ing	so'lo'ing
snuff	so'cio'ec'o'nom'ic	so'lar plex'us	so'lo'ist
snuff'box	so'cio'log'i'cal	sold	sol'stice
snuff'i'ness	so'cio'log'i'cal'ly	sol'der	sol'u'bil'i'ty
snuf'fle	so'ci'ol'o'gist	sol'dier	sol'u'ble
snuf'fled	so'ci'ol'o'gy	sol'dier'ly	sol'u'ble'ness
snuf'fling	so'cio'po'lit'i'cal	sole	sol'u'bly
snuffy	sock	sol'e'cism	sol'ute
snug	sock'et	sol'ecist	so'lu'tion
snugged	sock'eye	soled	solv'a'bil'i'ty
snug'ger	sod	sole'ly	solv'a'ble

solv'a'ble'ness
solve
solved
sol'ven'cy
sol'vent
solv'ing
so'mat'ic
som'bre
som'bre'ly
som'bre'ness
som'bre'ro
some
some'body
some'how
some'one
som'er'sault
some'thing
some'times
some'what
some'where
som'nam'bu'lant
som'nam'bu'late
som'nam'bu'lat'ed
som'nam'bu'lat'ing
som'nam'bu'la'tion
som'nam'bu'lism
som'nam'bu'list
som'no'lence
som'no'len'cy
som'no'lent
son
so'nant
so'nar
so'na'ta
son et lu'miére
song'bird
song'ster
song'stress
son'ic
son-in-law
son'net
son'nies
son'ny
so'nor'i'ty
so'no'rous
so'no'rous'ness
soon
soot
soothe
soothed
sooth'ing
sooth'ing'ly
sooth'say'er

soot'i'ness
sooty
sop
soph'ism
soph'ist
so'phis'tic
so'phis'ti'cal
so'phis'ti'cate
so'phis'ti'cat'ed
so'phis'ti'cat'ing
so'phis'ti'ca'tion
soph'ist'ries
soph'ist'ry
soph'o'more
soph'o'mor'ic
sop'o'rif'ic
sopped
sop'pi'er
sop'pi'est
sop'ping
sop'py
so'prano
sor'bet
sor'cer'er
sor'cer'ess
sor'cer'ous
sor'cery
sor'did
sor'did'ness
sore
sore'ly
sore'ness
sor'est
sor'ghum
so'ror'i'ties
so'ror'i'ty
sor'rel
sor'ri'er
sor'ri'est
sor'ri'ness
sor'row
sor'row'ful
sor'row'ful'ly
sor'ry
sort'a'ble
sor'tie
sot
sot'tish
sot'to vo'ce
sou
sou'brette
sou'bri'quet
souf'flé

souf'fléed
sough
sought
soul
soul'ful
soul'ful'ly
soul'less
soul-search'ing
sound
sound'able
sound'ing
sound'less
sound'less'ly
sound'ly
sound'ness
sound'proof
sound'track
soup
soup'çon
soup'i'er
soupy
sour
source
sour'ish
sour'ly
sour'ness
souse
soused
sous'ing
south
south'bound
south'east
south'east'er'ly
south'east'ern
south'er'ly
south'ern
south'ern'er
south'ern'most
south'paw
south'ward
south'west
south'west'er'ly
south'west'ern
sou've'nir
sou''west'er
sov'er'eign
sov'er'eign'ty
so'vi'et
so'vi'et'ism
sow
sowed
sow'ing
sown

soy'bean
soz'zled
space
space'craft
spaced
space'man
space'ship
spa'cial
spac'ing
spa'cious
spa'cious'ness
spade
spad'ed
spade'ful
spade'work
spad'ing
spa'ghet'ti
span
span'gle
span'gled
span'gling
Span'iard
span'iel
Span'ish
spank'ing
spanned
span'ner
span'ning
spar
spare
spared
spare'ness
spar'ing
spar'ing'ly
spar'ing'ness
spark
spar'kle
spar'kled
spar'kler
spar'kling
sparred
spar'ring
spar'row
sparse
sparse'ly
sparse'ness
spasm
spas'mod'ic
spas'mod'i'cal'ly
spas'tic
spas'ti'cal'ly
spat
spate

165

spa'tial
spa'ti'al'i'ty
spa'tial'ly
spat'ted
spat'ter
spat'ting
spat'u'la
spav'in
spawn
spay
speak
speak-easy
speak'er
speak'ing
spear
spear'head
spear'mint
spe'cial
spe'cial'ism
spe'cial'ist
spe'ci'al'ities
spe'ci'al'ity
spe'cial'i'za'tion
spe'cial'ize
spe'cial'ized
spe'cial'iz'ing
spe'cial'ly
spe'cie
spe'cies
spec'i'fi'able
spe'cif'ic
spe'cif'i'cal'ly
spec'i'fi'ca'tion
spec'i'fic'i'ty
spec'i'fied
spec'i'fy
spec'i'fy'ing
spec'i'men
spe'ci'os'i'ty
spe'cious
spe'cious'ness
speck
speck'le
speck'led
speck'ling
spec'ta'cle
spec'tac'u'lar
spec'tac'u'lar'ly
spec'ta'tor
spec'tra
spec'tral
spec'tre
spec'tro'scope

spec'tros'co'py
spec'trum
spec'u'la
spec'u'late
spec'u'lat'ed
spec'u'lat'ing
spec'u'la'tion
spec'u'la'tive
spec'u'la'tive'ly
spec'u'la'tor
spec'u'lum
sped
speech
speech'i'fy
speech'less
speed
speed'ed
speed'i'er
speed'i'est
speed'i'ly
speed'i'ness
speed'ing
speed'om'e'ter
speed'way
speed'well
speedy
spe'le'ol'o'gist
spe'le'ol'o'gy
spell
spell'bind'ing
spell'bound
spelled
spell'er
spell'ing
spelt
spe'lun'ker
spend
spend'a'ble
spend'er
spend'ing
spend'thrift
spent
sperm
sper'ma'ceti
sper'mat'ic
sper'ma'to'zo'a
sper'ma'to'zo'ic
sper'ma'to'zo'on
spew
spew'er
sphag'num
sphere
spher'ic

spher'i'cal
sphe'ric'ally
sphe'roid
sphe'roi'dal
sphinc'ter
sphinx
spice
spiced
spic'i'er
spic'i'est
spic'i'ly
spic'i'ness
spic'ing
spi'cule
spicy
spi'der
spi'dery
spied
spiel
spies
spiff'i'ness
spiffy
spig'ot
spike
spiked
spik'i'er
spik'i'est
spik'ing
spiky
spill
spil'lage
spilled
spill'ing
spilt
spin
spi'na bif'i'da
spin'ach
spi'nal
spin'dle
spin'dled
spin'dli'er
spin'dli'est
spin'dling
spin'dly
spine'less
spin'et
spin'i'ness
spin'na'ker
spin'ner
spin'ning
spin'ning
spin-off
spin'ster

spin'ster'hood
spiny
spi'ra'cle
spi'ral
spi'ralled
spi'ral'ling
spi'ral'ly
spire
spir'it
spir'it'ed
spir'it'ing
spir'it'less'ness
spir'i'tous
spir'it'u'al
spir'it'u'al'ism
spir'it'u'al'ist
spir'it'u'al'i'ty
spir'it'u'al'i'za'tion
spir'it'u'al'ize
spir'it'u'al'ized
spir'it'u'al'iz'ing
spir'it'u'al'ly
spir'it'u'os'i'ty
spir'it'u'ous
spi'ro'chete
spit
spite
spite'ful
spite'ful'ly
spit'ing
spit'ting
spit'tle
spit'toon
splash
splash'down
splash'i'ness
splashy
splat
splat'ter
splay
splay'foot
spleen
spleen'ful
splen'did
splen'did'ly
splen'dif'er'ous
splen'dour
sple'net'ic
splice
spliced
splic'ing
splin'ter
splin'tery

split
split-lev'el
split-sec'ond
split'ting
splotch
splotchy
splurge
splurged
splurg'ing
splut'ter
spoil
spoil'age
spoiled
spoil'er
spoil'ing
spoil'sport
spoilt
spoke
spo'ken
spokes'man
spokes'per'son
spokes'wom'an
spo'li'a'tion
spon'da'ic
spon'dee
sponge
sponged
spong'er
spong'i'er
spong'i'est
spon'gi'ness
spong'ing
spon'gy
spon'sor
spon'sored
spon'sor'ing
spon'sor'ship
spon'ta'ne'i'ty
spon'ta'ne'ous
spon'ta'ne'ous'ly
spon'ta'ne'ous'ness
spoof
spook
spook'i'er
spook'i'est
spook'i'ness
spooky
spool
spoon
spoon'er'ism
spoon-fed
spoon-feed
spoon-feed'ing

spoon'ful
spoor
spo'rad'ic
spo'rad'i'cal'ly
spo'ran'gi'um
spore
sport
sport'ful'ly
sport'i'ness
sport'ing
sport'ing'ly
spor'tive
sports'cast'er
sports'man
sports'man'like
sports'man'ship
sports'wear
sports'wom'an
sports'writ'er
sporty
spot
spot'less
spot'less'ly
spot'less'ness
spot'light
spot'lit
spot'ted
spot'ter
spot'ti'er
spot'ti'est
spot'ti'ly
spot'ti'ness
spot'ting
spot'ty
spouse
spout
sprain
sprained
sprang
sprat
sprawl
spray
spray'er
spread
spread-ea'gle
spread'er
spread'ing
spree
sprig
spright'li'er
spright'li'est
spright'li'ness
spright'ly

spring
spring'board
spring'bok
spring-clean'ing
spring'er
spring'i'er
spring'i'est
spring'i'ness
spring'ing
spring'time
springy
sprin'kle
sprin'kled
sprink'ler
sprin'kling
sprint
sprint'er
sprock'et
sprout
spruce
spruced
spruce'ly
spruc'ing
sprung
spry
spry'ness
spume
spum'ous
spun
spunk'i'er
spunk'i'est
spunk'i'ness
spunky
spur
spu'ri'ous
spu'ri'ous'ness
spurn
spurner
spurred
spur'ring
spurt
sput'nik
sput'ter
spu'tum
spy
spy'ing
squab'ble
squab'bled
squab'bling
squad
squad'ron
squal'id
squal'id'ness

squall
squally
squal'or
squan'der
square
squared
square-danc'ing
square'ly
square'ness
square-rigged
squar'ing
squar'ish
squash
squash'i'er
squash'i'est
squash'i'ness
squashy
squat
squat'ness
squat'ted
squat'ter
squat'ting
squat'ty
squaw
squawk
squawky
squeak
squeak'er
squeak'i'est
squeak'ing'ly
squeaky
squeal
squeal'er
squeam'ish
squeam'ish'ness
squee'gee
squeeze
squeezed
squeez'er
squeez'ing
squelch
squib
squid
squif'fy
squig'gle
squig'gled
squig'gling
squint
squint'er
squint'ing'ly
squinty
squire

squirm
squirmy
squir'rel
squirt
squish
squishy
stab
stabbed
stab'ber
stab'bing
sta'bile
sta'bil'i'ties
sta'bil'i'ty
sta'bi'li'za'tion
sta'bi'lize
sta'bi'lized
sta'bi'liz'er
sta'bi'liz'ing
sta'ble
sta'bled
sta'bling
stac'ca'to
stack
sta'dia
sta'di'um
staff
stag
stage
stage'coach
staged
stage-man'age
stage-man'aged
stage-man'ag'ing
stage-struck
stag'ger
stag'ger'ing
stag'ger'ing'ly
stag'i'er
stag'i'est
stag'ing
stag'nan'cy
stag'nant
stag'nate
stag'nat'ed
stag'nat'ing
stag'na'tion
stagy
staid
staid'ness
stain
stained
stain'less
stair

stair'case
stair'way
stair'well
stake
staked
stak'ing
sta'lac'tite
stal'ag
sta'lag'mite
stale
stale'mate
stale'mat'ed
stale'mat'ing
stale'ness
stalk
stalked
stalky
stall
stalled
stal'lion
stal'wart
sta'men
stam'i'na
stam'mer
stam'mer'ing'ly
stam'pede
stam'ped'ed
stam'ped'ing
stance
stan'chion
stand
stand'ard
stand'ard'i'za'tion
stand'ard'ize
stand'ard'ized
stand'ard'izing
stand'by
stand'ing
stand'off
stand'off'ish
stand'point
stand'still
stank
stan'za
staph'y'lo'coc'cus
sta'ple
sta'pled
sta'pler
sta'pling
star
star'board
starch
starch'i'er

starch'i'est
starch'i'ness
starchy
star'dom
stare
stared
star'gaze
star'gazed
star'gaz'ing
stark'ly
star'let
star'light
star'ling
starred
star'ri'ness
star'ring
star'ry
star'ry-eyed
star-span'gled
start'er
star'tle
star'tled
star'tling
start'ling'ly
star'va'tion
starve
starved
starve'ling
starv'ing
sta'sis
state
state'craft
stat'ed
state'hood
state'less
state'li'er
state'li'est
state'li'ness
state'ly
state'ment
state'room
states'man
states'man'like
states'man'ship
stat'ic
stat'i'cal'ly
stat'ing
sta'tion
sta'tion'ary
sta'tion'er
sta'tion'ery
stat'ism
stat'ist

sta'tis'tic
sta'tis'ti'cal
sta'tis'ti'cal'ly
stat'is'ti'cian
sta'tis'tics
sta'tor
stat'u'ary
stat'ue
stat'u'esque
stat'u'ette
stat'ure
sta'tus
sta'tus quo
stat'ute
stat'u'to'ri'ly
stat'u'to'ry
staunch
staunch'ly
stave
staved
stav'ing
stay
stayed
stay'ing
stay'sail
stead
stead'fast
stead'fast'ly
stead'fast'ness
stead'ied
stead'i'er
stead'i'est
stead'i'ly
stead'i'ness
steady
stead'y'ing
steak
steal
steal'ing
stealth
stealth'i'er
stealth'i'est
stealth'i'ly
stealth'i'ness
stealthy
steam
steam'er
steam'i'er
steam'i'est
steam'i'ness
steam'roll'er
steam'ship
steamy

168

sted'fast
steed
steel
steel'i'ness
steel'work'er
steel'works
steely
steep
steep'en
stee'ple
stee'ple'chase
stee'ple'jack
steep'ly
steep'ness
steer
steer'able
steer'age
stein
stel'lar
stem
stem'less
stemmed
stem'ming
stem-wind'ing
stench
sten'cil
sten'cilled
sten'cil'ling
Sten gun
ste'nog'ra'pher
sten'o'graph'ic
sten'o'graph'i'cal'ly
ste'nog'ra'phy
sten'to'ri'an
step
step'broth'er
step'child
step'child'ren
step'daugh'ter
step'fa'ther
step'lad'der
step'moth'er
step'par'ent
steppe
stepped
step'ping
step'ping'stone
step'sis'ter
ste'reo
ste'reo'phon'ic
ste'reo'phon'i'cal'ly
ste'reo'scope
ste'reo'scop'ic

ste'reo'type
ste'reo'typed
ste'reo'typ'ing
ster'ile
ste'ril'i'ty
ster'i'li'za'tion
ster'i'lize
ster'i'lized
ster'i'li'zer
ster'i'liz'ing
ster'ling
stern
ster'na
stern'ly
stern'ness
ster'num
ster'oid
ster'to'rous
stet
steth'o'scope
stet'son
stet'ted
stet'ting
ste've'dore
stew
stew'ard
stew'ard'ess
stew'ard'ship
stick
stick'er
stick'i'er
stick'i'est
stick'i'ness
stick'ing
stick'le'back
stick'ler
stick'pin
stick-up
sticky
sties
stiff
stiff'en
stif'fen'er
stiff'ly
stiff'ness
sti'fle
sti'fled
sti'fling
stig'ma
stig'ma'ta
stig'mat'ic
stig'mat'i'cal'ly
stig'ma'ti'za'tion

stig'ma'tize
stig'ma'tized
stig'ma'tiz'ing
stile
sti'let'to
still
still'birth
still'born
still'ness
still room
stilt'ed
stim'u'lant
stim'u'late
stim'u'lat'ed
stim'u'lat'ing
stim'u'la'tion
stim'u'la'tive
stim'u'li
stim'u'lus
sting
stin'gi'er
stin'gi'est
stin'gi'ness
sting'ing
sting'ray
stin'gy
stink
stink'ing
stinky
stint'ing
sti'pend
sti'pen'di'ar'ies
sti'pen'di'ary
stip'ple
stip'pled
stip'pling
stip'u'late
stip'u'lat'ed
stip'u'lat'ing
stip'u'la'tion
stip'u'la'to'ry
stir
stir-fried
stir-fry
stir-fry'ing
stirred
stir'rer
stir'ring
stir'rup
stitch
stoat
stock
stock'ade

stock'brok'er
stock'hold'er
stock'i'er
stock'i'est
stock'i'ly
stock'i'ness
stock'ing
stock'pile
stock'piled
stock'pil'ing
stock'room
stock'tak'ing
stocky
stodge
stodg'i'er
stodg'i'est
stodg'i'ness
stodgy
sto'ic
sto'i'cal
sto'i'cal'ly
sto'i'cism
stoke
stoked
stok'ing
stole
stol'en
stol'id
sto'lid'i'ty
stol'id'ly
stom'ach
stom'ach'ache
stone
stoned
stone'ma'son
stone'wall
stone'ware
stone'work
ston'i'er
ston'i'est
ston'i'ness
ston'ing
stony
stood
stooge
stool
stoop
stop
stop'cock
stop'gap
stop'page
stopped
stop'per

stop'ping
stop'watch
stor'age
store
stored
store'house
store'keeper
store'room
sto'rey
sto'ries
stor'ing
stork
storm'bound
storm'i'er
storm'i'est
storm'i'ness
stormy
story
sto'ry'book
sto'ry'tell'er
stoup
stout
stout-heart'ed
stout'ly
stout'ness
stove
stov'ing
stow
stow'age
stow'a'way
stra'bis'mus
strad'dle
strad'dler
strad'dling
strafe
strafed
straf'ing
strag'gle
strag'gled
strag'gler
strag'gli'er
strag'gli'est
strag'gling
strag'gly
straight
straight'away
straight'edge
straight'en
straight'for'ward
straight'way
strain
strain'er
strait

strait'en
strait'jack'et
strait-laced
strange
strange'ly
strange'ness
strang'er
strang'est
stran'gle
stran'gled
stran'gle'hold
stran'gler
stran'gles
stran'gling
stran'gu'late
stran'gu'lat'ed
stran'gu'lat'ing
stran'gu'la'tion
strap
strap'hang'er
strap'less
strapped
strap'ping
stra'ta
strat'a'gem
stra'te'gic
stra'te'gi'cal'ly
strat'e'gies
strat'e'gist
strat'e'gy
strat'i'fi'ca'tion
strat'i'fied
strat'i'fy
strat'i'fy'ing
stra'to'cu'mu'lus
strato'sphere
strato'spher'ic
stra'tum
stra'tus
straw
straw'ber'ries
straw'ber'ry
stray
stray'ing
streak
streak'er
streak'i'er
streak'i'est
streaky
stream
stream'er
stream'line
stream'lined

stream'lin'ing
street
street'light
street'walk'er
street'wise
strength
strength'en
stren'u'os'i'ty
stren'u'ous
stren'u'ous'ly
strep'to'coc'ci
strep'to'coc'cus
strep'to'my'cin
stress
stress'ful
stress'ful'ly
stretch
stretch'abil'i'ty
stretch'able
stretch'er
stretch'i'er
stretch'i'est
stretchy
strew
strewed
strew'ing
strewn
stria
stri'ae
stri'ate
stri'at'ed
stri'at'ing
stri'a'tion
strick'en
strict
strict'ly
strict'ness
stric'ture
strid'den
stride
stri'den'cy
stri'dent
stri'dent'ly
strid'ing
strid'u'late
strid'u'la'tion
strid'u'lous
strife
strike
strike'bound
strike'break'er
strik'er
strik'ing

strik'ing'ly
string
strin'gen'cy
strin'gent
strin'gent'ly
string'i'er
string'i'est
string'i'ness
string'ing
stringy
strip
strip crop'ping
stripe
striped
strip'i'er
strip'i'est
strip'ing
strip'ling
stripped
strip'per
strip'ping
strip'tease
stripy
strive
striv'en
striv'ing
strobe
stro'bo'scope
stro'bo'scop'ic
strode
stroke
stroked
strok'ing
stroll
stroll'er
strong
strong'hold
strong'ly
strong-mind'ed
strong'ness
stron'tium
strop
stropped
strop'ping
strove
struck
struc'tural
struc'tur'al'ism
struc'tur'al'ist
struc'tur'al'ly
struc'ture
struc'tured
struc'tur'ing

stru'del
strug'gle
strug'gled
strug'gler
strug'gling
strum
strummed
strum'ming
strum'pet
strung
strut
strut'ted
strut'ting
strych'nine
stub
stubbed
stub'bi'er
stub'bi'est
stub'bing
stub'ble
stub'bled
stub'bly
stub'born
stub'born'ly
stub'born'ness
stub'by
stuc'co
stuc'coed
stuc'co'ing
stuck
stud
stud'ded
stud'ding
stu'dent
stud'ied
stud'ied'ness
stud'ies
stu'dio
stu'di'ous
stu'di'ous'ly
stu'di'ous'ness
study
stud'y'ing
stuff
stuff'er
stuffi'er
stuffi'est
stuffi'ness
stuff'ing
stuffy
stul'ti'fi'ca'tion
stul'ti'fied
stul'ti'fy

stul'ti'fy'ing
stum'ble
stum'bled
stum'bling
stump
stump'i'er
stump'i'est
stumpy
stun
stung
stunk
stunned
stun'ner
stun'ning
stun'ning'ly
stunt
stunt'ed
stunt'ed'ness
stu'pe'fac'tion
stu'pe'fied
stu'pe'fy
stu'pe'fy'ing
stu'pen'dous
stu'pen'dous'ly
stu'pen'dous'ness
stu'pid
stu'pid'i'ties
stu'pid'i'ty
stu'pid'ly
stu'pid'ness
stu'por
stu'por'ous
stur'di'er
stur'di'est
stur'di'ly
stur'dy
stur'geon
stut'ter
stut'ter'er
stut'ter'ing'ly
sty
stye
style
styled
sty'li
styl'ing
styl'ish
styl'ish'ly
styl'ish'ness
styl'ist
sty'lis'tic
sty'lis'ti'cal
sty'lis'ti'cal'ly

styl'i'za'tion
styl'ize
styl'ized
styl'iz'ing
sty'lus
sty'mie
sty'mied
sty'mie'ing
styp'tic
sty'rene
suave
suave'ly
suave'ness
suav'i'ty
sub
sub'al'tern
sub'arc'tic
sub'as'sem'bler
sub'as'sem'bly
sub'atom'ic
sub'base'ment
subbed
sub'bing
sub'com'mit'tee
sub'con'scious
sub'con'scious'ly
sub'con'scious'ness
sub'con'ti'nent
sub'con'tract
sub'con'trac'tor
sub'cul'ture
sub'cu'ta'ne'ous
sub'di'vide
sub'di'vid'ed
sub'di'vid'ing
sub'di'vi'sion
sub'due
sub'dued
sub'du'ing
sub'en'tries
sub'en'try
sub'freez'ing
sub'group
sub'head'ing
sub'hu'man
sub'ject
sub'jec'tion
sub'jec'tive
sub'jec'tive'ly
sub'jec'tive'ness
sub'jec'tiv'i'ty
sub'join
sub ju'di'ce

sub'ju'gate
sub'ju'gat'ed
sub'ju'gat'ing
sub'ju'ga'tion
sub'junc'tive
sub'lease
sub'leased
sub'leas'ing
sub'let
sub'let'ting
sub'li'mate
sub'li'mat'ed
sub'li'mat'ing
sub'li'ma'tion
sub'lime
sub'lime'ly
sub'lime'ness
sub'lim'est
sub'lim'i'nal
sub'lim'i'nal'ly
sub'lim'i'ty
sub'ma'chine
sub'mar'gin'al
sub'ma'rine
sub'merge
sub'merged
sub'mer'gence
sub'mer'gi'ble
sub'merg'ing
sub'merse
sub'mersed
sub'mers'i'ble
sub'mers'ing
sub'mer'sion
sub'mi'cro'scop'ic
sub'mis'sion
sub'mis'sive
sub'mis'sive'ly
sub'miss'ive'ness
sub'mit
sub'mit'ted
sub'mit'ting
sub'nor'mal
sub'nor'mal'i'ty
sub'or'bit'al
sub'or'di'nate
sub'or'di'nat'ed
sub'or'di'nate'ly
sub'or'di'nate'ness
sub'or'di'nat'ing
sub'or'di'na'tion
sub'or'di'na'tive
sub'orn

sub'or'na'tion
sub'poe'na
sub'poe'naed
sub'poe'na'ing
sub're'gion
sub rosa
sub'scribe
sub'scribed
sub'scrib'er
sub'scrib'ing
sub'scrip'tion
sub'sec'tion
sub'se'quence
sub'se'quent
sub'se'quent'ly
sub'se'quent'ness
sub'ser'vi'ence
sub'ser'vi'en'cy
sub'ser'vi'ent
sub'ser'vi'ent'ly
sub'side
sub'sid'ed
sub'sid'ence
sub'sid'i'ar'ies
sub'sid'i'ary
sub'si'dies
sub'sid'ing
sub'si'di'za'tion
sub'si'dize
sub'si'dized
sub'si'diz'ing
sub'si'dy
sub'sist
sub'sist'ence
sub'soil
sub'son'ic
sub'spe'cies
sub'stance
sub'stand'ard
sub'stan'tial
sub'stan'ti'al'i'ty
sub'stan'tial'ly
sub'stan'tial'ness
sub'stan'ti'ate
sub'stan'ti'at'ed
sub'stan'ti'at'ing
sub'stan'ti'a'tion
sub'stan'ti'a'tive
sub'stan'ti'val
sub'stan'ti'val'ly
sub'stan'tive
sub'stan'tive'ly
sub'stan'tive'ness

sub'sta'tion
sub'sti'tut'able
sub'sti'tute
sub'sti'tut'ed
sub'sti'tut'ing
sub'sti'tu'tion
sub'sti'tu'tion'al
sub'stra'ta
sub'stra'tum
sub'struc'ture
sub'sum'a'ble
sub'sume
sub'sumed
sub'sum'ing
sub'sump'tion
sub'sump'tive
sub'sys'tem
sub'tend
sub'ter'fuge
sub'ter'ra'ne'an
sub'ter'ra'ne'ous
sub'ti'tle
sub'tle
sub'tle'ness
sub'tle'ties
sub'tle'ty
sub'tly
sub'tract
sub'tract'er
sub'trac'tion
sub'trac'tive
sub'tra'hend
sub'trop'ic
sub'trop'i'cal
sub'urb
sub'ur'ban
sub'ur'ban'ite
sub'ur'bia
sub'vene
sub'ven'tion
sub'ver'sion
sub'ver'sion'ary
sub'ver'sive
sub'ver'sive'ly
sub'ver'sive'ness
sub'vert
sub'vert'er
sub'way
suc'ceed
suc'ceed'ing
suc'cess
suc'cess'ful
suc'cess'ful'ly

suc'cess'ful'ness
suc'ces'sion
suc'ces'sion'al
suc'ces'sive
suc'ces'sive'ly
suc'ces'sive'ness
suc'ces'sor
suc'cinct
suc'cinct'ly
suc'cinct'ness
suc'cour
suc'cour'er
suc'cu'lence
suc'cu'len'cy
suc'cu'lent
suc'cu'lent'ly
suc'cumb
such
such'like
suck
suck'er
suck'le
suck'led
suck'ling
su'crose
suc'tion
Su'dan'ese
sud'den
sud'den'ly
sud'den'ness
suds'i'er
sud'sy
sue
sued
suede
su'er
su'et
suf'fer
suf'fer'able
suf'fer'ably
suf'fer'ance
suf'fer'er
suf'fer'ing
suf'fice
suf'ficed
suf'fi'cien'cies
suf'fi'cien'cy
suf'fi'cient
suf'fi'cient'ly
suf'fic'ing
suf'fix
suf'fo'cate
suf'fo'cat'ed

suf'fo'cat'ing
suf'fo'ca'tion
suf'fo'ca'tive
suf'fra'gan
suf'frage
suf'fra'gette
suf'frag'ist
suf'fuse
suf'fused
suf'fus'ing
suf'fu'sion
suf'fu'sive
sug'ar
sug'ar-coat
sug'ary
sug'gest
sug'gest'i'bil'i'ty
sug'gest'i'ble
sug'ges'tion
sug'ges'tive
sug'ges'tive'ly
sug'ges'tive'ness
su'i'cid'al
su'i'cide
su'ing
suit
suit'abil'i'ty
suit'able
suit'able'ness
suit'ably
suit'case
suite
suit'ing
suit'or
su'ki'ya'ki
sulk
sulk'i'er
sulk'i'est
sulk'i'ly
sulk'i'ness
sulky
sul'len
sul'len'ly
sul'len'ness
sul'lied
sul'ly
sul'ly'ing
sul'pha'nil'a'mide
sul'phate
sul'phide
sul'phon'a'mide
sulphur
sul'phur'ic

sul'phur'ous
sul'tan
sul'tana
sul'tan'ate
sul'tri'ly
sul'tri'ness
sul'try
sum
su'mac
sum'ma
sum'mand
sum'ma'ries
sum'mar'i'ly
sum'mar'i'ness
sum'ma'ri'za'tion
sum'ma'rize
sum'ma'rized
sum'ma'riz'ing
sum'ma'ry
sum'ma'tion
sum'ma'tion'al
summed
sum'mer
sum'mery
sum'ming
sum'ming-up
sum'mit
sum'mon
sum'mons
sump'tu'ary
sump'tu'ous
sump'tu'ous'ly
sump'tu'ous'ness
sun
sun'bathe
sun'bathed
sun'bath'er
sun'bath'ing
sun'beam
sun'bon'net
sun'burn
sun'burned
sun'burnt
sun'burst
sun'dae
sun'der
sun'der'ance
sun'di'al
sun'down
sun'dries
sun'dry
sun'fish
sun'flow'er

sung
sun'glass'es
sunk
sunk'en
sun'less
sun'light
sunned
sun'ni'er
sun'ni'est
sun'ni'ness
sun'ning
sun'ny
sun'shade
sun'shine
sun'spot
sun'stroke
sun'tan
sun'tanned
sup
su'per
su'per'a'bun'dance
su'per'a'bun'dant
su'per'an'nu'ate
su'per'an'nu'at'ed
su'per'an'nu'at'ing
su'per'an'nu'a'tion
su'perb
su'perb'ly
su'perb'ness
su'per'car'go
su'per'charge
su'per'charged
su'per'charg'er
su'per'charg'ing
su'per'cil'i'ous
su'per'cil'i'ous'ly
su'per'cil'i'ous'ness
su'per'ego
su'per'erog'a'to'ry
su'per'fi'cial
su'per'fi'ci'al'i'ties
su'per'fi'ci'al'i'ty
su'per'fi'cial'ly
su'per'fi'cial'ness
su'per'fine
su'per'flu'i'ty
su'per'flu'ous
su'per'flu'ous'ly
su'per'flu'ous'ness
su'per'high'way
su'per'hu'man
su'per'im'pose
su'per'im'posed

su'per'im'pos'ing
su'per'im'po'si'tion
su'per'in'duce
su'per'in'tend
su'per'in'tend'ence
su'per'in'tend'en'cy
su'per'in'tend'ent
su'pe'ri'or
su'pe'ri'or'i'ty
su'pe'ri'or'ly
su'per'la'tive
su'per'la'tive'ly
su'per'la'tive'ness
su'per'man
su'per'mar'ket
su'per'nal
su'per'nat'u'ral
su'per'nat'u'ral'ism
su'per'nat'u'ral'ly
su'per'nat'u'ral'ness
su'per'no'va
su'per'nu'mer'ary
su'per'phos'phate
su'per'pow'er
su'per'scribe
su'per'script
su'per'scrip'tion
su'per'sede
su'per'sed'ed
su'per'sed'ing
su'per'son'ic
su'per'son'i'cal'ly
su'per'star
su'per'sti'tion
su'per'sti'tious
su'per'sti'tious'ly
su'per'sti'tious'ness
su'per'struc'ture
su'per'tank'er
su'per'vene
su'per'vened
su'per'ven'ing
su'per'ven'tion
su'per'vise
su'per'vised
su'per'vis'ing
su'per'vi'sion
su'per'vi'sor
su'per'vi'so'ry
su'pine
su'pine'ness
supped
sup'per

sup'ping
sup'plant
sup'plan'ta'tion
sup'ple
sup'ple'ment
sup'ple'men'tal
sup'ple'men'ta'ry
sup'ple'men'ta'tion
sup'ple'ness
sup'plest
sup'pli'ant
sup'pli'cant
sup'pli'cate
sup'pli'cat'ed
sup'pli'cat'ing
sup'pli'ca'tion
sup'pli'ca'to'ry
sup'plied
sup'pli'er
sup'plies
sup'ply
sup'ply'ing
sup'port
sup'port'able
sup'port'ably
sup'port'er
sup'port'ive
sup'pos'able
sup'pos'ably
sup'pose
sup'posed
sup'pos'ed'ly
sup'pos'ing
sup'po'si'tion
sup'po'si'tion'al'ly
sup'pos'i'to'ries
sup'pos'i'to'ry
sup'press
sup'press'i'ble
sup'pres'sion
sup'pres'sor
sup'pu'rate
sup'pu'rat'ed
sup'pu'rat'ing
sup'pu'ra'tion
su'prem'a'cist
su'prem'a'cy
su'preme
su'preme'ly
su'preme'ness
sur'cease
sur'charge
sur'charged

sur'charg'ing
sur'cin'gle
sure
su're'al'is'ti'cal'ly
sure-foot'ed
sure'ly
sure'ness
sur'er
sur'est
sure'ties
sure'ty
surf
sur'face
sur'faced
sur'fac'ing
surf'board
sur'feit
surf'er
surf'ing
surge
surged
sur'geon
sur'ger'ies
sur'gery
sur'gi'cal
sur'gi'cal'ly
surg'ing
sur'li'er
sur'li'est
sur'li'ly
sur'li'ness
sur'ly
sur'mise
sur'mised
sur'mis'ing
sur'mount
sur'mount'able
sur'name
sur'pass
sur'pass'able
sur'pass'ing
sur'plice
sur'plus
sur'plus'age
sur'pris'al
sur'prise
sur'prised
sur'pris'ing
sur'pris'ing'ly
sur're'al
sur're'al'ism
sur're'al'ist
sur're'al'is'tic

sur'ren'der
sur'rep'ti'tious
sur'rep'ti'tious'ly
sur'rep'ti'tious'ness
sur'rey
sur'ro'gate
sur'ro'gat'ed
sur'ro'gat'ing
sur'round
sur'round'ings
sur'tax
sur'veil'lance
sur'veil'lant
sur'vey
sur'vey'ing
sur'vey'or
sur'viv'al
sur'vive
sur'vived
sur'viv'ing
sur'vi'vor
sus'cep'ti'bil'i'ties
sus'cep'ti'bil'i'ty
sus'cep'ti'ble
sus'cep'ti'ble'ness
sus'cep'ti'bly
su'shi
sus'pect
sus'pend
sus'pend'er
sus'pense
sus'pen'sion
sus'pi'cion
sus'pi'cious
sus'pi'cious'ly
sus'pi'cious'ness
sus'tain
sus'tain'a'ble
sus'tain'er
sus'tain'ment
sus'te'nance
sut'tee
su'ture
su'tured
su'tur'ing
su'ze'rain
svelte
svelte'ly
svelte'ness
swab
swabbed
swab'bing
swad'dle

swad'dled
swad'dling
swag'ger
swag'ger'ing
Swa'hi'li
swain
swal'low
swam
swa'mi
swamp
swamp'i'er
swamp'i'est
swamp'i'ness
swampy
swan
swan dive
swank
swank'i'ly
swank'i'ness
swanky
swap
swapped
swap'ping
sward
swarm
swarth'i'er
swar'thi'est
swarth'i'ness
swarthy
swash'buck'ler
swash'buck'ling
swas'ti'ka
swat
swathe
swathed
swath'ing
swat'ted
swat'ter
swat'ting
sway
sway'able
sway'backed
swear
swear'er
swear'ing
sweat
sweat'er
sweat'i'ly
sweat'i'ness
sweat'ing
sweat'shirt
sweat'suit
sweaty

Swede
Swed'ish
sweep
sweep'ing
sweep'ing'ness
sweep'stakes
sweet
sweet-and-sour
sweet'bread
sweet'en
sweet'en'er
sweet'heart
sweet'ie
sweet'ish
sweet'ly
sweet'meat
sweet'ness
swell
swelled
swell'ing
swel'ter
swel'ter'ing
swept
swerve
swerved
swerv'ing
swift
swift'ly
swift'ness
swig
swigged
swig'ging
swill
swim
swim'mer
swim'ming
swim'ming'ly
swim'suit
swin'dle
swin'dled
swin'dler
swin'dling
swine
swing
swing'a'ble
swing'er
swing'ing
swin'ish
swipe
swip'ed
swip'ing
swirl
swirl'ing'ly

swirly
swish
swishy
Swiss
switch
switch'back
switch'blade
switch'board
swiv'el
swiv'elled
swiv'el'ling
swiz'zle
swoll'en
swoon
swoon'ed
swoon'ing'ly
swoop
swop
swopped
swop'ping
sword
swords'man
swore
sworn
swum
swung
syc'a'more
syc'o'phan'cy
syc'o'phant
syc'o'phan'tic
syc'o'phan'ti'cal
syl'la'bi
syl'lab'ic
syl'lab'i'cate
syl'lab'i'ca'tion
syl'lab'i'fi'ca'tion
syl'lab'i'fied
syl'lab'i'fy
syl'la'ble
syl'la'bub
syl'la'bus
syl'la'bus'es
syl'lo'gism
syl'lo'gis'tic
sylph
sylph-like
syl'van
sym'bi'o'sis
sym'bi'ot'ic
sym'bol
sym'bol'ic
sym'bol'i'cal
sym'bol'i'cal'ly

sym'bol'ism
sym'bol'ist
sym'bol'i'za'tion
sym'bol'ize
sym'bol'ized
sym'bol'iz'ing
sym'met'ric
sym'met'ri'cal
sym'met'ri'cal'ly
sym'met'ries
sym'me'try
sym'pa'thet'ic
sym'pa'thet'i'cal'ly
sym'pa'thies
sym'pa'thize
sym'pa'thized
sym'pa'thiz'er
sym'pa'thiz'ing
sym'pa'thiz'ing'ly
sym'pa'thy
sym'phon'ic
sym'pho'nies
sym'pho'ny
sym'po'sia
sym'po'si'um
symp'tom
symp'to'mat'ic
symp'to'mat'i'cal
symp'to'mat'i'cal'ly
syn'a'gog'al
syn'a'gog'i'cal
syn'a'gogue
sync
synch
syn'chro'nism
syn'chro'nis'tic
syn'chro'nis'ti'cal
syn'chro'nis'ti'cal'ly
syn'chro'ni'za'tion
syn'chro'nize
syn'chro'nized
syn'chro'niz'er
syn'chro'niz'ing
syn'chro'nous
syn'chro'nous'ly
syn'chro'nous'ness
syn'chro'tron
syn'co'pate
syn'co'pat'ed
syn'co'pat'ing
syn'co'pa'tion
syn'co'pa'tor
syn'co'pe

syn'cre'tic
syn'cre'tism
syn'di'cate
syn'di'cat'ed
syn'di'cat'ing
syn'di'ca'tion
syn'di'ca'tor
syn'drome
syn'ec'do'che
syn'ecol'o'gy
syn'er'gism
syn'od
syn'od'al
syn'o'nym
syn'on'y'mous
syn'on'y'my
syn'op'ses
syn'op'sis
syn'op'tic
syn'tac'tic
syn'tac'ti'cal
syn'tax
syn'the'ses
syn'the'sis
syn'the'sist
syn'the'size
syn'the'sized
syn'the'siz'er
syn'the'siz'ing
syn'thet'ic
syn'thet'i'cal
syn'thet'i'cal'ly
syph'i'lis
syph'i'lit'ic
sy'phon
sy'ringe
sy'ringed
sy'ring'ing
syr'up
syr'upy
system
sys'tem'at'ic
sys'tem'at'i'cal
sys'tem'at'i'cal'ly
sys'tem'a'ti'za'tion
sys'tem'a'tize
sys'tem'a'tized
sys'tem'a'tiz'er
sys'tem'a'tiz'ing
sys'tem'ic
sys'tem'i'cal'ly
sys'to'le
sys'tol'ic

syzy'gy
tab
tab'ard
tabbed
tab'bies
tab'bing
tab'by
tab'er'na'cle
tab'er'nac'u'lar
ta'ble
tab'leau
ta'bleau vi'vant
ta'bleaux
ta'bled
tab'le d'hôte
ta'ble'spoon'fuls
tab'let
ta'bling
tab'loid
ta'boo
ta'booed
ta'boo'ing
ta'bor
tab'o'ret
tab'u'lar
tab'u'lar'ly
tab'u'late
tab'u'lat'ed
tab'u'lat'ing
tab'u'la'tion
tab'u'la'tor
ta'chom'e'ter
tac'it
tac'it'ly
tac'it'ness
tac'i'turn
tac'i'tur'ni'ty
tack
tacked
tack'i'er
tack'i'est
tack'i'ness
tack'ing
tack'le
tack'led
tack'ler
tack'ling
tacky
ta'co
ta'cos
tact
tact'ful
tact'ful'ly

tact'ful'ness
tac'ti'cal
tac'ti'cal'ly
tac'ti'cian
tac'tics
tac'tile
tac'til'i'ty
tact'less
tact'less'ly
tact'less'ness
tad'pole
taf'fe'ta
taf'fy
tag
tagged
tag'ging
Ta'hi'tian
tail
tail'back
tailed
tail'gate
tail'gat'ed
tail'gat'ing
tail'less
tai'lor
tai'lored
tai'lor'ing
taint
taint'ed
take
tak'en
take-off
take-over
tak'er
tak'ing
talc
tal'cum
tale
tal'ent
tal'ent'ed
tal'is'man
talk
talk'a'tive
talk'a'tive'ly
talk'a'tive'ness
talk'er
talk'ie
talk'i'er
talk'i'est
talky
tall
tal'lied
tal'lies

tall'ish
tal'low
tal'lowy
tal'ly
tal'ly'ho
tal'ly'ing
Tal'mud
Tal'mud'ic
Tal'mud'i'cal
tal'on
tal'oned
ta'ma'le
tam'a'rack
tam'a'rind
tam'a'risk
tam'bour
tam'bou'rine
tame
tame'able
tamed
tame'ly
tame'ness
Tam'il
tam'ing
tam-o'-shan'ter
tam'per
tam'pon
tan
tan'a'ger
tan'bark
tan'dem
tan'doori
tang
tan'ge'lo
tan'gen'cy
tan'gent
tan'gen'tial
tan'gen'tial'ly
tan'ge'rine
tan'gi'bil'i'ty
tan'gi'ble
tan'gi'ble'ness
tan'gi'bly
tang'i'er
tang'i'est
tan'gle
tan'gled
tan'gle'ment
tan'gling
tan'go
tan'goed
tan'go'ing
tangy

tank'age
tank'ard
tank'er
tanned
tan'nery
tan'nic
tan'nin
tan'ning
tan'ta'lize
tan'ta'lized
tan'ta'liz'ing
tan'ta'liz'ing'ly
tan'ta'mount
tan'trum
tap
tape
taped
ta'per
ta'per'ing'ly
tap'es'tried
tap'es'tries
tap'es'try
tape'worm
tap'ing
tap'i'o'ca
ta'pir
tapped
tap'pet
tap'ping
tar
tar'an'tel'la
ta'ran'tu'la
ta'ran'tu'lae
ta'ran'tu'las
tar'di'er
tar'di'est
tar'di'ly
tar'di'ness
tar'dy
tar'get
tar'get'ed
tar'get'ing
tar'iff
tar'mac'ad'am
tar'nish
tar'nish'a'ble
ta'ro
tar'ot
tar'pau'lin
tar'pon
tar'ra'gon
tarred
tar'ried

tar'ring
tar'ry
tar'ry'ing
tart
tar'tan
tar'tar
tar'tare
tar'tar'ic
tar'tar'ous
tart'ly
tart'ness
task
tas'sel
tas'selled
tas'sel'ling
taste
tast'ed
taste'ful
taste'ful'ly
taste'ful'ness
taste'less
taste'less'ly
taste'less'ness
tast'er
tast'i'er
tast'i'est
tast'i'ness
tast'ing
tasty
tat
tat'ted
tat'ter'de'ma'lion
tat'tered
tat'ters
tat'ti'er
tat'ti'est
tat'ting
tat'tle
tat'tled
tat'tle'tale
tat'tling
tat'too
tat'tooed
tat'too'ing
tat'too'ist
tat'ty
taught
taunt
taunt'ing'ly
taut
tau'ten
taut'ly
taut'ness

tau'to'log'i'cal
tau'to'log'i'cal'ly
tau'tol'o'gies
tau'tol'o'gy
tav'ern
taw'dri'er
taw'dri'est
taw'dri'ly
taw'dri'ness
taw'dry
taw'ni'er
taw'ni'est
taw'ni'ness
taw'ny
tax
tax'abil'i'ty
tax'able
taxa'tion
tax-ex'empt
taxi
taxi'cab
taxi'der'mic
taxi'der'mist
taxi'der'my
tax'o'nom'i'cal
tax'o'nom'i'cal'ly
tax'on'o'mies
tax'on'o'mist
tax'on'o'my
tax'pay'er
tea
teach
teach'abil'i'ty
teach'able
teach'able'ness
teach'er
teach'ing
teak
tea'ket'tle
teak'wood
teal
team
team-mate
team'ster
teamwork
tear
tear'ful
tear'ful'ly
tear'ful'ness
tear'ing
tear'jerk'er
teary
tease

teased
tea'sel
teas'er
teas'ing
tea'spoon
tea'spoon'ful
teat
tech'ne'tium
tech'ni'cal
tech'ni'cal'i'ties
tech'ni'cal'i'ty
tech'ni'cal'ly
tech'ni'cal'ness
tech'ni'cian
tech'nique
tech'no'cracies
tech'noc'ra'cy
tech'no'crat
tech'no'crat'ic
tech'no'log'ic
tech'no'log'i'cal
tech'no'log'i'cal'ly
tech'nol'o'gies
tech'nol'o'gist
tech'nol'o'gy
tec'ton'ic
ted'dies
ted'dy
te'di'ous
te'di'ous'ly
te'di'ous'ness
te'di'um
tee
teed
tee'ing
teem
teem'ing
teen'age
teen'ag'er
teen'i'er
teen'i'est
teens
teeny
teeny'bop'per
tee'pee
tee'ter
teeth
teethe
teethed
teeth'ing
tee'to'tal
tee'to'tal'ler
tee'to'tal'ism

tee'to'tal'ler
tee'to'tal'ly
teg'u'ment
tele'cast
tele'cast'er
tele'cast'ing
tele'gram
tele'graph
tele'graph'ese
tele'graph'ic
tele'graph'i'cal'ly
te'leg'ra'phy
tele'ki'ne'sis
tele'me'ter
te'lem'e'try
te'le'ol'o'gy
tele'path'ic
tele'path'i'cal'ly
te'lep'a'thist
te'lep'a'thy
tele'phone
tele'phoned
tele'phon'ic
tele'phon'ing
tele'pho'to
tele'pho'tog'ra'phy
tele'print'er
tele'scope
tele'scoped
tele'scop'ic
tele'scop'ical'ly
tele'scop'ing
tele'text
tele'thon
tele'vise
tele'vised
tele'vis'ing
tele'vi'sion
tel'ex
tell
tell'er
tell'ing
tell'tale
tel'lu'ri'um
te'mer'i'ty
tem'per
tem'pera
tem'per'a'bil'i'ty
tem'per'a'ble
tem'per'a'ment
tem'per'a'ment'al
tem'per'a'men'tal'ly
tem'per'ance

tem'per'ate
tem'per'ate'ly
tem'per'ate'ness
tem'per'a'ture
tem'pered
tem'per'er
tem'pest
tem'pes'tu'ous
tem'pes'tu'ous'ly
tem'pes'tu'ous'ness
tem'pi
tem'plate
tem'ple
tem'po
tem'po'ral
tem'po'ral'i'ty
tem'po'ral'ly
tem'po'ral'ness
tem'po'rar'i'ly
tem'po'rar'i'ness
tem'po'rary
tem'po'ri'za'tion
tem'po'rize
tem'por'ized
tem'po'riz'er
tem'pori'z'ing
tem'po'riz'ing'ly
tempt
tempt'able
temp'ta'tion
tempt'ing
tempt'ing'ly
tempt'ress
ten
ten'a'bil'i'ty
ten'a'ble
ten'a'ble'ness
ten'a'bly
te'na'cious
te'na'cious'ly
te'na'cious'ness
te'nac'i'ty
ten'an'cies
ten'an'cy
ten'ant
ten'ant'able
tench
ten'den'cies
ten'den'cy
ten'den'tious
ten'den'tious'ly
ten'den'tious'ness
ten'der

ten'der'foot
ten'der-heart'ed
ten'der'ize
ten'der'ized
ten'der'iz'er
ten'der'iz'ing
ten'der'loin
ten'der'ly
ten'der'ness
ten'don
ten'dril
te'neb'ri'ous
ten'e'ment
ten'et
ten'fold
ten'nis
ten'on
ten'or
tense
tensed
tense'ly
tense'ness
ten'sile
ten'sil'i'ty
tens'ing
ten'sion
ten'sion'al
ten'sion'less
ten'si'ty
ten'sive
ten'ta'cle
ten'ta'cled
ten'tac'u'lar
ten'ta'tive
ten'ta'tive'ly
ten'ta'tive'ness
ten'ter'hooks
tenth
te'nu'i'ty
ten'u'ous
ten'u'ous'ly
ten'u'ous'ness
ten'ure
ten'ured
ten'u'ri'al
ten'u'ri'al'ly
te'pee
tep'id
te'pid'i'ty
tep'id'ness
te'qui'la
ter'bi'um
ter'cen'te'na'ries

ter'cen'te'nary
ter'cen'ten'ni'al
ter'gi'ver'sate
ter'i'ya'ki
ter'ma'gant
ter'mi'na'ble
ter'mi'nal
ter'mi'nal'ly
ter'mi'nate
ter'mi'nat'ed
ter'mi'nat'ing
ter'mi'na'tion
ter'mi'na'tive
ter'mi'na'tor
ter'mi'ni
ter'mi'no'log'i'cal
ter'mi'no'log'i'cal'ly
ter'mi'nol'o'gies
ter'mi'nol'o'gy
ter'mi'nus
ter'mite
tern
ter'na'ry
terp'sich'o're'an
ter'race
ter'raced
ter'rac'ing
ter'ra-cot'ta
ter'ra fir'ma
ter'rain
ter'ra'pin
ter'rar'i'um
ter'raz'zo
ter'res'tri'al
ter'res'tri'al'ly
ter'ri'ble
ter'ri'ble'ness
ter'ri'bly
ter'ri'er
ter'rif'ic
ter'rif'i'cal'ly
ter'ri'fied
ter'ri'fy
ter'ri'fy'ing
ter'ri'fy'ing'ly
ter'ri'to'ri'al
ter'ri'to'ri'al'i'ty
ter'ri'to'ries
ter'ri'to'ry
ter'ror
ter'ror'ism
ter'ror'ist
ter'ror'is'tic

ter'ror'i'za'tion
ter'ror'ize
ter'ror'ized
ter'ror'iz'er
ter'ror'iz'ing
ter'ror'less
ter'ry
terse
terse'ly
terse'ness
ter'ti'ary
tes'sel'late
tes'sel'lat'ed
tes'sel'lat'ing
tes'sel'la'tion
tes'ta'ment
tes'ta'men'ta'ry
tes'tate
tes'ta'tor
tes'ta'trix
tes'tes
tes'ti'cle
tes'tic'u'lar
test'i'er
test'i'est
tes'ti'fied
tes'ti'fy
tes'ti'fy'ing
tes'ti'ly
tes'ti'mo'ni'al
tes'ti'mo'nies
tes'ti'mo'ny
tes'ti'ness
tes'tis
tes'tos'ter'one
tes'ty
tet'a'nus
tetchy
tête-à-tête
teth'er
tet'ra'eth'yl
tet'ra'he'dron
text
text'book
tex'tile
tex'tu'al
tex'tur'al
tex'tur'al'ly
tex'ture
tex'tured
Thai
tha'lid'o'mide
thal'li'um

than
thane
thank
thank'ful
thank'ful'ly
thank'ful'ness
thank'less
thank'less'ly
thank'less'ness
thanks'giv'ing
that
thatch
thatch'er
thatch'ing
thaw
the
the'atre
the'atre'go'er
the'at'ri'cal
the'at'ri'cal'ness
the'at'ri'cal'i'ty
the'at'ri'cal'ly
thee
theft
their
theirs
the'ism
the'ist
the'is'tic
the'mat'ic
the'mat'i'cal'ly
theme
them'selves
then
thence
thence'forth
the'oc'ra'cies
the'oc'ra'cy
theo'crat
theo'crat'ic
theo'crat'i'cal
theo'crat'i'cal'ly
the'od'o'lite
theo'lo'gian
theo'log'ic
theo'log'i'cal
theo'log'i'cal'ly
the'ol'o'gies
the'ol'o'gy
the'o'rem
the'o'rem'at'ic
the'o'ret'ic
the'o'ret'i'cal

the'o'ret'i'cal'ly

the'o're'ti'cian

the'o'ries

the'o'rist

the'o'ri'za'tion

the'o'rize

the'o'rized

the'o'riz'er

the'o'riz'ing

the'o'ry

theo'soph'ic

theo'soph'i'cal

theo'soph'i'cal'ly

the'os'o'phist

the'os'o'phy

ther'a'peu'tic

ther'a'peu'ti'cal

ther'a'peu'ti'cal'ly

ther'a'peu'tics

ther'a'peu'tist

ther'a'pist

ther'a'py

there

there'about

there'abouts

there'af'ter

there'by

there'fore

there'in

there'of

there'up'on

therm

ther'mal

ther'mal'ly

ther'mo'dy'nam'ic

ther'mo'e'lec'tric

ther'mom'e'ter

ther'mo'met'ric

ther'mo'nu'cle'ar

ther'mo'plas'tic

ther'mos

ther'mo'stat

ther'mo'stat'ic

ther'mo'stat'i'cal'ly

the'sau'rus

these

the'ses

the'sis

thes'pi'an

they

thi'a'mine

thick

thick'en

thick'en'er

thick'et

thick'et'ed

thick-head'ed

thick'ish

thick'ly

thick'ness

thick'set

thick-skinned

thief

thieve

thieved

thiev'ery

thieves

thiev'ing

thiev'ish

thiev'ish'ness

thigh

thim'ble

thim'ble'ful

thin

thine

thing

thing'a'ma'bob

thing'um'mies

thing'um'my

think

think'er

think'ing

thin'ly

thinned

thin'ner

thin'ness

thin'nest

thin'ning

thin-skinned

third

third'ly

thirst

thirst'i'er

thirst'i'est

thirst'i'ly

thirst'i'ness

thirsty

thir'teen

thir'teenth

thir'ties

thir'ti'eth

thirty

this

this'tle

this'tle-down

thith'er

thong

tho'ra'ces

tho'rac'ic

tho'rax

tho'ri'um

thorn

thorn'i'er

thorn'i'est

thorn'i'ness

thorny

thor'ough

thor'ough'bred

thor'ough'fare

thor'ough'go'ing

thor'ough'ly

thor'ough'ness

those

thou

though

thought

thought'ful

thought'ful'ly

thought'ful'ness

thought'less

thought'less'ly

thought'less'ness

thou'sand

thou'sandth

thrall

thral'dom

thrash

thrash'er

thrash'ing

thread

thread'bare

thread'i'ness

thready

threat

threat'en

threat'en'ing'ly

three

three-decker

three'fold

three'piece

three'quar'ter

three'score

three'some

three-wheeler

thren'o'dy

thresh

thresh'er

thresh'old

threw

thrice

thrift

thrift'i'er

thrift'i'est

thrift'i'ly

thrift'i'ness

thrift'less

thrifty

thrill

thril'ler

thrill'ing

thrive

thrived

thriven

thriv'ing

throat

throat'i'er

throat'i'est

throat'i'ly

throat'i'ness

throaty

throb

throbbed

throb'bing

throe

throm'bo'ses

throm'bo'sis

throne

throng

throt'tle

throt'tled

throt'tling

through

through'out

through'put

through'way

throve

throw

throw'away

throw'back

throw'ing

thrown

thrum

thrummed

thrum'ming

thrush

thrust

thrust'ing

thru'way

thud

thud'ded

thud'ding

thug

thug'gery
thug'gish
thu'li'um
thumb
thumb'nail
thumb'screw
thumb'tack
thump'ing
thun'der
thun'der'bolt
thun'der'clap
thun'der'cloud
thun'der'head
thun'der'ous
thun'der'show'er
thun'der'storm
thun'der'struck
thun'dery
thus
thwack
thwart
thy
thyme
thy'mus
thy'roid
thy'self
ti
ti'ara
Ti'bet'an
tib'ia
tic
tick
tick'er
tick'et
tick'ing
tick'le
tick'led
tick'ling
tick'lish
tick'lish'ness
tick-tack-toe
ti'dal
tid'dly'winks
tide
tide'land
tide'mark
tide'water
ti'died
ti'di'er
ti'di'est
ti'di'ly
ti'di'ness
ti'dings

ti'dy
ti'dy'ing
tie
tied
tier
tiff
ti'ger
ti'ger'ish
tight
tight'en
tight-fist'ed
tight-lipped
tight'ly
tight'ness
tight'rope
tight'wad
ti'gress
til'de
tile
tiled
til'ing
till
till'able
till'age
til'ler
tilt
tilt'ed
tim'bal
tim'ber
tim'bered
tim'ber'line
tim'bre
tim'brel
time
time-con'sum'ing
timed
time-hon'oured
time'keep'er
time'less
time'less'ness
time'ly
time'out
time'piece
tim'er
time'serv'er
time'share
time-shar'ing
time'ta'ble
time'worn
tim'id
tim'id'i'ty
tim'id'ly
tim'id'ness

tim'ing
tim'or'ous
tim'or'ous'ly
tim'or'ous'ness
tim'o'thy
tim'pa'ni
tim'pa'nist
tin
tinc'ture
tinc'tur'ing
tin'der
tin'der'box
tine
tin'foil
tinge
tinged
tinge'ing
tin'gle
tin'gled
tin'gling
tin'gly
ti'ni'er
ti'ni'ness
tink'er
tin'kle
tin'kled
tin'kling
tinned
tin'ni'er
tin'ni'est
tin'ni'ly
tin'ni'ness
tin'ning
tin'ny
tin'sel
tin'selled
tin'sel'ling
tint
tint'er
tint'ing
ti'ny
tip
tipped
tip'pet
tip'ping
tip'ple
tip'pled
tip'pler
tip'pling
tip'si'er
tip'si'est
tip'si'ly
tip'si'ness

tip'ster
tip'sy
tip'toe
tip'toed
tip'toe'ing
tip'top
ti'rade
tire
tired
tire'less
tire'less'ly
tire'some
tire'some'ness
tir'ing
tis'sue
ti'tan
ti'tan'ic
ti'ta'ni'um
tit'bit
tithe
tithed
tith'ing
ti'tian
tit'il'late
tit'il'lat'ed
tit'il'lat'ing
tit'il'la'tion
ti'tle
ti'tled
ti'tle-tat'tle
tit'mouse
tit'ter
tit'ter'ing
tit'u'lar
tiz'zy
to
toad
toad'ies
toad'stool
toady
toad'y'ing
toad'y'ism
toast
toast'er
toast'mas'ter
toast'mis'tress
to'bac'co
to'bac'co'nist
to'bog'gan
to'bog'ganed
to'bog'gan'ing
toc'ca'ta
toc'sin

to'day	to'ma'to	to'paz	tor'pid'i'ty
tod'dies	to'ma'toes	top'coat	tor'pid'ly
tod'dle	tomb	top-dress'ing	tor'por
tod'dled	tom'boy	tope	torque
tod'dler	tom'boy'ish	toped	tor'rent
tod'dling	tomb'stone	to'pee	tor'ren'tial
tod'dy	tom'cat	top'er	tor'rid
to-do	tome	top-heavy	tor'rid'i'ty
toe	tom'fool'ery	to'pi'ary	tor'rid'ly
toed	tom'my'rot	top'ic	tor'rid'ness
toe'hold	to'mor'row	top'i'cal	tor'sion
toe'ing	tom'tit	top'i'cal'i'ty	tor'sion'al
toe'nail	tom-tom	top'ing	tor'so
tof'fee	ton	top'knot	tort
tofu	ton'al	top'less	torte
tog	to'nal'i'ty	top'most	tor'til'la
to'ga	ton'al'ly	to'pog'ra'pher	tor'toise
to'geth'er	tone	top'o'graph'i'cal	tor'toise'shell
to'geth'er'ness	tone'less	top'o'graph'i'cal'ly	tor'to'ni
togged	tone'less'ly	to'pog'ra'phy	tor'tu'ous
tog'ging	tongue	top'o'log'i'cal	tor'tu'ous'ly
tog'gle	tongue-lash	to'pol'o'gy	tor'tu'ous'ness
tog'gled	tongue-tied	topped	tor'ture
tog'gling	ton'ic	top'per	tor'tured
toil	to'night	top'ping	tor'tur'er
toil'er	ton'nage	top'ple	tor'ture'some
toi'let	tonne	top'pled	tor'tur'ing
toi'let'ries	ton'neau	top'pling	toss
toi'let'ry	ton'sil	top'sail	toss'ing
toil'some	ton'sil'lec'to'my	top-se'cret	tot
to'ing and fro'ing	ton'sil'li'tis	top'soil	to'tal
to'ken	ton'so'ri'al	top'sy-tur'vy	to'tal'i'tar'i'an
to'ken'ism	ton'sure	toque	to'tal'i'tar'i'an'ism
told	ton'sured	tor	to'tal'i'ty
tole	ton'sur'ing	torch	to'tal'i'za'tor
tol'er'a'bil'i'ty	ton'tine	torch'bear'er	to'talled
tol'er'a'ble	too	torch'light	to'tal'ling
tol'er'a'ble'ness	took	tore	to'tal'ly
tol'er'a'bly	tool	tor'e'a'dor	tote
tol'er'ance	tool'mak'er	to're'ro	tot'ed
tol'er'ant	toot	tor'ment	to'tem
tol'er'ant'ly	tooth	tor'ment'ing	to'tem'ic
tol'er'ate	tooth'ache	tor'men'tor	to'tem'ism
tol'er'at'ed	tooth'brush	torn	to'tem'ist
tol'er'at'ing	tooth'i'er	tor'nad'ic	to'tem'is'tic
tol'er'a'tion	tooth'i'est	tor'na'do	tot'ing
tol'er'a'tive	tooth'i'ness	tor'na'does	tot'ted
toll	tooth'less	tor'na'dos	tot'ter
toll'booth	tooth'paste	tor'pe'do	tot'ter'ing
tolled	tooth'pick	tor'pe'doed	tot'ting
toll'house	tooth'some	tor'pe'does	tou'can
toll'ing	toothy	tor'pe'do'ing	touch
tom'a'hawk	top	tor'pid	touch'a'ble

touch'down
tou'ché
touched
touch'i'er
touch'i'est
touch'i'ness
touch'ing
touch'ing'ly
touch-type
touch-typed
touch-typ'ing
touchy
tough
tough'en
tough'ness
tou'pee
tour
tour de force
tour'ism
tour'ist
tour'isty
tour'ma'line
tour'na'ment
tour'ne'dos
tour'ney
tour'ni'quet
tou'sle
tou'sled
tout
tout'er
tow
tow'age
to'ward
towards
tow'boat
tow'el
tow'elled
tow'el'ling
tow'er
tow'ered
tow'er'ing
tow-head'ed
town
towns'folk
town'ship
towns'peo'ple
tox'aemia
tox'ic
tox'ic'i'ty
tox'i'co'log'i'cal
tox'i'co'log'i'cal'ly
tox'i'col'o'gist
tox'i'col'o'gy

tox'in
tox'oid
toy
trace
trace'a'ble
trace'a'bly
traced
trac'er
trac'ery
tra'chea
tra'che'ae
tra'che'ot'o'mies
tra'che'ot'o'my
tra'cho'ma
trac'ing
track
track-and-field
track'er
track'suit
tract
trac'ta'bil'i'ty
trac'ta'ble
trac'ta'ble'ness
trac'ta'bly
trac'tion
trac'tion'al
trac'tive
trac'tor
trade
trad'ed
trade'mark
trad'er
trades'man
trades'peo'ple
trad'ing
tra'di'tion
tra'di'tion'al
tra'di'tion'al'ism
tra'di'tion'al'ist
tra'di'tion'al'ly
tra'duce
tra'duced
tra'duce'ment
tra'duc'ing
traf'fic
traf'ficked
traf'fick'er
traf'fick'ing
tra'ge'di'an
tra'ge'di'enne
trag'e'dies
trag'e'dy
trag'ic

trag'i'cal
trag'i'cal'ly
tragi'com'e'dies
tragi'com'e'dy
tragi'com'ic
trail
trail'blaz'er
trail'blaz'ing
trail'er
train
train'able
train'ee
train'er
train'ing
traipse
traipsed
traips'ing
trait
trai'tor
trai'tor'ous
trai'tor'ous'ly
tra'jec'to'ries
tra'jec'to'ry
tram'mel
tram'melled
tram'mel'ling
tramp'ing
tram'ple
tram'pled
tram'pling
tram'po'line
tram'po'lin'ist
trance
tranche
tran'quil
tran'quil'li'ty
tran'quil'lize
tran'quil'lized
tran'quil'liz'er
tran'quil'liz'ing
tran'quil'ly
tran'quil'ness
trans'act
trans'ac'tion
trans'ac'tion'al
trans'ac'tor
trans'at'lan'tic
trans'ceiv'er
tran'scend
tran'scen'dence
tran'scend'ent
tran'scen'den'tal
tran'scen'den'tal'ly

trans'con'ti'nen'tal
tran'scribe
tran'scribed
tran'scrib'er
tran'scrib'ing
tran'script
tran'scrip'tion
tran'scrip'tion'al
tran'scrip'tive
tran'sect
tran'sept
tran'sep'tal
trans'fer
trans'fer'a'ble
trans'fer'al
trans'fer'ence
trans'ferred
trans'fer'ring
trans'fig'u'ra'tion
trans'fig'ure
trans'fig'ured
trans'fig'ure'ment
trans'fig'ur'ing
trans'fix
trans'fixed
trans'fix'ing
trans'fix'ion
trans'form
trans'form'able
trans'for'ma'tion
trans'form'a'tive
trans'form'er
trans'fus'able
trans'fuse
trans'fused
trans'fus'ible
trans'fus'ing
trans'fu'sion
trans'gress
trans'gres'sion
trans'gres'sive
trans'gres'sor
tran'sience
tran'sient
tran'sis'tor
tran'sis'tor'ize
tran'sis'tor'ized
tran'sis'tor'iz'ing
trans'it
tran'si'tion
tran'si'tion'al
tran'si'tion'al'ly
tran'si'tive

transitively   tribute

tran'si'tive'ly
tran'si'tive'ness
tran'si'tiv'i'ty
tran'si'to'ri'ly
tran'si'to'ri'ness
tran'si'to'ry
trans'lat'abil'i'ty
trans'lat'able
trans'late
trans'lat'ed
trans'lat'ing
trans'la'tion
trans'la'tion'al
trans'lat'or
trans'lit'er'ate
trans'lit'er'at'ed
trans'lit'er'at'ing
trans'lit'er'a'tion
trans'lu'cence
trans'lu'cen'cy
trans'lu'cent
trans'lu'cent'ly
trans'mi'grate
trans'mi'grat'ed
trans'mi'grat'ing
trans'mi'gra'tion
trans'mi'gra'tor
trans'mi'gra'to'ry
trans'mis'si'bil'i'ty
trans'mis'si'ble
trans'mis'sion
trans'mis'sive
trans'mis'siv'i'ty
trans'mit
trans'mit'ta'ble
trans'mit'tal
trans'mit'ted
trans'mit'ter
trans'mit'ting
trans'mut'a'bil'i'ty
trans'mut'a'ble
trans'mut'a'ble'ness
trans'mut'a'bly
trans'mu'ta'tion
trans'mute
trans'mut'ed
trans'mut'er
trans'mut'ing
trans'o'ce'an'ic
tran'som
tran'son'ic
trans'pa'cif'ic
trans'par'en'cies

trans'par'en'cy
trans'par'ent
trans'par'ent'ly
trans'par'ent'ness
tran'spi'ra'tion
tran'spire
tran'spired
tran'spir'ing
trans'plant
trans'plant'able
trans'plan'ta'tion
trans'port
trans'port'abil'i'ty
trans'port'able
trans'por'ta'tion
trans'port'er
trans'pos'able
trans'pose
trans'posed
trans'pos'ing
trans'po'si'tion
trans'ship
trans'ship'ment
trans'shipped
trans'ship'ping
trans'verse
trans'verse'ly
trans'ves'tism
trans'ves'tite
trap
trap'door
tra'peze
tra'pe'zia
tra'pe'zi'um
trap'e'zoid
trapped
trap'per
trap'ping
trap'pings
trap'shoot'ing
trash
trash'i'er
trash'i'est
trash'i'ness
trashy
trau'ma
trau'mat'ic
trau'mat'i'cal'ly
trau'ma'tize
tra'vail
tra'vel
trav'elled
trav'el'ler

trav'el'ling
trav'e'logue
tra'vers'able
tra'vers'al
trav'erse
trav'ersed
trav'ers'ing
trav'es'ties
trav'es'ty
trawl
trawl'er
tray
treach'er'ies
treach'er'ous
treach'er'ous'ly
treach'er'ous'ness
treach'ery
tread
tread'ing
trea'dle
tread'mill
trea'son
trea'son'able
trea'son'ably
trea'son'ous
treas'ur'able
treas'ure
treas'ured
treas'ur'er
treas'ur'ies
treas'ur'ing
treas'ury
treat
treat'able
trea'ties
trea'tise
treat'ment
trea'ty
tre'ble
tre'bled
tre'bling
tre'bly
tree
tree'less
tre'foil
trek
trekked
trek'king
trel'lis
trem'ble
trem'bled
trem'bling
trem'bly

tre'men'dous
tre'men'dous'ly
tre'men'dous'ness
trem'o'lo
trem'or
trem'or'ous
trem'u'lous
trem'u'lous'ly
trem'u'lous'ness
trench
trench'an'cy
trench'ant
trench'ant'ly
trench'er
trend
trend'i'er
trend'i'est
trend'set'ter
trendy
tre'pan
trep'an'a'tion
tre'panned
tre'pan'ning
tre'phine
trep'i'da'tion
tres'pass
tres'pass'er
tress
tress'es
tres'tle
tri'ad
tri'ad'ic
tri'al
tri'an'gle
tri'an'gu'lar
tri'an'gu'lar'i'ty
tri'an'gu'lar'ly
tri'an'gu'late
tri'an'gu'lat'ed
tri'an'gu'lat'ing
tri'an'gu'la'tion
trib'al
trib'al'ism
tribe
tribes'man
tribes'woman
trib'u'la'tion
tri'bu'nal
trib'une
trib'u'tar'ies
trib'u'tar'i'ly
trib'u'tary
trib'ute

183

trice
tri'ceps
trich'i'no'sis
tri'chot'o'my
trick
trick'ery
trick'i'er
trick'i'est
trick'i'ly
trick'i'ness
trick'le
trick'led
trick'ling
trick'ster
tricky
tri'col'our
tri'cus'pid
tri'cy'cle
tri'dent
tri'den'tate
tri'di'men'sion'al
tried
tri'en'ni'al
tri'en'ni'um
tri'er
tries
tri'fle
tri'fled
trif'ler
tri'fling
tri'fling'ness
tri'fo'cals
trig'ger
trig'o'no'met'ric
trig'o'no'met'ri'cal
trig'o'no'met'ri'cal'ly
trig'o'nom'e'try
tri'lin'gual
trill
tril'lion
tril'lionth
tril'o'gies
tril'o'gy
trim
tri'ma'ran
tri'mes'ter
tri'mes'tral
tri'mes'tri'al
trim'ly
trimmed
trim'mer
trim'mest
trim'ming

trim'ness
tri'month'ly
tri'ni'tro'tol'u'ene
trin'ket
trio
trip
tri'par'tite
tripe
trip'ham'mer
tri'ple
tri'pled
tri'plet
trip'li'cate
trip'li'cat'ed
trip'li'cat'ing
trip'li'ca'tion
tri'pling
tri'ply
tri'pod
tripped
trip'per
trip'ping
trip'tych
tri'sect
tri'sec'tion
tri'sec'tor
trite
trite'ly
trite'ness
tri'ti'um
trit'u'rate
tri'umph
tri'um'phal
tri'um'phant
tri'um'phant'ly
tri'um'vi'rate
triv'et
triv'ia
triv'i'al
triv'i'al'i'ties
triv'i'al'i'ty
triv'i'al'i'za'tion
triv'i'al'ize
triv'i'al'ized
triv'i'al'iz'ing
triv'i'al'ly
tri'week'ly
tro'cha'ic
tro'che
tro'chee
trod
trod'den
trog'lo'dyte

troi'ka
troll
trol'ley
trol'lop
trom'bone
trom'bon'ist
troop
troop'er
tro'phies
tro'phy
trop'ic
trop'i'cal
trop'o'sphere
trot
troth
trot'ted
trot'ter
trot'ting
trou'ba'dour
trou'ble
trou'bled
trou'ble'mak'er
trou'ble'mak'ing
trou'ble'shoot'er
trou'ble'some
trou'bling
trough
trounce
trounced
trounc'ing
troupe
trouped
troup'er
troup'ing
trou'sers
trous'seau
trous'seaux
trout
trove
trow'el
tru'an'cies
tru'an'cy
tru'ant
truce
truck
truck'age
truck'er
truck'ing
truckle
truck'led
truck'ling
truck'load
truc'u'lence

truc'u'lent
truc'u'lent'ly
trudge
trudged
trudg'ing
true
true'ness
tru'er
tru'est
truf'fle
tru'ism
tru'is'tic
tru'ly
trump
trump'er'y
trum'pet
trum'pet'ed
trum'pet'er
trum'pet'ing
trun'cate
trun'cat'ed
trun'cat'ing
trun'ca'tion
trun'cheon
trun'dle
trun'dled
trun'dling
trunk
truss
truss'ing
trust
trus'tee
trus'tee'ship
trust'ful
trust'ful'ly
trust'i'er
trust'i'est
trust'i'ness
trust'ing'ly
trust'wor'thi'ly
trust'wor'thi'ness
trust'wor'thy
trusty
truth
truth'ful
truth'ful'ly
truth'ful'ness
try
try'ing
try'sail
tryst
tsar
tsa'ri'na

tsar'ist
tset'se flies
tset'se fly
tsu'na'mi
tub
tu'ba
tu'bal
tub'bi'er
tub'bi'est
tub'bi'ness
tub'by
tube
tubed
tube'less
tu'ber
tu'ber'cle
tu'ber'cu'lar
tu'ber'cu'lin
tu'ber'cu'lo'sis
tube'rose
tu'ber'ous
tub'ing
tu'bu'lar
tu'bule
tuck
tuck-point
tuft
tuft'ed
tug
tugged
tug'ging
tu'i'tion
tu'la'rae'mia
tu'lip
tulle
tum'ble
tum'bled
tum'ble'down
tum'bler
tum'ble'weed
tum'bling
tum'brel
tum'bril
tu'mes'cent
tu'mid
tu'mid'i'ty
tum'mies
tummy
tu'mour
tu'mor'ous
tu'mult
tu'mul'tu'ous
tu'mul'tu'ous'ly

tu'mul'tu'ous'ness
tun
tu'na
tun'able
tun'dra
tune
tune'able
tuned
tune'ful
tune'less
tune'less'ly
tun'er
tung'sten
tu'nic
tun'ing
tun'nel
tun'nelled
tun'nel'ling
tun'nies
tunny
tuque
tur'ban
tur'baned
tur'bid
tur'bid'i'ty
tur'bid'ness
tur'bine
tur'bo
tur'bo'charged
tur'bo'fan
tur'bo'jet
tur'bo'prop
tur'bot
tur'bu'lence
tur'bu'len'cy
tur'bu'lent
tu'reen
turf
tur'gid
tur'gid'i'ty
tur'gid'ness
Turk
tur'key
Turk'ish
tur'mer'ic
tur'moil
turn
turn'about
turn'around
turn'coat
turn'ing
tur'nip
turn'key

turn'off
turn'out
turn'over
turn'pike
turn'stile
turn'ta'ble
tur'pen'tine
tur'pi'tude
turps
tur'quoise
tur'ret
tur'tle
tur'tle'dove
tur'tle'neck
turves
tusk
tusked
tus'sle
tus'sled
tus'sling
tus'sock
tu'te'lage
tu'tor
tu'tor'age
tu'tored
tu'to'ri'al
tu'tor'ing
tut'ti-frut'ti
tu'tu
tu-whit tu-whoo
tux'e'do
twad'dle
twain
twang
twang'ing
twangy
tweak
tweed
tweed'i'ness
tweedy
tweet
tweet'er
tweeze
tweezed
tweez'ers
tweez'ing
twelfth
twelve
twelve-month
twen'ties
twen'ti'eth
twen'ty
twerp

twice
twid'dle
twid'dled
twid'dling
twig
twig'gy
twi'light
twi'lit
twill
twilled
twin
twine
twined
twinge
twinged
twin'ing
twin'kle
twin'kled
twin'kling
twinned
twin'ning
twirl
twirl'er
twirly
twist
twist'er
twisty
twit
twitch
twitchy
twit'ted
twit'ter
twit'tery
'twixt
two
two-faced
two-fist'ed
two'fold
two-handed
two-ply
two-sid'ed
two-some
two-time
ty'coon
ty'ing
tym'pa'ni
tym'pan'ic
tym'pa'nist
tym'pa'num
type
type'cast
typed

type'face	uke'le'le	un'ac'knowl'edged	un'avoid'able
type'script	Ukrai'ni'an	un'ac'quaint'ed	un'avoid'ably
type'set	uku'le'le	un'adorned	un'aware
type'set'ter	ul'cer	un'adul'ter'at'ed	un'aware'ness
type'write	ul'cer'ate	un'ad'vised	un'awares
type'writ'er	ul'cer'at'ed	un'ad'vis'ed'ly	un'backed
type'writ'ing	ul'cer'at'ing	un'ad'vis'ed'ness	un'bal'anced
type'writ'ten	ul'cer'a'tion	un'af'fect'ed	un'bar
ty'phoid	ul'cer'ous	un'af'fect'ed'ly	un'barred
ty'phoon	ul'ster	un'af'fect'ed'ness	un'bar'ring
ty'phus	ul'te'ri'or	un'afraid	un'bear'able
typ'i'cal	ul'te'ri'or'ly	un'aid'ed	un'bear'able'ness
typ'i'cal'i'ty	ul'ti'ma	un'aligned	un'bear'ably
typ'i'cal'ly	ul'ti'mate	un'al'loyed	un'beat'able
typ'i'cal'ness	ul'ti'mate'ly	un'al'ter'able	un'beat'en
typ'i'fi'ca'tion	ul'ti'mate'ness	un'al'tered	un'be'com'ing
typ'i'fied	ul'ti'ma'tum	un'am'bi'tious	un'be'com'ing'ness
typ'i'fy	ul'ti'mo	un-Amer'i'can	un'be'known
typ'i'fy'ing	ul'tra	una'nim'i'ty	un'be'knownst
typ'ing	ul'tra'con'serv'a'tive	unan'i'mous	un'be'lief
typ'ist	ul'tra'ma'rine	unan'i'mous'ly	un'be'liev'able
ty'pog'ra'pher	ul'tra'mod'ern	unan'i'mous'ness	un'be'liev'ably
ty'po'graph'ic	ul'tra'son'ic	un'an'nounced	un'be'liev'er
ty'po'graph'i'cal	ul'tra'sound	un'an'swer'able	un'be'liev'ing
ty'po'graph'i'cal'ly	ul'tra'vi'o'let	un'an'swered	un'bend
ty'pog'ra'phy	ul'u'late	un'ap'peal'able	un'bend'ed
ty'pol'o'gy	ul'u'la'tion	un'ap'peal'ing	un'bend'ing
ty'ran'nic	um'bel	un'ap'pe'tiz'ing	un'bend'ing'ness
ty'ran'ni'cal	um'ber	un'ap'pre'ci'at'ed	un'bent
ty'ran'ni'cal'ly	um'bil'i'cal	un'ap'pre'ci'a'tive	un'bi'ased
tyr'an'nies	um'bra	un'ap'proach'able	un'bid'den
tyr'an'nize	um'brage	un'ap'pro'pri'at'ed	un'bind
tyr'an'nized	um'bra'geous	un'ar'gu'able	un'bind'ing
tyr'an'niz'er	um'bra'geous'ly	un'ar'gu'ably	un'bleached
tyr'an'niz'ing	um'bra'geous'ness	un'armed	un'blem'ished
tyr'an'nous	um'brel'la	un'a'shamed	un'blink'ing
tyr'an'ny	umi'ak	un'asham'ed'ly	un'block
ty'rant	um'laut	un'asked	un'blush'ing
tyre	um'pire	un'aspir'ing	un'bolt
ty'ro	um'pired	un'as'sail'able	un'bolt'ed
tzar	um'pir'ing	un'as'sailed	un'boned
tza'ri'na	ump'teen	un'as'sist'ed	un'born
tzar'ist	ump'teenth	un'as'sum'ing	un'bos'om
ubiq'ui'tous'ly	un'abashed	un'at'tached	un'bound
ubiq'ui'tous'ness	un'able	un'at'tain'able	un'bound'ed
ubiq'ui'ty	un'abridged	un'at'tained	un'bound'ed'ness
ubuiq'ui'tous	un'ac'cept'able	un'at'tended	un'bowed
ud'der	un'ac'cept'ably	un'at'trac'tive	un'brace
ug'li'er	un'ac'com'pa'nied	un'au'thor'ized	un'break'able
ug'li'est	un'ac'count'able	un'avail'able	un'bred
ug'li'ly	un'ac'count'a'bly	un'avail'ably	un'bri'dle
ug'li'ness	un'ac'count'ed	un'avail'ing	un'bri'dled
ug'ly	un'ac'cus'tomed	un'avoid'abil'i'ty	un'bro'ken

un'buck'le
un'buck'led
un'buck'ling
un'bur'den
un'bur'ied
un'but'ton
un'but'toned
un'but'ton'ing
un'called-for
un'can'ni'est
un'can'ni'ly
un'can'ni'ness
un'can'ny
un'cap
un'capped
un'cap'ping
un'cared-for
un'car'ing
un'ceas'ing
un'ceas'ing'ly
un'ceas'ing'ness
un'cer'e'mo'ni'ous
un'cer'tain
un'cer'tain'ly
un'cer'tain'ness
un'cer'tain'ties
un'cer'tain'ty
un'chain
un'chal'lenged
un'change'able
un'changed
un'chang'ing
un'char'ac'ter'is'tic
un'charged
un'char'i'ta'ble
un'char'i'ta'bly
un'chart'ed
un'chart'ered
un'checked
un'chris'tian
un'cial
un'ci'form
un'cir'cum'cised
un'ci'nate
un'ci'nus
un'civ'il
un'civ'i'lized
un'civ'il'ly
un'clad
un'claimed
un'clasp
un'class'i'fi'a'ble
un'clas'si'fied

un'cle
un'clean
un'clean'li'ness
un'clean'ly
un'clean'ness
un'clear
un'clench
un'clip
un'clothe
un'clothed
un'clut'tered
un'coil
un'col'oured
un'combed
un'com'fort'able
un'com'fort'ably
un'com'mit'ted
un'com'mon
un'com'mon'ly
un'com'mon'ness
un'com'mu'ni'ca'tive
un'com'plain'ing
un'com'plain'ing'ly
un'com'pli'cat'ed
un'com'pre'hend'ing
un'com'pro'mised
un'com'pro'mis'ing
un'con'cern
un'con'cerned
un'con'cern'ed'ly
un'con'cern'ed'ness
un'con'di'tion'al
un'con'di'tion'al'ly
un'con'firmed
un'con'for'mi'ty
un'con'ge'ni'al
un'con'nect'ed
un'con'quer'a'ble
un'con'quered
un'con'scion'a'ble
un'con'scion'a'bly
un'con'scious
un'con'scious'ly
un'con'scious'ness
un'con'sid'ered
un'con'sti'tu'tion'al
un'con'strained
un'con'test'ed
un'con'trol'la'ble
un'con'trol'la'bly
un'con'trolled
un'con'ven'tion'al
un'con'vinced

un'con'vinc'ing
un'con'vinc'ing'ly
un'cooked
un'co'op'er'a'tive
un'co'or'di'nat'ed
un'cork
un'count'ed
un'cou'ple
un'cour'te'ous
un'couth
un'couth'ly
un'couth'ness
un'cov'er
un'cov'ered
un'crit'i'cal
un'crit'i'cal'ly
un'crowned
unc'tion
unc'tu'ous
un'cul'ti'vat'ed
un'cul'tured
un'dam'aged
un'dat'ed
un'daunt'ed
un'daunt'ed'ly
un'daunt'ed'ness
un'de'ceived
un'de'ceiv'ing
un'de'cid'ed
un'de'cid'ed'ness
un'de'fin'a'ble
un'de'fined
un'de'mand'ing
un'dem'o'crat'ic
un'de'mon'stra'tive
un'de'ni'a'ble
un'de'ni'a'ble'ness
un'de'ni'a'bly
un'de'nied
un'de'pend'a'bil'i'ty
un'de'pend'a'ble
un'der
un'der'achiev'er
un'der'achieve'ment
un'der'act
un'der'age
un'der'arm
un'der'bel'lies
un'der'bel'ly
un'der'bid
under'bid'der
under'body
under'bodies

under'bred
under'breeding
under'buy
un'der'car'riage
un'der'charge
un'der'clothes
un'der'cloth'ing
un'der'coat
un'der'coat'ing
un'der'cov'er
un'der'cur'rent
un'der'cut
un'der'cut'ting
un'der'de'vel'oped
un'der'dog
un'der'done
un'der'em'ployed
un'der'es'ti'mate
un'der'es'ti'mat'ed
un'der'es'ti'mat'ing
un'der'es'ti'ma'tion
un'der'ex'pose
un'der'fed
un'der'foot
un'der'gar'ment
un'der'go
un'der'goes
un'der'go'ing
un'der'gone
un'der'grad'u'ate
un'der'ground
un'der'growth
un'der'hand
un'der'hand'ed
un'der'lain
un'der'lay
un'der'lie
un'der'line
un'der'lined
un'der'ling
un'der'lin'ing
un'der'ly'ing
un'der'manned
un'der'mine
un'der'mined
un'der'min'ing
un'der'most
un'der'neath
un'der'nour'ished
un'der'paid
un'der'pass
un'der'pin
un'der'pinned

187

un'der'pin'ning
un'der'play
un'der'pop'u'lat'ed
un'der'priv'i'leged
un'der'rate
un'der'rat'ed
un'der'rat'ing
un'der'score
un'der'scored
un'der'scor'ing
un'der'sea
un'der'sell
un'der'shirt
un'der'shoot
un'der'side
un'der'signed
un'der'sized
un'der'slung
un'der'sold
un'der'stand
un'der'stand'a'ble
un'der'stand'a'bly
un'der'stand'ing
un'der'state
un'der'stat'ed
un'der'state'ment
un'der'stat'ing
un'der'stood
un'der'stud'ied
un'der'stud'ies
un'der'study
un'der'stud'y'ing
un'der'take
un'der'tak'en
un'der'tak'er
un'der'tak'ing
un'der-the-coun'ter
un'der'tone
un'der'took
un'der'tow
un'der'val'ue
un'der'val'ued
un'der'val'u'ing
un'der'wa'ter
un'der'wear
un'der'weight
un'der'went
un'der'world
un'der'write
un'der'writ'er
un'der'writ'ing
un'der'writ'ten
un'der'wrote

un'de'served
un'de'sign'ing
un'de'sir'a'bil'i'ty
un'de'sir'a'ble
un'de'sir'a'ble'ness
un'de'sir'a'bly
un'de'tect'ed
un'de'ter'mined
un'de'vel'oped
un'did
un'dig'ni'fied
un'di'lut'ed
un'dip'lo'mat'ic
un'di'rec'ted
un'dis'ci'plined
un'dis'closed
un'dis'cov'ered
un'dis'guised
un'dis'mayed
un'dis'posed
un'dis'put'ed
un'dis'tin'guished
un'di'vid'ed
un'dis'turbed
un'do
un'does
un'do'ing
un'done
un'doubt'ed
un'doubt'ed'ly
un'doubt'ing
un'dress
un'dressed
un'dress'ing
un'due
un'du'lant
un'du'late
un'du'lat'ed
un'du'lat'ing
un'du'la'tion
un'du'la'tory
un'du'ly
un'dy'ing
un'earned
un'earth
un'earth'li'ness
un'earth'ly
un'ease
un'eas'i'ly
un'eas'i'ness
un'easy
un'eat'able
un'eco'nom'ic

un'eco'nom'i'cal
un'ed'u'cat'ed
un'emo'tion'al
un'emo'tion'al'ly
un'em'ploy'a'ble
un'em'ployed
un'em'ploy'ment
un'end'ing
un'en'dur'able
un'en'vi'able
un'equal
un'equalled
un'equal'ly
un'equiv'o'cal
un'equiv'o'cal'ly
un'err'ing
un'err'ing'ly
un'es'sen'tial
un'eth'i'cal
un'eth'i'cal'ly
un'even
un'even'ly
un'even'ness
un'event'ful
un'event'ful'ly
un'ex'am'pled
un'ex'cep'tion'a'ble
un'ex'cep'tion'al
un'ex'cit'ing
un'ex'pect'ed
un'ex'pect'ed'ly
un'ex'pect'ed'ness
un'ex'plained
un'ex'pres'sive
un'fail'ing
un'fail'ing'ly
un'fair
un'fair'ly
un'fair'ness
un'faith'ful
un'faith'ful'ly
un'faith'ful'ness
un'fa'mil'iar
un'fa'mil'i'ar'i'ty
un'fash'ion'able
un'fast'en
un'fath'om'able
un'fa'vour'able
un'fa'vour'a'bly
un'fed
un'feel'ing
un'feel'ing'ly
un'feel'ing'ness

un'feigned
un'fet'ter
un'fet'tered
un'fin'ished
un'fit
un'fit'ness
un'fit'ted
un'fit'ting
un'flag'ging
un'flap'pa'ble
un'flat'ter'ing
un'flinch'ing
un'fold
un'fore'seen
un'for'get'ta'ble
un'for'get'ta'bly
un'for'giv'able
un'for'giv'ing
un'formed
un'for'tu'nate
un'for'tu'nate'ly
un'for'tu'nate'ness
un'found'ed
un'fre'quent'ed
un'friend'li'er
un'friend'li'est
un'friend'li'ness
un'friend'ly
un'frocked
un'fruit'ful
un'furl
un'fur'nished
un'gain'li'ness
un'gain'ly
un'gen'er'ous
un'god'li'ness
un'god'ly
un'gov'ern'a'ble
un'grace'ful
un'gra'cious
un'gra'cious'ly
un'gra'cious'ness
un'gram'mat'i'cal
un'grate'ful
un'grate'ful'ly
un'grate'ful'ness
un'grudg'ing
un'guard'ed
un'guard'ed'ly
un'guent
un'ham'pered
un'handy
un'hap'pi'er

un'hap'pi'est
un'hap'pi'ly
un'hap'pi'ness
un'hap'py
un'harmed
un'health'i'er
un'health'i'est
un'health'i'ness
un'healthy
un'heard
un'heed'ed
un'heed'ful
un'heed'ing
un'help'ful
un'her'ald'ed
un'hes'i'tat'ing
un'hes'i'tat'ing'ly
un'hinge
un'hinged
un'hing'ing
un'ho'li'ness
un'ho'ly
un'hook
un'hur'ried
un'hur'ried'ly
un'hurt
un'hy'gien'ic
uni'cel'lu'lar
uni'corn
uni'cy'cle
un'iden'ti'fi'able
un'iden'ti'fied
uni'fi'ca'tion
uni'fied
uni'form
uni'formed
uni'form'i'ty
uni'form'ly
uni'form'ness
uni'fy
uni'fy'ing
uni'lat'er'al
uni'lat'er'al'ism
uni'lat'er'al'ly
un'imag'i'na'ble
un'imag'i'na'tive
un'im'paired
un'im'peach'a'ble
un'im'peach'a'bly
un'im'ped'ed
un'im'por'tance
un'im'por'tant
un'im'pressed

un'im'pres'sive
un'im'proved
un'in'hab'it'able
un'in'hab'it'ed
un'in'hib'it'ed
un'ini'ti'at'ed
un'in'spir'ing
un'in'tel'li'gent
un'in'tel'li'gi'ble
un'in'tel'li'gi'bly
un'in'ten'tion'al
un'in'ten'tion'al'ly
un'in'ter'est'ed
un'in'ter'est'ing
un'in'ter'rupt'ed
un'ion
un'ion'ism
un'ion'ist
un'ion'i'za'tion
un'ion'ize
un'ion'ized
un'ion'iz'ing
unique
unique'ly
unique'ness
uni'sex
uni'son
unit
unite
unit'ed
unit'ing
uni'ty
uni'va'lent
uni'valve
uni'ver'sal
uni'ver'sal'i'ty
uni'ver'sal'ly
uni'ver'sal'ness
uni'verse
uni'ver'si'ties
uni'ver'si'ty
un'just
un'jus'ti'fi'able
un'jus'ti'fi'ably
un'jus'ti'fied
un'just'ly
un'just'ness
un'kempt
un'kind
un'kind'ly
un'kind'ness
un'know'able
un'know'ing

un'know'ing'ly
un'known
un'law'ful
un'law'ful'ly
un'law'ful'ness
un'lead'ed
un'learn
un'learned
un'learn'ed
un'learnt
un'leash
un'leav'ened
un'less
un'let'tered
un'like
un'like'li'hood
un'like'li'ness
un'like'ly
un'like'ness
un'lim'ber
un'lim'it'ed
un'list'ed
un'lit
un'load
un'lock
un'looked-for
un'loose
un'loos'en
un'lov'able
un'loved
un'love'ly
un'lov'ing
un'luck'i'est
un'luck'i'ly
un'luck'i'ness
un'lucky
un'made
un'make
un'mak'er
un'mak'ing
un'man'ly
un'manned
un'man'ner'ly
un'marked
un'mar'ried
un'mask
un'matched
un'mean'ing
un'mean'ing'ly
un'men'tion'a'ble
un'mer'ci'ful
un'mer'ci'ful'ly
un'mind'ful

un'mis'tak'a'ble
un'mis'tak'a'bly
un'mit'i'gat'ed
un'mo'lest'ed
un'moved
un'mu'si'cal
un'named
un'nat'u'ral
un'nat'u'ral'ly
un'nat'u'ral'ness
un'nec'es'sar'i'ly
un'nec'es'sary
un'nerve
un'nerved
un'nerv'ing
un'no'ticed
un'num'bered
un'ob'jec'tion'a'ble
un'ob'served
un'ob'tain'able
un'ob'tru'sive
un'ob'tru'sive'ly
un'oc'cu'pied
un'of'fi'cial
un'of'fi'cial'ly
un'or'gan'ized
un'or'tho'dox
un'pack
un'paid
un'pala't'able
un'par'al'leled
un'par'don'a'ble
un'par'lia'men'ta'ry
un'pick
un'pleas'ant
un'pleas'ant'ly
un'pleas'ant'ness
un'plug
un'plugged
un'plug'ging
un'plumbed
un'pol'lut'ed
un'pop'u'lar
un'pop'u'lar'i'ty
un'prec'e'dent'ed
un'pre'dic'ta'bil'i'ty
un'pre'dict'able
un'pre'dic'ta'bly
un'prej'u'diced
un'pre'pared
un'pre'pos'sess'ing
un'pre'ten'tious
un'prin'ci'pled

un'print'a'ble
un'pro'duc'tive
un'pro'fes'sion'al
un'prof'it'a'ble
un'prom'is'ing
un'pro'nounce'able
un'pro'tect'ed
un'pro'voked
un'pun'ished
un'qual'i'fied
un'qual'i'fied'ly
un'ques'tion'able
un'ques'tion'ably
un'ques'tioned
un'ques'tion'ing
un'ques'tion'ing'ly
un'quote
un'rav'el
un'rav'elled
un'rav'el'ling
un'read
un'read'able
un'read'i'ness
un'ready
un're'al
un're'al'is'tic
un're'al'is'ti'cal'ly
un're'al'i'ty
un'rea'son'able
un'rea'son'able'ness
un'rea'son'a'bly
un'rea'son'ing
un'rec'og'niz'able
un'rec'og'nized
un're'con'struct'ed
un're'cord'ed
un're'fined
un're'gen'er'ate
un're'hearsed
un're'lat'ed
un're'lent'ing
un're'li'abil'i'ty
un're'li'able
un're'lieved
un're'mark'able
un're'mit'ting
un're'mit'ting'ly
unre'pen'tant
un'rep're'sen'ta'tive
un're'quit'ed
un're'served
un're'serv'ed'ly
un're'solved

un'rest
un're'strained
un're'strain'ed'ly
un're'strict'ed
un're'ward'ed
un're'ward'ing
un'ri'valled
un'roll
un'ruf'fled
un'ru'li'ness
un'ru'ly
un'sad'dle
un'sad'dled
un'sad'dling
un'safe
un'said
un'sale'able
un'san'i'ta'ry
un'sat'is'fac'to'ry
un'sat'is'fied
un'sat'is'fy'ing
un'sat'u'rat'ed
un'sa'voury
un'scathed
un'sched'uled
un'schooled
un'sci'en'tif'ic
un'scram'ble
un'screw
un'script'ed
un'scru'pu'lous
un'seal
un'sea'son'able
un'sea'son'ably
un'seat
un'see'ing
un'seem'li'ness
un'seem'ly
un'seen
un'seg're'gat'ed
un'self'ish
un'self'ish'ly
un'self'ish'ness
un'set'tle
un'set'tled
un'set'tling
un'shak'able
un'shake'able
un'shak'ably
un'shak'en
un'shav'en
un'sheathe
un'shod

un'sight'li'ness
un'sight'ly
un'signed
un'skilled
un'skil'ful
un'smil'ing
un'smil'ing'ly
un'snap
un'snapped
un'snap'ping
un'snarl
un'so'cia'ble
un'sold
un'so'lic'it'ed
un'solved
un'so'phis'ti'cat'ed
un'sought
un'sound
un'sound'ness
un'spar'ing
un'speak'able
un'speak'ably
un'spec'i'fied
un'spec'tac'u'lar
un'spoiled
un'spoilt
un'spok'en
un'sport'ing
un'spot'ted
un'sta'ble
un'sta'ble'ness
un'stat'ed
un'stead'i'ly
un'steady
un'stop
un'stop'pa'ble
un'stopped
un'stop'ping
un'stressed
un'struc'tured
un'strung
un'stuck
un'stud'ied
un'sub'stan'ti'at'ed
un'suc'cess'ful
un'suc'cess'ful'ly
un'suit'able
un'suit'ably
un'suit'ed
un'sul'lied
un'sung
un'sup'port'ed
un'sure

un'sur'passed
un'sur'pris'ing
un'sur'pris'ing'ly
un'sus'pect'ed
un'sus'pect'ing
un'sweet'ened
un'swerv'ing
un'sym'pa'the'tic
un'tamed
un'tan'gle
un'tan'gled
un'tan'gling
un'tapped
un'taught
un'ten'a'ble
un'think'able
un'think'ing
un'think'ing'ly
un'ti'di'er
un'ti'di'est
un'ti'di'ly
un'ti'di'ness
un'ti'dy
un'tie
un'tied
un'til
un'time'li'ness
un'time'ly
un'tir'ing
un'tir'ing'ly
un'to
un'told
un'touch'able
un'touched
un'to'ward
un'trained
un'tram'melled
un'treat'ed
un'tried
un'troub'led
un'true
un'trust'wor'thy
un'truth
un'truth'ful
un'truth'ful'ly
un'tu'tored
un'ty'ing
un'us'able
un'used
un'usu'al
un'usu'al'ly
un'usu'al'ness
un'ut'ter'able

un'ut'ter'ably
un'var'nished
un'vary'ing
un'veil
un'waged
un'want'ed
un'war'i'ness
un'war'rant'ed
un'wary
un'wa'ver'ing
un'wel'come
un'well
un'whole'some
un'wield'i'ness
un'wieldy
un'will'ing
un'will'ing'ly
un'will'ing'ness
un'wind
un'wind'ing
un'wise
un'wise'ly
un'wit'ting
un'wit'ting'ly
un'wont'ed
un'work'able
un'world'li'ness
un'world'ly
un'wor'thi'ly
un'wor'thi'ness
un'wor'thy
un'wound
un'wrap
un'wrapped
un'wrap'ping
un'writ'ten
un'yield'ing
un'zip
un'zipped
un'zip'ping
up
up-and-com'ing
up-and-down
up'beat
up'braid
up'bring'ing
up'com'ing
up'coun'try
up'date
up'dat'ed
up'dat'ing
up-front
up'grade

up'grad'ed
up'grad'ing
up'heav'al
up'heave
up'held
up'hill
up'hold
up'hold'er
up'hold'ing
up'hol'ster
up'hol'stery
up'keep
up'land
up'mar'ket
up'most
up'on
upped
up'per
up'per class
up'per'cut
up'per'most
up'ping
up'pish
up'pish'ness
up'pi'ty
up'raise
up'raised
up'rais'ing
up'rear
up'right
up'right'ness
up'ris'ing
up'roar
up'roar'i'ous
up'root
up'set
up'set'ting
up'shot
up'si'lon
up'stage
up'staged
up'stag'ing
up'stairs
up'stand'ing
up'start
up'state
up'stream
up'surge
up'swing
up'take
up'tight
up-to-date
up'town

up'turn
up'ward
up'wards
urae'mia
ura'ni'um
ur'ban
ur'bane
ur'bane'ly
ur'bane'ness
ur'ban'i'ty
ur'ban'i'za'tion
ur'ban'ize
ur'ban'ized
ur'ban'iz'ing
ur'chin
Ur'du
ure'ter
ure'thra
urge
urged
ur'gen'cy
ur'gent
ur'gent'ly
urg'ing
uri'nal
uri'nal'y'sis
uri'nary
uri'nate
uri'nat'ed
uri'nat'ing
uri'na'tion
urine
urn
uro'log'ic
urol'o'gy
us
us'a'bil'i'ty
us'a'ble
us'a'ble'ness
us'age
use
used
use'ful
use'ful'ly
use'ful'ness
use'less
use'less'ly
use'less'ness
us'er
ush'er
ush'er'ette
us'ing
usu'al

usu'al'ly
usu'rer
usu'ri'ous
usurp
usur'pa'tion
usurp'er
usu'ry
uten'sil
uter'us
util'i'tar'ian
util'i'ties
util'i'ty
uti'li'za'tion
uti'lize
uti'lized
uti'liz'ing
ut'most
ut'ter
ut'ter'able
ut'ter'ance
ut'ter'ly
ut'ter'most
uvu'la
uvu'lar
ux'o'ri'ous
ux'o'ri'ous'ness
va'can'cies
va'can'cy
va'cant
va'cant'ly
va'cate
va'cat'ed
va'cat'ing
va'ca'tion
vac'ci'nate
vac'ci'nat'ed
vac'ci'nat'ing
vac'ci'na'tion
vac'cine
vac'il'late
vac'il'lat'ed
vac'il'lat'ing
vac'il'la'tion
vac'il'la'tor
va'cu'i'ty
vac'u'ous
vac'u'ous'ness
vac'u'um
vag'a'bond
vag'a'bond'age
va'ga'ries
va'gar'i'ous
va'gary

va'gi'na
vag'i'nal
va'gran'cy
va'grant
vague
vague'ly
vague'ness
vain
vain'glo'ri'ous
vain'glo'ry
vain'ly
vain'ness
val'ance
val'anced
vale
val'e'dic'tion
val'e'dic'to'ri'an
val'e'dic'to'ry
va'lence
va'len'cies
va'len'cy
val'en'tine
val'et
val'iant
val'iant'ly
val'iant'ness
val'id
val'i'date
val'i'dat'ed
val'i'dat'ing
val'i'da'tion
va'lid'i'ty
val'id'ly
val'id'ness
va'lise
val'ley
val'leys
val'our
val'or'i'za'tion
val'or'ize
val'or'ous
val'or'ous'ly
val'u'a'ble
val'u'a'ble'ness
val'u'a'bly
val'u'a'tion
val'u'a'tion'al
val'ue
val'ued
val'ue'less
val'u'er
val'u'ing
valve

valve'less
val'vu'lar
va'moose
vam'pire
vam'pir'ic
va'na'di'um
van'dal
van'dal'ism
van'dal'ize
van'dal'ized
van'dal'iz'ing
vane
vaned
vane'less
van'guard
va'nil'la
van'ish
van'i'ties
van'i'ty
van'quish
van'quish'a'ble
van'quish'er
van'tage
vap'id
va'pid'i'ty
vap'id'ly
vap'id'ness
va'por'ize
va'por'iz'er
va'por'ous
va'por'ous'ly
va'pour
va'pour'er
va'pour'ish
va'pour'i'za'tion
vari'abil'i'ty
vari'able
vari'able'ness
vari'ably
vari'ance
vari'ant
vari'a'tion
vari'a'tion'al
vari'a'tion'al'ly
vari'col'oured
var'i'cose
var'i'cos'i'ty
var'ied
var'ied'ness
var'ie'gate
var'ie'gat'ed
var'ie'gat'ing
var'ie'ga'tion

va'ri'etal
va'ri'etal'ly
va'ri'eties
va'ri'ety
var'i'o'rum
var'i'ous
var'i'ous'ly
var'i'ous'ness
var'mint
var'nish
var'si'ties
var'si'ty
vary
vary'ing
vary'ing'ly
vas'cu'lar
vas'cu'lar'i'ty
vase
va'sec'to'mies
vas'ec'to'my
va'so'mo'tor
vas'sal
vas'sal'age
vast
vast'ly
vast'ness
vat
vat'ted
vat'ting
vaude'ville
vaude'vil'lian
vault
vault'ed
vault'er
vault'ing
vaunt
vaunt'er
veal
vec'tor
vec'to'ri'al
veer
veer'ing
ve'gan
veg'e'ta'ble
veg'e'tal
veg'e'tar'i'an
veg'e'tar'i'an'ism
veg'e'tate
veg'e'tat'ed
veg'e'tat'ing
veg'e'ta'tion
veg'e'ta'tion'al
veg'e'ta'tive

ve'he'mence
ve'he'men'cy
ve'he'ment
ve'he'ment'ly
ve'hi'cle
ve'hic'u'lar
veil
veiled
veil'ing
vein
vein'ing
veiny
veld
veldt
vel'lum
ve'loc'i'ties
ve'loc'i'ty
vel'our
ve'lum
vel'vet
vel'vet'een
vel'vet'like
vel'vety
ve'nal
ve'nal'i'ty
ve'nal'ly
ve'na'tion
ve'na'tion'al
vend'able
vend'er
ven'det'ta
vend'ibil'i'ty
vend'ible
vend'or
ve'neer
ve'neer'ing
ven'er'a'bil'i'ty
ven'er'a'ble
ven'er'a'ble'ness
ven'er'a'bly
ven'er'ate
ven'er'a'tion
ven'er'a'tor
ve'ne're'al
venge'ance
venge'ful
venge'ful'ness
ve'ni'al
ve'ni'al'i'ty
ve'ni'al'ly
ven'i'son
ven'om
ven'om'ous

ven'om'ous'ly
ven'om'ous'ness
ve'nous
ve'nous'ly
ve'nous'ness
vent
vent'ed
ven'ti'late
ven'ti'lat'ed
ven'ti'lat'ing
ven'ti'la'tion
ven'ti'la'tor
vent'ing
ven'tral
ven'tri'cle
ven'tri'lo'qui'al
ven'tril'o'quism
ven'tril'o'quist
ven'tril'o'quize
ven'tril'o'quized
ven'tril'o'quiz'ing
ven'ture
ven'tured
ven'ture'some
ven'tur'ing
ven'tur'ous
ven'ue
ve'ra'cious
ve'ra'cious'ness
ve'rac'i'ties
ve'rac'i'ty
ve'ran'da
ve'ran'dah
verb
ver'bal
ver'bal'i'za'tion
ver'bal'ize
ver'bal'ized
ver'bal'iz'ing
ver'bal'ly
ver'ba'tim
ver'be'na
ver'bi'age
ver'bose
ver'bose'ness
ver'bos'i'ty
ver'bo'ten
ver'dan'cy
ver'dant
ver'dict
ver'di'gris
ver'dure
ver'dured

ver'dur'ous
verge
verged
verg'er
verg'ing
ver'i'fi'abil'i'ty
ver'i'fi'able
ver'i'fi'able'ness
ver'i'fi'ca'tion
ver'i'fied
ver'i'fi'er
verify
ver'i'fy'ing
ver'i'ly
ver'i'si'mil'i'tude
ver'i'ta'ble
ver'i'ta'ble'ness
ver'i'ta'bly
ver'i'ties
ver'i'ty
ver'juice
ver'meil
ver'mi'cel'li
ver'mic'u'lar
ver'mic'u'late
ver'mi'form
ver'mi'fuge
ver'mil'ion
ver'min
ver'min'ous
ver'mouth
ver'nac'u'lar
ver'nac'u'lar'ism
ver'nal
ver'nal'ly
ver'ni'er
ver'ru'ca
ver'sa'tile
ver'sa'til'i'ty
verse
versed
ver'si'fi'ca'tion
ver'si'fied
ver'si'fy
ver'si'fy'ing
ver'sion
ver'sion'al
ver'so
ver'sus
ver'te'bra
ver'te'brae
ver'te'bral
ver'te'brate

ver'tex
ver'tex'es
ver'ti'cal
ver'ti'cal'i'ty
ver'ti'cal'ly
ver'ti'ces
ver'tig'i'nous
ver'ti'go
verve
very
ves'i'cant
ves'i'cle
ves'pers
ves'sel
ves'tal
vest'ed
ves'ti'bule
ves'tige
ves'tig'i'al
ves'tig'i'al'ly
vest'ment
vest-pock'et
ves'tries
ves'try
vet
vetch
vet'er'an
vet'er'i'nar'i'an
vet'er'i'nary
ve'to
ve'toed
ve'to'er
ve'toes
ve'to'ing
vet'ted
vet'ting
vex
vex'a'tion
vex'a'tious
vexed
vex'ing
via
vi'a'bil'i'ty
vi'a'ble
vi'a'bly
via'duct
vi'al
vi'and
vi'bran'cy
vi'brant
vi'bra'phone
vi'brate
vi'brat'ed

vi'brat'ing
vi'bra'tion
vi'bra'to
vi'bra'tor
vi'bra'to'ry
vi'bur'num
vic'ar
vic'ar'age
vi'car'i'ous
vi'car'i'ous'ly
vi'car'i'ous'ness
vice
vice ad'mi'ral
vice chan'cel'lor
vice-pres'i'den'cy
vice-pres'i'dent
vice-pres'i'den'tial
vice'regal
vice'roy
vice'roy'al'ty
vice ver'sa
vi'chys'soise
vi'cin'i'ties
vi'cin'i'ty
vi'cious
vi'cious'ly
vi'cious'ness
vi'cis'si'tude
vic'tim
vic'tim'i'za'tion
vic'tim'ize
vic'tim'ized
vic'tim'iz'ing
vic'tor
vic'to'ries
vic'to'ri'ous
vic'to'ri'ous'ly
vic'to'ri'ous'ness
vic'to'ry
vict'ual
vi'cu'na
vid'eo
vid'eo cas'sette
vid'eo tape
vie
vied
vi'er
Vi'et'nam'ese
view
view'er
view'find'er
view'point
vig'il

vig'i'lance
vig'i'lant
vig'i'lan'te
vig'i'lan'tism
vi'gnette
vig'or'ous
vig'or'ous'ly
vig'our
Vi'king
vile
vile'ly
vil'er
vil'est
vil'i'fi'ca'tion
vil'i'fied
vil'i'fy
vil'i'fy'ing
vil'la
vil'lage
vil'lag'er
vil'lain
vil'lain'ies
vil'lain'ous
vil'lain'ous'ly
vil'lain'ous'ness
vil'lainy
vil'lein
vil'lous
vim
vin'ai'grette
vin'ci'bil'i'ty
vin'ci'ble
vin'di'cate
vin'di'cat'ed
vin'di'cat'ing
vin'di'ca'tion
vin'di'ca'tor
vin'dic'tive
vin'dic'tive'ly
vin'dic'tive'ness
vin'e'gar
vin'e'gary
vin'er'ies
vin'ery
vine'yard
vi'ni'cul'ture
vi'nous
vin'tage
vint'ner
vi'nyl
vi'ol
vi'o'la
vi'o'la'bil'i'ty

vi'o'la'ble
vi'o'late
vi'o'lat'ed
vi'o'lat'ing
vi'o'la'tion
vi'o'la'tor
vi'o'lence
vi'o'lent
vi'o'lent'ly
vi'o'let
vi'o'lin
vi'o'lin'ist
vi'o'list
vi'o'lon'cel'list
vi'o'lon'cel'lo
vi'per
vi'ra'go
vi'ral
vir'eo
vir'gin
vir'gin'al
vir'gin'al'ly
vir'gin'i'ty
vir'gule
vir'ile
vi'ril'i'ty
vi'rol'o'gist
vi'rol'o'gy
vir'tu'al
vir'tu'al'ly
vir'tue
vir'tu'o'si
vir'tu'os'i'ty
vir'tu'o'so
vir'tu'ous
vir'tu'ous'ly
vir'tu'ous'ness
vir'u'lence
vir'u'len'cy
vir'u'lent
vir'u'lent'ly
vi'rus
vi'rus'es
vi'sa
vis'age
vis-à-vis
vis'cera
vis'cer'al
vis'cid
vis'cid'i'ty
vis'cid'ly
vis'cid'ness
vis'cose

vis'cos'i'ties
vis'cos'i'ty
vis'count
vis'count'ess
vis'cous
vis'i'bil'i'ty
vis'i'ble
vis'i'bly
vi'sion
vi'sion'ar'ies
vi'sion'ary
vis'it
vis'i'tant
vis'it'a'tion
vis'it'ed
vis'it'ing
vis'i'tor
vi'sor
vis'ta
vis'u'al
vis'u'al'iza'tion
vis'u'al'ize
vis'u'al'ized
vis'u'al'iz'ing
vis'u'al'ly
vi'tal
vi'tal'i'ty
vi'tal'iza'tion
vi'tal'ize
vi'tal'ized
vi'tal'iz'ing
vi'tal'ly
vi'tals
vi'ta'min
vi'ti'ate
vi'ti'at'ed
vi'ti'at'ing
vi'ti'a'tion
vit're'os'i'ty
vit're'ous
vit'ri'fi'a'ble
vit'ri'fi'ca'tion
vit'ri'fied
vit'ri'fy
vit'ri'fy'ing
vit'ri'ol
vit'ri'ol'ic
vi'tu'per'ate
vi'tu'per'at'ed
vi'tu'per'at'ing
vi'tu'per'a'tion
vi'tu'per'a'tive
vi'va

vi'va'cious
vi'va'cious'ly
vi'vac'i'ty
vi'var'i'um
vi'va vo'ce
viv'id
viv'id'ly
viv'id'ness
viv'i'fi'ca'tion
viv'i'fied
viv'i'fy
viv'i'fy'ing
vi'vip'ar'ous
vivi'sect
viv'i'sec'tion
vivi'sec'tion'ist
vix'en
viz
vi'zier
vi'zor
vo'cab'u'lar'ies
vo'cab'u'lary
vo'cal
vo'cal'ic
vo'cal'ist
vo'cali'za'tion
vo'cal'ize
vo'cal'ized
vo'cal'iz'ing
vo'ca'tion
vo'ca'tion'al
vo'ca'tion'al'ly
voc'a'tive
vo'cif'er'ate
vo'cif'er'ous
vo'cif'er'ous'ly
vod'ka
vogue
vogu'ish
voice
voiced
voice'less
voice-over
voice'print
voic'ing
void
void'able
voile
vol'a'tile
vol'a'til'i'ty
vol-au-vent
vol'can'ic
vol'can'i'cal'ly

vol'ca'no
vol'ca'noes
vol'ca'nos
vole
vo'li'tion
vol'ley
vol'ley'ball
vol'leyed
vol'ley'ing
vol'leys
volt
volt'age
vol'ta'ic
vol'u'bil'i'ty
vol'u'ble
vol'u'bly
vol'ume
vo'lu'mi'nous
vo'lu'mi'nous'ly
vo'lu'mi'nous'ness
vol'un'tar'i'ly
vol'un'tary
vol'un'teer
vo'lup'tu'ary
vo'lup'tu'ous
vo'lup'tu'ous'ly
vo'lup'tu'ous'ness
vo'lute
vom'it
vom'it'ed
vom'it'ing
voo'doo
voo'doo'ism
voo'doo'ist
voo'doo'is'tic
vo'ra'cious
vo'ra'cious'ly
vo'rac'i'ty
vor'tex
vor'tex'es
vor'ti'ces
vo'ta'ries
vo'ta'ry
vote
vot'ed
vot'er
vot'ing
vo'tive
vouch
vouch'er
vouch'safe
vouch'safed
vouch'saf'ing

vow
vow'el
vox po'pu'li
voy'age
voy'aged
voy'ag'er
voy'ag'ing
vo'yeur
vo'yeur'ism
voy'eur'is'tic
vul'can'i'za'tion
vul'can'ize
vul'can'ized
vul'can'iz'ing
vul'gar
vul'gar'ism
vul'gar'i'ty
vul'gar'iza'tion
vul'gar'ize
vul'gar'ized
vul'gar'iz'ing
vul'ner'a'bil'i'ty
vul'ner'a'ble
vul'ner'a'bly
vul'pine
vul'ture
vul'tur'ine
vul'tur'ous
vul'va
vul'val
vul'vi'form
vul'vi'tis
vy'ing
wab'ble
wab'bler
wab'bly
wack'i'er
wack'i'est
wack'i'ly
wack'i'ness
wacky
wad
wad'ded
wad'ding
wad'dle
wad'dled
wad'dler
wad'dling
wad'dly
wade
wad'ed
wad'er
wad'ing

wa'fer
waf'fle
waf'fled
waf'fling
waft
wag
waged
wa'ger
wagged
wag'gery
wag'ging
wag'gish
wag'gish'ly
wag'gle
wag'gled
wag'gling
wag'ing
wag'on
wag'tail
wa'hi'ne
waif
wail
wain'scot
wain'scot'ing
wain'wright
waist
waist'band
waist'coat
waist'line
wait
wait'er
wait'ing
wait'ress
waive
waived
waiv'er
waiv'ing
wake
waked
wake'ful
wake'ful'ly
wake'ful'ness
wak'en
wak'ing
wale
wal'ing
walk
walk'about
walk-away
walk'er
walk'ie-talk'ie
walk'out
walk'over

walk-up
walk'way
wall
wal'la'bies
wal'la'by
wall'board
wal'let
wall'flow'er
wal'lop
wal'loped
wal'lop'ing
wal'low
wall'pa'per
wall-to-wall
wal'nut
wal'rus
waltz
wam'pum
wan
wand
wan'der
wan'der'er
wan'der'lust
wane
waned
wan'gle
wan'gled
wan'gling
wan'ing
wan'ly
wan'ner
wan'ness
want
want'ing
wan'ton
wan'ton'ly
war
war'ble
war'bled
war'bler
war'bling
ward
war'den
ward'er
ward'ress
ward'robe
ware
ware'house
war'fare
war'head
war-horse
war'i'er
war'i'est

war'i'ly
war'i'ness
war'like
war'lock
warm
warm-blood'ed
warm'er
warm'est
warm-heart'ed
warm'ly
war'mong'er
warmth
warn
warn'ing
warp
war'path
war'rant
war'ran'ties
war'ran'ty
warred
war'ren
war'ring
war'ri'or
war'ship
wart
wart'hog
war'time
wary
was
wash
wash'able
wash'ba'sin
wash'bowl
wash'cloth
wash'er
wash'ing
wash'out
wash'room
wash'stand
wash'tub
washy
wasp
wasp'ish
was'pish'ness
was'sail
wast'age
waste
waste'bas'ket
wast'ed
waste'ful
waste'ful'ly
waste'land
waste'pa'per

wast'er
wast'ing
wast'rel
watch
watch'dog
watch'er
watch'ful
watch'ful'ly
watch'ful'ness
watch'man
watch'tow'er
watch'word
wa'ter
wa'ter'borne
wa'ter'col'our
wa'ter'course
wa'ter'cress
wa'tered
wa'ter'fall
wa'ter'fowl
wa'ter'front
wa'ter'i'ness
wa'ter'ing
wa'ter'less
wa'ter lev'el
wa'ter lil'ies
wa'ter lily
wa'ter'line
wa'ter'logged
wa'ter main
wa'ter'mark
wa'ter'mel'on
wa'ter moc'ca'sin
wa'ter'pow'er
wa'ter'proof
wa'ter-re'pel'lent
wa'ter-re'sis'tant
wa'ter'shed
wa'ter'side
wa'ter-ski
wa'ter-skied
wa'ter'ski'ing
wa'ter'spout
wa'ter'tight
wa'ter'way
wa'ter'wheel
wa'ter'works
wa'tery
watt'age
watt-hour
wat'tle
wat'tled
wave

waved
wave'length
wave'let
wa'ver
wav'i'er
wav'i'est
wav'i'ly
wav'i'ness
wav'ing
wavy
wax
waxed
wax'en
wax'i'er
wax'i'est
wax'i'ness
wax'ing
wax'wing
wax'work
waxy
way
way'far'er
way'far'ing
way'laid
way'lay
way'lay'ing
way-out
way'side
way'ward
we
weak
weak'en
weak-kneed
weak'li'er
weak'li'ness
weak'ling
weak'ly
weak-mind'ed
weak'ness
weal
wealth'i'er
wealth'i'est
wealth'i'ness
wealthy
wean
weap'on
weap'on'ry
wear
wear'able
wea'ried
wear'i'er
wear'i'est
wea'ri'ly

wea'ri'ness
wear'ing
wea'ri'some
wea'ry
wea'ry'ing
wea'sel
weath'er
weath'er'a'bil'i'ty
weath'er-beat'en
weath'er'cock
weath'er'glass
weath'er'ing
weath'er'man
weath'er'proof
weath'er'vane
weave
weaved
weav'er
weav'ing
web
webbed
web'bing
we'ber
web-foot'ed
wed
wed'ded
wed'ding
wedge
wedged
wedg'ing
wed'lock
weed
weed'i'er
weed'i'ness
weedy
week
week'day
week'end
week'lies
week'ly
wee'ni'er
wee'ni'est
wee'ny
weep
weep'ing
weepy
wee'vil
weft
weigh
weight
weight'i'er
weight'i'est
weight'i'ness

weight'less'ness
weighty
weir
weird
weird'er
weird'est
weird'ly
weird'ness
weirdo
wel'come
wel'comed
wel'com'ing
weld
weld'er
wel'fare
well
well-ad'vised
well-ap'point'ed
well-bal'anced
well-be'haved
well-be'ing
well-born
well-bred
well-brought-up
well-built
well-con'nect'ed
well-dis'posed
well-done
well-dressed
well-earned
well-fed
well-found'ed
well-groomed
well-ground'ed
well-heeled
well-in'formed
well-in'ten'tioned
well-kept
well-known
well-man'nered
well-mean'ing
well-meant
well-nigh
well-off
well-paid
well-pre'served
well-read
well-spo'ken
well'spring
well-thought-of
well-thought-out
well-thumbed
well-timed

well-to-do
well-turned
well-versed
well-wish'er
well-worn
Welsh
wel'ter
wel'ter'weight
wen
wench
wend
went
wept
were
were'wolf
were'wolves
west
west'bound
west'er'ly
west'ern
west'ern'i'za'tion
west'ern'ize
west'ern'ized
west'ern'iz'ing
west'ern'most
west'ward
west'wards
wet
wet'back
wet'ly
wet'ness
wet'ted
wet'ter
wet'test
wet'ting
whack
whale
whale'boat
whale'bone
whaled
whal'er
whal'ing
wharf
wharf'age
wharves
what
what'ev'er
what'not
what'so'ev'er
wheal
wheat
whee'dle
whee'dled

whee'dling
wheel
wheel'bar'row
wheel'base
wheel'chair
wheeled
wheel'er-deal'er
wheel'house
wheel'wright
wheeze
wheezed
wheez'i'ness
wheez'ing
wheezy
whelk
whelp
when
whence
when'ev'er
where
where'a'bouts
where'as
where'by
where'fore
where'in
where'of
where'on
where'so'ev'er
where'to
where'up'on
wher'ev'er
where'with
where'with'al
wher'ry
whet
wheth'er
whet'stone
whet'ted
whet'ting
whew
whey
which
which'ev'er
whiff
while
whiled
whil'ing
whim
whim'per
whim'si'cal
whim'sies
whim'sy
whine

whin'ed
whin'ing
whin'nied
whin'ny
whin'ny'ing
whip
whip'lash
whipped
whip'per'snap'per
whip'pet
whip'ping
whip'poor'will
whir
whirl
whirl'i'gig
whirl'pool
whirl'wind
whirr
whirred
whir'ring
whisk
whisk'er
whis'kery
whis'key
whis'keys
whis'kies
whis'ky
whis'per
whist
whis'tle
whis'tled
whis'tler
whis'tling
whit
white
white'bait
white-col'lar
whit'ed
white-faced
white-hot
whit'en
whit'ened
white'ness
whit'en'ing
white'out
whit'er
white'wash
whith'er
whit'ing
whit'ish
whit'tle
whit'tled
whit'tling

whiz
whizz
whizzed
whiz'zes
whiz'zing
who
whoa
who'dun'it
who'dun'nit
who'ev'er
whole
whole'heart'ed
whole'heart'ed'ly
whole'ness
whole'sale
whole'sal'er
whole'sal'ing
whole'some
whole-wheat
whol'ly
whom
whom'ev'er
whom'so'ev'er
whoop
whoop'ee
whoop'ing
whoosh
whop'per
whop'ping
whore
whore'house
whore'monger
whor'ish
whorl
whorled
whose
who'so'ev'er
why
wick
wick'ed
wick'ed'ly
wick'ed'ness
wick'er
wick'er'work
wick'et
wide
wide-an'gle
wide-awake
wide-eyed
wide'ly
wid'en
wid'er
wide-rang'ing

wide'spread
wid'est
widg'eon
wid'ow
wid'ow'er
wid'ow'hood
width
wield
wield'er
wieldy
wie'ner
wife
wife'li'ness
wife'ly
wig
wigged
wig'gle
wig'gled
wig'gli'est
wig'gling
wig'gly
wig'wag
wig'wagged
wig'wag'ging
wig'wam
wild
wild'cat
wil'de'beest
wil'der'ness
wild-eyed
wild'fire
wild'fowl
wild'life
wild'ly
wild'ness
wild'wood
wile
wil'ful
wil'ful'ly
will
willed
will'ing
wil'ling'ly
will'ing'ness
will-o'-the-wisp
wil'low
wil'lowy
will'pow'er
wil'ly-nil'ly
wilt
wily
wimp
wimp'le

wimpy
win
wince
winch
winc'ing
winc'ingly
wind
wind'bag
wind'blown
wind'break
wind'burnt
wind'cheater
wind'ed
wind'fall
wind'i'er
wind'i'est
wind'i'ness
wind'ing
wind'jam'mer
wind'lass
wind'mill
win'dow
win'dow'pane
win'dow-shop
win'dow-shopped
win'dow'sill
wind'pipe
wind'screen
wind'shield
wind'storm
wind'surf'er
wind'surf'ing
wind'up
wind'ward
windy
wine
wined
win'ery
winged
wing'span
wing'spread
win'ing
win'kle
win'na'ble
win'ner
win'ning
win'ning
win'now
win'some
win'ter
win'ter'green
win'ter'er
win'ter'ish

win'ter'time
win'ter'y
win'tri'ness
win'try
wipe
wiped
wip'er
wip'ing
wire
wired
wire-haired
wire'less
wire'tap
wire'tapped
wire'tap'per
wire'tap'ping
wir'i'er
wir'i'ness
wir'ing
wiry
wis'dom
wise
wise'crack
wised
wise'ly
wis'er
wis'est
wish'bone
wish'ful
wish'ful'ly
wishy-washy
wis'ing
wisp
wisp'i'er
wisp'i'est
wispy
wis'te'ria
wist'ful
wist'ful'ly
wist'ful'ness
wit
witch
witch'craft
witch'ery
witch ha'zel
witch'ing
with'al
with'draw
with'draw'al
with'draw'ing
with'drawn
with'drew
with'er

with'held
with'hold
with'hold'ing
with'in
with'out
with'stand
with'stand'ing
with'stood
wit'less
wit'ness
wit'ti'cism
wit'ti'er
wit'ti'est
wit'ti'ly
wit'ti'ness
wit'ting
wit'ting'ly
wit'ty
wives
wiz'ard
wiz'ard'ry
wiz'en
wiz'ened
woad
wob'ble
wob'bled
wob'bling
wob'bly
woe
woe'be'gone
woe'ful
woe'ful'ly
wok
woke
wok'en
wolf
wolf'hound
wolf'ram
wol'ver'ine
wolves
wom'an
wom'an'hood
wom'an'ish
wom'an'iz'er
wom'an'iz'ing
wom'an'kind
wom'an'li'ness
wom'an'ly
womb
wom'bat
wom'en
wom'en'folk
won

won'der
won'der'ful
won'der'ful'ly
won'der'land
won'der'ment
won'drous
wont
won't
wont'ed
woo
wood
wood'bine
wood'chuck
wood'cock
wood'craft
wood'cut'ter
wood'ed
wood'en
wood'en-head'ed
wood'en'ly
wood'i'er
wood'i'est
wood'land
wood lice
wood louse
wood'peck'er
wood'pile
wood'shed
woods'man
woodsy
wood'wind
wood'work
wood'worm
woody
woo'er
woof
woof'er
wool
wool'gath'er'ing
wool'len
wool'li'er
wool'lies
wool'li'est
wool'li'ness
wool'ly
wool'ly-head'ed
woo'zi'er
woo'zi'est
wooz'i'ly
wooz'i'ness
woozy
word
word'i'er

word'i'est
word'i'ly
word'i'ness
word'ing
word'less
word-per'fect
word'play
word pro'cess'ing
word pro'cess'or
wordy
wore
work
work'abil'i'ty
work'able
work'a'day
work'a'hol'ic
work'bench
work'book
work'day
worked-up
work'er
work'folk
work'force
work'horse
work'house
work'ing
work'ing'man
work'load
work'man
work'man'like
work'man'ship
work'out
work'room
work'shop
work'ta'ble
world
world-class
world'li'er
world'li'est
world'li'ness
world'ly
world'ly-wise
world-wea'ry
world'wide
worm
worm-eat'en
worm'i'er
worm'i'est
worm'wood
wormy
worn
worn-out
wor'ried

wor'ried'ly
wor'ri'er
wor'ries
wor'ri'some
wor'ry
wor'ry'ing
wor'ry'wart
worse
wors'en
worship
wor'ship'ful
wor'ship'fully
wor'ship'ped
wor'ship'per
wor'ship'ping
worst
wor'sted
worth
wor'thi'er
wor'thies
wor'thi'est
wor'thi'ly
wor'thi'ness
worth'less
worth'less'ness
worth'while
wor'thy
would
would-be
wound
wound'ed
wove
wov'en
wow
wrack
wraith
wran'gle
wran'gled
wran'gler
wran'gling
wrap
wrap'around
wrapped
wrap'per
wrap'ping
wrath
wrath'ful
wreak
wreath
wreathe
wreathed
wreath'ing
wreck

wreck'age
wreck'er
wren
wrench
wrest
wres'tle
wres'tled
wres'tler
wres'tling
wretch
wretch'ed
wretch'ed'ly
wretch'ed'ness
wri'er
wri'est
wrig'gle
wrig'gled
wrig'gler
wrig'gling
wrig'gly
wright
wring
wring'er
wring'ing
wrin'kle
wrin'kled
wrin'kling
wrin'kly
wrist
wrist band
wrist'watch
writ
write
writ'er
writhe
writhed
writh'ing
writ'ing
writ'ten
wrong
wrong'do'er
wrong'do'ing
wronged
wrong'ful
wrong'ful'ly
wrong-head'ed
wrong'ly
wrote
wrought
wrung
wry
wry'ly
wry'neck

wry'ness
wul'fen'ite
wun'der'kind
wun'der'kind'er
wurst
wych elm
wych hazel
wynd
wy'vern
xan'thate
xan'thene
xan'thic
xan'tho'ma
xan'thous
xe'bec
xe'non
xe'no'phobe
xe'no'pho'bia
xe'no'pho'bic
Xer'ox
xer'oxed
xer'ox'ing
x-ra'di'a'tion
x-ray
xy'lem
xy'lo'graph
xy'log'ra'phy
xy'loid
xy'lo'phone
xy'lo'phon'ist
x-rated
yacht
yacht'ing
yachts'man
yachts'wom'an
ya'hoo
yak
yam
yam'mer
yang
yank
yap
yapped
yap'ping
yard'age
yard'arm
yard'stick
yar'mul'ke
yarn
yar'row
yash'mak
yaw
yawl

yawn
ye
yea
yeah
year
year'book
year'ling
year'long
year'ly
year'lies
yearn
yearn'er
yearn'ing
year-round
yeast
yeasty
yell
yel'low
yel'low'bird
yel'low fe'ver
yel'low'ham'mer
yel'low'ish
yel'low jack'et
yelp
Ye'me'ni
yen
yenned
yen'ning
yeo'man
yes
ye'shi'va
yes-man
yes'ter'day
yes'ter'year
yet
ye'ti
yew
Yid'dish
yield
yield'ing
yield'ing'ly
yin
yin and yang
yo'delled
yo'del'ler
yo'del'ling
yo'ga
yog'hurt
yo'gi
yo'gurt
yoke
yoked
yo'kel

yok'ing
yolk
yon
yon'der
yore
you
young
young'er
young'ish
young'ling
young'ster
your
yours
your'self
your'selves
youth
youth'ful
youth'ful'ly
youth'ful'ness
yowl
yo-yo
yt'ter'bi'um
yt'tri'um
yuan
yuc'ca
Yu'go'slav
Yu'go'sla'vi'an
yule
yule'tide
yum'my
yup'pie
zeal
zeal'ot
zeal'ous
zeal'ous'ly
ze'bra
ze'bu
Zen
ze'nith
zeph'yr
zep'pe'lin
ze'ro
ze'roes
ze'ros
zest
zest'ful
zest'ful'ly
zesty
zig'zag
zig'zagged
zig'zag'ging
zinc
zin'cate

zinc'oid
zinc'ous
zincy
zinky
zin'nia
Zi'on
Zi'on'ism
Zi'on'ist
zip
zipped

zip'per
zip'pi'er
zip'pi'est
zip'ping
zip'py
zir'con
zir'co'ni'um
zith'er
zo'di'ac
zo'di'a'cal

zom'bie
zon'al
zon'al'ly
zone
zoned
zon'ing
zonked
zoo
zoo'ge'og'ra'phy
zo'o'log'ical

zo'ol'o'gist
zo'ol'o'gy
zoom
zoos
zuc'chet'to
zuc'chi'ni
Zu'lu
zwie'back
zy'gote

Grammar

A

a *see* **indefinite article.**

a-, an- A prefix derived from Greek, meaning 'not', 'without'. Older words using it include agnostic, anarchy, anonymous. Several modern words have been formed using it, as in apolitical, asexual, atypical.

abbreviation A shortened form of words, usually used as a space-saving technique and becoming increasingly common in modern usage. Abbreviations cause problems with regard to punctuation. The common question asked is whether the letters of an abbreviation should be separated by full stops. In modern usage the tendency is to omit full stops from abbreviations. This is most true of abbreviations involving initial capital letters, as in TUC, BBC, EC and USA. In such cases full stops should definitely not be used if one or some of the initial letters do not belong to a full word. Thus 'television' is abbreviated to TV and 'educationally subnormal' to ESN.

There are usually no full stops in abbreviations involving the first and last letters of a word (contractions)—Dr, Mr, Rd, St—but this is a matter of taste.

An abbreviation involving the first few letters of a word, as in 'Prof' (Professor), is the most likely to a have full stop, as in 'Feb.' (February), but again this is now a matter of taste.

Plurals of abbreviations are mostly formed by adding lower-case *s*, as in Drs, JPs, TVs. Note the absence of apostrophes.

See also ACRONYMS.

ablative A case in Latin grammar that expressed 'by, with or from'. In English this case does not exist, prepositional phrases being used its place.

-able A suffix meaning 'that can be', as in laughable, readable, washable. *See* ADJECTIVE.

abstract noun A noun which is the name of a thing that cannot be touched but refers to a quality, concept or idea. Examples of abstract nouns include 'anger', 'beauty', 'courage', 'Christianity', 'danger', 'fear', 'greed', 'hospitality', 'ignorance', 'jealousy', 'kudos', 'loyalty', 'Marxism', 'need', 'obstinacy', 'pain', 'quality', 'resistance', 'safety', 'truth', 'unworthiness', 'vanity', 'wisdom', 'xenophobia', 'youth', 'zeal'. *See also* CONCRETE NOUN.

accent (1) A regional or individual way of speaking or pronouncing words, as in 'a Glasgow accent'.

(2) A word meaning 'emphasis', as in 'In hotel the accent is on the second syllable of the word' or 'In fashion this year the accent is on longer skirts'.

(3) Any of certain symbols used on some foreign words adopted into English. In modern usage, which has a tendency to punctuate less than formerly was the case, accents are frequently omitted. For example, an actor's part in a play is now usually spelt 'role' but originally it was spelt 'rôle', the accent on *o* being called a circumflex. The accent is most likely to be retained if it affects the pronunciation. Thus 'cliché' and 'divorcé' usually retain the acute accent, as it is called, on the *e*. On the other hand, the accent known as the cedilla is frequently omitted from beneath the *c* in words such as 'façade/facade', although it is there to indicate that the *c* is soft, pronounced like an *s*, rather than a hard sound, pronounced like a *k*. The grave accent is retained in English in some words and phrases derived from French, as *mise en scène*.

accusative A case in Latin grammar, the equivalent of OBJECTIVE. It is sometimes used in English instead of objective.

acronym A word that, like some ABBREVIATIONS, is formed from the initial letters of several words. Unlike abbreviations, however, acronyms are pronounced as words rather than as just a series of letters. For example, OPEC (Organization of Petroleum Producing Countries) is pronounced *o-pek* and is thus an acronym, unlike USA (United States of America) which is pronounced as a series of letters and not as a word (*oo-sa* or *yoo-sa*) and is thus an abbreviation.

Acronyms are written without full stops, as in UNESCO (United Nations Educational, Scientific and Cultural Organization). Mostly acronyms are written in capital letters, as in NASA (National Aeronautics and Space Administration). However, very common acronyms, such as Aids (Acquired Immune Deficiency Syndrome), are written with just an initial capital, the rest of the letters being lower case.

Acronyms that refer to a piece of scientific or technical equipment are written like ordinary words in lower-case letters, as laser (light amplification by simulated emission of radiation).

active voice One of the two voices that verbs are divided into, the other being PASSIVE VOICE. In verbs in the active voice, commonly called **active verbs**, the subject of the verb performs the action described by the verb. Thus, in the sentence 'The boy threw the ball', 'throw' is in the active voice since the subject of the verb (the boy) is doing the throwing. Similarly, in the sentence 'Her mother was driving the car', 'driving' is in the active voice since it is the subject of the sentence (her mother) that is doing the driving. Similarly, in the sentence 'We saw the cows in the field', 'saw' is the active voice since it is the subject of the sentence (we) that is doing the seeing.

acute accent A mark placed over some letters in certain languages, such as French, to indicate vowel length, vowel quality, pronunciation, etc. It is found in English in some words that have been borrowed from the French, as in 'fiancé' and 'divorcé', to indicate pronunciation.

-ade A suffix meaning 'fruit drink', as in lemonade.

adjectival clause A kind of SUBORDINATE CLAUSE that describes or modifies a noun or pronoun. It is better known by the name RELATIVE CLAUSE.

adjective A word that describes or gives information about a noun or pronoun. It is said to qualify a noun or pronoun since it limits the word it describes in some way, by making it more specific. Thus, adding the adjective 'red' to 'book' limits 'book', since it means we can forget about books of any other colour. Similarly, adding 'large' to 'book' limits it, since it means we can forget about books of any other size.

Adjectives tell us something about the colour, size, number, quality or classification of a noun or pronoun, as in 'purple curtains', 'jet-black hair', 'bluish eyes'; 'tiny baby', 'large houses', 'biggish gardens', 'massive estates'; five children', 'twenty questions', 'seventy-five books'; 'sad people', 'joyful occasions', 'delicious food', 'civil engineering', 'nuclear physics', 'modern languages', 'Elizabethan drama'.

Several adjectives may modify one noun or pronoun, as in 'the small, black cat', 'an enormous, red-brick, Victorian house'. The order in which they appear is flexible and can vary according to the emphasis one wishes to place on the various adjectives. However, a common sequence is size, quality, colour and classification, as in 'a small, beautiful, pink wild rose' and 'a large, ugly, grey office building'.

Adjectives do not change their form. They remain the same whether the noun to which they refer is singular or plural, or masculine or feminine.

All the above examples of adjectives come before the noun, but not all adjectives do so. For information on the position of adjectives *see* ATTRIBUTIVE ADJECTIVE, PREDICATIVE ADJECTIVE, POST-MODIFIER.

Many adjectives are formed from either the past participles of verbs, and so end in *-ed*, or from the present participles and so end in *-ing*. Examples of adjectives ending in *-ed* include 'annoyed', 'blackened', 'coloured', 'damaged', 'escaped', 'fallen', 'guarded', 'heated', 'identified', 'jailed', 'knotted', 'labelled', 'mixed', 'numbered', 'opened', 'pleated', 'recorded', 'satisfied', 'taped', 'used', 'varied', 'walled', 'zoned'. Examples of adjectives ending in *-ing* include 'amusing', 'boring', 'captivating', 'demanding', 'enchanting', 'fading', 'grating', 'horrifying', 'identifying', 'jarring', 'kneeling', 'labouring', 'manufacturing', 'nursing', 'operating', 'parting', 'quivering', 'racing', 'satisfying', 'telling', 'undermining', 'worrying', 'yielding'.

Several adjectives end in *-ical* and are formed by adding *-al* to certain nouns ending in *-ic*. Examples include 'arithmetical', 'comical', 'critical', 'cynical', 'fanatical', 'logical', 'magical', 'musical', 'mystical' and 'sceptical'. Sometimes the adjectives ending in *-ical* are formed from nouns that end in *-ics*. These include 'acoustical', 'ethical', 'hysterical', 'statistical' and 'tropical'. Several adjectives end in *-ic* and are formed from nouns ending in *-ics*. These include 'acoustic', 'acrobatic', 'aerobic', 'athletic', 'economic', 'electronic', 'genetic', 'gymnastic', 'histrionic' and 'linguistic'.

Other common adjectival endings include *-ful*, as in 'beautiful', 'dreadful', 'eventful', 'graceful', 'hateful', 'tearful' and 'youthful'. They also include *-less*, as in 'clueless', 'graceless', 'hatless', 'meaningless' and 'sunless'.

Many adjectives end in *-able* and many end in *-ible*. There are often spelling problems with such adjectives. The following adjectives are likely to be misspelt:

Some adjectives ending in -*able*:

abominable	hearable
acceptable	immovable
adaptable	impassable
adorable	impeccable
advisable	implacable
agreeable	impracticable
amiable	impressionable
approachable	indescribable
available	indispensable
bearable	inimitable
bearable	insufferable
beatable	lamentable
believable	manageable
blameable	measurable
calculable	memorable
capable	nameable
changeable	non-flammable
comfortable	objectionable
commendable	operable
conceivable	palpable
definable	pleasurable
delectable	preferable
demonstrable	readable
dependable	recognizable
desirable	regrettable
discreditable	renewable
disreputable	reputable
durable	sizeable
durable	stoppable
enviable	tenable
excitable	tolerable
excusable	transferable
expendable	understandable
foreseeable	unmistakable
forgettable	usable

some adjectives ending in -ible:

forgivable
healable
washable
wearable

variable
viable
winnable
workable

Some adjectives ending in -ible:

accessible
admissible
audible
collapsible
combustible
compatible
comprehensible
contemptible
credible
defensible
destructible
digestible
discernible
divisible
edible
exhaustible
expressible
fallible
feasible
flexible

forcible
gullible
indelible
intelligible
irascible
negligible
perceptible
permissible
possible
repressible
reproducible
resistible
responsible
reversible
risible
sensible
susceptible
tangible
visible

See also COMPARISON OF ADJECTIVES, COMPOUNDS, DEMONSTRATIVE DETERMINERS, DETERMINER, FIRST PERSON, INTERROGATIVE ADJECTIVE, SECOND PERSON and THIRD PERSON.

adverb A word that adds to our information about a VERB, as in 'work rapidly'; about an ADJECTIVE, as in 'an extremely beautiful young woman'; or about another adverb, as in 'sleeping very soundly'. Adverbs are said to modify the words to which they apply since they limit the words in some way and make them more specific. Thus, adding 'slowly' to 'walk', as in 'They walked slowly down the hill', limits the verb 'walk' since all other forms of 'walk', such as 'quickly', 'lazily', etc, have been discarded.

There are several different kinds of adverbs, categorized according to the information they provide about the word they modify. They include adverbs of time, adverbs of place, adverbs of manner, adverbs of degree, adverbs of frequency, adverbs of probability, adverbs of duration and interrogative adverbs.

An **adverb of time** tells us when something happened, and they include such words as 'now', 'then', 'later', 'soon', 'afterwards', 'yesterday', etc, as in 'He is due to arrive now', I will call you later', 'She had a rest and went out afterwards', 'They left yesterday'.

An **adverb of place** tells us where something happened. Adverbs of place include such words as 'there', 'here', 'somewhere', 'anywhere', 'thereabouts', 'abroad', 'outdoors', 'overhead', 'underground', 'hither and thither', etc, as in 'I haven't been there', 'They couldn't see her anywhere', 'His family live abroad', and 'We heard a noise overhead'.

An **adverb of manner** tells us how something happens, and they include a wide range of possibilities. Frequently adverbs in this category are formed by adding -ly to an adjective. Examples of these include:

adjective	adverb
anxious	anxiously
bad	badly
cautious	cautiously

dumb	dumbly
elegant	elegantly
fashionable	fashionably
fearless	fearlessly
hot	hotly
interested	interestedly
joking	jokingly
lame	lamely
adjective	*adverb*
mean	meanly
narrow	narrowly
pale	palely
quick	quickly
soothing	soothingly
sound	soundly
tough	toughly
unwilling	unwillingly
vain	vainly
weak	weakly

Some adjectives have to be modified in some way before the suffix *-ly* is added to form the adverbs. For example, in adjectives ending in *-y*, the *y* changes to *i* before *-ly* is added. Examples of these include:

adjective	*adverb*
angry	angrily
busy	busily
canny	cannily
dry	drily
easy	easily
funny	funnily
adjective	*adverb*
happy	happily
merry	merrily
pretty	prettily
silly	sillily
tatty	tattily
weary	wearily

Note the exceptions 'shyly', 'slyly', 'wryly'.

Adjectives ending in *-e* frequently drop the *e* before adding *-ly*. Examples of these include:

adjective	*adverb*
able	ably
feeble	feebly
gentle	gently
peaceable	peaceably
adjective	*adverb*
true	truly
unintelligible	unintelligibly

Suffixes other than *-ly* that may be added to adjectives to form adverbs of manner include *-wards*, as in backwards, heavenwards; *-ways*, as in edgeways, sideways; *-wise*, as in clockwise, moneywise.

Some adverbs of manner may take the same form as the adjectives to which they correspond. These include 'fast', 'hard', 'solo', 'straight', 'wrong', as in 'She took the wrong book' and 'Don't get me wrong'.

An **adverb of degree** tells us the degree, extent or intensity of something that happens, and they include 'hugely', 'immensely', 'moderately', 'adequately', 'greatly', 'strongly', 'tremendously', 'profoundly', 'totally', 'entirely', 'perfectly', 'partially', 'practically', 'virtually', 'almost', as in 'They enjoyed the show hugely', 'The office was not adequately equipped', 'We strongly disapprove of such behaviour', 'He was totally unaware of the facts', 'They are virtually penniless'.

An **adverb of frequency** is used to tell us how often something happens, and they include 'never', 'rarely', 'seldom', 'infrequently', 'occasionally', 'periodically', 'intermittently', 'sometimes', 'often', 'frequently', 'regularly', 'normally', 'always', 'constantly', 'continually', as in 'She never eats breakfast', 'We go to the cinema occasionally', 'He goes to the dentist regularly', 'Normally they travel by bus', 'He is in pain constantly'.

An **adverb of probability** tells us how often something happens, and they include 'probably', 'possibly', 'conceivably', 'perhaps', 'maybe', 'presumably', 'hopefully', 'definitely', 'certainly', 'indubitably', 'doubtless', as in 'You will probably see them there', 'He may conceivably pass the exam this time', 'Presumably they know that she is leaving', 'Hopefully the news will be good', 'I am definitely not going', 'He is indubitably a criminal'.

An **adverb of duration** tells us how long something takes or lasts, and they include 'briefly', 'temporarily', 'long', 'indefinitely', 'always', 'permanently', 'forever', as in 'We stopped briefly for coffee', 'Have you known her long?', 'Her face is permanently disfigured', 'They have parted forever'.

An **adverb of emphasis** adds emphasis to the action described by the verb, and they include 'absolutely', 'certainly', 'positively', 'quite', 'really', 'simply', 'just', as in 'They absolutely detest each other', 'He positively adores her', 'She really wants to be forgiven', 'I simply must go now'

An **interrogative adverb** asks questions, and they include 'where', 'when', 'how', and 'why', as in 'Where are you going?', 'When will you be back?', 'How will you get there?', 'Why have they asked you to go?' They are placed at the beginning of sentences, and such sentences always end with a question mark.

adverbial clause A subordinate clause that modifies the main or principal clause by adding information about time, place, concession, condition, manner, purpose and result. Adverbial clauses usually follow the main clause but most of them can be put in front of the main clause for reasons of emphasis or style.

An **adverbial clause of time** indicates the time of an event and is introduced by a conjunction such as 'after', 'as', 'as soon as', 'before', 'once', 'since', 'the minute', 'the moment', 'till', 'until', 'when', 'whenever', while', 'whilst', as in 'He left after the meal was over', 'She arrived as I was leaving', 'Once I recognized him I spoke to him', 'I recognized him the minute I saw him', 'We won't know until tomorrow' and 'The thief ran away when he saw the police'.

An **adverbial clause of place** indicates the location of an event and is introduced by a conjunction such as 'where', 'wherever' or 'everywhere', as in 'He was miserable where he was', 'They left it where they found it', 'Wherever I went I saw signs of poverty' and 'Everywhere she goes she causes trouble'.

An **adverbial clause of concession** contains a fact that contrasts in some way with the main clause and is introduced by a CONJUNCTION such as 'although', 'even though', 'though', 'whereas', 'while', 'whilst', as in 'I have to admire his speech, although I disagree with what he said', 'He does his best at school work even though he is not very good at it' and 'Whilst I myself do not like him I can understand why he is popular'.

An **adverbial clause of condition** deals with possible situations and is introduced by the conjunctions 'if', 'only if', 'unless', 'as long as', 'providing', 'provided', as in 'If you had kept quiet they would not have known about the event', 'We cannot go unless we get permission', 'They can leave only if they have finished their work' and 'Provided he is feeling better he can leave hospital'. Inversion can be used in such clauses instead of a conjunction, as in 'Had you been present you would have been most amused' and 'Had he any sense he would leave now'.

An **adverbial clause of manner** describes the way that someone behaves or the way in which something is done, and is introduced by a conjunction such as 'as', 'as if', 'as though', 'like', 'the way', as in 'Why does he behave as he does', 'He slurred his speech as though he were drunk' and 'He looked at her as if he hated her'.

An **adverbial clause of purpose** indicates the intention someone has when doing something and is introduced by a conjunction such as 'to', 'in order to', 'so as to', 'so', 'so that', as in 'He did that just to upset her', 'They will have to work long hours in order to make that amount of money', 'They started to run so as to get home before it rained' and 'The firm reduced the number of staff in order that they might avoid bankruptcy'.

An **adverbial clause of reason** explains why something happens or is done and is introduced by a conjunction such as 'because', 'since' or 'as', as in 'We didn't go because the car broke down', 'As it was raining we had the party indoors' and 'since he has broken the school rules he should be punished'.

An **adverbial clause of result** indicates the result of an event or situation and is introduced by the conjunctions 'so' or 'so that', as in 'He fell awkwardly so that he broke his leg' and 'She stumbled over her words so that the audience had difficulty understanding her'. *See* COMPARISON OF ADVERBS and COMPOUNDS.

aero- A prefix meaning 'air', as in aerobics, aerodynamics, aeroplane and aerospace, or 'aircraft', as in aerodrome, aeronaut.

affix An element that is added to a base or root word to form another word. Affixes can be in the form of prefixes or suffixes. A **prefix** is an affix that is added to the beginning of a word. Thus *audio* in 'audiovisual' is both a prefix and an affix. A **suffix** is an affix that is added to the end of a word. Thus -*aholic* in 'workaholic' is a suffix and an affix.

agent noun A noun that refers to someone who is the 'doer' of the action of a verb. It is usually spelt ending in either -*er*, as 'enquirer', or in -*or*, as in 'investigator' and 'supervisor', but frequently either of these endings is acceptable, as 'adviser/advisor'.

agreement or **concord** The agreeing of two or more elements in a clause or sentence, i.e. they take the same number, person or gender. In English the most common form of agreement is that between subject and verb, and this usually involves NUMBER AGREE-MENT. This means that singular nouns are usually accompanied by singular verbs, as in 'She looks well', 'He is working late' and 'The boy has passed the exam', and that plural nouns are usually accompanied by plural verbs, as in 'They look well', 'They are working late' and 'The boys have passed the exam'.

Problems arise when the noun in question can be either singular or plural, for example, 'audience', 'committee', 'crowd', 'family', 'government', 'group'. Such nouns take a singular verb if the user is regarding the people or items referred to by the noun as a group, as in 'The family is moving house', or as individuals, as in 'The family are quarrelling over where to go on holiday'.

Compound subjects, that is two or more nouns acting as the subject, whether singular or plural, joined with 'and', are used with a plural noun, as in 'My friend and I are going to the cinema tonight' and 'James and John are leaving today', unless the two nouns together represent a single concept, as 'brandy and soda', in which case the verb is in the singular, as in 'Brandy and soda is his favourite drink' and 'cheese and pickle' in 'Cheese and pickle is the only sandwich filling available'.

In cases where two or more singular nouns acting as the subject are connected with such phrases as 'as well as', 'together with' and 'plus', as in 'His mother, as well as his father, is away from home' and 'The flat, together with the house, is up for sale', the verb is in the singular.

agro-

Indefinite pronouns such as 'anyone', 'everyone', 'no one', 'someone', 'either', 'neither' are singular and should be followed by a singular verb, as in 'Each of the flats is self-contained', 'Everyone is welcome', 'No one is allowed in without a ticket' and 'Neither is quite what I am looking for'.

When the subject is a singular noun, which is separated from the verb by a number of plural nouns, as in 'a list of dates and times of the next concerts', the verb is in the singular because 'list' is singular, as in 'A list of dates and times of the next concerts is available'.

Agreement with reference to both number and gender affects pronouns, as in 'She blames herself', 'He could have kicked himself' and 'They asked themselves why they had got involved'. Problems arise when the pronoun is indefinite and so the sex of the person is unspecified. Formerly in such cases the masculine pronouns were assumed to be neutral and so 'Each of the pupils was asked to hand in his work' was considered quite acceptable. The rise of feminism has led to a questioning of this assumption and alternatives have been put forward. These include 'Each of the pupils was asked to hand in his/her (or his or her) work', but some people feel that this is clumsy. Another alternative is 'Each of the pupils was asked to hand in their work'. Although it is ungrammatical, this convention is becoming quite acceptable in modern usage. To avoid both the clumsiness of the former and the ungrammatical-ness of the latter, it is possible to cast the whole sentence in the plural, as in 'All the pupils were asked to hand in their work'.

agro-, agri- A prefix derived from Greek meaning 'field', as in agriculture, agribusiness, agrobiology, agrochemicals.

-aholic A suffix meaning 'addicted to', formed on ANALOGY with 'alcoholic', as in worka-holic, shopaholic. It sometimes becomes **-oholic**, as in chocoholic.

allegory A kind of story that has deeper significance as well as the obvious surface meaning of the story. It is usually used to get a moral message across symbolically. Two of the most famous allegories in English literature are *The Pilgrim's Progress* by John Bunyan (1628–88) and *The Faerie Queene* by Edmund Spenser (*c*.1552–99).

alliteration A figure of speech in which a sequence of words begin with the same letter or sound, as in 'Round and round the rugged rocks the ragged rascal ran' and 'Peter Piper picked a peck of pickled peppers'. The given examples are both tongue twisters but alliteration is frequently used by poets for literary effect as in a 'red, red rose'.

also An adverb that should not be used as a CONJUNCTION instead of 'and'. Thus sentences such as 'Please send me some apples, also some pears' are grammatically incorrect.

although A conjunction that is used to introduce a subordinate adverbial clause of con-cession, as in 'They are very happy although they are poor', meaning 'Despite the fact they are poor they are happy'. 'Though' or 'even though' can be substituted for 'although', as in 'they are very happy even though they are poor'. *See* ADVERBIAL CLAUSE and CONJUNCTION.

ambi- A prefix derived from Greek 'two', 'both', as in ambidextrous, ambivalent.

an *see* **indefinite article.**

an- *see* **a-.**

-ana A suffix meaning 'things associated with', as in Victoriana, Americana.

anacoluthon A FIGURE OF SPEECH that refers to a change of construction in a sentence before the original structure is complete, as in 'My feeling is—but you must decide for yourself—how long did you say you have?' Anacoluthon is usually found in spoken English when someone is thinking aloud. Unlike many figures of speech, it is usually used accidentally rather than for literary or rhetorical effect.

anadiplosis A FIGURE OF SPEECH that refers to the repetition of a word or group at the end of one phrase or sentence and the beginning of the next for literary effect, as in 'sit and think about the past—the past which had been so warm and happy'.

analogy A FIGURE OF SPEECH, rather like the SIMILE, in which there is an inference of a resemblance between two items that are being compared, as in 'Mary's parties are a bit like Christmas—much looked forward to but often a bit of a disappointment'.

anastrophe A FIGURE OF SPEECH that refers to an inversion of the usual order of words in a sentence or phrase for emphasis, or literary or rhetorical effect, as in 'Many a foreign dawn has he seen'.

and A conjunction that is called a coordinating conjunction because it joins elements of language that are of equal status. The elements may be words, as in 'cows and horses', 'John and James', 'provide wine and beer'; phrases, as in 'working hard and playing hard' and 'trying to look after her children and her elderly parents'; clauses, as in 'John has decided to emigrate and his brother has decided to join him' and 'He has lost his job and he now has no money'. When a coordinating conjunction is used, the subject of the second clause can sometimes be omitted if it is the same as the subject of the first clause, as in 'They have been forced to sell the house and are very sad about it'. *See* CONJUNCTION.

The use of and at the beginning of a sentence is disliked by many people. It should be used only for deliberate effect, as in 'And then he saw the monster', or in informal contexts.

Other coordinating conjunctions include 'but', 'or', 'yet', 'both . . . and', 'either . . . or', and 'neither . . .nor', as in 'poor but honest' and 'the blue dress or the green one'.

Anglo- A prefix meaning 'English', as in Anglo-Irish, Anglo-Indian.

ante- A prefix derived from Latin meaning 'before', as in antedate, antenatal, anteroom.

antecedent A term that refers to the noun or noun phrase in a main clause to which a relative pronoun in a relative clause refers back. Thus in the sentence 'People who live dangerously frequently get hurt', 'people' is an antecedent. Similarly, in the sentence 'The child identified the old man who attacked her', 'the old man' is the antecedent. *See* RELATIVE CLAUSE.

anthropo- A prefix derived from Greek meaning 'human being', as in anthropoid, anthropology.

anti- A prefix derived from Greek meaning 'against'. It is used in many words that have been established in the language for a long time, as in antidote and antipathy, but it has also been used to form modern words, such as anti-establishment, antifreeze, anti-inflationary, anti-nuclear, anti-warfare.

anticlimax A FIGURE OF SPEECH in which there is a sudden descent from the lofty to the ridiculous or the trivial, as in 'She went home in a flood of tears and a taxi'. A well-known 19th-century example is in the couplet:

'And thou, Dalhousie, the great god of war,
Lieutenant-general to the earl of Mar'.

antiphrasis A FIGURE OF SPEECH in which a word or phrase is used in a sense that is opposite to the accepted sense. It is often used to achieve an ironic or humorous effect, as in 'His mother is ninety years young today'. Young is usually associated with youth but here it is associated with old age.

antithesis A FIGURE OF SPEECH in which contrasting ideas are balanced for effect, as in 'We need money, not advice', 'More haste, less speed' and 'Marry at haste, repent at leisure'. It is a common figure of speech in literature, as in Alexander Pope's 'To err is human, to forgive, divine' and John Milton's 'Better to reign in hell than to serve in heaven'.

antonomasia A FIGURE OF SPEECH indicating the use of a personal name or proper name to anyone belonging to a class or group, as in 'John is such an Einstein that the other members of the class are in awe of him', where the meaning is that 'John has such a brilliant mind that the other members of the class are in awe of him'.

antonym A word that is the opposite of another word. Thus 'black' is an antonym for 'white', 'cowardly' is an antonym for 'courageous', 'dull' is an antonym for 'bright', and 'fast' is an antonym for 'slow'.

any A pronoun that may take either a singular or plural verb, depending on the context. When a singular noun is used, a singular verb is used, as in 'Is any of the cloth still usable?' 'Are any of the children coming?' When a plural noun is used, either a plural or a singular verb can be used, the singular verb being more formal, as in 'Did you ask if any of his friends were/was there?'.

anyone A pronoun that should be used with a singular verb, as in 'Has anyone seen my book?' and 'Is anyone coming to the lecture?' It should also be followed, where relevant, by a singular, not plural, personal pronoun or possessive adjective, as in 'Has anyone left his/her book?' Because this construction, which avoids the sexist 'his', is considered by many people to be clumsy, there is a growing tendency to use 'their' and be ungrammatical.

aposiopesis A FIGURE OF SPEECH in which words are omitted or there is a sudden breaking off for dramatic effect, as in 'The door slowly opened and . . .' and 'There was the noise of gunshot and then . . .'

apostrophe¹ A FIGURE OF SPEECH that takes the form of a rhetorical address to an absent or dead person or to a personified thing, as in 'O Romeo! Romeo! wherefore art thou, Romeo?' and 'Oh Peace, why have you deserted us?'

apostrophe² A form of punctuation that is mainly used to indicate possession. Many spelling errors centre on the position of the apostrophe in relation to *s*.

Possessive nouns are usually formed by adding *'s* to the singular noun, as in 'the girl's mother', and Peter's car'; by adding an apostrophe to plural nouns that end in *s*, as in 'all the teachers' cars'; by adding *'s* to irregular plural nouns that do not end in *s*, as in 'women's shoes'.

In the possessive form of a name or singular noun that ends in *s*, *x* or *z*, the apostrophe may or may not be followed by *s*. In words of one syllable the final *s* is usually added, as in 'James's house', 'the fox's lair', 'Roz's dress'. The final *s* is most frequently omitted in names, particularly in names of three or more syllables, as in 'Euripides' plays'. In many cases the presence or absence of final *s* is a matter of convention.

The apostrophe is also used to indicate omitted letters in contracted forms of words, as in 'can't' and 'you've'. They are sometimes used to indicate missing century numbers in dates, as in 'the '60s and '70s', but are not used at the end of decades, etc, as in '1960s', not '1960's'.

Generally apostrophes are no longer used to indicate omitted letters in shortened forms that are in common use, as in 'phone' and 'flu'.

Apostrophes are often omitted wrongly in modern usage, particularly in the media and by advertisers, as in 'womens hairdressers', 'childrens helpings'. In addition, apostrophes are frequently added erroneously (as in 'potato's for sale' and 'Beware of the dog's'). This is partly because people are unsure about when and when not to use them and partly because of a modern tendency to punctuate as little as possible.

apposition A term for a noun or a phrase that provides further information about another noun or phrase. Both nouns and phrases refer to the same person or thing. In the phrase 'Peter Jones, our managing director', ' Peter Jones' and 'our managing director' are said to be in apposition. Similarly, in the phrase 'his cousin, the chairman of the firm', 'his cousin' and 'the chairman of the firm' are in apposition.

arch- A prefix derived from Greek meaning 'chief', as in archbishop, archduke, archenemy.

-arch A suffix derived from the Greek meaning 'chief, ruler', as in anarchy, hierarchy and monarchy.

-arian A suffix derived from Latin that means, in one of its senses, 'a supporter of', as in vegetarian, or 'one connected with', as in antiquarian and librarian.

article *see* **definite article** and **indefinite article.**

as A conjunction that can introduce either a subordinate adverbial clause of time, as in

'I caught sight of him as I was leaving', a subordinate adverbial clause of manner, as in 'He acted as he promised', and a subordinate adverbial clause of reason, as in 'As it's Saturday he doesn't have to work'. it is also used in the as . . . as construction, as in 'She doesn't play as well as her sister does'.

The construction may be followed by a subject pronoun or an object pronoun, according to sense. In the sentence 'He plays as well as she', which is a slightly shortened form of 'She plays as well as he does', 'he' is a subject pronoun. In informal English the subject pronoun often becomes an object pronoun, as in 'She plays as well as him'. In the sentence 'They hate their father as much as her', 'her' is an object and the sentence means 'They hate their father as much as they hate her', but in the sentence 'They hate their father as much as she', 'she' is a subject and the sentence means 'They hate their father as much as she does'. *See* ADVERBIAL CLAUSE and CONJUNCTION.

assonance A figure of speech in which vowel sounds are repeated to give a half-rhyme effect, as in 'with gun, drum, trumpet, blunderbuss and thunder'.

astro- A prefix derived from Greek meaning 'star', as in astrology, astronomy, astronaut, astrophysics.

asyndeton A figure of speech referring to the omission of conjunctions for dramatic or literary effect, as in 'I came, I saw, I conquered' and 'He entered, he looked round, he left'.

-athon, -thon A suffix meaning 'large scale or long-lasting contest or event', as in swimathon, telethon. These words are formed on analogy with the Greek derived word marathon, and they often refer to events undertaken for charity.

attributive adjective A term for an adjective that is placed immediately before the noun that it qualifies. In the phrases 'a red dress', 'the big house' and 'an enjoyable evening', 'red, 'big' and 'enjoyable' are attributive adjectives.

audio- A word derived from the Latin 'hear'. It is found in several words that have been established in the language for a long time, as in auditory, audition, but it is also used to form many modern words, as in audiotape, audio-cassette and audiovisual.

auto- A prefix derived from Greek meaning 'of or by itself', as in autobiography and autograph. It is also used to refer to things that work by themselves 'automatically', as in automobile, autocue, automaton, and to things that have to do with cars, as in automobiles, autosport, autotheft.

auxiliary verb A verb that is used in forming tenses, moods and voices of other verbs. These include 'be', 'do' and 'have'.

The verb 'to be' is used as an **auxiliary verb** with the *-ing* form of the main verb to form the continuous present tense, as in 'They are living abroad just now' and 'We were thinking of going on holiday but we changed our minds'.

The verb 'to be' is used as an auxiliary verb with the past participle of the main verb to form the passive voice, as in 'Her hands were covered in blood' and 'These toys are manufactured in China'.

The verb 'to have' is used as an auxiliary verb along with the past participle of the main verb to form the perfect tenses, as in 'They have filled the post', 'She had realized her mistake' and 'They wished that they had gone earlier'.

The verb 'to be' is used as an auxiliary verb along with the main verb to form negative sentences, as in 'She is not accepting the job'. The verb 'to do' is used as an auxiliary verb along with the main verb to form negative sentences, as in 'he does not believe her'. It is also used along with the main verb to form questions, as in 'Does he know that she's gone?' and to form sentences in which the verb is emphasized, as in 'She *does* want to go'. *See* MODAL VERB.

B

back formation The process of forming a new word by removing an element from an existing word. This is the reversal of the usual process since many words are formed by adding an element to a base or root word. Examples of back formation include 'burgle' from 'burglary'; 'caretake' from 'caretaker'; 'donate' from 'donation'; 'eavesdrop' from 'eavesdropper'; 'enthuse' from 'enthusiasm'; 'intuit' from 'intuition'; 'liaise' from 'liaison'; 'reminisce' from 'reminiscence'; 'televise' from 'television'.

base The basic uninflected form of a verb. It is found as the infinitive form, as in 'to go' and 'to take', and as the imperative form, as in 'Go away!' and 'Take it!' It is also the form that the verb in the present indicative tense takes, except for the third person singular, as in 'I always go there on a Sunday' and 'They go there regularly.'

Base also refers to the basic element in word formation. In this sense it is also known as 'root' or 'stem'. For example, in the word 'infectious' 'infect' is the base, in 'indescribable' 'describe' is the base and in 'enthusiastic' 'enthuse' is the base.

bathos A figure of speech consisting of sudden descent from the lofty or noble to the ridiculous or trivial. This descent can be either intentional for comic or satiric effect, as in Alexander Pope's 'When husbands or when lapdogs breathe their last', or it can be accidental, as in 'She collected her children and her coat'. Bathos and anticlimax mean the same. *See* ANTICLIMAX.

be *see* **auxiliary verb.**

both A word that can be used in several ways: as a determiner, as in 'He broke both his arms' and 'He lost both his sons in the war'; as a pronoun, as in 'I don't mind which house we rent, I like them both' and 'Neither of them work here. The boss sacked them both'; as a conjunction, as in 'He both likes and admires her' and 'She is both talented and honest'. Both can sometimes be followed by 'of'. 'Both their children are grown up' and 'Both of their children are grown up' are both acceptable. Care should be taken to avoid using both unnecessarily. In the sentence 'The two items are both identical', 'both' is redundant.

because A conjunction that introduces a subordinate adverbial clause of reason, as in 'They sold the house because they are going abroad' and 'Because she is shy she never goes to parties'. It is often used incorrectly in such constructions as 'The reason they went away is because they were bored'. This should be rephrased as either 'The reason that they went away is that they were bored' or 'They went away because they were bored'. *See* ADVERBIAL CLAUSE.

before A word that can either be a preposition, an adverb or a conjunction. As a preposition it means either 'coming or going in front of in time', as in 'He was the chairman before this one', or coming or going in front of in place, as in 'She went before him into the restaurant'. As an adverb it means 'at a time previously', as in 'I told you before' and 'He has been married before'. As a conjunction it introduces a subordinate adverbial clause of time, as in 'The guests arrived before she was ready for them' and 'Before I knew it they had arrived'. *See* ADVERBIAL CLAUSE.

bi- A prefix that is derived from Latin meaning 'two', as in bicycle, bifocal, bilingual, binoculars, bisect. Bi- forms words in English in which it means 'half', and other words in which it means 'twice'. This can give rise to confusion in such words as biweekly and bimonthly, where there are two possible sets of meanings. Biweekly can mean either 'every two weeks' or 'twice a week' so that one would not be able to be certain about the frequency of a 'biweekly publication'. Similarly, a 'bimonthly publication' might appear either twice a month or once every two months.

biblio- A prefix derived from Greek meaning 'book', as in bibliophile (a person who is fond of or collects books) and bibliography.

bio- A prefix derived from Greek meaning life or living material, as in biography, biology, biochemistry, biodegradable, biosphere, biopsy.

blend A word that is formed by the merging of two other words or elements, as in 'brunch' from 'breakfast' and 'lunch'; 'camcorder' from 'camera' and 'recorder'; 'chocoholic' from 'chocolate' and 'alcoholic'; 'motel' from 'motor' and 'hotel'; 'smog' from 'smoke' and 'fog'; 'televangelist' from 'television' and 'evangelist'.

bold or **bold face** A typeface that is thick and black. It is used for emphasis or to high-light certain words. The headwords, or entry words, in this book are set in bold type.

book titles These can cause problems as to punctuation. How they are treated in publications, business reports, etc, depends largely on the house style of the firm concerned. However, they are generally written in documents, letters, etc, as they appear on their title pages, that is with the first letter of the first word and of the following main words of the title in capital letters, and those of words of lesser importance, such as the articles, prepositions and coordinate conjunctions, in lowercase letters, as in The Guide to Yoga, Hope for the Best and In the Middle of Life.

Some people, and some house-style manuals, prefer to put the titles in italic, as in *A Room with a View* and *A Guide to Dental Health*. Others prefer to put book titles in quotation marks, as in 'Gardening for Beginners'. Such a convention can make use of either single or double quotation marks. Thus either 'Desserts for the Summer' or "Desserts for the Summer" is possible provided that the writer is consistent throughout any one piece of writing. If the title of a book is mentioned in a piece of direct speech in quotation marks it goes within the opposite style of quotation marks from the piece in direct speech. Thus if the direct speech is within single quotation marks, the book title goes within double quotation marks, as in 'Have you read "Wuthering Heights" or are you not a Bronte fan?' If the direct speech is within double quotation marks, the book title goes between single quotation marks, as in "Would you say that 'Animal Farm' was your favourite Orwell novel?"

It is even quite common for book titles to appear in documents both in italic type and with quotation marks. To some extent the punctuation of book titles is a matter of choice as long as they are consistent, but there is a growing tendency to have as little punctuation as possible and to have as uncluttered a page as possible.

borrowing The taking over into English of a word from a foreign language and also to the word so borrowed. Many words borrowed into English are totally assimilated as to spelling and pronunciation. Others remain obviously different and retain their own identity as to spelling or pronunciation, as *raison d'être*, borrowed from French. Many of them have been so long part of the English language, such as since the Norman Conquest, that they are no longer thought of as being foreign words. However the process goes on, and recent borrowings include *glasnost* and *perestroika* from Russian.

French, Latin and Greek have been the main sources of our borrowings over the centuries. However, we have borrowed extensively from other languages as well. These include Italian, from which we have borrowed many terms relating to music, art and architecture. These include *piano, libretto, opera, soprano, tempo, corridor, fresco, niche, parapet* and *grotto*, as well as many food terms, such as *macaroni, pasta, semolina* and *spaghetti*.

From the Dutch we have acquired many words relating to the sea and ships since they were a great sea-faring nation. These include *cruise, deck, skipper* and *yacht*. Through the Dutch/Afrikaans connection we have borrowed *apartheid, boss* and *trek*.

From German we have borrowed *dachshund, hamster, frankfurter, kindergarten* and *waltz*, as well as some words relating to World War II, for example, *blitz, flak* and *strafe*.

-bound

From Norse and the Scandinavian languages have come a wide variety of common words, such as *egg, dirt, glitter, kick, law, odd, skill, take, they, though*, as well as some more modern sporting terms such as *ski* and *slalom*.

From the Celtic languages have come *bannock, bog, brogue, cairn, clan, crag, slogan* and *whisky*, and from Arabic have come *algebra, alkali, almanac, apricot, assassin, cypher, ghoul, hazard, mohair, safari, scarlet* and *talisman*.

The Indian languages have provided us with many words, originally from the significant British presence there in the days of the British Empire. They include *bungalow, chutney, dinghy, dungarees, gymkhana, jungle, pundit* and *shampoo*. In modern times there has been an increasing interest in Indian food and cookery, and words such as *pakora, poppadom, samosa*, etc, have come into the language.

From the South American languages have come *avocado, chocolate, chilli, potato, tobacco* and *tomato*. From Hebrew have come *alphabet, camel, cinnamon* and *maudlin*, as well as more modern borrowings from Yiddish such as *bagel, chutzpah, schmaltz* and *schmuck*.

From the native North American languages have come *anorak, kayak, raccoon* and *toboggan*, and from the Aboriginal language of Australia have come *boomerang* and *kangaroo*.

Judo, *bonsai* and *tycoon* have come from Japanese, *rattan* from Malay and *kung-fu, sampan* and *ginseng* from Chinese.

The borrowing process continues. With Britain becoming more of a cosmopolitan and multi-cultural nation the borrowing is increasing.

-bound A suffix meaning 'confined or restricted', as in housebound, snowbound and spellbound. It can also mean 'obligated', as in duty-bound.

brackets A pair of characters that are used to enclose information that is in some way additional to a main statement. The information so enclosed is called **parenthesis** and the pair of brackets enclosing it can be known as **parentheses**. The information that is enclosed in the brackets is purely supplementary or explanatory in nature and could be removed without changing the overall basic meaning or grammatical completeness of the statement. Brackets, like commas and dashes, interrupt the flow of the main statement but brackets indicate a more definite or clear-cut interruption. The fact that they are more visually obvious emphasizes this.

Material within brackets can be one word, as in 'In a local wine bar we had some delicious crepes (pancakes)' and 'They didn't have the chutzpah (nerve) to challenge her'. It can also take the form of dates, as in 'Robert Louis Stevenson (1850–94) wrote *Treasure Island*' and '*Animal Farm* was written by George Orwell (1903–50)'.

The material within brackets can also take the form of a phrase, as in 'They served lasagne (a kind of pasta) and some delicious veal' and 'They were drinking Calvados (a kind of brandy made from apples)' or in the form of a clause, as in 'We were to have supper (or so they called it) later in the evening' and 'They went for a walk round the loch (as a lake is called in Scotland) before taking their departure'.

It can also take the form of a complete sentence, as in 'He was determined (we don't know why) to tackle the problem alone' and 'She made it clear (nothing could be more clear) that she was not interested in the offer'. Sentences that appear in brackets in the middle of a sentence are not usually given an initial capital letter or a full stop, as in 'They very much desired (she had no idea why) to purchase her house'. If the material within brackets comes at the end of a sentence the full stop comes outside the second bracket, as in 'For some reason we agreed to visit her at home (we had no idea where she lived)'.

If the material in the brackets is a sentence which comes between two other sentences it is treated like a normal sentence with an initial capital letter and a closing full stop, as in 'He never seems to do any studying. (He is always either asleep or watching television.) Yet he does brilliantly in his exams.' Punctuation of the main statement is unaffected by the presence of the brackets and their enclosed material except that any punctuation that would have followed the word before the first bracket follows the second bracket, as in 'He lives in a place (I am not sure exactly where), that is miles from anywhere.

There are various shapes of brackets. Round brackets are the most common type. Square brackets are sometimes used to enclose information that is contained inside other information already in brackets, as in '(Christopher Marlowe [1564–93] was a contemporary of Shakespeare)' or in a piece of writing where round brackets have already been used for some other purpose. Thus in a dictionary if round brackets are used to separate off the pronunciation, square brackets are sometimes used to separate off the etymologies.

Square brackets are also used for editorial comments in a scholarly work where the material within brackets is more of an intrusion to the flow of the main statement than is normerly the case with bracketed material. Angle brackets and brace brackets tend to be used in more scholarly or technical contexts.

buildings These can cause problems with regard to the style and punctuation of their names. The proper name attached to the building should have an initial capital, as should the common noun that may be part of it, as in The White House, The Saltire Building, The National Portrait Gallery and The Museum of Childhood.

businesses and **organizations** These often cause style and punctuation problems with regard to their names or titles. In general the initial letters of the main words of the title should be in capital letters and the words of lesser importance, such as the articles, coordinating conjunctions and prepositions, should be in lower case, except when they are the first word of the title, as in 'The Indian Carpet Company', 'Kitchens for All' and 'Capital Industrial Cleaners'. Obviously, when the names of people are involved these should have initial capital letters, as in 'Jones and Brown'.

but A conjunction that connects two opposing ideas. It is a coordinating conjunction in that it connects two elements of equal status. The elements may be words, as in 'not James but John'; phrases, as in 'working hard but not getting anywhere' and 'trying to earn a living but not succeeding'; clauses, as in 'He has arrived but his sister is late', 'I know her but I have never met him' and 'He likes reading but she prefers to watch TV'. It should not be used when no element of contrast is present. Thus the following sentence should be rephrased, at least in formal English—'She is not professionally trained but taught herself'. The two clauses are in fact agreeing, not disagreeing, with each other and so, strictly speaking, but should not be used.

The use of but at the beginning of a sentence is disliked by many people. It should be used only for deliberate effect or in informal contexts.

by- A prefix meaning 'subordinate', 'secondary', 'incidental', as in by-product, by-road, by-effect. It can also mean 'around', as in by-pass.

C

capital letters These are much less common than lower-case letters. They are used as the initial letters of proper nouns, the names of countries, rivers, mountains, cities, etc. Thus we find Africa, Mount Everest, River Nile, Paris, etc. The first names and surnames of people have initial capital letters, as in John Black and Mary Brown. Initial capital letters are used for the days of the week, as in Tuesday and Wednesday, for the months of the year, as in May and October, public and religious holidays, as in Easter Sunday, Ramadan and Hanaku. Initial capital letters are used for the books of the Bible.

Points of the compass are spelt with an initial capital letter if they are part of a specific geographical feature or region, as in South Africa.

Initial capital letters are usually used in the titles of books. Only the main words are capitalized. Prepositions, determiners and the articles are left in lower-case unless they form the first word of the title, as in *A Room with a View* and *For Whom the Bell Tolls*— *see* BOOK TITLES.

Initial capital letters are necessary in tradenames, as in Hoover, Jacuzzi, Xerox and Kodak. Note that verbs formed from trade names are not spelt with an initial capital letter.

The first word in a sentence is spelt with a capital letter, as in 'We heard them come in. They made very little noise. However, we are light sleepers.'

For capital letters in direct speech, *see* DIRECT SPEECH. For capital letters in abbreviation and acronyms, *see* ABBREVIATION and ACRONYM.

cardi- A prefix derived from Greek meaning 'heart', as in cardiology, cardiac.

cardinal number The numbers one, two three, four, etc, as opposed to ORDINAL NUMBERS, which refer to numbers such as first, second, third, fourth, etc.

case One of the forms in the DECLENSION of a noun, pronoun or adjective in a sentence.

clause A group of words containing a FINITE VERB which forms part of a compound or complex sentence. See MAIN CLAUSE, SUBORDINATE CLAUSES, ADVERBIAL CLAUSE, NOUN CLAUSE and RELATIVE CLAUSE.

clerihew A humorous four-line light verse in which the first two lines rhyme with each other and the last two rhyme with each other. The clerihew was popularized by Edward Clerihew Bentley (1875–1956). It usually deals with a person named in the first line and then describes him in a humorous way, as in

Mr Michael Foot
Had lots of loot
He loved to gloat
While petting his stoat

cliché A hackneyed stereotyped expression that is much overused. Examples of clichés include 'unaccustomed as I am to public speaking', 'the light at the end of the tunnel' and 'All's well that ends well'.

collective noun A singular noun that refers to a group of things or people. It is used when the whole group is being considered, as in 'flock of sheep', 'herd of cattle', 'team of oxen', 'shoal of herring', 'covey of partridges', 'unkindness of ravens', 'gaggle of geese', 'pride of lions', 'mutation of thrushes', 'exaltation of larks', 'convocation of eagles'.

colloquial A term used to describe informal language, such as that found in informal conversation.

colon A punctuation mark (:) that is used within a sentence to explain, interpret, clarify or amplify what has gone before it. 'The standard of school work here is extremely high: it is almost university standard', 'The fuel bills are giving cause for concern: they are almost double last year's'. 'We have some new information: the allies have landed'. A capital letter is not usually used after the colon in this context.

The colon is also used to introduce lists or long quotations, as in 'The recipe says we need: tomatoes, peppers, courgettes, garlic, oregano and basil', 'The boy has a huge list of things he needs for school: blazer, trousers, shirts, sweater, ties, shoes, tennis shoes, rugby boots, sports clothes and leisure wear' and 'One of his favourite quotations was: "If music be the food of love play on".'

The colon is sometimes used in numerals, as in '7:30 a.m.', '22:11:72' and 'a ratio of 7:3'. It is used in the titles of some books, for example where there is a subtitle or explanatory title, as in 'The Dark Years: the Economy in the 1930s'.

In informal writing, the dash is sometimes used instead of the colon, Indeed the dash tends to be overused for this purpose.

comma A very common punctuation mark (,). In modern usage there is a tendency to adopt a system of minimal punctuation and the comma is one of the casualties of this new attitude. Most people use the comma considerably less frequently than was formerly the case.

However there are certain situations in which the comma is still commonly used. One of these concerns lists. The individual items in a series of three or more items are separated by commas. Whether a comma is put before the 'and' which follows the second-last item is now a matter of choice. Some people dislike the use of a comma before 'and' in this situation, and it was formerly considered wrong. Examples of lists include—'at the sports club we can play tennis, squash, badminton and table tennis', 'We need to buy bread, milk, fruit and sugar', and 'They are studying French, German, Spanish and Russian'. The individual items in a list can be quite long, as in 'We opened the door, let ourselves in, fed the cat and started to cook a meal' and 'They consulted the map, planned the trip, got some foreign currency and were gone before we realized it'. Confusion may arise if the last item in the list contains 'and' in its own right, as in 'In the pub they served ham salad, shepherd's pie, pie and chips and omelette'. In such cases it as well to put a comma before the final 'and'.

In cases where there is a list of adjectives before a noun, the use of commas is now optional although it was formerly standard practice. Thus both 'She wore a long, red, sequinned dress' and 'She wore a long red sequinned dress' are used. When the adjective immediately before the noun has a closer relationship with it than the other adjectives no comma should be used, as in 'a beautiful old Spanish village'.

The comma is used to separate clauses or phrases that are parenthetical or naturally cut off from the rest of a sentence, as in 'My mother, who was of Irish extraction, was very superstitious'. In such a sentence the clause within the commas can be removed without altering the basic meaning. Care should be taken to include both commas. Commas are not normally used to separate main clauses and relative clauses, as in 'The woman whom I met was my friend's sister'. Nor are they usually used to separate main clauses and subordinate clauses, as in 'He left when we arrived' and 'They came to the party although we didn't expect them to'. If the subordinate clause precedes the main clause, it is sometimes followed by a comma, especially if it is a reasonably long clause, as in 'Although we stopped and thought about it, we still made the wrong decision'. If the clause is quite short, or if it is a short phrase, a comma is not usually inserted, as in 'Although it rained we had a good holiday' and 'Although poor they were happy'. The use of commas to separate such words and expression from the rest of the sentence to which they are related is optional. Thus one can write 'However, he could be right' or 'However he could be right'. The longer the expression is, the more likely it is to have a comma after it, as in 'On the other hand, we may decide not to go'.

Commas are always used to separate terms of address, interjections or question tags from the rest of the sentence, as in 'Please come this way, Ms Brown, and make yourself at home', 'Now, ladies, what can I get you?' and 'It's cold today, isn't it?'

Commas may be used to separate main clauses joined by a coordinating conjunction, but this is not usual if the clauses have the same subject or object, as in 'She swept the floor and dusted the table'. In cases where the subjects are different and the clauses are fairly long, it is best to insert a comma, as in 'They took all the furniture with them, and she was left with nothing'.

A comma can be inserted to avoid repeating a verb in the second of two clause, as in 'he plays golf and tennis, his brother rugby'.

commands These are expressed in the imperative mood, as in 'Be quiet!', 'Stop crying!', 'Go away!'

common noun Simply the name of an ordinary, everyday non-specific thing or person, as opposed to proper nouns, which refer to the names of particular individuals or specific places. Common nouns include 'baby', 'cat', 'girl', 'hat', 'park', 'sofa' and 'table'.

comparison of adjectives This is achieved in two different ways. Some adjectives form their comparative by adding *-er* to the positive or absolute form, as in 'braver', 'louder', 'madder', 'shorter' and 'taller'. Other adjectives form their comparative by using 'more' in conjunction with them, as in 'more beautiful', 'more realistic', 'more suitable' and 'more tactful'. Which is the correct form is largely a matter of length. One-syllable adjectives, such as 'loud', add *-er*, as 'louder'. Two-syllable adjectives sometimes have both forms as a possibility, as in 'gentler/more gentle', and 'cleverest/most clever'. Adjectives with three or more syllables usually form their comparatives with 'more', as in 'more comfortable', 'more gracious', 'more regular' and 'more understanding'. Some adjectives are irregular in their comparative forms, as in 'good/better', 'bad/worse', 'many/more'. Only if they begin with *un-* are they likely to end in *-er*, as in 'untrustworthier'.

Some adjectives by their very definitions do not normally have a comparative form, for example 'unique'.

complement The equivalent of the OBJECT in a clause with a LINKING VERB. In the sentence 'Jack is a policeman', 'a policeman' is the complement. In the sentence 'Jane is a good mother', 'a good mother' is the complement', and in the sentence 'His son is an excellent football player', 'an excellent football player' is the complement.

complex sentence A type of sentence in which there is a MAIN CLAUSE and one or more subordinate clauses. The sentence 'We went to visit him although he had been unfriendly to us' is a complex sentence since it is composed of a main clause and one subordinate clause ('although he had been unfriendly to us'). The sentence 'We wondered where he had gone and why he was upset' is a complex sentence since it has a main clause and two subordinate clauses ('where he had gone' and 'why he was upset').

compound sentence A type of sentence with more than one clause and linked by a coordinating conjunction, such as 'and' or 'but', as in 'He applied for a new job and got it' and 'I went to the cinema but I didn't enjoy the film'.

concord *see* **number agreement.**

concrete noun The name of something that one can touch, as opposed to an abstract noun, which one cannot. Concrete nouns include 'bag', 'glass', 'plate', 'pot', 'clothes', 'field', 'garden', 'flower', 'potato', 'foot' and 'shoe'. *See* ABSTRACT NOUN.

conjunction A word that connects words, clauses or sentences. Conjunctions are of two types. A **coordinating conjunction** joins units of equal status, as in 'bread and butter', 'We asked for some food and we got it'. A **subordinating conjunction** joins a dependent or subordinating clause to main verbs: in 'We asked him why he was there', 'why he was there' is a subordinate clause and thus 'why' is a subordinating conjunction.

content words *see* **function word.**

continuous tenses *see* **tense.**

contraction *see* **abbreviation.**

copula *see* **linking verb.**

copular verb *see* **equative** and **linking verb.**

count noun is the same as COUNTABLE NOUN.

countable noun is one which can be preceded by 'a' and can take a plural, as in 'hat/hats', 'flower/flowers'. *See also* UNCOUNTABLE NOUN.

D

dangling participle A participle that has been misplaced in a sentence. A participle is often used to introduce a phrase that is attached to a subject mentioned later in a sentence, as in 'Worn out by the long walk, she fell to the ground in a faint'. 'Worn out' is the participle and 'she' the subject. Another example is 'Laughing in glee at having won, she ordered some champagne'. In this sentence 'laughing' is the participle and 'she' is the subject. It is a common error for such a participle not to be related to any subject, as in 'Imprisoned in the dark basement, it seemed a long time since she had seen the sun'. This participle is said to be 'dangling'. Another example of a dangling participle is contained in 'Living alone, the days seemed long'.

It is also a common error for a participle to be related to the wrong subject in a sentence, as in 'Painting the ceiling, some of the plaster fell on his head', 'Painting' is the participle and should go with a subject 'he'. Instead it goes with 'some of the plaster'. Participles in this situation are more correctly known as **misrelated participles**, although they are also called dangling participles.

dash A punctuation mark in the form of a short line that indicates a short break in the continuity of a sentence, as in 'He has never been any trouble at school—quite the reverse', 'I was amazed when he turned up—I thought he was still abroad'. In such situations it serves the same purpose as brackets, except that it is frequently considered more informal. The dash should be used sparingly. Depending on it too much can lead to careless writing with ideas set down at random rather than turned into a piece of coherent prose.

The dash can be used to emphasize a word or phrase, as in 'They said goodbye then—forever'. It can also be used to add a remark to the end of a sentence, as in 'They had absolutely no money—a regular state of affairs towards the end of the month.' The dash can also be used to introduce a statement that amplifies or explains what has been said, as in 'The burglars took everything of value—her jewellery, the silver, the TV set, her hi-fi and several hundred pounds.' It can be used to summarize what has gone before, as in 'Disease, poverty, ignorance—these are the problems facing us.'

The dash is also used to introduce an afterthought, as in 'You can come with me—but you might not want to'. It can also introduce a sharp change of subject, as in 'I'm just making tea—what was that noise?' It can also be used to introduce some kind of balance in a sentence, as in 'It's going to take two of us to get this table out of here—one to move it and one to hold the door open.'

The dash is sometimes found in pairs. A pair of dashes acts in much the same way as a set of round brackets. A pair of dashes can be used to indicate a break in a sentence, as in 'We prayed—prayed as we had never prayed before—that the children would be safe', 'It was—on reflection—his best performance yet', and 'He introduced me to his wife—an attractive pleasant woman—before he left'.

Dashes are used to indicate hesitant speech, as in 'I don't—well—maybe—you could be right'. They can be used to indicate the omission of part of a word or name, as in 'It's none of your b— business', 'He's having an affair with Mrs D-'.

They can also be used between points in time or space, as in 'Edinburgh—London' and '1750—1790.'

dates These are usually written in figures, as in 1956, rather than in words, as in nineteen fifty-six, except in formal contexts, such as legal documents. There are various ways of writing dates. The standard form in Britain is becoming day followed by month followed by year, as in '24 February 1970'. In North America the standard form of this is 'February 24, 1970', and that is a possibility in Britain also. Alternatively, some people

dative case

write '24th February 1970'. Care should be taken with the writing of dates entirely in numbers, especially if one is corresponding with someone in North America. In Britain the day of the month is put first, the month second and the year third, as in '2/3/50', '2 March 1950'. In North America the month is put first, followed by the day of the month and the year. Thus in North America '2/3/50' would be 3 February 1950.

Centuries may be written either in figures, as in 'the 19th century', or in words, as in 'the nineteenth century'.

Decades and centuries are now usually written without apostrophes. as in '1980s' and '1990s'.

dative case The case that indicates 'to' or 'for'. This is applicable to Latin but not to English, where such meanings are expressed by prepositional phrases. In English the INDIRECT OBJECT is equivalent to the dative case in some situations.

deca- A prefix derived from Greek meaning 'ten', as in decade, decathlon and decahedron.

deci- A prefix derived from Latin meaning 'tenth', as in decibel, decimal, decimate and decilitre.

declarative sentence A sentence that conveys information. The subject precedes the verb in it. Examples include 'They won the battle', 'He has moved to another town', 'Lots of people go there' and 'There is a new person in charge'.

declarative mood the same as **indicative mood.**

declension The variation of the form of a noun, adjective or pronoun to show different cases, such as nominative and accusative. It also refers to the class into which such words are placed, as in first declension, second declension, etc. The term applies to languages such as Latin but is not applicable to English.

definite article A term for 'the', which is the most frequently used word in the English language. 'The' is used to refer back to a person or thing that has already been mentioned, as in 'Jack and Jill built a model. The model was of a ship' and 'We've bought a car. It was the cheapest car we could find'.

'The' can be used to make a general statement about all things of a particular type, as in 'The computer has led to the loss of many jobs' and 'The car has caused damage to the environment'. 'The' can be used to refer to a whole class or group, as in 'the Italians', 'the Browns' and 'the younger generation'.

'The' can also be used to refer to services or systems, as in 'They are not on the phone' and 'She prefers going by the bus'. It can be used to refer to the name of a musical instrument when someone's ability to play it is being referred to, as in 'Her son is learning to play the violin'.

'The' indicates a person or thing to be the only one, as in the Bible, the King of Spain, the White House, the Palace of Westminster and the President of the United States.

'The' can be used instead of a possessive determiner to refer to parts of the body, as in 'She took him by the arm' and 'The dog bit him on the leg'.

'The' is used in front of superlative adjectives, as in 'the largest amount of money' and 'the most beautiful woman'. It can also be used to indicate that a person or thing is unique or exceptional, as in 'the political debater of his generation'. In this last sense 'the' is pronounced 'thee'.

degree A level of comparison of gradable adjectives. The degrees of comparison comprise **absolute** or **positive**, as in 'big', 'calm', 'dark', 'fair', 'hot', 'late', 'short' and 'tall'; **comparative**, as in 'bigger', 'calmer', 'darker', 'fairest', 'hotter', 'late', 'shorter' and 'taller'; **superlative**, as in 'biggest', 'calmest', 'darkest', 'fairest', 'hottest', 'latest', 'shortest' and 'tallest'.

Degree can also refer to adverbs. Adverbs of degree include 'extremely', 'very', 'greatly', 'rather', 'really', 'remarkably', 'terribly', as in 'an extremely rare case', 'a very old man', 'He's remarkably brave' and 'We're terribly pleased'.

demi- A prefix derived from old French meaning 'half', as in demigod and demijohn.

224

demonstrative determiner A determiner that is used to indicate things or people in relationship to the speaker or writer in space or time. 'This' and 'these' indicate nearness to the speaker, as in 'Will you take this book home?' and 'These flowers are for you'. 'That' and 'those' indicate distance from the speaker, as in 'Get that creature out of here!' and 'Aren't those flowers over there beautiful!'

demonstrative pronoun A pronoun that is similar to a DEMONSTRATIVE DETERMINER except that it stands alone in place of a noun rather than preceding a noun, as in 'I'd like to give you this', 'What is that?', 'These are interesting books' and 'Those are not his shoes'.

dependent clause A clause that cannot stand alone and make sense, unlike an independent or MAIN CLAUSE. Dependent clauses depend on the main clause. The term is the same as SUBORDINATE CLAUSE.

derivation (1) The etymology of a word, as in 'The derivation of the expression is unknown'.
(2) The process of forming a new word by adding an AFFIX of some kind to an existing word or base, as in 'helpless' from 'help' and 'maker' from 'make'.

derivative A word that is formed by DERIVATION. For example, 'sweetly' is a derivative of 'sweet', 'peaceful' is a derivative from 'peace', 'clinging' is derived from from 'cling' and 'shortest' is derived from 'short'.

derm- A prefix derived from Greek meaning 'skin', as in dermatitis, dermatologist and dermatology.

determiner A word that is used in front of a noun or pronoun to tell us something about it. Unlike an ADJECTIVE, it does not, strictly speaking, 'describe' a noun or pronoun. Determiners are divided into the following categories: **articles** (a, an, the) as in 'a cat', 'an eagle', 'the book'; **demonstrative determiners** (this, that, these, those), as in 'this girl', 'that boy' and 'those people'; **possessive determiners** (my, your, his/her/its, our, their), as in 'my dog', 'her house', 'its colour', 'their responsibility'; **numbers** (one,two, three, four, etc, first, second, third, fourth, etc), as in 'two reasons', 'five ways', 'ten children'; and **indefinite** or **general determiners** (all, another, any, both, each, either, enough, every, few, fewer, less, little, many, most, much, neither, no, other, several, some), as in 'both parents', 'enough food', 'several issues'. Many words used as determiners are also pronouns. *See* ADJECTIVE; DEMONSTRATIVE DETERMINER; POSSESSIVE DETERMINER; NUMBERS; INDEFINITE DETERMINER.

di- A prefix derived from Greek meaning 'two' or 'double', as in dioxide, dilemma, diphthong and disyllabic.

dia- A prefix meaning 'through', as in diaphanous; 'apart', as in diacritical, diaphragm and dialysis; and 'across', as in diameter.

diacritic A mark placed over, under or through a letter to indicate a sound or stress value different from that of the same letter when it is unmarked. Diacritics include the cedilla, as in 'façade', the German umlaut, as in 'mädchen', and diaeresis, as in 'naïve'.

diaeresis A mark that is placed over a vowel to indicate that it is sounded separately from a neighbouring vowel, as in 'naïve', 'Chloë'.

dialect A variety of language that is distinct from other varieties in terms of pronunciation, accent, vocabulary, grammar and sentence structure. The term 'dialect' tends to imply a deviation from some standard form of language, usually the dialect used by educated upper-class or upper-middle-class people, known in English as 'standard' English.

Dialects may be regional in nature. Thus in Britain there is a Cornish dialect, a Liverpool dialect, a Glasgow dialect, and so on. Alternatively, they may be based on class differences, when they are sometimes known as 'social dialects'. These include working-class dialect, upper-class dialect, and so on.

At one time regional dialects were looked down on by people who spoke only standard English. People with regional accents, using regional dialects, were unlikely to get jobs in professions such as radio and television, where the use of language was a major consideration. People intent on such careers tried to change their accents to remove all traces of dialect. However, things have changed, and now it is quite common for people using regional accents and dialects to have jobs associated with radio and television.Note that the word 'dialect' is not appropriate if it is a global variety of English that is being referred to. For example, the English spoken in America is known as American English.

diction (1) The choice of words in writing or speech, especially with regard to correctness, clarity or effectiveness, as in 'The content of his essay was very interesting but his diction was poor'.

(2) The pronunciation and enunciation of words in speaking and singing, as in 'She has a beautiful natural singing voice but should take lessons in diction'.

dialogue The conversation in novels, etc, which is placed on a new line, often in a new paragraph, if there is a change of speaker, as in:

'We're going now', said John. 'Do you want to join us? If you do you'd better hurry. We can't wait.'

'Just go on', replied Mary. 'I'm not quite ready. I'll catch you up'.

digraph A group of two letters representing one sound, as in 'ay' in 'hay', 'ey' in 'key', 'oy' in 'boy', 'ph' in 'phone' and 'th' in 'thin'. When the digraph consists of two letters physically joined together, as 'ae', it is called a 'ligature'.

diminutive Something small or a small form or version of something, as in 'booklet', 'droplet', 'flatlet', 'auntie', 'doggy', 'islet', 'piglet', 'poppet', 'snippet', 'starlet', 'kitchenette', 'hillock', 'paddock', 'mannikin', 'lambkin', 'duckling', 'gosling', 'nestling', 'majorette', 'pipette'. Proper names often have diminutive forms, as in Alf for Alfred, Annie for Ann, Babs for Barbara, Bill for William, Charlie for Charles, Dot for Dorothy, Jimmy for James, Lizzie for Elizabeth, Meg for Margaret, Nell for Helen, Pat for Patrick and Teddy for Edward.

diphthong A speech sound that changes its quality within the same single syllable. The sound begins as for one vowel and moves on as for another. Since the sound glides from one vowel into another, a diphthong is sometimes called a **gliding vowel**. Examples include the vowels sounds in 'rain', 'weigh', 'either', 'voice', 'height', 'aisle', 'road', 'soul', 'know', 'house', 'care', 'pure', 'during', 'here' and 'weird'.

direct object The noun, noun phrase, noun or nominal clause or pronoun that is acted upon by the action of a transitive verb. In the sentence 'She bought milk', 'bought' is a transitive verb and 'milk' is a noun which is the direct object. In the sentence 'She bought loads of clothes', 'bought' is a transitive verb and 'loads of clothes' is the direct object. In the sentence 'He knows what happened', 'knows' is a transitive verb and 'what happened' is a 'noun clause' or 'nominal clause'. A direct object is frequently known just as object. *See* INDIRECT OBJECT.

direct speech The reporting of speech by repeating exactly the actual words used by the speaker. In the sentence 'Peter said, "I am tired of this"', "I am tired of this" is a piece of direct speech because it represents exactly what Peter said. Similarly, in the sentence 'Jane asked, "Where are you going?"', "Where are you going" is a piece of direct speech since it represents exactly what Jane said.

Quotation marks are used at the beginning and end of pieces of direct speech. Only the words actually spoken are placed within the quotation marks, as in '"If I were you," he said, "I would refuse to go"'. The quotation marks involved can be either single or double, according to preference or house style.

If there is a statement such as 'he said' following the piece of direct speech, a comma is placed before the second inverted comma, as in '"Come along," he said'. If the piece of direct speech is a question or exclamation, a question mark or exclamation mark is put instead of the comma, as in '"What are you doing?" asked John' and '"Get away from me!" she screamed'.

If a statement such as 'he said' is placed within a sentence in direct speech, a comma is placed after 'he said' and the second part of the piece of direct speech does not begin with a capital letter, as in '"I know very well," he said, "that you do not like me."'

If the piece of direct speech includes a complete sentence, the sentence begins with a capital letter, as in '"I am going away," she said, "and I am not coming back. I don't feel that I belong here anymore."' Note that the full stop at the end of a piece of direct speech that is a sentence should go before the closing inverted comma.

If the piece of direct speech quoted takes up more than one paragraph, quotation marks are placed at the beginning of each new paragraph. However, quotation marks are not placed at the end of each paragraph, just at the end of the final one.

When writing a story, etc, that includes dialogue or conversation, each new piece of direct speech should begin on a new line or sometimes in a new paragraph.

Quotation marks are not used only to indicate direct speech. For example, they are sometimes used to indicate the title of a book or newspaper. The quotation marks used in this way can be either single or double, according to preference or house style. If a piece of direct speech contains the title of a book, newspaper, etc, it should be put in the opposite type of quotation marks to those used to enclose the piece of direct speech. Thus, if single quotation marks have been used in the direct speech, then double quotation marks should be used for the title within the direct speech, as in "Have you read "Animal Farm" by George Orwell?' the teacher asked'. If double quotation marks have been used for the direct speech, single quotation marks should be used for the title, as in '"Have you read 'Animal Farm'?' by George Orwell?" the teacher asked'.

Sometimes titles are put in italic type instead of quotation marks. This avoids the clumsiness that can occur when both sets of quotation marks end on the same word, as in 'The pupil replied, 'No, I have not read "Animal Farm".''

dis- A prefix derived from Latin indicating 'opposite', 'not', as in disappear, disapprove, disband, disbelieve, disclaim, disconnect, discontinue, disenchant, disengage, disinherit, dislike, disobey, dispossess, distrust and disunite.

distributive pronoun A pronoun that refers to individual members of a class or group. These include 'each', 'either', 'neither', 'none', 'everyone', 'no one'. Such pronouns, where relevant, should be accompanied by singular verbs and singular personal pronouns, as in 'All the men are to be considered for the new posts. Each is to send in his application'. Problems arise when the sex of the noun to which the distributive pronoun refers back is either unknown or unspecified. Formerly it was the convention to treat such nouns as masculine and so to make the distributive pronoun masculine, as in 'All pupils must obey the rules. Each is to provide his own sports equipment'. Nowadays this convention is frequently considered to be unacceptably sexist and attempts have been made to get round this. One solution is to use 'him/her' (or 'him or her'), etc, as in 'The students have received a directive from the professor. Each is to produce his/her essay by tomorrow.' This convention is considered by many people to be clumsy. They prefer to be ungrammatical and use a plural personal pronoun, as in 'The pupils are being punished. Each is to inform their parents'. Where possible it is preferable to rephrase sentences to avoid being either sexist or ungrammatical, as in 'All of the pupils must tell their parents.'

Each, either, etc, in such contexts is fairly formal. In less formal situations 'each of', 'either of', etc, is more usual, as in 'Each of the boys will have to train really hard to win' and 'Either of the dresses is perfectly suitable'.

disyllabic A term that describes a word with two syllables. For example, 'window' is disyllabic, since it consists of the syllable 'win' and the syllable 'dow'. Similarly 'curtain' is disyllabic since it consists of the syllable 'cur' and 'tain'.

do

do An auxiliary verb that is used to form negative forms, as in, 'I do not agree with you', 'They do not always win', 'He does not wish to go' and 'She did not approve of their behaviour'. It is also used to form interrogative forms, as in 'Do you agree?', 'Does she know about it?', 'Did you see that?' and 'I prefer to go by train. Don't you?' Do is also used for emphasis, as in 'I do believe you're right' and 'They do know, don't they?'

-dom A suffix meaning 'state, condition', as in boredom, freedom, officialdom, martyr-dom. It can also mean 'rank or status', as in earldom, dukedom, or 'domain, territory' as in kingdom.

double negative The occurrence of two negative words in a single sentence or clause, as in 'He didn't say nothing' and 'We never had no quarrel'. This is usually considered incorrect in standard English, although it is a feature of some social or regional dialects. The use of the double negative, if taken literally, often has the opposite meaning to the one intended. Thus 'He didn't say nothing' conveys the idea that 'He said something'.

Some double negatives are considered acceptable, as in 'I wouldn't be surprised if they don't turn up', although it is better to restrict such constructions to informal contexts. The sentence quoted conveys the impression that the speaker will be quite surprised if 'they' do 'turn up'. Another example of an acceptable double negative is 'I can't not worry about the children. Anything could have happened to them'. Again this type of construction is best restricted to informal contexts.

It is the semi-negative forms, such as 'hardly' and 'scarcely', that cause most problems with regard to double negatives, as in 'We didn't have hardly any money to buy food' and 'They didn't have barely enough time to catch the bus'. Such sentences are incorrect.

double passive A clause that contains two verbs in the passive, the second of which is an infinitive, as in 'The goods are expected to be despatched some time this week'. Some examples of double passives are clumsy or ungrammatical and should be avoided, as in 'Redundancy notices are proposed to be issued next week'.

doubling of consonants These can cause spelling problems. There are a few rules that help to solve these problems. These include the following: In words of one syllable ending in a single consonant preceded by a single vowel, the consonant is doubled when an ending starting with a vowel is added, as in 'drop' and 'dropped', 'pat' and 'patting' and 'rub' and 'rubbing'.

In words of more than one syllable that end in a single consonant preceded by a single vowel, the consonant is doubled if the stress is on the last syllable, as in 'begin' and 'beginning', 'occur' and 'occurring', 'prefer' and 'preferred', 'refer' and 'referring' and 'commit' and 'committed'. In similar words where the stress is not on the last syllable, the consonant does not double, as in 'bigot' and 'bigoted' and 'develop' and 'developed'.

Exceptions to this rule include words ending in 'l'. The 'l' doubles even in cases where the last syllable containing it is unstressed, as in 'travel' and 'travelled' and 'appal' and 'appalling'. 'Worship', in which the stress is on the first syllable, is also an exception, as in 'worshipped'.

doubles Words that habitually go together, as in 'out and out', 'neck and neck', 'over and over', 'hale and hearty', 'rant and rave', 'fast and furious', 'hue and cry', 'stuff and non-sense', 'rough and ready', 'might and main', 'give and take', 'ups and downs', 'fair and square', 'high and dry' and 'wear and tear'. Doubles are also sometimes called **dyads**.

doublets Pairs of words that have developed from the same original word but now differ somewhat in form and usually in meaning. Examples include 'human' and 'humane', 'shade' and 'shadow', 'hostel' and 'hotel', 'frail' and 'fragile', and 'fashion' and 'faction'.

dramatic irony A situation in which a character in a play, novel, etc, says or does some-thing that has a meaning for the audience or reader, other than the obvious meaning, that he/she does not understand. Its use is common in both comedy and tragedy.

dual gender A category of nouns in which there is no indication of gender. The nouns referred to include a range of words used for people, and occasionally animals, which can be of either gender. Unless the gender is specified we do not know the sex of the person referred to. Such words include 'artist', 'author', 'poet', 'singer', 'child', 'pupil', 'student', 'baby', 'parent', 'teacher', 'dog'. Such words give rise to problems with accompanying singular pronouns. *See* EACH.

dummy subject A SUBJECT that has no intrinsic meaning but is inserted to maintain a balanced grammatical structure. In the sentences 'It has started to rain' and 'It is nearly midnight', 'it' is a dummy subject. In the sentences 'There is nothing else to say' and 'There is no reason for his behaviour', 'there' is a dummy subject.

dyads *see* **doubles.**

dynamic verb A verb with a meaning that indicates action, as 'work' in 'They work hard', 'play' in 'The boys play football at the weekend' and 'come' in 'The girls come here every Sunday'.

dys- A prefix derived from the Greek meaning 'bad', as in dyslexia, dysgraphia, dysmenorrhea, dyspepsia.

E

each A word that can be either a DETERMINER or a DISTRIBUTIVE PRONOUN. Each as a determiner is used before a singular noun and is accompanied by a singular verb, as in 'Each candidate is to reapply', 'Each athlete has a place in the final', 'Each country is represented by a head of state' and 'Each chair was covered in chintz'.

Each of can sometimes be used instead of each, as in 'each of the candidates'. Again a singular verb is used, as in 'Each of the books has pages missing', 'Each of the chairs has a broken leg' and 'Each of the pupils is to make a contribution to the cost of the outing'. Each of can also be used in front of plural pronouns, as in 'each of them'. Once again a singular verb is used, as in 'Each of them wants something different', 'Each of us is supposed to make a contribution' and 'Each of the words has several meanings'. If the user wishes to emphasize the fact that something is true about every member of a group, **each one of** should be used and not 'every', as in 'Each one of them feels guilty', 'Each one of us has a part to play' and 'Each one of the actors has improved'.

As a pronoun, each also takes a singular verb, as in 'They hate each other. Each is plotting revenge', 'These exercises are not a waste of time. Each provides valuable experience'. For emphasis **each one** can be used, as in 'We cannot leave any of these books behind. Each one of them is necessary' and 'We should not dismiss any of the staff. Each one has a part to play in the new firm'.

Each, where relevant, should be accompanied by a singular personal pronoun, as in 'Each girl has to provide her own sports equipment', 'Each of the men is to take a turn at working night shift', 'The boys are all well off and each can afford the cost of the holiday' and 'There are to be no exceptions among the women staff. Each one has to work full time'.

Problems arise when the noun that each refers back to is of unknown or unspecified sex. Formerly nouns in such situations were assumed to be masculine, as in 'Each pupil was required to bring his own tennis racket' and 'Each of the students has to

eco-

provide himself with a tape recorder'. Nowadays such a convention is regarded as being sexist and the use of 'he/her', 'his/her', etc, is proposed, as in 'Each pupil was required to bring his/her (or 'his or her') own tennis racket' and 'Each student has to provide himself/herself (or 'himself or herself') with a tape recorder'. Even in written English such a convention can be clumsy and it is even more so in spoken English. For this reason many people decide to be ungrammatical and opt for 'Each pupil was required to bring their own tennis racket' and 'Each student has to provide themselves with a tape recorder'.

Both sexism and grammatical error can be avoided by rephrasing such sentences, as in 'All pupils are required to bring their own tennis rackets' and 'All students have to provide themselves with tape recorders'.

Each is used rather than every when the user is thinking of the members of a group as individuals.

eco- A prefix indicating ecology. Following the increased awareness of the importance of the environment, there has been a growing interest in ecology and many words beginning with eco- have been added to the English language. Some of these are scientific terms such as ecotype, ecosystem or ecospecies. Others are more general terms, such as ecocatastrophe and ecopolitics, and some are even slang terms, such as ecofreak and econut.

-ectomy A suffix of Greek origin that indicates 'surgical removal', as in hysterectomy (the surgical removal of the womb), mastectomy (the surgical removal of a breast) and appendicectomy (the surgical removal of the appendix, the American English version of which is appendectomy).

-ed A suffix that forms the past tense and past participles of regular verbs, as in 'asked', 'blinded', 'caused', 'darkened', 'escaped', 'frightened', 'guarded', 'hunted', 'injured', 'jilted', 'kicked', 'landed', 'marked', 'noted', 'opened', 'painted', 'quarrelled', 'rattled', 'started', 'tormented', 'unveiled', 'washed', 'yielded'. Some past participles ending in '-ed' can act as adjectives, as in 'darkened room', 'escaped prisoners', 'frightened children', 'hunted animals', 'painted faces' and 'tormented souls'.

In the case of some verbs, the past tense and past participle may end in '-ed' or 't', according to preference. Such verbs include 'burn', 'dream', 'dwell', 'kneel', 'lean', 'leapt', 'smell', 'spell', 'spill' and 'spoil'. Thus 'burned' and 'burnt', 'dreamed' and 'dreamt', 'kneeled' and 'knelt', and 'learned' and 'learnt', etc, are acceptable forms.

-ee A suffix that is derived from French and is used as part of nouns that are the recipients of an action, as in deportee (a person who has been deported); employee (a person who is employed); interviewee (a person who is being interviewed); licensee (a person who has been licensed); trainee (a person who is being trained).

-Ee can also be used as part of a noun indicating a person who acts or behaves in a particular way, as absentee (a person who absents himself/herself) and escapee (a person who escapes).

e.g. The abbreviation of the Latin phrase *exempli gratia*, which means 'for example'. It is used before examples of what has previously been referred to, as in 'The tourists want to visit the historic sites of Edinburgh, e.g. Edinburgh Castle and Holyrood House'. By its very nature e.g. is mostly restricted to written English, becoming 'for example' in speech. Many writers also prefer to use 'for example' rather than use e.g. Both letters of the abbreviation usually have a full stop after them, as e.g., and it is usually preceded by a comma.

either A word that can be used as either a determiner or distributive pronoun. As a determiner it is used with a singular verb, as in 'Either hotel is expensive' and 'In principle they are both against the plan but is either likely to vote for it?'

Either of can be used instead of either. It is used before a plural noun, as in 'either of the applicants' and 'either of the houses'. It is accompanied by a singular verb, as in 'Either of the applicants is suitable' and 'Either of the houses is big enough for their family'.

Either can be used as a distributive pronoun and takes a singular verb, as in 'We have looked at both houses and either is suitable' and 'She cannot decide between the two dresses but either is appropriate for the occasion'. This use is rather formal.

In the **either . . . or** construction, a singular verb is used if both subjects are singular, as in 'Either Mary or Jane knows what to do' and 'Either my mother or my father plans to be present'. A plural verb is used if both nouns involved are plural, as in 'Either men or women can play' and 'Either houses or flats are available'.

When a combination of singular and plural subjects is involved, the verb traditionally agrees with the subject that is nearer to it, as in 'Either his parents or his sister is going to come' and 'Either his grandmother or his parents are going to come'.

As a pronoun, either should be used only of two possibilities.

electro- A prefix meaning 'electric, electrical' as in electrocardiograph, electromagnetic, electroscope, electrotherapy.

elision The omission of a speech sound or syllable, as in the omission of 'd' in one of the possible pronunciations of 'Wednesday' and in the omission of 'ce' from the pronunciation of 'Gloucester'.

ellipsis An omission of some kind. It can refer to the omission of words from a statement because they are thought to be obvious from the context. In many cases it involves using an auxiliary verb on its own rather than a full verb, as in 'Jane won't accept it but Mary will' and 'They would go if they could'. In such cases the full form of 'Jane won't accept it but Mary will accept it' and 'They would go if they could go' would sound unnatural and repetitive. This is common in spoken English.

Some sentences containing an ellipsis sound clumsy as well as ungrammatical, as in 'This is as good, or perhaps even better than that', where 'as' is omitted after 'good' and in 'People have and still do express their disapproval about it', where 'expressed' is omitted after 'have'. Care should be taken to avoid ellipsis if the use of it is going to be ambiguous or clumsy.

Ellipsis is often used to indicate an omission from a quoted passage. If part of a passage is quoted and there is a gap before the next piece of the same passage is required to be quoted, an ellipsis is used in the form of three dots (. . .). If the part of the passage quoted does not start at the beginning of a sentence the ellipsis precedes it.

emphasizing adjective An adjective that is used for emphasis. 'Very' is an emphasizing adjective in the sentence 'His very mother dislikes him' and 'own' is an emphasizing adjective in 'He likes to think that he is his own master'.

emphasizing adverb An adverb used for emphasis. 'Really' is an emphasizing adverb in the sentence 'She really doesn't care whether she lives or dies', and 'positively' is an emphasizing adverb in the sentence 'He positively does not want to know anything about it'.

emphatic pronoun A reflexive pronoun that is used for emphasis, as in 'He knows himself that he is wrong', 'She admitted herself that she had made a mistake' and 'The teachers themselves say that the headmaster is too strict'.

-en A suffix with several functions. In one sense it indicates 'causing to be', as in broaden, darken, gladden, lighten and sweeten. It also indicates a diminutive or small version of something, as in chicken and maiden. It also indicates what something is made of, as in silken, wooden and woollen. It is also used to form the past participle of many irregular verbs, such as 'broken', 'fallen', 'forgotten' and 'taken'.

en- A prefix indicating 'causing to be', as in enrich and enlarge, and 'putting into', as in endanger, enrage, enslave.

ending The final part of a word consisting of an inflection that is added to a BASE or root word. The '-ren' part of 'children' is an ending, the '-er' of 'poorer' is an ending and the '-ing' of 'falling' is an ending.

epic A word that originally referred to a very long narrative poem dealing with heroic deeds and adventures on a grand scale, as Homer's *Iliad*. In modern usage it has been extended to include novels or films with some of these qualities.

epigram A figure of speech consisting of a brief, pointed and witty saying, as in Jonathan Swift's 'Every man desires to live long; but no man would be old' and Oscar Wilde's 'A cynic is a man who knows the price of everything and the value of nothing'. 'Epigram' originally referred to a short poem inscribed on a public monument or tomb.

epithet An adjective that describes a quality of a noun, as in 'a beautiful dress', 'an amazing story' and 'an enjoyable occasion'. It is also used to indicate a term of abuse, as in 'The drunk man let out a stream of epithets at the policeman.'

eponym A person after whom something is named. The name of the thing in question can also be referred to as an eponym, or it can be said to be **eponymous**, eponymous being the adjective from eponym. English has several eponymous words. Some of these are listed below together with their derivations:

Bailey bridge, a type of temporary military bridge that can be assembled very quickly, called after Sir Donald **Bailey** (1901–85), the English engineer who invented it.

Bowie knife, a type of hunting knife with a long curving blade, called after the American soldier and adventurer, James **Bowie** (1799–1836), who made it popular.

cardigan, a knitted jacket fastened with buttons called after the Earl of **Cardigan** (1797–1868) who was fond of wearing such a garment and was the British cavalry officer who led the unsuccessful Charge of the Light Brigade during the Crimean War (1854).

Celsius the temperature scale, called after the Swedish astronomer, Anders **Celsius** (1701–44).

freesia, a type og sweet-smelling flower, called after the German physician, Friedrich Heinrich Theodor **Freese** (died 1876).

garibaldi, a type of biscuit with a layer of currants in it, called after Giuseppe **Garibaldi** (1807–1882), an Italian soldier patriot who is said to have enjoyed such biscuits.

Granny Smith, a variety of hard green apple, called after the Australian gardener, Maria Ann Smith, known as **Granny Smith** (died 1870), who first grew the apple in Sydney in the 1860s.

greengage, a type of greenish plum, called after Sir William **Gage** who introduced it into Britain from France (1777–1864).

leotard, a one-piece, close-fitting garment worn by acrobats and dancers, called after the French acrobat, Jules **Leotard** (1842–70), who introduced the costume as a circus garment.

mackintosh, a type of raincoat, especially one made of rubberized cloth, called after the Scottish chemist, Charles **Mackintosh** (1766–1843), who patented it in the early 1820s.

praline, a type of confectionery made from nuts and sugar, is called after Count Plessis-**Praslin** (1598–1675), a French field marshal, whose chef is said to have been the first person to make the sweet.

plimsoll, a type of light rubber-soled canvas shoe, called after the English shipping reform leader, Samuel **Plimsoll** (1824–98). The shoe is so named because the upper edge of the rubber was thought to resemble the **Plimsoll** Line, the set of markings on the side of a ship which indicate the levels to which the ship may be safely loaded. The Plimsoll Line became law in 1876.

salmonella, the bacteria that causes some diseases such as food poisoning, called after Daniel Elmer **Salmon** (1850–1914), the American veterinary surgeon who identified it.

sandwich, a snack consisting of two pieces of buttered bread with a filling, called after the Earl of **Sandwich** (1718–92) who was such a compulsive gambler that he would not leave the gaming tables to eat, but had some cold beef between two slices of bread brought to him.

saxophone, a type of keyed brass instrument often used in jazz music, called after Adolphe **Sax** (1814–94), the Belgium instrument-maker who invented it.

shrapnel, an explosive projectile that contains bullets or fragments of metal and a charge that is exploded before impact, called after the British army officer, Henry **Shrapnel** (1761–1842), who invented it.

stetson, a type of wide-brimmed, high-crowned felt hat, called after its designer, the American hat-maker, John Batterson **Stetson** (1830–1906).

trilby, a type of soft felt hat with an indented crown, called after 'Trilby', the dramatized version of the novel by the English writer, George du Maurier. The heroine of the play, Trilby O'Ferrall, wore such a hat.

wellington, a waterproof rubber boot that extends to the knee, called after the Duke of **Wellington** (1769–1852), who defeated Napoleon at Waterloo (1815).

equative A term that indicates that one thing is equal to, or the same as, another. The verb 'to be' is sometimes known as an **equative verb** because it links a subject and complement that are equal to each other, as in 'He is a rogue' ('he' and 'rogue' refer to the same person) and 'His wife is a journalist' ('his wife' and 'journalist' refer to the same person). Other equative verbs include 'appear', 'become', 'look', 'remain' and 'seem', as in 'She looks a nasty person' and 'He became a rich man'. Such verbs are more usually known as **copular verbs**.

-er A suffix with several functions. It can indicate 'a person who does something', as in bearer, cleaner, employer, farmer, manager. Some words in this category can also end in '-or', as in adviser/advisor. It can also indicate 'a person who is engaged in something', as in lawyer. It also indicates 'a thing that does something', as in blender, cooker, mower, printer and strainer. It can also indicate the comparative form of an adjective, as in darker, fairer, older, shorter and younger. It can also indicate 'someone that comes from somewhere', as in Londoner.

-esque A suffix of French origin that means 'in the style or fashion of', as in Junoesque, statuesque, Picassoesque, Ramboesque.

-ese A suffix that indicates 'belonging to, coming from' and is used of people and languages, as Chinese, Japanese and Portuguese. By extension it refers to words indicating some kind of jargon, as computerese, journalese and officialese.

Esq. A word that can be used instead of 'Mr' when addressing an envelope to a man, as in 'John Jones, Esq.'. It is mostly used in formal contexts. Note that Esq. is used instead of 'Mr', not as well as it. It is usually spelt with a full stop.

-ess A suffix that was formerly widely used to indicate the feminine form of a word, as authoress from 'author', poetess from 'poet', editress from 'editor', and sculptress from 'sculptor'. In many cases the supposed male form, such as 'author', is now considered a neutral form and so is used of both a woman and a man. Thus a woman as well as a man may be an author, a poet, an editor and a sculptor, etc. Some words ending in -ess remain, as princess, duchess, heiress and hostess. Actress and waitress are still also fairly widespread.

-est A suffix that indicates the superlative forms of adjectives, as in biggest, hardest, lowest, smallest, ugliest.

etc The abbreviation of a Latin phrase *et cetera*, meaning 'and the rest, and other things'. It is used at the end of lists to indicate that there exist other examples of the kind of thing that has just been named, as in 'He grows potatoes, carrots, turnips, etc', 'The girls can play tennis, hockey, squash, etc', 'The main branch of the bank can supply francs, marks, lire, kroner, etc'. Etc is preceded by a comma and is also spelt with a full stop.

-ette A suffix indicating a diminutive or smaller version, as cigarette, kitchenette, rosette, serviette. It can also indicate 'imitation', as in flannelette, leatherette, satinette. It can also indicate 'female', as in majorette, usherette, suffragette. In this last sense it is sometimes used disparagingly, as in jockette (a derogatory word for a female jockey) and hackette (a derogatory word for a female journalist).

etymology The source of the formation of a word and the development of its meaning, as in 'What is the etymology of the word "biochemistry"?' It also means the branch of language studies that deals with the origin and development of words, as in 'He specializes in etymology'. In addition it refers to an account or statement of the formation of a word or phrase, as in 'Does that dictionary have etymologies?' In larger dictionaries it is usual to include etymologies, often at the end of each entry. These indicate which language the relevant word has been derived from, for example, whether it has come from Old English, Norse, Latin, Greek, French, German, Dutch, Italian, Spanish, etc. Alternatively they indicate which person, place, etc, the word has been named after. Some dictionaries also include the date at which the relevant word entered the English language. *See* BORROWING.

 Many words and phrases in the English language are of unknown or uncertain origin. In such cases much guesswork goes on and various suggestions put forward, most of which cannot be proved.

euphemism A term given to an expression that is a milder, more pleasant, less direct way of saying something that might be thought to be too harsh or direct. English has a great many euphemisms, many of these referring to certain areas of life. Euphemisms range from the high-flown, to the coy, to slang. Some examples of euphemisms and of the areas in which they tend to occur are listed below:

euphemisms for 'die' or 'be dead': be in the arms of Jesus, be laid to rest, be with one's maker, be no longer with us, be with the Lord, be written out of the script, bite the dust, cash in one's chips, croak, depart this life, go to a better place, go the way of all flesh, go to one's long home, go to the happy hunting grounds, have been taken by the grim reaper, have bought it, have breathed one's last, have gone to a better place, kick the bucket, meet one's end, pass away, pay the supreme sacrifice, pop off, push up the daisies, rest in peace, shuffle off this mortal coil, slip one's rope, turn up one's toes.

euphemisms for 'old': getting on a bit, not as young as one was, not in the first flush of youth, in the sunset years, in the twilight years, of advanced years, so many years young (as in '90 years young').

euphemisms for 'suicide': do away with oneself, die by one's own hand, end it all, make away with oneself, take one's own life, take the easy way out, top oneself.

euphemisms for 'to dismiss': declare (someone) redundant, deselect, dispense with (someone's) services, give early retirement to, give (someone) a golden handshake, give (someone) his/her marching orders, let (someone) go, not to renew (someone's) contract.

euphemisms for 'drunk': blotto, feeling no pain, happy, half-cut, legless, merry, one over the eight, plastered, three sheets to the wind, tiddly, tipsy, tired and emotional, squiffy, well-oiled.

euphemisms for 'naked': in a state of nature, in one's birthday suit, in the buff, in the nuddy, in the raw, starkers, without a stitch, wearing only a smile.

euphemisms for 'pregnant': awaiting the patter of tiny feet, expecting, expecting a happy event, in a delicate condition, in an interesting condition, in the club, in the family way, in the pudding club, up the pole, up the spout, with a bun in the oven.

euphemisms for 'to have sexual intercourse': be intimate with, do it, get one's end away, go to bed with, have it off with, make love, make out, sleep with, score.

euphemisms for 'sexual intercourse': hanky panky, intimacy, nookie, roll in the hay, rumpy pumpy/rumpty pumpty.

euphemisms for 'to go to the toilet': answer the call of nature, freshen up, go somewhere, pay a visit, powder one's nose, spend a penny, take a slash, wash one's hands.

euphemisms for 'toilet': bathroom, bog, can, john, karzy, powder room, rest room, the facilities, the conveniences, the geography of the house, the little boys' room/the little girls' room, the littlest room, the smallest room, the plumbing, wash room.

euphemisms and political correctness: Many of the expressions advocated by the politically correct movement for viewing physical and mental disabilities in a more positive light are in fact euphemisms. These include 'aurally challenged' for 'deaf', 'optically challenged' for 'blind', and 'uniquely abled' for 'physically disabled'.

Euro- A prefix meaning either 'referring to Europe', as in 'Eurovision', but more commonly now 'referring to the European Community', as in Euro-MP, Eurocrat, Eurocurrency.

every A word used with a singular noun to indicate that all the members of a group are being referred to. It takes a singular verb, as in 'Every soldier must report for duty', 'Every machine is to be inspected' and 'Every house has a different view'. Every should also be accompanied, where relevant, by a singular pronoun, as in 'Every boy has his job to do', 'Every girl is to wear a dress' and 'Every machine is to be replaced'. Problems arise when the sex of the noun to which every refers is unknown or unspecified. Formerly it was the custom to assume such a noun to be masculine and to use masculine pronouns, as in 'Every pupil is to behave himself properly. This assumption is now regarded as sexist, and to avoid this 'he/she', 'him/her' and 'his/her' can be used. Many people feel that this convention can become clumsy and prefer to be ungrammatical by using 'they', 'them' and 'their', as in 'Every pupil is to behave themselves properly.' Many sentences of this kind can be rephrased to avoid being either sexist or ungrammatical, as in 'All pupils are to behave themselves properly'. *See* EACH.

everyone A pronoun that takes a singular verb, as in 'Everyone is welcome' and 'Everyone has the right to a decent standard of living'. In order to be grammatically correct, it should be accompanied, where relevant, by a singular personal pronoun but it is subject to the same kind of treatment as EVERY.

ex- A prefix meaning 'former', as in ex-chairman, ex-president, ex-wife.

exclamation A word, phrase or sentence called out with strong feeling of some kind. It is marked by an **exclamation mark** which occurs at the end of the exclamation, as in 'Get lost!', 'What a nerve!', 'Help!', 'Ouch!' 'Well I never!', 'What a disaster!', 'I'm tired of all this!' and 'Let me out of here!' An **exclamatory question** is a sentence that is interrogative in form but is an exclamation in meaning, as in 'Isn't the baby beautiful!' and 'Isn't it lovely!'.

extra- A prefix meaning 'beyond, outside' as in extra-marital, extra-terrestrial, extra-curricular.

F

fable A story that is intended to convey a moral lesson. Fables frequently feature animals that speak and act like human beings. Most famous are those of Aesop, a Phrygian slave (620–560 BC), who wrote such fables as 'The Hare and the Tortoise' and 'The Fox and the Grapes'.

false friends A term for words that have the same or similar forms in different languages but have different meanings in each. For example, the French word *abusif* and the English word 'abusive' are false friends. *Abusif* does not mean 'abusive' but 'incorrect, illegal, unauthorized, excessive'. Similarly, the French word *actuel* and the English 'actual' are false friends. *Actuel* does not mean 'actual' but 'present-day'. Similarly, the

French *eventuel* and Italian *eventuale* are false friends with the English 'eventual'. *Eventuel* and *eventuale* do not mean 'eventual' but 'possible', while *sensible* in French and *sensibile* in Italian do not mean 'sensible, having good sense or judgement' but 'sensitive, tender, touchy'.

feminine The term for the GENDER that indicates female persons or animals. It is the opposite of 'masculine'. The feminine gender demands the use of the appropriate pronoun, including 'she', 'her', 'hers' and 'herself', as in 'The girl tried to save the dog but *she* was unable to do so', 'The woman hurt *her* leg', 'Mary said that the book is *hers*', and 'The waitress cut *herself*'.

The feminine forms of words, formed by adding *—ess*, used to be common but many such forms are now thought to be sexist. Words such as 'author', 'sculptor', 'poet' are now considered to be neutral terms that can be used to refer to a man or a woman. Some *-ess* words are either still being used or are in a state of flux, as in 'actress'. See -ESS.

few and **a few** These are not interchangeable. Both expressions mean 'some, but not many', but they convey different impressions. **Few** is the opposite of 'many', as in 'We have few resources' and 'We have few ideas left'. **A few** conveys a more positive impression and is the opposite of 'none', as in 'We have a few pounds set aside for Christmas' and 'We have not reached a definite decision but we have a few ideas in hand'. The sentence 'We have few ideas left' indicates a negative situation, that 'we' are running out of 'ideas', but the sentence 'We have a few ideas in hand' conveys a positive impression.

fewer and **less** These are liable to be used wrongly. **Fewer** means 'a smaller number of' and should be used with plural nouns, as in 'fewer problems', 'fewer resources', 'fewer fears', 'fewer boxes', 'fewer books', 'fewer bottles' and 'fewer chairs'. **Less** means 'a smaller amount of' and should be used with singular nouns, as in 'less responsibility', 'less anxiety', 'less work', 'less milk', 'less wood' and 'less material'. It is a very common error to use less where fewer is correct, as in 'less bottles' and 'less queues'.

figurative A term that refers to words that are not used literally. For example, 'mine' in the sense of 'excavation in the earth from which coal, tin, etc, is taken' is a literal use of the word. 'Mine' in the sense of 'He is a mine of information' is a figurative use of the word. There are many figurative expressions in English. These include 'take the bull by the horns', 'put one's shoulder to the wheel', 'hide one's light under a bushel', 'be in seventh heaven', 'count one's chickens', 'change horses in mid-stream', 'blow hot and cold', 'run with the hare and hunt with the hounds', 'make the feathers fly', 'put the cat among the pigeons', 'cut corners', 'cry over spilt milk', 'jump on the bandwagon', 'let the grass grow under one's feet', 'drop a brick', 'burn the midnight oil', 'show a clean pair of heels', 'turn one's coat', 'drive a coach and horses through' and 'take coals to Newcastle'.

figure of speech A form of expression used to heighten the effect of a statement. The most commonly known are SIMILES and METAPHORS, but there are many more, such as PERSONIFICATION. *See* individual entries for further information.

finite clause A clause that contains a FINITE VERb, as in 'when she sees him', 'after she had defeated him', and 'as they were sitting there'.

finite verb A verb that has a tense and has a subject with which it agrees in number and person. For example 'cries' is finite in the sentence 'The child cries most of the time', and 'looks' is finite in the sentence 'The old man looks ill'. However 'go' in the sentence 'He wants to go' is non-finite since it has no variation of tense and does not have a subject. Similarly in the sentence 'Sitting on the river-bank, he was lost in thought', 'sitting' is non-finite.

first person This refers to the person who is speaking or writing when referring to himself or herself. The **first person pronouns** are 'I', 'me', 'myself' and 'mine', with the plural forms being 'we', 'us', 'ourselves' and 'ours'. Examples include 'She said, "*I* am going home"', "*I* am going shopping," he said', "*We* have very little money left," she said to her husband' and 'He said, "*We* shall have to leave now if we are to get there on time"'. The **first person determiners** are 'my' and 'our', as in 'I have forgotten to bring *my* notebook' and 'We must remember to bring *our* books home.'

fixed phrase, also called **set phrase** A phrase that has no, or virtually no, variants, as in 'from bad to worse', 'to and fro', 'hither and thither', 'horse and cart', 'this and that', 'alas and alack' and 'rough and ready'.

-fold A suffix meaning 'times, multiplied by', as in fourfold, a hundredfold.

for- A prefix derived from Old English with several meanings. These include 'prohibition', as in forbid; 'abstention' as in forbear, forgo and forswear; 'neglect', as in forsake; 'excess, intensity', as in forlorn; and 'away, off, apart', as in forgive.

fore- A prefix derived from Old English meaning 'before', as in forecast, forestall, foretell, forewarn, foregoing and forefathers. It can also mean 'front', as in foreleg, forehead, forepart.

foreign plural A plural of a word in English that has retained the plural form of the foreign word from which the English word has been derived. Examples include 'phenomena' from 'phenomenon', 'crises' from 'crisis' and 'criteria' from 'criterion'. There is a modern tendency to anglicize some of the foreign plural forms. In some cases the foreign plural form and the anglicized form exist alongside each other as 'formulae/formulas', 'thesauri/thesauruses', 'radii/radiuses', 'indices/indexes' and 'bureaux/bureaus'.

foreign expression An expression that has been adopted into English but not 'naturalized' and is sometimes written in italic type, as in *bête noire* (a fear or obsession), *rara avis* (a rarity), *en passant* (in passing), *hors de combat*, (out of the contest, disabled), *en route* (on the way), *bon mot* (witty saying), *in toto* (completely), *in flagrante delicto* (in the very act of committing an offence), *enfant terrible* (a person who causes embarrassment by indiscreet or outrageous behaviour), *en famille* (with one's family) and *inter alia* (among other things).

-form A suffix meaning 'having the form of', as in cruciform, or 'having such a number of', as in uniform, multiform.

formal The term used to refer to speech and writing that is characterized by more complicated and more difficult language and by more complicated grammatical structures. Short forms and contractions are avoided in formal speech and writing. *See* INFORMAL.

formula A set phrase that is used in certain conventions, as in 'How do you do?', 'Yours faithfully', 'Yours sincerely', 'Kind regards', 'See you later', 'Nice to see you!' and 'Many happy returns'.

form word *see* **function word.**

fragmentary sentence *see* **major sentence.**

-free A suffix used to form adjectives indicating 'absence of, freedom from', as in carefree, trouble-free, anxiety-free, tax-free, duty-free, additive-free, lead-free.

-friendly A modern suffix formed on analogy with 'user-friendly' to mean 'helpful to, supporting', as in child-friendly, environment-friendly and ozone-friendly.

frequentative A term referring to a verb that expresses frequent repetition of an action. In English the verb endings *-le* and *-el* sometimes indicate the frequentative form, as in 'waddle' from 'wade', 'sparkle' from 'spark', 'crackle' from 'crack' and 'dazzle' from 'daze'. The ending *-er* can also indicate the frequentative form, as in 'stutter', 'spatter' and 'batter'.

-ful A suffix indicating 'the amount that fills something', as in bucketful, basinful, handful, spoonful, bagful and pocketful. It can also mean 'full of', as in beautiful, truthful and scornful. It can also mean 'having the qualities of', as in masterful, and 'apt to, able to', as in forgetful, mournful and useful.

full stop A punctuation mark consisting of a small dot (.). Its principal use is to end a sentence that is not a question or an exclamation, as in 'They spent the money.', 'She is studying hard.', 'He has been declared redundant and is very upset.' and 'Because she is shy, she rarely goes to parties.'

The full stop is also used in decimal fractions, as in '4.5 metres', '6.3 miles' and '12.2 litres'. It can also be used in dates, as in '22.2.94', and in times, as in '3.15 tomorrow afternoon'.

In modern usage the tendency is to omit full stops from abbreviations. This is most true of abbreviations involving initial capital letters as in TUC, BBC, EEC and USA. In such cases full stops should definitely not be used if one or some of the initial letters do not belong to a full word. Thus, television is abbreviated to TV and educationally subnormal to ESN.

There are usually no full stops in abbreviations involving the first and letters of a word (contractions) Dr, Mr, Rd, St, but this is a matter of taste.

Abbreviations involving the first few letters of a word, as in 'Prof' (Professor) are the most likely to have full stops, as in 'Feb.' (February), but again this is now a matter of taste.

For the use of the full stop in direct speech *see* DIRECT SPEECH. The full stop can also be called **point** or **period**.

function word A word that has very little meaning but is primarily of grammatical significance and merely performs a 'function' in a sentence. Function words include determiners, and prepositions such as in, on and up. Words that are not function words are sometimes known as **content words**.

Function word is also known as **form word** or **structure word**.

future perfect tense The TENSE of a verb that is formed by 'will' or 'shall' together with the perfect tense, as in 'They will have been married ten years next week', 'You will have finished work by this time tomorrow' and 'By the time Jane arrives here she will have been travelling non-stop for forty-eight hours'.

future tense The TENSE of a verb that describes actions or states that will occur at some future time. It is marked by 'will' and 'shall'. Traditionally 'shall' was used with subjects in the first person, as in 'I shall see you tomorrow' and 'We shall go there next week', and 'will' was used with subjects in the second and third person, as in 'You will find out next week', 'He will recognize her when he sees her' and 'They will be on the next train'. Formerly 'will' was used with the first person and 'shall' with the second and third person to indicate emphasis or insistence, as in 'I *will* go on my own' and 'We *will* be able to afford it'; 'You *shall* pay what you owe' and 'The children *shall* get a holiday'. In modern usage 'shall' is usually used only for emphasis or insistence, whether with the first, second or third person, except in formal contexts. Otherwise 'will' is used, as in 'I will go tomorrow', 'We will have to see', 'You will be surprised', and 'They will be on their way by now'.

The future tense can also be marked by 'be about to' plus the infinitive of the relevant verb or 'be going to' plus the infinitive of the relevant verb. Examples include 'We are about to leave for work', 'They are about to go on holiday', 'She is going to be late' and 'They are going to demolish the building'.

G

-gate A modern suffix that is added to a noun to indicate something scandalous. Most of the words so formed are short-lived and forgotten about almost as soon as they are invented. In modern usage they are frequently used to apply to sexual scandals, but originally -gate was restricted to some form of political scandal. The suffix is derived from Watergate, and refers to a political scandal in the United States during President Richard Nixon's re-election campaign in 1972, when Republican agents were caught breaking into the headquarters of the Democratic Party in Washington, which were in a building called the Watergate Building. The uncovering of the attempts to cover up the break-in led to Richard Nixon's resignation.

gemination The doubling of consonants before a suffix. *See* DOUBLING OF CONSONANTS.

gender In the English language this usually refers to the natural distinctions of sex (or absence of sex) that exist, and nouns are classified according to these distinctions— masculine, feminine and neuter. Thus, 'man', 'boy', 'king', 'prince', 'emperor', 'duke', 'heir', 'son', 'brother', 'father', 'nephew', 'husband', 'bridegroom', 'widower', 'hero', 'cock', 'drake', 'fox' and 'lion' are masculine nouns. Similarly, 'girl', 'woman', 'queen', 'princess', 'empress', 'duchess', 'heiress', 'daughter', 'sister', 'mother', 'niece', 'wife', 'bride', 'widow', 'heroine', 'hen', 'duck', 'vixen' and 'lioness' are feminine nouns. Similarly, 'table', 'chair', 'desk', 'carpet', 'window', 'lamp', 'car', 'shop', 'dress', 'tie', 'newspaper', 'book', 'building' and 'town' are all neuter.

Some nouns in English can refer either to a man or a woman, unless the sex is indicated in the context. Such neutral nouns are sometimes said to have DUAL GENDER. Examples include 'author', 'singer', 'poet', 'sculptor', 'proprietor', 'teacher', 'parent', 'cousin', 'adult' and 'child'. Some words in this category were formerly automatically assumed to be masculine and several of them had feminine forms, such as 'authoress', 'poetess', 'sculptress' and 'proprietrix'. In modern times this was felt to be sexist and many of these feminine forms are now rarely used, for example, 'authoress' and 'poetess'. However some, such as actress and waitress, are still in common use. *See* - ESS.

In many languages grammatical gender plays a major part. In French, for example, all nouns are divided into masculine and feminine, and there is no neuter classification. Masculine nouns are preceded by *le* (definite article). Thus 'ceiling' is masculine (*le plafond*), 'hat' is masculine (*le chapeau*) and 'book' is masculine (*le livre*). Feminine nouns are preceded by *la* (definite article). Thus 'door' is feminine (*la porte*), 'dress' is feminine (*la robe*), and 'window' is feminine (*la fenêtre*).

In German there are three grammatical genders—masculine, feminine and neuter. Masculine nouns are preceded by *der* (definite article) as *der Stuhl* (the chair); feminine nouns are preceded by *die* (definite article) as *die Brücke* (the bridge); neuter nouns are preceded by *das*, as *das Brot* (bread).

Grammatical gender in English is not relevant except in the third personal singular pronouns, as 'he/him/his/himself', 'she/her/hers/herself' and 'it/it/its/itself'. Traditionally 'he', etc, was considered an acceptable pronoun not just for nouns of the masculine gender, but also for those of neutral or dual gender as well. Thus 'Every student must check that he has registered for the exam' was considered acceptable, as was 'Each passenger must be responsible for his own luggage'. Nowadays such sentences are considered sexist. In order to avoid this, some people use the 'he/she', 'his/her', etc, convention, as in 'Every employee must supply his/her own transport' and 'Each candidate must hand in his/her application form now'. People who feel this is clumsy sometimes prefer to be ungrammatical and use a plural pronoun, as in 'Every writer was told to collect their manuscripts in person' and 'Every pupil was told that they would have to be back in school by four o'clock'. It is sometimes possible to avoid being both sexist and ungrammatical by rephrasing such sentences in the plural, as in 'All pupils were told that they would have to be back in school by four o'clock'.

genitive case A case that indicates possession or ownership. It is usually marked by *s* and an apostrophe. Many spelling errors centre on the position of the *s* in relation to the apostrophe.

Nouns in the genitive case are usually formed by adding *'s* to the singular noun, as in 'the girl's mother', and Peter's car'; by adding an apostrophe to plural nouns that end in *s*, as in 'all the teachers' cars' and 'the doctors' surgeries'; by adding *'s* to irregular plural nouns that do not end in *s*, as in 'women's shoes'.

In the genitive form of a name or singular noun that ends in *s*, *x* or *z*, the apostrophe may or may not be followed by *s*. In words of one syllable the final *s* is usually added, as in 'James's house', 'the fox's lair', 'Roz's dress'.

The final *s* is most frequently omitted in names, particularly in names of three or more syllables, as in 'Euripides' plays'.

In many cases the presence or absence of final *s* is a matter of convention.

Apostrophes are often omitted wrongly in modern usage, particularly in the media and by advertisers, as in 'womens hairdressers', 'childrens helpings'. In addition, apostrophes are frequently added erroneously (as in 'potato's for sale' and 'Beware of the dog's'). This is partly because people are unsure about when and when not to use them and partly because of a modern tendency to punctuate as little as possible.

A group genitive occurs when more than one noun is involved, as in 'Gilbert and Sullivan's operas'. Note there is only one apostrophe *s*.

The alternative genitive construction involves the use of 'of', as in 'the mother of the girl', 'the uncle of the little girl', 'the pages of the newspaper' and 'the leg of the chair'. In general, proper nouns and animate beings tend to take the apostrophe and *s* ending and inanimate objects tend to take the 'of' construction.

geo- A prefix derived from Greek indicating 'earth', as in geography, geology, geomagnetic and geophysics.

geographical features These should be written with initial capital letters. They include the common nouns that are part of the name of the feature, as in Niagara Falls, Atlantic Ocean, River Thames, Mount Everest and Devil's Island.

gerund The *-ing* form of a verb when it functions as a noun. It is sometimes known as a **verbal noun**. It has the same form as the present participle but has a different function. For example, in the sentence 'He was jogging down the road', 'jogging' is the present participle in the verb phrase 'was jogging', but in the sentence 'Running is his idea of relaxation', 'running' is a gerund because it acts as a noun as the subject of the sentence. Similarly, in the sentence 'We were smoking when the teacher found us', 'smoking' is the present participle in the verb phrase 'were smoking', but in the sentence 'We were told that smoking is bad for our health', 'smoking' is a gerund since it acts as a noun as the subject of the clause.

get This verb is sometimes used to form the passive voice instead of the verb 'to be'. The use of the verb 'to get' to form the passive, as in 'They get married tomorrow', 'Our team got beaten today' and 'We got swindled by the con man' is sometimes considered to be more informal than the use of 'be'. Often there is more action involved when the get construction is used than when be is used, since get is a more dynamic verb, as in 'She was late leaving the pub because she got involved in an argument' and in 'It was her own fault that she got arrested by the police. She hit one of the constables'.

Get is frequently overused. Such overuse should be avoided, particularly in formal contexts. Get can often be replaced by a synonym such as 'obtain', 'acquire', 'receive', 'get hold of', etc. Thus, 'If you are getting into money difficulties you should get some financial advice. Perhaps you could get a bank loan' could be rephrased as 'If you are in financial difficulty you should obtain some financial help. Perhaps you could receive a bank loan'.

Got, the past tense of get, is often used unnecessarily, as in 'She has got red hair and freckles' and 'We have got enough food to last us the week'. In these sentences 'has' and 'have' are sufficient on their own.

gliding vowel means the same as **diphthong**.

goal This can be used to describe the recipient of the action of a verb, the opposite of 'agent' or 'actor'. Thus, in the sentence 'The boy hit the girl', 'boy' is the 'agent' or 'actor' and 'girl' is the goal. Similarly, in the sentence 'The dog bit the postman', 'dog' is the 'agent' or 'actor' and 'postman' is the goal.

gobbledygook A noun that is used informally to refer to pretentious and convoluted language of the type that is found in official documents and reports. It is extremely difficult to understand and should be avoided and 'plain English' used instead.

govern A term that is used of a verb or preposition in relation to a noun or pronoun to indicate that the verb or preposition has a noun or pronoun depending on it. Thus, in the phrase 'on the table', 'on' is said to govern 'table'.

gradable A term that is used of adjectives and adverbs to mean that they can take degrees of comparison. Thus 'clean' is a gradable adjective since it has a comparative form (cleaner) and a superlative form (cleanest). 'Soon' is a gradable adverb since it has a comparative form (sooner) and a superlative form (soonest). Such words as 'supreme', which cannot normally have a comparative or superlative form, are called **non-gradable**.

-gram A suffix derived from Greek indicating 'writing' or 'drawing', as in telegram, electrocardiogram and diagram. It is also used in modern usage to indicate a 'greeting' or 'message', as in kissogram.

-graph A suffix derived from Greek indicating 'written, recorded, represented', as in autograph, monograph, photograph. It is also used to indicate 'an instrument that records', as in seismograph, tachograph and cardiograph.

group noun means the same as **collective noun.**

gynaec-, gynaeco- A prefix derived from Greek indicating 'female, woman', as in gynaecology, gynaecium.

H

habitual A term used to refer to the action of a verb that occurs regularly and repeatedly. The **habitual present** is found in such sentences as 'He goes to bed at ten every night', 'She always walks to work' and 'The old man sleeps all day'. This is in contrast to the **stative present**, which indicates the action of the verb that occurs at all times, as in 'Cows chew the cud', 'Water becomes ice when it freezes', 'Children grow up' and 'We all die'. Examples of the **habitual past** tense include; 'They travelled by train to work all their lives', 'We worked twelve hours a day on that project' and 'She studied night and day for the exams'.

-hand A suffix meaning 'worker', as in deckhand, farmhand and cowhand. It can also mean 'position', as in right-hand and left-hand.

haem-, haemo- A prefix derived from Greek meaning 'blood', as in haemorrhage, haematology and haematoma.

haiku A short Japanese poem in three unrhymed lines with an exact number of syllables per line, the syllable pattern being 5-7-5. The traditional subject matter is usually something to do with nature. A master of the form was the 17th-century Japanese poet Basho, and the following is one of his haiku:

> The | white | chry|san|themum
> Even | when | lif|ted | to | the | eye
> Re|mains | im|macu|late.

half and **halve** These are liable to be confused. **Half** is a noun and **halve** is a verb. Half is followed by a singular noun when it is referring to an amount, as in 'Half of the milk has gone sour' and 'Half the money is hers'. It is followed by a plural verb when it is referring to a number, as in 'Half of the people are still undecided' and 'Half of the sweets are for the younger children'. The plural of half is **halves**, as in 'They cut the

hanged

oranges in two and distributed the halves to the members of the two teams'.

The plural noun halves is liable to be confused with the verb **halve**. Examples of the noun halves include 'They served halves of grapefruit for breakfast' and 'He split the estate into halves and left it to his son and daughter'. Examples of the verb halve include 'halve the grapefruit for breakfast' and 'He decided to halve his estate between his son and daughter'.

hanged and **hung** These are both past tense and past participles of the verb 'to hang' but they are not interchangeable. **Hung** is the more usual form, as in 'The children hung their outdoor clothes on pegs outside the classroom', 'They hung the portrait of her father in the dining room', 'Dark clouds of smoke hung over the city' and 'The boy has hung around with the same crowd of friends for years'.

Hanged is restricted to the meaning 'suspended by the neck until dead', as in 'They hanged him for the murder of his wife in the 1920s', 'The murderer took his own life before he could be hanged', 'They had to break the news to the children that their father had hanged himself' and 'She hanged herself while the balance of her mind was disturbed'

hanging participle *see* **dangling participle.**

have A verb that has several functions. A major use is its part in forming the 'perfect tense' and 'past perfect tense', or 'pluperfect tense', of other verb tenses. It does this in conjunction with the 'past participle' of the verb in question.

The perfect tense of a verb is formed by the present tense of the verb have and the past participle of the verb. Examples include 'We have acted wisely', 'They have beaten the opposition', 'The police have caught the thieves', 'The old man has died', 'The child has eaten all the food', 'The baby has fallen downstairs', 'They have grabbed all the bargains', 'You have hated him for years' and 'He has indicated that he is going to retire'. The past perfect or pluperfect is formed by the past tense of the verb have and the past participle of the verb in question, as in 'He had jumped over the fence', 'They had kicked in the door', 'The boy had led the other children to safety', 'His mother had made the cake', 'The headmaster had punished the pupils' and 'They had rushed into buying a new house'. Both perfect tenses and past perfect or pluperfect tenses are often contracted in speech or in informal written English, as in 'We've had enough for today', 'You've damaged the suitcase', 'You've missed the bus', 'He's lost his wallet', 'She's arrived too late', 'They'd left before the news came through', 'She'd married without telling her parents', 'He'd packed the goods himself' and 'You'd locked the door without realizing it'.

Have is often used in the phrase **have to** in the sense that something must be done. In the present tense have to can be used instead of 'must', as in 'You have to leave now', 'We have to clear this mess up', 'He has to get the next train' and 'The goods have to be sold today'. If the 'something that must be done' refers to the future the verb **will have to** is used, as in 'He will have to leave now to get there on time', 'The old man will have to go to hospital' and 'They'll have to move out of the house when her parents return'. If the 'something that must be done' refers to the past, **had to** is used, as in 'We had to take the injured man to hospital', 'They had to endure freezing conditions on the mountain', 'They'd to take a reduction in salary' and 'We'd to wait all day for the workman to appear'.

Have is also used in the sense of 'possess' or 'own', as in 'He has a swimming pool behind his house ', 'She has a huge wardrobe', 'We have enough food' and 'They have four cars'. In spoken or in informal English 'have got' is often used, as in 'They've got the largest house in the street', 'We've got problems now', 'They haven't got time'. This use should be avoided in formal English.

Have is also used to indicate suffering from an illness or disease, as in 'The child has measles', 'Her father has flu' and 'She has heart disease'. Have can also indicate that an activity is taking place, as in 'She's having a shower', 'We're having a party', 'She is having a baby' and 'They are having a dinner party'.

he A personal pronoun that is used as the subject of a sentence or clause to refer to a man, boy, etc. It is thus said to be a 'masculine' personal pronoun. Since he refers to a third party and does not refer to the speaker or the person being addressed, it is a third-person pronoun. Examples include 'James is quite nice but he can be boring', 'Bob has got a new job and he is very pleased' and 'He is rich now but his parents are still very poor'.

He traditionally was used not only to refer to nouns relating to the masculine sex but also to nouns that are now regarded as being neutral or of DUAL GENDER. Such nouns include 'architect', 'artist', 'athlete', 'doctor', 'passenger', 'parent', 'pupil', 'singer', 'student'. Without further information from the context it is impossible to know to which sex such nouns are referring. In modern usage it is regarded as sexist to assume such words to be masculine by using he to refer to one of them unless the context indicates that the noun in question refers to a man or boy. Formerly it was considered acceptable to write or say 'Send a message to the architect who designed the building that he is to attend the meeting' whether or not the writer or speaker knew that the architect was a man. Similarly it was considered acceptable to write or say 'Please tell the doctor that he is to come straight away' whether or not the speaker or writer knew that the doctor was in fact a man. Nowadays this convention is considered sexist. In order to avoid sexism it is possible to use the convention 'he/she', as in 'Every pupil was told that he/she was to be smartly dressed for the occasion', 'Each passenger was informed that he/she was to arrive ten minutes before the coach was due to leave' and 'Tell the doctor that he/she is required urgently'. However this convention is regarded by some people as being clumsy, particularly in spoken English or in informal written English. Some people prefer to be ungrammatical and use the plural personal pronoun 'they' instead of 'he/she' in certain situations, as in 'Every passenger was told that they had to arrive ten minutes before the coach was due to leave' and 'Every student was advised that they should apply for a college place by March'. In some cases it may be possible to rephrase sentences and avoid being either sexist or ungrammatical, as in 'All the passengers were told that they should arrive ten minutes before the coach was due to leave' and 'All students were advised that they should apply for a college place by March'.

heading A word, phrase or sentence put at the top of a page, chapter, section, etc, of a book or other printed document. These are sometimes written with initial capital letters (except for articles or prepositions), as in 'Annual Report', 'Department Budget for the Year', 'The Year Ahead', 'What Went Wrong', 'Company Plans', 'Trading Outlook Overseas', but this is a matter of taste or of house style of the company or organization involved. Some people prefer to use lower-case letters except for the first word, as in 'Sales targets for the year', 'A review of export markets', and 'The way forward'. Headings can be underlined or placed in italic type or bold type to highlight them on the page.

headline The name given to the title of a newspaper article. From the very nature of headlines they are short, partly because of shortage of space and partly to capture the attention of the would-be reader. In order to achieve this, the definite and indefinite articles and other minor words tend to be omitted, the future tense represented by a to-infinitive, as in 'Prescription charges to rise', and the present tenses used for past events. **Headline language**, particularly that of tabloid newspapers which has to be especially succinct and eye-catching, can have an effect on the general language. Thus expressions such as 'tug-of-love', which describes the state of a child whose custody is being bitterly fought over by both parents, is now quite common in the general language but started out as a headline term. Other expressions that are typical of the language of the headlines include 'killing spree', which describes someone who loses control and kills, usually by shooting, several people indiscriminately, as in 'Local gunman goes on killing spree'. Another one is 'have-a-go', which describes an attempt by a member of the public to try and catch a criminal, as in 'Pensioner in have-a-go with bank-raider'. The language and style of headlines is frequently known as **headlinese**.

headword A word that is at the head of an entry in a dictionary or other reference book. It is also known as 'entry word' and is usually written in bold type so that it stands out on the page and is readily identifiable.

helping verb another name for **auxiliary verb**.

hemi- A prefix derived from Greek meaning 'half', as in hemisphere and hemiplegia.

hendiadys A figure of speech in which two nouns joined by 'and' are used to express an idea that would normally be expressed by the use of an adjective and a noun, as in 'through storm and weather' instead of 'through stormy weather'.

he/she *see* **he**.

her A personal pronoun. It is the third person singular, is feminine in gender and acts as the object in a sentence, as in 'We saw her yesterday', 'I don't know her', 'He hardly ever sees her', 'Please give this book to her', 'Our daughter sometimes plays with her' and 'We do not want her to come to the meeting'. *See* HE; SHE.

hers A personal pronoun. It is the third person singular, feminine in gender and is in the poassessive case. 'The car is not hers', 'I have forgotten my book but I don't want to borrow hers', 'This is my seat and that is hers', and 'These clothes are hers'. *See* HIS; HER and POSSESSIVE.

hetero- A prefix derived from Greek meaning 'other, another, different', as in heterodox and heterosexual.

hexa- A prefix derived from Greek meaning 'six', as in hexagram and hexagon.

hiatus A break in pronunciation between two vowels that come together in different syllables, as in 'Goyaesque' and 'cooperate'.

him The third person masculine personal pronoun when used as the object of a sentence or clause, as in 'She shot him', 'When the police caught the thief they arrested him' and 'His parents punished him after the boy stole the money'. Traditionally him was used to apply not only to masculine nouns, such as 'man' and 'boy', but also to nouns that are said to be 'of dual gender'. These include 'architect', 'artist', 'parent', 'passenger', 'pupil' and 'student'. Without further information from the context, it is not possible for the speaker or writer to know the sex of the person referred to by one of these words. Formerly it was acceptable to write or say 'The artist must bring an easel with him' and 'Each pupil must bring food with him'. In modern usage this convention is considered sexist and there is a modern convention that 'him/her' should be used instead to avoid sexism, as in 'The artist must bring an easel with him/her' and 'Each pupil must bring food with him/her'. This convention is felt by some people to be clumsy, particularly in spoken and in informal English, and some people prefer to be ungrammatical and use the plural personal pronoun 'them' instead, as in 'The artist must bring an easel with them' and 'Each pupil must bring food with them'. In some situations it is possible to avoid being either sexist or ungrammatical by rephrasing the sentence, as in 'All artists must bring easels with them' and 'All pupils must bring food with them'. *See* HE.

him/her *see* **him**.

his The third personal masculine pronoun when used to indicate possession, as in 'He has hurt his leg', 'The boy has taken his books home' and 'Where has your father left his tools?' Traditionally his was used to refer not only to masculine nouns, such as 'man', 'boy', etc, but to what are known as nouns 'of dual gender'. These include 'architect', 'artist', 'parent', 'passenger', 'pupil' and 'student'. Without further information from the context it is not possible for the speaker or the writer to know the sex of the person referred to by one of these words. Formerly it was considered acceptable to use his in such situations, as in 'Every pupil has to supply his own sports equipment' and 'Every passenger is responsible for his own luggage'. In modern usage this is now considered sexist and there is a modern convention that 'his/her' should be used instead to avoid sexism, as in 'Every pupil has to supply his/her own sports equipment' and 'Every passenger is responsible for his/her own luggage'. This convention is felt by some people to be clumsy, particularly when used in spoken or informal written English. Some people prefer to be ungrammatical and use the plural personal pronoun 'their', as in 'Every pupil must supply their own sports equipment' and 'Every passenger is to be responsible for their own luggage'. In some situations it is possible to avoid being sexist, clumsy and ungrammatical by rephrasing the sentence, as in 'All pupils must supply their own sports equipment' and 'All passengers are to be responsible for their own luggage.

his/her see **his.**

holidays These, in the sense of public holidays or festivals, should be written with an initial capital letter, as in Christmas Day, Easter Sunday, New Year and Independence Day.

holo- A prefix meaning 'complete, whole', as in holistic.

homo- A prefix derived from Greek meaning 'same', as in homogenous, homonym, homograph, homology, homophone and homosexual.

homograph A word that is spelt the same as another word but has a different meaning and pronunciation. Homographs include:

bow, pronounced to rhyme with 'how', a verb meaning 'to bend the head or body as a sign of respect or in greeting, etc', as in 'The visitors bowed to the emperor' and 'The mourners bowed their heads as the coffin was lowered into the grave'.

bow, pronounced to rhyme with 'low', a noun meaning 'a looped knot, a ribbon tied in this way', as in 'She tied her hair in a bow' and 'She wears blue bows in her hair'.

lead, pronounced 'leed', a verb meaning 'to show the way', as in 'The guide will lead you down the mountain'.

lead, pronounced 'led', a noun meaning 'a type of greyish metal', as in 'They are going to remove any water pipes made from lead'.

row, pronounced to rhyme with 'low', a noun meaning 'a number of people or things arranged in a line', as in 'The princess sat in the front row'.

row, pronounced to rhyme with 'how', a noun meaning 'a quarrel, a disagreement', as in 'He has had a row with his neighbour over repairs to the garden wall'.

slough, pronounced to rhyme with 'rough', a verb meaning 'to cast off', as in 'The snake had sloughed off its old skin'.

slough, pronounced to rhyme with 'how', a noun meaning 'a swamp', as in 'Get bogged down in a slough' and 'in the Slough of Despond'.

sow, pronounced to rhyme with 'low', a verb meaning 'to scatter seeds in the earth', as in 'In the spring the gardener sowed some flower seeds in the front garden'.

sow, pronounced to rhyme with 'how', a noun meaning 'a female pig', as in 'The sow is in the pigsty with her piglets'.

homonym A word that has the same spelling and the same pronunciation as another word but has a different meaning from it. Examples include:

bill, a noun meaning 'a written statement of money owed', as in 'You must pay the bill for the conversion work immediately', or 'a written or printed advertisement', as in 'We were asked to deliver handbills advertising the play'.

bill, a noun meaning 'a bird's beak', as in 'The seagull has injured its bill'.

fair, an adjective meaning 'attractive', as in 'fair young women'; 'light in colour', as in 'She has fair hair'; 'fine, not raining', as in 'I hope it keeps fair'; 'just, free from prejudice', as in 'We felt that the referee came to a fair decision'.

fair, a noun meaning 'a market held regularly in the same place, often with stalls, entertainments and rides' (now often simply applying to an event with entertainments and rides without the market), as in 'He won a coconut at the fair'; 'a trade exhibition', as in 'the Frankfurt Book Fair'.

pulse, a noun meaning 'the throbbing caused by the contractions of the heart', as in 'The patient has a weak pulse'.

pulse, a noun meaning 'the edible seeds of any of various crops of the pea family, as lentils, peas and beans', as in 'Vegetarians eat a lot of food made with pulses'.

row, a verb meaning 'to propel a boat by means of oars', as in 'He plans to row across the Atlantic single-handed'.

row, a noun meaning 'a number of people or things arranged in a line', as in 'We tried to get into the front row to watch the procession' and 'The gardener has planted rows of cabbages'.

homophone The term for a word that is pronounced in the same way as another but is spelt in a different way and has a different meaning. Some examples of homophones include the following:

aisle, a noun meaning 'a passage between rows of seats in a church, theatre, cinema etc', as in 'The bride walked down the aisle on her father's arm'.

isle, a noun meaning 'an island', as in 'the Isle of Wight'.

alter, a verb meaning 'to change', as in 'They have had to alter their plans'.

altar, a noun meaning 'in the Christian church, the table on which the bread and wine are consecrated for Communion and which serves as the centre of worship', as in 'The priest moved to the altar, from where he dispensed Communion', 'There is a holy painting above the altar'; or 'a raised structure on which sacrifices are made or incense burned in worship', as in 'The Druids made human sacrifices on the altar of their gods'.

ail, a verb meaning 'to be ill', as in 'The old woman is ailing'; 'to be the matter, to be wrong', as in 'What ails you?'

ale, a noun meaning 'a kind of beer', as in 'a pint of foaming ale'.

blew, a verb, the past tense of the verb 'blow', as in 'They blew the trumpets loudly'.

blue, a noun and adjective meaning 'a colour of the shade of a clear sky', as in 'She wore a blue dress'.

boar, a noun meaning 'a male pig', as in 'a dish made with wild boar'.

bore, a verb meaning 'to make tired and uninterested', as in 'The audience was obviously bored by the rather academic lecture'.

bore, a verb, the past tense of the verb 'bear', as in 'They bore their troubles lightly'.

cereal, a noun meaning 'a plant yielding grain suitable for food', as in 'countries which grow cereal crops' and 'a prepared food made with grain', as in 'We often have cereal for breakfast'.

serial, a noun meaning 'a story or television play which is published or appears in regular parts, as in 'the final instalment of the magazine serial which she was following'.

cite, a verb meaning 'to quote or mention by way of example or proof', as in 'The lawyer cited a previous case to try and get his client off'.

sight, a noun meaning 'the act of seeing', as in 'They recognized him at first sight'.

site, a noun meaning 'a location, place', as in 'They have found a site for the new factory'.

feat, a noun meaning 'a notable act or deed', as in 'The old man received an award for his courageous feat'.

feet, a noun, the plural form of 'foot', as in 'The child got her feet wet from wading in the puddle'.

none, a pronoun meaning 'not any', as in 'They are demanding money but we have none'.

nun, a noun meaning 'a woman who joins a religious order and takes vows of poverty, chastity and obedience', as in 'She gave up the world to become a nun'.

know, a verb meaning 'to have understanding or knowledge of', as in 'He is the only one who knows the true facts of the situation', and 'to be acquainted with', as in 'I met her once but I don't really know her'.

no, an adjective meaning 'not any', as in 'We have no food left'.

rite, a noun meaning 'a ceremonial act or words,' as in 'rites involving witchcraft'.

right, an adjective meaning 'correct', as in 'Very few people gave the right answer to the question'.

write, a verb meaning 'to form readable characters', as in 'he writes regularly for the newspapers'.

stare, a verb and noun meaning 'to look fixedly' and 'a fixed gaze', as in 'She stared at him in disbelief when he told her the news' and 'He has the stare of a basilisk'.

stair, a noun meaning 'a series of flights of stairs', as in 'The old lady is too feeble to climb the stairs to her bedroom'.

-hood A suffix meaning 'state, condition', as in babyhood, childhood, manhood, priest-hood, womanhood and widowhood.

hybrid A word that is formed from words or elements derived from different languages, such as 'television'.

hydro- A prefix derived from Greek meaning 'water, as in hydro-electric and hydropho-bia. It also means 'hydrogen', as in hydrochloride.

hyper- A prefix derived from Greek meaning 'over, above', as in hyperbole, hyperactive, hypercritical, hyperinflation and hypersensitive.

hyperbole A figure of speech consisting of exaggeration or over-statement, used for emphasis, as in 'I could eat a horse' and in 'I am boiling in this heat'.

hyphen A small stroke (-) that is used to join two words together or to indicate that a word has been broken at the end of a line because of lack of space. It is used in a variety of situations.

The hyphen is used as the prefixed element in a proper noun, as in 'pre-Christian', 'post-Renaissance', 'anti-British', 'anti-Semitic', 'pro-French' and 'pro-Marxism'. It is also used before dates or numbers, as in 'pre-1914', 'pre-1066', 'post-1920', 'post-1745'. It is also used before abbreviations, as in 'pro-BBC', 'anti-EEC' and 'anti-TUC'.

The hyphen is used for clarification. Some words are ambiguous without the presence of a hyphen. For example, 're-cover', as in 're-cover a chair', is spelt with a hyphen to differentiate it from 'recover', as in 'The accident victim is likely to recover'. Similarly, it is used in 're-form', meaning 'to form again', as in 'They have decided to re-form the society which closed last year', to differentiate the word from 'reform', meaning 'to improve, to become better behaved', as in 'He was wild as a young man but he has reformed now'. Similarly 're-count' in the sense of 'count again', as in 're-count the number of votes cast', is spelt with a hyphen to differentiate it from 'recount' in the sense of 'tell', as in 'recount what happened on the night of the accident'.

The hyphen was formerly used to separate a prefix from the main element of a word if the main element begins with a vowel, as in 'pre-eminent', but there is a growing tendency in modern usage to omit the hyphen in such cases. At the moment both 'pre-eminent' and 'preeminent' are found. However, if the omission of the hyphen results in double *i*, the hyphen is usually retained, as in 'anti-inflationary' and 'semi-insulated'.

The hyphen was formerly used in words formed with the prefix *non-*, as in 'non-functional', 'non-political', 'non-flammable' and 'non-pollutant'. However there is a growing tendency to omit the hyphen in such cases, as in 'nonfunctional' and 'non-pollutant'. At the moment both forms of such words are common.

The hyphen is usually used with 'ex-' in the sense of 'former', as in 'ex-wife' and 'ex-president'.

The hyphen is usually used when 'self-' is prefixed to words, as in 'self-styled', 'a self-starter' and 'self-evident'.

Use or non-use of the hyphen is often a matter of choice, house style or frequency of usage, as in 'drawing-room' or 'drawing room', and 'dining-room' or 'dining room'. There is a modern tendency to punctuate less frequently than was formerly the case and so in modern usage use of the hyphen in such expressions is less frequent. The length of compounds often affects the inclusion or omission of the hyphen. Compounds of two short elements that are well-established words tend not to be hyphenated, as in 'bedroom' and 'toothbrush'. Compound words with longer elements are more likely to be hyphenated, as in 'engine-driver' and 'carpet-layer'.

Some fixed compounds of two or three or more words are always hyphenated, as in 'son-in-law', 'good-for-nothing' and 'devil-may-care'

Some compounds formed from phrasal verbs are sometimes hyphenated and sometimes not. Thus both 'take-over' and 'takeover' are common, and 'run-down' and 'rundown' are both common. Again the use of the hyphen is a matter of choice. However some words formed from phrasal verbs are usually spelt without a hyphen, as in 'breakthrough'.

Compound adjectives consisting of two elements, the second of which ends in -*ed*, are usually hyphenated, as in 'heavy-hearted', 'fair-haired', 'fair-minded' and 'long-legged'.

Compound adjectives when they are used before nouns are usually hyphenated, as in 'gas-fired central heating', 'oil-based paints', 'solar-heated buildings' and 'chocolate-coated biscuits'.

Compounds containing some adverbs are usually hyphenated, sometimes to avoid ambiguity, as in 'his best-known opera', a 'well-known singer', 'an ill-considered venture' and 'a half-planned scheme'.

Generally adjectives and participles preceded by an adverb are not hyphenated if the adverb ends in -*ly*, as in 'a highly talented singer', 'neatly pressed clothes' and 'beautifully dressed young women'.

In the case of two or more compound hyphenated adjectives with the same second element qualifying the same noun, the common element need not be repeated but the hyphen should be, as in 'two- and three-bedroom houses' and 'long- and short-haired dogs'.

The hyphen is used in compound numerals from 21 to 99 when they are written in full, as in 'thirty-five gallons', 'forty-four years', 'sixty-seven miles' and 'two hundred and forty-five miles'. Compound numbers such as 'three hundred' and 'two thousand' are not hyphenated.

Hyphens are used in fractions, as in 'three-quarters', 'two-thirds', and 'seven-eighths'.

Hyphens are also used in such number phrases as 'a seventeenth-century play', 'a sixteenth-century church', 'a five-gallon pail', 'a five-year contract' and a 'third-year student'.

The other use of hyphens is to break words at the ends of lines. Formerly people were more careful about where they broke words. Previously, words were broken up according to etymological principles, but there is a growing tendency to break words according to how they are pronounced. Some dictionaries or spelling dictionaries give help with the division and hyphenation of individual words. General points are that one-syllable words should not be divided and words should not be broken after the first letter of a word or before the last letter. Care should be taken not to break up words, for example by forming elements that are words in their own right, in such a way as to mislead the reader. Thus divisions such as 'the-rapist' and 'mans-laughter' should be avoided.

hypo- A prefix derived from Greek meaning 'under', as in hypothermia, hypodermic.

I

I and me These are liable to be confused. They are both parts of the first person singular pronoun, but I acts as the subject of a sentence and me as the object. People often assume wrongly that me is less 'polite' than I. This is probably because they have been taught that in answer to such questions as 'Who is there?' the grammatically correct reply is 'It is I'. In fact, except in formal contexts, 'It is me' is frequently found in modern usage, especially in spoken contexts. Confusion arises as to whether to use I or me after 'between'. Since 'between' is followed by an object, me is the correct form. Thus it is correct to say 'Just between you and me, I think he is dishonest'. On the other hand, me, being an object, should not be used in such sentences as 'You and I have both been invited', 'May Jane and I play?' and 'The children and I are going to join you'. Me should, however, be used in such sentences as 'The cake was made by Mary and me', 'They were sitting in front of my son and me at the cinema' and 'My brother and father played against my mother and me', since in all these cases it is the object form of the first person singular that is required.

-ian A suffix either indicating 'a profession, job or pastime', as in comedian, musician, optician, physician, or indicating 'proper names', as in Dickensian, Orwellian and Shakesperian.

-iana A suffix form of -ANA, indicating 'memorabilia or collections relating to people or places of note', as in Victoriana and Churchilliana.

-ible *see* **adjectives.**

-ics A suffix indicating 'science' or 'study', as in 'acoustics', 'electronics', 'genetics', 'obstetrics', 'politics' and 'physics'.

ideogram A written character that symbolizes a word or phrase without indicating the pronunciation, such as £, &, +.

idiolect The speech habits, knowledge and command of language of an individual. This can vary considerably from person to person. For example, one person might have a much more formal idiolect than another.

idiom An expression whose meaning cannot be easily deduced from the individual meanings of the words it contains. Thus, in the expression 'know the ropes' one can know what 'know' means and know what 'ropes' means without being able to deduce the meaning of 'know the ropes'. In fact, 'know the ropes' is a nautical idiom. If a sailor was being taught the basics of seamanship in the days of sailing ships, he would have to be taught the mechanics of ropes which were an important part of sailing in those days. Hence, 'know the ropes' has come to mean 'to understand the procedures and details involved in something', as in 'When he first started the job the trainee mechanic felt really awkward and useless, but he when he knew the ropes he felt more confident and happier'.

Similarly, one can easily understand the meanings of the various individual words in the expression 'out on a limb', but it is not at all obvious that it means idiomatically 'in a risky and often lonely position', this being a reference to someone being stuck in an isolated and precarious position on the branch of a tree. This idiom is found in sentences such as 'The young designer has gone out on a limb and produced clothes that his boss says are too experimental for the mass market'. Literally it refers to a person or animal that has crawled so far out on a branch of a tree that he/she is in danger of falling or of not being able to crawl back to the main tree.

Similarly, in the expression 'throw someone to the lions' one can easily understand the meanings of the various individual words without realizing that the expression means 'deliberately to put someone in a difficult or dangerous position', as in 'All the teachers were responsible for the change in policy with regard to school uniform but they threw the deputy head to the lions when they asked him to address a parents' meeting on the subject'. In order to appreciate the meaning of the idiom fully, the reader or listener has to understand that the idiom refers to a supposed form of entertainment in ancient Rome in which prisoners were thrown to hungry wild animals to be attacked and killed (while spectators looked on enthusiastically).

Similarly, in the expression 'throw in the towel' one can easily understand the meanings of the various individual words without realizing that the phrase means 'to give in, to admit defeat', as in 'She tried to stand up to the bullies in her school but finally she threw in the towel and asked her parents to send her to another school'. This idiom comes from the world of boxing in which 'throwing in the towel' indicates a method of conceding defeat.

Similarly, understanding the individual words of the expression 'sell someone down the river' will not help one to understand that it means 'to betray or be disloyal to someone', as in 'The bank robber who was caught by the police refused to sell his associates down the river'. The origin here is slightly more obscure in that it refers historically to slave owners in the Mississippi states of the United States, who sold their slaves to buyers downstream in Louisiana where living and working conditions were much harder.

Such idioms as 'sell someone down the river' are known as 'opaque idioms' since there is no resemblance between the meaning of the individual words of the idiom and the idiom itself. Idioms such as 'keep a straight face' are known as 'transparent idioms' since, although they are not to be interpreted literally, it is reasonably obvious what they mean.

i.e. The abbreviation of the Latin phrase *id est*, which is used before explanations or amplifications of what has just been mentioned, as in 'He was a mercenary in the war, i.e. he fought for money' and 'She is agoraphobic, i.e. she is afraid of open spaces' and 'He is a bibliophile, i.e. he loves books'. It is usually spelt with a full stop after each of the letters.

if A CONJUNCTION that is often used to introduce a subordinate ADVERBIAL CLAUSE of condition, as in 'If he is talking of leaving he must be unhappy', 'If you tease the dog it will bite you', 'If he had realized that the weather was going to be so bad he would not have gone on the expedition', 'If I had been in charge I would have sacked him' and 'If it were a better organized firm things like that would not happen'.

If can also introduce a 'nominal' or 'noun clause', as in 'He asked if we objected' and 'She inquired if we wanted to go'.

-ify A suffix indicating 'making or becoming', as in beautify, clarify, dignify, purify, satisfy and simplify.

imperative mood The verb mood that expresses commands. The verbs in the following sentences are in the imperative mood: 'Go away!', 'Run faster!', 'Answer me!', 'Sit down!', 'Please get out of here!'. All of these expressions with verbs in the imperative mood sound rather imperious or dictatorial and usually end with an exclamation mark, but this is not true of all expressions with verbs in the imperative mood. For example, the following sentences all have verbs in the imperative mood: 'Have another helping of ice cream', 'Help yourself to more wine', 'Just follow the yellow arrows to the X-ray department', and 'Turn right at the roundabout'. Sentences with verbs in the imperative mood are known as **imperative sentences**.

imperfect A TENSE that denotes an action in progress but not complete. The term derives from the classification in Latin grammar and was traditionally applied to the 'past imperfect', as in 'They were standing there'. The imperfect has now been largely superseded by the progressive/continuous tense, which is marked by the use of 'be' plus the present participle. Continuous tenses are used when talking about temporary situations at a particular point in time, as in 'They were waiting for the bus'.

impersonal A verb that is used with a formal subject, usually 'it', as in 'It is raining' and 'They say it will snow tomorrow'.

indefinite article A and **an** are the forms of the indefinite article. The form a is used before words that begin with a consonant sound, as 'a box', 'a garden', 'a road', 'a wall'. The form an is used before words that begin with a vowel sound, as 'an apple', 'an easel', 'an ostrich', 'an uncle'. Note that it is the sound of the initial letter that matters and not the spelling. Thus a is used before words beginning with a *u* when they are pronounced with a *y* sound as though it were a consonant, as 'a unit', 'a usual occurrence'. Similarly, an is used, for example, before words beginning with the letter *h* where this is not pronounced, as in 'an heir', 'an hour', 'an honest man'.

Formerly it was quite common to use an before words that begin with an *h* sound and also begin with an unstressed syllable, as in 'an hotel (*ho-tel*)', 'an historic (*his-tor-ik*) occasion', 'an hereditary (*her-ed-it-ary*) disease'. It is now more usual to use a in such cases and ignore the question of the unstressed syllable.

indefinite pronouns These are used refer to people or things without being specific as to exactly who or what they are. They include 'everyone', 'everybody', 'everything', 'anyone', 'anybody', 'anything', 'somebody', 'someone', 'something' and 'nobody', 'no one', 'nothing', as in 'Everyone is to make a contribution', 'Anyone can enter', 'Something will turn up' and 'Nobody cares'.

independent clause A clause that can stand alone and make sense without being dependent on another clause, as in 'The children are safe'. MAIN CLAUSES are independent clauses. Thus in the sentence 'She is tired and she wants to go home', there are two independent clauses joined by 'and'. In the sentence 'She will be able to rest when she gets home', 'She will be able to rest' is an independent clause and 'when she gets home' is a DEPENDENT CLAUSE. In the sentence 'Because she is intelligent she thinks for herself', 'she thinks for herself' is an independent clause and 'because she is intelligent' is a dependent clause.

indicative mood The MOOD of a verb which denotes making a statement. The following sentences have verbs in the indicative mood: 'We go on holiday tomorrow', 'He was waiting for her husband', 'They have lost the match' and 'She will arrive this afternoon'. The indicative mood is sometimes known as the **declarative mood**. The other moods are THE IMPERATIVE MOOD and SUBJUNCTIVE MOOD.

indirect object An object that can be preceded by 'to' or 'for'. The indirect object usually refers to the person who benefits from an action or receives something as the result of it. In the sentence 'Her father gave the boy food', 'boy' is the indirect object and 'food' is the DIRECT OBJECT. The sentence could be rephrased as 'Her father gave food to the boy'. In the sentence 'He bought his mother flowers', 'his mother' is the indirect object and 'flowers' is the direct object. The sentence could have been rephrased as 'He bought flowers for his mother'. In the sentence 'They offered him a reward', 'him' is the indirect object and 'reward' is the direct object. The sentence could be rephrased as 'They offered a reward to him'.

indirect question A question that is reported in INDIRECT SPEECH, as in 'We asked them where they were going', 'They inquired why we had come' and 'They looked at us curiously and asked where we had come from'. Note that a question mark is not used.

indirect speech also known as **reported speech** A way of reporting what someone has said without using the actual words used by the speaker. There is usually an introductory verb and a subordinate 'that' clause, as in 'He said that he was going away', 'They announced that they were leaving next day' and 'She declared that she had seen him there before'. In DIRECT SPEECH these sentences would become 'He said, "I am going away"', 'They announced, "We are leaving tomorrow"' and 'She declared, "I have seen him there before"'. When the change is made from direct speech to indirect speech, the pronouns, adverbs of time and place and tenses are changed to accord with the viewpoint of the person doing the reporting.

infinitive The BASE form of a verb when used without any indication of person, number or tense. There are two forms of the infinitive. One is the **to infinitive** form, as in 'They wished to leave', 'I plan to go tomorrow', 'We aim to please' and 'They want to emigrate', 'To know all is to forgive all', 'To err is human', 'Pull the lever to open', 'You should bring a book to read', 'The child has nothing to do', 'She is not very nice to know' and 'It is hard to believe that it happened'. The other form of the infinitive is called the **bare infinitive**. This form consists of the base form of the verb without 'to', as in 'We saw him fall', 'She watched him go', 'They noticed him enter', 'She heard him sigh', 'They let him go', 'I had better leave' and 'Need we return' and 'we dare not go back'. See SPLIT INFINITIVE.

inflect When applied to a word, this means to change form in order to indicate differences of tense, number, gender, case, etc. Nouns inflect for plural, as in 'ships', 'chairs', 'houses' and 'oxen'; nouns inflect for possessive, as in 'boys'', 'woman's', 'teachers'', and 'parents''; some adjectives inflect for the comparative form, as in 'brighter', 'clearer', 'shorter' and 'taller'; verbs inflect for the third person singular present tense, as in 'hears', 'joins', 'touches' and 'kicks'; verbs inflect for the present participle, as in 'hearing', 'joining', 'touching' and 'kicking'; verbs inflect for the past participle, as in 'heard', 'joined', 'touched' and 'kicked'.

inflection The act of inflecting—*see* INFLECT. It also refers to an inflected form of a word or a suffix or other element used to inflect a word.

informal The term to describe a spoken or written style of language that has a simpler grammatical structure and simpler vocabulary, often involving vocabulary that is colloquial in nature or even slang.

infra- A prefix derived from Latin indicating 'below, beneath', as in infrared and infrastructure.

-ing form This form of a verb can be either a PRESENT PARTICIPLE or A gerund. Present participles are used in the formation of the progressive or continuous TENSES, as in 'We were looking at the pictures', 'Children were playing in the snow', 'They are waiting for the bus', 'Parents were showing their anger', 'He has been sitting there for hours'. Present participles can also be used in non-finite clauses or phrases, as in 'Walking along, she did not have a care in the world', 'Lying there, he thought about his life', 'Sighing, he left the room' and 'Smiling broadly he congratulated his friend'.

A large number of adjectives end in -ing. Many of these have the same form as the present participle of a transitive verb and are similar in meaning. Examples include 'an amazing spectacle', 'a boring show', 'an interesting idea', 'a tiring day', 'an exhausting climb' and 'aching limbs'. Some -ing adjectives are related to intransitive verbs, as 'existing problems', 'increasing responsibilities', 'dwindling resources', 'an ageing work force' and 'prevailing circumstances'. Some -ing adjectives are related to the forms of verbs but have different meanings from the verbs, as in 'becoming dress', 'an engaging personality', 'a dashing young man' and 'a retiring disposition'. Some -ing adjectives are not related to verbs at all. These include 'appetizing', 'enterprising', 'impending' and 'balding'. Some -ing adjectives are used informally for emphasis, as in 'a blithering idiot', 'a stinking cold' and 'a flaming cheek'.

Gerunds act as nouns and are sometimes known as **verbal nouns**. Examples include 'Smoking is bad for one's health', 'Cycling is forbidden in the park' and 'Swimming is his favourite sport'.

intensifier The term for an adverb that affects the degree of intensity of another word. Intensifiers include 'thoroughly' in 'We were thoroughly shocked by the news', 'scarcely' in 'We scarcely recognized them' and 'totally' in 'She was totally amazed'.

inter- A prefix of Latin origin indicating 'between', as in intercity, intercontinental and interstate.

interjection A kind of EXCLAMATION. Sometimes they are formed by actual words and sometimes they simply consist of sounds indicating emotional noises. Examples of interjections include 'Oh! I am quite shocked', 'Gosh! I'm surprised to hear that!', 'Phew! It's hot!', 'Ouch! That was my foot!', 'Tut-tut! He shouldn't have done that!' and 'Alas! She is dead.'

International Phonetic Alphabet A system of written symbols designed to enable the speech sounds of any language to be consistently represented. Some of the symbols are the ordinary letters of the Roman alphabet but some have been specially invented. The alphabet was first published in 1889 and is commonly known a **IPA**.

interrogative adjective or **determiner** An adjective or determiner that asks for information in relation to the nouns which it qualifies, as in 'What dress did you choose in the end?', 'What kind of book are you looking for?', 'Which house do you like best?', 'Which pupil won the prize?', 'Whose bike was stolen?' and 'Whose dog is that?'

interrogative adverb An adverb that asks a question, as in 'When did they leave?', 'When does the meeting start?', 'Where do they live?', 'Where was the stolen car found?', 'Where did you last see her?', 'Why was she crying?', 'Why have they been asked to leave?', 'How is the invalid?', 'How do you know that she has gone?' and 'Wherever did you find that?'

interrogative pronoun A pronoun that asks a question, as in 'Who asked you to do that?', 'Who broke the vase?', 'What did he say?, 'What happened next?', 'Whose are those books?', 'Whose is that old car?', 'To whom was that remark addressed?' and 'To whom did you address the package?'

interrogative sentence A sentence that asks a question, as in 'Who is that?', 'Where is he?', 'Why have they appeared?', 'What did they take away?, 'Which do you prefer?' and 'Whose baby is that?'. Sentences that take the form of an interrogative question do not always seek information. Sometimes they are exclamations, as in 'Did you ever see anything so beautiful?', 'Isn't she sweet?' and 'Aren't they lovely?'. Sentences that take the form of questions may really be commands or directives, as in 'Could you turn down that radio?', 'Would you make less noise?' and 'Could you get her a chair?'. Sentences that take the form of questions may function as statements, as in 'Isn't there always a reason?' and 'Haven't we all experienced disappointment?'. Some interrogative sentences are what are known as RHETORICAL QUESTIONS, which are asked purely for effect and require no answer, as in 'Do you think I am a fool?', 'What is the point of life?' and 'What is the world coming to?'.

intra- A prefix of Latin origin indicating 'within', as intramuscular, intra-uterine and intravenous.

intransitive verb A verb that does not take a DIRECT OBJECT, as in 'Snow fell yesterday', 'The children played in the sand', 'The path climbed steeply', 'Time will tell', 'The situation worsened', 'Things improved' and 'Prices increased'. Many verbs can be either TRANSITIVE or intransitive, according to the context. Thus 'play' is intransitive in the sentence 'The children played in the sand' but transitive in the sentence 'The boy plays the piano'. Similarly 'climb' is intransitive in the sentence 'The path climbs steeply' but transitive in the sentence 'The mountaineers climbed Everest'. Similarly 'tell' is intransitive in the sentence 'Time will tell' but transitive in the sentence 'He will tell his life story'.

introductory it The use of 'it' as the subject of a sentence in the absence of a meaningful subject. It is used particularly in sentences about time and the weather, as in 'It is midnight', 'It is dawn', 'It is five o'clock', 'It is twelve noon', 'It is raining', 'It was snowing', 'It was windy' and 'It was blowing a gale'.

intrusive r The pronunciation of the *r* sound between two words or syllables where the first of these ends in a vowel sound and the second begins with a vowel sound and where there is no 'r' in the spelling. It appears in such phrases as 'law and order', which is frequently pronounced as 'lawr and order'.

invariable A word whose form does not vary by inflection. Such words include 'sheep' and 'but'.

inversion The reversal of the usual word order. It particularly refers to subjects and verbs. Inversion is used in questions, in some negative sentences, and for literary effect. In questions, an AUXILIARY VERB is usually put in front of the subject and the rest of the verb group is put after the subject, as in 'Are you going to see her?' and 'Have they inspected the goods yet?'. The verb 'to do' is frequently used in inversion, as in 'Did he commit the crime?' and 'Do they still believe that?'. Examples of the use of inversion in negative sentences include 'Seldom have I witnessed such an act of selfishness', 'Never had she experienced such pain' and 'Rarely do we have time to admire the beauty of the countryside'. This use in negative sentences is rather formal.

Inversion frequently involves adverbial phrases of place, as in 'Beyond the town stretched field after field', 'Above them soared the eagle' and 'Along the driveway grew multitudes of daffodils'.

Inversion is also found in conditional clauses that are not introduced by conjunction, as in 'Had you arrived earlier you would have got a meal' and 'Had we some more money we could do more for the refugees'.

inverted commas or **quotation marks** or **quotes** These are used to enclose material that is part of DIRECT SPEECH. They can also be used instead of italic type in the titles of books, newspapers, magazines, plays, films, musical works, works of art, etc, as in 'The Times', 'Northanger Abbey' by Jane Austen, 'Two Gentlemen of Verona', 'The Silence of the Lambs' and 'The Mikado'. Inverted commas can also be used to emphasize or draw attention to a particular word or phrase, as in 'She wants to know how to spell "picnicked"'. Inverted commas can either be single or double. If a word, phrase or passage is already contained within quotes, one should use the opposite style of inverted commas to the set already in use, as in 'She asked how to pronounce "controversy"' or "She asked how to pronounce 'controversy'".

IPA *see* **International Phonetic Alphabet.**

irony The use of a word or words to convey something that is completely different from the literal meaning, as in 'I don't suppose you'd be interested to hear that your house has been burgled', 'So you've crashed the car. Thanks! That's a great help!' *See also* DRAMATIC IRONY.

irregular adjective An adjective that does not conform to the usual rules of forming the comparative and superlative (*see* COMPARISON OF ADJECTIVES). Many adjectives either add -*er* for the comparative and -*est* for the superlative, as in 'taller', 'shorter' and 'tallest', 'shortest' from 'tall' and 'short'. Some adjectives form their comparatives with 'more' and their superlatives with 'most', as in 'more beautiful', 'more practical' and 'most beautiful', 'most practical'. Irregular adjectives do not form their comparatives and superlatives in either of these ways. Irregular adjectives include:

positive	comparative	superlative
good	better	best
bad	worse	worst
little	less	least
many	more	most

irregular plural The plural form of a noun that does not form its plural in the regular way. Most nouns in English add -*s* to the singular form to form the plural form, as in 'boy' to 'boys'. Some add -*es* to the singular form to form the plural, as in 'church' to 'churches'. Nouns ending in a consonant followed by -*y* have -*ies* as a regular plural ending. Thus 'fairy' becomes 'fairies' and 'berry' becomes 'berries'. The foregoing are all examples of regular plurals.

Irregular plurals include words that are different in form from the singular forms and do not simply add an ending. These include 'men' from 'man', 'women' from 'woman' and 'mice' from 'mouse'. Some irregular plurals are formed by changing the vowel of the singular forms, as in 'feet' from 'foot', 'geese' from 'goose' and 'teeth' from 'tooth'. Some irregular plural forms are formed by adding -*en*, as 'oxen' from 'ox' and 'children' from 'child'. Some nouns ending in -*f* form plurals in -*ves*, as in 'loaf' to 'loaves', 'half' to 'halves', 'wife' to 'wives' and 'wolf' to 'wolves', but some have alternative endings, as 'hoof' to either 'hoofs' or 'hooves', and some form regular plurals unchanged, as 'roof' to 'roofs'. Some irregular plural forms are the original foreign plural forms of words adopted into English, for example 'stimuli' from 'stimulus', 'phenomena' from 'phenomenon', 'criteria' from 'criterion', 'larvae' from 'larva'. In modern usage there is a growing tendency to anglicize the plural forms of foreign words. Many of these co-exist with the plural form, for example 'thesauruses' and 'thesauri', 'formulas' and 'formulae', 'gateaus' and 'gateaux' and 'indexes' and 'indices'. Sometimes the anglicized plural formed according to the regular English rules differs slightly in meaning from the irregular foreign plural. Thus 'indexes' usually applies to guides in books and 'indices' is usually used in mathematics. Some nouns have irregular plurals in that the plural form and the singular form are the same. These include 'sheep', 'grouse' (the game-bird) and 'salmon'. Some nouns have a regular plural and an irregular plural form. Thus 'brother' has the plural forms 'brothers' and 'brethren', although 'brethren' is now mainly used in a religious context and is archaic in general English.

irregular sentence *see* **major sentence.**

irregular verb A verb that does not conform to the usual pattern of verbs in that some of its forms deviate from what one would expect if the pattern of regular verbs was being followed. There are four main forms of a **regular verb**—the INFINITIVE or base form, as in 'hint', 'halt', 'hate' and 'haul'; the third-person singular form, as 'hints', 'halts', 'hates' and 'hauls'; the -ING form or present participle, as 'hinting', 'halting', 'hating' and 'hauling'; the -*ed* form or 'past tense' or 'past participle', as 'hinted', 'halted', 'hated' and 'hauled'.

Irregular verbs deviate in some way from that pattern, in particular from the pattern of adding -*ed* to the past tense and past participle. They fall into several categories.

One category concerns those that have the same form in the past tense and past participle forms as the infinitive and do not end in -*ed*, like regular verbs. These include:

infinitive	past tense	past participle
bet	bet	bet
burst	burst	burst
cast	cast	cast
cost	cost	cost
cut	cut	cut
hit	hit	hit
hurt	hurt	hurt
let	let	let
put	put	put
run	run	run
set	set	set
shed	shed	shed
shut	shut	shut
slit	slit	slit
split	split	split
spread	spread	spread

Some irregular verbs have two past tenses and two past participles which are the same, as in:

infinitive	past tense	past participle
burn	burned, burnt	burned, burnt,
hang	hanged, hung,	hanged, hung,
kneel	kneeled, knelt,	kneeled, knelt

lean	leaned, leant	learned, learnt
leap	leaped, leapt,	leaped, leapt
learn	learned, learnt	learned, learnt
light	lighted, lit	lighted, lit
smell	smelled, smelt	smelled, smelt
speed	speeded, sped	speeded, sped
spill	spilled, spilt	spilled, spilt
spoil	spoiled, spoilt	spoiled, spoilt
wet	wetted, wet	wetted, wet

Some irregular verbs have past tenses that do not end in *-ed* and have the same form as the past participle. These include:

become	became	became
bend	bent	bent
bleed	bled	bled
breed	bred	bred
build	built	built
cling	clung	clung
come	came	came
dig	dug	dug
feel	felt	felt
fight	fought	fought
find	found	found
flee	fled	fled
fling	flung	flung
get	got	got
grind	ground	ground
hear	heard	heard
hold	held	held
keep	kept	kept
lay	laid	laid
lead	led	led
leave	left	left
lend	lent	lent
lose	lost	lost
make	made	made
mean	meant	meant
meet	met	met
pay	paid	paid
rend	rent	rent
say	said	said
seek	sought	sought
sell	sold	sold
send	sent	sent
shine	shone	shone
shoe	shod	shod
sit	sat	sat
sleep	slept	slept
slide	slid	slid
sling	slung	slung
slink	slunk	slunk
spend	spent	spent
spin	spun	spun

stand	stood	stood
stick	stuck	stuck
sting	stung	stung
strike	struck	struck
string	strung	strung
sweep	swept	swept
swing	swung	swung
teach	taught	taught
tell	told	told
think	thought	thought
understand	understood	understood
weep	wept	wept
win	won	won
wring	wrung	wrung

Some irregular verbs have regular past tense forms but two possible past participles, one of which is regular. These include:

infinitive	*past tense*	*past participle*
mow	mowed	mowed, mown
prove	proved	proved, proven
sew	sewed	sewn, sewed
show	showed	showed, shown
sow	sowed	sowed, sown
swell	swelled	swelled, swollen

Some irregular verbs have past tenses and past participles that are different from each other and different from the infinitive. These include:

infinitive	*past tense*	*past participle*
arise	arose	arisen
awake	awoke	awoken
bear	bore	borne
begin	began	begun
bid	bade	bidden
bite	bit	bitten
blow	blew	blown
break	broke	broken
choose	chose	chosen
do	did	done
draw	drew	drawn
drink	drank	drunk
drive	drove	driven
eat	ate	eaten
fall	fell	fallen
fly	flew	flown
forbear	forbore	forborne
forbid	forbade	forbidden
forgive	forgave	forgiven
forget	forgot	forgotten
forsake	forsook	forsaken
freeze	froze	frozen
forswear	forswore	forewarn
give	gave	given
go	went	gone

grow	grew	grown
hew	hewed	hewn
hide	hid	hidden
know	knew	known
lie	lay	lain
ride	rode	ridden
ring	rang	rung
saw	sawed	sawn
see	saw	seen
rise	rose	risen
shake	shook	shaken
shrink	shrank	shrunk
slay	slew	slain
speak	spoke	spoken
spring	sprang	sprung
steal	stole	stolen
stink	stank	stunk
strew	strewed	strewn
stride	strode	stridden
strive	strove	striven
swear	swore	sworn
swim	swam	swum
take	took	taken
tear	tore	torn
throw	threw	thrown
tread	trod	trodden
wake	woken	woke
wear	wore	worn
write	written	wrote

-ise and **-ize** These are both verb endings. In British English there are many verbs that can be spelt ending in either **-ise** or **-ize**, as 'computerise/ize', 'economise/ize', 'finalist/ize', 'hospitalise/ize', 'modernise/ize', 'organise/ize', 'realise/ize', 'theorise/ize'. There are a few verbs which cannot be spelt -ize. These include 'advertise', 'advise', 'comprise', 'despise', 'exercise', 'revise', 'supervise' and 'televise'.

-ish A suffix indicating 'somewhat', as in baldish, biggish, smallish, youngish, and 'nationality', as in Spanish, Turkish and Polish.

-ism A suffix indicating 'state, condition', as in absenteeism, alcoholism, fatalism, heroism and plagiarism, or indicating 'doctrine, movement, system, theory', as in Catholicism, Marxism and Thatcherism. It now also indicates 'discrimination', as in ageism, sexism, racism.

iso- A prefix indicating 'equal', as in isobar, isotherm and isosceles.

-ist A suffix indicating 'believer, supporter, practitioner', as in atheist, fascist, feminist and Methodist.

italic type A sloping typeface that is used for a variety of purposes. It is used to differentiate a piece of text from the main text, which is usually in Roman type. For example, it is used sometimes for the titles of books, newspapers, magazines, plays, films, musical works and works of art, as in 'he is a regular reader of *The Times*', 'She reads *Private Eye*', 'Have you read *Animal Farm* by George Orwell', 'He has never seen a production of Shakespeare's *Othello*', 'We went to hear Handel's *Messiah*', '*Mona Lisa* is a famous painting'. Sometimes such titles are put in quotation marks rather than in italic.

Italic type is also sometimes used for the names of ships, trains, etc, as in 'the launch of *The Queen Elizabeth II*', 'She once sailed in *The Queen Mary*' and 'Their train was called *The Flying Scotsman*'.

Italic type is also used for the Latin names of plants and animals, as in 'of the genus *Lilium*', 'trees of the genus *Pyrus*', '*Panthera pardus*' and '*Canis lupus*'.

Italic type is sometimes used for foreign words that have been adopted into the English language but have never been fully integrated. Examples include *bête noire*, *raison d'être*, *inter alia* and *Weltschmerz*.

Italic type can also sometimes be used to draw attention to a particular word, phrase or passage, as in 'How do you pronounce formidable?', or to emphasize a word or phrase, as in 'Is he *still* in the same job?'

-ite A suffix that can indicate 'believer, supporter, practitioner', as in Thatcherite and Trotskyite.

-itis A suffix indicating 'illness or disease', as in bronchitis, hepatitis and meningitis.

its and **it's** These are liable to be confused. **Its** is an adjective meaning 'belonging to it', as in 'The house has lost its charm' and 'The dog does not like its kennel'. **It's** means 'it is', as in 'Do you know if it's raining?' and 'It's not fair to expect her to do all the chores'.

-ize *see* **-ise.**

J

jargon A technical or specialist language used among members of a particular profession or area. It is often used as a derogatory term to describe unnecessarily obscure or pretentious language, used within a profession, that is incomprehensible to members of the public who might come into contact with it and require to know what is being talked about. Jargon should be avoided in any document or situation involving lay people who have no specialist knowledge of the subject being referred to or of the language associated with it. Jargon in some professions easily becomes GODDLEDEGOOK.

journalese A derogatory name for the style of writing and choice of vocabulary supposedly found in newspapers. It is usually the style of writing in tabloid newspapers, such as widespread use of clichés, sensational language and short sentences, that is meant by the term. *See* HEADLINE.

jussive A type of clause or sentence that expresses a command, as in 'Do be quiet! I'm trying to study', 'Let's not bother going to the party. I'm too tired', 'Would you pass me that book' and 'Look at that everybody! The river has broken its banks'.

just An adverb that indicates that something happened a short time previously. In British English it is usually used with the perfect tense of the verb that it accompanies, as in 'I have just finished work', 'We have just decided to buy a new car', 'You've just missed the bus' and 'She's just passed her driving test'.

In American English, just usually accompanies the past tense of the verb, and some speakers of British English do also, especially in an informal context, as in 'I just saw a bad accident on the motorway', 'We just noticed that it's snowing' and 'He just left'.

Just has more than meaning. It can also mean 'only' and 'exactly'. In the sense of 'only', care should be taken to position it in the correct place in the sentence. For example, in the sentence 'He drank just two glasses of wine', it means that he drank only two glasses of wine, but in the sentence 'He just drank two glasses of wine' it means that he very recently drank two glasses of wine. To add to the confusion, although people may be careful about the positioning of just in formal writing they tend not to be in informal writing or speech. Thus someone could say in reply to the questions 'How much has he had to drink? Is he fit to drive?', 'He just had two glasses of wine', meaning that that was all he had drunk. In speech the meaning is usually obvious from intonation and context.

Just can also be used in the sense of 'only' in such sentences as 'Just Peter went on holiday with his parents. The other children stayed at home' and 'Just one coat was left. The rest were sold early on'. Again care should be taken to place just before the word it refers to in order to avoid ambiguity.

Just can also mean 'exactly', as in 'I see you have a food processor. That's just what I need' and 'Where did you find that cape? That's just what I've been looking for'.

K

kibbutzim An example of an IRREGULAR PLURAL form. Most nouns in English form plurals by adding -s or -es to the singular form, as in 'book and books' and 'church and churches'. However several words of foreign origin which have been adopted into English but not fully integrated retain the plural form found in the foreign language. 'Kibbutz', meaning a communal settlement in Israel, is one such word. Of Hebrew origin, it retains the plural form kibbutzim. In some cases there is a growing tendency for foreign plurals to be anglicized, or to exist alongside an anglicized plural, as in 'thesauruses/thesauri', but this is not yet the case with kibbutzim.

kilo- A prefix indicating 'a thousand', as in kilogram, kilohertz, kilolitre, kilometre and kilowatt.

-kin A suffix that indicates 'a diminutive or smaller version', as in lambkin and mannikin.

kind A noun that can cause grammatical problems. It is used to refer to a class of people or things. Since it is a COUNTABLE NOUN, it should take the plural form 'kinds' after words such as 'all' and 'many', as in 'He met all kinds of people when he was travelling round the world', 'We found all kinds of treasure when we were clearing out the attic' and 'We found all kinds of wild flower in the meadows'. A singular noun should follow 'kinds of', as in 'We found all kinds of treasure', but it is quite common for people to use a plural noun instead, as in 'We found all kinds of treasures'. This is best restricted to informal or spoken use.

'These' and 'those' are frequently found preceding **kind of**, as in 'She doesn't like these kind of cakes' and 'My mother used to make those kind of biscuits' but this is incorrect, and 'this' and 'that' should be used, as in 'I don't like that kind of joke' and 'My mother prefers this kind of holiday'.

The use of kind of to mean 'somewhat' or 'rather', as in 'I'm kind of hungry', 'She's kind of rude to him' and It's kind of cold in there', should be restricted to informal speech or dialect. This phrase is sometimes written 'kinda', as in 'We're kinda bored'.

Kind is also used as an adjective meaning 'caring' or 'generous', as in 'A kind old lady lent the children money to get a bus home', 'It was kind of you to let them borrow your car' and 'Children should be taught to be kind to animals'.

-kind A suffix indicating 'a group of people', as in humankind, mankind, womankind.

kindly A word that looks like an adverb but can be either an adverb or an adjective. As an adverb it means 'in a kind or caring manner' or 'generously', as in 'They treated us kindly during our stay', 'Her parents kindly treated us to a meal in a restaurant' and 'They very kindly offered us a lift'. The adverb kindly is also used in rather an ironic way when the user is annoyed, as in 'Would you kindly stop allowing your dog to foul the pavement'. It is also used in the phrase 'not to take kindly to', meaning 'to be unwilling to accept', as in 'The new pupil doesn't take kindly to discipline', 'He won't take kindly to being kept waiting' and 'The candidate was so confident that he is unlikely to take kindly to being rejected'.

Kindly is more common as an adjective and means 'kind, warm, friendly', as in 'a kindly old lady who was always helping her neighbours' and 'She gave the children a kindly smile'.

kneel One of several verbs in English that have more than one past participle and past tense form. The past participle and past tense can both be either 'kneeled' or 'knelt', as in 'The child knelt in prayer', 'She kneeled before the altar' and 'She had knelt at her dying husband's bedside every night' and 'They had kneeled in supplication before the emperor but he spurned them'. Although both 'knelt' and 'kneeled' are acceptable forms in British English, 'knelt' is the more common form.

L

laid and **lain** Words that are liable to be confused. **Laid** is the past tense and past participle of the verb 'lay', meaning 'to place or put', as in 'She laid the antique vase carefully on the table', 'He laid the new carpet tiles in the hall', 'They have laid the baby on a mat on the floor' and 'We have laid vinyl tiles on the kitchen floor'. **Lain** is the past participle of the verb 'lie', 'to rest in a horizontal position', as in 'Those letters have lain on his desk all week', 'The dead man had lain in the empty house for several days', and 'They had lain on the beach in the midday sun'.

language The means by which human beings communicate using words, as in 'Children acquire language at different rates. Some speak much earlier than others'. Language can refer either to spoken or written communication. It can also refer to the variety of communication used by a particular nation or state, as in 'He visits France regularly but makes no attempt to understand the French language', 'He won't start to learn a foreign language until he goes to secondary school' and 'People in other parts of Europe tend to speak more languages than the British'. The language that a person speaks from birth is known as his/her 'first language' or 'mother tongue'. He/she is said to be a native speaker of this language.

Language can also be used to refer to the style and vocabulary of a piece of writing, as in 'The language of his novels is very poetic'.

Language can also apply to the particular style and variety of language that is used in a particular profession or among a particular group of people with some common interest, as in 'legal language', 'scientific language', 'technical language', etc. Such technical or specialist language is sometimes referred to rather pejoratively as JARGON or as 'legalese', 'medicalese', 'computerese', etc.

A person's own style of language with regard to vocabulary, structure, etc, is known as IDEOLECT, as in 'He is the son of academic parents and has rather a formal ideolect'.

The language of a region or community with regard to vocabulary, structure, grammar and pronunciation is known as DIALECT, as in 'the dialect of the Northeast of England', 'the dialects of the Southern states of the USA'.

last A word that can be an adverb or an adjective. As an adjective it can give rise to ambiguity. It can mean 'coming after all others, final', as in 'He was the last runner to hit the finishing tape', 'That was the last novel he wrote before he died', 'He did not die until he was 90 but he wrote his last novel at the age of 40'. Ambiguity arises when last takes on other meanings. For example, it is frequently used as a synonym for 'latest', as in 'I really enjoyed his last novel and I'm looking forward to the next'. In this particular sentence it is clear that last means 'latest' not 'final' but this is not always the case. For example, in the sentence 'He was 60 when he directed his last film', it is not at all clear from the evidence of the sentence alone whether it is his 'final' or 'latest' film that is being referred to. Thus it is better to use either 'final' or 'latest' rather than 'last' in order to clarify the meaning.

Confusion can arise also between last, meaning 'final', and last, meaning 'preceding', as in 'I did not quite understand the last chapter'. On the evidence of the sentence alone, it is not clear whether last refers to the preceding chapter or to the final chapter. Again it is best to avoid ambiguity by using a synonym for last.

Yet more confusion can be caused with regard to last when it is used to refer to days of the week. It varies from person to person whether 'last Saturday' refers to the Saturday that has just gone or to the one before that. To some extent it depends which day of the week it is when the statement is made. To avoid ambiguity it is best to specify the date.

Last is also used as an adverb, as in 'They last saw their father when he was going to war', 'When the family go to the dentist my brother always wants to go in last' and 'If you are adding cream to the soup you add it last'. The adverbial use does not suffer from problems of ambiguity.

latest An adjective that is liable to be confused with LAST. It can also mean 'most up-to-date', 'most fashionable', as in 'the very latest dresses from the Paris designers'. Latest is also found in this meaning in the phrase 'the very latest', as in 'she always dresses in the very latest'. It can also mean 'most late', the superlative of 'late', in the sense of 'far on in the day or night', as in 'The latest train which you can get from that station leaves at ten o' clock'. In this sense latest is also found in the phrase 'at the latest' and in the phrase 'at the very latest', meaning 'most late time', as in 'You must arrive at the station at ten o'clock at the latest' and 'The students' essays must be handed in by Friday at the very latest'.

lay and **lie** These are liable to be confused. This is because **lay** as well as being a verb in its own right is also one of the principal parts of **lie**—the past tense, as in 'They lay on the beach in the sun', 'The books lay on the table gathering dust' and 'She lay on her bed and wept'.

Lay is a TRANSITIVE VERB meaning 'to place or put', as in 'She asked him to lay new tiles in the kitchen' and 'She had to lay down her shopping to open the door'. The principal parts of lay are 'lays' (third person singular present), as in 'She always lays the baby on the grass to play'; 'laying' (present participle), as in 'Laying her shopping down she put her key in the lock'; 'laid' (past participle and past tense), as in 'She laid the package on the table' and 'He had laid his car keys on the table and forgotten about them'.

Lie is an INTRANSITIVE VERB whose principal parts are 'lies' (third person singular present), as in 'Their house lies to the north of the village'; 'lying' (present participle), as in 'Lying on the grass they looked up at the sky'; 'lay' (past tense), as in 'The climbers lay on the summit exhausted'; 'lain' (past participle), as in 'Those books have lain there for weeks'.

Lie has another totally unrelated meaning. It means 'to say or write something that is untrue', as in 'You didn't have to lie about your part in the affair'. The principal parts of the verb lie are 'lies' (third person singular present), as in 'lies about why he arrives home late from work'; 'lying' (present participle), as in 'Lying, he looked her straight in the face'; 'lied' (past participle and past tense), as in 'He lied to his employers about his qualifications' and 'she suddenly realized that he had lied all the time'.

lean One of several verbs in English that have two forms of the past tense and the past participle, 'leaned' and 'leant', as in 'She leaned over the fence to talk to her neighbour', 'He leaned over his desk to catch the attention of his colleagues', 'They have leaned over backwards to help her' and 'She has leant down to pick something up and hurt her back'. The two forms are interchangeable.

leap One of several verbs in English that have two forms of the past tense and past participle, 'leaped' and 'leapt', as in 'The children leaped around the park in high spirits', 'She leapt up in surprise when she heard the news', 'She had leaped over a high fence and broken her leg' and 'The child has leapt over the steam and run off'. The two forms are virtually interchangeable but 'leapt' is more common in British English.

learn One of several verbs in English that have two forms of the past tense and past participle, 'learned' and 'learnt', as in 'They learned French at school', 'She learnt to ski in Austria', 'I think the boys have learned their lesson' and 'He had learnt to be grateful for what he was given'. The forms are interchangeable. 'Learned' as a past tense or past participle should not be confused with 'learned', the adjective meaning 'erudite, well-read, intellectual', as in 'Students filled the lecture hall to listen to the learned professor' and 'The company publishes learned journals'. This adjective is pronounced with two syllables—*ler-nid*—whereas 'learned', the past tense and past participle, is pronounced as one syllable—*lernd*.

length mark A mark used in phonetics in relation to a vowel to indicate that it is long. This can take the form of a 'macron', a small horizontal stroke placed above a letter, or a symbol resembling a colon placed after a vowel in the IPA pronunciation system.

-less A suffix meaning 'without, lacking' added to nouns to form adjectives, as in characterless, clueless, expressionless, fearless, flawless, harmless, homeless, hopeless, passionless, toothless and useless. It can also mean 'without being able to be measured', as in ageless, countless, priceless and timeless.

less and **fewer** Two words that are liable to be confused. *See* FEWER.

-let A suffix indicating a diminutive or smaller form of something, as in booklet, coverlet, droplet, islet, piglet, starlet and streamlet.

letter-writing This has become something of a dying art in view of the widespread use of the telephone. However, all of us from time to time have to write some form of letter and many of these are business letters. There are a few conventions in formal letters that should be observed.

One's own address, including one's postcode, should be placed at the right-hand side of the page. Each line of one's own address should be indented slightly below the one above and the date put below the last line of the address, as in:

23 Park Drive
Raleigh
Blackshire
RA14 2TY
5 June 1993

Whether one puts a comma at the end of the various lines of the address is a matter of taste. It is becoming common in modern usage not to do so. Note that there should be no full stop after the postcode.

One's telephone number can either be placed between the postcode and the date or at the other side of the page on the same line as the first line of the address.

If one is writing a business letter one should also put the address of the person to whom one is writing. It should be placed at the other side of the page below one's own address and the lines of this should be placed directly below each other without being indented, as in:

                                                              23, Park Drive
                                                                  Raleigh
                                                                Blackshire
                                                                RA 14 2TY
                                                              5 June 1993

The Manager Eastlands Bank
33 West Street
Northlands
Blackshire
NR15 3RJ

With regard to deciding how to address the person to whom one is writing it is best to find out his/her name. Having done so then one can start the letter off, as in:

Dear Mr White,

If one is writing to a woman the situation is slightly more problematic. Formerly it was considered acceptable to address the person written to as 'Miss' if one knew her to be unmarried or as 'Mrs' if one knew her to be married. If one did not know her marital status one could either use 'Miss' or use the 'Madam' convention. In modern usage 'Ms' is the acceptable term if one does not know the marital status of the woman to whom one is writing. Many people prefer to use this designation even if they do know the person's marital status and many women prefer to be addressed in this way. On the other hand, some women, especially older women, do not like the 'Ms' designation.

In modern usage some people prefer to put the first name and surname of the relevant person instead of the surname preceded by Mr, etc, as in:

Dear John White,

The above style of address is considered rather informal by some people.

If it is not easy to ascertain the name of the person to whom one wishes to write then it is perfectly acceptable to address him/her in terms of their position or job, as in:

Dear manager,
Dear Personnel Manager,
Dear Area Manager,

In formal letters it is also acceptable to use 'Sir' or 'Madam', as in:

Dear Sir,
Dear Madam,
Dear Sir/Madam,

Obviously the above style of address is used in cases where one does not know the sex of the person to whom one is writing.

In ending a formal letter it was traditionally the custom to write 'Yours faithfully' before one's signature, if one had addressed the person written to as 'Dear sir' or 'Dear madam', as in:

Yours faithfully,
Jane Black

It was also the custom to end the letter with 'Yours sincerely' if the letter was either informal in nature or a formal letter which began with 'Dear Mr White' etc, as in:

Yours sincerely,
Mary Brown

In modern usage it is now considered acceptable to end a letter with 'Yours sincerely' even if one has begun it with 'Dear sir', etc. These days 'Yours faithfully' is considered to be exceptionally formal.

It is common to end even business letters with 'Kind regards', especially if the person written to is known to one.

On the envelope the lines can be indented or not, according to taste. Each line, except the last one, can have a comma after or not. However, in modern usage there is an increasing tendency to punctuate as little as possible and the commas are frequently omitted, as in:

Ms Mary Brown
29 Lower Forth Street
Redwood
Blackshire
RD16 5YP

The same comments on Mrs, Miss and Ms apply to envelopes as apply to the opening greeting in letters. *See above*. Anything that can be done to make the address as clear as possible should be done. It is important always to put the postcode in the address as failure to do so slows down delivery of the letter. It is also advisable to highlight the town one is sending the letter to, either by putting it in capital letters, or by underlining it, as in:

Mr James Green
45 Park Avenue
BOSTON
Blackshire
BT16 6GH

In modern usage it is becoming increasingly common to write the full name of the person written to on the envelope, as in:

James Black
36 High Street
BLANKTON
Blankshire
BL13 9T2

It is considered formal or old-fashioned to use 'Esq.', usually spelt with a full stop at the end and preceded by a comma. If used, 'Esq.' should be placed after the mans's name and there should be no accopmanying 'Mr', as in:

John Brown, Esq
43 Queen Street
Whiteoaks
Blankshire
WH12 TY

lexicography The art and practice of defining words, selecting them and arranging them in dictionaries and glossaries.

licence and **license** These are liable to be confused. **Licence** is a noun referring to 'a document indicating that official permission or authorization has been given to do something', as in 'He does not have a current driving licence', 'You need a trading licence to sell goods there' and 'The pub owner lost his licence'. Licence also means 'too great freedom, disregard for rules of behaviour, social acceptability, morals, etc', as in 'The organizers of the concert objected to the licence shown by the young people in their dress'. In this sense the word licence is usually used in formal situations.

License is a verb meaning 'to give a licence to, to give official permission or authorization to', as in 'He is licensed to sell alcohol', 'She is not licensed to sell goods in the market' and 'The restaurant is not licensed but you can bring your own wine'. Licence is often misspelt as license.

The above comments refer to British English. In American English license is used for both the noun and the verb.

lie *see* **lay.**

ligature A printed character combining two letters in one, as in æ and œ. It is sometimes called a DIGRAPH.

-like A suffix indicating similarity, as in childlike, cowlike, dreamlike, ladylike, lifelike and warlike.

-ling A suffix indicating a diminutive or smaller version of something, as in duckling, gosling and nestling.

-logue A suffix derived from Greek meaning 'indicating 'conversation, discussion', as in dialogue, epilogue, monologue, prologue and travelogue.

limerick A humorous five-lined piece of light verse, with the first two lines rhyming with each other, the third and fourth lines rhyming with each other, and the fifth line rhyming with the first line. Usually there are three stressed beats in the first, second and fifth lines and two stressed beats on the third and fourth lines. Traditionally the name of a place is mentioned in the first line and may be repeated in the last line. Edward Lear made the form popular in the nineteenth century. Limerick is a town in Ireland but the name of the verse is probably derived from a Victorian custom of singing nonsense songs at parties where 'Will you come up to Limerick' was a common refrain. An example is:

> There once was a man from Nantucket
> Who kept all his cash in a bucket;
> But his daughter named Nan
> Ran away with a man,
> And as for the bucket, Nantucket.

lingua franca A language defined as 'a language adopted as a common language by speakers whose mother tongues or native languages are different'. This enables people to have a common medium of communication for various purposes, such as trading. Examples include Swahili in East Africa, Hausa in West Africa and Tok Pisin in Papua New Guinea. The term historically referred to 'a language that was a mixture of Italian, French, Greek, Spanish and Arabic, used for trading and military purposes.'

linguistics The systematic, scientific study of language. It describes language and seeks to establish general principles rather than to prescribe rules of correctness.

line-break The division of a word at the end of a line for space purposes. This is marked by a HYPHEN.

linking adverbs and **linking adverbials** Words and phrases that indicate some kind of connection between one clause or sentence and another. Examples include 'however', as in 'The award had no effect on their financial situation. It did, however, have a marked effect on their morale'; 'moreover', as in 'He is an unruly pupil. Moreover, he is a bad influence on the other pupils'; 'then again', as in 'She does not have very good qualifications. Then again, most of the other candidates have even fewer'; 'in the meantime', as in 'We will not know the planning committee's decision until next week. In the meantime we can only hope'; 'instead', as in 'I thought he would have reigned. Instead he seems determined to stay'.

linking verb A verb that 'links' a subject with its complement. Unlike other verbs, linking verbs do not denote an action but indicate a state. Examples of linking verbs include 'He is a fool', 'She appears calm', 'He appeared a sensible man', 'You seemed to become anxious', 'They became Buddhists', 'The child feels unwell', 'It is getting rather warm', 'It is growing colder', 'You look well', 'She remained loyal to her friend', 'She lived in America but remained a British citizen' and 'You seem thoughtful' and 'She seems a nice person'. Linking verbs are also called **copula** or **copular verbs**.

literary criticism The formal study, discussion and evaluation of a literary work, as in 'The students who are studying literary criticism have been asked to write a critical analysis of *Ulysses* by James Joyce.'

litotes A kind of understatement in which a statement is conveyed by contradicting or denying its opposite, as in 'It will be no easy task to look after their children for a week' (meaning that it will be a difficult task), 'She's not exactly communicative' (meaning she is silent or reserved).

loanword A word that has been taken into one language from another. From the point of view of the language taking the word in, the word is known as a BORROWING. Some loanwords become naturalized or fully integrated into the language and have a pronunciation and spelling reflecting the conventions of the language which has borrowed it. Other loanwords retain the spelling and pronunciation of the language from which they have been borrowed. These include 'Gastarbeiter', borrowed from German and meaning 'a foreign worker'.

localism A word or expression the use of which is restricted to a particular place or area. The area in question can be quite small, unlike DIALECT words or 'regionalism'.

lower-case letter The opposite of CAPITAL LETTER. It is also known informally as 'small letter'. Lower-case letters are used for most words in the language. It is capital letters that are exceptional in their use.

-ly A common adverbial ending. *See* ADVERBS.

M

macro- A prefix derived from the Greek meaning 'large in size or scope', as in macrobiotic, macrocosm, macroeconomics, macromolecular and macrostructure.

macron *see* **length mark.**

main clause The principal clause in a sentence on which any SUBORDINATE CLAUSES depend for their sense. The main clause can stand alone and make some sense but the subordinate clauses cannot. In the sentence 'I left early because I wanted to catch the 6 o'clock train', 'I left early' is the principal clause and 'because I wanted to catch the 6 o'clock train' is the subordinate clause. In the sentence 'When we saw the strange man we were afraid', the main clause is 'we were afraid' and the subordinate clause is 'when we saw the strange man'. In the sentence 'Because it was late we decided to start out for home as soon as we could', the main clause is 'we decided to start out for home' and the subordinate clauses are 'because it was late' and 'as soon as we could'. A main clause can also be known as a **principal clause** or an INDEPENDENT CLAUSE.

mal- A prefix derived from French meaning 'bad, unpleasant', as in malodorous, or 'imperfect, faulty', as in malabsorption, maladjusted, maladministration,

malapropism

malformation, malfunctioning, malnutrition, malpractice and maltreatment.

malapropism The incorrect use of a word, often through confusion with a similar-sounding word. It often arises from someone's attempt to impress someone else with a knowledge of long words or of technical language. Examples include 'The doctor says the old man is not in possession of all his facilities'. Here 'facilities' has been wrongly used instead of 'faculties'. Another example is 'My friend lives in a computer belt'. Here 'computer' has been wrongly used instead of 'commuter'. Another example is 'Her husband's had a vivisection'. Here 'vivisection' has been used instead of 'vasectomy'. 'Ah! It's wonderful to be on terracotta again. I hate sailing'. Here 'terracotta' has been wrongly used instead of 'terra firma'. The effect of malapropism is often humorous. Sometimes people use it deliberately for a comic effect, as in 'He was under the affluence of incahol'.

Malapropism is called after Mrs Malaprop, a character in a play called *The Rivals* (1775), a comedy by R. B. Sheridan. Her name is derived from the French *mal à propos*, 'not apposite, inappropriate'. Some of her malapropisms in the play include 'She's as headstrong as an allegory on the banks of the Nile'. She has used 'allegory' wrongly instead of 'alligator'. Another of Mrs Malapropism's malapropisms is 'Illiterate him quite from your mind'. Here she has used 'illiterate' wrongly instead of 'obliterate'.

major sentence A sentence that contains at least one SUBJECT and a FINITE VERB, as in 'We are going' and 'They won'. They frequently have more elements than this, as in 'They bought a car', 'We lost the match', 'They arrived yesterday' and 'We are going away next week'. They are sometimes described as **regular** because they divide into certain structural patterns: a subject, finite verb, adverb or adverbial clause, etc. The opposite of a major sentence is called a **minor sentence**, **irregular sentence** or **fragmentary sentence**. These include interjections such as 'Ouch!' and 'How terrible'; formula expressions, such as 'Good morning' and 'Well done'; and short forms of longer expressions, as in 'Traffic diverted', 'Shop closed', 'No dogs' and 'Flooding ahead'. Such short forms could be rephrased to become major sentences, as in 'Traffic has been diverted because of roadworks', 'The shop is closed on Sundays', 'The owner does not allow dogs in her shop' and 'There was flooding ahead on the motorway'.

-man A suffix used with nouns to form nouns indicating someone's job, as in barman, chairman, clergyman, coalman, fireman, policeman, postman, salesman.

In modern usage, when attempts are being made to remove sexism from the language, alternatives have been sought for any words ending in -man. Formerly, words ending in -man were often used whether or not the person referred to was definitely known to be a man. Different ways have been found to avoid the sexism of -man. 'Salesman' has been changed in many cases to 'salesperson', 'chairman' often becomes 'chairperson' or 'chair'. Similarly, 'fireman' has become 'fire-fighter' and 'policeman' frequently becomes 'police officer'. *See* -PERSON.

-mania A suffix indicating abnormal or obsessional behaviour, as in kleptomania, nymphomania and pyromania.

manner, adverbs of *see* **adverb.**

manner, adverbial clause of *see* **adverbial clause.**

masculine In grammatical terms, one of the GENDERS that nouns are divided into. Nouns in the masculine gender include words that obviously belong to the male sex, as in 'man', 'boy', 'king', 'prince' 'bridegroom', 'schoolboy' and 'salesman'. Many words now considered to be of DUAL GENDER formerly were assumed to be masculine. These include such words as 'author', 'sculptor' and 'engineer'. Gender also applies to personal pronouns, and the third personal singular pronoun masculine is 'he' (subject), 'him' (object) and 'his' (possessive). For further information *see* HE; SHE.

mass noun the same as **uncountable noun.**

-mate A suffix referring to 'someone who shares something with someone', as in bedmate, classmate, room-mate, schoolmate, shipmate, team-mate and workmate.

mega- A prefix derived from Greek meaning 'very large', as in megabid, megabucks, megaproduction and megastar. Many words using mega- in this way are modern and many are also informal or slang. In technical language mega- means 'a million times bigger than the unit to which it is attached, as in megabyte, megacycle, megahertz and megawatt.

meiosis A figure of speech using understatement to emphasize the size or importance of something, as in 'He's a decent enough bloke' and 'He's rather a decent tennis player'.

melted and **molten** Words that are liable to be confused. **Melted** is the past tense and past participle of the verb 'to melt', as in 'The chocolate melted in the heat' and 'The ice cream had melted by the time they got home'. Melted is also used as an adjective, as in 'melted chocolate'. **Molten** is used only as an adjective but it is not synonymous with melted. It means 'melted or made liquid at high temperatures', as in 'molten lava' and 'molten metal'.

meta- A prefix derived from Greek indicating 'alteration or transformation', as in metamorphosis, metaphor and metaphysics.

metaphor A figure of speech that compares two things by saying that one thing is another, as in 'He was a lion in the fight' (meaning that he was as brave as a lion), 'She is a mouse whenever he is present' (meaning that she is very timid), 'He is a giant among men' (meaning that he is a great man), 'She was a shining light to us all' (meaning she was a source of inspiration) and 'Life was not a bed of roses' (meaning life was not easy and enjoyable). By extension, metaphor refers to a word or phrase used in a sentence where it does not have a literal meaning, as in 'a butter mountain', 'a wine lake', 'My colleague is a snake in the grass', 'She always sits on the fence at committee meetings', 'They walked home with leaden feet' and 'He was rooted to the spot when he saw the man with the gun'. *See* MIXED METAPHOR and SIMILE.

-meter A suffix indicating 'a measuring instrument', as in altimeter, barometer, pedometer, calorimeter, speedometer, thermometer.

metonym A figure of speech in which a word or expression is used to indicate something with which it has a close relationship, as in 'The position of the Crown is more uncertain than it was formerly' (meaning that the position of the monarchy is not as stable as it once was), 'The City is nervously awaiting the announcement of this month's trade figures' (meaning that the people who work in London's financial sector are nervously awaiting the announcement of this month's trade figures) and 'The Kremlin began to adopt a more enlightened approach to foreign visitors' (meaning that the Russian government began to adopt a more enlightened approach to foreign visitors), 'The White House has yet to comment on the proposal' (meaning that the President of the United States has yet to reply to the proposal).

-metre A suffix indicating 'meter, the unit of length', as in centimetre, kilometre and millimetre.

micro- A prefix derived from Greek meaning 'very small', as in microbiology, microfiche, microfilm, microscope, microsurgery.

milli- A prefix derived from Latin meaning 'thousand', as in millisecond, millennium.

mini- A prefix derived from Latin meaning 'very small, least', as in minimum, minimal, and miniature. Mini- is frequently used to form modern words, as in minibus, minicab, mini-computer, mini-cruise, mini-golf, mini-market and miniskirt. Modern words beginning with mini- can be spelt either with a hyphen or without.

minor sentence *see* **major sentence.**

mis- A prefix indicating 'badly, wrongly', as in misbehave, miscalculate, misdirect, mishandle, mishear, misjudge, mismanage, mispronounce, misspell, mistreat, mistrust, misunderstanding and misuse.

misrelated participle *see* **dangling participle.**

mixed metaphor The situation that occurs when unrelated METAPHORS are put in the

modal verb

same sentence. Examples include 'She sailed into the room with both guns blazing'. Here the use of the word 'sail' belongs to nautical metaphors but the 'guns blazing' belongs to cowboy or Wild West metaphors. Another example is 'The company's new flagship did not get off the ground'. Here 'flagship' is a nautical term while 'get off the ground' refers to an aircraft taking off. Another example is 'They were caught red-handed with their trousers down'. Here 'caught red-handed' is a metaphorical reference to a murderer caught with blood on his/her hands but 'caught with one's trousers down' is either a reference to the embarrassing experience of being caught unawares in the toilet or else caught in an embarrassing sexual situation.

modal verb A type of AUXILIARY VERB that 'helps' the main verb to express a range of meanings including, for example, such meanings as possibility, probability, wants, wishes, necessity, permission, suggestions, etc. The main modal verbs are 'can', 'could'; 'may'; 'might'; 'will', 'would'; 'shall', 'should'; 'must'. Modal verbs have only one form. They have no -s form in the third person singular, no infinitive and no participles. Examples of modal verbs include 'He cannot read and write', 'She could go if she wanted to' (expressing ability); 'You can have another biscuit', 'You may answer the question' (expressing permission); 'We may see her on the way to the station', 'We might get there by nightfall' (expressing possibility); 'Will you have some wine?', 'Would you take a seat?' (expressing an offer or invitation); 'We should arrive by dawn', 'That must be a record' (expressing probability and certainty); 'You may prefer to wait', 'You might like to leave instructions' (expressing suggestion); 'Can you find the time to phone him for me?', 'Could you give him a message?' (expressing instructions and requests); 'They must leave at once', 'We must get there on time' (expressing necessity).

modifier A word, or group of words, that 'modifies' or affects the meaning of another word in some way, usually by adding more information about it. Modifiers are frequently used with nouns. They can be adjectives, as in 'He works in the *main* building' and 'They need a *larger* house'. Modifiers of nouns can be nouns themselves, as in 'the *theatre* profession', 'the *publishing* industry' and '*singing* tuition'. They can also be place names, as in 'the *Edinburgh* train', 'a *Paris* café' and 'the *London* underground', or adverbs of place and direction, as in 'a *downstairs* cloakroom' and 'an *upstairs* sitting room.

Adverbs, adjectives and pronouns can be accompanied by modifiers. Examples of modifiers with adverbs include 'walking *amazingly* quickly' and 'stopping *incredibly* abruptly'. Examples of modifiers with adjectives include 'a *really* warm day' and 'a *deliriously* happy child'. Examples of modifiers with pronouns include '*almost* no one there' and '*practically* everyone present'.

The examples given above are all premodifiers. *See also* POSTMODIFIER.

molten *see* **melted.**

-monger A suffix derived from Old English meaning 'dealer, trader', as in fishmonger and ironmonger. As well as being used for occupations in which people sell things, it is used for people who 'trade' in less tangible things, as in gossipmonger, rumourmonger, scaremonger and warmonger.

mono- A prefix derived from Greek meaning 'one, single', as in monochrome, monocracy, monogamy, monologue, monoplane, monosyllabic and monoxide.

months of the year These are spelt with initial capital letters, as in January, February, March, April, May, June, July, August, September, October, November and December.

mood One of the categories into which verbs are divided. The verb moods are indicative, imperative and subjunctive. The **indicative** makes a statement, as in 'He lives in France', 'They have two children' and 'It's starting to rain'. The **imperative** is used for giving orders or making requests, as in 'Shut that door!', 'Sit quietly until the teacher arrives' and 'Please bring me some coffee'. The **subjunctive** was originally a term in Latin grammar and expressed a wish, supposition, doubt, improbability or other non-factual statement. It is used in English for hypothetical statements and certain formal 'that' clauses, as in 'If I were you I would have nothing to do with it', 'If you were to go now you would arrive on time', 'Someone suggested that we ask for more money' and 'It was his solicitor who suggested that he sue the firm'. The word 'mood' arose because it was said to indicate the verb's attitude or viewpoint.

more An adverb that is added to some adjectives to make the comparative form (*see* COMPARISON OF ADJECTIVES). In general it is the longer adjectives that have more as part of their comparative form, as in 'more abundant', 'more beautiful', 'more catastrophic', 'more dangerous', 'more elegant', 'more frantic', 'more graceful', 'more handsome', 'more intelligent', 'more luxurious', 'more manageable', 'more opulent', 'more precious', 'more ravishing', 'more satisfactory', 'more talented', 'more unusual', 'more valuable'. Examples of adverbs with more in their comparative form include 'more elegantly', 'more gracefully', 'more energetically', 'more dangerously' and 'more determinedly'.

most An adverb added to some adjectives and adverbs to make the superlative form. In general it is the longer adjectives that have most as part of their superlative form, as in 'most abundant', 'most beautiful', 'most catastrophic', 'most dangerous', 'most elegant', 'most frantic', 'most graceful', 'most handsome', 'most intelligent', 'most luxurious', 'most manageable', 'most noteworthy', 'most opulent', 'most precious', 'most ravishing', 'most satisfactory', 'most talented', 'most unusual', 'most valuable'. Examples of adverbs with most in their superlative form include 'most elegantly', 'most gracefully', 'most energetically', 'most dangerously' and 'most determinedly'.

mother tongue The language that one first learns, the language of which one is a 'native speaker'. It means the same as 'native tongue'.

ms, miss and **miss** *see* **letter-writing.**

mow A verb that has two possible past participles—'mowed' and 'mown'—as in 'He has not yet mowed the grass' and 'We have mown the grass several times this summer'. The two participles are interchangeable. Only **mowed**, however, can be used as the past tense, as in 'They mowed the grass yesterday' and 'If they mowed the grass more often the garden would be tidier'. **Mown** can also be an adjective, as in 'the smell of freshly mown hay'.

multi- A prefix derived from Latin meaning 'many', as in multiply, multitude and multitudinous. Multi- is frequently used to form new modern words, as in multi-married, multi-media, multi-publicized, multi-purpose, multi-storey, multi-talented and multi-travelled.

multi-sentence A sentence with more than one clause, as in 'She tripped over a rock and broke her ankle' and 'She was afraid when she saw the strange man'.

N

-naut A suffix derived from Greek 'sailor' and meaning 'navigator', as in astronaut and cosmonaut.

negative sentence A sentence that is the opposite of a **positive sentence**. 'She has a dog' is an example of a positive sentence. 'She does not have a dog' is an example of a negative sentence. The negative concept is expressed by an AUXILIARY VERB accompanied by 'not' or 'n't'. Other words used in negative sentences include 'never', 'nothing' and 'by no means', as in 'She has never been here' and 'We heard nothing'.

neither An adjective or a pronoun that takes a singular verb, as in 'Neither parent will come' and 'Neither of them wishes to come'. In the **neither . . . nor** construction, a singular verb is used if both parts of the construction are singular, as in 'Neither Jane nor Mary was present'. If both parts are plural the verb is plural, as in 'Neither their parents nor their grandparents are willing to look after them'. If the construction involves a mixture of singular and plural, the verb traditionally agrees with the subject that is nearest it, as in 'Neither her mother nor her grandparents are going to come' and 'Neither her grandparents nor her mother is going to come'. If pronouns are used, the nearer one governs the verb as in 'Neither they nor he is at fault' and 'Neither he nor they are at fault'.

neologism A word that has been newly coined or newly introduced into the language, as 'camcorder', 'Jacuzzi' and 'karaoke'.

neuro- A prefix derived from Greek meaning 'nerve', as in neuritis, neurology, neuron and neurosurgery.

neuter One of the grammatical GENDERS. The other two grammatical genders are MASCULINE and FEMININE. Inanimate objects are members of the neuter gender. Examples include 'table', 'desk', 'garden', 'spade', 'flower' and 'bottle'.

nominal clause *see* **noun clause.**

non-finite clause A clause which contains a NON-FINITE VERB. Thus in the sentence 'He works hard to earn a living', 'to earn a living' is a non-finite clause since 'to earn' is an infinitive and so a non-finite verb. Similarly in the sentence 'Getting there was a problem', 'getting there' is a non-finite clause, 'getting' being a present participle and so a non-finite verb.

non-finite verb A verb that shows no variation in tense and has no subject. The non-finite verb forms include the infinitive form, as in 'go', the present participle and gerund, as in 'going', and the past participle, as in 'gone'.

non-gradable *see* **gradable.**

noun The name of something or someone. Thus 'anchor', 'baker', 'cat', 'elephant', 'foot', 'gate', 'lake', 'pear', 'shoe', 'trunk' and 'wallet' are all nouns. There are various categories of nouns. *See* ABSTRACT NOUN, COMMON NOUN, CONCRETE NOUN, COUNTABLE NOUN, PROPER NOUN and UNCOUNTABLE NOUN.

noun clause A SUBORDINATE CLAUSE that performs a function in a sentence similar to a noun or noun phrase. It can act as the subject, object or complement of a MAIN CLAUSE. In the sentence 'Where he goes is his own business', 'where he goes' is a noun clause. In the sentence 'They asked why he objected', 'why he objected' is a noun clause. A noun clause is also known as a **nominal clause.**

noun phrase A group of words containing a noun as its main word and functioning like a noun in a sentence. Thus it can function as the SUBJECT, OBJECT or COMPLEMENT of a sentence. In the sentence 'The large black dog bit him', 'the large black dog' is a noun phrase, and in the sentence 'They bought a house with a garden', 'with a garden' is a noun phrase. In the sentence 'She is a complete fool', 'a complete fool' is a noun phrase.

number In grammar this is a classification consisting of 'singular' and 'plural'. Thus the number of the pronoun 'they' is 'plural' and the number of the verb 'carries' is singular. *See* NUMBER AGREEMENT.

number agreement or **concord** The agreement of grammatical units in terms of NUMBER. Thus a singular subject is followed by a singular verb, as in 'The girl likes flowers', 'He hates work' and 'She was carrying a suitcase'. Similarly a plural subject should be followed by a plural verb, as in 'They have many problems', 'The men work hard' and 'The girls are training hard'.

numbers These can be written in either figures or words. It is largely a matter of taste which method is adopted. As long as the method is consistent it does not really matter.

Some establishments, such as a publishing house or a newspaper office, will have a house style. For example, some of them prefer to have numbers up to 10 written in words, as in 'They have two boys and three girls'. If this system is adopted, guidance should be sought as to whether a mixture of figures and words in the same sentence is acceptable, as in 'We have 12 cups but only six saucers', or whether the rule should be broken in such situations as 'We have twelve cups but only six saucers'.

numeral A word for 'number', as in 'print all the numerals in bold type'. Numeral is often used to refer to 'one, two, three, etc' in grammar since NUMBER is used to refer to the singular/plural category.

O

object The part of a sentence that is acted upon or is affected by the verb. It usually follows the verb to which it relates. There are two forms of object—the DIRECT OBJECT and INDIRECT OBJECT. A direct object can be a noun, and in the sentence 'The girl hit the ball', 'ball' is a noun and the object. In the sentence 'They bought a house', 'house' is a noun and the object. In the sentence 'They made an error', 'error' is a noun and the object. A direct object can be a noun phrase, and in the sentence 'He has bought a large house', 'a large house' is a noun phrase and the object. In the sentence 'She loves the little girl', 'the little girl' is a noun phrase and the object. In the sentence 'They both wear black clothes', 'black clothes' is a noun phrase and the object'. A direct object can be a noun clause, and in the sentence 'I know what he means', 'what he means' is a noun phrase and the object. In the sentence 'He denied that he had been involved', 'that he had been involved' is a noun phrase and the object. In the sentence 'I asked when he would return', 'when he would return' is a noun phrase and the object. A direct object can also be a pronoun, and in the sentence 'She hit him', 'him' is a pronoun and the object. In the sentence 'They had a car but they sold it', 'it' is a pronoun and the object. In the sentence 'She loves them', 'them' is a pronoun and the object.

objective case The case expressing the OBJECT. In Latin it is known as the ACCUSATIVE case.

oblique A diagonal mark (/) that has various uses. Its principal use is to show alternatives, as in 'he/she', 'Dear Sir/Madam', 'two/three-room flat' and 'the budget for 1993/4'. The oblique is used in some abbreviations, as in 'c/o Smith' (meaning 'care of Smith'). The word 'per' is usually shown by means of an oblique, as in 60km/h (60 kilometres per hour).

officialese A derogatory term for the vocabulary and style of writing often found in official reports and documents and thought of as being pretentious and difficult to understand. It is usually considered to be the prime example of GOBBLEDEGOOK.

-oholic *see* **-aholic.**

-ology A suffix derived from Greek indicating 'study of', as in biology, geology and technology.

omni- A prefix derived from Latin indicating 'all', as in omnipotent and omnivorous.

onomatopoeia A figure of speech that uses words whose sound suggests their meaning, as in 'The sausages sizzled in the pan', 'The fire crackled in the grate' and 'The water gurgled in the pipes'.

ordinal numbers The numbers 'first', 'second', 'third', etc, as opposed to CARDINAL NUMBERS, which are 'one', 'two, 'three', etc.

orthographic A term that refers to spelling, as in 'words which give rise to orthographic problems'.

orthography The study or science of how words are spelt, as in 'make a survey of the orthography and the pronunciation of Scandinavian languages'.

-osis A suffix derived from Greek indicating either 'a disease', as in cirrhosis and thrombosis, or a develoment, as in metamorphosis.

oxymoron A figure of speech that is based on the linking of incongruous or contradictory words, as in 'and honour rooted in dishonour stood' (Tennyson) and 'the wisest fool in Christendom'.

P

paragraph A subdivision of a piece of prose. Many people find it difficult to divide their work into paragraphs. Learning to do so can be difficult but it is an area of style that improves with practice.

A paragraph should deal with one particular theme or point of the writer's writing or argument. When that has been dealt with, a new paragraph should be started. However, there are other considerations to be taken into account. If the paragraph is very long it can appear offputting visually to the would-be reader and can be difficult to make one's way through. In such cases it is best to subdivide themes and shorten paragraphs. On the other hand, it is best not to make all one's paragraphs too short as this can create a disjointed effect. It is best to try to aim for a mixture of lengths to create some variety.

Traditionally it was frowned upon to have a one-sentence paragraph but there are no hard and fast rules about this. Usually it takes more than one sentence to develop the theme of the paragraph, unless one is a tabloid journalist or copywriter for an advertising firm, and it is best to avoid long, complex sentences.

The opening paragraph of a piece of writing should introduce the topic about which one is writing. The closing paragraph should sum up what one has been writing about. New paragraphs begin on new lines and they are usually indented from the margin. In the case of dialogue in a work of fiction, each speaker's utterance usually begins on a new line for the clarification of the reader.

parenthesis *see* **brackets.**

participle A part of speech, so called because, although a verb, it has the character both of verb and adjective and is also used in the formation of some compound tenses. *See also* -ING WORDS and PAST PARTICIPLE.

part of speech Each of the categories (e.g. verb, noun, adjective, etc) into which words are divided according to their grammatical and semantic functions.

passive voice The voice of a verb whereby the subject is the recipient of the action of the verb. Thus, in the sentence 'Mary was kicked by her brother', 'Mary' is the receiver of the 'kick' and so 'kick' is in the passive voice. Had it been in the active voice it would have been 'Her brother kicked Mary'. Thus 'the brother' is the subject and not the receiver of the action.

past participle This is formed by adding *-ed* or *-d* to the base words of regular verbs, as in 'acted', ' alluded', 'boarded', 'dashed', 'flouted', 'handed', 'loathed', 'tended' and 'wanted', or in various other ways for IRREGULAR VERBS.

past tense This TENSE of a verb is formed by adding *-ed* or *-d* to the base form of the verb in regular verbs, as in 'added', 'crashed', 'graded', 'smiled', 'rested' and 'yielded', and in various ways for IRREGULAR VERBS.

perfect tense *see* **tense.**

period *see* **full stop.**

personification A form of METAPHOR that represents an inanimate object or abstract notion as possessing the attributes of a person. For example, Uncle Sam is a personification of the United States of America, while John Bull is a personification of England.

personal pronoun A pronoun that is used to refer back to someone or something that has already been mentioned. The personal pronouns are divided into subject pronouns, object pronouns and possessive pronouns. They are also categorized according to 'person'. *See* FIRST PERSON, SECOND PERSON and THIRD PERSON.

philology The science, especially comparative, of languages and their history and structure.

phonetics The science connected with pronunciation and the representation of speech sounds.

phrasal verb A usually simple verb that combines with a preposition or adverb, or both, to convey a meaning more than the sum of its parts, e.g. to phase out, to come out, to look forward to.

phrase Two or more words, usually not containing a FINITE VERB, that form a complete expression by themselves or constitute a portion of a sentence.

plural noun The form of a noun referring to 'more than one' and contrasted with a SINGULAR NOUN. Singular nouns form plural forms in different ways. Most singular nouns add *s*, as in 'bat/bats', 'monkey/monkeys', 'table/tables', 'umbrella/umbrellas', or add *es*, as in 'church/churches' or 'torch/torches'. Singular nouns ending in a consonant followed by *y* add *ies*, as in 'fairy/fairies' and 'story/stories'. Some plural forms are formed irregularly (*see* IRREGULAR PLURALS). Some nouns are encountered in their plural form only. These include scissors, trousers and vermin.

point *see* **full stop.**

positive sentence *see* **negative sentence.**

possessive apostrophe *see* **apostrophe².**

possessive pronoun *see* **personal pronoun; first person; second person** and **third person.**

postmodifier A MODIFIER that comes after the main word of a NOUN PHRASE, as in 'of stone' in 'tablets of stone'.

predicate All the parts of a clause or sentence that are not contained in the subject. Thus in the sentence 'The little girl was exhausted and hungry', 'exhausted and hungry' is the predicate. Similarly, in the sentence 'The tired old man slept like a top', 'slept like a top' is the predicate.

predicative adjective An adjective that helps to form the PREDICATE and so comes after the verb, as 'tired' in 'She was very tired' and 'mournful' in 'The music was very mournful'.

prefix *see* **affix.**

premodifier A MODIFIER that comes before the main word of a NOUN PHRASE, as 'green' in 'green dress' and 'pretty' in 'pretty houses'.

preposition A word that relates two elements of a sentence, clause or phrase together. Prepositions show how the elements relate in time or space and generally precede the words that they 'govern'. Words governed by prepositions are nouns or pronouns. Prepositions are often very short words, as 'at', 'in', 'on', 'to', 'before' and 'after'. Some complex prepositions consist of two words, as 'ahead of', 'instead of', 'apart from', and some consist of three, as 'with reference to', 'in accordance with' and 'in addition to'.

present continous

Examples of prepositions in sentences include 'The cat sat on the mat', 'We were at a concert', 'They are in shock', 'We are going to France', 'She arrived before me', 'Apart from you she has no friends' and 'We acted in accordance with your instructions'.

present continuous *see* **tense.**

present participle *see* **-ing words.**

present tense *see* **tense.**

principal clause *see* **main clause.**

progressive present *see* **tense.**

pronoun A word that takes the place of a NOUN or a NOUN PHRASE. *See* PERSONAL PRONOUNS, HE, HER, HIM and HIS, RECIPROCAL PRONOUNS, REFLEXIVE PRONOUNS, DEMONSTRATIVE PRONOUNS, RELATIVE PRONOUNS, DISTRIBUTIVE PRONOUNS, INDEFINITE PRONOUNS and INTERROGATIVE PRONOUNS.

proper noun A noun that refers to a particular individual or a specific thing. It is the 'name' of someone or something', as in Australia, Vesuvius, John Brown, River Thames, Rome and Atlantic Ocean. *See* CAPITAL LETTERS.

punctuation The use of punctuation marks within a written text to enhance its meaning or fluency or to indicate aspects of pronuncation.

punctuation mark One of the standardized symbols used in punctuation, as the FULL STOP, COLON, SEMICOLON, COMMA, QUESTION MARK, etc.

Q

question mark The punctuation mark (?) that is placed at the end of a question or interrogative sentence, as in 'Who is he?', 'Where are they?', 'Why have they gone?', 'Whereabouts are they?', 'When are you going?' and 'What did he say?'. The question mark is sometimes known as the **query**.

question tag A phrase that is interrogative in form but is not really asking a question. It is added to a statement to seek agreement, etc. Examples include 'That was a lovely meal, wasn't it?', 'You will be able to go, won't you?', 'He's not going to move house, is he?' and 'She doesn't drive, does she?' Sentences containing question tags have question marks at the end.

quotation marks or **inverted commas** or **quotes**

Punctuation marks that are used in DIRECT SPEECH. Quotation marks are also used to enclose titles of newspapers, books, plays, films, musical works and works of art, as in 'The Times', 'Animal Farm', 'Othello', 'My Fair Lady' and 'Portrait of the Artist'. Quotation marks may consist of a set of single inverted comas (' ') or a set of double inverted commas (" "). If a title, etc, is to be enclosed in quotation marks and the title is part of a piece of writing already in quotation marks for some other reason, such as being part of direct speech, then the quotation marks round the title should be in the type of quotation marks opposite to the other ones. Thus, if the piece of writing is in single quotation marks then the title should be in double quotation marks. If the piece of prose is in double quotation marks the title should be in single quotation marks. Examples include 'Have you read "Wuthering Heights"?' and "Did you go to see 'My Fair Lady'?"

R

re- A common prefix, meaning 'again', in verbs. In most cases it is not followed by a hyphen, as in 'to retrace one's footsteps', 'a retrial ordered by the judge' and 'reconsider his decision'. However, it should be followed by a hyphen if its absence is likely to lead to confusion with another word, as in 're-cover a chair'/'recover from an illness', 're-count the votes'/'recount a tale of woe', 'the re-creation of a 17th-century village for a film set'/'play tennis for recreation' and 're-form the group'/'reform the prison system'. In cases where the second element of a word begins with *e*, re- is traditionally followed by a hyphen, as in 're-educate', 're-entry' and 're-echo', but in modern usage the hyphen is frequently omitted.

reciprocal pronoun A pronoun used to convey the idea of reciprocity or a two-way relationship. The reciprocal pronouns are 'each other' and 'one another'. Examples include 'They don't love each other any more', 'They seem to hate each other', 'We must try to help each other', 'The children were calling one another names', 'The two families were always criticizing one another' and 'The members of the family blame one another for their mother's death'.

reciprocal verb A verb such as 'consult', 'embrace', 'marry', 'meet', etc, that expresses a mutual relationship, as in 'They met at the conference', 'She married him in June'.

reduplication The process by which words are created by repetition or by semi-repetition. These include 'argy-bargy', 'dilly-dally', 'shilly-shally', 'flimflam', 'heebie-jeebies', 'hocus-pocus', 'hugger-mugger', 'knick-knack', and 'mish-mash'.

reflexive pronoun A pronoun that ends in '-self' or '-selves' and refers back to a noun or pronoun that has occurred earlier in the same sentence. The reflexive pronouns include 'myself', 'ourselves'; 'yourself', 'yourselves'; 'himself', 'herself', 'itself', 'themselves'. Examples include 'The children washed themselves', 'He cut himself shaving', 'Have you hurt yourself?' and 'She has cured herself of the habit'.

Reflexive pronouns are sometimes used for emphasis, as in 'The town itself was not very interesting' and 'The headmaster himself punished the boys'. They can also be used to indicate that something has been done by somebody by his/her own efforts without any help, as in 'He built the house himself', 'We converted the attic ourselves'. They can also indicate that someone or something is alone, as in 'She lives by herself' and 'The house stands by itself'.

reflexive verb A verb that has as its direct object a REFLEXIVE PRONOUN, e.g. 'They pride themselves on their skill as a team'.

regular sentence *see* **major sentence.**

regular verb *see* **irregular verb.**

relative clause A SUBORDINATE CLAUSE that has the function of an adjective. It is introduced by a RELATIVE PRONOUN.

relative pronoun A pronoun that introduces a RELATIVE CLAUSE. The relative pronouns are 'who', 'whom', 'whose', 'which' and 'that'. Examples of relative clauses introduced by relative pronouns include 'There is the man who stole the money', 'She is the person to whom I gave the money', 'This is the man whose wife won the prize', 'They criticized the work which he had done' and 'That's the house that I would like to buy'. Relative pronouns refer back to a NOUN or NOUN PHRASE in the MAIN CLAUSE. These nouns and noun phrases are known as ANTECEDENTS. The antecedents in the example sentences are respectively 'man', 'person', 'man', 'work' and 'house'.

Sometimes the relative clause divides the parts of the main clause, as in 'The woman whose daughter is ill is very upset', 'The people whom we met on holiday were French' and 'The house that we liked best was too expensive'.

reported speech *see* **indirect speech.**

retro- A prefix derived from Latin meaning 'back, backwards', as in retrograde, retrospect, retrorocket.

retronym A word or phrase that has had to be renamed slightly in the light of another invention, etc. For example, an ordinary guitar has become 'acoustic guitar' because of the existence of 'electric guitar'. Leather has sometimes become 'real leather' because of the existence of 'imitation leather'.

rhetorical question A question that is asked to achieve some kind of effect and requires no answer. Examples include 'What's this country coming to?', 'Did you ever see the like', 'Why do these things happen to me?', 'Where did youth go?', 'Death, where is thy sting?' and 'Where does time go?'. *See also* INTERROGATIVE SENTENCE.

Roman type The normal upright type used in printing, not BOLD or ITALIC type.

root means the same as **base.**

S

second person The term used for the person or thing to whom one is talking. The term is applied to PERSONAL PRONOUNS. The second person singular whether acting as the subject of a sentence is 'you', as in 'I told you so', 'We informed you of our decision' and 'They might have asked you sooner'. The second person personal pronoun does not alter its form in the plural in English, unlike in some languages. The possessive form of the second person pronoun is 'yours' whether singular or plural, as in 'These books are not yours'and 'This pen must be yours'.

semicolon A rather formal form of punctuation. It is mainly used between clauses that are not joined by any form of conjunction, as in 'We had a wonderful holiday; sadly they did not', 'She was my sister; she was also my best friend' and 'He was a marvellous friend; he is much missed'. A DASH is sometimes used instead of a semicolon but this more informal.

    The semicolon is also used to form subsets in a long list or series of names so that the said list seems less complex, as in 'The young man who wants to be a journalist has applied everywhere. He has applied to *The Times* in London; *The Globe and Mail* in Toronto; *The Age* in Melbourne; *The Tribune* in Chicago'.

    The semicolon is also sometimes used before 'however', 'nevertheless' 'hence', etc, as in 'We have extra seats for the concert; however you must not feel obliged to come'.

sentence This is at the head of the hierarchy of grammar. All the other elements, such as words, phrases and clauses, go to make up sentences. It is difficult to define a sentence. In terms of recognizing a sentence visually it can be described as beginning with a capital letter and ending with a full stop, or with an equivalent to the full stop, such as an exclamation mark. It is a unit of grammar that can stand alone and make sense and obeys certain grammatical rules, such as usually having a SUBJECT and a PREDICATE, as in 'The girl banged the door', where 'the girl' is the subject and 'the door' is the predicate. *See* MAJOR SENTENCE, SIMPLE SENTENCE, COMPLEX SENTENCE.

set phrase *see* **fixed phrase.**

sexism The domination of male values, which was formerly widespread in the English language whether this was intentional or not. Efforts are now being made to rectify this situation, although some of the suggestions made are rather extreme. Sensible progress has, however, been made. *See* HE; EACH; -MAN and -PERSON.

simile A figure of speech in which something is compared with another and said to be like it. This is in contradistinction to METAPHOR. where one thing is said actually to be another. Examples of similes include 'She is like an angel', 'Her hair is like silk', 'The old man's skin is like leather', He swims like a fish'.

simple sentence A SENTENCE that cannot be broken down into other clauses. It generally contains a FINITE VERB. Simple sentences include 'The man stole the car', 'She nudged him' and 'He kicked the ball'. *See* COMPLEX SENTENCE and COMPOUND SENTENCE.

singular noun A noun that refers to 'one' rather than 'more than one', which is the PLURAL form. *See also* IRREGULAR PLURAL.

spelling *see* **Appendix 1.**

split infinitive An infinitive that has had another word in the form of an adverb placed between itself and 'to', as in 'to rudely push' and 'to quietly leave'. This was once considered a a great grammatical sin but the split infinitive is becoming acceptable in modern usage. In any case it sometimes makes for a clumsy sentence if one slavishly adheres to the correct form.

spoonerism The accidental or deliberate transposition of the initial letters of two or more words, as in 'the queer old dean' instead of 'the dear old queen', 'a blushing crow' instead of a 'crushing blow' and 'a well-boiled icicle' instead of a 'well-oiled bicycle'. Spoonerisms are called after the Reverend William Archibald Spooner (1844–1930) of Oxford University.

stative present *see* **habitual and tense.**

stem *see* **base.**

strong verb The more common term for IRREGULAR VERB.

structure word *see* **function word.**

subject That which is spoken of in a sentence or clause and is usually either a NOUN, as in 'Birds fly' (birds is the noun as subject); a NOUN PHRASE, as in 'The people in the town dislike him' (the people in the town' is the subject); a PRONOUN, as in 'She hit the child' (she is the pronoun as subject); a PROPER NOUN, as in 'Paris is the capital of France'. *See* DUMMY SUBJECT.

subjunctive *see* **mood.**

subordinate clause A clause that is dependent on another clause, namely the MAIN CLAUSE. Unlike the main clause, it cannot stand alone and make sense. Subordinate clauses are introduced by CONJUNCTIONS. Examples of conjunctions that introduce subordinate clauses include 'after', 'before', 'when', 'if', 'because' and 'since'. *See* ADVERBIAL CLAUSE; NOUN CLAUSE.

subordinating conjunction *see* **conjunction.**

suffix An AFFIX that goes at the end of a word. The affix '-ness' is a suffix in 'softness' and 'prepreparedness'.

superlative form The form of an adjective or adverb that expresses the highest or utmost degree of the quality or manner of the word. The superlative forms follow the same rules as comparative forms except that they end in *-est* instead of *-er* and the longer ones use 'most' instead of 'more'. *See also* COMPARISON OF ADJECTIVES.

syllepsis is another word for **zeugma.**

synecdoche A figure of speech in which the part is put for the whole. For example, in 'The power of the sceptre is fading', 'sceptre' is used for 'monarch'; in 'The country has a fleet of a hundred sail', 'sail' is used for 'ship'; In 'The actor had a very successful career on the boards', 'boards' is used for 'stage'.

T

tautology Unnecessary repetition, as in 'new innovations', 'a see-through transparent material' and 'one after the other in succession'.

techno- A prefix derived from Greek meaning 'craft, skill', as in technical, technology, technique, etc.

tele- A prefix derived from Greek meaning 'distance', as in telephone, telescope and television, etc.

tense The form of a verb that is used to show the time at which the action of the verb takes place. One of the tenses in English is the **present tense**. It is used to indicate an action now going on or a state now existing. A distinction can be made between the **habitual present**, which marks habitual or repeated actions or recurring events, and the **stative present**, which indicates something that is true at all times. Examples of habitual present include 'He works long hours' and 'She walks to work'. Examples of the stative tense include 'The world is round' and 'Everyone must die eventually'.

The **progressive present** or **continuous present** is formed with the verb 'to be' and the present participle, as in, 'He is walking to the next village', 'She was driving along the road when she saw him' and 'They were worrying about the state of the economy'

The **past tense** refers to an action or state that has taken place before the present time. In the case of regular verbs it is formed by adding -ed to the base form of the verb, as in 'fear/feared', 'look/looked', and 'turn/turned'. *See also* IRREGULAR VERBS.

The **future tense** refers to an action or state that will take place at some time in the future. It is formed with 'will' and 'shall'. Traditionally 'will' was used with the second and third person pronouns ('you', 'he/she/it', 'they') and 'shall' with the first person ('I' and 'we'), as in 'You will be bored', 'He will soon be home', 'They will leave tomorrow', 'I shall buy some bread' and 'We shall go by train'. Also traditionally 'shall' was used with the second and third persons to indicate emphasis, insistence, determination, refusal, etc, as in 'You shall go to the ball' and 'He shall not be admitted'. 'Will' was used with the first person in the same way, as in 'I will get even with him'.

In modern usage 'will' is generally used for the first person as well as for second and third, as in 'I will see you tomorrow' and 'We will be there soon' and 'shall' is used for emphasis, insistence, etc, for first, second and third persons.

The future tense can also be formed with the use of 'be about to' or 'be going to', as in 'We were about to leave' and 'They were going to look for a house'.

Other tenses include the **perfect tense**, which is formed using the verb 'to have' and the past participle. In the case of regular verbs the past participle is formed by adding *ed* to the base form of the verb. *See also* IRREGULAR VERBS. Examples of the perfect tense include 'He has played his last match', 'We have travelled all day' and 'They have thought a lot about it'.

The **past perfect tense** or **pluperfect tense** is formed using the verb 'to have' and the past participle, as in 'She had no idea that he was dead' and 'They had felt unhappy about the situation'.

The **future perfect** is formed using the verb 'to have' and the past participle, as in 'He will have arrived by now'.

the The definitive article, which usually refers back to something already identified or to something specific, as in 'Where is the key?', 'What have you done with the book that I gave you?' and 'We have found the book that had we lost'. It is also used to denote someone or something as being the only one, as in 'the House of Lords', 'the King of Spain' and 'the President of Russia' and to indicate a class or group, as in 'the aristocracy', 'the cat family' and 'the teaching profession'. The is sometimes pronounced 'thee' when it is used to identify someone or something unique or important, as in 'Is that the John Frame over there?' and 'She is the fashion designer of the moment'.

they *see* **he.**

third person A third party, not the speaker or the person or thing being spoken to. Note that 'person' in this context can refer to things as well as people. 'Person' in this sense applies to personal pronouns. The third person singular forms are 'he', 'she' and 'it' when the subject of a sentence or clause, as in 'She will win' and 'It will be fine'. The third person singular forms are 'him', 'her','it' when the object, as in 'His behaviour hurt her' and 'She meant it'. The third person plural is 'they' when the subject, as in 'They have left' and 'They were angry' and 'them' when the object, as in 'His words made them angry' and 'We accompanied them'.

The possessive forms of the singular are 'his', 'hers' and 'its', as in 'he played his guitar' and 'The dog hurt its leg', and the the possessive form of the plural is theirs, as in 'That car is theirs' and 'They say that the book is theirs'. *See* HE.

to-infinitive The INFINITIVE form of the verb when it is accompanied by 'to' rather than when it is the bare infinitive without 'to'. Examples of the to-infinitive include 'We were told to go', 'I didn't want to stay' and 'To get there on time we'll have to leave now'.

transitive verb A verb that takes a DIRECT OBJECT. In the sentence 'The boy broke the window', 'window' is a direct object and so 'broke' (past tense of break) is a transitive verb. In the sentence 'She eats fruit', 'fruit' is a direct object and so 'eat' is a transitive verb. In the sentence 'They kill enemy soldiers' 'enemy soldiers' is a direct object and so 'kill' is a transitive verb. *See* INTRANSITIVE VERB.

U

ultra- A prefix derived from Latin meaning 'beyond', as in ultraviolet and ultramodern.

umlaut The DIACRITIC, which indicates a change of vowel sound in German, as in *mädchen*.

un- A prefix with two meanings. It can mean either 'not', as in unclean, untrue and unwise. it can also mean 'back, reversal', as in undo, unfasten, unlatch and untie.

uncountable noun or **uncount noun** A noun that is not usually pluralized or 'counted'. Such a noun is usually preceded by 'some', rather than 'a'. Uncountable nouns often refer to substances or commodities or qualities, processes and states. Examples of uncountable nouns include butter, china, luggage, petrol, sugar, heat, information, poverty, richness and warmth. In some situations it is possible to have a countable version of what is usually an uncountable noun. Thus 'sugar' is usually considered to be an uncountable noun but it can be used in a countable form in contexts such as 'I take two sugars in my coffee please'. Some nouns exist in an uncountable and countable form. Examples include 'cake', as in 'Have some cake' and 'She ate three cakes' and 'She could not paint for lack of light' and 'the lights went out'.

uni- A prefix derived from Latin meaning 'one', as in unicycle, unilateral and unity.

V

verb The part of speech often known as a 'doing' word. Although this is rather restrictive, since it tends to preclude AUXILIARY VERBS, MODAL VERBS, etc, the verb is the word in a sentence that is most concerned with the action and is usually essential to the structure of the sentence. Verbs 'INFLECT' and indicate TENSE, voice, mood, number, number and person. Most of the information on verbs has been placed under related entries. *See* ACTIVE VOICE, AUXILIARY VERB, FINITE VERB, -ING FORMS, INTRANSITIVE VERB, IRREGULAR VERBS, LINKING VERB, MODAL VERB, MOOD, NON-FINITE VERB, PASSIVE VOICE and TRANSITIVE VERB.

verbal noun *see* **gerund** and **-ing form.**

verb phrase A group of verb forms that have the same function as a single verb. Examples include 'have been raining', 'must have been lying', 'should not have been doing' and 'has been seen doing'.

virgule A rare word for an oblique. *See* OBLIQUE.

vocative case A case that is relevant mainly to languages such as Latin which are based on cases and inflections. In English the vocative is expressed by addressing someone, as 'John, could I see you for a minute', or by some form of greeting, endearment or exclamation.

voice One of the categories that describes verbs. It involves two ways of looking at the action of verbs. It is divided into ACTIVE VOICE and PASSIVE VOICE.

W

-ways A suffix that to some extent acts as an alternative to -WISE in its first two meanings, as in lengthways.

weak verb A less common term for a regular verb, in which inflection is effected by adding a letter or syllable (dawn, dawned) rather than a change of vowel (rise, rose). *See* IRREGULAR VERB.

who and **whom** Who is the SUBJECT of a verb or clause, as in 'Who told you?' and 'the girls who took part in the play'. **Whom** is the OBJECT of a verb or preposition, as 'Whom did he tell?' and ' the people from whom he stole'.

whose and **who's** These are liable to be confused because they sound the same. However they are not at all the same. **Who's** is a contraction of 'who is' and is used in speech and informal written contexts, as in 'Who's going to the cinema?' and 'Who's afraid of spiders'. **Whose** is a possessive pronoun or possessive adjective, as in 'That's the woman whose house was burgled' and 'Whose hat is this?'

-wise A suffix with several meanings. It can mean 'indicating manner or way', as in clockwise. It can also mean 'in the position or direction of' as in lengthwise and breadthwise. It can also mean 'with reference to', as in careerwise. It can also mean 'clever, sensible', as in streetwise.

Z

zero plural A plural form that has the same form as the singular. Examples include 'cod', 'deer', 'grouse' (game-bird) and 'sheep'. Some nouns have ordinary plurals and zero plurals as alternatives, as in 'fish/fishes'. Nouns of measurement often have zero plurals, as in 'She is five foot three' and 'Six dozen eggs'.

zeugma or **syllepsis** A figure of speech that uses a single word to apply to two words that are not appropriate to each other, as in 'We collected our coats and our baby', 'She left the building and her job' and 'She left in a taxi and a fit of hysterics'. Zeugma is similar to BATHOS.

Usage

A

a and **an** are the forms of the indefinite article. The form **a** is used before words that begin with a consonant sound, as in *a* box, *a* garden, *a* road, *a* wall. The form **an** is used before words that begin with a vowel sound, as in *an* apple, *an* easel, *an* ostrich, *an* uncle. Note that it is the *sound* of the initial letter that matters and not the *spelling*. Thus **a** is used before words beginning with a *u* when they are pronounced with a *y* sound as though it were a consonant, as *a* unit, *a* usual occurrence. Similarly **an** is used, for example, before words beginning with the letter *h* where this is not pronounced, as in *an* heir, *an* hour, *an* honest man.

Formerly it was quite common to use **an** before words that begin with an *h* sound and also begin with an unstressed syllable, as in *an* hotel (ho-*tel*), *an* historic (his-*tor*-ik) occasion, *an* hereditary (her-*ed*-it-ary) disease. It is more usual nowadays to use **a** in such cases, ignoring the question of the unstressed syllable.

abbreviations are shortened forms of words, usually used as a space-saving technique and are becoming increasingly common in modern usage. They frequently take the form of the initial letters of several words as, for example, in the title of an organization, person, etc, e.g. TUC (Trade Union Council) or BBC (British Broadcasting Corporation), JP (Justice of the Peace). Note that, unlike acronyms, abbreviations are not pronounced as words even when this would be possible. Thus TUC is not pronounced *tuk*.

Abbreviations may also be formed from the first and last letters of a word (when they are known as contractions), e.g. Dr (Doctor), Rd (Road), St (Street or Saint), pd (paid). Many of these are found mainly in written, rather than spoken, form.

Abbreviations may also be formed from the first few letters of a word, e.g. Feb (February), Prof (Professor), Rev (Reverend). In modern usage the tendency is to omit full stops from abbreviations. This is most true of abbreviations involving initial capital letters, as in TUC, BBC, EEC and USA. In such cases full stops should definitely not be used if one or some of the initial letters do not belong to a full word. Thus 'television' is abbreviated to TV.

There are usually no full stops in abbreviations involving the first and last letters of a word (contractions), as in Dr, Mr, Rd, St, but this is a matter of taste.

Abbreviations involving the first few letters of a word, as in Prof for 'Professor', are the most likely to have full stops, as Feb. for 'February', but again this is now a matter of taste.

Plurals in abbreviations are mostly formed by adding lower-case *s*, as in Drs, JPs, TVs. Note the absence of apostrophes.

See also **acronyms**.

abdomen is now usually pronounced with the emphasis on the first syllable (*ab*-do-men).

aberration is frequently misspelt. Note the single *b* and double *r*. It means deviation or departure from what is considered normal, as in 'mental aberration'.

-able and **-ible** are both used to form adjectives. It is easy to confuse the spelling of words ending in these, and the best way to get them right is to memorize them, unless you have a good knowledge of Latin. Words ending in **-ible** are usually formed from Latin words ending in *-ibilis*, and some words ending in **-able** are formed from Latin words ending in *-abilis*.

In addition, some words ending in **-able** are derived from French, and words formed from English words end in **-able** rather than **-ible**. The form **-able** is what is known as a 'living suffix' and is the form that is used when coining modern words, as 'a sackable offence', 'washable materials', 'a jailable crime', 'a kickable ball', 'a catchable ball'.

Some words ending in **-able**:

abominable	healable	manageable	sizeable
acceptable	hearable	measurable	solvable
agreeable	identifiable	memorable	stoppable
bearable	impeccable	nameable	storable
beatable	immutable	nonflammable	tenable
blameable	impracticable	objectionable	tolerable
comfortable	inapplicable	operable	touchable
commendable	inappreciable	palpable	undoable
delectable	incalculable	passable	usable
discreditable	indispensable	purchasable	variable
disreputable	indescribable	rateable	viable
enviable	indisputable	readable	washable
forgettable	lamentable	reviewable	wearable
forgivable	laudable	saleable	winnable
governable	likeable	shakeable	workable

Some words ending in **-ible**:

accessible	discernible	indelible	repressible
admissible	divisible	intelligible	reproducible
audible	edible	irascible	resistible
collapsible	exhaustible	legible	responsible
combustible	expressible	negligible	reversible
compatible	fallible	ostensible	risible
comprehensible	feasible	perceptible	sensible
contemptible	flexible	permissible	susceptible
credible	forcible	plausible	tangible
defensible	gullible	possible	visible
digestible			

-abled is a suffix meaning 'able-bodied'. It is most usually found in such phrases as 'differently abled', a 'politically correct', more positive way of referring to people with some form of disability, as in 'provide access to the club building for differently abled members'. In common with many politically correct terms, it is disliked by many people, including many disabled people.

ableism or **ablism** means discrimination in favour of able-bodied people as in 'people in wheelchairs unable to get jobs because of ableism'. Also known as **able-bodiedism** and **able-bodism**. Note that the suffix '-ism' is often used to indicate discrimination against the group to which it refers, as in 'ageism'.

Aboriginal rather than **Aborigine** is now the preferred term for an original inhabitant of Australia, especially where the word is in the singular.

abscess, meaning an inflamed swelling with pus in it, is frequently misspelt. Note the *c* after the first *s*.

abuse and **misuse** both mean wrong or improper use or treatment. However, **abuse** tends to be a more condemnatory term, suggesting that the wrong use or treatment is morally wrong or illegal. Thus we find 'misuse of the equipment' or 'misuse of one's talents', but 'abuse of a privileged position' or 'abuse of children'. 'Child abuse' is usually used to indicate physical violence or sexual assault.

Abuse is also frequently applied to the use of substances that are dangerous or injurious to health, as 'drug abuse', 'solvent abuse', or 'alcohol abuse'. In addition, it is used to describe insulting or offensive language, as in 'shout abuse at the referee'.

academic is used to describe scholarly or educational matters, as 'a child with academic rather than sporting interests'. From this use it has come to mean theoretical rather than actual or practical, as in 'wasting time discussing matters of purely academic concern'. In modern use it is frequently used to mean irrelevant, as in 'Whether you vote for him or not is academic. He is certain of a majority of votes'.

accelerate, meaning 'to go faster', is a common word that is frequently misspelt. Note the double *c* but single *l*.

accent commonly refers to a regional or individual way of speaking or pronouncing words, as in 'a Glasgow accent'. The word is also used to mean emphasis, as in 'In hotel the accent is on the second syllable of the word', or 'In fashion this year the accent is no longer on shirts'.

Accent also refers to certain symbols used on some foreign words adopted into English. In modern usage, which has a tendency to punctuate less than was formerly the case, accents are frequently omitted. For example, an actor's part in a play is now usually spelt 'role' but originally it was spelt 'rôle', the accent on *o* being called a circumflex. The accent is most likely to be retained if it affects the pronunciation. Thus 'cliché' and 'divorcé' usually retain the acute accent, as it is called, on the *e*. On the other hand, the accent known as the cedilla is frequently omitted from beneath the *c* in words such as 'façade/facade', although it is there to indicate that the *c* is soft, pronounced like an *s*, rather than a hard sound pronounced like a *k*.

access is commonly misspelt. Note the double *c* and double *s*. The word is usually a noun meaning 'entry or admission', as in 'try to gain access to the building', or 'the opportunity to use something', as in 'have access to confidential information'. It is also used to refer to the right of a parent to spend time with his or her children, as in 'Father was allowed access to the children at weekends'.

However **access** can also be used as a verb. It is most commonly found in computing, meaning obtaining information from, as in 'accessing details from the computer file relating to the accounts'. In modern usage many technical words become used, and indeed overused, in the general language. Thus the verb **access** can now be found meaning to obtain information not on a computer, as in 'access the information in the filing cabinet'. It can also be found in the sense of gaining entry to a building, as in 'Their attempts to access the building at night were unsuccessful'.

accessory and **accessary** are interchangeable as regards only one meaning of **accessory**. A person who helps another person to commit a crime is known either as an **accessory** or an **accessary**, although the former is the more modern term. However, only **accessory** is used to describe a useful or decorative extra that is not strictly necessary, as in 'Seat covers are accessories that are included in the price of the car' and 'She wore a red dress with black accessories' ('accessories' in the second example being handbag, shoes and gloves).

accompany can be followed either by the preposition 'with' or 'by'. When it means 'to go somewhere with someone', 'by' is used, as in 'She was accompanied by her parents to church' Similarly, 'by' is used when **accompany** is used in a musical context, as in 'The singer was accompanied on the piano by her brother'. When **accompany** means 'to go along with something' or 'supplement something', either 'by' or 'with' may be used, as in 'The roast turkey was accompanied by all the trimmings', 'His words were accompanied by/with a gesture of dismissal', and 'The speaker accompanied his words with expressive gestures'.

accommodation is one of the most commonly misspelt words. Note the double *c*, and double *m*.

acetic is a common misspelling of **ascetic** although it is a word in its own right. **Acetic** refers to the acid used in vinegar and is used to mean sour. **Ascetic** means 'self-denying' or 'self-disciplined' and is used to refer to a person (or to his/her lifestyle) who abstains from many of life's pleasures and who is often a recluse. A person who has such a lifestyle is known as an **ascetic.**

acknowledgement and **acknowledgment** are both acceptable spellings.

acoustics can take either a singular or plural verb. When it is being thought of as a branch of science it is treated as being singular, as in 'Acoustics deals with the study of sound', but when it is used to describe the qualities of a hall, etc, with regard to its sound-carrying properties, it is treated as being plural, as in 'The acoustics in the school hall are very poor'.

acquaint is often misspelt. It is a common error to omit the *c*. It means 'to become familiar with' or 'to inform'. The same problem arises in the word **acquaintance**, which means 'someone whom one knows slightly'.

acquire, **acquirement** and **acquisition** are all frequently misspelt. It is a common error to omit the *c*.

acronyms, like some **abbreviations,** are formed from the initial letters of several words. Unlike **abbreviations,** however, **acronyms** are pronounced as words rather than as just a series of letters. For example OPEC (Organization of Petroleum Producing Countries) is pronounced *o*-pek and is thus an acronym, unlike USA (United States of America) which is pronounced as a series of letters and *not* as a word (*oo*-sa or *yoo*-sa) and is thus an **abbreviation.**

Acronyms are written without full stops, as in UNESCO (United Nations Educational, Scientific and Cultural Organization). Mostly **acronyms** are written in capital letters, as in NASA (National Aeronautics and Space Administration). However, very common **acronyms,** such as Aids (Acquired Immune Deficiency Syndrome), are written with just an initial capital, the rest of the letters being lower case.

Acronyms that refer to a piece of scientific or technical equipment are written like ordinary words in lower-case letters, as 'laser' (light amplification by simulated emission of radiation).

A fashion originated in the mid 1980s for inventing **acronyms** relating to lifestyles or categories of society. These included 'yuppie', also spelt 'yuppy', which is an acronym of 'young urban (or upwardly mobile) professional'. 'Yuppie' became an established part of the language, as to a certain extent did 'nimby' (not in my back yard), an **acronym** that indicates people's reluctance to have any new developments, such as a hostel for ex-prisoners, in the vicinity of their homes, even if they are in theory in general favour of such developments. The majority of **acronyms** coined at this time were short-lived and are no longer commonly used. These included 'dinky' ('dual or double income, no kids') and 'woopie' ('well-off older person'). The fashion in forming such acronyms became rather silly, resulting in such words as 'pippie' ('person inheriting parents' property') and 'whanny' ('we have a nanny').

acrylic refers to the fibre used in a kind of man-made textile. The word is commonly misspelt. Note the *y*, not *i*, before the *l*.

activate and **actuate** both mean 'make active' but are commonly used in different senses. **Activate** refers to physical or chemical action, as in 'The terrorists activated the explosive device'. **Actuate** means 'to move to action' and 'to serve as a motive', as in 'The murderer was actuated by jealousy'.

acute and **chronic** both refer to disease. **Acute** is used of a disease that is sudden in onset and lasts a relatively short time, as in 'Flu is an acute illness'. **Chronic** is used of a disease that may be slow to develop and lasts a long time, possibly over several years, as in 'Asthma is a chronic condition'.

acumen is now usually pronounced *ak*-yoo-men, with the emphasis on the first syllable, although formerly the stress was usually on the second syllable (yoo). It means 'the ability to make good or shrewd judgements, as in 'a woman of excellent business acumen'.

actress is still widely used as a term for a woman who acts in plays or films, although many people prefer the term 'actor', regarding this as a neutral term rather than simply the masculine form. The **-ess** suffix, used to indicate the feminine form of a word, is generally becoming less common as these forms are regarded as sexist or belittling. *See also* **-ess**.

AD and **BC** are abbreviations that accompany year numbers. **AD** stands for 'Anno Domini', meaning 'in the year of our Lord' and indicates that the year concerned is one occurring after Jesus Christ was born. Traditionally **AD** is placed before the year number concerned, as in 'Their great-grandfather was born in AD 1801', but in modern usage it sometimes follows the year number, as in 'The house was built in 1780 AD.' **BC** stands for 'Before Christ' and indicates that the year concerned is one occurring before Jesus Christ was born. It follows the year number, as in 'The event took place in Rome in 55 BC'.

adagio is a musical direction indicating that a piece or passage of music should be played slowly. It is an Italian word meaning 'at ease' and is pronounced a-*dah*-jee-o.

adapter and **adaptor** can be used interchangeably, but commonly **adapter** is used to refer to a person who adapts, as in 'the adapter of the stage play for television and **adaptor** is used to refer to a thing that adapts, specifically a type of electrical plug.

ad hoc is a Latin phrase commonly used in English to mean 'for a particular purpose only', as in 'An ad hoc committee was formed to deal with the flooding of the town'.

adjourn is commonly misspelt. Note the *d* before the *j*. It means either 'to postpone or stop for a short time', as in 'The meeting will adjourn for lunch', and 'to go', as in 'They adjourned to another room'.

admissible is frequently misspelt. Note the -IBLE ending.

admission and **admittance** both mean 'permission or right to enter'. **Admission** is the more common term, as in 'They refused him admission to their house', and, unlike **admittance**, it can also mean 'the price or fee charged for entry' as in 'Admission to the football match is £3'. **Admittance** is largely used in formal or official situations, as in 'They ignored the notice saying "No Admittance" '. **Admission** also means 'confession' or 'acknowledgement of responsibility', as in 'On her own admission she was the thief'.

admit may be followed either by the preposition 'to' or the preposition 'of', depending on the sense. In the sense of 'to confess', **admit** is usually not followed by a preposition at all, as in 'He admitted his mistake' and 'She admitted stealing the brooch'. However, in this sense **admit** is sometimes followed by 'to', as in 'They have admitted to their error' and 'They have admitted to their part in the theft'.

In the sense of 'to allow to enter', **admit** is followed by 'to', as in 'The doorman admitted the guest to the club'. Also in the rather formal sense of 'give access or entrance to', **admit** is followed by 'to', as in 'the rear door admits straight to the garden'. In the sense of 'to be open to' or 'leave room for', **admit** is followed by 'of', as in 'The situation admits of no other explanation'.

admittance *see* **admission**.

adolescence is frequently misspelt. Note the letters *sc* in the middle of the word. Adolescence refers to the period of life between puberty and adulthood.

adopted and **adoptive** are liable to be confused. **Adopted** is applied to children who have been adopted, as in 'The couple have two adopted daughters'. **Adoptive** is applied to a person or people who adopt a child, as in 'Her biological parents tried to get the girl back from her adoptive parents'.

adult may be pronounced with the emphasis on either of the two syllables. Thus *a*-dult and a-*dult* are both acceptable although the pronunciation with the emphasis on the first syllable (*a*-dult) is the more common. The adjective **adult** means 'mature', as in 'a very adult young man' and 'for adults' as in 'courses in adult education'. However it can also mean 'pornographic', as in 'adult movies'.

adversary is commonly pronounced with the emphasis on the first syllable (*ad*-ver-sar-i) although in modern usage it is also found with the emphasis on the second syllable (ad-*ver*-sar-i).

adverse and **averse** are often confused because they sound and look rather alike, although they are different in meaning. **Adverse** means 'unfavourable' or 'hostile', as in 'Her actions had an adverse effect on her career' and 'The committee's proposals met with an adverse reaction'. **Averse** means 'unwilling' or 'having a dislike', as in 'The staff are not averse to the reconstruction plans', 'Her mother is totally averse to her marrying him'. Note that **averse** is followed by the preposition 'to'.

Adverse is usually pronounced with the emphasis on the first syllable (*ad*-vers) and **averse** is always pronounced with the emphasis on the second syllable (a-*vers*).

advertise is commonly misspelt. It is not one of those verbs that can end in either -*ise* or -*ize*. 'Advertize' is an erroneous spelling.

advice and **advise** are sometimes confused. **Advice** is a noun meaning 'helpful information or guidance', as in 'She asked her sister's advice on clothes' and 'She should seek legal advice'. **Advise** is a verb meaning 'to give advice', as in 'The career's office will advise you about educational qualifications'. It can also mean to 'inform', as in 'The officer advised the men of the change of plan'. It is usually used in a formal or official context. Note that it is wrong to spell advise with a *z*.

adviser and **advisor** are both acceptable spellings. The word is applied to someone who gives advice, usually in a professional or official capacity, as in 'He is a financial adviser/advisor'.

aerial is commonly misspelt. Note the *ae* at the beginning of the word. **Aerial** as an adjective means either 'of the air', as in 'aerial changes', or 'from the air or an aircraft', as in 'an aerial view'.

aeroplane is commonly abbreviated to **plane** in modern usage. In American English **aeroplane** becomes **airplane.**

affect and **effect** are often confused. **Affect** is a verb meaning 'to have an effect on', 'to influence or change in some way', as in 'His health was affected by his poor working conditions', 'Their decision was affected by personal prejudice'. It is often confused with **effect**, a noun meaning 'result or consequence' or 'influence', as in 'Their terrible experiences will have an effect on the children'. **Effect** is also a verb used mostly in formal contexts and means 'to bring about', as in 'The company plans to effect major changes'. **Affect** can also mean 'to pretend or feign' as in 'She affected an appearance of poverty although she was very wealthy'.

affinity may be followed by the preposition 'with' or 'between', and means 'close relationship', 'mutual attraction' or similarity, as in 'the affinity which twins have with each other' and 'There was an affinity between the two families who had lost children'. In modern usage it is sometimes followed by 'for' or 'towards', and means 'liking', as in 'She has an affinity for fair-haired men'.

aficionado is frequently misspelt. Note the single *f* and single *n*. It means a fan or supporter as in 'an aficionado of jazz', 'an opera aficionado', and is pronounced a-fiss-eon-*ah*-do. The plural is **aficionados**.

afters *see* **dessert**.

aged has two possible pronunciations depending on the sense. When it means 'very old', as in 'aged men with white beards', it is pronounced *ay*-jid. When it means 'years of age', as in 'a girl aged nine', it is pronounced with one syllable, *ayjd*.

ageing in modern usage may also be spelt **aging.**

ageism means discrimination on the grounds of age, as in 'By giving an age range in their job advert the firm were guilty of ageism'. Usually it refers to discrimination against older or elderly people, but it also refers to discrimination against young people.

agenda in modern usage is a singular noun having the plural **agendas**. It means 'a list of things to be attended to', as in 'The financial situation was the first item on the committee's agenda'. Originally it was a plural noun, derived from Latin, meaning 'things to be done'.

aggravate literally means 'to make worse', as in 'Her remarks simply aggravated the situation'. In modern usage it is frequently found meaning 'to irritate or annoy', as in 'The children were aggravating their mother when she was trying to read'. It is often labelled as 'informal' in dictionaries and is best avoided in formal situations.

agnostic and **atheist** are both words meaning 'disbeliever in God', but there are differences in sense between the two words. **Agnostics** believe that it is not possible to know whether God exists or not. **Atheists** believe that there is no God.

agoraphobia is frequently misspelt. Note the *o*, not *a*, after *g*. The word means 'fear of open spaces'.

alcohol abuse is a modern term for alcoholism. *See* **abuse**.

alibi is derived from the Latin word for 'elsewhere'. It is used to refer to a legal plea that a person accused or under suspicion was somewhere other than the scene of the crime at the time the crime was committed. In modern usage **alibi** is frequently used to mean simply 'excuse' or 'pretext', as in 'He had the perfect alibi for not going to the party—he was ill in hospital'.

align is frequently misspelt. Note the single *l*. The word means either 'to bring into (a straight) line', as in 'align the wheels of a car', or 'to support, be on the side of', as in 'He aligned himself with the rebels'.

all right is frequently misspelt as 'alright'. Although 'alright' is commonly found, it is still regarded as an error.

allude should be used only in the meaning of 'to refer indirectly to', as in 'When he spoke of people who had suffered from mental illness he was alluding to himself'. It should not be used simply to mean 'to refer to', as in 'In his speech he alluded frequently to the fact that he was retiring', although this is commonly found nowadays in informal contexts.

allusion and **illusion** are liable to be confused because of the similarity in their pronunciation, but they are completely different in meaning. **Allusion** means 'an indirect reference', as in 'His remarks on poverty in the area were an allusion to the hardship of his own childhood there'. *See* **allude**. **Illusion** means 'a false or misleading impression', as in 'Putting a screen round her part of the room gave at least the illusion of privacy'.

alternate and **alternative** are liable to be confused. **Alternate** means 'every other' or 'occurring by turns', as in 'They visit her mother on alternate weekends' and 'between alternate layers of meat and cheese sauce'. **Alternative** means 'offering a choice' or 'being an alternative', as in 'If the motorway is busy there is an alternative route'. **Alternative** is found in some cases in modern usage to mean 'not conventional, not traditional', as in 'alternative medicine' and 'alternative comedy'.

Alternative as a noun refers to the choice between two possibilities, as in 'The alternatives are to go by train or by plane'. In modern usage, however, it is becoming common to use it to refer also to the choice among two or more possibilities, as in 'He has to use a college from five alternatives'.

although and **though** are largely interchangeable but **though** is slightly less formal, as in 'We arrived on time although/though we left late'.

all together and **altogether** are not interchangeable. **All together** means 'at the same time' or 'in the same place', as in 'The guests arrived all together' and 'They kept their personal papers all together in a filing cabinet'. **Altogether** means 'in all, in total' or 'completely', as in "We collected £500 altogether' and 'The work was altogether too much for him'.

a.m. and **p.m.** are liable to be confused. **A.M.**, which is short for Latin 'ante meridiem' meaning 'before noon', is used to indicate that the time given occurs between the hours of midnight and midday, as in 'She asked friends for coffee at 11 a.m'. **P.M.**, which is short for *post meridiem*, meaning 'after noon', is used to indicate that the time given occurs during the hours between midday and midnight, as in 'The shop stays open until 10 p.m.' Full stops are usually used both in **a.m.** and **p.m.**; in the case of **a.m.** to

amend

distinguish it from the verb 'am'. Usually both **a.m.** and **p.m.** are spelt with lower-case letters.

amend and **emend** are liable to be confused. Both words mean 'to correct', but **emend** has a more restricted use than **amend**. **Emend** means specifically 'to remove errors from something written or printed', as in 'The editor in the publishing office emended the author's manuscript'. **Amend** means 'to correct', 'to improve' or 'to alter', as in 'We have overcharged you but we shall amend the error', and 'The rules for entry are old-fashioned and have to be amended'.

amiable and **amicable** both refer to friendliness and goodwill. **Amiable** means 'friendly' or 'agreeable and pleasant', and is mostly used of people or their moods, as in 'amiable neighbours', 'amiable travelling companions', 'of an amiable temperament' and 'be in an amiable mood'. **Amicable** means 'characterized by friendliness and goodwill' and is applied mainly to relationships, agreements, documents, etc, as in 'an amicable working relationship', 'reach an amicable settlement at the end of the war' and 'send an amicable letter to his former rival'.

among and **amongst** are interchangeable, as in 'We searched among/amongst the bushes for the ball,' 'Divide the chocolate among/amongst you', and 'You must choose among/amongst the various possibilities'.

among and **between** may be used interchangeably in most contexts. Formerly **between** was used only when referring to the relationship of two things, as in 'Share the chocolate between you and your brother', and **among** was used when referring to the relationship of three or more things, as in 'Share the chocolate among all your friends'. In modern usage **between** may be used when referring to more than two things, as in 'There is agreement between all the countries of the EC' and 'Share the chocolate between all of you'. However, **among** is still used only to describe more than two things.

amoral and **immoral** are not interchangeable. **Amoral** means 'lacking moral standards, devoid of moral sense', indicating that the person so described has no concern with morals, as in 'The child was completely amoral and did not know the difference between right and wrong'. **Immoral** means 'against or breaking moral standards, bad'. 'He knows he's doing wrong but he goes on being completely immoral' and 'commit immoral acts'. Note the spelling of both words. **Amoral** has only one *m* but **immoral** has double *m*.

an *see* **a**.

anaesthetic and **analgesic** are liable to be confused. As an adjective, **anaesthetic** means 'producing a loss of feeling', as in 'inject the patient with an anaesthetic substance', and as a noun it means 'a substance that produces a loss of feeling', as in 'administer an anaesthetic to the patient on the operating table'. A local anaesthetic produces a loss of feeling in only part of the body, as in 'remove the rotten tooth under local anaesthetic'. A **general anaesthetic** produces loss of feeling in the whole body and induces unconsciousness, as in 'The operation on his leg will have to be performed under general anaesthetic'. As an adjective **analgesic** means 'producing a lack of or reduction in, sensitivity to pain, pain-killing', as in 'aspirin has an analgesic effect'. As a noun **analgesic** means 'a substance that produces a lack of, or reduction in, sensitivity to pain', as in 'aspirin, paracetamol, and other analgesics'.

analyse is frequently misspelt. Note that it is not one of those verbs that can end in *-ize*. However, in American English 'analyze' is the accepted spelling.

annex and **annexe** are not interchangeable. Annex is a verb meaning 'to take possession of', as in 'The enemy invaders annexed the country' or 'to add or attach', as in 'She annexed a note to the document'. **Annexe** is a noun meaning 'a building added to, or used as an addition to, another building', as in 'build an annexe to the house as a workshop' and 'some school classes taking place in an annexe'.

antihistamine is sometimes misspelt. Note the *i*, not *y*, after *h*. **Antihistamine** is used to treat allergies.

apostrophe is a form of punctuation that is mainly used to indicate possession. Many spelling errors centre on the position of the apostrophe in relation to *s*.

Possessive nouns are usually formed by adding *'s* to the singular noun, as in 'the girl's mother', and Peter's car'; by adding an apostrophe to plural nouns that end in *s*, as in 'all the teachers' cars'; by adding *'s* to irregular plural nouns that do not end in *s*, as in 'women's shoes'.

In the possessive form of a name or singular noun that ends in *s*, *x* or *z*, the apostrophe may or may not be followed by *s*. In words of one syllable the final *s* is usually added, as in 'James's house', 'the fox's lair', 'Roz's dress'. The final *s* is most frequently omitted in names, particularly in names of three or more syllables, as in 'Euripides' plays'. In many cases the presence or absence of final *s* is a matter of convention.

The apostrophe is also used to indicate omitted letters in contracted forms of words, as in 'can't' and 'you've'. They are sometimes used to indicate missing century numbers in dates, as in 'the '60s and '70s', but are not used at the end of decades, etc, as in '1960s', not '1960's'.

Generally apostrophes are no longer used to indicate omitted letters in shortened forms that are in common use, as in 'phone' and 'flu'.

Apostrophes are often omitted wrongly in modern usage, particularly in the media and by advertisers, as in 'womens hairdressers', 'childrens helpings'. In addition, apostrophes are frequently added erroneously (as in 'potato's for sale' and 'Beware of the dog's'). This is partly because people are unsure about when and when not to use them and partly because of a modern tendency to punctuate as little as possible.

appal is very frequently misspelt. Note the double *p* and single *l*. Note also the double *ll* in **appalled** and **appalling**.

arbiter and **arbitrator**, although similar in meaning, are not totally interchangeable. **Arbiter** means 'a person who has absolute power to judge or make decisions', as in 'Parisian designers used to be total arbiters of fashion'. **Arbitrator** is 'a person appointed to settle differences in a dispute', as in 'act as arbitrator between management and workers in the wages dispute'. **Arbiter** is occasionally used with the latter meaning also.

archaeology is liable to be misspelt. Note the order of the three vowels in the middle—*aeo*.

artist and **artiste** are liable to be confused. **Artist** refers to 'a person who paints or draws,' as in 'Renoir was a great artist'. The word may also refer to 'a person who is skilled in something', as in 'The mechanic is a real artist with an engine'. **Artiste** refers to 'an entertainer, such as a singer or a dancer', as in 'a list of the artistes in the musical performances'. The word is becoming a little old-fashioned.

asphyxiate is frequently misspelt. Note that it has *y*, not *i*, before *x*. It means 'to suffocate', as in 'asphyxiate his victim with a pillow'.

assassinate is frequently misspelt. Note the two sets of double *s*. It means 'to murder, especially someone of political importance', as in 'Rebels assassinated the president'. Note also the spelling of **assassin**, 'a person who assassinates someone'.

asthma is frequently misspelt. Note the *th*, which is frequently wrongly omitted. The word refers to 'a chronic breathing disorder'.

atheist *see* **agnostic**.

at this moment in time is an overused phrase meaning simply 'now'. In modern usage there is a tendency to use what are thought to be grander-sounding alternatives for simple words. It is best to avoid such overworked phrases and use the simpler form.

au fait is French in origin but it is commonly used in English to mean 'familiar with' or 'informed about', as in 'not completely au fait with the new office system'. It is pronounced *o* fay.

aural and **oral** are liable to be confused because they sound similar and are both related to parts of the body. **Aural** means 'of the ear' or 'referring to the sense of hearing', as in 'aural faculties affected by the explosion' and 'The children were given an aural comprehension test (that is, one that one was read out to them) in French'. **Oral** means 'of the mouth' or 'referring to speech', as in 'oral hygiene' and 'an oral examination' (that is, one in which questions and answers are spoken, not written).

aurally challenged means 'deaf' or 'hard of hearing'. It is part of the 'politically correct' movement to make a personal problem or disadvantage appear in a positive rather than a negative light. Although the intention behind it is a good one, the phrase, and others like it, have not really caught on, and such phrases are indeed subject to ridicule because they sound rather high-flown.

authoress is not used in modern usage since it is considered sexist. **Author** is regarded as a neutral term to describe both male and female authors.

averse *see* **adverse**.

avoid *see* **evade**.

avoidance *see* **evasion**.

B

bachelor is frequently misspelt, it being common, and wrong, to include a *t* before the *c*. Note that the term **bachelor girl** is objected to by many women for the same reason that they object to adding *-ess* to the masculine to make a feminine form, as in 'authoress'.

backward and **backwards** in British English are respectively adjective and adverb. Examples of **backward** include 'take a backward step' and 'The child is rather backward for his age'. Examples of **backwards** include 'take a step backwards'. In American English **backward** is frequently used as a adverb.

bacteria is a plural noun, the singular form being **bacterium**, which is found mainly in scientific or medical texts. Thus it is correct to say 'a stomach infection caused by bacteria in the water' but quite wrong to say 'an infection caused by a bacteria'.

bail and **bale** are liable to be confused. **Bail** as a noun means 'the security money deposited as a guarantee that an arrested person will appear in court', as in 'Her family provided money for her bail' and 'Her brother stood bail for her.' It also has a verb form, as in 'His friends did not have enough money to bail him'. This verb often takes the form **bail out**. **Bale** is a noun meaning 'a bundle', as in 'a bundle of hay'.

    Bail and **bale** are both acceptable forms of the verb meaning 'to scoop', as in 'The fishermen had to bail/bale water out of the bottom of the boat'. Similarly, both forms of the verb are acceptable when they mean 'to make an emergency parachute jump from a plane', as in 'The plane caught fire and the pilot had to bail/bale out'.

baited *see* **bated**.

bale *see* **bail**.

balk and **baulk** are both acceptable spellings of the verb meaning 'to refuse or be reluctant to do something', as in 'She balked/baulked at paying such a high price for a dress' and 'to obstruct or prevent', as in 'She was balked/baulked in her attempt at swimming the Channel by bad weather'.

banal is frequently mispronounced. It should rhyme with 'canal', with the emphasis on the second syllable (ba-*nal*).

banister, meaning 'the handrail supported by posts fixed at the side of a staircase', may be spelt **bannister** but it is a less common form.

barmaid is disliked by many people on the grounds that it sounds a belittling term and is thus sexist. It is also disliked by people who are interested in political correctness. However the word continues to be quite common, along with **barman**, and efforts to insist on **bar assistant** or **barperson** have not yet succeeded.

basis, meaning 'something on which something is founded', as in 'The cost of the project was the basis of his argument against it', has the plural form **bases** although it is not commonly used. It would be more usual to say 'arguments without a firm basis' than 'arguments without firm bases'.

basically means literally 'referring to a base or basis, fundamentally', as in 'The scientist's theory is basically unsound', but it is frequently used almost meaninglessly as a fill-up word at the beginning of a sentence, as in 'Basically he just wants more money'. Overuse of this word should be avoided.

bated, as in 'with bated breath' meaning 'tense and anxious with excitement', is frequently misspelt **baited**. Care should be taken not to confuse the two words.

bath and **bathe** are not interchangeable. **Bath** as a verb means 'to have a bath', as in 'He baths every morning' or 'to wash someone in a bath', as in 'The mother bathed the baby in a small tin bath'. **Bathe**, on the other hand, is used to mean 'to wash (a wound, etc)', as in 'She bathed the boy's grazed knee with warm water' or 'to swim in the sea', as in 'too cold to bathe today'. In American English **bathe** is used in the sense of 'have a bath', as in 'prefer to bathe than take a shower'.

bathroom *see* **toilet**.

baulk *see* **balk**.

BC *see* **AD**.

beat and **beaten** are frequently used wrongly. **Beat** is the past tense of the verb 'to beat', as in 'Our team beat the opposition easily' and 'His father used to beat him when he was a child'. **Beaten** is the past participle of the verb 'to beat', as in 'We should have beaten them easily' and 'He thought the child should have been beaten for his bad behaviour'.

beautiful is frequently misspelt. Note the order of the vowels (*eau*). Note also the single *l*.

because means 'for the reason that', as in 'He left because he was bored', and is sometimes misused. It is wrong to use it in a sentence that also contains 'the reason that', as in 'The reason she doesn't say much is that she is shy'. The correct form of this is 'She doesn't say much because she is shy' or 'The reason she doesn't say much is that she is shy'.

because of *see* **due to**.

beg the question is often used wrongly. It means 'to take for granted the very point that has to be proved', as in 'To say that God must exist because we can see all his wonderful creations in the world around us begs the question'. The statement assumes that these creations have been made by God although this has not been proved and yet this fact is being used as evidence that there is a God. **Beg the question** is often used wrongly to mean 'to evade the question', as in 'The police tried to get him to say where he had been but he begged the question and changed the subject'.

beige, meaning 'a pale brown colour', is frequently misspelt. Note the order of *e* and *i*. The pronunciation of the word may also cause difficulties. It is pronounced *bayzh*.

benefit causes problems with the parts of the verb. The past tense is **benefited**, as in 'They benefited from having had an excellent education'. The present participle is **benefiting**, as in 'Benefiting from the will of their late uncle they were able to buy a bigger house'. Note the single *t*.

benign means 'kindly, well-disposed' when applied to people, as in 'fortunate enough to have a benign ruler'. This meaning may also be used of things, as in 'give a benign smile' and 'live in a benign climate'. As a medical term **benign** means 'nonmalignant, non-cancerous'. **Innocent** is another word for **benign** in this sense.

beside and **besides** are not interchangeable. **Beside** is a preposition meaning 'by the side of', as in 'The little girl wants to sit beside her friend' and 'They walked beside each other all the way'. **Beside** is also found in the phrase **'beside oneself'**, meaning 'extremely agitated', as in 'The children were beside themselves with excitement waiting to go on a picnic' and 'He was beside himself with rage when his rival won the prize'.

Besides has several meanings. It means 'moreover, in addition', as in 'The house is overpriced. Besides, it's too far from the village'. It also means 'as well as, in addition to', as in 'We have visited many countries besides France', and 'other than, except for', as in 'They are interested in nothing besides work' and 'I have told no one besides you'.

bet is the common form of the past tense and past participle of the verb 'to bet', as in 'He bet me he could run faster than me' and 'He would have bet hundreds of pounds that the horse he fancied would win'. 'Placed a bet' is an alternative form, as in 'He has never placed a bet in his life' as an alternative to 'He has never bet in his life'. The form **betted** exists but it is rare.

bête noire refers to 'something that one detests or fears', as in 'Loud pop music is her father's bête noire, although she sings with a pop group'. Note the spelling, particularly the accent (circumflex) on **bête** and the *e* at the end of **noire.** The phrase is French in origin and the plural form is **bêtes noires**, as in 'A bearded man is one of her many bêtes noires'.

betted *see* **bet**.

better should be preceded by 'had' when it means 'ought to' or 'should', as in 'You had better leave now if you want to arrive there by nightfall' and 'We had better apologize for upsetting her'. In informal contexts, especially in informal speech as in 'Hey Joe, Mum says you better come now', the 'had' is often omitted but it should be retained in formal contexts. The negative form is 'had better not', as in 'He had better not try to deceive her'.

between *see* **among**.

between is often found in the phrase 'between you and me' as in 'Between you and me I think he stole the money'. Note that 'me' is correct and that 'I' is wrong. This is because prepositions like 'between' are followed by an object, not a subject. 'I' acts as the subject of a sentence, as in 'I know her', and 'me' as the object, as in 'She knows me'.

bi- Of the words beginning with the prefix bi-, biannual and biennial are liable to be confused. **Biannual** means 'twice a year' and **biennial** means 'every two years'.

Bicentenary and **bicentennial** both mean 'a 200th anniversary', as in 'celebrating the bicentenary/bicentennial of the firm'. **Bicentenary** is, however, the more common expression in British English, although **bicentennial** is more common in American English.

Biweekly is a confusing word as it has two different meanings. It means both 'twice a week' and 'once every two weeks'. Thus there is no means of knowing without other information whether 'a bi-weekly publication' comes out once a week or every two weeks. The confusion arises because the prefix 'bi-', which means 'two', can refer both to doubling, as in 'bicycle', and halving, as in 'bisection'.

biannual *see* **bi-**.

bias should become **biased** and **biasing** in the past tense and past participle, and the present participle, respectively, as in 'The behaviour of some of the competitors biased the judges against them' and in 'The behaviour of some of the competitors seem to be biasing the judges against them.'. However in modern usage **biassed** and **biassing** respectively are acceptable alternative spellings.

bicentenary and **bicentennial** *see* **bi-**.

biennial *see* **bi-**.

billion traditionally meant 'one million million' in British English, but in modern usage it has increasingly taken on the American English meaning of 'one thousand million'. When the number of million pounds, etc, is specified, the number immediately precedes the word 'million' without the word 'of', as in 'The firm is worth five billion dollars', but if no number is present then 'of' precedes 'dollars, etc', ' as in 'The research project cost the country millions of dollars'. The word **billion** may also be used loosely to mean 'a great but unspecified number', as in 'Billions of people in the world live in poverty'.

birth name is a suggested alternative for **maiden name**, a woman's surname before she married and took the name of her husband. **Maiden name** is considered by some to be inappropriate since maiden in one of its senses is another name for 'virgin' and it is now not at all usual for women to be virgins when they marry. Another possible name alternative is **family name.**

biweekly *see* **bi-**.

bizarre, meaning 'odd, weird', is frequently misspelt. Note the single *z* and double *r*.

black is the word now usually applied to dark-skinned people of Afro-Caribbean origins and is the term preferred by most black-skinned people themselves. **Coloured** is considered by many to be offensive since it groups all non-Caucasians together. In America, African-American is becoming increasingly common as a substitute for **black**.

blackguard, meaning 'a wicked or dishonourable person, a scoundrel', has an unusual pronunciation. It is pronounced *blagg*-ard.

blind is objected to by those concerned with 'political correctness' on the grounds that it concentrates on the negative aspect of being without sight. They suggest 'optically challenged' although this has not become widely used.

bloc and **block** are liable to be confused. **Bloc** refers to 'a group of people, parties or countries that get together for a particular purpose, often a political one', as in 'Those countries were formerly members of the communist bloc'. **Block** has a wide range of meanings, as in 'a block of wood', 'a block of cheese', 'an office block', 'a road block'.

blond and **blonde** are both used to mean 'a fair-haired person', but they are not interchangeable. **Blond** is used to describe a man or boy, **blonde** is used to describe a woman or girl. They are derived from the French adjective, which changes endings according to the gender of the noun.

boat and **ship** are often used interchangeably, but usually **boat** refers to a smaller vessel than a ship.

bona fide is an expression of Latin origin meaning literally 'of good faith'. It means 'genuine, sincere' or 'authentic', as in 'a bona fide member of the group', 'a bona fide excuse for not going', or 'a bona fide agreement'.

born-again was originally applied to an evangelical Christian who had been converted. Although this use still exists, the meaning has extended to refer to a conversion to a belief or cause, especially when this is extremely enthusiastic and fervent, as in 'a born-again nonsmoker', 'a born-again conservationist'.

bottom line is an expression from accountancy that has become commonly used in the general language. In accountancy it refers to the final line of a set of company accounts, which indicates whether the company has made a profit or a loss, obviously a very important line. In general English, **bottom line** has a range of meanings, from 'the final outcome or result', as in 'The bottom line of their discussion was that they decided to sell the company', through 'the most important point of something', as in 'The bottom line was whether they could get there on time or not', to 'the last straw', as in 'His affair with another woman was the bottom line of their stormy relationship and she left him'.

bouquet is frequently misspelt and mispronounced. Note the *ou* and *qu* in the spelling. It is pronounced boo-*kay*.

bourgeois, a word meaning middle-class that is usually derogatory, is frequently misspelt. Note the *our* in the first syllable and the *e* before the *ois*.

boycott, meaning 'to refuse to having anything to do with', is frequently misspelt. Note the double *t* at the end of the word.

brackets may be used to enclose any material of a supplementary or explanatory nature that interrupts the flow of a sentence. The material inside the brackets may be removed without altering the central meaning of the sentence. Commas or dashes may be used to serve the same purpose, when the interruption to the flow of the sentence is not quite so marked. Round brackets are more commonly used than square brackets. Examples of brackets include 'Pablo Picasso (1881–1973) was a famous artist'; 'There are a great many people with her family name (Brown) listed in the telephone directory'; 'He has a yucca (a kind of plant) in his study'. **Brackets** are also known as **parentheses** (singular **parenthesis**).

breach and **breech** are liable to be confused. **Breach** means 'a break or gap', as in 'cows getting through a breach in the fence', and 'the breaking or violation of', as in 'commit a breach of the peace', 'a breach of the local bye-laws'. **Breech**, on the other hand, means 'the rear part of the body' as in 'It was a breech delivery (i.e. the baby was delivered bottom first)', or 'the part of a gun behind the barrel', as in 'a breech-loading gun'.

broach and **brooch** are liable to be confused. They are pronounced alike but have different meanings. **Broach** is a verb meaning either to 'introduce or mention (a subject)', as in 'She did not like to broach the subject of money at the interview', or 'to open (a bottle)', as in 'broach a bottle of champagne to celebrate the baby's birth'. **Brooch** is a noun that means 'a piece of jewellery that one pins on a blouse, sweater, etc.'

brochure is usually pronounced *bro*-sher, despite the *ch* spelling, rather than bro-*shoor*, which is French-sounding. The word is French in origin.

brooch *see* **broach**.

buffet has two different pronunciations according to sense. In the sense of 'a counter or sideboard from which food is served' and 'self-service food set out on tables', as in 'They are having a buffet rather than a sit-down meal at the wedding', **buffet** is pronounced *boo*-fay. **Buffet** also has the meaning of 'to strike', as in 'ships buffeted by the wind', and 'a blow', as in 'give the boy a buffet across the ear', when it is pronounced buf-fet.

buoyant, meaning either 'able to float', as in 'Rubber is a buoyant substance', or 'cheerful', as in 'in buoyant mood', is frequently misspelt. The most common error is to put the *u* and *o* in the wrong order.

bureaucracy is frequently misspelt. Note the *eau* combination and the *c*, not *s*, before *y*.

burned and **burnt** may be used interchangeably as the past tense and the past participle of the verb 'to burn', as in 'They burned/burnt the rubbish in the back garden' and 'She has burned/burnt her arm on the stove'.

business is frequently misspelt. The most common error is to omit letter *i* since it is not pronounced.

bus was originally an abbreviation for omnibus but it is no longer spelt with an apostrophe before it. Thus **bus**, not **'bus.** The plural is **buses**.

bylaw and **bye-law** are both acceptable spellings. The word means a law or rule applying to a local area.

C

caffeine, a stimulant found in coffee and tea, is frequently misspelt. Note the double *f* and the *ei* combination. Note also the pronunciation (*kaf*-feen).

calendar, **calender** and **colander**: **calendar** is often misspelt as **calender**, which is the name of 'a machine used to smooth paper or cloth', or as **calander**, simply an erroneous spelling. **Calendar** is also sometimes confused with **colander**, a perforated bowl used for straining.

can and **may** both mean in one of their senses 'to be permitted'. In this sense **can** is much less formal than **may** and is best restricted to informal contexts, as in '"Can I go to the park now?" asked the child'. **May** is used in more formal contexts, as in 'May I please have your name?' Both **can** and **may** have other meanings. **Can** has the meaning 'to be able', as in 'They thought his legs were permanently damaged but he can still walk'. **May** has the additional meaning 'to be likely', as in 'You may well be right'.

  The past tense of **can** is **could**, as in 'The children asked if they could (= be permitted to) go to the park'. 'The old man could (= be unable to) not walk upstairs'. The past tense of **may** is **might**, as in 'The child asked if he might have a piece of cake (= be permitted to)'. 'They might (= be likely to) well get here tonight'.

cannon and **canon** are liable to be confused although they mean completely different things. **Cannon** means 'a large gun', as in 'large cannons placed on the castle ramparts', or 'a kind of shot in billiards', as in 'His opponent won the match with a superb cannon'. **Canon** refers to 'a ruling, particularly one laid down by the church', as in 'accused of breaking the canons of his church' and 'refuse to obey the traditional moral canons', or to 'a title given to some clergymen' as in 'one of the cathedral canons'.

cannot, **can not**, and **can't** all mean the same thing but they are used in different contexts. **Cannot** is the most usual form, as in 'The children have been told that they cannot go' and 'We cannot get there by public transport'. **Cannot** is written as two words only for emphasis, as in 'No, you can not have any more' and 'The invalid certainly can not walk to the ambulance'. **Can't** is used in less formal contexts and often in speech, as in 'I can't be bothered going out' and 'They can't bear to be apart'.

canvas and **canvass** are liable to be confused. **Canvas** is 'a type of heavy cloth', as in 'tents made of canvas', 'trousers made of canvas', and 'paint on canvas'. **Canvass** is a verb meaning 'to solicit votes, orders, etc, from', as in 'members of various political parties canvassing people in the high street' and 'encyclopedia salesmen canvassing our neighbours', and also meaning 'to find out how people are going to vote in an election, etc', as in 'Party workers canvassed our street the night before the election'. **Canvass** may also be a noun, as in 'an eve-of-election canvass'.

capital letters are used in a number of different situations. The first word of a sentence or a direct quotation begins with a **capital letter**, as in 'They left early', 'Why have they gone?' and 'He said weakly, "I don't feel very well"'.

  The first letter of a name or proper noun is always a **capital letter**, as in 'Mary Brown', 'John Smith', 'South America', 'Rome', 'speak Italian', 'Buddhism', 'Marxism'. **Capital letters** are also used in the titles of people, places or works of art, as in 'Uncle Fred', 'Professor Jones', 'Ely Cathedral', 'Edinburgh University', 'reading *Wuthering Heights*', 'watching *Guys and Dolls*', 'listen to Beethoven's Third Symphony' and 'a copy of *The Potato Eaters* by van Gogh'. They are also used in the titles of wars and historical, cultural and geological periods, as in 'the Wars of the Roses', 'the Renaissance', 'the Ice Age'.

  Note that only the major words of titles, etc, are in **capital letters**, words, such as 'the', 'on', 'of', etc, being in lower-case letters.

A **capital letter** is used as the first letter of days of the week, months of the year, and religious festivals, as in 'Monday', 'October', 'Easter', 'Yom Kippur'. It is a matter of choice whether the seasons of the year are given capital letters or not, as in 'spring/Spring', 'autumn/Autumn'.

Apart from 'I', pronouns are lower-case except when they refer to God or Christ, when some people capitalize them, as in 'God asks us to trust in Him'.

Trade names should be spelt with an initial **capital letter**, as in 'Filofax', 'Jacuzzi', 'Xerox', 'Biro', 'Hoover'. When verbs are formed from these, they are spelt with an initial lower-case letter, as 'xerox the letter', 'hoover the carpet'.

carburettor is frequently misspelt. Note the single *r* and double *t*.

carcass and **carcase** are both acceptable spellings for the word for the body of a dead animal. The dead body of a human is called a **corpse**.

cardinal and **ordinal** numbers refer to different aspects of numbers. **Cardinal** is applied to those numbers that refer to quantity or value without referring to their place in the set, as in 'one', 'two', 'fifty' 'one hundred'. **Ordinal** is applied to numbers that refer to their order in a series, as in 'first', 'second', 'fortieth', 'hundredth'.

cardigan, jersey, jumper and **sweater** all refer to knitted garments for the top part of the body. **Cardigan** refers to a jacket-like garment with buttons down the front. **Jersey, jumper** and **sweater** refer to a knitted garment pulled over the head to get it on and off.

carer has recently taken on the meaning of 'a person who looks after a sick, handicapped or old relative or friend', as in 'carers requiring a break from their responsibilities'.

caring has recently been used to apply to professions such as social workers, nurses and doctors, and others who are professionally involved in the welfare of people, as in 'the members of the caring professions'.

carpet and **rug** both refer to forms of floor covering. Generally a rug is smaller than a carpet, and the fitted variety of fabric floor covering is always known as carpet.

caster and **castor** are mainly interchangeable. Both forms can be applied to 'a swivelling wheel attached to the base of a piece of furniture to enable it to be moved easily' and 'a container with a perforated top from which sugar is sprinkled'. The kind of sugar known as **caster** can also be called **castor**, although this is less usual. The lubricating or medicinal oil known as **castor oil** is never spelt **caster**.

catarrh is frequently misspelt. Note the single *t*, double *r*, and *h*.

Catholic and **catholic** have different meanings. **Catholic** as an adjective refers to the Roman Catholic Church, as in 'The Pope is head of the Catholic Church', or to the universal body of Christians. As a noun it means 'a member of the Catholic Church', as in 'She is a Catholic but he is a Protestant'. Catholic with a lower-case initial letter means 'general, wide-ranging', as in 'a catholic selection of essays', and ' broad-minded, liberal', as in 'a catholic attitude to the tastes of others'.

ceiling is frequently misspelt. Note the *e* before *i*. As well as its literal use, **ceiling** is used to mean 'upper limit', as in 'impose a ceiling on rent increases'.

celibate means 'unmarried' or 'remaining unmarried and chaste, especially for religious reasons', as in 'Roman Catholic priests have to be celibate'. In modern usage, because of its connection with chastity, **celibate** has come to mean 'abstaining from sexual intercourse', as in 'The threat of Aids has made many people celibate'. The word is frequently misspelt. Note the *i* after *l*.

Celsius, centigrade and **Fahrenheit** are all scales of temperature. **Celsius** and **centigrade** mean the same and refer to a scale on which water freezes at O° and boils at 100°. This scale is now the principal unit of temperature. **Celsius** is now the more acceptable term. **Fahrenheit** refers to a scale on which water freezes at 32° and boils at 212°. It is still used, informally at least, of the weather, and statements such as 'The temperature reached the nineties today' are still common.

Note the initial capital letters in **Celsius** and **Fahrenheit**. This is because they are named after people, namely the scientists who devised them.

Celtic is usually pronounced kel-tik. It refers to the 'language, people or culture of Scotland, Ireland, Wales and Brittany', as in 'try to preserve the Celtic tradition'.

censor, **censure** and **censer** are liable to be confused. **Censor** means 'to examine letters, publications, etc, and remove anything whose inclusion is against official policy, or is obscene or libellous', as in 'In wartime, soldiers' letters were often censored in case the enemy got hold of useful information' and in 'Parts of the film had to be censored in order to make it suitable for children'. **Censure** means 'to blame or criticize severely', as in 'The police were censured by the press for not catching the murderer of the child' and in 'The pupils were censured by the headmaster for bullying younger children'. **Censure** may also be a noun, as in 'They encountered strong censure from their neighbours for reprimanding the children'. The spelling of **censor** is often confused with that of **censer**, 'a vessel used for burning incense'.

centenary and **centennial** are both used to refer to a 'one-hundredth anniversary'. **Centenary** is the more common term in British English, as in 'celebrate the town's centenary', whereas **centennial** is more common in American English. **Centennial** may be used as an adjective, as in 'organize the town's centennial celebrations'.

centigrade *see* **Celsius**.

centre and **middle** mean much the same, but **centre** is used more precisely than **middle** in some cases, as in 'a line through the centre of the circle' and 'She felt faint in the middle of the crowd'.

centre on and **centre around** are often used interchangeably, as in 'Her world centres on/around her children'. **Centre around** is objected to by some people on the grounds that **centre** is too specific to be used with something as vague as **around**. When it is used as a verb with place names, **centre** is used with 'at', as in 'Their business operation is centred at London'.

centuries are calculated from 1001, 1501, 1901, etc, not 1000, 1500, 1900, etc. This is because the years are counted from AD 1, there being no year 0.

cervical has two possible pronunciations. Both *ser*-vik-al, with the emphasis on the first syllable, and ser-*vik*-al, with the emphasis on the second syllable which has the same sound as in Viking. The word means 'referring to the neck or the constricted part of an organ, e.g. of the uterus', as in 'cervical cancer'.

chair is often used to mean 'a person in charge of a meeting, committee, etc', as in 'The committee has a new chair this year'. Formerly **chairman** was always used in this context, as in 'He was appointed chairman of the fund-raising committee' but this is disapproved of on the grounds that it is sexist. Formerly, **chairman** was sometimes used even if the person in charge of the meeting or committee was a woman, and sometimes **chairwoman** was used in this situation. **Chairperson**, which also avoids sexism, is frequently used instead of **chair**. **Chair** is also a verb meaning 'to be in charge of a meeting, committee, etc'.

-challenged is a modern suffix that is very much part of politically correct language. It is used to convey a disadvantage, problem or disorder in a more positive light. For example, 'visually challenged' is used in politically correct language instead of 'blind' or 'partially sighted' and 'aurally challenged' is used instead of 'deaf' or 'hard of hearing'. **-Challenged** is often used in humorous coinages, as in 'financially challenged', meaning 'penniless', and 'intellectually challenged', meaning 'stupid'.

chamois is frequently both misspelt and mispronounced. In the sense of 'a kind of cloth (made from the skin of the chamois antelope) used for polishing or cleaning' it is pronounced *sham*-mi. In the sense of 'a kind of antelope', it is pronounced *sham*-wa.

changeable is frequently spelt wrongly. Note the *e* after the *g*.

chaperon and **chaperone** are both acceptable spellings. The word means 'an older woman who accompanies or supervises a young unmarried woman on social occasions', as in 'in Victorian times young unmarried women did not go out with young men without a chaperon/chaperone'. The word may also be a verb, as in 'She was asked to chaperon/chaperone her niece to the ball'.

charisma was formerly a theological word used to mean 'a spiritual gift', such as the gift of healing, etc. In modern usage it is used to describe 'a special quality or power that influences, inspires or stimulates other people, personal magnetism', as in 'The president was elected because of his charisma'. The adjective from **charisma** is **charismatic**, as in 'his charismatic style of leadership'.

charted and **chartered** are liable to be confused. **Charted** is formed from the verb 'to chart', meaning 'to make a chart or map of', as in 'few charted areas of the continent'. It is more common in the negative, as in 'uncharted areas of the interior of the country'. **Chartered** has two meanings. One is formed from the verb 'to charter', meaning 'to hire', as in 'a chartered yacht'. The other is usually found in such phrases as 'chartered accountant/surveyor/engineer, etc', and means 'an accountant, etc, who has passed the examinations of the Institute of Chartered Accountants, etc'. The institutes in question have received a royal charter or 'document granting certain official rights or privileges'.

chauvinism originally meant 'excessive patriotism', being derived from the name of Nicolas Chauvin, a soldier in the army of Napoleon Bonaparte, who was noted for his excessive patriotism. In modern usage **chauvinism** has come to mean 'excessive enthusiasm or devotion to a cause' or, more particularly, 'an irrational and prejudiced belief in the superiority of one's own cause'. When preceded by 'male', it refers specifically to attitudes and actions that assume the superiority of the male sex and thus the inferiority of women, as in 'accused of not giving her the job because of male chauvinism'. **Chauvinism** is frequently used to mean **male chauvinism**, as in 'He shows his chauvinism towards his female staff by never giving any of them senior jobs'. The adjective formed from **chauvinism** is **chauvinistic**.

check and **cheque** are liable to be confused. **Check** as a verb means 'to make sure that something is in order', as in 'check the tread of the tyres', or 'to make sure', as in 'check you locked the windows', or 'to slow down, stop or control', as 'check the growth of drug-related offences'. As a noun **check** means 'an examination to make sure that something is in order, as in 'conduct checks on all tyre treads', or 'a slowing-down or stopping', as in 'ordering a check on public expenditure', or 'a curb, restraint or check', as in 'His common sense acted as a check on their extravagance'. **Cheque** means 'a money order', as in 'pay his bill by cheque'. In American English **check** is used for 'money order' as well as the other meanings.

chemist and **pharmacist** have the same meaning in one sense of **chemist** only. **Chemist** and **pharmacist** are both words for 'one who prepares drugs ordered by medical prescription'. **Chemist** has the additional meaning of 'a scientist who works in the field of chemistry', as in 'He works as an industrial chemist'.

cheque *see* **check**.

chilblain is frequently misspelt. Note the single *l*.

childish and **childlike** both refer to someone being like a child but they are used in completely different contexts. **Childish** is used in a derogatory way about someone to indicate that he or she is acting like a child in an immature way, as in 'Even though she is 20 years old she has childish tantrums when she does not get her own way' and 'childish handwriting for an adult'. **Childlike** is a term of approval or a complimentary term used to describe something that has some of the attractive qualities of childhood, as in 'She has a childlike enthusiasm for picnics' and 'He has a childlike trust in others'.

chiropodist, meaning 'a person who treats minor disorders of the feet, is usually pronounced kir-*op*-od-ist with an initial *k* sound, but the pronunciation shir-*op*-od-ist with an initial *sh* sound is also possible.

chord and **cord** are liable to be confused because they sound alike. The spelling **chord** is used in the musical sense, as in 'play the wrong chord', and in the mathematical sense, as in 'draw a chord joining the points on the circumference of a circle'. The spelling **cord** is used to mean 'a kind of string', as in 'tie up the bundle with cord' and 'use a piece of nylon cord as a washing line'. Cord is also used with reference to certain parts of the body, as in 'spinal cord', 'vocal cords', umbilical cord'.

Christian name is used to mean someone's first name as opposed to someone's **surname**. It is increasingly being replaced by **first name** or **forename** since Britain has become a multicultural society where there are several religions as well as Christianity.

chronic *see* **acute**.

cirrhosis is liable to be misspelt. Note the *rrh* combination. The word refers to 'a disease of the liver'.

city and **town** in modern usage are usually distinguished on grounds of size and status, a city being larger and more important than a town. Originally in Britain a **city** was a town which had special rights conferred on it by royal charter and which usually had a cathedral.

clandestine, meaning 'secret or furtive', usually has the emphasis on the second syllable, as klan-*des*-tin', but it is acceptable to pronounce it with the emphasis on the first syllable, as *klan*-des-tin.

classism means 'discrimination on the grounds of class, snobbism', as in 'Not letting her children play with the children of her housekeeper was classism'. **Classist** refers to 'a person who practises classism, a snob', as in 'She's such a classist that she is always rude to shop assistants'.

claustrophobia, fear of confined spaces, is frequently misspelt. Note the *au* and the *o* before *p*.

clean and **cleanse** as verbs both mean 'to clean', as in 'clean the house' and 'cleanse the wound'. However, **cleanse** tends to indicate a more thorough cleaning than **clean** and sometimes carries the suggestion of 'to purify', as in 'prayer cleansing the soul'.

cliché is 'a phrase that has been used so often that it has become stale'. Some examples include 'unused to public speaking as I am', 'time heals everything', 'a blessing in disguise', 'keep a low profile', 'conspicuous by their absence', 'part and parcel', 'at death's door'. Sometimes the phrase in question was quite apt when first used but overuse has made it trite and frequently almost meaningless.

client and **customer**, although closely related in meaning, are not interchangeable. **Client** refers to 'a person who pays for the advice or services of a professional person', as in 'They are both clients of the same lawyer', 'a client waiting to see the bank manager' and 'hairdressers who keep their clients waiting'. **Customer** refers to 'a person who purchases goods from a shop, etc', as in 'customers complaining to shopkeepers about faulty goods' and 'a regular customer at the local supermarket'. **Client** is used in the sense of 'customer' by shops who regard it as a more superior word, as in ' clients of an exclusive dress boutique'.

clientele, meaning a group of clients, is frequently both mispronounced and misspelt. It is pronounced klee-on-*tel*. Note the *le*, not double *ll*.

climate no longer refers just to weather, as in 'go to live in a hot climate', 'Britain has a temperate climate'. It has extended its meaning to refer to 'atmosphere', as in 'live in a climate of despair' and to 'the present situation', as in 'businessmen nervous about the financial climate'.

clone originally was a technical word meaning 'one of a group of offspring that are asexually produced and which are genetically identical to the parent and to other members of the group'. In modern usage **clone** is frequently used loosely to mean 'something that is very similar to something else', as in 'In the sixties there were many Beatles' clones', and 'grey-suited businessmen looking like clones of each other'.

collaborate and **cooperate** are not interchangeable in all contexts. They both mean 'to work together for a common purpose', as in 'The two scientists are collaborating/cooperating on cancer research' and 'The rival building firms are collaborating/cooperating

coloured

on the new shopping complex'. When the work concerned is of an artistic or creative nature **collaborate** is the more commonly used word, as in 'The two directors are collaborating on the film' and 'The composers collaborated on the theme music'. **Collaborate** also has the meaning of 'to work with an enemy, especially an enemy that is occupying one's country', as in 'a Frenchman who collaborated with the Germans when they installed a German government in France'.

coloured *see* **black**.

coloration, meaning 'arrangement or mode of colouring', as in 'the unusual coloration of the bird', is frequently misspelt. Unlike **colour**, it has no *u* before the *r*.

columnist, meaning 'a person who writes a column, or regular feature, in a newspaper or magazine', as in 'a columnist with the *New York Times*', is liable to be mispronounced. The *n* is pronounced, unlike in **column** where the *n* is silent.

commemorate means 'to remember, or mark the memory of, especially with some kind of ceremony', as in 'commemorate the soldiers who died in the war with an annual church service'. When applied to a plaque, piece of sculpture, etc, it means 'to serve as a memorial to', as in 'The statue in the village square commemorates those who gave their lives in World War II.

commence, **begin** and **start** mean the same, but **commence** is used in a more formal context than the other two words, as in 'The legal proceedings will commence tomorrow' and 'The memorial service will commence with a hymn'. **Begin** and **start** are used less formally, as 'The match begins at 2 p.m.' and 'The film has already started'.

commensurate is followed by 'with' to form a phrase meaning 'proportionate to, appropriate to', as in 'a salary commensurate with her qualifications' and 'a price commensurate with the quality of the goods'.

commitment, meaning 'dedication or loyalty', as in 'his commitment to the socialist cause' and 'unable to make the commitment that marriage demands', is frequently misspelt. Note the double *m* but single *t*. Note that **committed** has double *t*.

committee is frequently misspelt. Note the double *m*, double *t* and double *e*. It may be either a singular or plural noun, and so takes either a singular or plural verb, as in 'The committee meets tomorrow' and 'The committee have reached a decision'.

comparable is liable to be mispronounced. The emphasis should be on the first syllable, as in *kom*-par-able. It is often mispronounced with the emphasis on the second syllable.

comparatively means 'relatively, in comparison with a standard', as in 'The house was comparatively inexpensive for that area of the city' and 'In an area of extreme poverty they are comparatively well off'. In modern usage it is often used loosely to mean 'rather' or 'fairly' without any suggestion of reference to a standard, as in 'She has comparatively few friends' and 'It is a comparatively quiet resort'.

compare may take either the preposition 'to' or 'with'. 'To' is used when two things or people are being likened to each other or being declared similar, as in 'He compared her hair to silk' and 'He compared his wife to Helen of Troy'. 'With' is used when two things or people are being considered from the point of view of both similarities and differences, as in 'If you compare the new pupil's work with that of the present class you will find it brilliant', and 'If you compare the prices in the two stores you will find that the local one is the cheaper'. In modern usage the distinction is becoming blurred because the difference is rather subtle.

comparison is usually followed by the preposition 'with', as in 'In comparison with hers his work is brilliant'. However, when it means 'the action of likening something or someone to something or someone else', it is followed by 'to', as in 'the comparison of her beauty to that of Garbo'.

complacent and **complaisant** are liable to be confused because they are pronounced similarly, as kom-*play*-sint and kom-*play*-zint. However, they have slightly different meanings. **Complacent** means 'smug, self-satisfied', as in 'He knows that he has passed the

306

exam and he is very complacent' and 'She gave a complacent smile when she realized that she had won'. **Complaisant** is rather a formal word meaning 'willing to go along with the wishes of others, acquiescent', as in ''She will not raise any objections—she is so complaisant'. 'She indicated her agreement with a complaisant gesture'.

complement and **compliment** are liable to be confused since they sound alike. However, they have totally different meanings. **Complement** refers to 'something that makes something complete', as in 'The wine was the perfect complement to the meal' and 'Her hat and shoes were the ideal complement to her outfit'. It also refers to 'the complete number or quantity required or allowed', as in 'We have our full complement of staff' and 'a full complement of passengers'. When trying to distinguish between **complement** and **compliment** it is helpful to remember the connection between complement and complete since both have *ple* in the middle. **Compliment** is 'an expression of praise, admiration, approval, etc', as in 'pay her a compliment on her hair' and 'receive compliments on the high standard of their work'. **Complement** and **compliment** are also verbs, as in 'The wine complemented the meal very well' and 'He complimented her on her musical performance'.

complementary medicine is a term applied to the treatment of illness or disorders by techniques other than conventional medicine. These include homoeopathy, osteopathy, acupuncture, acupressure, iridology, etc. The word **complementary** suggests that the said techniques complement and work alongside conventional medical techniques. **Alternative medicine** means the same as **complementary medicine**, but the term suggests that they are used instead of the techniques of conventional medicine rather than alongside them.

complex in one of its senses is used rather loosely in modern usage. It refers technically to 'an abnormal state caused by unconscious repressed desires or past experiences', as in 'an inferiority complex'. In modern usage it is used loosely to describe 'any obsessive concern or fear', as in 'She has a complex about her weight', 'He has a complex about his poor background'. **Complex** is also used to refer to 'a group of connected or similar things'. It is now used mainly of a group of buildings or units connected in some way, as in 'a shopping complex' or 'a sports complex'.

   Complex is also an adjective meaning 'complicated', as in 'His motives in carrying out the crime were complex' and 'The argument was too complex for most people to understand'.

compose, **comprise** and **constitute** are all similar in meaning but are used differently. **Compose** means 'to come together to make a whole, to make up'. It is most commonly found in the passive, as in 'The team was composed of young players' and 'The group was composed largely of elderly people'. It can be used in the active voice, as in 'the tribes which composed the nation' and 'the members which composed the committee', but this use is rarer. **Constitute** means the same as **compose** but it is usually used in the active voice, as in 'the foodstuffs that constitute a healthy diet' and 'the factors that constitute a healthy environment'. **Comprise** means 'to consist of, to be made up of', as in 'The firm comprises six departments' and 'The team comprises eleven players and two reserve players'. It is frequently used wrongly instead of **compose**, as in 'The team is comprised of eleven players' and instead of **constitute**, as in 'the players that comprise a team'.

compulsory and **compulsive** are liable to be confused. They are both adjectives derived from the verb 'to compel', meaning 'to force', but they are used differently. **Compulsory** means 'obligatory, required by a rule, law, etc', as in 'Foreign languages are not compulsory in that school' and 'It is compulsory to wear school uniform in some schools'. **Compulsive** means 'caused by an obsession or internal urge', as in 'a compulsive gambler' and 'a compulsive eater'. It is also used to mean 'fascinating' in some situations, as in 'A compulsive novel' and 'a compulsive TV series'.

concave and **convex** are liable to be confused. **Concave** means 'curved inwards', as in

'The inside of a spoon would be described as concave'. **Convex** means 'curved outwards, bulging', as in 'The outside or bottom of a spoon would be described as convex'.

conducive, meaning 'leading to, contributing to', is followed by the preposition 'to', as in 'conditions conducive to health growth'.

confidant and **confident** are liable to be confused. They sound alike but have different meanings. **Confidant** is rather a rare formal noun referring to 'a person in whom one confides', as in 'The king used two of his most trusted nobles as confidants'. It is derived from French and adds an *e* at the end if the person being confided in is female, as in 'ladies-in-waiting who were the queen's confidantes'. It has two possible pronunciations. The older pronunciation has the emphasis on the last syllable (kon-fi-*dant*). The more modern pronunciation has the emphasis on the first syllable (*kon*-fi-dant). **Confident** is a common adjective meaning 'self-assured, having confidence', as in 'She looks confident but she is rather an uncertain person', 'give a confident smile', and 'be confident that he will get the job'.

conform may be followed by the preposition 'to' or the preposition 'with'. It is followed by 'to' when it means 'to keep to or comply with', as in 'conform to the conventions' and 'refuse to conform to the company regulations', and with 'with' when it means 'to agree with, to go along with', as in 'His ideas do not conform with those of the rest of the committee'.

conjurer and **conjuror**, meaning a person who does conjuring tricks, are both acceptable spellings.

connection and **connexion** are different forms of the same word, meaning 'a relationship between two things'. In modern usage **connection** is much the commoner spelling, as in 'no connection between the events' and 'a fire caused by a faulty connection'.

connoisseur is liable to be misspelt. Note the double *n* and double *s*, and the *oi*. The word means 'a person having specialized knowledge and judgement on a subject' as in 'a connoisseur of French wines' and 'a connoisseur of Italian opera'.

conscientious, meaning 'diligent and careful', as in 'conscientious pupils doing their home work', is commonly misspelt. Note the *t*, which is frequently wrongly omitted.

connote and **denote** are liable to be confused. **Connote** means 'to suggest something in addition to the main, basic meaning of something', as in 'the fear that the word cancer connotes' and 'The word 'home' connotes security and love'. **Denote** means 'to mean or indicate', as in 'The word cancer denotes a malignant illness' and 'The word "home" denotes the place where one lives'.

consequent and **consequential** are liable to be confused. **Consequent** means 'following as a direct result', as in 'He was badly wounded in the war and never recovered from the consequent lameness'. In one of its senses **consequential** has a meaning similar to that of **consequent** in that it means 'following as a indirect result', as in 'She was injured and suffered a consequential loss of earnings'. In this sense **consequential** is usually used in a legal or formal context. **Consequential** also means 'important', as in 'a grave and consequential meeting' and is sometime applied to people when it means 'self-important', as in 'a pompous, consequential little man'.

consequent and **subsequent** are liable to be confused. **Consequent** means 'following as a direct result', as in 'his accident and consequent injuries', while **subsequent** means simply 'happening or occurring after', as in 'their arrival and subsequent speedy departure'.

    Consequent is sometimes followed by the preposition 'on' or 'upon', as in 'The court requires him to prove that his disability was consequent upon his accident at work'. **Subsequent** is sometimes followed by the preposition 'to', as in 'He was a security man subsequent to his retirement from the police'.

conservative when spelt with a lower-case *c* means 'supporting established traditions, institutions, etc, and opposed to great or sudden change', as in 'Some of the members of the amateur dramatics group wanted to stage a modern play this year but the more conservative members opted for a Shakespearian play instead', and 'She would like to go somewhere exotic on holiday but her conservative husband likes to go to the same place every year'. **Conservative** with an initial capital *C* refers to 'a person who is a member or supporter of the Conservative party', as in 'His wife votes Labour but he is a Conservative'. **Conservative** also means 'cautious, moderate', as in 'At a conservative estimate there must have been a thousand people there.

consist can be followed either by the preposition 'of' or by the preposition 'in', depending on the meaning. **Consist of** means 'to be made up of, to comprise', as in 'The team consists of eleven players and two reserve players'. **Consist in** means 'to have as the chief or only element or feature, to lie in', as in 'The charm of the village consists in its isolation' and 'The effectiveness of the plan consisted in its simplicity'.

constitute *see* **compose**.

contagious and **infectious** both refer to diseases that can be passed on to other people but they do not mean the same. **Contagious** means 'passed on by physical contact', as in 'He caught a contagious skin disease while working in the clinic' and 'Venereal diseases are contagious'. **Infectious** means 'caused by airborne or water-borne microorganisms', as in 'The common cold is highly infectious and is spread by people sneezing and coughing'.

contemporary originally meant 'living or happening at the same time', as in 'Shakespeare and Marlowe were contemporary playwrights' and 'Marlowe was contemporary with Shakespeare'. Later it came to mean also 'happening at the present time, current', as in 'What is your impression of the contemporary literary scene?' and 'Contemporary moral values are often compared unfavourably with those of the past'. These two uses of **contemporary** can cause ambiguity. In modern usage it is also used to mean 'modern, up-to-date', as in 'extremely contemporary designs'.

contemptible and **contemptuous** are both adjectives formed from the noun 'contempt', but they are different in meaning. **Contemptible** means 'deserving contempt, despicable', as in 'The contemptible villain robbed the blind man' and 'It was contemptible of her to swindle an old woman'. **Contemptuous** means 'feeling or showing contempt', as in 'their contemptuous attitude to the people they employ' and 'have a contemptuous disregard for the law of the land'.

continual and **continuous** are not interchangeable. **Continual** means 'frequently repeated', as in 'Tired of the continual interruptions he took the telephone off the hook' and 'There were continual complaints from the school about the truancy of their children'. **Continuous** means 'without a break or interruption', as in 'a continuous period of ill health', 'machines giving off a continuous high-pitched whine' and 'a continuous roll of paper'.

contrary has two possible pronunciations. When it means 'opposite', as in 'hold contrary views', 'traffic going in contrary directions' and 'On the contrary, I would like to go very much', it is pronounced with the emphasis on the first syllable (*kon*-trar-i). When it means 'perverse, stubborn', as in 'contrary children' it is pronounced with the emphasis on the second syllable, which is pronounced to rhyme with 'Mary'.

controversy is usually pronounced with the emphasis on the first syllable (*kon*-tro-ver-si). In modern usage there is a growing tendency to place the emphasis on the second syllable (kon-*tro*-ver-si).

convalescence is commonly misspelt. Note the *sc* combination. The word means 'recovery after an illness', as in 'She will have to undergo a long convalescence after her operation'.

convertible is commonly misspelt. Note the *-ible* spelling.

convex *see* **concave**.

cooperate *see* **collaborate**.

cord *see* **chord**.

co-respondent *see* **correspondent**.

correspondence

correspondence is frequently misspelt. Note the *ence*. This is often misspelt as *ance*.

correspondent and **co-respondent** are liable to be confused. **Correspondent** refers either to 'a person who communicates by letter', as in 'They were correspondents for years but had never met', or to 'a person who contributes news items to a newspaper or radio or television programme', as in 'the foreign correspondent of the *Times*'. A **co-respondent** is 'a person who has been cited in a divorce case as having committed adultery with one of the partners'.

council and **counsel** sound alike but have different meanings. **Council** refers to 'an assembly of people meeting for discussion, consultation, administrative purposes, etc', as in 'the town council' and 'a community council'. **Counsel** means 'advice', as in 'She received wise counsel from her parents but ignored it'. **Counsel** is also a verb meaning 'to give advice to', as in he counselled him on possible careers', 'She was counselled against leaving school without qualifications'.

councillor and **counsellor** sound alike but have different meanings. **Councillor** is a member of a council, as in 'town councillors'. **Counsellor** refers to 'a person who gives advice, especially professional advice on a social issue', as in 'a debt counsellor' and 'a career counsellor'.

cousin can cause confusion. The children of brothers and sisters are **first cousins** to each other. The children of **first cousins** are **second cousins** to each other. The child of one's **first cousin** and the **first cousin** of one's parents is one's **first cousin first removed**. The grandchild of one's **first cousin** or the **first cousin** of one's grandparent is one's **second cousin twice removed**.

credible, **creditable** and **credulous** are liable to be confused. **Credible** means 'believable', as in 'a scarcely credible story' and 'I do not find her account of the accident credible'. **Creditable** means 'deserving praise', as in 'Despite his injury the athlete gave a very creditable performance'. **Credulous** means 'too ready to believe, gullible', as in 'She was so credulous that she was taken in by the swindler' and 'a credulous young girl believing everything her new boyfriend said'.

crisis literally means 'turning point' and should be used to refer to 'a turning point in an illness', as in 'The fever reached a crisis and she survived' and 'a decisive or crucial moment in a situation, whose outcome will make a definite difference or change for better or worse', as in 'The financial situation has reached a crisis—the firm will either survive or go bankrupt'. In modern usage **crisis** is becoming increasingly used loosely for 'any worrying or troublesome situation', as in 'There's a crisis in the kitchen. The cooker's broken down'. The plural is **crises**.

criterion, meaning 'a standard by which something or someone is judged or evaluated', as 'What criterion is used for deciding which pupils will gain entrance to the school?' and 'The standard of play was the only criterion for entrance to the golf club'. It is a singular noun of which **criteria** is the plural, as in 'They must satisfy all the criteria for entrance to the club or they will be refused'.

critical has two main meanings. It means 'finding fault', as in 'His report on her work was very critical'. It also means 'at a crisis, at a decisive moment, crucial', as in 'It was a critical point in their relationship'. This meaning is often applied to the decisive stage of an illness, as in 'the critical hours after a serious operation', and is used also to describe an ill person who is at a crucial stage of an illness or dangerously ill. **Critical** also means 'involved in making judgements or assessments of artistic or creative works', as in 'give a critical evaluation of the author's latest novel'.

crucial means 'decisive, critical', as in 'His vote is crucial since the rest of the committee is split down the middle'. In modern usage it is used loosely to mean 'very important', as in 'It is crucial that you leave now'. **Crucial** is derived from crux, meaning 'a decisive point', as in 'the crux of the situation'.

cuisine is liable to be misspelt. Note the *u* before the first *i*. It is rather a formal word and means 'cooking' or 'a style of cooking', as in 'The cuisine at the new restaurant is outstanding'; 'She prefers Italian cuisine to French cuisine'. Note that it is pronounced kwee-*zeen*.

curb and **kerb** are not interchangeable although they sound similar. **Curb** is both a noun and a verb. As a noun it means 'control, check, restraint', as in 'act as a curb on his extravagance'. As a verb it means 'to control, to restrain', as in 'She must learn to curb his anger' and 'If he does not learn to curb his expenditure he will become bankrupt'. **Kerb** is a noun meaning 'the edge of a pavement', as in 'The child stood on the kerb waiting to cross the road'. In American English **curb** is used instead of **kerb**.

curriculum is commonly misspelt. Note the double *r* and single *l*. The word means 'a programme of educational courses', as in 'The government is making changes to the primary school curriculum' and 'There is a wide range of options on the sixth form curriculum'. **Curriculum** is derived from Latin and originally took the plural form **curricula**, but in modern usage the plural form **curriculums** is becoming common.

curriculum vitae refers to 'a brief account of a person's qualifications and career to date'. It is often requested by an employer when a candidate is applying for a job. **Vitae** is pronounced *vee*-ti, the second syllable rhyming with my.

curtsy and **curtsey** are both acceptable spellings. The word refers to 'a sign of respect in which a woman puts one foot behind the other and bends her knees, sometimes holding her skirt out'.

customer *see* **client**.

D

dais, meaning 'platform' or 'stage', is now usually pronounced as two syllables, as day-is. Formerly it was pronounced as one syllable, as days.

data was formerly used mainly in a scientific or technical context and was always treated as a plural noun, taking a plural verb, as in 'compare the data which were provided by the two research projects'. The singular form was **datum**, which is now rare. In modern usage the word **data** became used in computing as a collective noun meaning 'body of information' and is frequently used with a singular verb, as in 'The data is essential for our research'. This use has spread into the general language.

dates are usually written in figures rather than in words except in formal contexts, such as legal documents. There are various ways of writing dates. The standard form in Britain is becoming day followed by month followed by year, as in '24 February 1970'. In America the standard form of this is 'February 24 1970' and that is a possibility in Britain also. Alternatively, some people write '24th February 1970'. Care should be taken with the writing of dates entirely in numbers, especially if one is corresponding with someone in America. In Britain the day of the month is put first, the month second and the year third, as in '2/3/50', '2 March 1950'. In America the month is put first, followed by the day of the month and the year. Thus in America '2/3/50', would be 3 February 1950.

Centuries may may be written either in figures, as in 'the 19th century' or in words, as in 'the nineteenth century'. Decades and centuries are now usually written without apostrophes, as in '1980s' and '1900s'.

datum

datum *see* **data**.

deadly and **deathly** both refer to death but they have different meanings. **Deadly** means 'likely to cause death, fatal', as in 'His enemy dealt him a deadly blow with his sword' and 'He contracted a deadly disease in the jungle'. **Deathly** means 'referring to death, resembling death', as in 'She was deathly pale with fear'.

decade is pronounced with the emphasis on the first syllable as *dek*-ayd. An alternative but rare pronunciation is dek-*ayd*.

decimate literally means 'to kill one in ten' and is derived from the practice in ancient Rome of killing every tenth soldier as a punishment for mutiny. In modern usage it has come to mean 'to kill or destroy a large part of', as in 'Disease has decimated the population'. It has also come to mean 'to reduce considerably', as in 'the recession has decimated the jobs in the area'.

decry and **descry** are liable to be confused. **Decry** means 'to express criticism or disapproval of, to disparage', as in 'The neighbours decried their treatment of their children' and 'The local people decried the way the police handled the situation'. **Descry** means 'catch sight of', as in 'descry a herd of deer on the horizon'.

defective and **deficient** are similar in meaning but are not interchangeable. **Defective** means 'having a fault, not working properly', as in 'return the defective vacuum cleaner to the shop', 'The second-hand car proved to be defective' and 'He cannot be a pilot as his eyesight is defective'. **Deficient** means 'having a lack, lacking in', as in 'The athlete is very fast but he is deficient in strength' and 'Her diet is deficient in vitamin C.

defence, as in 'soldiers losing their lives in defence of their country' is commonly misspelt. Note the *c*. The word is frequently wrongly spelt with an *s* along the lines of **defensive**. In American English **defence** is spelt **defense**.

deficient *see* **defective**.

definitely is frequently misspelt. Note the *i* before the *t*. It is a common error to put *a* in that position.

delicatessen is liable to be misspelt. Note the single *l*, single *t* and double *s*. It refers to 'a shop selling prepared foods, such as cooked meats, cheeses, etc', as in 'buy some quiche from the local delicatessen'.

deliverance and **delivery** are both nouns formed from the verb 'to deliver' but they are used in different senses. **Deliverance** refers to 'the act of delivering from danger etc, to rescue or save', as in 'thank God for their child's deliverance from the evil kidnappers' and 'pray for their deliverance from evil'. This word is now used only in literary or very formal contexts. **Delivery** has several meanings. It refers to 'the act of delivering letters, goods, etc', as in 'There is no delivery of mail on Sundays' and 'awaiting delivery of a new washing machine'; 'the pro-cess of birth', as in 'Her husband was present at the delivery of their son'; 'manner of speaking', as in 'The lecturer's subject was interesting but his delivery was poor'.

delusion and **illusion** in modern usage are often used interchangeably but they are not quite the same. **Delusion** means 'a false or mistaken idea or belief', as in 'He is under the delusion that he is brilliant' and 'suffer from delusions of grandeur'. It can be part of a mental disorder, as in 'He suffers from the delusion that he is Napoleon. **Illusion** means 'a false or misleading impression', as in 'There was no well in the desert—it was an optical illusion', 'The conjurer's tricks were based on illusion' and 'the happy childhood illusions that everyone lived happy ever after'.

demise is a formal word for death, as in 'He never recovered from the demise of his wife'. In modern usage it applies to the ending of an activity, as in 'The last decade saw the demise of coal-mining in the area'. In modern usage it has come to mean also 'the decline or failure of an activity', as in 'the gradual demise of his business'.

demonstrable is most commonly pronounced di-*mon*-strabl, with the emphasis on the second syllable, in modern usage. Previously the emphasis was on the first syllable as *dem*-on-strabl.

dénouement is commonly misspelt. Note the *oue* combination. The first *e* was originally always spelt with an acute accent, as *é*, but in modern usage it is frequently written without the acute. The word means 'the final outcome', as in 'The novel had a unexpected denouement'. It is pronounced day-*noo*-mon.

dependant and **dependent** are frequently confused. **Dependant** is a noun meaning 'a person who depends on someone else for financial support', as in 'He has four dependants—his wife and three children'. **Dependent** is an adjective meaning 'reliant on', as in 'dependent on drugs'; 'relying on someone else for financial support', as in 'have several dependent relatives'; 'decided by, affected by', as in 'Success in that exam is dependent on hard work'.

deprecate and **depreciate** are liable to be confused although they have totally different meanings. **Deprecate** means 'to express disapproval of', as in 'It was unsporting of him to deprecate his rival's performance' and 'deprecate their choice of furnishings'. **Depreciate** means 'to reduce in value', as in 'New cars depreciate very quickly'. It also means 'to belittle or disparage', as in 'They made great efforts to help but she depreciated them', 'Management depreciated the role the deputy manager played in the firm'. In modern usage **deprecate** is sometimes used with the second meaning of **depreciate**, as in 'He was always praising his elder son's work and deprecating that of his younger son although the latter was the cleverer pupil'.

deprived means 'having something removed', as in 'The prisoner was punished by being deprived of his privileges' and 'The fire deprived the children of their home'. In modern usage it has come to mean 'not having what are considered to be basic rights, standard of living, etc', as in 'deprived children sent to school in worn-out clothes' and 'deprived people living in substandard accommodation'.

derisive and **derisory** are both adjectives connected with the noun 'derision' but they have different meanings. **Derisive** means 'expressing derision, scornful, mocking' as in 'give a derisive smile' and 'His efforts were met with derisive laughter'. Derisory means 'deserving derision, ridiculous' as in 'Their attempts at playing the game were derisory'. **Derisory** is frequently used to mean 'ridiculously small or inadequate', as in 'The salary offered was derisory'.

descry *see* **decry**.

desert and **dessert** are frequent confused. **Desert** as a noun refers to 'a large area of barren land with very little water or vegetation and often sand-covered', as in 'the Sahara Desert'. **Deserts** is a plural noun meaning 'what someone deserves', as in 'The thief who mugged the old lady got his just deserts when he was sent to prison'. As a verb **desert** means 'to abandon', as in 'desert his wife and children' and 'soldiers deserting their post', or 'to fail', as in 'his courage deserted him'. **Dessert** means the last (and sweet) course of a meal, as in 'She served apple pie and cream for dessert'. *See* **dessert**.

desiccated is frequently misspelt. Note the single *s* and double *c*. It means 'dried', as in 'desiccated coconut', or 'lacking animation', as in 'a desiccated old bachelor'.

despatch and **dispatch** are interchangeable. It is most common as a verb meaning 'to send', as in 'despatch/dispatch an invitation'. It is rarer as a noun. It means 'a message or report, often official', as in 'receive a despatch/dispatch that the soldiers were to move on'. It also means 'rapidity, speed', as in 'carry out the orders with despatch/dispatch'.

desperate is frequently misspelt. Note the *e* before the *r*. It is a common error to put *a* instead.

dessert, **pudding**, **sweet** and **afters** all mean the same thing. They refer to the last and sweet course of a meal. **Dessert** has relatively recently become the most widespread of these terms. **Pudding** was previously regarded by the upper and middle classes as the most acceptable word of these, but it is now thought of by many as being rather old-fashioned or as being more suited to certain types of dessert than others—thus syrup sponge would be a pudding, but not fresh fruit salad. **Sweet** is a less formal word

detach

and is regarded by some people as being lower-class or regional. **Afters** is common only in very informal English. *See also* **desert**.

detach is often misspelt. Note that there is no *t* before the *ch*.

detract and **distract** are liable to be confused. **Detract** means 'to take away from', as in 'Nothing he could say could detract from her reputation as a writer'. 'The new high-rise buildings detracted from the old-fashioned charm of the village'. **Distract** means 'to take someone's mind off something, to divert someone's attention', as in 'The golf-player said he lost the match because he was distracted by a dog running on the course'.

device and **devise** are liable to be confused. **Device** is a noun and refers to 'a gadget or tool', as in 'a device for taking stones out of horses' hoofs'. **Devise** is a verb meaning 'to plan, to bring about', as in 'He succeeded in devising a scheme that was certain to succeed'.

devil's advocate is a phrase that is often misunderstood. It means 'someone who points out the possible flaws or faults in an argument etc', as in 'He played the devil's advocate and showed her the weakness in her argument so that she was able to perfect it before presenting it to the committee'. The phrase is sometimes wrongly thought of as meaning 'someone who defends an unpopular point of view or person'.

devise *see* **device**.

diagnosis and **prognosis** are liable to be confused. Both are used with reference to disease but have different meanings. **Diagnosis** refers to 'the identification of a disease or disorder', as in 'She had cancer but the doctor failed to make the correct diagnosis until it was too late'. **Prognosis** refers to 'the prediction of the likely course of a disease or disorder', as in 'According to the doctor's prognosis, the patient will be dead in six months'.

dialect refers to an established form of language confined to an area of a country or to a particular class of people. It includes pronunciation, vocabulary, grammar or sense structure.

dialogue refers to 'a discussion between two or more people'. It usually refers to an exchange of views of people who are involved in a conflict of interest and are trying to reach a compromise, as in 'management and union leaders in dialogue over the factory wages structure' and 'The leaders are engaged in a dialogue to try to prevent a war'.

diarrhoea is frequently misspelt. Note the *rrh* combination and the *oea* combination. The word refers to a very loose bowel movement.

dice was originally the plural form of the singular noun **die**, but **die** is now rarely used. Instead, **dice** is used as both a singular and a plural noun, as in 'throw a wooden dice' and 'use three different dice in the same game'.

dietician and **dietitian** are both acceptable spellings. The word means 'a person who specializes in the principles of nutrition', as in 'hospital dieticians drawing up menus for the patients'.

different is most usually followed by the preposition 'from', as in 'Their style of living is different from ours'. **Different from** is considered to be the most correct construction, particularly in formal English. **Different to** is used in informal situations, as in 'His idea of a good time is different to ours'. **Different than** is used in American English.

differently abled *see* **disabled**.

dilatation and **dilation** are both acceptable forms of the same word formed from the verb 'dilate', meaning 'to expand', as in 'Note the dilatation/dilation of the patient's pupils'.

dilapidated is frequently misspelt. Common errors include putting *t* instead of the middle *d* and substituting *de* at the beginning for *di*.

dilemma is frequently used wrongly. It refers to 'a situation in which one is faced with two or more equally undesirable possibilities', as in 'I can't decide which of the offers to accept. It's a real dilemma'.

dinghy and **dingy** are liable to be confused. **Dinghy** refers to 'a type of small boat', as in

'They went out for a sail in their dinghy'. **Dingy** means 'dirty-looking, gloomy', as in 'colourful curtains to cheer up a dingy room'.

dinner, **lunch**, **supper** and **tea** are terms that can cause confusion. Their use can vary according to class, region of the country and personal preference. Generally speaking, people who have their main meal in the evening call it **dinner**. However, people who have their main meal in the middle of the day frequently call this meal **dinner**. People who have **dinner** in the evening usually refer to their midday meal, usually a lighter meal, as **lunch**. A more formal version of this word is **luncheon**, which is now quite a rare word. **Supper** has two meanings, again partly dependent on class and region. It can refer either to the main meal of the day if it is eaten in the evening—when it is virtually a synonym for **dinner**. Alternatively, it can refer to a light snack, such as cocoa and toasted cheese, eaten late in the evening before going to bed. **Tea** again has two meanings when applied to a meal. It either means a light snack-type meal of tea, sandwiches and cakes eaten in the late afternoon. Alternatively, it can refer to a cooked meal, sometimes taken with tea, and also referred to as **high tea**, eaten in the early evening, rather than **dinner** later in the evening.

diphtheria can cause problems both with spelling and pronunciation. Note the *phth* combination in the spelling. The word, which refers to a type of infectious disease, should be pronounced with an *f* at the end of the first syllable (*dif*) but it is often pronounced with a *p* (*dip*).

disabled is objected to by some people on the grounds that it is a negative term, but it is difficult to find an acceptable alternative. In politically correct language **physically challenged** has been suggested as has **differently abled**, but neither of these has gained widespread use. It should be noted that the use of 'the disabled' should be avoided. 'Disabled people' should be used instead.

disablism and **disableism** mean 'discrimination against disabled people', as in 'He felt his failure to get a job was because of disablism'. **Disablist** and **disableist** are adjectives meaning 'showing or practising disablism', as in 'guilty of disablist attitudes'. They also refer to 'a person who discriminates on the grounds of disability', as in 'That employer is a disablist'.

disadvantaged and **disadvantageous** are both formed from disadvantage but they are used in different senses. **Disadvantaged** means 'not having the standard of living, living conditions or basic rights that others enjoy', as in 'disadvantaged families living in slum conditions'. It means much the same as deprived. **Disadvantageous** means 'causing a disadvantage, unfavourable', as in 'At the end of the first round of the competition the former champion was in a disadvantageous position'.

disappoint is very frequently misspelt. Note the single *s* and double *p*. A common error is to put double *s* and single *p*.

disastrous is frequently misspelt. Note that, unlike **disaster** from which it is derived, it has no *e*.

discoloration is frequently misspelt. Note, unlike **colour**, the absence of *u*.

discomfit and **discomfort** are liable to be confused. **Discomfit** is a verb which means 'to disconcert, to embarrass', as in 'They were discomfited by her direct questions', or 'to thwart, to defeat', as in 'He succeeded in discomfiting his opponent'. **Discomfort** is most commonly a noun, although it does exist as a verb. It means 'lack of comfort, lack of ease', as in 'the discomfort of their holiday conditions'.

discover and **invent** are not interchangeable. **Discover** means 'to find something that is already in existence but is generally unknown', as in 'discover a new route to China' and 'discover the perfect place for a holiday'. **Invent** means 'to create something that has never before existed', as in 'invent the telephone' and 'invent a new form of heating system'.

discriminating and **discriminatory** are both formed from **discrimination** but they have different meanings. **Discriminating** means 'able to tell the difference between good and poor quality, etc, having good judgement', as in 'a discriminating collector of antiques'

disempowered

and 'discriminating in their choice of wines'. **Discriminatory** means 'showing or practising discrimination or prejudice', as in 'have a discriminatory attitude towards people of a different race' and 'employers accused of being discriminatory towards women'.

disempowered in modern usage does not mean only 'having one's power removed', as in 'The king was disempowered by the invading general', but also means the same as 'powerless', as in 'We are disempowered to give you any more money'. **Disempowered** is seen in politically correct language as a more positive way of saying **powerless**.

disinterested and **uninterested** are often used interchangeably in modern usage to mean 'not interested, indifferent', as in 'pupils totally *disinterested/uninterested* in school work'. Many people dislike **disinterested** being used in this way and regard it as a wrong use, but it is becoming increasingly common. **Disinterested** also means 'impartial, unbiased', as in 'ask a disinterested party to settle the dispute between them'.

disorient and **disorientate** are used interchangeably. 'The town had changed so much since his last visit that he was completely disoriented/disorientated' and 'After the blow to her head she was slightly disoriented/disorientated'.

disassociate and **dissociate** are used interchangeably, as in 'She wished to disassociate/dissociate herself from the statement issued by her colleagues', but **dissociate** is the more usual.

distinct and **distinctive** are liable to be confused. **Distinct** means 'definite, easily heard, seen, felt, etc', as in 'I got the distinct impression that I had offended him', or 'different, separate', as in 'an artistic style quite distinct from that of his father'. **Distinctive** means 'distinguishing, characteristic', as in 'The zebra has distinctive markings'.

distract *see* **detract**.

divorcee refers to 'a divorced person', as in 'a club for divorcees'. **Divorcé** refers to 'a divorced man', and **divorcée** to 'a divorced woman'.

doubtful and **dubious** can be used interchangeably in the sense of 'giving rise to doubt, uncertain', as in 'The future of the project is dubious/doubtful', and in the sense of 'having doubts, unsure', as in 'I am doubtful/dubious about the wisdom of going'. **Dubious** also means 'possibly dishonest or bad', as in 'of dubious morals'.

downward and **downwards** are not used interchangeably. **Downward** is an adjective, as in 'a downward slope' and 'in a downward direction'. **Downwards** is an adverb, as in 'look downwards from the top of the hill'.

draft and **draught** are liable to be confused. **Draft** as a noun in British English has several meanings. It can mean 'a preliminary version', as in 'present a rough draft of their proposals'; 'a money order', as in 'a draft drawn on a foreign bank'; 'a group of soldiers or other people chosen for a special purpose', as in 'a draft of new recruits sent to the front' and 'a draft of nurses and doctors despatched to the scene of the disaster'. **Draught** as a noun in British English refers to 'a current of air', as in 'a draught from an ill-fitting window', or to 'a drink, a swallow of liquid', as in 'long for a draught of cool beer'. In American English **draught** is spelt **draft**.

drawing room *see* **sitting room**.

draught *see* **draft**.

draughtsman/woman and **draftsman/woman** are not the same. **Draughtsman/woman** refers to 'a person who draws detailed plans of a building, etc', as in 'study the plans of the bridge prepared by the draughtsman'. **Draftsman/woman** refers to 'a person who prepares a preliminary version of plans, etc', as in 'several draftswomen working on the draft parliamentary bills'.

dreamed and **dreamt** are interchangeable both as the past tense and the past participle of the verb 'dream', as in 'She *dreamed/dreamt* about living in the country' and in 'He has dreamed/dreamt the same dream for several nights'.

drier and **dryer** can both be used to describe 'a machine or appliance that dries', as in 'hair-drier/hair-dryer' and 'tumbler drier/dryer'. As an adjective meaning 'more dry', **drier** is the usual word, as in 'a drier summer than last year'.

drunk and **drunken** both mean 'intoxicated' but they are used rather differently. When someone is temporarily intoxicated **drunk** is used, as in 'The drunk men staggered home'. **Drunken** tends to be used to describe someone who is in the habit of being intoxicated, as in 'drunken creatures who are rarely sober'. Otherwise **drunk** is usually used after a verb, as in 'They were all drunk at the party'. **Drunken** is usually used before a noun as in 'take part in a drunken party'.

dryer *see* **drier**.

dubious *see* **doubtful**.

dual and **duel** are liable to be confused since they sound alike. **Dual** is an adjective meaning 'double, twofold', as in 'He played a dual role in the team as captain and trainer' and 'a dual carriageway'. **Duel** is a noun meaning ' a formal fight between two people, using swords or pistols', as in 'He challenged a fellow officer to a duel because he had called him a liar'. **Duel** can also be a verb. The *l* doubles before '-ing', '-ed', or '-er' is added, as in 'duelling at dawn'.

due to, **owing to** and **because of** should not be used interchangeably. Strictly speaking, **due to** should be used only adjectivally, as in 'His poor memory is due to brain damage' and 'cancellations due to bad weather'. When a prepositional use is required **owing to** and **because of** should be used, as in 'the firm was forced to close owing to a lack of capital' and 'The train was cancelled because of snow on the line'. In modern usage it is quite common for **due to** to be used instead of **owing to** or **because of** because the distinction is rather difficult to comprehend.

dyeing and **dying** sound alike but are completely different in meaning. **Dyeing** is formed from the verb 'to dye' and is used in such contexts as 'dyeing white dresses blue'. **Dying** is formed from the verb 'to die' and is used in such contexts as 'dying from starvation'.

E

each, when it is the subject of a sentence, should be followed by a singular verb and, where relevant, by a pronoun in the singular, as in 'Each boy brought his own lunch'. In order to avoid sexism in language some people advocate using a plural pronoun instead, as in 'Each pupil had their own books'. Before sexism in language became an issue, the assumption was that words such as pupil, which can indicate members of either sex, should take a male pronoun, as in 'Each pupil had his own books'. People who dislike using a plural pronoun with **each** on the grounds that it is ungrammatical but do not wish to be sexist can use 'his/her', as in 'Each pupil had his/her own books' although this device can be clumsy. It is often possible to avoid the problem by rephrasing the sentence, as in 'All the pupils had their own books'. When **each** follows a plural noun or pronoun, the verb should be plural as in 'The houses each have a red door' and 'They each have black hair'.

each other and **one another** used not to be used interchangeably. It was taught that **each other** should be used when only two people are involved and that **one another** should be used when more than two people are involved, as in 'John and Mary really love each other' and 'All the members of the family love one another'. In modern use this restriction is often ignored.

earthly

earthly and **earthy** are both adjectives formed from 'earth' but they have different meanings. **Earthly** is used to refer to this world rather than to heaven or the spiritual world, as in 'He is interested only in earthly pleasures but his brother is interested in spiritual satisfaction'. It is also used informally to mean 'possible', as in 'What earthly reason could she have for leaving?' **Earthy** refers to earth in the sense of 'soil', as in 'the earthy smell of a garden after rain'. It can also mean 'unrefined, coarse', as in 'an earthy sense of humour'.

EC and **EEC** both refer to the same thing, but **EC**, the abbreviation for **Economic Community** has now replaced **EEC**, the abbreviation for **European Economic Community.**

economic and **economical** are both connected with the noun 'economy' but they have different meanings. **Economic** means 'referring to or relating to the economy or economics', as in 'the government's economic policies' and 'studying economic theory'. **Economical** means 'thrifty, avoiding waste', as in 'She is a very economical housekeeper', and 'cheap', as in 'It is more economical for four of us to go by car than by train'. The phrase **economical with the truth** is a less forthright way of saying 'lying', as in 'politicians accused of being economical with the truth'.

ecstasy, meaning 'great joy', is frequently misspelt. Note the *cs* and *as*. Ecstasy, spelt with a capital *E*, is also the name of a non-medicinal drug, associated with raves, professionally organized large-scale parties for young people.

effect *see* **affect**.

effeminate *see* **female**.

e.g. means 'for example' and is an abbreviation of the Latin phrase *exempli gratia*. It is used before examples of something just previously mentioned, as in 'He cannot eat dairy products, e.g. milk, butter and cream'. A comma is usually placed just before it and, unlike some abbreviations, it has full stops.

egoist and **egotist** are frequently used interchangeably in modern usage. Although they are not, strictly speaking, the same, the differences between them are rather subtle. **Egoist** refers to 'a person intent on self-interest, a selfish person', as in 'an egoist who never gave a thought to the needs of others'. **Egotist** refers to 'a person who is totally self-centred and obsessed with his/her own concerns', as in 'a real egotist who was always talking about herself'.

eighth is frequently misspelt. Note the *h* before the *t*.

either should be used only when referring to two people or things, as in 'He hasn't been in touch with either of his parents for several years', but 'He hasn't been in touch with any of his four brothers'.

Either as an adjective or a pronoun takes a singular verb, as in 'Either parent will do' and 'Either of you can come'.

In the **either . . . or** construction, a singular verb is used if both parts of the construction are singular, as in 'Either Jane or Mary is in charge'. If both parts are plural the verb is plural, as in 'Either their parents or their grandparents are in charge.' If the construction involves a mixture of singular and plural the verb traditionally agrees with the subject that is nearer it, as in 'Either her mother or her grandparents are in charge' and 'Either her grandparents or her mother is in charge'. If pronouns are used, the nearer one governs the verb, as in 'Either they or he is at fault' and 'Either she or they are at fault'. *See* **neither**.

eke out originally meant 'to make something more adequate by adding to it or supplementing it', as in 'The poor mother eked out the small amount of meat with a lot of vegetables to feed her large family'. It can now also mean 'to make something last longer by using it sparingly', as in 'try to eke out our water supply until we reach a town', and 'to succeed or make with a great deal of effort', as in 'eke out a meagre living from their small farm'.

elder and **older** are not interchangeable. **Elder** is used only of people, as in 'The smaller boy is the elder of the two'. It is frequently used of family relationships, as in 'His elder brother died before him'. **Older** can be used of things as well as people, as in 'The church looks ancient but the castle is the older of the buildings' and 'The smaller girl is the older of the two'. It also can be used of family relationships, as in 'It was his older brother who helped him'. **Elder** used as a noun suggests experience or worthiness as well as age, as in 'Important issues used to be decided by the village elders' and 'Children should respect their elders and betters'.

elderly, as well as meaning 'quite or rather old', as in 'a town full of middle-aged and elderly people', is a more polite term than 'old', no matter how old the person referred to is, as in 'a residential home for elderly people'. **Elderly** is used only of people, except when used humorously, as in 'this cheese is getting rather elderly'.

eldest and **oldest** follow the same pattern as **elder** and **older**, as in 'The smallest boy is the eldest of the three', 'His eldest brother lived longer than any of them', 'The castle is the oldest building in the town' and 'He has four brothers but the oldest one is dead'.

elemental and **elementary** are both connected with the noun 'element' but they are not interchangeable. **Elemental** means 'like the elements (in the sense of forces of nature), powerful, uncontrolled', as in 'give way to elemental passion'. It also means 'basic, essential', as in 'the elemental truths of Buddhism'. **Elementary** means 'basic, introductory', as in 'teaching elementary maths', and 'easy, simple', as in 'He cannot carry out the most elementary of tasks' and 'The test is very elementary'.

embarrass is very frequently misspelt. Note the double *r* and double *s*. Note also **embarrassed** and **embarrassing**. The word means 'to cause to feel self-conscious, confused or ashamed', as in 'His extravagant compliments embarrassed her'.

emigrant and **immigrant** are liable to be confused. **Emigrant** refers to 'a person who leaves his/her native land to go and live elsewhere', as in 'go down to the docks to say farewell to the emigrants on the ship'. **Immigrant** refers to 'a person who arrives to live in another country, having left his/her native land', as in 'go down to the docks to welcome the immigrants arriving on the ship'. Both terms can apply to the same person, viewed from different points of view.

emotional and **emotive** are both connected with the noun 'emotion' but they have different meanings. **Emotional** means 'referring to emotion', as in 'emotional problems', 'expressing emotion or excessive emotion', as in 'an emotional farewell', and 'having emotions that are easily excited', as in 'The rest of the family are very calm but she is so emotional that she is always either in tears or laughing with joy'. **Emotive** means 'causing emotion', as in 'Child abuse is often an emotive subject'.

empathy and **sympathy** are liable to be confused although they are not interchangeable. **Empathy** means 'the ability to imagine and share another's feelings, experiences, etc', as in 'As a single parent herself, the journalist has a real empathy with women bringing up children on their own' and 'The writer felt a certain empathy with the subject of his biography since they both came from a poverty-stricken childhood'. **Sympathy** means 'a feeling of compassion, pity or sorrow towards someone', as in 'feel sympathy for homeless children' and 'show sympathy towards the widow'.

encyclopaedia and **encyclopedia** are now both acceptable spellings in modern British English. **Encyclopaedia** is the traditional spelling in British English but the traditional spelling in American English, **encyclopedia**, is now becoming more and more common in British English.

endemic is usually used to describe a disease and means 'occurring in a particular area', as in 'a disease endemic to the coastal areas of the country' and 'difficult to clear the area of endemic disease'.

enervate is a word that is frequently misused. It means 'to weaken, to lessen in vitality', as in 'she was enervated by the extreme heat' and 'Absence of funding had totally enervated the society'. It is often wrongly used as though it meant the opposite.

enormity and **enormousness** are liable to be confused but mean different things.

Enormity means 'outrageousness or wickedness', as in 'The whole village was shocked by the enormity of his crime'. **Enormousness** means 'the quality of being enormous or extremely large', as in 'The little boy was scared by the enormousness of the elephant' and 'the enormousness of their estates'.

enquiry and **inquiry** are frequently used interchangeably, as in 'make enquiries/inquiries about her health'. However some people see a distinction between them and use **enquiry** for ordinary requests for information, as in 'make enquiries about the times of trains'. They use **inquiry** only for 'investigation', as in 'The police have begun a murder inquiry' and 'launch an inquiry into the hygiene standards of the food firm'.

enrol is frequently misspelt. Note the single *l*, but note also that the *l* doubles in the past tense and past participle and the present participle, as **enrolled, enrolling**. However, the noun **enrolment**, as in 'The enrolment of students takes place tomorrow', has a single *l*. In American English the word is spelt **enroll**. **Enrol** means 'to become a member of a class, society, etc, as in 'She plans to enrol in an aerobics class' and 'to make a member of a class, society, etc, as in 'The tutor will enrol more students next week'.

enthral is frequently misspelt. Note the single *l*, but note that the *l* doubles in the past tense and past participle and the present participle, as **enthralled** and **enthralling**. However, note the single *l* in **enthralment**. In American English the word is spelt **enthrall**. **Enthral** means 'to bewitch, to capture the attention of', as in 'Her performance will enthral the critics'.

envelop and **envelope** are not interchangeable. **Envelop** means 'to wrap up, to enclose, to surround completely', as in 'He enveloped his daughter in his arms' and 'Mist enveloped the mountain tops'. **Envelope** means 'a paper wrapper for a letter, etc', as in 'put the sheets of paper in a large envelope'. **Envelop** is pronounced en-*vel*-op. The preferred pronunciation of envelope is *en*-vel-op although some people pronounce it *on*-vel-op.

enviable and **envious** are both formed from the noun 'envy' but they mean different things. **Enviable** means 'arousing envy, desirable', as in 'an enviable lifestyle' and 'an enviable optimistic attitude to life'. **Envious** means 'showing or expressing envy', as in 'envious eyes following the expensively dressed woman' and 'They were envious of her lifestyle'.

equable and **equitable** are liable to be confused. **Equable** means 'moderate, not given to extremes', as in 'live in an equable climate' and 'have an equable temperament'. **Equitable** means 'fair, just', as in 'We felt that the judge had come to an equitable decision'.

equal can be followed either by the preposition 'with' or the preposition 'to', but the two constructions are not interchangeable. **Equal to** is used in such sentences as 'He wished to climb the hill but his strength was not equal to the task'. **Equal with** is used in such sentences as 'After many hours of playing the two players remained equal with each other' and 'The women in the factory are seeking a pay scale equal with that of men'.

equally should not be followed by 'as'. Examples of it used correctly include 'Her brother is an expert player but she is equally talented' and 'He is trying hard but his competitors are trying equally hard'. These should not read 'but she is equally as talented' nor 'but his competitors are trying equally as hard'.

Esq. is the abbreviation for 'Esquire'. It is sometimes used rather formally when addressing a letter to a man, as in 'Peter Jones, Esq.' It should not be used with Mr. 'Mr Peter Jones, Esq.' is wrong.

-ess is a suffix that used routinely to be added to a noun to form the femine form, as in 'authoress, editress, poetess, sculptress'. This practice is now often seen as patronizing to women and sexist, and **-ess** is being used less and less. What were once considered masculine forms, as 'author, editor, poet, sculptor', are now considered to be neutral forms applying to either sex. The suffix is still found in such words as 'princess', 'countess', 'hostess' and 'waitress', and sometimes in 'actress'.

et al is the abbreviation of the Latin phrase *et alii*, meaning 'and others'. It is used in lists to indicate that there are more of the same, as in 'She loves Bach, Beethoven, Mozart et al'. The phrase is usually used in a formal context, but it is sometimes used humorously in informal contexts as in 'Uncle Fred, Uncle Jim et al'.

etc is the abbreviation of the Latin phrase *et cetera*, meaning 'and other things, and the rest', as in 'potatoes, carrots, turnips, etc', 'curtains, carpets, rugs, etc'. It can also be spelt **etc.** (with a full stop).

ethnic is a word that causes some confusion. It means 'of a group of people classified according to race, nationality, culture, etc', as in 'a cosmopolitan country with a wide variety of ethnic groups'. It is frequently used loosely to mean 'relating to race', as in 'violent clashes thought to be ethnic in origin', or 'foreign' as in 'prefer ethnic foods to British foods'.

euphemism is 'a more indirect, pleasanter, milder, etc, way of saying something'. 'To join one's forefathers' is a **euphemism** for 'to die'. 'To be tired and emotional' is a euphemism for 'to be drunk'.

evade and **avoid** are similar in meaning but not identical. **Evade** means 'to keep away from by cunning or deceit', as in 'The criminal evaded the police by getting his friend to impersonate him'. **Avoid** means simply 'to keep away from', as in 'Women avoid that area of town at night'.

evasion and **avoidance** are frequently applied to the non-payment of income tax but they are not interchangeable. Tax **avoidance** refers to 'the legal nonpayment of tax by clever means'. Tax **evasion** refers to 'the illegal means of avoiding tax by cunning and dishonest means'.

even should be placed carefully in a sentence since its position can influence the meaning. Compare 'He didn't even acknowledge her' and 'He didn't acknowledge even her'. and 'He doesn't even like Jane , let alone love her' and 'He hates the whole family—he doesn't like even Jane'. This shows that **even** should be placed immediately before the word it refers to in order to avoid ambiguity. In spoken English people often place it where it feels most natural, before the verb as in 'He even finds it difficult to relax on holiday'. To be absolutely correct this should be 'He finds it difficult to relax even on holiday' or 'Even on holiday he finds it difficult to relax'.

ever is sometimes added to 'who', 'what', where, etc, as a separate word for emphasis, as in 'Who ever did that terrible thing?' and 'Where ever did you find that?'. Where there is no question of emphasis, **ever** is joined on to the relevant pronoun. Examples include 'Whoever she is, she must be a bad mother' and 'Wherever he goes she goes'.

every is used with singular nouns. Related words, such as verbs and pronouns, are in the singular too, as in 'Every man must provide his own work clothing'. Some people use a plural pronoun in certain situations in order to avoid sexism in language, as in 'Every worker must supply their own work clothing'. This is to avoid the sexism of 'Every worker must supply his own clothing'. It is possible to avoid both sexism and ungrammatical constructions by using 'Every worker must supply his/her clothing', which can be rather clumsy. Alternatively, the whole sentence can be put in the plural, as in 'All the workers must supply their own work clothing'.

everybody and **everyone** can be used interchangeably. They both take singular verbs, as in 'Everyone has expressed the wish to stay' and 'Everybody wishes the war to end'. **Every one** as two words is used when emphasis is required, as in 'Every one of the workers wanted to stay' and 'Every one of the machines was damaged'.

ex- as a prefix means 'former', as in 'the ex-manager' and 'his ex-wife'. It is usually attached to the noun it describes with a hyphen. As a noun, used informally, **ex** means 'former wife, husband or partner'. as in 'He still visits his ex'. **Ex-directory** means 'not listed in the telephone directory', as in 'choose to have an ex-directory number after having received a series of nuisance calls'.

exaggerate is liable to be misspelt. Note the double *g* and single *r*. Note also the *e* before the *r*. The word means 'to describe as being larger, greater, etc, than is the case', as in 'exaggerate the difficulty of the job' and 'exaggerate how poor he is'.

exceedingly and **excessively** are not the same. **Exceedingly** means 'extremely, to a very great extent', as in 'She was exceedingly beautiful' and 'It was exceedingly kind of them to help'. **Excessively** means 'immoderately, to too great an extent, beyond measure', as in 'It was excessively annoying of him to interfere' and 'He was excessively fond of alcohol'.

except is commoner than **except for**. **Except** is used in such sentences as 'They are all dead except his father', 'He goes every day except Sunday'. **Except for** is used at the beginning of sentences, as in 'Except for Fred, all the workers were present', and where **except** applies to a longish phrase, as in 'There was no one present except for the maid cleaning the stairs' and 'The house was silent except for the occasional purring of the cat'. When followed by a pronoun, this should be in the accusative or objective, as in 'There was no one there except *him*' and 'Everyone stayed late except *me*'.

exceptionable and **exceptional** are both related to the noun 'exception' but they mean different things. **Exceptionable** describes something that someone might take exception to or object to, as in 'They found his behaviour exceptionable' and 'behaviour that was not at all exceptionable'. **Exceptional** means 'out of the ordinary, unusual', as in 'an exceptional talent'. It often means 'unusually good, superior', as in 'have an exceptional singing voice' and 'serve exceptional food and drink'.

excessively *see* **exceedingly**.

exercise and **exorcise** are liable to be confused because they sound alike. However, they are completely different in meaning. **Exercise** as a noun means 'physical exertion', as in 'sitting in front of the television taking little exercise' or 'a set of energetic movements' as in 'doing exercises in the morning'. It can also mean 'a piece of school work', as in 'pupils completing maths exercises'.

It is as a verb that **exercise** is most likely to be confused with **exorcise**. **Exercise** as a verb means 'to take part in physical exertion', 'to perform a series of energetic movements', as in 'The girls liked to exercise to music'. It also means 'to make use of, to employ', as in 'He was charged with the offence but exercised his right to remain silent'. **Exorcise** means 'to rid of evil spirits', as in 'ask a priest to exorcise the haunted house'. **Exercise** and **exorcise** are both frequently misspelt. It is a common error to put a *c* after the *x* in both words. Note that **exercise** is not one of the verbs that can end in *-ize*.

exhausting and **exhaustive** are both formed from the verb 'exhaust' but they mean different things. **Exhausting** means 'extremely tiring', as in 'an exhausting climb up the hill' and 'have an exhausting day at the office'. **Exhaustive** means 'thorough, comprehensive', as in 'police making an exhaustive search of the grounds for the murder weapon'.

exhilarate is often misspelt. Note the *lar* combination. It is a common error to put *ler*. The word means 'to make excited, to rouse, to thrill', as in 'exhilarated by a drive in a fast car', 'exhilarated by their walk in the hills'.

expeditious and **expedient** are liable to be confused but have quite different meanings. Expeditious means 'rapid', as in 'send the parcel by the most expeditious method possible'. **Expedient** means 'most convenient, most advantageous', as in 'The government was only interested in what was politically expedient' and 'choose the most expedient method, no matter how immoral'.

explicable is now usually pronounced with the emphasis on the second syllable (ex-*plik*-ibl). Formerly it was commonly pronounced with the emphasis on the first syllable (*ex*-plikibl).

explicit and **implicit** are liable to be confused although they are virtually opposites. **Explicit** means 'direct, clear', as in 'The instructions were not explicit enough' and 'Give explicit reasons for your decision'. **Explicit** is often used in modern usage to mean 'with nothing hidden or implied', as in 'explicit sex scenes'. **Implicit** means 'implied, not directly expressed', as in 'There was an implicit threat in their warning' and 'an implicit criticism in his comments on their actions'. **Implicit** also means 'absolute and unquestioning', as in 'an implicit faith in his ability to succeed' and 'an implicit confidence in her talents'.

exquisite has two possible pronunciations. It is most usually pronounced with the emphasis on the first syllable (*ex*-kwis-it) but some prefer to put the emphasis on the second syllable (iks-*kwis*-it). The word means 'beautiful, delicate', as in 'exquisite jewellery' and 'exquisite workmanship'. It can also mean 'acute', as in 'the exquisite pain of rejected love'.

extant and **extinct** are liable to be confused although they are opposites. **Extant** means 'still in existence', as in 'customs of ancient origin that are still extant in the village', 'a species of animal that is no longer extant'. **Extinct** means 'no longer in existence', as in 'Dinosaurs have been extinct for millions of years', and 'no longer active', as in 'extinct volcanoes' and 'extinct passion'. Note the spelling of **extinct**, which is frequently misspelt.

extinct *see* **extant**.

extinguish is frequently misspelt. Note the *gui* combination. The word means 'to put out, to cause to stop burning', as in 'firemen extinguishing the flames' and 'extinguish the passion'.

extraordinary can cause problems with pronunciation and spelling. The *a* is silent in the pronunciation. Note the *a* before *o* in the spelling. Remember it is made up of 'extra' and 'ordinary'.

extravagant is frequently misspelt. Note the single *g*.

extrovert and **introvert** are liable to be confused although they are opposites. **Extrovert** refers to 'a person who is more interested in what is going on around him/her than in his/her own thoughts and feelings, such a person usually being outgoing and sociable', as in 'She is a real extrovert who loves to entertain the guests at parties'. **Introvert** refers to 'a person who is more concerned with his/her own thoughts and feelings than with what is going around him/her, such a person usually being shy and reserved', as in 'an introvert who hates having to speak in public' and 'introverts who prefer to stay at home than go to parties'. Both **extrovert** and **introvert** can be adjectives as well as nouns, as in 'extrovert behaviour' and 'introvert personality. Note the spelling of **extrovert.** It was formerly spelt with an *a* instead of an *o*.

F

façade can cause problems both with regard to spelling and pronunciation. It is French in origin and, although it has been part of the English language for some time, it still usually retains the cedilla under the *c* (*ç*). In modern usage there is a growing tendency to punctuate less and less, and as this tendency also applies to the use of accents **facade**

facetious

is also found. The word is pronounced fa-*sahd* and means 'front', as in 'a building with an imposing façade', and 'outward appearance', as in 'hide her grief behind a façade of happiness'.

facetious is commonly misspelt. Note that the vowels appear in alphabetical order (*aeiou*). It means 'humorous, flippant', as in 'You shouldn't make facetious remarks about so grave a subject' and 'a facetious young woman who does not take anything seriously'.

facility and **faculty** are liable to be confused in the sense of 'ability'. **Facility** means 'ease or skill in doing something', as in 'admire his facility with words'. **Faculty** means 'a particular natural talent or power', as in 'her faculty for learning foreign languages'. **Facility** also means 'something that makes it possible or easier to do something'. In this sense it is usually plural (**facilities**), when it often refers to equipment or buildings, as in 'sports facilities'. **Facilities** is sometimes used to mean 'toilet', as in 'Ask the garage owner if we can use his facilities'.

fahrenheit *see* **Celsius**.

family name is used in politically correct language instead of **maiden name** since this is thought to imply that all women are virgins before they are married. Thus 'Her family name was Jones' would be used instead of 'Her maiden name was Jones'. Another politically correct term is **birth name**, as in 'Her birth name was Jones'.

faint and **feint** are sometimes confused. **Faint** as an adjective means either 'not clear, not strong', as in 'hear a faint noise' and 'bear a faint resemblance', or 'giddy, feeling as though one were about to lose consciousness', as in 'She asked if she could sit down as she felt faint'. As a verb it means 'to lose consciousness', as in 'She turned pale and fainted'. As an adjective **feint** is used on stationery to mean 'with faintly printed fine lines', as in 'a pad with feint pages'. In this sense **feint** is sometimes spelt **faint**. **Feint** as a noun means 'a pretended movement intended to distract someone', as in 'His opponent was misled when the boxer made a feint with his left fist'.

fait accompli is a French phrase that has been adopted into English. It refers to 'something that has been done and cannot be undone or changed', as in 'Her parents disapproved of him but by the time they found about the wedding it was a fait accompli and there was nothing they could do about it'. It is pronounced fayt a-kom-*plee*.

fantastic literally means 'relating to fantasy, fanciful, strange', as in 'fantastic dreams' and 'tales of fantastic events'. In modern usage it is often used informally to mean 'exceptionally good, excellent', as in 'have a fantastic holiday' and 'be a fantastic piano player'. It can also mean in informal usage 'very large', as in 'pay a fantastic sum of money'.

farther and **further** are not used interchangeably in all situations in modern usage. **Farther** is mainly restricted to sentences where physical distance is involved, as in 'It is farther to Glasgow from here than it is to Edinburgh'. **Further** can also be used in this sense, as in 'It is further to the sea than I thought'. When referring to time or extent, **further** is used, as in 'Further time is required to complete the task' and 'The police have ordered further investigations'. It can also mean 'additional', as in 'We shall require further supplies'. **Further**, unlike **farther**, can be used as a verb to mean 'to help the progress or development about', as in 'further the cause of freedom'.

fascinate is often misspelt. Note the *c* after the *s*. The word means 'to attract greatly, to capture the attention of', as in 'They were fascinated by the explorer's tales of adventure'.

fatal and **fateful** are liable to be confused although they mean different things. **Fatal** means 'causing death', as in 'involved in a fatal accident' and 'contract a fatal illness', or 'causing ruin or disaster', as in 'His plans for expansion proved fatal to the company' and 'The thief made a fatal mistake and was caught by the police'. **Fateful** means 'important and decisive, having important consequences', as in 'He never arrived home on that fateful night' and 'They eventually got married after that first fateful meeting'.

faux pas is a French phrase that has been adopted into the English language. It means 'a social blunder, an indiscreet or embarrassing remark or deed', as in 'The hostess made a faux pas when she asked after her guest's wife, not knowing that they had divorced last year'. **Faux** is pronounced to rhyme with *foe*, and **pas** is pronounced *pa*.

fax is an abbreviation of 'facsimile' and refers to 'an electronic system for transmitting documents using telephone lines'. As a noun **fax** can refer to the machine transmitting the documents, as in 'the fax has broken down again'; to the system used in the transmission, as in 'send the report by fax'; and the document or documents so transmitted, as in 'He replied to my fax at once'.

faze and **phase** are liable to be confused because they sound alike. However, they have totally different meanings. **Faze** is a verb meaning 'to fluster or disconcert', as in 'He was completely fazed by the interviewer's question—he could think of nothing to say'. **Phase** is primarily a noun meaning 'stage', as in 'the next phase of the development plans' and 'teachers going through a defiant phase'. **Phase** can also be a verb, found principally in the phrases **phase in** and **phase out**, which mean respectively 'to introduce gradually' and 'to withdraw gradually', as in 'The changes in the educational system are to be phased in over three years' and 'The old system of staffing will be phased out over the next few months'.

fearful and **fearsome** are both adjectives derived from the noun 'fear' but they mean different things. **Fearful** means 'scared, nervous', as in 'fearful children stumbling through the dark woods' and 'The burglars were fearful of being sent to prison'. It also means informally 'very bad, terrible', as in 'what a fearful mess he's in!' **Fearsome** means 'causing fear, frightening', as in 'fearsome wild animals' and 'It was a fearsome sight to behold'.

feasible is liable to be misspelt. Note the '-*ible*' ending. It means 'capable of being done or achieved, practicable', as in 'trials being carried out to find out if the suggested project is feasible'. In modern usage it is frequently used rather loosely to mean 'possible, probable or likely', as in 'It is just feasible that it might rain'.

February causes problems both with spelling and pronunciation. With reference to spelling note the first *r* between the *b* and *u*. It is a common error to omit this. The correct pronunciation is *feb*-roo-ari, but this is often simplified in informal speech to *feb*-ra-ri.

feint *see* **faint**.

ferment and **foment** can both mean 'to excite, to stir up', as in 'Troublemakers out to ferment discontent' and 'People out to foment trouble in the crowd'. Both words have other meanings that do not relate to each other. **Ferment** means 'to undergo the chemical process known as fermentation', as in 'home-made wine fermenting in the basement'. **Foment** means 'to apply warmth and moisture to in order to lessen pain or discomfort', as in 'foment the old man's injured hip'.

fetid has two possible pronunciations and two possible spellings. The first syllable can rhyme either with 'met' or 'meet'. With reference to spelling, **foetid** is a rarer alternative spelling.

fête is French in origin and is usually spelt, even in English, with a circumflex over the first *e*. It means 'an outdoor entertainment with the sale of goods, amusement stalls, etc, often held to make money for charity or a good cause', as in 'The proceeds of the village fête went towards the repair of the church roof'. It can be pronounced either to rhyme with 'mate' or 'met'. **Fête** can also be a verb meaning 'to honour or entertain lavishly', as in 'the winning football team were fêted by the whole town when they returned home'.

fetus *see* **foetus**.

female, **feminine** and **feminist** all relate to women but they are by no means interchangeable. **Female** refers to the sex of a person, animal or plant, as in 'the female members of the group', 'the female wolf and her cubs' and 'the female reproductive cells'. It refers to the childbearing sex and contrasts with 'male'. **Feminine** means 'having qualities that are considered typical of women or are traditionally associated with women', as in 'wear feminine clothes', 'take part in supposedly feminine pursuits, such as cooking and sewing' and 'feminine hairstyles'. It is the opposite of 'masculine'. It can be used of men as well as women, when it is usually derogatory, as in 'He has a very feminine voice' and 'He walks in a very feminine way'. When applied in a derogatory way to a man, **feminine** means much the same as **effeminate**. **Feminine** also applies to the gender of words, as in 'Lioness is the feminine form of lion'. **Feminist** means 'referring to feminism', 'feminism' being 'a movement based on the belief that women should have the same rights, opportunities, etc', as in 'management trying to avoid appointing anyone with feminist ideas' and 'Equal opportunities is one of the aims of the feminist movement'.

few and **a few** do not convey exactly the same meaning. **Few** is used to mean the opposite of 'many', as in 'We expected a good many people to come but few did' and 'Many people entered the competition but few won a prize'. The phrase **a few** is used to mean the opposite of 'none', as in 'We didn't expect anyone to turn up but a few did' and 'We thought that none of the students would get a job but a few did'.

fewer *see* **less**.

fiancé and **fiancée** are respectively the masculine and feminine forms of 'the person to whom one is engaged', as in 'She introduced her fiancé to her parents' and 'He gave his fiancée a magnificent engagement ring'. **Fiancé** and **fiancée** are derived from French and follow the French spelling. Note the acute accent on the *é* of **fiancé** and **fiancée** and the additional *e* on **fiancée**. Both words are pronounced in the same way—fi-*on*-say.

fictional and **fictitious** are both derived from the noun 'fiction' and are interchangeable in the sense of 'imagined, invented', as in 'a fictional character based on an old man whom he used to know' and 'The events in the novel are entirely fictitious'. However, **fictitious** only is used in the sense of 'invented, false', as in 'an entirely fictitious account of the accident' and 'think up fictitious reasons for being late'.

fill in and **fill out** are both used to mean 'to complete a form, etc, by adding the required details', as in 'fill in/fill out an application form for a passport'. In British English **fill in** is the more common term, although **fill out** is the accepted term in American English.

finance can be pronounced in two ways. The commoner pronunciation has the emphasis on the second syllable and the first syllable pronounced like the fin of a fish (fin-*ans*). The alternative pronunciation has emphasis on the first syllable, which then is pronounced as fine (*fin*-ans). As a noun the word means 'money, capital, funding', as in 'provide the finance for the project'. As a verb it means 'to provide the money for, to pay for', as in 'expect her parents to finance her trip round the world'.

first and **firstly** are now both considered acceptable in lists, although formerly **firstly** was considered unacceptable. Originally the acceptable form of such a list was as in 'There are several reasons for staying here. First, we like the house, secondly we have pleasant neighbours, thirdly we hate moving house'. Some users now prefer to use the adjectival forms of 'second' and 'third' when using **first**, as in 'He has stated his reasons for going to another job. First, he has been offered a higher salary, second, he has more opportunities for promotion, third, he will have a company car'. As indicated, **firstly** is now quite acceptable and is the form preferred by many people, as in 'They have several reasons for not having a car. Firstly they have very little money, secondly, they live right next to the bus-stop, thirdly, they feel cars are not environmentally friendly'.

fish and **fishes** are both found as plural forms of 'fish', but **fish** is by far the more widely used form, as in 'He keeps tropical fish', 'Some fish live in fresh water and some in the sea' and 'there are now only three fish in the tank'. **Fishes** is rarely used but when it is, it is usually used to refer to different species of fish, as in 'He is comparing the fishes of the Pacific Ocean with those of the Indian Ocean'. **Fish** can also be used in this case.

first name *see* **Christian name**.

flaccid, meaning 'soft and limp', as in 'repelled by the sight of his flaccid flesh' causes problems both with reference to spelling and pronunciation. In spelling note the double *c*. As for pronunciation, **flaccid** is usually pronounced *flak*-sid but *flas*-id is a rarer alternative.

flair and **flare** are liable to be confused because they sound alike. However, they mean entirely different things. **Flair** refers to 'a natural aptitude or talent', as in 'She has a real flair for dress designing', or to 'stylishness or attractiveness', as in 'She always dresses with flair, although she does not spend much money on clothes'. As a noun, **flare** refers to a 'bright, sudden unsteady flame', as in 'From the sea they caught sight of the flare of the bonfire on the hilltop', or 'a signal in the form of light used at sea', as in 'The captain of the sinking ship used flares to try to attract the attention of passing vessels'. As a verb **flare** means either 'to burn brightly and unsteadily', as in 'The match flared in the darkness', or 'to burst into activity', as in 'Tempers flare when the two families get together'. It also means 'to become wider at the bottom', as in 'skirts flaring at the knee'.

flak originally referred to 'gunfire aimed at enemy aircraft', as in 'Pilots returning across the English Channel encountered heavy flak'. In modern usage it is also applied to 'severe criticism', as in 'the government receiving flak for raising taxes'.

flammable and **inflammable** both mean 'easily set on fire, burning easily', as in 'Children's nightclothes should not be made of flammable/inflammable material' and 'The chemical is highly flammable/inflammable'. **Inflammable** is frequently misused because some people wrongly regard it as meaning 'not burning easily', thinking that it is like such words as 'incredible', 'inconceivable' and 'intolerant' where the prefix 'in' means 'not'.

flare *see* **flair**.

flaunt and **flout** are liable to be confused although they mean different things. **Flaunt** means 'to show off, to display in an ostentatious way', as in 'flaunting her new clothes in front of the other children who were envious of her' and 'flaunting her generous bust'. **Flout** means 'to disobey or disregard openly or scornfully', as in 'expelled for flouting school rules' and 'flout convention by not wearing evening dress'.

fleshly and **fleshy** are not interchangeable although they are both derived from the noun 'flesh'. **Fleshly** means 'referring to the body as opposed to the spirit', as in 'more interested in fleshly pleasure than in prayer'. **Fleshy** means either 'soft and pulpy, as in 'ripe, fleshy peaches', or 'plump', as in 'Women with fleshy upper arms should avoid sleeveless dresses'.

flounder and **flounce** are liable to be confused although they have different meanings. **Flounder** means 'to move with difficulty or clumsily, to struggle helplessly', as in 'walkers floundering in the swampy ground' and 'to hesitate or make mistakes', as in 'The politician answered the first few questions easily but floundered when the interviewer asked him about his policies'. **Founder** means 'to sink', as in 'The ship hit some rocks and foundered' and 'to fail, to collapse', as in 'His business foundered for lack of enough capital' and 'The campaign foundered when the mayor withdrew his support'.

flout *see* **flaunt**.

flotsam and **jetsam** are often used together to refer to 'miscellaneous objects, odds and ends', as in 'We have moved most of the furniture to the new house—there's just the flotsam and jetsam left', and 'vagrants, tramps', as in 'people with no pity in their hearts for the flotsam and jetsam of society'. In the phrase **flotsam and jetsam** they are used as though they meant the same thing but this is not the case. Both words relate to the remains of a wrecked ship, but **flotsam** refers to 'the wreckage of the ship found floating in the water', as in 'The coastguards knew the ship must have broken up when they

flounder

saw bits of flotsam near the rocks', while **jetsam** refers to 'goods and equipment thrown overboard from a ship in distress in order to lighten it', as in 'The coastguards were unable to find the ship although they found the jetsam'.

flounder *see* **founder**.

flu and **flue** are liable to be confused although they have entirely different meanings. **Flu** is a shortened form of 'influenza', as in 'He is off work with flu', 'She caught flu and had to cancel her skiing trip'. It is much more commonly used than 'influenza', which is restricted to very formal or technical contexts, as in 'an article on the dangers of influenza in a medical journal'. Note that **flu** is no longer spelt with an initial apostrophe although the spelling **'flu** was formerly common. **Flue** means 'a channel or pipe through which smoke, hot air or fumes pass from a boiler, etc, usually to a chimney', as in 'The boiler is not working properly as the flue needs to be cleaned'.

fluorescent, as in 'fluorescent lighting' or 'fluorescent paint', is frequently misspelt. Note the *uo* combination, the *sc* and *ent*.

focus as a verb has two possible spellings in its past participle and past tense. Formerly only **focused** was considered acceptable but in modern usage **focussed** is also considered acceptable. The same applies to the present participle and so **focusing** and **focussing** are both acceptable. **Focus** as a verb means 'to adjust the focus of', as in 'focus a camera'; 'to become able to see clearly', as in 'His eyes gradually began to focus in the darkened room'; 'to cause to be concentrated at a point', as in 'focus the sun's rays through a magnifying glass'; 'to concentrate (one's attention or mind) on', as in 'unable to focus his mind on the problem' and 'the committee should focus on improving the financial situation'.

As a noun **focus** has two possible plural forms. Of these **focuses** (not **focusses**) is the more common in modern usage except in very technical contexts when **foci** is used. **Focus** as a noun means 'the point at which rays of light or sound meet', as in 'the focus of the sun's rays'; 'the point at which the outline of something is most clearly seen', as in 'The trees on the horizon are not yet in focus'; 'a device or adjustment on a lens to produce a clearer image', as in 'a camera with a faulty focus'; 'centre of interest, attention, etc', as in 'The focus of the meeting was on getting the plans for the new road rejected' and 'In that dress she was the focus of attention'.

foetid *see* **fetid**.

foetus and **fetus** are both possible spellings of a word meaning 'a young human or animal that has developed within the womb but has not yet reached the stage of being born', as in 'doctors worrying about giving the pregnant woman a drug that might harm the foetus'. Originally **fetus** was restricted to American English but it is becoming increasingly used in British English also, as in 'a fetus liable to abort'. The adjective formed from **foetus/fetus** is **foetal/fetal.**

foment *see* **ferment**.

forbear and **forebear** are interchangeable in one meaning of **forbear** only. **Forbear** is a verb meaning 'to refrain from', as in 'I hope she can forbear from pointing out that she was right' and this cannot be spelt **forebear**. However, **forebear** meaning 'ancestor' can also be spelt **forbear**, as in 'One of his *forebears/forbears* received a gift of land from Henry VIII'.

The verb **forbear** is pronounced with the emphasis on the second syllable as for-*bair*. The nouns **forbear** and **forebear** are pronounced alike with the emphasis on the first syllable as *for*-bair. the past tense of the verb **forbear** is **forbore**, as in 'He forbore to mention that he was responsible for the mistake'.

forever can be spelt as two words when it means 'eternally, for all time', as in 'doomed to separate forever/for ever' and 'have faith in the fact that they would dwell forever/for ever with Christ'. In the sense of 'constantly or persistently', only **forever** is used, as in 'His wife was forever nagging' and 'the child was forever asking for sweets'.

formally and **formerly** are liable to be confused because they sound alike. **Formally**

means 'in a formal way', as in 'dress very formally for the dinner' and 'address the meeting formally'. **Formerly** means 'previously, before, at an earlier time', as in 'Formerly the committee used to meet twice per month' and 'He was formerly chairman of the board'.

former and **latter** are opposites. **Former** refers to 'the first of two people or things mentioned' while **latter** refers to 'the second of two people or things mentioned', as in 'He was given two options, either to stay in his present post but accept less money or to be transferred to another branch of the company. He decided to accept the former/latter option'. **Former** also means 'previous, at an earlier time', as in 'He is a former chairman of the company' and 'She is a former holder of the championship title'.

formerly *see* **formally**.

formidable may be pronounced with the emphasis on the first syllable as *for*-mid-ibl or with the emphasis on the second syllable as for-*mid*-ibl. The first of these is the more widely used. The word means 'causing fear or apprehension', as in 'The sight of the raging torrent was a formidable prospect'; 'difficult to deal with', as in 'a formidable task'; 'arousing respect', as in 'a formidable opponent' and 'a formidable list of qualifications'.

forte causes problems with pronunciation. The usual pronunciation in is *for*-tay but it can also be pronounced as single syllable fort. The word means 'someone's strong point', as in 'Putting people at their ease is not her forte' and 'The chef's forte is desserts'. There is also a musical word **forte** meaning 'loud' or loudly'. It is of Italian origin and is pronounced either *for*-ti or *for*-tay.

forward and **forwards** are not interchangeable in all contexts. They are interchangeable in the adverbial sense of **forward** meaning 'towards the front', as in 'He took a step forward/forwards' and 'facing forward/forwards'. **Forwards** is never used as an alternative for **forward** as an adjective, as in 'forward planning'. Nor is **forwards** ever used in idiomatic phrasal verbs such as 'look forward', 'put forward', 'come forward', as in 'look forward to a happy retirement', 'put forward new proposals' and 'appeal to witnesses to come forward'.

founder *see* **flounder**.

foyer causes pronunciation problems. The most widely used pronunciation is foi-ay but it can also be pronounced fwah-yay following the original French pronunciation. It means 'an entrance hall in a hotel, theatre, etc'.

fulfil is frequently misspelt. Note that neither *l* is doubled. However the second *l* is doubled in the past tense and past participle as **fulfilled** and in the present participle as **fulfilling**. In American English the usual spelling is **fulfill**.

further *see* **farther**.

G

gaff and **gaffe** are liable to be confused because they sound alike. **Gaff** means 'a rod with an iron hook for pulling a large fish out of the water', as in 'The anglers in the boat reached for the gaff when they saw the size of the fish'. It is more commonly found in the slang phrase **blow the gaff**, meaning 'to reveal a secret', as in 'The thieves refused to tell the police where they had hidden the stolen money but the wife of one of them blew the gaff'. **Gaffe** means 'a social blunder, an indiscreet remark or deed', as in 'He wore a sports jacket to the dinner party and realized that he had made a gaffe when he saw everyone else in evening dress'.

gallop, meaning to go or ride fast, as in 'try to get the horse to gallop', is frequently misspelt. Note the double *l* and single *p*. The past tense, past participle and present participle are even more likely to be misspelt. The *p* does not double, as **galloped** and **galloping**. Thus we have 'horses which galloped across the plains' and 'watch the ponies galloping'.

gamble and **gambol** are liable to be confused because they sound alike although they mean different thing. **Gamble** is much more common than **gambol** and means 'to play games of chance for money', as in 'He gambles all night at the casino', or 'to bet, wager or risk money on something uncertain', as in 'He gambled all his money on the horse in the last race' and 'He gambled all his savings on a risky business venture'. **Gambol** means 'to skip about', as in 'Lambs used to gambol in the fields here'. The single *l* doubles in the past tense, past participle and present participle as **gambolled** and **gambolling**. Thus 'The lion cubs gambolled around their mother' and 'Watch the children gambolling on the beach'.

gaol *see* **jail**.

-gate is a modern suffix which is added to a noun to indicate something scandalous. Most of the words so formed are short-lived and forgotten about almost as soon as they are invented. In modern usage they are frequently used to apply to sexual scandals, but originally **-gate** was restricted to some form of political scandal. The suffix is derived from **Watergate**, and refers to a political scandal in the United States during President Richard Nixon's re-election campaign in 1972 when Republican agents were caught breaking into the headquarters of the Democratic Party in Washington, called the Watergate Building. The uncovering of the attempts to cover up the break-in led to Richard Nixon's resignation.

gauge, meaning 'measure, standard', as in 'petrol gauge' and 'a gauge of his intelligence', is frequently misspelt. Note that the *a* comes before the *u*. It is a common error to put them the wrong way round.

gay originally meant 'merry, light-hearted', as in 'the gay laughter of children playing' and 'everyone feeling gay at the sight of the sunshine'. Although this meaning still exists in modern usage, it is rarely used since **gay** has come to be an accepted word for 'homosexual', as in 'gay rights' and 'gay bars'. Although the term can be applied to men or women it is most commonly applied to men, the corresponding word for women being **lesbian**. There is a growing tendency among homosexuals to describe themselves as **queer**, a term that was formerly regarded as being offensive.

geriatric is frequently found in medical contexts to mean 'elderly' or 'old', as in 'an ever-increasing number of geriatric patients' and 'a shortage of geriatric wards'. In such contexts **geriatric** is not used in a belittling or derogatory way, **geriatrics** being the name given to the branch of medicine concerned with the health and diseases of elderly people. However, **geriatric** is often used in the general language to refer to old people in a derogatory or scornful way, as in 'geriatric shoppers getting in the way' or 'geriatric drivers holding up the traffic'.

gibe and **jibe** both mean 'to jeer at, mock, make fun of', as in 'rich children gibing/jibing at the poor children for wearing out-of-date clothes'. **Gibe** and **jibe** are nouns as well as verbs as in 'politicians tired of the gibes/jibes of the press'.

gipsy and **gypsy** are both acceptable spellings, as in 'gipsies/gypsies travelling through the country in their caravans'. Some people object to the word **gipsy** or **gypsy**, preferring the word traveller, as in 'councils being asked to build sites for travellers'. The term **traveller** is used to apply to a wider range of people who travel the country, as in 'New

Age travellers', and not just to gipsies, who are Romany in origin.

girl means 'a female child or adolescent', as in 'separate schools for girls and boys' and 'Girls tend to mature more quickly than boys'. However it is often applied to a young woman, or indeed to a woman of any age, as in 'He asked his wife if she was going to have a night out with the girls from the office'. Many women object to this use, regarding it as patronizing, although the user of the term does not always intend to convey this impression.

glamorous is frequently misspelt. Note that there is no *u* before the *r*, although there is one in **glamour**. **Glamorous** means 'beautiful, stylish, elegant', as in 'glamorous filmstars'.

glutton *see* **gourmand**.

gobbledygook and **gobbledegook** are both acceptable spellings of a word meaning 'pretentious language that is difficult to understand, often found in official documents', as in 'The leaflets were meant to explain how to apply for a grant but they were written in gobbledygook'.

gorilla and **guerilla** are liable to be confused because they sound alike. They are completely different in meaning. **Gorilla** is a type of large African ape, as in 'The zoo has several gorillas'. It is also used informally to describe a large, powerful, often ugly and brutal man, as in 'The gangster has a gang of gorillas to protect him'. **Guerilla**, which can also be spelt **guerrilla**, means 'a member of an irregular army who fights in small, secret groups', as in 'The army were shot at by guerillas hiding in the hills'. Both words are pronounced alike as gir-*il*-a.

gourmand and **gourmet** and **glutton** all have reference to food but they do not mean quite the same thing. **Gourmand** refers to 'a person who likes food and eats a lot of it', as in 'Gourmands tucking into huge helpings of the local food'. It means much the same as **glutton**, but **glutton** is a more condemnatory term, as in 'gluttons stuffing food into their mouths'. **Gourmet** is a more refined term, being used to refer to 'a person who enjoys food and who is discriminating and knowledgeable about it', as in 'gourmets who spend their holidays seeking out good local restaurants and produce'. In modern usage **gourmet** is often used as an adjective to mean 'high-class, elaborate, expensive', as in 'gourmet restaurants' and 'gourmet foods'.

graffiti is frequently misspelt. Note the double *f* and single *t*. The word is used of 'unofficial writing and drawings, often of an obscene nature, on the walls of public places', as in 'trying to clean the graffiti from the walls of the public toilets'. Graffiti is Italian in origin and is actually the plural form of **graffito**, meaning a single piece of writing or drawing, but this is now hardly ever used in English.

gratuitous is liable to be misspelt and misunderstood. Note the *ui* combination. The word means 'uncalled-for, without good reason, unwarranted, unnecessary', as in 'resent her gratuitous advice' and 'upset by her gratuitous insults'.

gray *see* **grey**.

green is used to mean 'conserved with the conservation of the environment', as in 'a political party concerned with green issues' and 'buy as many green products as possible'. The word is derived from German *grün*, the political environmental lobby having started in West Germany, as it was then called.

grievous causes problems with reference to both spelling and pronunciation. Note the *ie* combination and the absence of *i* before *ou*. It is pronounced *gree*-vus. **Grievous** means 'causing grief or suffering', as in 'grievous bodily harm', or 'serious, grave', as in 'a grievous crime'.

grey and **gray** are both acceptable spellings. In British English, however, **grey** is the more common, as in 'different shades of grey' and 'grey hair', but **gray** is the standard form in American English.

guarantee is frequently misspelt. Note the *u* before the *a* and the *a* after the *r*. It means 'a promise or assurance that certain conditions will be fulfilled', as in 'under the terms of the manufacturer's guarantee'.

guerilla

guerilla, guerrilla *see* gorilla.

gynaecology is frequently misspelt. Note the *y* after the *g* and the *ae* combination after the *n*. Gynaecology refers to 'the study and treatment of disorders of women, specially of the female reproductive system', as in 'have an appointment at the gynaecology department'. The American English spelling is gynecology.

gypsy *see* gipsy.

H

haemorrhage is frequently misspelt. Note the *ae* and the *rrh* combinations. It can be either a noun meaning 'excessive loss of blood', as in 'a haemorrhage from the womb after the birth of the baby', or a verb meaning 'to bleed heavily', as in 'haemorrhaging badly after the birth of the baby'. In American English the word is spelt hemorrhage.

hail and hale are liable to be confused. They are pronounced alike but have different meanings. Hail refers to frozen rain, as in 'get caught in a storm of hail', or to 'something coming in great numbers and with force', as in 'a hail of bullets'. As a verb it means 'to fall as hail', as in 'It began to hail', or 'to come down fast and with force', as in 'Bullets hailed down on them'. There is another word hail, which is a verb that means 'to call to in order to attract attention', as in 'He hailed a friend on the other side of the street'; 'to acknowledge enthusiastically as in 'hail him as their new leader' and 'hail his new painting as a masterpiece'; 'to come from', as in 'She hails from a small town up north'. Hale means 'healthy and strong' and is frequently found in the phrase 'hale and hearty', as in 'he was very ill but he is hale and hearty again'.

hallo, hello and hullo are all acceptable spellings of a word used in greeting, as in 'Hallo/hello/hullo, I didn't expect to see you here' and 'He was in a hurry and didn't stop to say "hallo/hello/hullo"'.

handicap is frequently misspelt in the past tense, past participle and present participle, as in 'physically handicapped people' and 'handicapping circumstances'. The word handicap is disliked by some people because they feel it is too negative a term. There is as yet no widespread alternative apart from disabled, although various suggestions have been made as part of the politically correct language movement, such as physically challenged and differently abled.

hangar and hanger are liable to be confused since they sound alike. However, they have totally different meanings. Hangar refers to 'a building for housing aircraft', as in 'a hangar holding four small aircraft'. Hanger refers to 'an apparatus on which clothes are hung', as in 'The hotel didn't provide enough hangars for their clothes'.

hanged and hung are both past participles and past tenses of the verb 'to hang' but they are used in different contexts. Hanged is restricted to the sense of 'hang' that means 'to suspend by the neck until dead', as in 'He was hanged for murder' and 'She hanged herself while depressed'. Hung is used in the other sense of 'hang', as in 'They hung the picture on the wall by the door' and 'A towel hung from the rail'.

hanger *see* hangar.

harass causes problems with reference both to spelling and pronunciation. Note the single *r* and the double *s*. It is a common error to put double *r* and single *s*. There are two possible pronunciations. Traditionally it is pronounced with the stress on the first syllable, as *har*-as. However, in modern usage there is an increasing tendency to put the emphasis on the second syllable, as har-*as*, which is how the word is pronounced in America.

hard and **soft** are both terms applied to drugs. **Hard drugs** refer to 'strong drugs that are likely to be addictive', as in 'Heroin and cocaine are hard drugs'. **Soft drugs** refer to 'drugs that are unlikely to cause addiction', as in 'cannabis and other soft drugs'.

hardly is used to indicate a negative idea. Therefore a sentence or clause containing it does not require another negative. Sentences, such as 'I couldn't hardly see him' and 'He left without hardly a word' are *wrong*. They should read 'I could hardly see him' and 'He left with hardly a word'. **Hardly** is followed by 'when', not 'than', as in 'Hardly had he entered the house when he collapsed', although the 'than' construction is very common.

hare-brained is frequently misspelt as 'hair-brained'. It means 'foolish', as in 'a hare-brained scheme to make money'.

height is a simple word that is frequently misspelt. Note the *ei* and the *gh* combination. As well as meaning 'the distance from the bottom to the top of a person or object', as in 'measure the child's height', it can mean 'the highest point of something', as in 'at the height of his career', or 'the most intense or extreme point of something', as in 'at the height of their passion'.

heinous, meaning 'very wicked', as in 'a heinous crime', causes problems both with reference to spelling and pronunciation. Note the *ei*. It is most commonly pronounced *hay*-nis, although *hee*-nis also exists.

hello *see* **hallo**.

he/she is a convention used to avoid sexism. Before the rise of feminism anyone referred to, whose sex was not specified, was assumed to be male, as in 'Each pupil must take his book home' and 'Every driver there parked his car illegally'. The only exception to this occurred in situations that were thought to be particularly appropriate to women, as in 'The cook should make her own stock' and 'The nurse has left her book behind'. In modern usage where attempts are made to avoid sexism either **he/she** or 'he or she' is frequently used, as in 'Each manager is responsible for his/her department' or 'It is a doctor's duty to explain the nature of the treatment to his or her patient'. People who regard this convention as being clumsy should consider restructuring the sentence or putting it in the plural, as in 'All managers are responsible for their departments'. Some users prefer to be ungrammatical and use a plural pronoun with a singular noun, as in 'Every pupil should take their books home'.

hereditary and **heredity** are liable to be confused. **Hereditary** is an adjective meaning 'passed on from parent to child, genetically transmitted', as in 'suffer from a hereditary disease', or 'passed on from parent to child, inherited', as in 'a hereditary title'. **Heredity** is the noun from which **hereditary** is derived, as in 'part of his genetic heredity' and 'The disease can be put down to heredity'.

heterosexism refers to 'discrimination and prejudice by a heterosexual person against a homosexual one', as in 'He was convinced that he had not got the job because he was gay—that the employer had been guilty of heterosexism'.

historic and **historical** are both adjectives formed from the noun history' but they are not interchangeable. **Historic** refers to events that are important enough to earn, or have earned, a place in history, as in 'Nelson's historic victory at Trafalgar' and 'the astronaut's historic landing on the moon'. It can be used loosely to mean 'extremely memorable', as in 'attend a historic party'. **Historical** means 'concerning past events', as in 'historical studies', or 'based on the study of history, as in 'take into consideration only historical facts' and 'produce historical evidence'.

hoard and **horde** are liable to be confused. They sound alike but they have completely different meanings. **Hoard** refers to 'a collected and reserved store', as in 'the miser's hoard of money' and 'a hoard of old comics'. It can also be a verb meaning 'to collect and store', as in 'hoarding food because they thought it was going to be rationed' and 'squirrels hoarding nuts for the winter'. **Horde** refers to 'a large crowd of people, a multitude', as in 'Hordes of people arrived to see the pop star arriving at the theatre'.

honorary and **honourable** are liable to be confused. They are both derived from the noun **honour**, but they mean different things. **Honorary** means 'given as an honour rather than acquired through the usual channels', as in 'an honorary degree', or 'unpaid', as in 'the honorary secretary' and 'an honorary post'. **Honourable** means 'showing honour', as in 'an honourable man' and 'the honourable thing to do', and 'worthy of honour', as in 'perform honourable deeds in battle'.

hopefully has two meanings. The older meaning is 'with hope', as in 'The child looked hopefully at the sweet-shop window' and 'It is better to travel hopefully than to arrive'. A more recent meaning, which is disliked by some people, means 'it is to be hoped that', as in 'Hopefully we shall soon be there'.

horde see **hoard**.

hospitable can be pronounced in two ways. The more traditional pronunciation has the emphasis on the first syllable, as *hos*-pit-ibl. In modern usage it is sometimes pronounced with the emphasis on the second syllable, as hos-*pit*-ibl. The word means 'showing or giving hospitality, generous to guests', as in 'He is very hospitable and is always having people to stay' and 'a most hospitable hostess who fed her guests very well'.

hullo see **hallo**.

human and **humane** are liable to be confused. **Human** means either 'referring to human beings', as in 'not fit for human habitation', or 'kindly', as in 'He holds a very important position but he is a very human person'. **Humane** means 'showing kindness, sympathy or understanding', as in 'their humane attitude to prisoners of war' and 'Be humane and put the dying animal to sleep'.

humanism and **humanitarianism** are liable to be confused. **Humanism** is a philosophy that values greatly human beings and their rôle, and rejects the need for religion, as in 'She was brought up as a Christian but she decided to embrace humanism in later life'. **Humanitarianism** refers to the philosophy and actions of people who wish to improve the lot of their fellow human beings and help them, as in 'humanitarians trying to help the refugees by taking them food and clothes'.

humorous is frequently misspelt. Note the *o* before the *r*. It is liable to be confused with 'humour' and an extra *u* added before the *r*.

hung see **hanged**.

hygiene is liable to be misspelt. Note the *y* after the *h*, not *i*. It means 'the study and practice of cleanliness and good health', as in 'poor standards of hygiene in the hotel kitchens'.

hyper- and **hypo-** are liable to be confused. They sound rather similar but they are opposites. **Hyper-** means 'above, excessively', as in 'hyperactive', 'hyperexcitable'. **Hypo-** means 'under, beneath', as in 'hypothermia'.

I

-ible *see* **-able**.

identical in modern usage can be followed by either 'with' or 'to'. Formerly only 'with' was considered correct, as in 'His new suit is identical with the one he bought last year'. Now 'to' is also considered acceptable, as in 'a brooch identical to one which he bought for his wife'.

idioms are expressions the meanings of which are different from the literal meanings of the individual words that they contain. Thus 'straight from the shoulder', 'have a finger in every pie' and 'have one's back to the wall' are all idioms.

idiosyncrasy is frequently misspelt. Note the *y* after the *s*, and the *asy* combination, not *acy*. It means 'a particular and individual way of behaving, thinking, etc', as in 'It was one of his idiosyncrasies always to buy yellow cars'.

idle and **idol** are liable to be confused since they sound alike. They mean entirely different things. **Idle** is an adjective meaning 'inactive, not functioning', as in 'machines lying idle', and 'lazy', as in 'too idle to get up and do any work'. **Idol** refers to 'something or someone that one worships or admires', as in 'worship idols carved from wood', 'Her elder brother was her idol' and 'pop stars who are the idols of teenagers'.

idyllic causes problems both with reference to spelling and pronunciation. Note the *y* and double *l*. It is pronounced with the emphasis on the second syllable and the first syllable is usually pronounced to rhyme with 'lid', as in id-*il*-ik. The first syllable is sometimes pronounced with 'wide', as in *id*-il-ik. The word means 'peaceful and pleasant, perfect', as in 'a cottage in an idyllic setting'.

i.e. is the abbreviation of a Latin phrase *id est*, meaning 'that is', as in 'He is a lexicographer, i.e. a person who edits dictionaries'. It is mostly used in written, rather than formal contexts.

illegible and **eligible** are liable to be confused although they have completely different meanings. **Illegible** means 'impossible to decipher, make out or read', as in 'unable to understand the message because of her totally illegible handwriting'. **Eligible** means 'qualified, suitable', as in 'several candidates who were eligible for the post' and 'eligible bachelors'. **Illegible** is pronounced with the emphasis on the the second syllable (il-*lej*-ibl) but **eligible** is pronounced with the emphasis on the first syllable (*el*-ij-ibl).

illegible and **unreadable** are not totally interchangeable. **Illegible** refers to something that is impossible to make out or decipher, as in 'her handwriting is practically illegible'. **Unreadable** can also mean this, as in 'unreadable handwriting', but it can also mean 'unable to be read with understanding or enjoyment', as in 'His writing is so full of jargon that it is unreadable'.

illicit and **elicit** are liable to be confused. They sound alike although they have totally different meanings. **Illicit** means 'unlawful', as in 'the sale of illicit drugs', or 'against the rules of society', as in 'His wife did not know about his illicit affair with his secretary'. **Elicit** means 'to draw out, often with difficulty', as in 'We finally succeeded in eliciting a response from them' and 'All attempts at eliciting the truth from the boy failed'. Both words sound alike, with the emphasis on the second syllable as il-*lis*-it.

illusion *see* **allusion**.
illusion *see* **delusion**.

imaginary and **imaginative** are liable to be confused. They are related but do not mean the same thing. **Imaginary** means 'existing only in the imagination, unreal', as in 'The child has an imaginary friend'. **Imaginative** means 'having a vivid or creative imagination', as in 'An imaginative child who was always inventing her own games', and 'indi-

imbroglio

cating or using a vivid or creative imagination', as in 'an imaginative adventure story'.

imbroglio means 'a confused, complicated or embarrassing situation', as in 'politicians getting involved in an international imbroglio during the summit conference'. It is liable to be misspelt and mispronounced. Note the g which is liable to be omitted erroneously as it is not pronounced. It is pronounced im-*bro*-lio with emphasis on the second syllable which rhymes with 'foe'. **Imbroglio** is used only in formal or literary contexts.

immigrant *see* **emigrant**.

immoral *see* **amoral**.

impasse causes problems with reference to meaning, spelling and pronunciation. It means 'a difficult position or situation from which there is no way out, deadlock', as in 'The negotiations between management and workers have reached an impasse with neither side being willing to compromise'. Note the final e in the spelling. The first syllable can be pronounced 'am', or 'om' in an attempt at following the original French pronunciation, although in modern usage it is frequently totally anglicized as 'im'.

impeccable is frequently misspelt. Note the -*able*, not -*ible*, and the double c. The word means 'faultless, free from error or defect', as in 'The pianist gave an impeccable performance' and 'It was a difficult situation but his behaviour was impeccable'.

impious is frequently misspelt. The emphasis should be on the first syllable as *im*-pi-us. This is unlike 'impiety' where the stress is on the second syllable. **Impious** means 'showing a lack of respect for God or religion'.

implicit *see* **explicit**.

imply and **infer** are often used interchangeably but they in fact are different in meaning. **Imply** means 'to suggest, to hint at', as in 'We felt that she was implying that he was lying' and 'She did not actually say that there was going to be a delay but she implied it'. **Infer** means 'to deduce, to conclude', as in 'From what the employer said we inferred that there would be some redundancies' and 'From the annual financial reports observers inferred the company was about to go bankrupt'. Note that **infer** doubles the r when adding '-ed' or '-ing' to form the past tense, past participle or present participle as **inferred** and **inferring**.

impracticable and **impractical** are liable to be confused. **Impracticable** means 'impossible to put into practice, not workable', as in 'In theory the plan is fine but it is impracticable in terms of costs'. **Impractical** means 'not sensible or realistic', as in 'It is impractical to think that you will get there and back in a day'; 'not skilled at doing or making things', as in 'He is a brilliant academic but he is hopelessly impractical'.

inapt and **inept** are similar in meaning in one sense of **inept**. **Inapt** means 'inappropriate, unsuitable', as in 'The speaker's remarks were totally inapt', 'make a few inapt comments on the situation' and 'inapt behaviour'. **Inept** can mean much the same as this except that it suggests also clumsiness', as in 'embarrassed by his inept remarks'. **Inept** also means 'unskilful, clumsy', as in 'his inept handling of the situation' and 'make an inept attempt at mending the roof'.

incomparable is liable to be mispronounced. The emphasis should be on the second syllable and not the third. It should be pronounced in-*kom*-pir-ibl. **Incomparable** means 'without compare', as in 'her incomparable kindness' and in 'his incomparable rendition of the song'.

incredible and **incredulous** are liable to be confused although they mean different things. **Incredible** means 'unbelievable' or 'difficult to believe', as in 'I find his account of the accident totally incredible' and 'It is incredible that everyone accepts his story'. It also means 'amazing', as in 'earn an incredible amount of money'. **Incredulous** means 'not believing, disbelieving', as in 'His incredulous listeners stared at him'.

indefinite article *see* **a**.

indefinitely is frequently misspelt. Note the i before the t. Many people wrongly put an

336

a. It means 'for an unspecified time', as in 'You could wait indefinitely for a car exactly like that'.

independent is frequently misspelt. Note the final *e*. It is never spelt with an *a*. *See* **dependant**.

indexes and **indices** are both plural forms of 'index'. In modern usage **indexes** is the more common form in general language, as in 'Indexes are essential in large reference books'. An **index** in this sense is 'an alphabetical list given at the back of a book as a guide to its contents'. The form **indices** is mostly restricted to technical contexts, such as mathematical information. **Indices** is pronounced in-dis-is and is the Latin form of the plural.

indict and **indite** are liable to be confused since they are pronounced alike but they have different meanings. **Indict** means 'to charge, to accuse', as in 'He has been indicted on a charge of murder'. **Indite** is a rarer word meaning 'to write down', as in 'The headmaster indited the names of the culprits on an official report'. The words are both pronounced with the emphasis on the second syllable which rhymes with 'light' as in *-dit*.

indispensable is frequently misspelt. Note the *-able* ending, not *-ible*. It means 'absolutely essential', as in 'He now finds his computer indispensable' and 'Since both parents work full time a good nanny is indispensable'.

indite *see* **indict**.

individual refers to 'a single person as opposed to a group', as in 'The rights of the community matter but so do the rights of the individual'. **Individual** is also sometimes used instead of 'person', but in such cases it is often used in a disapproving or belittling way, as in 'What an unpleasant individual she is!' and 'The individual who designed that building should be shot'.

indoor and **indoors** are not interchangeable. **Indoor** is an adjective, as in 'have an indoor match' and 'indoor games'. **Indoors** is an adverb, as in 'children playing outdoors instead of watching television indoors' and 'sleep outdoors on warm evenings instead of indoors'.

inequality and **inequity** are liable to be confused although they mean different things. **Inequality** means 'lack of equality, the state of being unequal or different', as in 'an inequality in the pay structures of the male and female workers' and 'fight against racial inequalities in the job market'. **Inequity** means 'unfairness, unjustness', as in 'feel that there was a certain inequity in the judge's decision'.

infectious *see* **contagious**.

infer *see* **imply**.

infinite and **infinitesimal** are similar in meaning but are not interchangeable. **Infinite** means 'without limit', as in 'infinite space', or 'very great', as in 'have infinite patience' and 'He seems to have an infinite capacity for hard work'. **Infinitesimal** means 'very small, negligible', as in 'an infinitesimal difference in size' and 'an infinitesimal increase'. **Infinitesimal** is pronounced with the emphasis on the fourth syllable in-fin-it-*es*-im-il.

inflammable *see* **flammable**.

influenza *see* **flu**.

informer and **informant** both refer to 'a person who provides information' but they are used in different contexts. **Informer** is used to refer to 'a person who gives information to the police or authorities about a criminal, fugitive, etc', as in 'The local police have a group of informers who tell them what is going on in the criminal underworld' and 'The resistance worker was caught by the enemy soldier when an informer told them about his activities'. An **informant** provides more general information, as in 'My informant keeps me up-to-date with changes in personnel'.

ingenious and **ingenuous** are liable to be confused. They look rather alike but they mean completely different things. **Ingenious** means 'clever, inventive', as in 'an ingenious device for opening wine bottles' and 'It was ingenious of her to find a quick way to get to the new house'. **Ingenuous** means 'innocent' or 'naive', as in 'so ingenuous as to believe his lies'.

in-law is usually found in compounds such as 'mother-in-law' and 'father-in-law'. When these compounds are in the plural the *s* should be added to the first word of the compound, not to **in-law**, as in 'mothers-in-law' and 'fathers-in-law'.

in lieu, which means 'instead of', as in 'receive extra pay in lieu of holidays', causes problems with pronunciation. It may be pronounced in lew or in loo.

innocuous is frequently misspelt. Note the double *n* and the *ouo* combination. It means 'harmless', as in 'He has a reputation for fierceness but he seems fairly innocuous' and 'It seemed an innocuous remark but she was upset by it'.

input used to be a technical term with particular application to computers. This meaning still exists and **input** can refer to the data, power, etc, put into a computer. As a verb it means 'to enter data into a computer', as in 'input the details of all the travel resorts in the area'. In modern usage it is frequently used in general language to mean 'contribution', as in 'Everyone is expected to provide some input for tomorrow's conference'. It is even found in this sense as a verb, as in 'input a great deal to the meeting'.

inquiry *see* **enquiry**.

install and **instal** are now both considered acceptable spellings. **Install** was formerly considered to be the only correct spelling and it is still the more common. The *l* is doubled in **instal** in the past participle, past tense and present participle as **installed**, **installing**. It means 'to put in', as in 'he installed a new television set'. The noun is spelt **instalment**.

instantaneously and **instantly** are interchangeable. Both mean 'immediately, at once', as in 'They obeyed instantaneously/instantly' and 'The accident victims were killed instantly/instantaneously'.

instil is often misspelt 'instill'. Note the single *l*. It means 'to introduce gradually', as in 'instil a sense of responsibility into children'. The *l* doubles in the past participle, past tense and present participle as **instilled** and **instilling**.

intense and **intensive** are not interchangeable. Intense means 'very strong, extreme', as in 'an intense desire to scream' and 'unable to tolerate the intense cold on the icy slopes'. **Intensive** means 'thorough', as in 'conduct an intensive search', and 'concentrated', as in 'an intensive course in first aid' and 'intensive bombing'.

interment and **internment** mean different things. **Interment** means 'burial', as in 'delay the interment of the bodies until a post mortem takes place'. **Internment** means 'imprisonment, especially of prisoners-of-war, etc', as in 'released at the end of the war after several years of internment'. In both **interment** and **internment** the emphasis is on the second syllable.

interpretative and **interpretive** are both forms of the same word. They mean 'interpreting', as in 'an interpretative/interpretive study of his poetry'.

introvert *see* **extrovert**.

invalid refers to two different words. If it is pronounced with the emphasis on the second syllable, as in-*val*-id it means 'not valid, no longer valid', as in 'This visa becomes invalid after six months'. If it is pronounced with the emphasis on the first syllable, as *in*-val-id, it means 'a person who is ill', as in 'The doctor has arrived to see the invalid'.

invent *see* **discover**.

inventory is liable to be pronounced wrongly. Unlike the word 'invention', the emphasis is on the first syllable as *in*-ven-tri or *in*-ven-tor-i. **Inventory** means 'a detailed list of goods in a house, etc,' as in 'Take an inventory of the furniture before you rent the house'.

inward and **inwards** are not used interchangeably. **Inward** is an adjective, as in 'an inward curve' and 'No one could guess her inward feelings'. **Inwards** is an adverb, as in 'toes turning inwards' and 'thoughts turning inwards'. **Inward** can be used as an adverb in the same way as **inwards.**

IQ is the abbreviation of 'intelligence quotient', as in 'He has a high IQ. It is always written in capital letters and is sometimes written with full stops and sometimes not, according to preference.

irascible is frequently misspelt. Unlike 'irritable' it has a single *r*. Note the *c* and the *-ible* ending. It means 'easily roused to anger', as in 'The children were told not to disturb the irascible old man'.

irony is 'the expression of one's meaning by saying the direct opposite of one's thoughts', as in 'This is a fine state of affairs' when in fact things have gone wrong. The adjective is **ironic**, as in 'make ironic remarks'.

irrelevant is frequently misspelt. Note the double r and the *-ant* ending.

irreparable is frequently both mispronounced and misspelt. Note the double *r*, the *a* before the *r* and the *-able* ending. It should be pronounced with the emphasis on the second syllable, as ir-*rep*-ar-abl. The word means 'unable to be put right', as in 'Being abused as a child inflicted irreparable mental damage on him'. It is usually applied to abstract nouns, **unrepairable** being used for objects, as in 'shoes that are unrepairable'. **Unrepairable** is pronounced with the emphasis on the third syllable (*pair*) which rhymes with 'care'.

irrespective is followed by the preposition 'of'. The phrase means 'not taking account of, not taking into consideration', as in 'All can go on the trip, irrespective of age'.

irrevocable is frequently misspelt and mispronounced. Note the double *r* and the *-able* ending. It is pronounced with the emphasis on the second syllable, as ir-*rev*-ok-ibl. When applied to legal judgements, etc, it is sometimes pronounced with the emphasis on the third syllable, as ir-rev-*ok*-ibl. The word means 'unable to be changed or revoked', as in 'Their decision to get divorced is irrevocable' and 'The jury's decision is irrevocable'.

-ise and **-ize** are both verb endings. In British English there are many verbs that can be spelt ending in either **-ise** or **-ize**, as 'computerise/ize', 'economise/ize', 'finalise/ize', 'hospitalise/ize', 'modernise/ize', 'organise/ize', 'realise/ize', 'theorise/ize'. There are a few verbs that cannot be spelt **-ize**. These include 'advertise', 'advise', 'comprise', 'despise', 'exercise', 'revise', 'supervise' and 'televise'.

-ism is a suffix originally used to form nouns indicating doctrine or system, as in 'Thatcherism' and 'Marxism'. This use is still current but **-ism** is now commonly used to indicate discrimination, as in 'ageism', 'racism', 'sexism'. The agent nouns from nouns ending in **-ism** in the latter sense end in **-ist**, as 'ageist', 'racist', 'sexist'.

itinerary is frequently misspelt. Note the *e* before the first *r*, and the *a* before the second *r*.

its and **it's** are liable to be confused. **Its** is an adjective meaning 'belonging to it', as in 'The house has lost its charm' and 'The dog does not like its kennel'. **It's** means 'it is', as in 'Do you know if it's raining?' and 'It's not fair to expect her to do all the chores'.

-ize *see* **-ise**.

J

jail and **gaol** are both acceptable spellings although jail is the more common. They mean 'prison' and can be both nouns and verbs, as in 'sent to jail/gaol for killing his wife' and 'jail/gaol him for his part in the bank robbery'.

jargon refers to the technical or specialized language used by a particular group, e.g. doctors, computer engineers, sociologists, etc, to communicate with each other within their specialty. It should be avoided in the general language as it will not be clear to the ordinary person exactly what is meant.

jersey *see* **cardigan**.

jeopardize is liable to be misspelt. Note the *o*. It is pronounced *jep*-er-dise and means 'to put at risk', as in 'He jeopardizes his career by his unpunctuality.'

jetsam *see* **flotsam**.

jettison is frequently misspelt. Note the double *t* and single *s*. In the past tense, past participle and present participle the *n* is not doubled, as **jettisoned** and **jettisoning**. It means 'to throw out, especially in order to make a ship, aircraft, etc, lighter', as in 'The ship's captain decided to jettison most of the cargo'. It also means 'to abandon, reject', as in 'They have had to jettison their plans for expansion because of lack of money'.

jewellery and **jewelry** are both acceptable spellings, as in 'A great deal of jewellery/jewelry was stolen in the robbery', but **jewellery** is the more common spelling in British English.

jibe *see* **gibe**.

jodhpurs, meaning 'trousers worn when horse-riding', is frequently misspelt. Note the *h*, which is liable to be omitted since it is silent, or put in the wrong place. The word is pronounced *jod*-purs.

judgement and **judgment** are both acceptable spellings, as in 'accept the judgement/judgment of the referee', although in British English **judgement** is slightly more common. **Judgment** is used in legal contexts.

judicial and **judicious** are liable to be confused but they are completely different in meaning. **Judicial** means 'referring to a court of law', as in 'judicial proceedings' and 'a judicial inquiry'. **Judicious** means 'having or showing good sense or judgement, wise', as in ' a judicious choice of words' and 'a judicious course of action'.

just is liable to be put in the wrong place in a sentence. It should be placed before the word it refers to, as in 'He has just one book left to sell', not 'He just has one book left to sell'. **Just** in the sense of 'in the very recent past' is used with the perfect tense, as in 'They have just finished the job', not 'They just finished the job'.

K

kaleidoscope is frequently misspelt. Note the *ei* and the first *o*. It is pronounced with the emphasis on the second syllable, which rhymes with 'my', as kal-*i*-do-skop. **Kaleidoscope** refers to 'a kind of toy consisting of a tube containing small loose pieces of coloured glass and mirrors which reflect the glass pieces to form changing patterns when the tube is turned', as in 'The child was fascinated by the changing colours of the kaleidoscope'. It also means 'a constantly and rapidly changing pattern', as in 'The Eastern market was a kaleidoscope of colour', or 'a succession of changing phases', as in 'the kaleidoscope of international politics'.

kerb *see* **curb**.

khaki is frequently misspelt. Note the *h* after the first *k*. It is liable either to be omitted in error or put in the wrong place. **Khaki** is pronounced kah-ki and refers to 'a yellowish brown colour', as in 'Military uniforms are often khaki in colour'.

kidnap is liable to be misspelt in the past tense, past participle and present participle when it doubles the *p* as **kidnapped, kidnapping.** The agent noun, 'one who kidnaps', is spelt **kidnapper**. **Kidnap** means 'to take away by force and illegally, often with a view to obtaining money or having specified demands met', as in 'The president's daughter was kidnapped by a gang who asked her father for a huge ransom' and 'The terrorists kidnapped the foreign diplomat and would not let him go unless some of their number were released from prison in his country'.

kilometre has two possible pronunciations in modern usage. It can be pronounced with the emphasis on the first syllable, as *kil*-o-meet-er, or with the emphasis on the second syllable, as kil-*om*-it-er. The first of these is the more traditional pronunciation but the second is becoming common. The word means 'the metric unit of length', as in 'It is 200 kilometres from there to Paris'.

kind should be used with a singular noun, as 'This kind of accident can be avoided'. This should not read 'These kind of accidents can be avoided'. Similarly 'The children do not like that kind of film' is correct, not 'The children do not like those kind of films'. A plural noun can be used if the sentence is rephrased as 'Films of that kind are not liked by children'.

Kind of, meaning 'rather', as in 'That restaurant's kind of dear' and 'She's kind of tired of him', is informal and should be avoided in formal contexts.

kindly can be either an adjective or adverb. The adjective means 'kind, friendly, sympathetic', as in 'A kindly lady took pity on the children and lent them some money to get home' and 'She gave them a kindly smile'. The adverb means 'in a kind manner', as in 'We were treated kindly by the local people' and 'They will not look kindly on his actions'.

kneeled and **knelt**, the past tense and past participle of the verb 'to kneel', are both acceptable spellings although **knelt** is more common, as in 'He knelt and asked for forgiveness' and 'She knelt down to look under the car'.

knit in modern usage is becoming increasingly used as a noun to mean 'a knitted garment', as in 'a shop selling beautifully coloured knits'.

knowledgeable is frequently misspelt. Note the *d*, which is often omitted in error, the *e* after the *g*, which is also liable to be omitted in error, and the *-able* ending. **Knowledgeable** means 'knowing a lot, well-informed', as in 'take advice from people more knowledgeable than himself' and 'He is extremely knowledgeable on the subject of ancient Greece'.

L

laboratory is frequently mispronounced. It should be pronounced with the emphasis on the second syllable, as lab-*or*-a-tor-i or lab-*or*-a-tri. In American English the emphasis is on the first syllable. The word refers to a 'room or building where scientific work, such as research and experiments, is carried out', as in 'collect the results of the blood tests from the laboratory'.

laborious is frequently misspelt. Note that there is no *u* before *r*. It is not spelt like 'labour'. It means 'needing much effort', as in 'It was a laborious task to move all the books from the attic', or 'showing signs of effort, not fluent or flowing', as in 'His laborious style of prose is difficult to read'.

labyrinth is liable to be misspelt. Note the *y* before the *r* and the *i* after *r*. It means 'a network of winding paths, passages, etc, through which it is difficult to find one's way', as in 'a labyrinth of underground passages underneath the castle' and 'unable to find one's way around the labyrinth of regulations'.

lady and **woman** cause controversy. **Lady** is objected to by many people when it is used instead of **woman**. Formerly, and still in some circles, it was regarded as a polite form of **woman**, as in '"Please get up and give that lady a seat", said the mother to her son'. Indeed, **woman** was thought to be rather insulting. For many people **woman** is now the preferred term and **lady** is seen as classist, because it is associated with nobility, privilege, etc, or condescending. However, **lady** is still quite commonly used, particularly when women are being addressed in a group, as in '"Ladies, I hope we can reach our sales target", said the manager' and 'Come along, ladies the bus is about to leave'. Phrases, such as **dinner lady** and **cleaning lady** are thought by some to be condescending but others still find **woman** rather insulting.

laid and **lain** are liable to be confused. **Laid** is the past participle and past tense of **lay**, 'to put, place', as in 'They have laid a new carpet in the dining room' and 'We laid the blanket on the ground'. **Lain** is the past participle of **lie**, 'to rest in a horizontal position', as in 'He had lain there for hours before they found him'. *See* also **lay**.

lama and **llama** are liable to be confused although they have completely different meanings. **Llama** means 'a kind of South American animal', as in 'go to see the llama enclosure in the zoo'. **Lama** refers to a monk who is member of the order of Lamaism, a form of Buddhism in Tibet and Mongolia, as in 'lamas gathering for prayer'.

lamentable is frequently mispronounced. It should be pronounced with the emphasis on the first syllable, as *lam*-en-tabl. However it is becoming common to place the emphasis on the second syllable in the same way that 'lament' does. It means 'deplorable, regrettable', as in 'showing a lamentable lack of consideration for other people's feelings'.

languor is frequently misspelt. Note the *uo* combination and note that there is not a *u* before the *r*. It means 'weariness, listlessness, laziness', as in 'people full of languor on that hot, still afternoon'. The adjective from **languor** is **languorous**, as in 'feeling languorous after drinking so much wine at lunch'.

last is liable to cause confusion because it is not always clear which meaning is meant. **Last** as an adjective has several meanings. It can mean 'final', as in 'That was the musician's last public appearance—he died shortly after'; 'coming after all others in time or order', as in 'December is the last month in the year', 'The last of the runners reached the finishing tape'; 'latest, most recent', as in 'Her last novel is not as good as her earlier ones'; 'previous, preceding', as in 'This chapter is interesting but the last one was boring'. In order to avoid confusion it is best to use a word other than **last** where ambiguity is likely to arise. An example of a sentence which could cause confusion is 'I cannot remember the title of his last book', which could mean either 'his latest book' or 'his final book'.

latter *see* **former**.

lavatory *see* **toilet**.

lay and **lie** are liable to be confused. They are related but are used in different contexts. **Lay** means 'to put or place' and is a transitive verb, i.e. it takes an object. It is found in such sentences as 'Ask them to lay the books carefully on the table' and 'They are going to lay a new carpet in the bedroom'. **Lie**, meaning 'to rest in a horizontal position', is an intransitive verb, i.e. it does not take an object. It is found in such sentences as 'They were told to lie on the ground' and 'Snow is apt to lie on the mountain tops for a long time'. The confusion between the two words arises from the fact that **lay** is also the past tense of **lie**, as in 'He lay still on the ground' and 'Snow lay on the mountain tops'. The past tense of **lay** is **laid**, as in 'They laid the books on the table'. There is another verb **lie**, meaning 'to tell falsehoods, not to tell the truth', as in 'He was told to lie to the police'. The past tense of **lie** in this sense is **lied**, as in 'We suspect that he lied but we cannot prove it'. *See also* **laid**.

lead and **led** are liable to be confused. **Lead**, pronounced to rhyme with 'feed', is a verb meaning 'to guide, to show the way to, especially by going in front of', as in 'He lead the police to the spot where he had found the murdered man'. **Lead**, pronounced to rhyme with 'fed, means 'a kind of metal', as in 'replace water pipes made of lead'. **Led**, which also rhymes with fed, is thus pronounced in the same way as **lead** in the sense of metal. It is the past participle and past tense of the verb **lead**, as in 'He had led the search party to the wrong place' and 'The guide led the climbers to the top of the mountain'.

leading question is often used wrongly. It should be used to mean 'a question that is so worded as to invite (or lead to) a particular answer desired by the questioner', as in 'The judge refused to allow the barrister to ask the witness the question on the grounds that it was a leading question'. However, it is often used wrongly to mean 'a question that is difficult, unfair or embarrassing'.

leaned and **leant** are both acceptable forms of the past participle and past tense of the verb 'to lean', as in 'He had *leaned/leant* the ladder against the garage wall' and he *leaned/leant* on the gate and watched the cows'. **Leaned** is pronounced leend or lent, and **leant** is pronounced lent.

leaped and **leapt** are both acceptable forms of the past participle and past tense of the verb 'to leap', as in 'He *leaped /leapt* to his feet and shouted out' and 'The dog had *leaped/leapt* over the fence'. **Leaped** is pronounced either leept or leapt, and **leapt** is pronounced lept.

learn and **teach** are liable to be confused. **Learn** means 'to gain information or knowledge about', as in 'She learnt Spanish as a child', or 'to gain the skill of', as in 'She is learning to drive'. **Teach** means 'to give instruction in, to cause to know something or be able to do something', as in 'She taught her son French' and 'She taught her son to swim'. **Learn** is frequently used wrongly instead of **teach**, as in 'She learnt us to drive'.

learned and **learnt** are both acceptable forms of the past participle and past tense of the verb 'to learn', as in 'She has now *learned/learnt* to drive' and 'They *learned/learnt* French at school'. **Learned** in this sense can be pronounced either lernd or leant. However, **learned** can also be an adjective, meaning 'having much knowledge, erudite', as in 'an learned professor', or 'academic', as in 'learned journals'. It is pronounced *ler*-ned.

leave and **let** are not interchangeable. **Leave go** should not be substituted for **let go** in such sentences as 'Do not let go of the rope'. 'Do not leave go of the rope' is considered to be incorrect. However both **leave alone** and **let alone** can be used in the sense of 'to stop disturbing or interfering with', as in '*Leave/let* the dog alone or it will bite you' and '*leave/let* your mother alone—she is not feeling well'. **Leave alone** can also mean 'leave on one's own, cause to be alone', as in 'Her husband went away and left her alone', but **let alone** cannot be used in this sense. **Let alone** can also mean 'not to mention, without considering', as in 'They cannot afford proper food, let alone a holiday', but **leave alone** should not be used in this sense.

led *see* **lead**.

legible and **readable** are not interchangeable. **Legible** means 'able to be deciphered or made out', as in 'His writing is scarcely legible'. **Readable** can also be used in this sense, as in 'His handwriting is just not readable'. However **readable** is also used to mean 'able to be read with interest or enjoyment', as in 'He is an expert on the subject but I think his books are simply not readable' and 'I find her novels very readable but my friend does not like her style'.

legion has three meanings. It refers to 'a unit of the ancient Roman army', as in 'Caesar's legions', and to 'a very large number', as in 'the pop star has legions of admirers'. As an adjective **legion** means 'very many, numerous', as in 'His faults are legion'.

legionnaire is frequently misspelt. Note the double *n*. The word refers to 'a member, or former member, of a military legion, for example, the French Foreign Legion'. In modern usage it is most likely to be found in the phrase **legionnaires' disease**, a kind of pneumonia first discovered in 1976 at a meeting of the American Legion.

leisure is frequently misspelt. Note the *ei* combination. It is pronounced *lezh*-er. In American English it is pronounced *leezh*-er. **Leisure** means 'time spent away from work or duties', as in 'He works a lot of overtime and has very little leisure'. It is frequently used as an adjective, as in 'leisure time' and 'leisure pursuits'.

lend and **loan** can cause confusion. **Lend** is used as a verb in British English to mean 'to allow someone the use of temporarily', as in 'Can you lend me a pen?' and 'His father refused to lend him any money'. **Loan** is a noun meaning 'something lent, the temporary use of', as in 'They thanked her for the loan of her car'. In American English **loan** is used as a verb to mean **lend**, and this use is becoming common in Britain although it is still regarded as not quite acceptable.

length, as in 'measure the length of the room', is frequently misspelt. Note the *g*, which is sometimes wrongly omitted.

lengthways and **lengthwise** are used interchangeably, as in 'fold the tablecloth lengthways/lengthwise' and 'measure the room lengthwise/lengthways'.

lengthy and **long** are not interchangeable. **Lengthy** means 'excessively long', as in 'We had a lengthy wait before we saw the doctor' and 'It was such a lengthy speech that most of the audience got bored'. **Lengthy** is frequently misspelt. Note the *g*.

leopard is frequently misspelt. Note the *o*. It is the name of a wild animal of the cat family, as in 'leopards stalking deer'.

less and **fewer** are often confused. Less means 'a smaller amount or quantity of' and is the comparative form of 'little'. It is found in sentences such as 'less milk', 'less responsibility' and 'less noise'. **Fewer** means 'a smaller number of' and is the comparative of 'few'. It is found in sentences such as 'buy fewer bottles of milk', 'have fewer responsibilities', have fewer opportunities' and 'hear fewer noises'. **Less** is commonly wrongly used where **fewer** is correct. It is common but ungrammatical to say or write 'less bottles of milk' and 'less queues in the shops during the week'.

leukaemia is frequently misspelt. Note the *eu*, *ae* and *ia* combinations. It is pronounced with the emphasis on the second syllable, as loo-*kee*-mia. The word refers to 'a type of cancer in which there is an abnormal increase in the number of white corpuscles', as in 'children suffering from leukaemia'.

liable to and **likely to** both express probability. They mean much the same except that **liable to** suggests that the probability is based on past experience or habit. 'He is liable to lose his temper' suggests that he has been in the habit of doing so in the past. 'He is likely to lose his temper' suggests that he will probably lose his temper, given the situation, but that the probability is not based on how he has reacted in the past. This distinction is not always adhered to, and some people use the terms interchangeably.

liaison, meaning 'communication and cooperation', as in 'Liaison between departments is essential', is frequently misspelt. Note the *i* before the *s*. This is often omitted in error. Note also the *i* before the *s* in **liaise**, which means 'to act as a link or go-between', as in 'You must liaise with your colleague in the other department'.

libel and **slander** both refer to defamatory statements against someone but they are not interchangeable. **Libel** refers to defamation that is written down, printed or drawn, as in 'The politician sued the newspaper for libel when it falsely accused him of fraud'.

Slander refers to defamation in spoken form, as in 'She heard that one of her neighbours was spreading slander about her'. Both **libel** and **slander** can act as verbs, as in 'bring a suit against the newspaper for libelling him' and 'think that one of her neighbours was slandering her'. Note that the verb **libel** doubles the *l* in the past participle, past tense and present participle, as in **libelled** and **libelling**.

library, meaning a collection of books or the place where it is kept, should be pronounced *lib*-ra-ri although it is quite often pronounced *lib*-ri.

licence and **license** are liable to cause confusion in British English. **Licence** is a noun meaning 'an official document showing that permission has been given to do, use or own something', as in 'require a licence to have a stall in the market', 'have a licence to drive a car', and 'apply for a pilot's licence'. **License** is a verb meaning 'to provide someone with a licence', as in 'The council have licensed him as a street trader', 'The restaurant has been licensed to sell alcohol'. Note **licensed grocer** and **licensing laws** but **off-licence**. In American English both the noun and verb are spelt **license**.

lie *see* **lay**.

lieu *see* **in lieu**.

lieutenant is often misspelt. Note the *ieu* combination. In British English the word is pronounced lef-*ten*-ant. The word originally referred to an army or naval rank but is also used to mean 'a deputy, a chief assistant', as in 'The owner of the factory was unavailable but we talked to some of his lieutenants'.

lifelong and **livelong** are liable to be confused. **Lifelong** means 'lasting a lifetime', as in 'He never realized his lifelong ambition of going to Australia' and 'her lifelong membership of the society'. **Livelong** is found in rather literary contexts and means 'whole, entire', as in 'The children played on the beach the livelong day'. In **livelong** the first syllable is pronounced like 'live', as in 'live a long time'.

lighted and **lit** can both be used as the past participle and past tense of the verb 'to light'. **Lit** is the more common form, as in 'We lit the fire early' and 'They lit the birthday candles'. **Lighted** is used when the past participle is used as an adjective, as in 'children playing with lighted matches' and 'The fire was started by a lighted match being thrown away'.

lightning and **lightening** are liable to be confused because they sound alike. **Lightning** refers to 'flashes of light produced by atmospheric electricity', as in 'The child was afraid of thunder and lightning' and 'He was hit by lightning and was killed'. **Lightning** is also used as an adjective meaning 'happening very quickly, suddenly or briefly', as in 'The police made a lightning strike on the nightclub', 'She made a lightning decision to go on holiday', and 'The visitors made a lightning tour of the factory'. **Lightening** is the present participle of the verb 'to lighten', as in 'lightening her hair with peroxide' and 'Lightening his work load is a priority'.

light years are a measure of distance, not time. A **light year** is the distance travelled by light in one year (about six million, million miles) and is a term used in astronomy. **Light years** are often referred to in an informal context when time, not distance, is involved, as in 'Owning their own house seemed light years away' and 'It seems light years since we had a holiday'.

likable *see* **likeable**.

like tends to cause confusion. It is a preposition meaning 'resembling, similar to', as in 'houses like castles', gardens like jungles', 'actors like Olivier', 'She looks like her mother', 'She plays like an expert', 'The child swims like a fish' and 'Like you, he cannot stand cruelty to animals'. To be grammatically correct **like** should not be used as a conjunction. Thus 'The house looks like it has been deserted' is incorrect. It should read 'The house looks as though/if it has been deserted'. Similarly, 'Like his mother said, he has had to go to hospital' should read 'As his mother said, he has had to go to hospital'.

likeable and **likable** are both acceptable spellings. The word means 'pleasant, agreeable, friendly', as in 'He is a likeable/likable young man'.

likely

likely to *see* **liable to**.

lineage and **linage** do not mean the same thing. **Lineage** refers to 'line of descent, ancestry', as in 'a family of noble lineage'. **Linage** is rather a specialist term meaning 'number of written or printed lines', as in 'The freelance journalist was paid on a linage basis'. **Linage** can also be spelt **lineage**.

liqueur and **liquor** are liable to be confused. **Liqueur** refers to 'a sweet alcoholic drink taken after dinner', as in 'have a liqueur with one's coffee'. **Liquor** refers to 'any strong alcoholic drink', as in 'prefer soft drinks to liquor'.

liquidate and **liquidize** are liable to be confused. **Liquidate** is frequently used in a financial context. It means 'to settle or pay', as in 'to liquidate a debt'; 'to terminate the operations of a firm by assessment of debts and use the assets towards paying off the debts', as in 'forced to liquidate the firm'; 'to convert into cash', as in 'liquidate one's assets'. In an informal context **liquidate** means 'to kill', as in 'paid to liquidate a member of the enemy gang'. **Liquidize** means 'to make liquid, especially to pulverize into a pulp', as in 'liquidize the vegetables to make a soup'.

liquor *see* **liqueur**.

lit *see* **lighted**.

literal, **literary** and **literate** are liable to be confused. **Literal** means 'word for word, exact', as in 'a literal translation', 'a literal interpretation of the words'. **Literary** means 'referring to literature', as in 'come from a literary background', 'have literary interests' and 'literary criticism'. **Literate** means 'able to read and write', as in 'children who are leaving school scarcely literate', and 'well-educated', as in 'a very literate family'.

literally is frequently used simply to add emphasis to an idea rather than to indicate that the word, phrase, etc, used is to be interpreted word for word. Thus, 'She was literally tearing her hair out' does not mean that she was pulling her hair out by the handful but that she was very angry, anxious, frustrated, etc.

literary *see* **literal**.

livelong *see* **lifelong**.

livid and **lurid** are liable to be confused although they mean different things. **Livid** means 'discoloured, of a greyish tinge', as in 'a livid bruise on her face', and 'furious', as in 'When he saw his damaged car he was livid'. **Lurid** means 'sensational, shocking', as in 'give the lurid details about finding the body', and 'garish, glaringly bright', as in 'wear a lurid shade of green'.

living room *see* **sitting room**.

loan *see* **lend**.

loath, **loathe** and **loth** are not all interchangeable. **Loath** and **loth** mean 'reluctant, unwilling', as in 'We were loath/loth to punish the children' and 'They are loath/loth to move house again'. **Loathe** means 'to hate very much, to detest', as in 'She loathes dishonesty' and 'The rivals loathe each other'. The *th* in **loath** and **loth** is pronounced as the *th* in 'bath', but the *th* in **loathe** is pronounced like the *th* in 'bathe'.

longevity, meaning 'long life', is liable to be mispronounced. It should be pronounced lon-*jev*-iti. Some people pronounce it lon-*gev*-iti, but this is rarer.

loo *see* **toilet**.

loose, **loosen** and **lose** are liable to be confused. **Loose** and **loosen** are related but not **lose**. **Loose** is an adjective meaning 'not tight', as in 'His clothes are loose now that he has lost weight', and 'free, not confined', as in 'The cows are loose'. It is also a verb meaning 'to undo', as in 'loose the knot', or 'set free', as in 'loose the pack of hounds'. **Loosen** means 'to make less tight', as in 'He has put on weight and so he has had to loosen his belt'. **Lose** is a verb meaning 'not to be able to find, to mislay', as in 'I always lose one glove' and 'They may lose their way'. **Loose** is pronounced loos, but **lose** is pronounced looz.

lose *see* **loose**.

lots of and **a lot of**, meaning 'many' and 'much', should be used only in informal contexts', as in '"I've got lots of toys," said the child' and 'You're talking a lot of rubbish'. They should be avoided in formal prose.

loth *see* **loath**.

lounge *see* **sitting room**.

low and **lowly** are not interchangeable. **Low** means 'not high', as in 'a low fence', 'a low level of income', 'speak in a low voice' and 'her low status in the firm'. It can also mean 'despicable, contemptible', as in 'That was a low trick' or 'He's a low creature'. **Lowly** means 'humble', as in 'of lowly birth' and 'the peasant's lowly abode'.

lowly *see* **low**.

lunch and **luncheon** both refer to a meal eaten in the middle of the day. **Lunch**, as in 'a business lunch' and 'have just a snack for lunch', is by far the more usual term. **Luncheon**, as in 'give a luncheon party for the visiting celebrity', is a very formal word and is becoming increasingly uncommon. *See also* **dinner**.

lurid *see* **livid**.

luxuriant, **luxurious** and **luxury** are liable to be confused. They have completely different meanings. **Luxuriant** means 'profuse, growing thickly and strongly', as in 'the luxuriant vegetation of the area' and 'her luxuriant hair'. **Luxurious** means 'referring to or characterized by luxury', as in 'a luxurious lifestyle' and 'live in luxurious surroundings'. **Luxury** is a noun meaning 'great ease or comfort based on wealth', as in 'live in luxury' and 'a hotel providing luxury'. It also means 'something that is enjoyable but is not essential and is usually expensive', as in 'no money for luxuries' and 'spend money on luxuries such as champagne'. **Luxury** can be used as an adjective, as in 'a luxury hotel' and 'a shop selling luxury goods'.

M

macabre, meaning 'connected with death' or 'gruesome', as in 'a macabre tale about attacks on people in the graveyard' and 'policemen sickened by a particularly macabre murder', is liable to be misspelt. Note the *re* ending.

machinations, meaning 'devious plots or schemes', as in 'They were plotting to kill the king but their machinations were discovered', should be pronounced mak-in-*ay*-shunz but mash-in *ay*-shunz is becoming increasingly common in modern usage.

madam and **madame** are liable to be confused. **Madam** is the English-language form of the French **madame**. It is a form of formal of address for a woman, as in 'Please come this way, madam'. It is used in formal letters when the name of the woman being written to is not known, as in 'Dear Madam'. **Madam** can be written either with a capital letter or a lower-case letter. **Madam** is pronounced *mad*-am, with the emphasis on the first syllable. **Madame**, which is the French equivalent of 'Mrs', is occasionally found in English, as in Madame Tussaud's, and is pronounced in the same way as **madam**. In French **madame** is pronounced ma-*dam*.

majority and **minority** are opposites. **Majority** means 'more than half the total number of', as in 'The majority of the pupils live locally' and 'the younger candidate received the majority of the votes'. **Minority** means less than half the total number of', as in 'A small minority of the football fans caused trouble' and 'Only a minority of the committee voted against the motion'. **Majority** and **minority** should not be used to describe the greater or lesser part of a single thing. Thus it is wrong to say 'The majority of the book is uninteresting'.

male, **masculine** and **mannish** all refer to the sex that is not female but the words are used in different ways. **Male** is the opposite of 'female' and refers to the sex of a person or animal, as in 'no male person may enter', 'a male nurse', 'a male elephant' and 'the male reproductive system'. **Masculine** is the opposite of 'feminine' and refers to people or their characteristics. It refers to characteristics, etc, that are traditionally considered to be typically **male**. Examples of its use include 'a very masculine young man', 'a deep, masculine voice'. It can be used of women, as in 'She has a masculine walk' and 'She wears masculine clothes'. When used of women it is often derogatory and is sometimes replaced with **mannish**, which is derogatory, as in 'women with mannish haircuts'. **Male** can also be used as a noun, as in 'the male of the species' 'of the robins, the male is more colourful' and 'the title can be held only by males'.

man causes a great deal of controversy. To avoid being sexist it should be avoided when it really means 'person'. 'We must find the right man for the job' should rèad 'We must find the right person for the job'. Similarly, 'All men have a right to a reasonable standard of living' should read 'All people have a right to a reasonable standard of living' or 'Everyone has a right to a reasonable standard of living'. Problems also arise with compounds, such as 'chairman'. In such situations 'person' is often used, as in 'chairperson'. Man is also used to mean 'mankind, humankind', as in 'Man is mortal' and 'Man has the power of thought'. Some people also object to this usage and consider it sexist. They advocate using 'humankind' or 'the human race'.

manageable is liable to be misspelt. Note the *e* before the ending *-able*. It means 'able to be controlled, easily controlled', as in 'a task of scarcely manageable proportions' and 'The nanny will not take the job unless the children are manageable'.

mandatory is liable to be mispronounced. The emphasis should be on the first syllable, as *man*-da-tor-i. It means 'required by law, compulsory', as in 'A visa is mandatory for some countries' and 'He was fined for not making the mandatory payment'.

manoeuvre is frequently misspelt. Note the *oeu* combination and the *-re* ending. In American English the *o* is omitted and the ending is *er*. It means 'a movement or action, especially one requiring skill and dexterity', as in 'We were admiring the manoeuvres of the skaters', and 'a skilful, and often complicated and deceptive plan', as in 'his manoeuvres to discredit his boss and obtain his job'. **Manoeuvre** is also a verb meaning 'to move or position, especially with skill or dexterity', as in 'racing drivers manoeuvring their cars on a muddy circuit', and 'to guide or manipulate skilfully and usually cunningly', as in 'She manoeuvred herself into a position of trust'.

mantel and **mantle** are liable to be confused. **Mantel** is more usually called **mantelpiece** and refers to 'a shelf above a fireplace', as in 'a vase of flowers on the mantelpiece'. **Mantelpiece** is frequently misspelt as 'mantlepiece'. **Mantle** is an old word for a cloak and is now found mostly in the sense of 'covering', as in 'a mantle of autumn leaves on the grass'.

many is used in more formal contexts rather than 'a lot of' or 'lots of', as in 'The judge said the accused had had many previous convictions'. **Many** is often used in the negative in both formal and informal contexts, as in 'They don't have many friends' and 'She won't find many apples on the trees now'.

margarine causes confusion with reference to pronunciation. Formerly the usual pronunciation was mar-ga-reen but now the most common pronunciation is mar-ja-reen. It refers to 'a substitute for butter'.

masculine *see* **male**.

masterful and **masterly** are liable to be confused although they mean different things. **Masterful** means 'able to control others, dominating', as in 'She likes masterful men' and 'The country needs a masterful ruler'. **Masterly** means 'very skilful', as in 'admire his masterly handling of the situation' and 'their masterly defeat of the opposing team'.

mattress is often misspelt. Note the double *t* and double *s*. The word means 'a fabric case filled with soft or springy material used for sleeping on', as in 'He likes to sleep on a firm mattress'.

may *see* **can**.

maybe and **may be** are liable to be confused although they have different meanings. **Maybe** means 'perhaps', as in 'Maybe they lost their way' and 'He said, "Maybe" when I asked him if he was going'. It is used in more informal contexts than 'perhaps'. **May be** is used in such sentences as 'He may be poor but he is very generous' and 'They may be a little late'.

mayoress means 'the wife or partner of a male mayor', as in 'an official dinner for the mayor and mayoress'. A mayor who is a woman is called either 'mayor' or 'lady mayor'.

meaningful originally meant 'full of meaning', as in 'make very few meaningful statements' and 'There was a meaningful silence'. In modern usage it has come to mean 'important, significant, serious', as in 'not interested in a meaningful relationship' and 'seeking a meaningful career'. The word now tends to be very much over-used.

means in the sense of 'way, method' can be either a singular or plural noun, as in 'The means of defeating them is in our hands' and 'Many different means of financing the project have been investigated'. **Means** in the sense of 'wealth' and 'resources' is plural, as in 'His means are not sufficient to support two families'.

media gives rise to confusion. In the form of **the media** it is commonly applied to the press, to newspapers, television and radio, as in 'The politician claimed that he was being harassed by the media'. **Media** is a plural form of 'medium', meaning 'means of communication', as in 'television is a powerful medium'. In modern usage **media** is beginning to be used as a singular noun, as in 'The politician blamed a hostile media for his misfortunes', but this is still regarded as being an incorrect use.

mediaeval and **medieval** are both acceptable spellings. **Mediaeval** was formerly the only acceptable spelling in British English and **medieval** was considered the American spelling. However, in modern usage **medieval** is the more common term in British English. The word means 'relating to the Middle Ages', as in 'medieval knights' and 'medieval castles'.

mediocre is liable to be misspelt. Note the *-re* ending It is a common error to make this *-er*. It means 'not very good, of indifferent quality', as in 'a mediocre pupil unlikely to do well in the exam' and 'His work is at best mediocre'. It is pronounced meed-i-*ok*-er, with the emphasis on the third syllable.

melted and **molten** are not interchangeable although they are both formed the verb 'to melt'. **Melted** is the past participle and the past tense of 'melt', as in 'The ice cream had melted all over the child's clothes' and 'The chocolate melted in the heat'. **Molten** means 'melted or made liquid by heating to very high temperature', as in 'molten rock' and 'molten lava'.

memento is liable to be misspelt. Note the *e* following the first *m*. It is a common error to put *o* instead. The plural form is either **mementos** or **mementoes**. **Memento** refers to 'something kept as a reminder', as in 'He bought her a scarf as a memento of their trip to Paris'.

metal and **mettle** are liable to be confused because they sound alike. **Metal** refers to 'a member of a group of mineral substances that are opaque and good conductors of heat and electricity', as in 'appliances made of metal' and 'cutlery made of plastic, not metal'. **Mettle** means 'endurance, courage, strength of character', as in 'show his mettle by learning to walk again' and 'give the candidates a chance to prove their mettle'.

metaphor is a figure of speech in which a word or phrase is used to suggest a similarity to something else. The similarity is not introduced by 'like' or 'as' as it is in the case of

meter

a 'simile'. Examples include 'She was a rose among thorns' and 'Their new product is the jewel in the firm's crown', 'He is a pillar of the community' and 'His mother is a clinging vine'.

meter *see* **metre**.

mettle *see* **metal**.

middle *see* **centre**.

migraine causes problems with regard to pronunciation. It is pronounced *mee*-grayn in British English but the American pronunciation of *mi*-grayn, in which the first syllable rhymes with 'eye', is sometimes used in Britain. **Migraine** refers to 'a severe and recurrent type of headache, often accompanied by vomiting', as in 'She had to lie down in a darkened room because of her migraine'.

mileage and **milage** are both acceptable spellings for 'the distance travelled or measured in miles', as in 'The car is a bargain, given the low mileage'. However **mileage** is much more common than **milage**. The word also means informally 'benefit, advantage', as in 'The politician got a lot of mileage from the scandal surrounding his opponent' and 'There's not much mileage in pursuing that particular line of inquiry'.

militate and **mitigate** are liable to be confused. **Militate** means 'to have or serve as a strong influence against', as in 'Their lack of facts militated against the success of their application' and 'His previous record will militate against his chances of going free'. **Mitigate** means 'to alleviate', as in 'try to mitigate the suffering of the refugees', or 'moderate', as in 'mitigate the severity of the punishment'.

millenium is liable to be misspelt. Note the double *n* which is frequently omitted in error. The plural form is **millennia**. **Millennium** refers to 'a period of 1000 years', as in 'rock changes taking place over several millennia'. In religious terms it refers to 'the thousand-year reign of Christ prophesied in the Bible'.

millionaire is liable to be misspelt. Note the single *n*. It means 'a person who has a million pounds or dollars' or 'a very wealthy person', as in 'millionaires who spend all their time travelling around the world'.

mimic is liable to be misspelt in its past participle, past tense and present tense. These are respectively **mimicked** and **mimicking**. Note the *k* in these forms. The word means 'to imitate', as in 'The pupil was mimicking the teacher when she walked into the room'. Note that the noun **mimicry** does not have a *k*.

miniature is frequently misspelt. Note the *i* after the *n*. This is often omitted in error. It means 'very small in size', as in 'beautiful miniature coffee cups' and 'a miniature bottle of whisky'. It can also be a noun meaning 'a very small copy or model', as in 'a miniature of the Tower of London', or 'a very small detailed painting', as in 'admire the miniatures in the art gallery'.

minority *see* **majority**.

minuscule is liable to be misspelt. Note the *u* before the *s*. It is a common error to put an *i*. The word is pronounced *min*-iskyool. It means 'extremely small, tiny', as in 'only a minuscule amount of coffee left'.

miscellaneous is very frequently misspelt. Note the *c* after the *s*, the double *l* and the -*eous* ending. The word means 'of various kinds', as in 'a miscellaneous collection of articles for the jumble sale' and 'Some money will have to be allocated for miscellaneous expense'.

mischievous is frequently misspelt and mispronounced. Note the *ie* combination and the absence of *i* before *ous*. It is pronounced *mis*-chiv-is, not mis-*cheev*-is.

Miss *see* **Ms**.

misspelled and **misspelt** are often wrongly spelt. Note the double *s*. Both **misspelled** and **misspelt** are acceptable spellings of the past tense and past participle of the verb 'to misspell'. **Misspell** means 'to spell wrongly'.

misuse *see* **abuse**.

mitigate *see* **militate**.

mnemonic refers to 'something that aids the memory'. For example, some people use a **mnemonic** in the form of a verse to remind them how to spell a word or to recall a date. The word is liable to be misspelt and mispronounced. Note the initial *m*, which is silent. **Mnemonic** is pronounced nim-*on*-ik, with the emphasis on the second syllable.

moccasin is frequently misspelt. Note the double *c* and single *s*. The word refers to 'a flat-soled shoe made of soft leather', as in 'She was wearing moccasins and so he did not hear her approach'.

modern and **modernistic** are not quite the same. **Modern** means 'referring to the present time or recent times', as in 'the politics of modern times' and 'a production of Shakespeare's *Twelfth Night* in modern dress'. It also means 'using the newest techniques, equipment, buildings, etc, as in 'a modern shopping centre' and 'a modern office complex'. **Modernistic** means 'characteristic of modern ideas, fashions, etc, and is often used in a derogatory way, as in 'She says she hates that modernistic furniture'.

modus vivendi refers to 'a practical, sometimes temporary, arrangement or compromise by which people who are in conflict can live or work together', as in 'The two opposing parties on the committee will have to reach a modus vivendi if any progress is to be made'. It is a Latin phrase that literally means 'a way of living' and is pronounced *mo*-dus viv-*en*-di.

molten *see* **melted**.

momentary and **momentous** are liable to be confused. They look rather similar but they are completely different in meaning. **Momentary** means 'lasting for a very short time', as in 'There was a momentary pause' and 'enjoy a momentary success'. It is derived from the noun 'moment' in the sense of 'a very brief period of time'. **Momentous** means 'very important, of great significance', as in 'a momentous incident that led to war'. It is derived from the noun 'moment' in the sense of 'importance, significance', as in 'a meeting of moment'. In **momentary** the emphasis is on the first syllable, as *mom*-en-tar-i or *mom*-en-tri. In **momentous** the stress is on the second syllable, as mom-*en*-tus.

moral and **morale** are liable to be confused although they are different in meaning. **Moral** means 'concerning the principles of right and wrong', as in 'the decline of moral standards' and 'criticize his actions on moral grounds'. **Morale** means 'state of confidence, enthusiasm, etc', as in 'It was a blow to his morale when he failed to get the job' and 'The morale of the country was very low during the recession'. **Moral** is pronounced with the emphasis on the first syllable, as in *mor*-al. **Morale** is pronounced with the emphasis on the second syllable'.

more is used to form the comparative of adjectives and adverbs that do not form the comparative by adding *-er*. This usually applies to longer adjectives, as in 'more beautiful', 'more gracious', 'more useful', and 'more flattering'. **More** should not be used with adjectives that have a comparative ending already. Thus it is wrong to write 'more happier'. **Most** is used in the same way to form the superlative of adjectives and adverbs, as in 'most beautiful', 'most gracious' etc.

Moslem *see* **Muslim**.

most *see* **more**.

motif and **motive** are liable to be confused although they have entirely different meanings. **Motif** refers to 'a theme or idea that is repeated and developed in a work of music or literature', as in 'a motif of suicide runs through the whole novel'. It also means 'a decorative design or pattern', as in 'curtains with a flower motif'. **Motive** refers to 'the reason for a course of action', as in 'There appears to have been no motive for the murder' and 'What was her motive in telling lies about him?' **Motif** is pronounced with the emphasis on the second syllable, as mo-*teef*. **Motive** is pronounced with the emphasis on the first syllable, as *mo*-tiv.

motive *see* **motif**.

movable and **moveable** are both possible spellings but **movable** is the more common, as in 'movable possessions' and 'machines with movable parts'.

Ms, **Mrs** and **Miss** are all used before the names of women in addressing them and in letter-writing. Formerly **Mrs** was used before the name of a married woman and **Miss** before the name of an unmarried woman or girl. In modern usage **Ms** is often used instead of **Miss** or **Mrs**. This is sometimes because the marital status of the woman is not known and sometimes from a personal preference. Many people feel that since no distinction is made between married and unmarried men when they are being addressed, no distinction should be made between married and unmarried women. On the other hand some people, particularly older women, object to the use of **Ms**.

much, except in negative sentences, is used mainly in rather formal contexts, as in 'They own much property'. 'A great deal of' is often used instead, as in 'They own a great deal of property'. In informal contexts 'a lot of' is often used instead of **much**, as in 'a lot of rubbish' not 'much rubbish'. **Much** is used in negative sentences, as in 'They do not have much money'.

Muslim and **Moslem** refer to to 'a follower of the Islamic faith'. In modern usage **Muslim** is the preferred term rather than the older spelling **Moslem**.

N

naïve causes problems with reference to both spelling and pronunciation. It can be spelt either **naïve** or **naive** and is pronounced ni-*eev*, with the emphasis on the second syllable, and the first syllable rhyming with 'my'. The accent on the *ï* (called a diaeresis) indicates that the two vowels *a* and *i* are to be pronounced separately. **Naive** means either 'innocent' or 'too ready to believe what one is told', as in 'You would have to be incredibly naive to believe his excuses'.

naturalist and **naturist** are liable to be confused. They look rather similar but have completely different meanings. **Naturalist** refers to 'a person who studies animals, birds and plants', as in 'naturalists collecting some of the local wild flowers'. **Naturist** refers to 'a person who practises naturism or nudism', as in 'naturists with their own secluded beaches'. **Naturist** can also be an adjective, as in 'naturist beaches'.

naught and **nought** are not totally interchangeable. **Naught** means 'nothing', as in 'All his projects came to naught', and is rather a formal or literary word in this sense. **Naught** is also a less usual spelling of **nought**, which means 'zero' when it is regarded as a number, as in 'nought point one (0.1)'.

naval and **navel** are liable to be confused. They sound alike but they have entirely different meanings. **Naval** means 'referring to the navy', as in 'a naval base' and 'naval personnel'. **Navel** refers to 'a small hollow in the middle of the abdomen where the umbilical cord was attached at birth', as in 'The baby has an infection in the navel'.

nearby and **near by** can cause problems. **Nearby** can be either an adjective, as in 'the nearby village', or an adverb, as in 'Her mother lives nearby'. **Near by** is an adverb, as in 'He doesn't have far to go—he lives near by'. In other words, the adverbial sense can be spelt either **nearby** or **near by**.

necessarily is traditionally pronounced with the emphasis on the first syllable, but this is often very difficult to say except when one is speaking exceptionally carefully. Because of this difficulty it is often pronounced with the emphasis on the third syllable although it is considered by many people to be incorrect.

necessary is frequently misspelt. Note the single *c* and double *s*. It means 'that cannot be done without', as in 'make only necessary purchases' and 'It may be necessary to take him to hospital'.

née is used to indicate the maiden or family name of a married woman, as in 'Jane Jones, née Smith'. It is derived from French, being the feminine form of the French word for 'born'. It can be spelt either with an acute accent or not—**née** or **nee**.

negligent and **negligible** are liable to be confused. **Negligent** means 'not giving proper attention, careless', as in 'mothers accused of being negligent by not making sure their children attend school' and 'He said that his wife had died because of a negligent doctor'. **Negligible** means 'extremely small', as in 'a negligible difference between the prices' and 'lose a negligible amount of weight'. Note the *-ible* ending in **negligible**.

neither as an adjective or a pronoun takes a singular verb, as in 'Neither parent will come' and 'Neither of them wishes to come'. In the **neither . . . nor** construction, a singular verb is used if both parts of the construction are singular, as in 'Neither Jane nor Mary was present'. If both parts are plural the verb is plural, as in 'Neither their parents nor their grandparents are willing to look after them'. If the construction involves a mixture of singular and plural, the verb traditionally agrees with the subject that is nearest it, as in 'Neither her mother nor her grandparents are going to come' and 'Neither her grandparents nor her mother is going to come'. If pronouns are used, the nearer one governs the verb as in 'Neither they nor he is at fault' and 'Neither he nor they are at fault'.

never in the sense of 'did not', as in 'He never saw the other car before he hit it', should be used in only very informal contexts. **Never** means 'at no time, on no occasion', as in 'He will never agree to their demands' and 'She has never been poor'. It is also used as a negative for the sake of emphasis, as in 'He never so much as smiled'.

nevertheless and **none the less** mean the same thing, as in 'He has very little money. Nevertheless/none the less he gives generously to charity'. **None the less** is usually written as three words but **nevertheless** is spelt as one word. In modern usage **none the less** is sometimes written as one word, as **nonetheless**.

next and **this** can cause confusion. **Next** in one of its senses is used to mean the day of the week, month of the year, season of the year, etc, that will follow next, as in 'They are coming next Tuesday', 'We are going on holiday next June' and 'They to be married next summer'. **This** can also be used in this sense and so ambiguity can occur. Some people use **this** to refer to the very next Tuesday, June, summer, etc, and use **next** for the one after that. Thus someone might say on Sunday, 'I'll see you next Friday', meaning the first Friday to come, but someone else might take that to mean a week on from that because they would refer to the first Friday to come as 'this Friday'. The only solution is to make sure exactly which day, week, season, etc, the other person is referring to.

nice originally meant 'fine, subtle, requiring precision', as in 'There is rather a nice distinction between the two words', but it is widely used in the sense of 'pleasant, agreeable, etc', as in 'She is a nice person' and 'We had a nice time at the picnic'. It is overused and alternative adjectives should be found to avoid this, as in 'She is an amiable person' and 'We had an enjoyable time at the picnic'.

niceness and **nicety** are both nouns formed from 'nice' but they do not mean the same thing. **Niceness** is the noun from 'nice' in the sense of 'pleasant, agreeable', as in 'They appreciated the niceness of the old lady' and 'The niceness of the climate is the best part of the holiday resort'. **Nicety** is the noun from 'nice' in the sense of 'fine, subtle', as in 'the nicety of the distinction between the two words'.

niche causes problems with reference to both pronunciation and spelling'. The most common pronunciation is *nitch*, but *neech*, following the French pronunciation, is also a possibility. Note the absence of *t* in the spelling.

nimby *see* **acronym**.

nobody *see* **no one**.

none can be used with either a singular verb or plural verb. Examples of sentences using a singular verb include 'There is none of the food left' and 'None of the work is good enough' and 'None of the coal is to be used today'. In sentences where none is used with a plural noun the verb was traditionally still singular, as in 'None of the books is suitable' and 'None of the parcels is undamaged'. This is still the case in formal contexts but, in the case of informal contexts, a plural verb is often used in modern usage, as in 'None of these things are any good'.

none the less *see* **nevertheless**.

no one and **no-one** are interchangeable but the word is never written 'noone', unlike 'everyone'. **No one** and **no-one** are used with a singular verb, as in 'No one is allowed to leave' and 'No one is anxious to leave'. They are used by some people with a plural personal pronoun or possessive case when attempts are being made to avoid sexism, as in 'No one is expected to take their child away', although the singular form is grammatically correct, as in 'No one is expected to take his/her child away'. 'No one is expected to take his child away' is sexist. Nobody is interchangeable with no one, as in 'You must tell no one/nobody about this'.

nor is used as part of the **neither . . . nor** construction, and this is dealt with under **neither**. It is also used in such constructions as 'He plays neither golf nor tennis' and 'We were given neither food nor drink' and 'He does not watch television. Nor does he go to the cinema'. In some contexts **nor** is interchangeable with **or**, as in 'The shop is not open on Saturday nor/or Sunday' and 'They have no food nor/or drink'. **Nor** can be used at the start of a sentence, as in 'He does not believe her. Nor does he trust her'.

notable *see* **noticeable**.

noticeable and **notable** are liable to be confused. They are both related to 'note' but they mean different things. **Noticeable** means 'obvious', as in 'She had a noticeable bruise on her cheek' and 'The hostile atmosphere between them was noticeable to everyone'. **Notable** means 'of note, remarkable', as in 'his notable achievements in the world of business' and 'one of the most notable poets of the century'.

not only is frequently used in a construction with 'but also', as in 'We have not only the best candidate but also the most efficient organization' and 'The organizers of the fete not only made a great deal of money for charity but also gave a great many people a great deal of pleasure'.

nought *see* **naught**.

noxious and **obnoxious** are liable to be confused. They both refer to unpleasantness or harmfulness but they are used in different contexts. **Noxious** is used of a substance, fumes, etc, and means 'harmful, poisonous', as in 'firemen overcome by noxious fumes' and 'delinquent children having a noxious influence on the rest of the class'. **Obnoxious** means 'unpleasant, nasty, offensive', as in 'He has the most obnoxious neighbours' and 'The child's parents let him off with the most obnoxious behaviour'. **Noxious** is used in formal and technical contexts rather than **obnoxious**.

nubile originally meant 'old enough to marry, marriageable' as in 'he has five nubile daughters'. In modern usage **nubile** is frequently used in the sense of 'sexually attractive', as in 'admiring the nubile girls sunbathing on the beach' and 'nubile models posing for magazine illustrations'.

numbers can be written in either figures or words. It is largely a matter of taste which method is adopted. As long as the method is consistent it does not really matter. Some establishments, such as a publishing house or a newspaper office, will have a house style. For example, some of them prefer to have numbers up to 10 written in words, as in 'They have two boys and three girls'. If this system is adopted, guidance should be sought as to whether a mixture of figures and words in the same sentence is acceptable, as in 'We have 12 cups but only six saucers', or whether the rule should be broken in such situations as 'We have twelve cups but only six saucers'.

nutritional and **nutricious** are liable to be confused. They both refer to 'nutrition, the process of giving and receiving nourishment' but mean different things. **Nutritional** means 'referring to nutrition', as in 'doubts about the nutritional value of some fast foods' and 'people who do not receive the minimum nutritional requirements'. **Nutritious** means 'nourishing, of high value as a food', as in 'nourishing homemade soups' and 'something slightly more nourishing than a plate of chips'.

O

O and **Oh** are both forms of an exclamation made at the beginning of a sentence. O**h** is the usual spelling, as in 'Oh well. It's Friday tomorrow' and 'Oh dear, the baby's crying again'. **O** is considerably rarer and is used in literary contexts in poetry, hymns etc, as in 'O come all ye faithful'. Both **Oh** and **O** are always spelt with an initial capital letter.

object refers to the noun, pronoun or phrase that is affected by the action of the verb. In the sentence 'He eventually married the girl', 'girl' is the object. In the sentence 'They beat him up badly', 'him' is the object. In the sentence 'She received a bunch of flowers', 'bunch of flowers' is the object. An object may be *direct* or *indirect*. The examples shown above are all *direct objects*. In the sentence 'She gave the child a book', 'book' is the *direct object* and 'the child' is the *indirect object*. In the sentence 'I bought him an apple', 'him' is the *indirect object*. In the case of *indirect objects*, it is usually possible to rephrase the sentences in which they appear, putting 'to' or 'for' before the *indirect object*, as in 'She gave a book to the child' and 'I bought an apple for him'. *See* **subject**.

Object can also mean 'aim, goal'—*see* **objective** and **subjective**.

Object is also a verb meaning 'to say that one is not in favour of something, to protest', as in 'They objected to the fact that the decision was taken in their absence'. In the verb sense, **object** is pronounced with the emphasis on the second syllable, as ob-*ject*.

objective and **subjective** are opposites. **Objective** means 'not influenced by personal feelings, attitudes, or prejudices', as in 'She is related to the person accused and so she cannot give an objective view of the situation' and 'It is important that all members of a jury are completely objective'. **Subjective** means 'influenced by personal feelings, attitudes and prejudices', as in 'It is only natural to be subjective in situations regarding one's children' and 'She wrote a very subjective report on the conference and did not stick to the facts'. **Objective** can also be a noun in the sense of 'aim, goal', as in 'Our objective was to make as much money as possible'. **Object** can also be used in this sense, as in 'Their main object is to have a good time'.

oblivious means 'unaware of, unconscious of, not noticing'. Traditionally it is followed by the preposition 'of', as in 'The lovers were oblivious of the rain' and 'When he is reading he is completely oblivious of his surroundings'. In modern usage its use with the preposition 'to' is also considered acceptable, as in 'They were oblivious to the fact that he was cheating them' and 'sleep soundly, oblivious to the noise'.

obnoxious *see* **noxious**.

obscene and **pornographic** are not interchangeable. **Obscene** means 'indecent, especially in a sexual way, offending against the accepted standards of decency', as in 'obscene drawings on the walls of the public toilet' and 'When his car was damaged he let out a stream of obscene language'. **Pornographic** means 'intended to arouse sexual excitement', as in 'pornographic videos' and 'magazines with women shown in pornographic poses'. **Obscene** is frequently misspelt. Note the *c* after the *s*.

observance and **observation** are liable to be confused. They are both derived from the verb 'to observe' but from different senses of it. **Observance** is derived from 'observe' in the sense of 'obey, comply with', as in 'the observance of school rules' and 'the observance of local customs'. It also refers to 'a ritual act or practice', as in 'religious observances'. **Observation** is derived from the verb 'to observe' meaning 'to see, to notice', as in 'keep the patient under observation' and 'From his observation of them they appeared to be acting strangely'. **Observation** also means 'a remark', as in 'The inspector made a few critical observations about the state of the restaurant's kitchens'.

occasion is frequently misspelt. Note the double *c* and single *s*. It is a common error to put a single *c* and double *s*. **Occasion** is a noun meaning 'a particular time', as in 'happen on more than one occasion', and 'a special event or celebration', as in 'the dinner was a formal occasion'. More rarely **occasion** can be used as a verb but it should be restricted to rather formal situations. It means 'to cause, to bring about', as in 'His remarks occasioned a family feud'.

occurrence is very frequently misspelt. Note the double *c*, double *r* and *-ence* ending. It comes from the verb **occur**, 'to happen'. Note also **occurred** and **occurring**. **Occurrence** means 'an event, incident, happening', as in 'Robbery is an everyday occurrence there' and 'The occurrence of tuberculosis is on the increase'.

oculist *see* **optician**.

of is sometimes wrongly used instead of the verb 'to have', as in 'He must of known she was lying' instead of 'He must have known she was lying'. The error arises because the two constructions sound alike when not emphasized.

off is liable to be misspelt as 'of'. Note 'run off', 'keep off the grass', 'take one's coat off', 'a house off the main street'. The spelling 'of' is totally wrong in phrases such as these. **Off** is used by some people instead of 'from', as in 'He bought the radio off a street trader'. This use should be avoided except in informal contexts.

offence is liable to be misspelt. Note the *c*. It is a common error to put *s* in the British English spelling. **Offense** is the standard American spelling.

officious and **official** are liable to be confused. They sound and look rather alike but they have different meanings. **Official** means 'authorized', as in 'receive an official pass to the conference' and 'The police have released an official statement', and 'formal', as in 'an official reception for the visiting diplomat'. **Officious** means 'too ready to give orders, offer advice, bossy, interfering, self-important', as in 'told by the officious woman behind the desk that I would have to provide other documentation' and 'The child who had lost the money for her fare was put off the bus by an officious inspector'.

Oh *see* **O**.

OK and **okay** are both acceptable spellings of an informal word indicating agreement or approval, as in 'OK/okay, I'll come with you', 'We've at last been given the OK/okay to begin building'. When the word is used as a verb it is more usually spelt **okay** because of the problem in adding endings, as in 'They've okayed our plans at last'. **OK** is sometimes written with full stops as **O.K.**

older *see* **elder**.

omelette is frequently misspelt. Note the double *t* and first *e*. This *e* is not sounded in the pronunciation. It is pronounced with the emphasis on the first syllable, as *om*-lit. **Omelet** is the American English spelling.

omission is frequently misspelt. Note the single *m*. The word means 'the act of leaving out', as in 'the accidental omission of his name from the list of invitations'.

one is used in formal situations to indicate an indefinite person where 'you' would be used in informal situations, as in 'One should not believe all one hears' and 'One should be kind to animals'. This construction can sound rather affected. Examples of the informal 'you' include 'You would've thought he would've had more sense' and 'You wouldn't think anyone could be so stupid'. **One** when followed by 'of the' and a plural noun takes a singular verb, as in 'One of the soldiers was killed' and 'One of the three witnesses has died'. However, the constructions 'one of those . . . who' and one of the . . . that' take a plural verb, as in 'He is one of those people who will not take advice' and 'It is one of those houses that are impossible to heat'.

only must be carefully positioned in written sentences to avoid confusion. It should be placed before, or as close as possible before, the word to which it refers. Compare 'She drinks only wine at the weekend', 'She drinks wine only at the weekend' and 'Only she drinks wine at the weekend'. In spoken English, where the intonation of the voice will indicate which word **only** applies to it may be placed in whichever position sounds most natural, usually between the subject and the verb, as in 'She only drinks wine at the weekend'.

onomatopoeia refers to 'the combination of sounds in a word that imitates or suggests the sound of what the word refers to'. 'Crackle', as in 'The fire crackled', 'hiss', as in 'The snake began to hiss', 'rumble', as in 'The thunder rumbled' are all examples of **onomatopoeia**. The word is frequently misspelt. Note the *oeia* combination.

onto and **on to** are both acceptable forms in sentences such as 'The cat leapt onto/on to the table' and 'He jumped from the plane onto/on to the ground'. However, in sentences such as 'It is time to move on to another city' **onto** is not a possible alternative'.

onward and onwards are not interchangeable. **Onward** is an adjective, as in 'onward motion' and 'onward progress'. **Onwards** is an adverb, as in 'march onwards' and 'proceed onwards'.

optician, **ophthalmologist**, **optometrist** and **oculist** all refer to 'a person who is concerned with disorders of the eyes' but they are not interchangeable. **Dispensing optician** refers to 'a person who makes and sells spectacles or contact lenses'. **Ophthalmic optician** refers to 'a person who tests eyesight and prescribes lenses'. **Optometrist** is another term for this. **Ophthalmologist** refers to 'a doctor who specializes in disorders of the eyes' and **oculist** is another name for this. **Ophthalmologist** is frequently misspelt. Note the *h* after the *p*. It is pronounced of-thal-mol-*ol*-oj-ist.

optimum means 'the most favourable or advantageous condition, situation, amount, degree, etc', as in 'A temperature of 20° is optimum for these plants'. It is mostly used as an adjective meaning 'most favourable or advantageous', as in 'the optimum speed to run the car at', 'the optimum time at which to pick the fruit' and 'the optimum amount of water to give the plants'. It should not be used simply as a synonym for 'best'.

optometrist *see* **optician**.

or is accompanied by a singular verb when it connects singular subjects, as in 'Dessert will be ice cream or fruit salad' and 'Tuesday or Wednesday would be a suitable day'. A plural verb is used if the subjects are plural, as in 'Oranges or peaches are suitable' and 'Roses or carnations are possibilities'. If there is a combination of singular and plural subjects the verb agrees with the subject that is nearest to it, as in 'One very large cake or several small ones have been ordered' and 'Several small cakes or one very large one has been ordered'.

oral *see* **aural**.

orientate and **orient** are both acceptable forms of the same word. **Orientate** is the more common in British English but the shorter form, **orient**, is preferred by some people and is the standard form in American English. They are verbs meaning 'to get one's bearings', as in 'difficult to orientate/orient themselves in the mist on the mountain'; 'to adjust to new surroundings', as in 'It takes some time to orientate/orient oneself in a new job'; 'to direct at', as in 'The course is orientated/oriented at older students'; 'to direct the interest of to', as in 'try to orientate/orient students towards the sciences'.

orthopaedic and **paediatric** are liable to be confused. They both apply to medical specialties but they are different. **Orthopaedic** means 'referring to the treatment of disorders of the bones', as in 'attend the orthopaedic clinic with an injured back'. **Paediatric** means 'referring to the treatment of disorders associated with children', as in 'Her little boy is receiving treatment from a paediatric consultant'. In American English these are respectively spelt **orthopedic and pediatric**.

other than can be used when **other** is an adjective or pronoun, as in 'There was no means of entry other than through a trap door' and 'He disapproves of the actions of anyone other than himself'. Traditionally it should not be used as an adverbial phrase, as in 'It was impossible to get there other than by private car'. In such constructions **otherwise than** should be used, as in 'It is impossible to get there otherwise than by private car.' However, **other than** used adverbially is common in modern usage.

otherwise traditionally should not be used as an adjective or pronoun, as in 'Pack your clothes, clean or otherwise' and 'We are not discussing the advantages, or otherwise, of the scheme at this meeting'. It is an adverb, as in 'We are in favour of the project but he obviously thinks otherwise' and 'The hours are rather long but otherwise the job is fine'. *See* **other than**.

outdoor and **outdoors** are not interchangeable. **Outdoor** is an adjective, as in 'encourage the children to take part in outdoor activities' and 'have an outdoor party'. **Outdoors** is an adverb, as in 'children going outdoors to play' and 'hold the party outdoors'.

outrageous is liable to be misspelt. Note the *e*. The word means 'shocking, offensive', as in 'their outrageous behaviour at the church service', and 'unconventional', as in 'wearing outrageous hats'.

outward and **outwards** are not completely interchangeable. **Outward** is an adjective, as in 'the outward journey', but it is also a possible alternative to **outwards**, the adverb, as in 'toes turned outwards/outward'.

owing to *see* **due to**.

P

p *see* **pence**.

pace is a Latin word adopted into English where it means 'with due respect to', usually preceding a statement of disagreement, as in 'Pace Robert Louis Stevenson, but I do not think it is better to travel hopefully than to arrive' and 'Pace your parents, but you might well find that school days are not the happiest days of your life'. It is used in formal, literary or facetious contexts and is pronounced *pah*-chay.

paediatric *see* **orthopaedic**.

palate, **palette** and **pallet** are liable to be confused. They sound alike but they have completely different meanings. **Palate** means either 'the top part of the inside of one's mouth', as in 'have a sore throat and palate' and 'a cleft palate', or 'sense of taste, the ability to distinguish one taste from another', as in 'Sweet things do not appeal to my palate' and 'His wine merchant complimented him on his palate'. **Palette** refers to 'the board on which an artist's colours are mixed', as in 'mix a beautiful shade of purple on his palette'. **Pallet** refers to 'a large platform for carrying or storing goods', as in 'put a pallet of books on the fork-lift truck', or 'a hard bed or straw mattress', as in 'wounded soldiers lying on pallets'.

panacea and **placebo** are liable to be confused. **Panacea** means 'a universal remedy for all ills and troubles', as in 'The new government does not have a panacea for the country's problems'. It is often used loosely to mean any remedy for any problem, as in 'She thinks that a holiday will be a panacea for his unhappiness'. **Panacea** is pronounced pan-a-*see*-a. **Placebo** refers to 'a supposed medication that is just a harmless substance given to a patient as part of a drugs trial etc', as in 'She was convinced the pills were curing her headaches but the doctor has prescribed her a placebo'. It is pronounced pla-*see*-bo.

panic causes spelling problems with reference to the past participle, past tense and present participle as **panicked** and **panicking**, as in 'They panicked when they smelt the smoke' and 'The panicking audience rushed for the exit'. Note also **panicky**, as in 'She got a bit panicky when she heard the footsteps behind her'.

paraffin is frequently misspelt. Note the single *r* and double *f*. The word refers to 'a type of oil used in heaters and lights', as in 'paraffin lamps'.

parallel is frequently misspelt. Note the single *r* and double *l* and single *l*. Note also that the *l* does not double in the past participle and present participle, as **paralleled** and **paralleling**. The word means 'of lines having the same distance between them at every point' and 'exactly corresponding', as in 'a parallel case'. As a verb it means 'to be equal to', as in 'His comparison has never been paralleled', and 'to be comparable to or similar to', as in 'His experience of the firm paralleled hers'.

paralyse is frequently misspelt. Note the *yse* ending. In American English it is spelt **paralyze**. The word means 'to prevent from moving', as in 'The accident paralysed him from the waist down' and 'to prevent from functioning', as in 'The strike paralysed the factory for weeks'.

parameter is a mathematical term that is very loosely used in modern usage to mean 'limit, boundary, framework' or 'limiting feature or characteristic', as in 'work within the parameters of our budget and resources'. The word is over-used and should be avoided where possible. The emphasis is on the second syllable as par-*am*-it-er.

paranoid is an adjective meaning 'referring to a mental disorder, called **paranoia**, characterized by delusions of persecution and grandeur', as in 'a paranoid personality'. In modern usage it is used loosely to mean 'distrustful, suspicious of others, anxious etc', as in 'It is difficult to get to know him—he's so paranoid' and 'paranoid about people trying to get his job', when there is no question of actual mental disorder. **Paranoia** is pronounced par-a-*noy*-a.

paraphernalia means 'all the bits and pieces of equipment required for something', as in 'all the paraphernalia needed to take a baby on holiday', 'put his angling paraphernalia in the car'. Strictly speaking it is a plural noun but it is now frequently used with a singular verb, as in 'The artist's paraphernalia was lying all over the studio'. **Paraphernalia** is liable to be misspelt. Note the *er* before the *n*.

parentheses *see* **brackets**.

parliament is liable to be misspelt. Note the *i* before the *a*. It is pronounced *par*-la-ment. It refers to 'a legislative assembly or authority'. When it refers to a particular assembly, such as the British one, it is usually spelt with a capital letter.

parlour *see* **sitting room**.

particular means 'special, exceptional', as in 'a matter of particular importance', or 'individual', as in 'Have you a particular person in mind?', and 'concerned over details, fastidious', as in 'very particular about personal hygiene'. **Particular** is often used almost meaninglessly, as in 'this particular dress' and 'this particular car', when **particular** does not add much to the meaning.

partner can be used to indicate one half of an established couple, whether the couple are married or living together, as in 'Her partner was present at the birth of the child'.

passed and **past** are liable to be confused. **Passed** is the past participle and past tense of the verb 'to pass', as in 'She has already passed the exam' and 'They passed an old man on the way'. **Past** is used as a noun, as in 'He was a difficult teenager but that is all in the past now' and 'He has a murky past'. It is also used as an adjective, as in 'I haven't seen him in the past few weeks' and 'Her past experiences affected her opinion of men'. **Past** can also be a preposition, as in 'We drove past their new house', 'It's past three o'clock' and 'He's past caring'. It can also be an adverb, as in 'He watched the athletes running past' and 'The boat drifted past'.

patent, in British English, is usually pronounced *pay*-tent, as in 'patent leather dancing shoes'. **Patent** in the sense of 'obvious', as in 'his patent dislike of the situation' and 'It was quite patent that she loved him' is also pronounced in that way. **Patent** in the sense of 'a legal document giving the holder the sole right to make or sell something and preventing others from imitating it', as in 'take out a patent for his new invention', can be pronounced either *pay*-tent or *pat*-ent. **Patent** in this last sense can also be a verb, as in 'He should patent his invention as soon as possible'.

peaceable and **peaceful** are interchangeable in some meanings. Both **peaceable** and **peaceful** can mean 'not quarrelsome or aggressive, peace-loving', as in 'He is a peaceable person but his neighbours are always trying to pick a quarrel' and 'peaceful nations unwilling to go to war'. They can also both mean 'without fighting or disturbance, non-violent', as in 'try to reach a peaceable settlement' and 'take part in a peaceful demonstration'. **Peaceful** means 'characterized by peace, calm, quiet', as in 'a peaceful spot for a quiet holiday' and 'peaceful country scene'. **Peaceable** is frequently misspelt. Note the *e* before the second *a* and note the *-able*, not *-ible*, ending.

pedal and **peddle** are liable to be confused. They sound alike but have different meanings. **Pedal** refers to a 'foot-operated lever', as in 'The pedal on his bicycle broke' and 'the soft pedal on a piano'. It is also a verb meaning 'to operate a pedal', as in 'pedal the bicycle slowly uphill'. **Peddle** is a verb meaning 'to sell small articles from house to house or from place to place, to hawk', as in 'tinkers peddling clothes pegs and paper flowers around the village'. It also means 'to put forward or spread', as in 'peddle his agnostic theories'. In modern usage **peddle** is often used of selling drugs, as in 'evil men peddling hard drugs to young people'.

peddle *see* **pedal**.

peddler and **pedlar** are not interchangeable in British English. **Peddler** refers particularly to 'a person who peddles drugs', as in 'drug-peddlers convicted and sent to prison'. **Pedlar** refers to 'a person who sells small articles from house to house or from place to place', as in 'pedlars selling ribbons at the fair'.

pedlar *see* **peddler**.

pejorative is liable to be mispronounced. In modern usage it is pronounced with the emphasis on the second syllable, as in pi-*jor*-at-iv. It means 'expressing criticism or scorn, derogatory, disparaging', as in 'It was unsportsmanlike to make pejorative remarks about his rival'.

pence, **p** and **pennies** are liable to be confused. **Pence** is the plural form of 'penny', as in 'There are a hundred pence in the pound'. It is commonly found in prices, as in 'apples costing 10 pence each'. **Pence** has become much more common than 'pennies', which tends to be associated with pre-decimalization money (the British currency was decimalized in 1972), as in 'There were twelve pennies in one shilling'.

Pence is sometimes used as though it were singular, as in 'have no one-pence pieces'. In informal contexts **p** is often used, as in 'Have you got a 10p (pronounced ten pee) piece' and 'Those chocolate bars are fifteen p'. **Pence** in compounds is not pronounced in the same way as pence was pronounced in compounds before decimalization. Such words as 'ten pence' are now pronounced *ten pens*, with equal emphasis on each word. In pre-decimalization days it was pronounced *ten*-pens, with the emphasis on the first word.

pennies *see* **pence**.

people is usually a plural noun and so takes a plural verb, as in 'The local people were annoyed at the stranger's behaviour' and 'People were being asked to leave'. In the sense of 'nation', 'race' or 'tribe' it is sometimes treated as a singular noun, as in 'the nomadic peoples of the world'. **People** acts as the plural of 'person', as in 'There's room for only one more person in that car but there's room for three people in this one'. In formal or legal contexts **persons** is sometimes used as the plural of 'person', as in 'The lift had a notice saying "Room for six persons only"'.

per means 'for each' and is used to express rates, prices, etc, as in 'driving at 60 miles per hour', 'cloth costing £5 per square metre', 'The cost of the trip is £20 per person' and 'The fees are £1000 a term per child'. It can also mean 'in each', as in 'The factory is inspected three times per year'.

per capita is a formal expression meaning 'for each person', as in 'The cost of the trip will be £300 per capita'. It is a Latin phrase which has been adopted into English and literally means 'by heads'. It is pronounced per *ka*-pi-ta.

per cent is usually written as two words. It is used adverbially in combination with a number in the sense of 'in or for each hundred', as in '30 per cent of the people are living below the poverty line'. The number is sometimes written in figures, as in 'Fifty per cent of the staff are married'. The symbol % is often used instead of the words 'per cent', especially in technical contexts, as in 'make savings of up to 30%'. **Per cent** in modern usage is sometimes used as a noun, as in 'They have agreed to lower the price by half a per cent'.

percentage refers to 'the rate, number or amount in each hundred', as in 'the number of unemployed people expressed as a percentage of the adult population' and 'What percentage of his salary is free?'. It is also used to mean proportion, as in 'Only a small percentage of last year's students have found jobs' and 'A large percentage of the workers are in favour of a strike' 'In modern usage it is sometimes used to mean 'a small amount' or 'a small part', as in 'Only a percentage of the students will find work'.

perceptible and **perceptive** are liable to be confused. They look and sound rather similar but they mean different things. **Perceptible** means 'noticeable, recognizable', as in 'There was no perceptible difference in her appearance even after all those years' and 'There has been a perceptible improvement in her work'. **Perceptive** means 'quick to notice and understand', as in 'She was perceptive enough to realize that she was not welcome, although her hosts tried to hide the fact', and 'having or showing understanding or insight, discerning', as in 'She wrote a perceptive analysis of his poetry'.

perpetrate and **perpetuate** are liable to be confused. **Perpetrate** means 'to commit, to perform', as in 'perpetrate a crime' and 'perpetrate an act of violence'. **Perpetuate** means 'to cause to continue', as in 'perpetuate the myth that women are helpless' and 'His behaviour will simply perpetuate his reputation as a villain'.

perquisite *see* **prerequisite**.

per se is a Latin phrase that has been adapted into English and means 'in itself', as in 'The substance is not per se harmful but it might be so if it interacts with other substances' and 'Television is not per se bad for children'. It should be used only in formal contexts.

persecute and **prosecute** are liable to be confused. They look and sound rather similar but they mean different things. **Persecute** means 'to treat cruelly, to oppress, to harass', as in 'The Christians in ancient Rome were persecuted for their beliefs' and 'Some of the pupils persecuted the new boy because he was so different from them'. **Prosecute** means 'to take legal action against', as in 'He was prosecuted for embezzling money from the company' and 'Shoplifters will be prosecuted'. It also means 'to follow, to continue to be occupied with', as in 'prosecute a new line of inquiry' and 'prosecute his musical career'. This meaning should be restricted to formal contexts.

person is now used in situations where 'man' was formerly used to avoid sexism in language'. It is used when the sex of the person being referred to is either unknown or not specified, as in 'They are advertising for another person for the warehouse'. It often sounds more natural to use 'someone', as in 'They are looking for someone to help out in the warehouse'. **Person** is often used in compounds, as in **chairperson, spokesperson** and **salesperson**, although some people dislike this convention and some compounds, such as **craftsperson**, have not really caught on. **Person** has two possible plurals. *See* **people**. **Person with** and **people with** are phrases advocated in 'politically correct' language to avoid negative terms such as 'victim', 'sufferer', as in 'person with Aids'.

personal and **personnel** are liable to be confused. **Personal** is an adjective meaning 'of or affecting a person', as in 'carry out the scheme for personal gain' and 'her personal belongings'; 'of or belonging to a particular person rather than a group', as in 'state her personal opinion rather than the official company policy'; 'done in person', as in 'thanks to her personal intervention'; 'of the body', as in 'personal hygiene'; 'critical of a person's character, etc', as in 'upset by her personal remarks'. **Personnel** refers to 'the people employed in a workplace, such as an an office, shop, factory, etc, considered collectively', as in 'personnel officer, 'personnel department', 'Some of the local firms are beginning to recruit more personnel' and 'cut back on personnel during the recession'. It is rather a formal word and is best restricted to a business situation, such as recruitment advertisements. Words such as 'staff', 'workers' and 'employees' can be used instead. **Personnel** is liable to be misspelt. Note the double *n* and single *l*.

phase *see* **faze**.

phenomenal means 'referring to a phenomenon'. It is often used to mean 'remarkable, extraordinary', as in 'a phenomenal atmospheric occurrence', and in modern usage it is also used loosely to mean 'very great', as in 'a phenomenal increase in the crime rate' and 'a phenomenal achievement'. This use is usually restricted to informal contexts.

phenomenon is a singular noun meaning 'a fact, object, occurrence, experience, etc, that can be perceived by the senses rather than by thought or intuition', as in 'She saw something coming out of the lake but it remained an unexplained phenomenon', and 'a strange, unusual or remarkable fact, event or person of some particular significance', as in 'Single parenthood is one of the phenomena of the 1990s'. The plural is **phenomena**, as in 'natural phenomena'. It is a common error to treat **phenomena** as a singular noun. Note the spelling of **phenomenon** as it is liable to be misspelt.

phlegm causes problems with reference to both spelling and pronunciation. Note the *g*, which is often omitted in error. The word is pronounced *flem* and refers to 'a thick mucus secreted by respiratory passages, especially when one has a cold etc', as in 'cough up phlegm'. It also refers to 'slowness to act, react or feel, indifference', as in 'She seemed to face the crisis with an amazing amount of phlegm'. The adjective from this is phlegmatic, meaning 'slow to act, react or feel, indifferent, calm', as in 'require a phlegmatic temperament to cope with all the crises in the office'.

phobia refers to 'an abnormal or irrational fear or aversion', as in 'She is consulting a psychiatrist about her phobia about birds' and 'try to cure his phobia about flying'. It is often used loosely in modern usage to mean 'dislike', as in 'a phobia about people with red hair', or 'obsession', as in 'She has a phobia about her weight.' **Phobia** is liable to be misspelt. Note the *ph*.

phone, which is a short form of 'telephone', is not regarded as being as informal as it once was. It is quite acceptable in sentences such as 'He is going to buy a mobile phone',

'There is an extension phone in the kitchen'. It can also be used as a verb, as in 'Could you phone back tomorrow?' and 'Phone the doctor—it's an emergency'. Telephone is used only in very formal or official contexts', as in 'Please telephone for an application form'. 'If you wish to make an appointment with Mr Jones you will have to telephone his secretary'. Note that **phone** is now spelt without an apostrophe.

phoney and **phony** are both acceptable spellings but **phoney** is the more common in British English. The word means 'pretending or claiming to be what one is not, fake', as in 'He has a phoney American accent' and 'There's something phoney about him'.

photo is an abbreviation of 'photograph' which is usually used in an informal context, as in 'His mother is showing his girlfriend his baby photos', 'He's boring everybody with his holiday photos'. In more formal and official contexts 'photograph' is used, as in 'Assemble the children for the school photograph' and 'Enclose the photographs with the passport application form'. The plural of **photo** is **photos**. It is not generally used as a verb.

picnic causes problems with regard to the past participle, past tense and present participle. They add a *k* after the final *c* before the endings are added, as **picnicked** and **picnicking**, as in 'They picnicked by the river' and 'We were picnicking on wine'. Note also **picnicker**, as in 'Picnickers should not leave litter'.

pidgin and **pigeon** are liable to be confused. **Pidgin** refers to 'a language that is a mixture of two other languages', as in 'unable to understand the local people who were speaking pidgin English'. **Pigeon** is 'a type of bird of the dove family', as in 'pigeons eating crumbs as we were eating our sandwiches'.

pièce de résistance is a French phrase that has been adopted into English meaning 'the most important or impressive item', as in 'His portrait of his wife was the pièce de résistance of the exhibition'. The phrase is liable to be misspelt. Note the accent on the *e* of **pièce** which should not be omitted or it becomes 'piece'. Note also the accent on the first *e* of **résistance**. The phrase is pronounced pyes-de-re-*zist*-ahns.

pigeon *see* **pidgin**.

placebo *see* **panacea**.

plain and **plane** are liable to be confused since they sound alike. However, they have completely different meanings. **Plain** can be an adjective with several meanings. It means 'easy to see, hear or understand, clear', as in 'It was plain that she was unhappy' and 'speak in plain English so that you will be understood'; 'frank, not trying to deceive', as in 'the plain truth'; 'simple, not decorated or fancy', as in 'a plain style of dressing' and 'plain food'; 'without a pattern', as in 'prefer a plain material'; 'not beautiful', as in 'People said that she was the plain one of the family'. **Plain** as a noun refers to 'a large area of flat, treeless land', as in 'grow wheat on the plains'. **Plane** as a noun means 'the shortened form of aeroplane', as in 'Travelling by plane will be quicker'; 'a flat or level surface', as in 'create a plane by levelling the surface'; 'a level or standard', as in 'His mind is on a different plane from ours' and 'reach a higher plane of development'; 'a tool for smoothing surfaces', as in 'use a plane to smooth out the imperfections in the wood'. Note the **plain** in the phrase **plain sailing**, as in 'She thought it would be plain sailing once she got a place of her own but there were problems'. It is a common error to put **plane**. *See* **plane**.

plaintiff and **plaintive** are liable to be confused because they sound similar. However, they have completely different meanings. **Plaintiff** refers to 'a person who brings a legal action against someone', as in 'It was the accused's mother who was the plaintiff'. **Plaintive** means 'sounding sad, mournful', as in 'the plaintive cries of hungry children' and 'the plaintive sound of the bagpipes'.

plane and **aeroplane** mean the same thing, both referring to a 'a machine that can fly and is used to carry people and goods'. In modern usage **plane** is the usual term, as in 'The plane took off on time' and 'nearly miss the plane'. **Aeroplane** is slightly old-fashioned or unduly formal, as in 'Her elderly parents say that they refuse to travel by aeroplane'.

The American English spelling is **airplane**. Note that **plane** is not spelt with an apostrophe although it is a shortened form. *See also* **plain**.

pleaded and **pled** mean the same thing, both being the past tense and past participle of the verb 'to plead'. **Pleaded** is the usual form in British English, as in 'They pleaded with the tyrant to spare the child's life' and 'The accused was advised to plead guilty'. **Pled** is the usual American spelling.

plenty is used only informally in some contexts. It is acceptable in formal and informal contexts when it is followed by the preposition 'of', as in 'We have plenty of food', or when it is used as a pronoun without the 'of' construction, as in 'You can borrow some food from us—we have plenty'. Some people think its use as an adjective, as in 'Don't hurry—we have plenty time' and 'There's plenty food for all in the fridge', should be restricted to informal contexts. As an adverb it is a acceptable in both formal and informal contexts in such sentences as 'Help yourself—we have plenty more'. However, such sentences as 'The house is plenty big enough for them' is suitable only for very informal or slang contexts'.

plurals cause many problems. Most words in English add *s* to form the plural, as in 'cats', 'machines' and 'boots'. However, words ending in *-s*, *-x*, *-z*, *-ch* and *-sh* add *es*, as in 'buses', 'masses', 'foxes', 'fezzes or fezes', 'churches' and 'sashes'. Nouns ending in a consonant followed by *y* have *-ies* in the plural, as 'fairies' and 'ladies', but note 'monkey', where the *y* is preceded by a vowel and becomes 'monkeys'. Proper nouns ending in *y* add *s*, as in 'the two Germanys'. Some words ending in *f* have *ves* in the plural, as 'wives' and 'halves', but some simply add *s* to the singular form, as 'beliefs'. Some words ending in *f* can either add *s* or change to *ves*, as 'hoofs or hooves'. Words ending in *o* cause problems as some end in *oes* in the plural, as 'potatoes' and 'tomatoes', and some end in *s*, as in 'pianos', while some can be spelt either way and have to be learned or looked up in a dictionary etc. Shortened forms, such as 'photo' and 'video', add simply *s*, as 'photos', 'videos'. Some words have the same form in the plural as they do in the singular, such as 'sheep' and 'deer'. Some are plural in form already and so do not change,. These include 'trousers' and 'scissors'. Several words in English have irregular plural forms which just have to be learned or looked up in a dictionary, etc. These include 'men', 'mice' and 'feet'. Some foreign words adopted into English used to retain the foreign plural form in English but this is becoming less common and, at the very least there is now often an English-formed alternative, as 'gateaux/gateaus', 'index/indices', 'formulae/formulas', 'appendixes/appendices'. However, several nouns of foreign extraction retain the foreign-style plural in English, such as 'criteria' and 'crises'.

p.m. *see* **a.m.**

poignant is liable to be misspelt. Note the *g*, which is silent. It is pronounced *poy*-nyant. The word means 'affecting one's feelings deeply, distressing', as in 'a poignant tale of an orphan child'.

politic and **political** are liable to be confused although they are completely different in meaning. **Politic** means 'prudent, wise', as in 'He thought it politic not to mention that he knew that his boss had been fined for speeding'. **Political** means 'referring to politics', as in 'political parties' and 'the end of his political career'. **Politic** is pronounced with the emphasis on the first syllable, as *pol*-it-ik, but **political** is pronounced with the emphasis on the second syllable as pol-*it*-ic-al.

political correctness is a modern movement aiming to remove all forms of prejudice in language, such as sexism, racism and discrimination against disabled people. Its aims are admirable but in practice many of the words and phrases suggested by advocates of political correctness are rather contrived or, indeed, ludicrous. The adjective is **politically correct**.

pore and **pour** are liable to be confused because they sound alike. **Pore** as a verb means 'to look at or study intently', as in 'They pored over the old document looking for the site of the treasure'. **Pour** means 'to cause to flow', as in 'she poured milk from the jug', or 'to flow in large amounts', as in 'Water poured from the burst pipe'. **Pore** can also be a noun when it means 'one of the tiny openings on the surface of the skin', as in 'clogged pores'.

portrait is liable to be misspelt. Note the first *r*. The word means 'a painting, drawing or photograpgh of a person or animal, particularly one which concentrates on the face', as in 'portraits of his ancestors hanging on the walls of the dining room'.

portray is liable to be misspelt. Note the first *r*. It means 'to paint or draw', as in 'The queen was portrayed in her coronation robes'; 'to describe', as in 'In his autobiography his father is portrayed as a bully'; 'and to act the part of', as in 'The actress portrayed Desdemona in *Othello*'.

Portuguese is liable to be misspelt. Note the *u* after the *g*. It is the adjective from 'Portugal'.

possessives are indicated in English by either apostrophes or the preposition 'of', as in 'the boy's books', Jim's car', the dogs' kennels', 'the key of the back door' and 'The soldiers of the king'. When the 'of' construction is used of people, an apostrophe is often used as well, as in 'a colleague of her husband's'. The 'of' construction is usually used of things rather than people, as in 'The catch of the garden gate is broken', and it is usually used when geographical regions are being referred to, as in 'the forests of Scandinavia'. If the possession in question refers to more than one person the apostrophe goes on the last owner mentioned, as in 'John and Mary's beautiful house'. In the case of compound nouns, the apostrophe goes on the last word, as in 'the lady-in-waiting's role'. For the position of the apostrophe in **possessives** *see* **apostrophe**.

posthumous causes problems with both spelling and pronunciation. Note the *h*, which is often omitted in error since it is silent in pronunciation. The word is pronounced *post*-ewmus with the emphasis on the first syllable, which rhymes with 'lost'. The word means 'happening or given after death', as in 'a posthumous novel' and 'a posthumous medal'. The adverb **posthumously** means 'after one's death', as in 'The soldier's son was born posthumously'.

pour *see* **pore**.

practicable and **practical** should not be used interchangeabably. **Practicable** means 'able to be done or carried out, able to be put into practice', as in 'His schemes seem fine in theory but they are never practicable'. **Practical** has several meanings, such as 'concerned with action and practice rather than with theory', as in 'He has studied the theory but has no practical experience of the job'; 'suitable for the purpose for which it was made', as in 'practical shoes for walking'; 'useful', as in 'a practical device with a wide range of uses'; 'clever at doing and making things', as in 'She's very practical when it comes to dealing with an emergency'; 'virtual', as in 'He's not the owner but he's in practical control of the firm'.

practically can mean 'in a practical way', as in 'Practically, the scheme is not really possible', but in modern usage it is usually used to mean 'virtually', as in 'He practically runs the firm although he is not the manager', and 'almost', as in 'The driver of that car practically ran me over'.

practice and **practise** are not interchangeable. **Practice** is a noun, as in 'She has gone to netball practice', 'It is time to put the plan into practice', 'It is accepted practice to tip the waiters', 'object to some of the practices of the religious sect' and 'Our doctor has retired from the practice'. **Practise** is the verb form, as in 'He practises the piano every evening', 'We must practise economy if we are to remain solvent', 'He is a medical doctor but he has not practised for years' and 'He is a Catholic but he no longer practises his religion'. Note that **practise** is not one of the verbs that can end in *-ize*. In American English both the noun and the verb are spelt **practice**.

pray and **prey** are liable to be confused. They sound alike but they have completely different meanings. **Pray** means 'to speak to God, to make requests of God', as in 'pray and sing hymns in church on Sundays' and 'pray to God that the pardon will arrive in

precede

time', or 'to ask a favour from, to beg', as in 'They prayed to the tyrant to release their brother'. **Prey** is a noun meaning 'an animal or bird hunted and killed by another animal or bird', as in 'The lion had its prey, a deer, in its mouth'. It also means 'a person who is exploited or harmed by another, a victim', as in 'The old lady was easy prey for the con man'. **Prey** is also a verb meaning 'to hunt and kill as prey', as in 'Eagles prey on small animals', and 'to trouble greatly, to obsess', as in 'His part in the crime preyed on his mind'.

precede and **proceed** are liable to be confused because they sound alike but they mean different things. **Precede** means 'to go in front of', as in 'The guide preceded us into the room', 'to come in front of', as in 'The text is preceded by a long introduction' and 'He preceded her as chairman'. **Proceed** means 'to go on, to continue', as in 'Work is proceeding at an even pace' and 'We were told to proceed with our work', or 'to make one's way, to go', as in 'They were proceeding up the street in a drunken manner'.

precipitate and **precipitous** are liable to be confused. **Precipitate** as an adjective means 'violently hurried', as in 'When the thief saw the policeman he made a precipitate dash from the room', 'sudden', as in 'Her precipitate disappearance from the firm', and 'rash, impulsive', as in 'We thought his action in leaving the firm was rather precipitate'. **Precipitous** means 'very steep, like a precipice', as in 'It was almost impossible to climb the precipitous slope'. **Precipitate** is also a verb meaning to cause something to happen suddenly or sooner than expected, to hasten', as in 'His setting fire to the bicycle shed precipitated his expulsion from the school', or 'to throw', as in 'His sudden departure precipitated the whole office into a state of confusion'. In the pronunciation of both the verb and the adjective, the emphasis is on the second syllable, but in the case of the verb the last syllable rhymes with 'gate' whereas in the case of the adjective the last syllable is pronounced to rhyme with 'hat'. Thus the pronunciation of the adjective is pri-*sip*-i-tat, and that of the verb pri-sip-it-ayt.

prefer is followed by the preposition 'to' not 'than', as in 'She prefers dogs to cats', 'They prefer Paris to London' and 'They prefer driving to walking'. **Prefer** causes spelling problems with regard to the past participle, past tense and present participle. Note that the final *r* of **prefer** doubles before the '-ed' and '-ing' are added, as **preferred** and **preferring**. The word means 'to like better', as in 'She preferred the country to the town'.

premier and **première** are liable to be confused. **Premier** means 'leading, principle', as in 'He is the premier authority on genetic engineering in the country'. **Première** refers to 'the first performance of a film, play, etc', as in 'attend the world première of his latest film'. It is now also a verb, as in 'His latest film was premiered in London'. **Premier** is pronounced *prem*-ier. Première is pronounced *prem*-i-ay or *prem*-i-ayr. **Première** is liable to be misspelt. Note the final *e*. The word is usually spelt with a grave accent over the second *e*.

premise *see* **premises**.

premises and **premise**. are liable to be confused. **Premises** refers to 'a building including any outbuildings and grounds', as in 'the car sales showroom has moved to new premises'. **Premises** is a plural noun and so takes a plural verb, as in 'Their present premises are too small for the volume of business'. **Premise** is a singular noun meaning 'assumption, hypothesis', as in 'His advice was based on the premise that they had enough capital for the project'. It is also spelt **premiss**.

premiss *see* **premises**.

prerequisite and **perquisite** are liable to be confused although they are completely different in meaning. **Perquisite** means 'money or goods given as a right in addition to one's pay', as in 'various perquisites such as a company car'. It is frequently abbreviated to 'perks', as in 'The pay's not very much but the perks are good'. **Prerequisite** refers to 'something required as a condition for something to happen or exist', as in 'Passing the exam is a prerequisite for his getting the job' and 'A certain amount of studying is a prerequisite of passing the exam'.

prescribe and **proscribe** are liable to be confused. They sound similar but are completely different in meaning. **Prescribe** means 'to advise or order the use of, especially a medicine or remedy', as in 'The doctor prescribed antibiotics' and 'The doctor prescribed complete bed rest'. It also means 'to lay down as a rule or law', as in 'School regulations prescribe that all pupils wear school uniform'. **Proscribe** means 'to prohibit', as in 'proscribe the carrying of guns', and 'to outlaw or exile', as in 'proscribe the members of the clan who betrayed the chief'. In some cases the words are virtually opposite in meaning. Compare 'The lecturer has prescribed several books which must be read by the end of term' and 'The government has proscribed several books that are critical of them'.

prestige is liable to be mispronounced. It is pronounced prez-*teezh* and means 'the respect, status or renown derived from achievement, distinction, wealth, glamour etc', as in 'He suffered a loss of prestige when he lost all his money' and 'He enjoys the prestige of being chairman of the company'.

prevaricate and **procrastinate** are liable to be confused although they have completely different meanings. **Prevaricate** means 'to try to avoid telling the truth by speaking in an evasive or misleading way', as in 'She prevaricated when the police asked her where she had been the previous evening'. **Procrastinate** means 'to delay or postpone action', as in 'The student has been procrastinating all term but now he has to get to grips with his essay'.

preventative and **preventive** both mean 'preventing or intended to prevent, precautionary', as in 'If you think the staff are stealing from the factory you should take preventative/preventive measures' and 'Preventative/preventive medicine seeks to prevent disease and disorders rather than cure them'. **Preventive** is the more frequently used of the two terms.

prey *see* **pray**.

prima facie is a Latin phrase that has been adopted into English. It means 'at first sight, based on what seems to be so' and is mainly used in legal or very formal contexts, as in 'The police say they have prima facie evidence for arresting him but more investigation is required'. The phrase is pronounced *pri*-ma *fay*-shee.

primarily is traditionally pronounced with the emphasis on the first syllable, as *prim*-ar-el-i. Since this is difficult to say unless one is speaking very slowly and carefully, it is becoming increasingly common to pronounce it with the emphasis on the second syllable, as prim-*err*-el-i. It means 'mainly', as in 'He was primarily interested in the creative side of the business' and 'The course is primarily a practical one'.

primeval and **primaeval** are both acceptable forms of the word meaning 'of the earliest period in the history of the world, very ancient', as in 'primeval rocks'. In modern usage **primeval** is the more common term although **primaeval** was formerly the more usual term.

principal and **principle** are liable to be confused. They sound alike but they have different meanings. **Principal** means 'chief, main', as in 'his principal reason for leaving' and 'her principal source of income'. **Principal** is also a noun meaning 'head', as in 'the principal of the college'. **Principle** means 'a basic general truth', as in 'according to scientific principles', and 'a guiding rule for personal behaviour', as in 'It is against his principles to lie'.

principle *see* **principal**.

prise and **prize** are liable to cause confusion. The verb 'to force open' can be spelt either **prise** or **prize**, as in 'prise/prize open the chest with an iron bar'. **Prise** is the more common spelling. **Prize** has another meaning for which prise cannot be substituted. It means 'an award or reward', as in 'He won first prize in the tennis competition', and 'something won in a lottery etc', as in 'He won first prize on the football pools'. **Prize** can also be a verb meaning 'to value highly', as in 'She prizes her privacy'.

privilege is liable to be misspelt. Note the *i* before the *l*, and the *e* before the *g*. It refers to 'a special right or advantage', as in 'the privileges conferred on ambassadors' and 'enjoy the privileges of being a senior executive'.

procrastinate *see* **prevaricate**.

professor is liable to be misspelt. Note the single *f* and the double *s*. The word means 'a senior university lecturer', as in 'The professor is retiring from the chair of English this year'.

prognosis *see* **diagnosis**.

programme and **program** are liable to cause confusion. In British English **programme** is the acceptable spelling in such senses as in 'a television programme', 'put on a varied programme of entertainment' 'buy a theatre programme' and 'launch an ambitious programme of expansion'. However, in the computing sense **program** is used. **Programme** can also be a verb meaning 'to plan, to schedule', as in 'programme the trip for tomorrow'; 'to cause something to conform to a particular set of instructions', as in 'programme the central heating system'; or 'to cause someone to behave in a particular way, especially to conform to particular instructions', as in 'Her parents have programmed her to obey them implicitly'. In the computing sense of 'to provide with a series of coded instructions', the verb is spelt **program** and the *m* is doubled to form the past participle, past tense and present participle, as **programmed** and **programming**. In American English **program** is the accepted spelling for all senses of both noun and verb.

prophecy and **prophesy** are liable to confused. **Prophecy** is a noun meaning 'prediction', as in 'Some of the old woman's prophecies came true'. **Prophesy** is a verb meaning 'to predict', as in 'The old woman had prophesied the disaster that befell the village' and 'They prophesied that the recession would be over in a year'. **Prophecy** is pronounced with the emphasis on the first syllable, as *pro*-fi-si. **Prophesy** is also pronounced with the emphasis on the first syllable, but the last syllable rhymes with 'eye' as *pro*-fi-si.

proscribe *see* **prescribe**.

prosecute *see* **persecute**.

prostate and **prostrate** are liable to be confused although they are completely different in meaning. **Prostate** refers to 'a gland around the neck of the bladder in men', as in 'have a prostate complaint' and 'contract cancer of the prostate'. **Prostrate** means 'lying face downwards', as in 'The injured rider was lying prostrate on the ground', 'overcome by', as in 'prostrate with grief', and 'exhausted, helpless', as in 'a country competely prostrate after the war'. **Prostrate** is also a verb meaning 'to throw oneself face down on the ground, for example, as a sign of submission', as in 'The soldiers prostrated themselves before the emperor', 'to overcome', as in 'Grief prostrated her', and 'to make helpless or exhausted', as in 'prostrated following a bout of flu'.

protagonist was originally a term for 'the chief character in a drama', as in 'Hamlet is the protagonist in the play that bears his name'. It then came to mean also 'the leading person or paticipant in an event, dispute, etc', as in 'The protagonists on each side of the dispute had a meeting'. In modern usage it can now also mean 'a leading or notable supporter of a cause, movement, etc,' as in 'She was one of the protagonists of the feminist movement'.

protein is liable to be misspelt. Note the *ei* combination. It is an exception to the 'i before e' rule. **Protein** refers to 'a substance that is an important body-building part of the diet of humans and animals', as in 'Meat, eggs and fish are sources of protein'.

provided and **providing** are used interchangeably, as in 'You may go, provided/providing that you have finished your work' and 'He can borrow the car provided/providing he pays for the petrol'. 'That' is optional. The phrases mean 'on the condition that'.

psychiatry is liable to be misspelt. Note the initial *p* and the *y* after the *s*. It is pronounced si-*ki*-i-tri and refers to 'the branch of medicine that deals with disorders of the mind'.

publicly is liable to be misspelt. There is no *k* before the *l*. It is a common error to spell it 'publically'. The word means 'not in private, in front of other people', as in 'He publicly admitted that he was at fault'.

pudding *see* **dessert**.

pupil and **student** are not interchangeable. **Pupil** refers to 'a child or young person who is at school', as in 'primary school pupils and secondary school pupils', **Student** refers to 'a person who is studying at a place of further education, at a university or college', as in 'students trying to find work during the vacations'. In modern usage senior **pupils** at secondary school are sometimes known as **students**. In American English student refers to people at school as well as to people in further education. **Pupil** can also refer to 'a person who is receiving instruction in something from an expert' as in 'The piano teacher has several adult pupils'. **Student** can also refer to 'a person who is studying a particular thing', as in 'In his leisure time he is a student of local history'.

purposefully and **purposely** are not interchangeable. **Purposefully** means 'determinedly', as in 'He strode purposefully up to the front of the hall and addressed the meeting'. **Purposely** means 'on purpose, deliberately', as in 'He didn't leave his book behind by accident—he did it purposely'.

Q

quasi- is Latin in origin and means 'as if, as it were'. In English it is combined with adjectives in the sense of 'seemingly, apparently, but not really', as in 'He gave a quasi-scientific explanation of the occurrence which convinced many people but did not fool his colleagues', or 'partly, to a certain extent but not completely', as in 'It is a quasi-official body which does not have full powers'. **Quasi-** can also be combined with nouns to mean 'seeming, but not really', as in 'a quasi-socialist who is really a capitalist' and 'a quasi-Christian who will not give donations to charity'. **Quasi-** has several possible pronunciations. It can be pronounced *kway*-zi, *kway*-si or *kwah*-si

quay is liable to be mispronounced. The spelling of the word does not suggest the pronunciation, which is *key*. It means 'a landing place', as in 'ships unloading at the quay'.

queer in the sense of 'homosexual' was formerly used only in a slang and derogatory or offensive way. However, it is now used in a non-offensive way by homosexual people to describe themselves, as an alternative to 'gay'.

question *see* **beg the question**; **leading question**.

questionnaire is liable to be misspelt. Note the double *n*. Formerly the acceptable pronunciation was kes-tyon-*air*, but in modern usage kwes-chon-*air* is more common. The word refers to 'a list of questions to be answered by a number of people as part of a survey or collection of statistics', as in 'People entering the supermarket were asked to fill in a questionnaire on their shopping habits' and 'Householders were asked to complete a questionnaire on their electrical equipment'.

quick is an adjective meaning 'fast, rapid', as in 'a quick method', 'a quick route' and 'a quick walker'. It should not be used as an adverb, as in 'Come quick', in formal contexts since this is grammatically wrong.

quite has two possible meanings when used with adjectives. It can mean 'fairly, rather, somewhat', as in 'She's quite good at tennis but not good enough to play in the team' and 'The house is quite nice but it's not what we're looking for'. Where the indefinite article is used, **quite** precedes it, as in 'quite a good player' and 'quite a nice house'.

'**Quite** can also mean 'completely, totally', as in 'We were quite overwhelmed by their generosity' and 'It is quite impossible for him to attend the meeting'.

R

rack and **wrack** are liable to be confused. **Rack** refers to 'a framework for storing and displaying things', as in 'a luggage rack' and 'a vegetable rack'. It is also the name given historically to an instrument of torture, consisting of a frame on which a person lay with wrists and ankles tied and had their arms stretched in one direction and their legs in the other, as in 'prisoners on the rack'. The verb **rack** means 'to cause to suffer pain or great distress to', as in 'cancer patients racked with agony', 'racked with uncertainty' and 'nerve-racking'. The phrase 'rack one's brains' means 'to try hard to think of or remember', as in 'racking his brains to remember their address'. **Wrack** is a rarer word that refers to 'a kind of seaweed' or 'a remnant of something that has been destroyed'. **Rack** and **wrack** are interchangeable in the phrase **rack/wrack and ruin**—'neglect, decay, destruction', as in 'Since the owner has been ill the business has gone to rack/wrack and ruin'.

racket and **racquet** are liable to be confused. Either **racket** or **racquet** may be used to indicate 'a kind of implement with a stringed frame used in sport for striking the ball', as in 'tennis racket/racquet' and 'badminton racket/racquet'. **Racket** also means 'a loud noise', as in 'neighbours complaining about the racket made by the party guests' and 'children making a racket running up and down stairs'. **Racket** also refers to 'a dishonest or illegal way of making money', as in 'a drug racket' and 'a racket involving forged currency'.

raise and **raze** are liable to be confused. They sound alike but have completely different meanings. **Raise** means 'to move to a higher position', as in 'raise the flag', 'raise prices' and 'raise morale'. **Raze** means 'to destroy completely', as in 'The invading army razed the village to the ground'.

raison d'être is French in origin and is used in English to mean 'a reason, a justification for the existence of', as in 'Her children are her raison d'être' and 'His only raison d'être is his work'. The phrase is liable to be misspelt. Note the accent (^) on the first *e*. It is pronounced *ray*-zon detr.

rang and **rung** are liable to be confused. **Rang** is the past tense of the verb 'to ring', as in 'She rang the bell', and **rung** is the past participle, as in 'They had rung the bell'.

rara avis is French in origin and means literally 'rare bird'. In English it is used to refer to 'a rare or unusual person or thing', as in 'a person with such dedication to a company is a rara avis'. It is pronounced *ray*-ra *ayv*-is or *ra*-ra *ay*-vis.

ravage and **ravish** are liable to be confused. They sound rather similar although they have different meanings. **Ravage** means 'to cause great damage to, to devastate', as in 'low-lying areas ravaged by floods' and 'a population ravaged by disease', or 'to plunder, to rob', as in 'neighbouring tribes ravaging their territory'. **Ravish** means either 'to delight greatly, to enchant', as in 'The audience were ravished by the singer's performance'. It also means 'to rape', as in 'The girl was ravished by her kidnappers', but this meaning is rather old-fashioned and is found only in formal or literary contexts.

raze see **raise.**

re, meaning 'concerning, with reference to', as in 'Re your correspondence of 26 November', should be restricted to business or formal contexts.

re- is a common prefix, meaning 'again', in verbs. In most cases it is not followed by a hyphen, as in 'retrace one's footsteps', 'a retrial ordered by the judge' and 'reconsider his decision'. However, it should be followed by a hyphen if its absence is likely to lead to confusion with another word, as in 're-cover a chair'/'recover from an illness', 're-count the votes'/'recount a tale of woe', 'the re-creation of a 17th-century village for a film set'/'play tennis for recreation' and 're-form the group'/'reform the prison system'. In cases where the second element of a word begins with *e*, **re-** is traditionally followed by a hyphen, as in 're-educate', 're-entry' and 're-echo', but in modern usage the hyphen is frequently omitted.

readable *see* **legible**.

receipt is frequently misspelt. Note the *ei* combination in line with the '*i* before *e* except after *c*' rule. Note also *p*, which is not pronounced. **Receipt** is pronounced ri-*seet* and means either 'the act of receiving', as in 'on receipt of your letter', or 'a written statement that money, goods, etc, have been received', as in 'Keep the receipt in case you want to return the goods'.

recommend is frequently misspelt. Note the single *c* and double *m*. The word means 'to suggest as suitable, to praise as suitable', as in 'I can thoroughly recommend this brand of face cream', and 'to suggest as advisable, to advise', as in 'He recommends that we reduce expenditure'.

reconnaissance is frequently misspelt. Note the single *c*, double *n*, and double *s*. It is pronounced ri-*kon*-i-sins and means 'an exploration or survey of an area', as in 'troops engaged in reconnaissance' and 'undertake an aerial reconnaissance of the area where the child was lost'.

re-cover, recover *see* **re-**.

re-creation, recreation *see* **re-**.

refer causes problems with regard to its past participle, past tense and present participle. The *r* doubles before the addition of '-ed' or '-ing', as in **referred** and **referring**, as in 'He referred to her good work in his speech' and 'He was not referring to the present holder of the post'. Note, however, **reference** with a single *r*.

referendum causes problems with regard to its plural form. It has two possible plural forms, **referendums** or **referenda**. In modern usage **referendums** is the more usual plural. **Referendum** means 'the referring of an issue of public importance to a general vote by all the people of a country', as in 'hold a referendum on whether to join the EC'.

re-form, reform *see* **re-**.

refrigerator is frequently misspelt. Note the *-or* ending, the *er* in the middle and the absence of *d*. It is a common error to include a *d* because of confusion with 'fridge'.

registry office and **register office** are interchangeable, although **registry office** is the more common term in general usage. The words refer to 'an office where civil marriage ceremonies are performed and where births, marriages and deaths are recorded', as in 'She wanted to be married in church but he preferred a registry office ceremony' and 'register the child's birth at the local registry office'.

reign and **rein** are liable to be confused. **Reign** is the time during which a king or queen reigns', as in 'during the reign of George V'. **Rein** refers to 'one of the leather straps that control a horse', as in 'The coachman let go of the reins and the horse bolted'. **Reins**, the plural of **rein**, refers to 'a means of control or restraint', as in 'The deputy president held the reins of power'. Both **reign** and **rein** can also be verbs. **Reign** means 'to rule as king or queen', as in 'a monarch who reigned for more than fifty years'. **Rein** as a verb is found in the phrase **rein in**, meaning 'to restrain or stop', as in 'rein in the horse'.

relevant is liable to be misspelt. Note the *-ant* ending. It means 'connected with what is being discussed, happening, done, etc', as in 'collect all the relevant information' and 'police noting details relevant to the case'.

reminiscences is frequently misspelt. Note the *sc* combination. The word refers to 'remembered experiences', as in 'listening to the old woman's reminiscences of her childhood days'. **Reminiscent** is an adjective meaning either 'thinking or talking about past events', as in 'in reminiscent mood', or 'reminding one of, suggesting someone or something', as in 'The style of the artist is reminiscent of Monet'.

requisite *see* **perquisite**.

rhyme and **rime** are liable to be confused. They sound alike but have completely different meanings. **Rhyme** refers to 'a word which is like another in its final sound', as in 'tailor and sailor are rhymes', 'rough and puff are rhymes' and 'dilatory and military are rhymes'. **Rhyme** can also be a verb, as in 'tailor rhymes with sailor'. **Rime** refers to 'a thick white frost', as in 'fields covered with rime'.

rhythm is frequently misspelt. Note the first *h* and the *y*. It means 'a regular repeated pattern of sounds or beats', as in 'the fast rhythm of the dance music'.

rigorous is frequently misspelt. Note the absence of *u* before the second *r*. It is unlike **rigour** in this respect. **Rigorous** means 'severe, strict', as in 'the rigorous discipline of the army', 'harsh, unpleasant', as in 'rigorous weather conditions', and 'strict, detailed', as in 'with rigorous attention to the small print of the agreement'.

rigour and **rigor** are liable to be confused. They look similar but they have completely different meanings. **Rigour** means 'severity, strictness', as in 'the rigour of the punishment', and 'harshness, unpleasantness', as in 'the rigour of the climate' (in this sense it is often in the plural, **rigours**), and 'strictness, detailedness', as in 'the rigour of the editing'. **Rigor** is a medical term meaning 'rigidity', as in 'muscles affected by rigor', or 'a feeling of chilliness often accompanied by feverishness', as in 'infectious diseases of which rigor is one of the symptoms'. **Rigor** is also short for **rigor mortis**, meaning 'the stiffening of the body that occurs after death'. The first syllable of **rigour** is pronounced to rhyme with 'big', but **rigor** can be pronounced either in this way or with the *i* pronounced as in 'ride'

role can be spelt either with a circumflex, as **rôle**, or not, as **role**. **Role** is the more common spelling in modern usage. The word means 'part', as in 'play the role of Hamlet' and 'She had to play the role of mother and of father.' It can also be used to mean 'function, position', as in 'the role of play in a child's development'.

roof causes problems with regard to its plural form. The usual plural is **roofs**, which can be pronounced either as it is spelt, to rhyme with 'hoofs', or to rhyme with 'hooves'.

rout and **route** are liable to be confused. They look similar but are pronounced differently and have completely different meanings'. **Rout** as a noun means 'overwhelming defeat', as in 'the rout of the opposing army', and as a verb 'to defeat utterly', as in 'Their team routed ours last time'. **Route** refers to 'a way of getting somewhere', as in 'the quickest route' and 'the scenic route'. **Route** can also be a verb meaning 'to arrange a route for, to send by a certain route', as in 'route the visitors along the banks of the river'. **Rout** is pronounced to rhyme with 'shout'. **Route** is pronounced to rhyme with 'brute'.

rug *see* **carpet**.

rung *see* **rang**.

S

's and **s'** *see* **apostrophe**.

sacrilegious is frequently misspelt. Note the *i* before the *l* and the *e* before the g. It is a common error to confuse it with the pattern of 'religious'. **Sacrilegious** is the adjective from 'sacrilege' and means 'showing disrespect for something holy', as in 'the sacrilegious act of destroying the altar'.

salon and **saloon** are liable to be confused. **Salon** in modern usage is most frequently found as a name given to certain businesses, as 'own a hairdressing salon' and 'visit a beauty salon'. Formerly it was used to refer to a room in a large house where guests were received and also to 'a regular gathering of notable guests at the house of a noble lady or wealthy lady', as in 'hold a literary salon'.

sank, **sunk** and **sunken** are liable to be confused. **Sank** is the past tense of the verb 'to sink', as in 'The ship sank without trace'. **Sunk** is also used in this sense, as in 'The dog sunk its teeth into the postman's leg', but **sank** is the more common form. The past participle of 'sink' is **sunk**, as in 'We have sunk all our money in the business'. **Sunken** is a form of the past participle usually used as an adjective, as in 'sunken treasure' and 'sunken cheeks'.

scarfs and **scarves** are both acceptable spellings of the plural of 'scarf', meaning a piece of cloth worn around the neck or the head', as in 'a silk scarf at her neck' and 'wearing a head scarf'.

sceptic and **septic** are liable to be confused, particularly with regard to their pronunciation. **Sceptic** is pronounced *skep*-tik and refers to 'a person who has doubts about accepted beliefs, principles, etc', as in 'The rest of the family are deeply religious but he is a sceptic'. **Septic** is pronounced *sep*-tik and means 'infected with harmful bacteria', as in 'a wound that turned septic' and 'have a septic finger'.

schedule, meaning 'plan or timetable', as in 'work that is behind schedule' and 'try to work out a revision schedule well before the exams', is usually pronounced *shed*-yool in British English. However, the American English pronunciation *sked*-yool is now sometimes found in British usage.

Scotch, **Scots** and **Scottish** are liable to be confused. **Scotch** is restricted to a few set phrases, such as 'Scotch whisky', 'Scotch broth' and 'Scotch mist'. As a noun **Scotch** refers to 'Scotch whisky', as in 'have a large Scotch with ice'. **Scots** as an adjective is used in such contexts as 'Scots accents', 'Scots people' and 'Scots attitudes'. As a noun **Scots** refers to the Scots language, as in 'He speaks standard English but he uses a few words of Scots.' The noun **Scot** is used to refer to 'a Scottish person', as in 'Scots living in London'. **Scottish** is found in such contexts as 'Scottish literature', 'Scottish history' and 'Scottish culture'.

sculpt and **sculpture** are interchangeable as verbs meaning 'to make sculptures, to practise sculpting', as in 'commissioned to sculpt/sculpture a bust of the chairman of the firm' and 'She both paints and sculpts/sculptures.

seasonal and **seasonable** are liable to be confused. They are both adjectives formed from the noun 'season' but they have different meanings. **Seasonal** means 'happening during a particular season, varying with the seasons', as in 'Hotel work is often seasonal' and 'a recipe that uses seasonal vegetables'. **Seasonable** means 'suitable for or appropriate to', as in 'seasonable weather'.

start *see* **commence**.

secretary is liable to be misspelt. Note the *-ary* ending. It is pronounced *sek*-re-tri and refers to 'a person employed to deal with correspondence, typing, filing, making appointments, etc', as in 'Her secretary is dealing with all her phone calls today'. It also

seize

refers to 'a person appointed in a society, club, etc, to deal with correspondence, take minutes, keep records, etc, as in 'elected secretary of tennis club'.

seize, meaning 'to take hold of suddenly and by force, to grab', as in 'The kidnappers seized the child' and 'seize the opportunity to escape', is frequently misspelt. Note the *ei* combination, which is an exception to the '*i* before *e* except after *c*' rule.

sensual and **sensuous** are liable to be confused. **Sensual** means 'relating to physical (often sexual) pleasure, enjoying or giving physical pleasure', as in 'the sensual pleasures of eating and drinking'. **Sensuous** means 'relating to the senses, giving pleasure to the senses', as in 'the sensuous feel of silk' and 'the sensuous appeal of the music'.

sentiment and **sentimentality** are liable to be confused. They are related but have different shades of meaning. **Sentiment** means 'feeling, emotion', as in 'His actions were the result of sentiment not rationality'. It also means 'attitude, opinion', as in 'a speech full of anti-Christian sentiments'. **Sentimentality** is the noun from the adjective **sentimental** and means 'over-indulgence in tender feelings', as in 'dislike the sentimentality of the love songs' and 'She disliked her home town but now speaks about it with great sentimentality'.

separate, is frequently misspelt. Note the *a* following the *p*. It is a common error to put *e* in that position. As an adjective **separate** means 'forming a unit by itself, existing apart', as in 'occupy separate rooms' and 'lead separate lives'. It also means 'distinct, different', as in 'happening on five separate occasions' and 'separate problems'. As a verb **separate** means 'to divide', as in 'The roads separate further up'; 'to cause to divide', as in 'separate the group'; 'to keep apart', as in 'A river separates the two parts of the estate'; 'to stop living together', as in 'The child's parents have recently separated'.

sewed and **sewn** are interchangeable as the past participle of the verb 'to sew', as in 'She has sewed/sewn patches on the torn parts of the trousers'. When the participle is used as an adjective, **sewn** is the more common form, as in 'badly sewn seams'. **Sewed** is also the past tense of 'to sew', as in 'She sewed the garment by hand'.

sexism in language has been an issue for some time, and various attempts have been made to avoid it. For example, 'person' is often used where 'man' was traditionally used and 'he/she' substituted for 'he' in situations where the sex of the relevant person is unknown or unspecified.

ship *see* **boat**.

siege is frequently misspelt. Note the *ie* combination. It follows the '*i* before *e* except after *c*' rule, but it is a common error to put *ei* instead. **Siege** means 'the surrounding of a town, fortress, etc, in order to capture it'.

sine qua non is a Latin phrase that has been adopted into English and means 'essential condition, something that is absolutely necessary', as in 'It is a sine qua non of the agreement that the rent is paid on time'. It is used only in formal or legal contexts.

sitting room, **living room**, **lounge** and **drawing room** all refer to 'a room in a house used for relaxation and the receiving of guests'. Which word is used is largely a matter of choice. Some people object to the use of **lounge** as being pretentious but it is becoming increasingly common. **Drawing room** is a more formal word and applies to a room in rather a grand residence.

skilful, as in 'admire his skilful handling of the situation' is frequently misspelt. Note the single *l* before the *f*. In American English the word is spelt **skillful**.

slander *see* **libel**.

sometime and **some time** are liable to be confused. **Sometime** means 'at an unknown or unspecified time', as in 'We must get together sometime' and 'I saw her sometime last year'. There is a growing tendency in modern usage to spell this as **some time**. Originally **some time** was restricted to meaning 'a period of time', as in 'We need some time to think'.

spelled and **spelt** are both acceptable forms of the past tense and past participle of the verb 'to spell', as in 'They spelled/spelt the word wrongly' and 'He realized that he had spelled/spelt the word wrongly'.

spoiled and **spoilt** are both acceptable forms of the past tense and past participle of the verb 'to spoil', as in 'They spoiled/spoilt that child' and 'They have spoiled/spoilt that house with their renovations'. When the past participle is used adjectivally, **spoilt** is the usual form, as in 'a spoilt child'.

stadium causes problems with regard to its plural form. **Stadiums** and **stadia** are both acceptable. **Stadium** is derived from Latin and the original plural form followed the Latin and was **stadia**. However, anglicized plural forms are becoming more and more common in foreign words adopted into English, and **stadiums** is now becoming the more usual form.

stanch and **staunch** are both acceptable spellings of the word meaning 'to stop the flow of', as in 'stanch/staunch the blood from the wound in his head' and 'try to stanch/staunch the tide of violence'. **Staunch** also means 'loyal, firm', as in 'the team's staunch supporters'.

stank and **stunk** are liable to be confused. **Stank** and **stunk** can both act as the past tense of the verb 'to stink', as in ' The rotten cheese stank' and 'He stunk of stale beer'. **Stunk** can also act as the past participle, as in 'This room has stunk of cigarette smoke for days'.

stationary and **stationery** are liable to be confused. They sound alike but have completely different meanings. **Stationary** means 'not moving, standing still', as in 'stationary vehicles'. **Stationery** refers to 'writing materials', as in 'office stationery'. An easy way to differentiate between them is to remember that **stationery** is bought from a 'stationer', which, like 'baker' and 'butcher', ends in -*er*.

staunch *see* **stanch**.

stimulant and **stimulus** are liable to be confused. Formerly the distinction between them was quite clear but now the distinction is becoming blurred. Traditionally **stimulant** refers to 'a substance, such as a drug, that makes a person more alert or more active', as in 'Caffeine is a stimulant'. **Stimulus** traditionally refers to 'something that rouses or encourages a person to action or greater effort', as in 'The promise of more money acted as a stimulus to the work force and they finished the job in record time'. In modern usage the words are beginning to be used interchangeably. In particular, **stimulus** is used in the sense of **stimulant** as well as being used in its own original sense.

storey and **story** are liable to be confused. They sound alike but have completely different meanings. **Storey** means 'level of a building, floor', as in 'a multi-storey car park' and 'They live on the second storey of the house'. **Story** means 'a tale', as in 'tell the children a bedtime story'. The plural of **storey** is **stories** and the plural of **story** is **stories**. In American English, **story** is used for both meanings.

straight away and **straightaway** are both acceptable ways of spelling the expression for 'without delay, at once', as in 'attend to the matter straight away/straightaway'.

straitened and **straightened** are liable to be confused. They sound alike but have completely different meanings. **Straitened** means 'severely restricted' and is most commonly found in the phrase 'in straitened circumstances', which means 'in extremely difficult financial circumstances'. **Straightened** is the past tense and participle of the verb 'to straighten', as in 'They have straightened the road out' and 'with her straightened hair'.

strata *see* **stratum**.

stratagem and **strategy** are liable to be confused. They look and sound similar but they have different meanings. **Stratagem** means 'a scheme or trick', as in 'think of a stratagem to mislead the enemy' and 'devise a stratagem to gain entry to the building'. **Strategy** refers to 'the art of planning a campaign', as in 'generals meeting to put together a battle strategy', and 'a plan or policy, particularly a clever one, designed for a particular purpose', as in 'admire the strategy which he used to win the game'.

stratum and **strata** are liable to be confused. **Stratum** is the singular form and **strata** is the plural form of a word meaning 'a layer or level', as in 'a stratum of rock' and 'different strata of society'. It is a common error to use **strata** as a singular noun.

student *see* **pupil**.

subconscious and unconscious are used in different contexts. **Subconscious** means 'concerning those areas or activities of the mind of which one is not fully aware', as in 'a subconscious hatred of her parents' and 'a subconscious desire to hurt her sister'. **Unconscious** means 'unaware', as in 'She was unconscious of his presence' and 'unconscious of the damage which he had caused', and 'unintentional', as in 'unconscious humour' and 'an unconscious slight'. **Unconscious** also means 'having lost consciousness, insensible', as in 'knocked unconscious by the blow to his head'.

subjective *see* **objective**.

subsequent *see* **consequent**.

subsidence has two acceptable pronunciations. It can be pronounced either sub-*sid*-ens, with the emphasis on the middle syllable which rhymes with 'hide', or *sub*-sid-ens, with the emphasis on the first syllable and with the middle syllable rhyming with 'hid'. **Subsidence** means 'falling or sinking', as in 'the subsidence of houses in that street'.

such and **like** are liable to be confused. **Such** is used to introduce examples, as in 'herbs, such as chervil and parsley' and 'citrus fruits, such as oranges and lemons'. **Like** introduces comparisons. 'She hates horror films like *Silence of the Lambs*', and 'Very young children, like very old people, have to be kept warm.'

suit and **suite** are liable to be confused. They look similar but they have completely different meanings. **Suit** has several meanings. These include 'a set of clothes', as in 'He was wearing a tweed three-piece suit' (a jacket, trousers and waistcoat in the same material) and 'She was married in a white suit, rather than a dress'; 'one of the four sets of playing cards', as in 'Which suit is trump?'; and 'an action in a court of law', as in 'bring a suit against her ex-husband for non-payment of maintenance'. **Suite** refers to 'a set of furniture', as in 'prefer non-matching chairs to the traditional three-piece suite' (a sofa and two armchairs in the same material); 'a set of rooms', as in 'book a suite at an expensive hotel' and 'the hotel's honeymoon suite'; and 'a musical composition consisting of three or more related parts', as in 'a ballet suite'. Note the *e* at the end of **suite**. **Suit** is pronounced *soot* or *syoot*. **Suite** is pronounced *sweet*.

supercilious is liable to be misspelt. Note the *c* and single *l*. It means 'condescending, disdainful', as in 'She treats unemployed people in a very supercilious way'.

supersede is frequently misspelt. Note the -*sede* ending. It is a common error to put -*cede* here, along the lines of 'precede'. **Supersede** means 'to take the place of, to replace', as in 'Word processors have superseded typewriters in many offices'.

supervise is frequently misspelt. Note the -*ise* ending. This is not one of the verbs that can be spelt ending in -*ize*. **Supervise** means 'to oversee', as in 'the teacher who was supervising the children in the playground' and 'a senior worker supervising the work of the trainees'.

supper *see* **dinner**.

susceptible is frequently misspelt. Note the *sc* combination and the -*ible*, not -*able*, ending. **Susceptible** means 'easily affected or influenced' and is frequently followed by the preposition 'to', as in 'children who are susceptible to colds' and 'people who are susceptible to political propaganda'.

swam and **swum** are not interchangeable. **Swam** is the past tense of the verb 'to swim', as in 'They swam ashore'. **Swum** is the past participle of the same verb, as in 'The children have swum for long enough'.

swingeing and **swinging** are liable to be confused. They look similar but they have completely different meanings. **Swinging** is simply the present participle of the verb 'to swing', as in 'children swinging on the gate'. It is also rather a dated term for 'lively and modern', as in 'the swinging sixties'. **Swingeing** means 'severe', as in 'swingeing cuts in public spending'. Note the *e* in **swingeing**. Note also the pronunciation of **swinge-ing**. It is pronounced *swin*-jing, not like swinging.

syndrome in its original meaning refers to 'a set of symptoms and signs that together indicate the presence of a physical or mental disorder', as in 'Down's syndrome'. In modern usage it is used loosely to indicate 'any set of events, actions, characteristics, attitudes that together make up, or are typical of, a situation', as in 'He suffers from the "I'm all right Jack" syndrome and doesn't care what happens to anyone else' and 'They seem to be caring people but they are opposing the building of an Aids hospice in their street—a definite case of "the not in my back yard" syndrome'.

T

target in its verb form, meaning 'to aim at', causes spelling problems with regard to its past participle, past tense and present participle. They are respectively **targeted** and **targeting**, as in 'resources targeted at the poorest section of the community' and 'the need for targeting their advertising campaign at young people.'

tariff is liable to be misspelt. Note the single *r* and double *f*. It means either 'duty to be paid on imported goods', as in 'the tariff payable on imported cars', or 'a list of fixed charges in a hotel, restaurant, etc', as in 'The hotel tariff is hanging behind the bedroom door' and 'the lunch tariff hanging outside the restaurant'.

tea *see* **dinner**.

teach *see* **learn**.

telephone *see* **phone**.

televise is frequently misspelt. Note the *-ise* ending. It is a common error to spell it with an *-ize* ending. It is helpful to remember the *s* of 'television'.

terminal and **terminus** in some contexts are interchangeable. They both refer to 'the end of a bus route, the last stop on a bus route, the building at the end of a bus route', as in 'The bus doesn't go any further—this is the terminus/terminal', but **terminus** is the more common term in this sense. They can also both mean 'the end of a railway line, the station at the end of a railway line', but **terminal** is the more common term in this sense. **Terminal** can refer to 'a building containing the arrival and departure areas for passengers at an airport' and 'a building in the centre of a town for the arrival and departure of air passengers'. **Terminal** also refers to 'a point of connection in an electric circuit', as in 'the positive and negative terminals', and 'apparatus, usually consisting of a keyboard and screen, for communicating with the central processor in a computing system', as in 'He has a dumb terminal so he can read information but not input it'. As an adjective **terminal** means 'of, or relating to, the last stage in a fatal illness', as in 'a terminal disease' and 'terminal patients'.

terminus *see* **terminal**.

tête-à-tête, meaning 'an intimate conversation between two people', as in 'have a tête-à-tête with her best friends about her marital problems', is liable to be misspelt. Note the circumflex accent on the first *e* of each **tête** and the accent on the *a*. The phrase has been adopted into English from French.

than is used to link two halves of comparisons or contrasts, as in 'Peter is considerably taller than John is', 'He is older than I am' and 'I am more informed about the situation than I was yesterday'. Problems arise when the relevant verb is omitted. In order to be grammatically correct, the word after 'than' should take the subject form if there is an implied verb, as in 'He is older than I (am)'. However this can sound stilted, as in 'She works harder than he (does)', and in informal contexts this usually becomes 'She works harder than him'. If there is no implied verb, the word after **than** is in the object form, as in 'rather you than me!'

their and **there** are liable to be confused because they sound similar. **There** means 'in, to or at that place', as in 'place it there' and 'send it there'. **Their** is the possessive of 'they', meaning 'of them, belonging to them', as in 'their books' and 'their mistakes'.

their and **they're** are liable to be confused because they sound similar. **Their** is the possessive of 'they', meaning 'of them, belonging to them', as in 'their cars' and 'their attitudes'. **They're** is a shortened form of 'they are', as in 'They're not very happy' and 'They're bound to lose'.

they, used in conjunction with 'anyone', everyone', 'no one' and 'someone', is increasingly replacing 'he' or 'she', although to do so is ungrammatical. The reason for this is to avoid the sexism of using 'he' when the sex of the person being referred to is either unknown or unspecified, and to avoid the clumsiness of 'he/she' or 'he or she'. Examples of **they** being so used include 'Everyone must do their best' and 'No one is to take their work home'.

they're *see* **their**.

this *see* **next**.

threshold is liable to be misspelt. Note the single *h*. It is a common error to put double *h*. **Threshold** means either 'doorway', as in 'meet the other visitor on the threshold', or 'the beginning', as in 'on the threshold of a new career'.

till and **until** are more or less interchangeable except that **until** is slightly more formal, as in 'They'll work till they drop' and 'Until we assess the damage we will not know how much the repairs will cost'.

tobacconist is frequently misspelt. Note the single *b*, the double *c* and the single *n*. A **tobacconist** refers to 'a person or shop that sells tobacco, cigarettes and cigars'.

toilet, **lavatory**, **loo** and **bathroom** all have the same meaning but the context in which they are used sometimes varies. **Toilet** is the most widely used of the words and is used on signs in public places. The informal **loo** is also very widely used. **Lavatory** is less common nowadays although it was formerly regarded by all but the working class and lower-middle class as the most acceptable term. **Bathroom** in British English usually refers to 'a room containing a bath', but in American English it is the usual word for **toilet**. **Ladies** and **gents** are terms for **toilet**, particularly in public places. **Powder room** also means this, as does the American English **rest room**.

town *see* **city**.

trade names should be written with a capital letter, as in 'Filofax' and 'Jacuzzi'. When trade names are used as verbs they are written with a lower case letter, as in 'hoover the carpet'.

trafficker is frequently misspelt. Note the *k*. The word means 'a person who deals in or trades in something, particularly something illegal or dishonest', as in 'drugs traffickers'. Note also **trafficked** and **trafficking** but **traffic**.

trait is traditionally pronounced *tray* but *trayt* is also an acceptable pronunciation in modern usage. It means an element or quality in someone's personality', as in 'One of his least attractive traits is his habit of blaming other people for his mistakes'.

tranquillity, meaning 'peace, peaceful state', as in 'disturb the tranquillity of the countryside', is liable to be misspelt. Note the double *l*.

travel causes problems with regard to the past participle, past tense and present participle. The *l* doubles before '-ed' and '-ing' are added, as **travelled** and **travelling**, as in 'They travelled to many parts of the world' and 'nervous when travelling by car'. Note also **traveller**, as in 'travellers in foreign lands'. In American English the *l* is not doubled, as **traveled, traveling** and **traveler**.

troop and **troupe** are liable to be confused. **Troop** refers to 'a military unit', as in 'the officer in charge of the troop', or to 'a group or collection of people or animals', as in 'Troops of people arrived at the demonstration from all over the country'. **Troupe** refers to 'a company of actors or performers', as in 'a troupe of acrobats'.

try to and **try and** are interchangeable in modern usage. Formerly **try and** was considered suitable only in spoken and very informal contexts, but it is now considered acceptable in all but the most formal contexts, as in 'Try to/and do better' and 'They must try to/and put the past behind them'.

twelfth, as in 'December is the twelfth month of the year', is liable to be both mispronounced and misspelt. The *f* is frequently omitted in error in pronunciation and spelling.

U

ultra is used as a prefix meaning 'going beyond', as in 'ultraviolet' and 'ultrasound', or 'extreme, very', as in 'ultra-sophisticated', ultra-modern, and 'ultra-conservative'. Compounds using it may be spelt with or without a hyphen. Words such as 'ultrasound' and 'ultraviolet' are usually spelt as one word, but words with the second sense of **ultra**, such as 'ultra-sophisticated', are often hyphenated.

unaware and **unawares** are not interchangeable. **Unaware** is an adjective meaning 'not aware, not conscious of', as in 'He was unaware that he was being watched' and 'She was unaware of his presence', and 'ignorant, having no knowledge of', as in 'politically unaware'. **Unawares** is an adverb meaning 'without being aware, without noticing, unintentionally', as in 'I must have dropped my keys unawares' and 'The child dropped her gloves unawares', or 'by surprise, unexpected, without warning', as in 'The enemy attack took them unawares' and 'The snowstorm caught the climbers unawares'.

unconscious *see* **subconscious**.

underhand and **underhanded** are interchangeable in the sense of 'sly, deceitful', as in 'He used underhand/underhanded methods to get the job' and 'It was underhand/underhanded of him to not to tell her that he was leaving'. **Underhand** is the more common of the two terms.

under way, meaning 'in progress', is traditionally spelt as two words, as in 'Preparations for the conference are under way'. In modern usage it is frequently spelt as one word, as in 'The expansion project is now underway'. It is a common error to write 'under weigh'.

undoubtedly, as in 'He is undoubtedly the best player in the team' and 'Undoubtedly we shall be a little late', is liable to be misspelt. A common error is to spell it 'Undoubtably', probably in confusion with 'indubitably'. **Undoubtedly** means the same as 'without a doubt'.

unexceptionable and **unexceptional** are liable to be confused. They look and sound rather similar but they have different meanings. **Unexceptionable** means 'not liable to be criticized or objected to, inoffensive, satisfactory', as in 'His behaviour was quite unexceptionable' and 'I found her remarks quite unexceptionable'. **Unexceptional** means 'ordinary, not outstanding or unusual', as in 'She was supposed to be a brilliant player but her performance was unexceptional' and 'an unexceptional student'.

uninterested *see* **disinterested**.

unique traditionally means 'being the only one of its kind', as in 'a unique work of art' and 'everyone's fingerprints are unique' and so cannot be modified by such words as 'very', 'rather', 'more', etc, although it can be modified by 'almost' and 'nearly'. In modern usage **unique** is often used to mean 'unrivalled, unparalleled, outstanding', as in 'a unique opportunity' and 'a unique performance'.

unreadable *see* **illegible**.

unrepairable *see* **irreparable**.

until *see* **till**.

unwanted and **unwonted** are liable to be confused. They sound alike but they have completely different meanings. **Unwanted** means 'not wanted', as in 'give unwanted furniture to a charity shop', 'an unwanted pregnancy' and 'feel unwanted'. **Unwonted** means 'not customary, not usual', as in 'behave with unwonted courtesy' and 'a feeling of unwonted optimism'. **Unwonted** is not pronounced in the same way as **unwanted**. It is pronounced un-*wont*-ed with the second syllable pronounced as 'won't'.

up and **upon** mean the same and are virtually interchangeable, except that **upon** is slightly more formal. Examples include 'sitting on a bench', 'the carpet on the floor', 'the stamp on the letter', caught with the stolen goods on him' and 'something on his mind'; and 'She threw herself upon her dying mother's bed', 'a carpet of snow upon the ground' and 'Upon his arrival he went straight upstairs'.

upward and **upwards** are not interchangeable. **Upward** is used as an adjective, as in 'on an upward slope' and 'an upward trend in prices'. **Upwards** is an adverb, as in 'look upwards to see the plane'.

urban and **urbane** are liable to be confused. They look similar but they have completely different meanings. **Urban** means 'of a town or city', as in 'urban dwellers' and 'in an urban setting'. **Urbane** means 'smoothly elegant and sophisticated', as in 'an urbane wit' and 'an urbane man of the world'.

usable and **useable** are both acceptable spellings, as in 'furniture which is no longer usable/useable' and 'crockery which is scarcely usable/useable'. **Usable** is more common.

V

vacation, meaning 'holiday', in British English is mostly restricted to a university or college situation, as in 'students seeking paid employment during their vacation'. In American English it is the usual word for 'holiday'.

vaccinate is liable to be misspelt. Note the double *c* and single *n*. The word means 'to inject a vaccine into to prevent a particular disease', as in 'vaccinate the children against tuberculosis'. **Vaccine** refers to 'a substance that is injected into the bloodstream and protects the body against a disease by making it have a mild form of the disease', as in 'a vaccine against smallpox'.

vacuum is liable to be misspelt. Note the single *c* and double *u*. It refers to 'a space that is completely empty of all matter and gases', as in 'create a total vacuum'.

variegated is liable to be misspelt. Note the *e* between the *i* and the *g*. It means 'varied in colour, speckled or mottled with different colours', as in 'variegated leaves'. It is pronounced *vayr*-i-gayt-ed.

verbal and **oral** are liable to be confused. **Oral** means 'expressed in speech', as in 'an oral, rather than a written examination'. **Verbal** means 'expressed in words', as in 'He asked for an instruction diagram but he was given verbal instructions' and 'They were going to stage a protest match but they settled for a verbal protest'. It is also used to mean 'referring to the spoken word, expressed in speech', as in 'a verbal agreement'. Because of these two possible meanings, the use of **verbal** can lead to ambiguity. In order to clarify the situation, **oral** should be used when 'expressed in speech' is meant. **Verbal** can also mean referring to verbs, as in 'verbal endings'. For more information on **oral** *see* **aural**.

vice versa means 'the other way round, with the order reversed', as in 'He will do his friend's shift and vice versa' and 'Mary dislikes John and vice versa'. It is pronounced vis-e ver-sa, vi-si ver-sa or vis ver-sa and is derived from Latin.

vigorous is liable to be misspelt. Note the absence of *u* before *r*, unlike the noun **vigour**. It means 'strong and energetic', as in 'vigorous young men playing football', or 'forceful', as in 'vigorous debate' and 'vigorous criticism'.

vis-à-vis means 'in relation to', as in 'their performance vis-à-vis their ability' and 'the company's policy vis-à-vis early retirement'. It is pronounced vee-za-vee and is derived from French. Note the accent on the *a*.

vitamin is pronounced vit-a-min, with the first syllable rhyming with 'lit' in British English. In American English the first syllable rhymes with 'light'. The word refers to 'one of a group of substances which are essential for healthy life, different ones occurring in different foods', as in a 'sufferer from a deficiency of vitamin B6' and 'Citrus fruits are a source of vitamin C'.

victuals, meaning 'food', as in 'children requiring nourishing victuals', is liable to be mispronounced. It is pronounced vitlz.

W

-ways *see* **-wise**.

weaved, **wove** and **woven** can cause problems. **Wove** is the usual past tense of the verb 'to weave', as in 'She wove the cloth on a hand loom', 'The spider wove a web' and 'The children wove a garland of flowers'. However, in the sense of 'to move along by twisting and turning' **weaved** is the past tense, as in 'The cyclist weaved in and out of the traffic' and 'The drunks weaved their way home'. **Woven** is the past participle of all but 'the twisting and turning' sense, as in 'She had woven the cloth herself' and 'The children had woven garlands'. **Weaved** is the past participle, as in 'She has weaved her way through the traffic'.

weird is liable to be misspelt. Note the *ei* combination. The word means 'strange, uncanny, unnatural', as in 'see weird figures in the mist' and 'hear weird cries in the night'. It also means 'unusual, bizarre, unconventional', as in 'wear weird clothes' and 'have a weird sense of humour'.

wet and **whet** are liable to be confused. **Wet** means 'to cover with moisture', as in 'Wet the clay before using it' and 'wet one's lips'. **Whet** means 'to sharpen', as in 'whet the blade of the sword', and 'to stimulate, excite', as in 'whet his appetite for adventure'.

what ever and **whatever** are not interchangeable. **What ever** is used when 'ever' is used for emphasis, as in 'What ever does he think he's doing?' and 'What ever is she wearing'. **Whatever** means 'anything, regardless of what, no matter what', as in 'Help yourself to whatever you want' and 'Whatever he says I don't believe him'.

whet *see* **wet**.

which and **what** can cause problems. In questions **which** is used when a limited range of alternatives is suggested, as in 'Which book did you buy in the end?' and **what** is used in general situations, as in 'What book did you buy?'

whisky and **whiskey** both refer to a strong alcoholic drink distilled from grain. **Whisky** is made in Scotland and **whiskey** in Ireland and America. **Whisky** is the usual British English spelling.

who and **whom** cause problems. **Who** is the subject of a verb, as in 'Who told you?', 'It was you who told her' and 'the girls who took part in the play'. **Whom** is the object of a verb or preposition, as in 'Whom did he tell?', 'To whom did you speak?' and 'the people from whom he stole'. In modern usage **whom** is falling into disuse, especially in questions, except in formal contexts. **Who** is used instead even although it is ungrammatical, as in 'Who did you speak to?' **Whom** should be retained when it is a relative pronoun, as in 'the man whom you saw', 'the person to whom he spoke' and 'the girl to whom she gave the book'.

whose and **who's** are liable to be confused. They sound alike but have different meanings. **Whose** means 'of whom' or 'of which', as in 'the woman whose child won', 'the boy whose leg was broken', 'Whose bicycle is that?' and 'the firm whose staff went on strike'. **Who's** is a shortened form of 'who is', as in 'Who's that?', 'Who's first in the queue?' and 'Who's coming to the cinema?'

wilful is liable to be misspelt. Note the single *l* before *f*, and the final single *l*. It means 'done deliberately, unintentional', as in 'wilful damage done to the phone box', or 'headstrong, obstinate', as in 'a wilful child'. In American English the word is spelt with a double *l*, as 'willful'.

-wise and **-ways** cause problems. Added to nouns, **-wise** can form adverbs of manner indicating either 'in such a position or direction', as in 'lengthwise' and 'clockwise', and 'in the manner of', as in 'crabwise'. In modern usage **-wise** is frequently used to mean 'with reference to', as in 'Weatherwise it was fine', 'Workwise all is well' and 'Moneywise they're not doing too well'. The suffix **-ways** has a more limited use. It means 'in such a way, direction or manner of', as in 'lengthways' and 'sideways'.

withhold is sometimes misspelt. Note the double *h*. It means 'to keep back', as in 'withhold evidence'.

woman *see* **lady**.

worship causes problems with regard to the past tense, past participle and present participle as **worshipped, worshipping**. Note also **worshipper** but **worshipful**.

wove *see* **weaved**.

wrack *see* **rack**.

X

Xerox causes problems with regard to both spelling and pronunciation. It is a registered trademark for 'a type of photographic process used for copying documents, etc', as in 'a Xerox photocopier', or 'a copy made using this process', as in 'a Xerox of the contract'. Since it is a registered trademark the noun must be spelt with a capital letter. **Xerox** can also be a verb meaning 'to copy a document using the Xerox process' and can be spelt with either a capital letter or a lower-case letter, as in 'Please Xerox/xerox these letters before posting them'.

Xmas is sometimes used as an alternative and shorter form of 'Christmas'. It is common only in a written informal context and is used mainly in commercial situations, as in 'Xmas cards on sale here' and 'Get your Xmas tree here'. When pronounced it is the same as 'Christmas'. The X derives from the Greek *chi*, the first letter of *Christos*, the Greek word for Christ.

X-ray is usually written with an initial capital letter when it is a noun meaning 'a photograph made by means of X-rays showing the bones or organs of the body', as in 'take an X-ray of the patient's chest'. Another term for the noun **X-ray** is 'radiograph'. As a verb it is also usually spelt with an initial capital, as 'After the accident he had his leg X-rayed', but it is sometimes spelt with an initial lower-case letter, as in 'have his chest x-rayed'.

Y

yoghurt is the most usual spelling of the word for 'a type of semi-liquid consisting of milk fermented by added bacteria', as in 'have yoghurt and fruit for breakfast', but **yogurt** and **yoghourt** are also acceptable spellings. It is usually pronounced yog-ert, but yoh-gert is also a possible pronunciation and is the standard one in American English.

yoke and **yolk** are liable to be confused. They sound alike but have completely different meanings. **Yolk**, referring to 'the yellow part of an egg', as in 'The yolk of this egg is too soft', is the commoner of the two words. **Yoke** has several meanings. It means 'a connecting bar', as in 'the yoke across the necks of the oxen' and 'a peasant carrying two pails of water on a yoke'; 'a pair of oxen', as in 'owning three yoke of oxen'; 'an oppressive control', as in 'under the yoke of the cruel tyrant'; 'the part of a garment fitting round the shoulders or hips from which the rest of the garment hangs', as in 'a sweater with a contrasting-coloured yolk'. Both words are pronounced yok to rhyme with 'poke'.

you is used in informal or less formal situations to indicate an indefinite person referred to as 'one' in formal situations. Examples include 'You learn a foreign language more quickly if you spend some time in the country where it is spoken', 'You would think that they would make sure that their staff are polite', 'You can get used to anything in time' and 'You have to experience the situation to believe it'. **You** in this sense must be distinguished from **you** meaning the second person singular', as in 'You have missed

your

your bus', 'You must know where you left your bag' and 'You have to leave now'. *See* **one**.

your and **you're** are liable to be confused. **Your** is a possessive adjective meaning 'belonging to you, of you', as in 'That is your book and this is mine', 'Your attitude is surprising' and 'It is your own fault'. **You're** is a shortened form of 'you are', as in 'You're foolish to believe him', 'You're going to be sorry' and 'You're sure to do well. Note the spelling of the pronoun **yours**, as in 'This book is yours' and 'Which car is yours?' It should not be spelt with an apostrophe as it is not a shortened form of anything.

yours *see* **your**.

yuppie *see* **acronyms**.